THE OLDER AMERICAN'S HANDBOOK

Practical information and help on··
Medical and Nursing Care
Housing • Recreation
Legal Services • Employment
In-Home Services • Food
Associations and Organizations
Transportation
Mental Health and Counseling
···for older and retired Americans

Craig & Peter Norback

Bernard E. Nash
Consulting Editor

(Formerly Executive Director of the American Association of Retired Persons)

VNR VAN NOSTRAND REINHOLD COMPANY
NEW YORK   CINCINNATI   ATLANTA   DALLAS   SAN FRANCISCO
LONDON   TORONTO   MELBOURNE

Van Nostrand Reinhold Company Regional Offices:
New York   Cincinnati   Atlanta   Dallas   San Francisco

Van Nostrand Reinhold Company International Offices:
London   Toronto   Melbourne

Copyright © 1977 by Litton Educational Publishing, Inc.

Library of Congress Catalog Card Number: 77-11945
ISBN: 0-442-26062-8

All rights reserved. No part of this work covered by the copyright hereon may be reproduced or used in any form or by any means — graphic, electronic, or mechanical, including photocopying, recording, taping, or information storage and retrieval systems — without permission of the publisher.

Manufactured in the United States of America

Published by Van Nostrand Reinhold Company
450 West 33rd Street, New York, N.Y. 10001

Published simultaneously in Canada by Van Nostrand Reinhold Ltd.

15 14 13 12 11 10 9 8 7 6 5 4 3 2 1

Library of Congress Cataloging in Publication Data

Norback, Craig T
   The older American's handbook.

  Includes index.
  1. Aged—United States—Handbooks, manuals, etc.
2. Old age assistance—United States—Directories.
I. Norback, Peter G., joint author. II. Title.
HQ1064.U5N58   362.6   77-11945
ISBN 0-442-26062-8

Our sincere thanks to Betty Junna for helping us with this handbook.

Preface

One thing is certain, every single one of us must eventually live with those terrible, horrible expressions, *old age, the elderly, senior citizen,* and *the golden years*. But is it really so terrible? Personally, we can't think of anything worse than being teenagers. That period of life has got to be the most dreadful time of all because everything — and we mean everything — is uncomfortable, unpleasant, and generally miserable. So aging isn't so bad when compared with other circumstances and other problems.

We have read thousands and thousands of pages of advice for the elderly in pamphlets, articles, brochures, and books. And, although a lot of the material was good, the thought kept coming back to us that only *you* know what you want and need.

Therefore, unlike other publications in the field of aging, this book does not tell you what you should do, rather, it gives you the best sources to go to in every facet of human activity, so that you can take care of yourself. It is the first do-it-yourself book for older Americans.

We learned many things from the year-long research necessary to prepare this book. One of them was that there are not enough jobs for the elderly.

As we stated in the preface, 2.9 million or 14 percent of all older Americans are in the labor force. This figure varies somewhat during any given year, but even at slightly higher levels, it is a small percentage of the 23 million older Americans living in the United States today.

Why are so few working? The reasons are primarily two: (1) mandatory retirement and (2) the Social Security laws, which require that recipients pay Uncle Sam 50 cents on every dollar they earn in one year over approximately $3,400. This is like forced welfare.

During the last few years, Congress has helped by tying Social Security payments to the cost-of-living index. However, this does not solve the real problem — that is, the limitations placed upon the elderly with respect to the amount of money they can earn in a given year.

Private enterprise does not seem to help much either. Forced retirement, which is not a law, but rather a business practice forced upon the elderly by both the Social Security system and pension plans, serves only one purpose; to move up younger, supposedly more effective and aggressive management. It is often devastating to people who, having spent their lives actively participating *in* the system, one day find themselves out, and out for good.

What the Government Should Do

It's our belief that more older Americans receiving Social Security benefits would work if the federal government would (1) raise the amount a person could earn annually to substantially higher levels than exist today and (2) reduce the amount of tax on this money. This would give them an added incentive to work — in addition to their desire to remain involved, productive, and, above all, independent. And, in the long run, this plan would reduce the financial burden on all taxpayers.

Also, the entire Social Security program should be voluntary. Under such a system, we believe that those who want to work will not elect to participate in the Social Security system until much later in their lives. People could decide, in their mid-forties, for example, whether to participate at the age of 62 or 65 years, or to remain independent and working until much later. Should they have to change their minds, for some reason, they would be given the opportunity, with certain time stipulations, to participate in the system.

In all, we believe that Social Security should be an alternative, and not the only way for older Americans to survive.

What Business Should Do

In order to encourage business to hire the elderly, the government could offer such programs as tax-break incentives and shared costs. This might encourage business to treat each prospective retiree on an individual basis, rather than copping-out and blaming forced retirement on the system. Forced retirement is the result of obsolete insurance mortality and disability statistics, which, along with the entire system, need revising.

The issue here is whether business and government are going to be responsive to the needs of the largest single age group in the United States, older Americans. They want to remain productive and useful for as long as they are able, and only enlightened management and legislature can help accomplish this goal.

You, the reader, can help foster these changes. Write to your congressional representative; write to the American Association of Retired Persons, 1909 K Street, NW, Washington, DC 20049; write to Senator Frank Church who heads the Special Committee on Aging in the U.S. Senate, Washington, DC 20510; or write to the authors in care of Van Nostrand Reinhold Company, 450 W. 33rd St., New York, New York 10001.

We want to hear from you, and we will make certain that your ideas reach the right people.

Because of the enormous changes taking place in the field of aging, the authors may have missed some programs or services afforded the elderly. Don't hesitate to write or inquire about a program or service you might have heard about in your investigations. The authors welcome all inquiries and suggestions.

CRAIG AND PETER NORBACK

Contents

Preface/v
Introduction/1

1. Administration on Aging (AOA)/3
2. American Association of Retired Persons (AARP) and National Retired Teachers Association (NRTA)/6
3. Area Agencies on Aging/12
4. Associations and Organizations/22
5. Audio Visual Material/28
6. Books for the Blind and Physically Handicapped/29
7. Employment/36
    Paid Employment/38
    Volunteer Work/39
8. Foundations/41
9. Friendly Visiting/42
10. Fund Raising for Nonprofit Organizations/43
11. Government Programs/45
12. Health/90
13. Home Health Agencies/99
14. Homemaker-Home Health Aide Service/140
15. Housing/144
16. In-Home Services/223
17. Legal Services/225
18. Medicare and Medicaid/236
19. Mental Health Centers/242
20. National Alliance of Businessmen/258
21. National Nutrition Program/263
22. Nursing Homes/278
23. Outreach Services/281
24. Preretirement Planning – Information Sources/282
25. Publications/285

26. Publishers/294
27. Recreation/295
28. Revenue Sharing/297
29. Senior Centers/298
30. Shows and Conventions/299
31. State Agencies on Aging/302
32. Telephone Reassurance/304
33. Transporation Projects Serving the Elderly/305
34. YMCA and YWCA/311

Introduction

How many older Americans are there?

In 1975, one in every 10 persons in the United States — 22.4 million men and women — was 65 years of age or over. This number is about the same as the total population of the 20 smallest states and the District of Columbia.

The proportion of the population 65 years old and over varies by race and ethnic origin: 11% for whites, 7% for blacks, and 4% for persons of Hispanic origin.

Between 1900 and 1975, the percentage of the United States population aged 65+ more than doubled (4.1% in 1900 and 10.5% in 1975), while the number increased about sevenfold (from 3 million to 22 million).

Where do older Amercians live?

In 1975, about half (45.5%) of all persons aged 65+ lived in the seven most populated states: California, Illinois, New York, Ohio, Pennsylvania, Texas, and Florida. Each of these states had more than 1 million older persons. The 65+ population in two states, California and New York, is over 2 million. Nine states had an unusually high proportion of older persons, 12% or more, in their total populations: Florida, 16.1%; Arkansas, 12.8%; Iowa, 12.7%; Missouri and Kansas, 12.6% each; Nebraska, 12.5%; South Dakota, 12.4%; Oklahoma, 12.3%; and Rhode Island, 12.2%.

Has life expectancy changed?

A child born in 1900 could expect to live an average of about 47 years; a child born in 1974 could expect to live 25 years longer, or an average of 72 years. The major part of the increase occurred because of reduced death rates among children and young adults. More people now reach old age; however, they do not live much longer than did their ancestors who reached age 65 in 1900.

At age 65, life expectancy is 15.5 years; 13 years for men, 18 years for women. As a result of this sex difference in life expectancy, there were 144 older women per 100 older men in 1974, and the disparity continues to grow with age. Assuming that the 1974 death rates do not change, 81% of female infants will live to age 65, compared with only 67% of male infants.

More than 1.2 million older people died in 1974, a rate of 56.8 per 1,000 (70 for men, 48 for women). The death rate for the under-65 group was 4 per 1,000. Three-fifths of all deaths of older persons resulted from heart disease (45%), and cancer (17%).

What are the costs of health care?

In 1974, Americans spent approximately $90 billion for personal health care. About 30% of this amount was spent on older persons. The *per capita* health-care cost for an older person was $1,218, nearly three times as much as the $420 spent for younger adults. Benefits from government programs such as Medicare accounted for three-fifths of the health expenditures of older persons, compared with three-tenths for adults under 65.

What are the living arrangements of older persons?

About 5%, or approximately 1 million older persons, lived in institutions of all kinds in 1975. That figure increased slightly in 1976.

Most older persons lived in a family setting. Nevertheless, the proportion living in family settings decreases rapidly with advancing age.

In the noninstitutional population, the numbers of older men and women living in a family setting were about the same: 7.3 million men, 7.4 million women. However, since there are many more older women than older men (144 per 100), the proportion of older men in family settings was 83% while that of women was 59%.

More than one-third of all older persons (6.5 million, or 1.5 and 5.0 million men and women, respectively) lived alone or with nonrelatives. This accounts for 41% of all older women but only 17% of all older men.

What is the marital status of older persons?

In 1975, 79% of older men were married; most older women (53%) were widows. There were more than five times as many widows as widowers.

One-third (37.7%) of the older married men had wives who were under 65 years of age. In 1973, forty-one states and the District of Columbia reported the marriages of a total of 16,407 brides and 33,020 grooms aged 65+. These were first marriages for about 5% of both the men and women. Most were remarriages of older persons who were previously widowed.

What about income?

One of every five couples with a husband 65+ had incomes of less than $4,000 in 1974. At the other end of the income scale, one of every four elderly couples had incomes of $10,000 or more.

The income of elderly persons living alone or with nonrelatives was more skewed to the lower end of the income distribution. Half received incomes under $3,000 while only one out of six received more than $6,000.

Are most older people poor?

About 15.7 percent, or 3.3 million persons 65+, were living below the poverty level. Among elderly whites, one out of every seven was poor; over one-third of elderly blacks were living below the poverty level. The proportion below the poverty level was much higher for elderly persons living alone or with nonrelatives (32%) than for those living in families (9%). Persons 65+ who resided outside the nation's metropolitan areas were more likely to be poor (20%) than were elderly city dwellers (13%).

Of the 8 million families headed by a person 65+, some 760,000 or 10% were below the poverty level. The income received by such families was almost entirely derived from public sources such as Social Security, Supplemental Security, and public assistance. For nonpoor families with a head who was 65+, only one-third of the income was from public sources. About 40% was received in the form of wages, salaries, and self-employment income.

Three-fifths, or 2.1 million, of the elderly poor were living alone or with nonrelatives. About 1.9 million of these people lived alone. As with elderly families, nearly all (92%) of the income received by poor individuals who were 65+ was from public sources.

Among nonpoor individuals, only half of the income was received from public sources. One-sixth was from earnings and about one-third was from all other sources.

Of the 4.5 million families with a head who was 65+ and that received more than half of their income from public sources, only 14% were poor. However, about 38% of elderly individuals who received over half of their income from public sources were below the poverty level.

How many older persons work?

In 1975, more than 2.9 million older people (14%) were in the labor force, either working or actively seeking work. They now make up 3.1% of the United States labor force. Slightly more than one-fifth of the older men (1.9 million) and about 8% of the older women (1.0 million) are in the labor force.

Only 5.3%, or 1 in 19 older people in the labor force, were unemployed. A large proportion of older men who work are in low-paying agricultural jobs.

The male labor-force participation rate has decreased steadily, from 2 in 3 older men in 1900 to 1 in 5 in 1975; the rate for females rose slightly, from 1 in 12 in 1900 to 1 in 10 in 1972, but dropped to 1 in 12 in 1975.

How healthy are older Americans? How often do they use health-care services?

Chronic conditions are more prevalent among older persons than younger. In 1974, about 39% of older persons were limited in their major activity (e.g., working, keeping house), due to such conditions, compared to only 7% for younger persons.

In 1972, chronic conditions interfered with the mobility of about 18% of the 65+ group: 6% had some trouble getting around alone, 7% needed a mechanical aid to get around, and 5% were homebound.

In 1974, older people had about a 1 in 6 chance of being hospitalized during a year, whereas persons under 65 had a 1 in 10 chance. The proportion with more than one hospitalization during a year was also greater for older people, 4.1% versus 1.5%. Once in the hospital, older people stayed about 4 days longer than younger patients.

On the average, older people had over one-third more physician visits in 1974 than did persons under 65, with a higher proportion of visits occurring within the last 6 months of the year.

Half of the older population either had not seen a dentist for 5 or more years or had never visited a dentist. In 1971, dental visits of older persons were much more likely to be for denture work and less likely to be for examinations or teeth cleaning than were visits of younger persons.

In 1971, older people were twice as likely, when compared to those under 65, to wear glasses and 13 times as likely to use a hearing aid. About 92% of persons 65+ wore eyeglasses or contact lenses, and 5% used hearing aids.

1
Administration on Aging (AOA)

The Administration on Aging (AOA) was established by the Older Americans Act of 1965. The act, which has been amended by Congress a number of times, lists federal objectives for older people and authorizes funds for the following programs:

- State and Community Grants Program
- Nutrition Program for the Elderly
- Model Projects Program
- Research and Development Program
- Manpower Development and Training Program

The 1973 amendments to the act specify that every federal agency proposing to initiate a program for older people should consult with the AOA and that every federal agency operating such a program should cooperate with AOA.

The amendments required that AOA establish a National Clearinghouse on Aging to collect, store, and disseminate information about older people. They also provide for a 15-member Federal Council on the Aging appointed by the president with the consent of Congress, and with the secretary of HEW and the commissioner on aging as *ex officio* members. Although the council is a separate governmental agency, it is staffed by the AOA.

Located in the Office of Human Development, Office of the Secretary, U.S. Department of Health, Education and Welfare, AOA is headed by a commissioner on aging, who also serves as the chairman of the Interdepartmental Working Group of the White House Domestic Council Committee on Aging.

The State and Community Grants Program is a formula-grants program, under which federal funds are allocated to states in relation to their numbers of older people. The funds must be matched by varying amounts at the state or local level in accordance with ratios established by law.

Each of the 50 states, the District of Columbia, Guam, Puerto Rico, Samoa, the Trust Territories of the Pacific, and the Virgin Islands have an agency on aging charged with developing comprehensive and coordinated service systems for older persons at the local level to help them remain in their homes and out of institutions as long as they are able and wish to do so. By July 1, 1975, area agencies, and state agencies on aging in areas where there are no area agencies, must have identified an information and referral source reasonably available to older people in their area. Information and referral services can help older people and their families find the services they need, or, if a needed service is lacking, they can alert the state or area agencies to the need for it.

Area agencies on aging are planning bodies and, unless they were providing services before they became area agencies, are not service providers. They develop annual plans for approval by the state agencies on aging, under which, with their state's approval, they can fund service programs for older people operated by local service providers. Much of their effort is directed toward coordinating existing service programs, tapping unused resources, and acting as advocates for older people in their areas.

The Nutrition Program for the Elderly is a formula-grants program, under which money appropriated by congress is allocated to states on the basis of the number of persons 60 and older in their populations. The program's purpose is to assist communities to meet the nutritional and social needs of elderly persons who do not eat adequately because:

1. They cannot afford to do so.
2. They lack the skills to select and prepare nourishing, well-balanced meals.
3. They have limited mobility, which makes it difficult for them to shop and cook for themselves.
4. They have feelings of rejection and loneliness, which destroy their incentives to prepare and eat meals alone.

The state agencies on aging make grants to public or nonprofit agencies or organizations for up to 90 percent of the cost of large nutrition projects serving meals in several sites.

The 665 projects now funded serve a hot, nutritious meal once a day, 5 days a week. They also include outreach to find older people who need the meals, transportation to help them reach the meal sites, and supportive services such as information and referral, health and welfare counseling, consumer and nutrition education, and opportunities for recreation and volunteer services to others.

Most of the meals are served to groups of older people at sites such as churches, schools, senior centers, or community centers. Up to 10 percent of the meals served by any one project can be home-delivered; however, the program's purpose is basically to get older people out of their homes and into group settings where they can find companionship and receive other services.

People 60 years of age or older and their spouses are eligible. The law specifically requires that each project serve primarily low-income older persons and minority, American Indian, and limited-English-speaking persons at least in proportion to their numbers within the state.

There is no means test. Participants pay only what they can afford. If they cannot afford to pay, they are still eligible for the meals.

Since the delivery of low-cost meals and related service is one component of a comprehensive service system for older people, state and area agencies on aging are encouraged to work out with nutrition project directors mutually satisfactory agreements that are designed to integrate nutrition projects into area service systems.

The Model Projects Program supports projects that promise to provide information that will make a national impact on the improvement of social services or otherwise promote the well-being of older persons. Approval of the projects follows review by the state agency on aging in the state where a project will be conducted and by a review committee appointed by the commissioner.

The Older Americans Act specifies that, in awarding grants or contracts under this program, the commissioner shall give special consideration to projects that will:

1. assist in meeting the special housing needs of older persons
2. provide continuing education that is designed to enable them to lead more productive lives
3. provide preretirement education, information, and relevant services to persons planning retirement
4. provide services to assist in meeting the particular needs of physically and mentally impaired older persons.

The commissioner will also give consideration to other projects that show promise of superior contribution to the achievement of the intent of the program. From time to time, the commissioner published guidelines to indicate priorities for meeting unmet needs and, which, in his judgment, represent the most advantageous use of funds available.

The Research and Demonstration Program supports research designed to:

1. increase both the amount of knowledge about the elderly and the effectiveness of services for them
2. identify needs and assess the adequacy of resources to meet the needs of the elderly
3. identify ways and means to increase coordination of existing state and area resources and pooling of available but untapped resources that can be used in comprehensive service systems to meet the needs of the elderly
4. identify ways and means to increase availability and quality of services for the elderly, including access services such as information and referral
5. develop ways to promote participation of older people in the planning, coordination, and implementation by state and area agencies on aging of improved service delivery for the elderly
6. develop ways of increasing the coordination and utilization of federal resources for meeting the needs of the elderly
7. improve and increase the dissemination and utilization of information on the elderly and the services provided to them.

AOA also funds investigator-initiated research for which support, however limited, would be a worthwhile investment, and dissertation research in the form of small grants to encourage recognition and interest in the field of aging by graduate students in educational institutions.

The Manpower Development and Training Program awards grants to public or nonprofit private agencies, organizations, or institutions, or to state agencies on aging, and enters into contracts for training projects. The program's purpose is to increase the number of trained personnel in the field of aging and thus improve the quality of services to older people.

In 1975, AOA funded projects to:

1. provide short-term training for state and area agency on aging staff, and new nutrition project directors, professional and paraprofessional personnel delivering services, older persons serving other older persons, and volunteers working in programs for the elderly
2. provide continued professional training in aging through educational institutions
3. attract qualified persons from a variety of professions to enter the field of aging.

Interagency Agreements. AOA is the federal focal point for planning and advocacy for older people. At the state and local level, state and area agencies on aging perform the same functions. At the federal level, AOA is developing interagency agreements, which are to be paralleled at the state and local levels and which are designed to lead to more effective and efficient utilization of resources on behalf of all the elderly.

A list of the AOA regional offices follows.

ADMINISTRATION ON AGING REGIONAL OFFICES

REGION I (Connecticut, Maine, Massachusetts, New Hampshire, Rhode Island, Vermont)
J. F. Kennedy Federal Building
Government Center
Boston, MA 02203
(617) 223-6885

REGION II (New Jersey, New York, Puerto Rico, Virgin Islands)
26 Federal Plaza
Broadway & Lafayette St.
New York City, NY 10007
(212) 264-4592

REGION III (Delaware, Maryland, Pennsylvania, Virginia, West Virginia, Washington, DC)
3535 Market St.
Philadelphia, PA 19101
(215) 596-6891

REGION IV (Alabama, Florida, Georgia, Kentucky, Mississippi, North Carolina, South Carolina, Tennessee)
50 Seventh St., NE
Atlanta, GA 30323
(404) 526-2042

REGION V (Illinois, Indiana, Michigan, Minnesota, Ohio, Wisconsin)
300 S. Wacker Drive
Chicago, IL 60606
(312) 353-4904

REGION VI (Arkansas, Louisiana, New Mexico, Oklahoma, Texas)
Fidelity Union Tower Building
1507 Pacific Ave.
Dallas, TX 75201
(214) 749-7286

REGION VII (Iowa, Kansas, Missouri, Nebraska)
601 E. 12th St.
Kansas City, MO 64106
(816) 374-2955

REGION VIII (Colorado, Montana, North Dakota, South Dakota, Utah, Wyoming)
19th & Stout Sts.
Denver, CO 80202
(303) 837-2951

REGION IX (Arizona, California, Hawaii, Nevada, Samoa, Guam, Trust Territory)
50 U.N. Plaza
San Francisco, CA 94102
(415) 556-6003

REGION X (Alaska, Idaho, Oregon, Washington)
Arcade Plaza Building
1321 Second Ave.
Seattle, WA 98101
(206) 442-5341

# 2
American Association of Retired Persons (AARP)

1909 K Street, NW, Washington, DC 20049 (202) 872-4700

The AARP is the nation's largest and most experienced organization of older persons. The NRTA is a companion organization of the AARP.

Local Chapters
For interested members, there are more than 2,400 chapters of the AARP, which work for local community welfare, and carry on programs to support the goals of the national organization, as well as educational and social programs for members. Most likely there's a chapter near you.

Legislative Role
One of AARP's most significant services is to inform members about legislative issues of special concern to older persons that are being considered by Congress and state legislatures. AARP has worked effectively in supporting increased Social Security and Medicare benefits and is working to educate legislators about the need for improved pension coverages, a national health insurance program, the elimination of mandatory retirement, and tax reform.

Publications
Modern Maturity is an illustrated, full-color bimonthly magazine written especially for AARP members. Articles on such subjects as health, food, travel, sports, books, humor, legislation, and personalities regularly appear in its issues.

The AARP News Bulletin is published monthly to report news of national developments and local AARP activities and to provide information of practical value to retired men and women.

Available on request are free guides on subjects of great importance to people in the age group of AARP members: choosing a retirement locale, financial planning, second careers, and nutrition, to name a few.

Pharmacy Service
Members may have prescriptions, vitamins, medical appliances, sickroom supplies, and health aids delivered directly to their homes, promptly, with no postage or handling charges or prepayment necessary, at realistic prices. Registered AARP pharmacies are located in St. Petersburg, Florida; Long Beach, California; Kansas City, Missouri; Hartford, Connecticut; Indianapolis, Indiana; Washington, D.C.; and Portland, Oregon. These pharmacies maintain a complete inventory of nationally known brands as well as comparable items prepared under the AARP Pharmacy Service label.

Tax-Aide Program
For help in preparing income tax returns, AARP members across the country may call upon volunteer counselors. The volunteers are trained by the Internal Revenue Service to assist in answering questions about preparing tax forms and to advise on eligibility for special tax considerations.

Consumer-Aide Program
The AARP consumer-aide program serves as a clearinghouse for information on consumer affairs; to conduct consumer-education programs; to acquaint members with basic economic principles, budgeting, price comparison, installment purchasing, and consumer frauds; and to assist members with consumer inquiries on complaints.

Institute of Lifetime Learning
With classroom programs offered at extension centers in communities around the country, the institute offers members a full educational program. It covers music appreciation, psychology, creative writing, government, literature, speech improvement, and a variety of other subjects.

Health Education Program

Called "VIM" (Vigor in Maturity), this program is devised to help members maintain their health and well-being. It consists of five sessions dealing with health, safety, disease, food, and adjustment to new life patterns. In addition, special programs and workshops are arranged upon request.

Purchase Privilege Program

Significant courtesy discounts are granted to AARP members by Sheraton, Marriott, Rodeway, Howard Johnson's, Treadway, Holiday Inns, and Days Inns. Almost all individual motel or hotel units of these chains participate in the discounts. Details are available in the special brochure for AARP members.

Auto Insurance

Recognizing the need for automobile insurance for mature drivers, AARP and a progressive insurance company created Driverplan Plus. Information about this policy, which contains guaranteed lifetime protection, is offered to all members.

Employment Service

Mature Temps is now serving older persons and members in a number of major metropolitan areas across the country. This totally free service has assisted thousands of mature persons to supplement their retirement incomes through temporary or part-time employment.

Life Insurance

Members in most states receive information about the additional life insurance protection they may need in times of rising prices and shrinking assets. AARP was influential in making it possible for mature men and women to obtain, without medical examination, life insurance issued by an established American insurance company.

Travel Service

Thousands of members enjoy the pleasures of traveling here and abroad — even around the world — on trips created by the AARP Travel Service to meet the needs and tastes of the mature traveler. There are a wide variety of quality tours and cruises ranging from luxury to economy, most of them escorted by experienced AARP Travel Service tour directors. The warm friendly atmosphere of these tours adds to the travel enjoyment of AARP members.

Health Insurance Plans

A very important service for which AARP members are eligible, is group health insurance sponsored by AARP under group policies issued by a leading insurance company. The AARP Health Insurance Plans were expressly designed to give members extra protection, whether as a supplement to Medicare or as additional security when illness or injury create financial need. They include two unusual Nursing Home and Home-Nursing Care Plans, worthwhile in-hospital protection, and valuable out-of-hospital coverage. The plans are available only to AARP members and their spouses, with the opportunity for enrollment guaranteed to all members.

NRTA/AARP Andrus Foundation

The Andrus Foundation, through the tax-deductible gifts of members, provides broad support to programs and research designed to have immediate impact on improving the quality of life for older persons.

AARP Eligibility Requirement and Fees

Persons who are 55 years of age or older, and actively employed, semiretired, or retired, are eligible to join AARP. The $3.00 annual fee includes AARP membership for both you and your spouse. A 3-year membership costs $8.00.

COMMUNITY SERVICE PROGRAMS

To assist NRTA units and AARP chapters in their community service work, the national associations have developed a series of programs. Some are in the form of courses and include complete presentation manuals and materials. Others include only resource materials and program suggestions. The following descriptions provide information about what is available from the national and regional offices and what is required of the unit and chapter. The program staff of the associations welcomes suggestions for other program concepts and is available for consultation and assistance on community-service projects initiated at the local level. Information about AARP and NRTA programs should be requested from the address included with each description. Regional office addresses are listed at the end of the chapter.

Church Relations

PURPOSE: The NRTA-AARP Church Relations Office assists religious organizations of all denominations and faiths with programs involving older persons.

METHOD: The church relations staff provides consultation and assistance to religious organizations of all denominations and faiths that sponsor programs involving older persons in activities of the congregation or community. Bulletin covers and inserts with a special message for older persons are available at no charge from the Washington office for congregations to use throughout the year and especially during May, which is designated as Older Americans Month. The church relations staff also assists NRTA units and AARP chapters that wish to sponsor voluntary programs on spiritual well-being.

PROCEDURE: For program information write to the church relations office. You might also suggest that your pastor, priest, or rabbi request samples of the bulletin covers and inserts.

ADDRESS:
NRTA-AARP Church Relations Office
1909 K Street, NW
Washington, DC 20049

Consumer Program

PURPOSE: The NRTA-AARP consumer office helps older persons prevent and resolve consumer problems.

METHOD: The National Consumer Assistance Center in the Washington office helps resolve individual consumer complaints. On the local level, the consumer staff offers program suggestions to NRTA units and AARP chapters and provides single-session programs on such consumer topics as food and money.

PROCEDURE: For information about single-session programs or consultation about local consumer programs, write to the consumer office. Individuals with consumer complaints should write to the National Consumer Assistance Center (NCAC) in the consumer office.

ADDRESS:
NRTA-AARP Consumer Office
1909 K Street, NW
Washington, DC 20049

Crime Prevention Program

PURPOSE: The crime prevention program helps members and other older persons to avoid becoming victims of crime and to reduce unnecessary fear about crimes that do not affect them.

METHOD: The program offers a course consisting of four 2-hour sessions covering street crime, burglary, fraud/bunco, and community-police relations. Any of these subjects can also be presented separately.

PROCEDURE: Appoint a program coordinator who will request a convening date from the regional office, secure a meeting place, obtain resource persons, arrange for a projector, and publicize the program. The regional office provides scripts, a guidebook, and films.

ADDRESS: For information, contact the NRTA-AARP regional office.

Driver Improvement Program

PURPOSE: To help older drivers update driving skills and prevent accidents through "defensive driving."

METHOD: A classroom course for licensed drivers, consisting of 8 hours of sessions, is taught by qualified volunteer instructors certified by the National Safety Council.

COST: For members of NRTA, AARP, and AIM, a fee of $1.00 covers the price of the student workbook.

PROCEDURE: To arrange for a course instructor to conduct the program, write to the NRTA-AARP regional office. The regional office will supply workbooks, films, and other visual aids. Members interested in becoming instructors should request information about the instructor training program from the regional office or the National Driver Improvement Office in Washington, D.C.

ADDRESS:
NRTA-AARP Driver Improvement Office
1909 K Street, NW
Washington, DC 20049

Also contact the NRTA-AARP regional office.

Health Education Program

PURPOSE: The health education program helps members and other older persons to maintain and improve their health.

METHOD: Vigor in Maturity (VIM) is a program of five 2-hour sessions on safety, personal health, chronic disease, nutrition, and adjustments in life patterns. Each session features films, printed materials, and resource persons from the local community.

COST: A 50¢ fee for each VIM participant covers program and handling costs.

METHOD: Single-session programs on arthritis and diabetes are available to chapters and units. These 1-hour sessions include films and local resource persons, and are free.

PROCEDURE: Appoint a health-education coordinator to secure a meeting place, arrange for a projector, confirm a convening date from the Washington office of NRTA-AARP, and secure local resource persons. Films, a coordinator's manual, and other program materials are sent from the Washington office.

ADDRESS:
NRTA-AARP Health Education Office
1909 K Street, NW
Washington, DC 20049

Housing Program

PURPOSE: The housing program provides members and other older persons with information and advice about housing matters.

METHOD: The housing staff provides advice and counsel to individuals about housing matters, assists AARP chapters and RTA units in developing programs on housing, and serves as liaison with other organizations and government agencies that deal with housing for the elderly.

PROCEDURE: For consultation, write to the housing office.

ADDRESS:
NRTA-AARP Housing Office
1909 K Street, NW
Washington, DC 20049

Senior Community Service Aides Project (SCSAP)

PURPOSE: SCSAP assists disadvantaged older persons with job training and placement in permanent employment.

METHOD: The program, which maintains offices in many major cities to provide employment assistance to disadvantaged older persons, is funded under contracts from the U.S. Department of Labor. Applicants are referred by local state Employment Security offices, Social Security offices, and other appropriate agencies.

PROCEDURE: For information, write to the SCSAP office in Washignton or contact a state Employment Security office.

ADDRESS:
NRTA-AARP Senior Community Service Aides Project
1909 K Street, NW
Washington, DC 20049

Widowed Persons Service Program

PURPOSE: To assist newly widowed persons in adjusting to new life patterns.

METHOD: The Widowed Persons Service staff encourages and assists volunteer groups in establishing programs in which widowed persons contact the newly widowed. The booklet, "On Being Alone — A Guide for Widowed Persons," is available free to NRTA units and AARP chapters that wish to provide it to the widowed. The booklet includes information and advice about living through bereavement, as well as about financial and legal affairs, employment, and housing.

PROCEDURE: For information about establishing a widowed persons program or to request copies of "On Being Alone," write to the Washington office.

ADDRESS:
NRTA-AARP Widowed Persons Service
1909 K Street, NW
Washington, DC 20049

Institute of Lifetime Learning

PURPOSE: To provide all older adults with opportunities for continuing education and "lifetime learning."

METHOD: The Institute of Lifetime Learning maintains program development centers in Washington, D.C., and Long Beach, California, and Extension Institutes in cities throughout the country. The institutes offer minimally priced, nongraded courses on a variety of topics. The courses are especially adapted to the needs and interests of the older adult. Consultation services are also provided for schools, colleges, and universities on request.

PROCEDURE: For information about establishing an Extension Institute, write to the Institute in Washington, D.C., or Long Beach, California. To develop an Extension Institute, NRTA units and AARP chapters should elect an Extension Institute advisory committee, a chairperson, and program coordinator. Then they should contact a national office for full instructions and assistance.

ADDRESS:
Institute of Lifetime Learning
1346 Connecticut Avenue, NW
Washington, DC 20036

or

215 Long Beach Boulevard
Long Beach, CA 90802

Tax-Aide Program *(A Program of the Institute of Lifetime Learning)*

PURPOSE: To provide volunteer counselors to assist older persons in preparing income tax forms.

METHOD: In the tax-aide program, volunteer counselors trained by the Internal Revenue Service meet individually with older persons to assist them with tax forms. Counselors do not fill in or sign tax forms, but they advise older persons of special tax considerations and credits for which they might be eligible.

PROCEDURE: Local chapters appoint a tax-aide coordinator and notify the national tax-aide coordinator at the Institute of Lifetime Learning. The local coordinator recruits volunteer counselors, establishes a training schedule with the IRS, secures a convenient counseling location, and arranges publicity for the program. The national tax-aide office works directly with local coordinators and supplies a coordinator's handbook and other materials needed for the program.

ADDRESS:
Tax-Aide Coordinator
Institute of Lifetime Learning
1346 Connecticut Avenue, NW
Washington, DC 20036

NRTA-AARP REGIONAL OFFICES

Andrus Building 215 Long Beach Blvd. Long Beach, CA 90801 (213) 432-5781 Contact: Fred H. Dewey	1346 Connecticut Ave., NW Suite 632 Washington, DC 20036 (202) 872-4820 Contact: Mary Chenoweth	6580 34th St., N. P.O. Box 14457 St. Petersburg, FL 33733 (813) 522-9461 Contact: Sally Kelling

1819 Peachtree St., NE
Suite 313
Atlanta, GA 30309
(404) 352-3232
Contact: Paul Gerlock

2720 Des Plaines Ave.
Suite 113
Des Plaines, IL 60018
(312) 298-2852
Contact: Eugene H. Molenaur

Park Square Building 434
31 St. James Ave.
Boston, MA 02116
(617) 426-1185
Contact: Myra L. Herrick

2400 Pershing Rd.
Suite 680
Kansas City, MS 64108
(816) 842-3959
Contact: Boris Steiman

555 Madison Ave., 2nd Floor
New York, NY 10022
(212) 758-1411
Contact: Martha J. Morgan

312 Noel Page Building
6400 N. Central Expressway
Dallas, TX 75206
(214) 369-9206
Contact: D. Ned Linegar

609 Kerns Building
136 S. Main St.
Salt Lake City, UT 84101
(801) 328-0691
Contact: Robert J. Utzinger

ACTION FOR INDEPENDENT MATURITY (AIM), a Division of AARP

Action for Independent Maturity offers people between the ages of 50 and 65 and still busy with a job and career, a wealth of useful information about leisure possibilities, money management, health matters, and other topics that can make their life now more enjoyable and satisfying. As a division of AARP, the nation's largest and most experienced organization of older persons, AIM also provides practical advice on how to take advantage of countless opportunities to improve the prospects for a happy, comfortable life after retirement.

AIM Publication

AIM members receive the colorful, bimonthly *Dynamic Maturity* magazine, the nation's only publication edited exclusively for persons in the 50-65 age bracket. Its articles run the gamut of preretirement living, offering tips on leisure activities...handling legal affairs...the pros and cons of various retirement locales and types of housing... how to build satisfying second careers. And, since many preretirees are involved in changing family situations, which may make the financial load lighter, *Dynamic Maturity* spotlights investment opportunities to help them plan for a secure retirement.

Guidebooks

AIM publishes a series of guidebooks offering detailed information about specific aspects of preretirement planning and other issues. These booklets are available to all AIM members upon request. "Guide to Home and Personal Security" describes how to burglar-proof your home, avoid home accidents and fires, and develop neighborhood security plans. "Guide to Dynamic Fitness" offers advice on ways to maintain maximum good health through diet, exercise, weight control, and regular medical examinations. "Guide to housing Security" provides guidance on whether to own or rent, kinds of retirement housing, desirable features to look for, climate conditions, and tax considerations. "Guide to Leisure Years" offers suggestions for second careers, volunteer activities, and hobbies, which can give added meaning to retirement years. "Guide for Widowed Persons" takes a sensitive and understanding approach to bereavement, immediate actions required, and suggestions for personal and household management.

Preretirement Services

Retirement years can be as active and interesting as you make them, but it helps to plan ahead. Retirement always brings many changes in lifestyle. AIM'S Retirement Planning Seminars, sponsored by many employers, community service organizations, and local colleges, can provide useful and practical information to help you adjust to changes more easily.

Pharmacy Service

AIM members may have prescription medicines, vitamins, medical appliances, sickroom supplies, and health aids delivered directly to their homes (postage paid) at realistic prices. A complete inventory is maintained of nationally known brands as well as comparable items prepared under AIM's Pharmacy Service label.

Group Health Insurance Plan

One of AIM's most important services is a group Health Insurance Plan, under a group policy issued by a national insurance company. The plan is designed to give members the extra protection they need. AIM Health Insurance provides benefits payable directly to them, no matter what other health insurance they may have.

Legislative Role

AIM acts as a watchdog for the interests of older citizens where issues affecting the lives of mature Americans come up before Congress and state legislatures. AARP has represented the interests of retired Americans by lobbying to increase Social Security and Medicare benefits. In a similar way, AIM is acting to improve the pension situation, through legislation that vests employees with pension credits that will accumulate even though they may change jobs. Members of AIM are kept informed of everything concerning their future.

Life Insurance

The AIM-Recommended Life Insurance can help provide members with the additional life insurance protection they need. This policy features premium reductions of 50% when members reach 65 or have been insured for 3 years, whichever is later.

Auto Insurance

Recognizing the need for automobile insurance for experienced drivers, AIM recommends Driverplan Plus, a policy with limited cancellation and guaranteed renewable features offering a broad range of coverages. This program is designed to provide mature drivers with the coverage they need, at a reasonable cost.

Purchase Privilege Plan

When traveling, AIM members can save on rates at certain motor inns and hotels, one of the privileges of AIM membership. And if members rent a car for their journey, AIM can save them money on cars rented from both Hertz and Avis.

Travel Service

AIM members can enjoy the opportunity to travel here and abroad, even around the world, through the AIM travel program. A warm, friendly atmosphere adds to the travel enjoyment of AIM members.

Eligibility Requirement and Fees

You are eligible to join AIM if you are between 50 and 65 years of age and still employed. The $3.00 annual fee includes AIM membership for both you and your spouse.

3
Area Agencies on Aging

The agencies listed in this chapter serve the elderly as the primary source of all activities in the community. They are concerned not only with government programs and activities, but they keep tabs on all private programs and services offered the elderly. You should contact these agencies for specific answers to questions on transportation, recreation, medical care, state and local programs, senior center locations, housing, financial help, legal help, educational opportunities, volunteer work, food, and so on.

ALABAMA

East Alabama Planning & Development Commission
700 Quintard Ave.
Anniston, AL 36201

Birmingham Regional Planning Commission
2112 11th Ave., S.
Birmingham, AL 35203

Jefferson County AAA
United Way — Community Chest
3600 Eighth Ave.
Birmingham, AL 35222

Alabama — Tombigbee Rivers Regional Planning & Development Commission
Clifton Street
Camden, AL 36726

North Central Alabama Area Agency
402 Lee St.
Decatur, AL 35601

Top of Alabama Regional Council of Governments
Central Bank Building
Huntsville, AL 35801

South Alabama Regional Planning Commission
International Trade Center
250 N. Water St.
Mobile, AL 36601

Central Alabama Aging Consortium
303 Washington Ave.
Montgomery, AL 36104

South Central Alabama Area Agency on Aging
2823-27 E. South Blvd.
Montgomery, AL 36111

Northwest Alabama Council of Local Governments
P.O. Box 2358
Muscle Shoals, AL 35660

West Alabama Planning & Development Council
P.O. Box 28
Tuscaloosa, AL 35401

ARIZONA

Southeastern Arizona Governments Organization
P.O. Box 204
Bisbee, AZ 85603

Northern Arizona Council of Government
P.O. Box 57
Flagstaff, AZ 86001

Pinal-Gila Council of Senior Citizens
P.O. Box 518
Florence, AZ 85232

District IV Council of Government
114 Tucker
Kingman, AZ 86401

Maricopa Community Council Co.
1515 E. Osborn Rd.
Phoenix, AZ 85014

Pima Council on Aging
100 E. Alameda
Tucson, AZ 85701

ARKANSAS

White River Area Agency on Aging
North Central Planning & Development District
P.O. Box 2396
Batesville, AR 72501

Western Arkansas Area Agency on Aging
Western Arkansas Planning & Development District
523 Garrison
Fort Smith, AR 72901

Northwest Arkansas Area Agency on Aging
Northwest Arkansas Economic Development District
P.O. Box 668
Harrison, AR 72601

West Central Area Agency on Aging
West Central Planning & Development District
2814 Malvern St.
Hot Springs, AR 71901

East Arkansas Area Agency on Aging
Eastern Planning & Development District
P.O. Box 1403
Jonesboro, AR 72401

Central Arkansas Area Agency on Aging
Central Arkansas Planning & Development District
1700 W. 13th St.
Little Rock, AR 72202

Southwest Area Agency on Aging
Southwest Planning & Development District
Municipal Building
Magnolia, AR 71753

Southeast Arkansas Area Agency on Aging
Southeast Arkansas Planning & Development District
1108 Popular
Pine Bluff, AR 71601

CALIFORNIA

Senior Information & Referral Center
P.O. Box 3583
Chico, CA 95926

Area 7 Agency on Aging
Department of Social Services
2450 Stanwell Drive
Concord, CA 94520

City of Los Angeles
Mayor's Office on Aging
200 N. Soring St.
Los Angeles, CA 90012

Los Angeles County Department of Senior Citizens Affairs
601 South Kingsley Drive
Los Angeles, CA 90005

Area Technical Agency for Aging Programs
1100 Kansas Ave.
Modesto, CA 95351

Tri County Commission for Senior Citizens
Area Agency on Aging
1270-A Coast Village Circle
Montecity, CA 93103

North Bay Senior Planning Council
920 Sherman Ave.
Novato, CA 94947

Alameda County Human Resources Agency
Human Relations Department
Office of Aging
401 Broadway
Oakland, CA 94607

San Mateo County Area Agency on Aging
704 Winston St.
Redwood City, CA 94063

Office on Aging County of Riverside
21160 Box Springs Rd.
Riverside, CA 92507

Community Service Planning Council, Inc.
1832 Tribute Rd.
Sacramento, CA 95815

Plan Action for Senior Citizens
San Bernardino County Council of Community Services
365 North E Street
San Bernardino, CA 92405

San Diego County Office of Senior Citizens Affairs
1955 Fourth Ave.
San Diego, CA 92101

Commission on Aging
City & County of San Francisco
1095 Market St.
San Francisco, CA 94103

Council on Aging of Santa Clara County, Inc.
277 W. Hedding St.
San Jose, CA 95110

Orange County Council on Aging, Inc.
801C N. Broadway
Santa Ana, CA 92701

COLORADO

Department of Aging
Adams State College
Alamosa, CO 81101

Pikes Peak Area Agency on Aging
27 E. Vermijo St.
Colorado Springs, CO 80903

Region III Office on Aging
1776 South Jackson
Denver, CO 80210

San Juan Basin Area Agency on Aging
1911 North Ave.
Durango, CO 81301

Rocky Mountain Area Agency on Aging
125 North Eighth
Grand Junction, CO 81501

Lower Arkansas Valley Area Agency on Aging
Bent County Courthouse
Las Animas, CO 81504

Larimer-Weld Area Agency on Aging
201 E. Fourth St.
Loveland, CO 80537

The District 7 and 13 Area Agency on Aging
426 W. Tenth St.
Pueblo, CO 81003

Northeastern Colorado Area Agency on Aging
P.O. Box 1782
Starling, CO 80758

East Central Council of Gerontology
Region V
Stralton, CO 80836

CONNECTICUT

Regional IV Area Agency on Aging
328 Park Ave.
Bridgeport, CT 06604

Area II Agency on Aging
999 Asylum Ave.
Hartford, CT 06105

Area III Agency on Aging
317 Main St.
Norwich, CT 06360

South Central Connecticut Agency on Aging, Inc.
4 S. Main St.
Wallingford, CT 04692

Area I Agency on Aging, Inc.
20 E. Main St.
Waterbury, CT 06702

DELAWARE

Division of Aging
Department of Health & Social Services
2413 Lancaster Ave.
Wilmington, DE 19805

WASHINGTON, D.C.

Division of Services to the Aged
Department of Human Resources
1329 E Street, NW
Washington, DC 20004

FLORIDA

Areawide Council on Aging of Broward County, Inc.
13 SW 16th St.
Fort Lauderdale, FL 33315

Gulfstream Areawide Agency on Aging
Indian River Community College
3209 Virginia Ave.
Fort Pierce, FL 33450

Northeast Florida Area Agency on Aging, Inc.
1045 Riverside Ave.
Jacksonville, FL 32204

United Way of Dade County
955 SW Second Ave.
Miami, FL 33130

Tampa Bay Regional Planning Council
3151 Third Ave., N.
St. Petersburg, FL 33713

East Central Florida Regional Planning Council
1011 Wymore Road
Winter Park, FL 32789

GEORGIA

Northeast Georgia Area Planning & Development Commission
305 Research Drive
Athens, GA 30601

Atlantic Regional Commission
100 Peachtree Street NW
Atlanta, GA 30303

Central Savannah River Area Planning & Development Commission
2123 Wrightsboro Road
Augusta, GA 30904

Coastal Georgia Area Planning & Development Commission
P.O. Box 1316
Brunswick, GA 31520

Southwest Georgia Area Planning & Development Commission
P.O. Box 346
Camillia, GA 31730

Georgia Mountains Area Planning & Development Commission
P.O. Box 1720
Gainesville, GA 30501

Coastal Plains Area Planning & Development Commission
P.O. Box 1223
Valdosta, Georgia 31601

HAWAII

Hawaii County Office of Aging
34 Rainbow Drive
Hilo, HI 96720

Honolulu Area Agency on Aging
51 Merchant St.
Honolulu, HI 96813

Kauai County Office of Elderly Affairs
P.O. Box 111
Lihue, HI 96766

Marie County Committee on Aging
200 S. High St.
Wailuku, HI 96793

ILLINOIS

East Central Illinois Agency on Aging
501 S. Sixth St.
Bloomington, IL 61701

Midland Area Agency on Aging
140 S. Locust
Centralia, IL 62801

Southern Illinois Agency on Aging
P.O. Box 556
Carbondale, IL 62901

Mayor's Office for Senior Citizens
330 South Wells St.
Chicago, IL 60606

Suburban Cook County Area on Aging
223 W. Jackson Blvd.
Chicago, IL 60606

Southwestern Illinois Area Agency on Aging
8787 State St.
East St. Louis, IL 62203

Four Rivers Area Agency on Aging
Kankakee Community College
Rural Route 1
River Road
Kankakee, IL 60901

Western Illinois Agency on Aging
1518 Fifth Ave.
Moline, IL 61265

Central Illinois Agency on Aging
234 N. Madison
Peoria, IL 61602

West Central Illinois Area Agency on Aging
Lampe Highrise
Fifth & Broadway
Quincy, IL 62301

Northwestern Illinois Area Agency on Aging
4223 E. State St.
Rockford, IL 61108

Project Life Area Agency on Aging, Inc.
325 W. Edwards
Springfield, IL 62704

INDIANA

Area 12 Agency on Aging
P.O. Box 66
Dillsboro, IN 47018

Southwest Indiana Regional Council on Aging, Inc.
528 Main
Evansville, IN 47708

Allen County Planning for Aged
Department of Human Resources
City-County Building
Fort Wayne, IN 46802

Lake County Economic Opportunity Council
5518 Calumet Ave.
Hammond, IN 46320

Central Indiana Council on Aging, Inc.
146 E. Washington St.
Indianapolis, IN 46204

Area 4 Council on Aging
533 Main St.
Lafayette, IN 47901

South Central Council for Aging and Aged, Inc.
317 E. Fifth St.
New Albany, Indiana 47150

Area 15 Agency on Aging
P.O. Box 296
Salem, IN 47157

Real Services of St. Joseph County, Inc.
521 W. Colfax Ave.
South Bend, IN 46601

West Central Indiana Economic Development District
P.O. Box 627
Terre Haute, IN 47808

Vincennes University
Box 14
Vincennes, IN 47591

IOWA

Heritage Area Agency on Aging
Kirkwood Community College
6301 Kirkwood Blvd., SW
Cedar Rapids, IA 52406

Area XIII Agency on Aging
409 First National Bank Building
Council Bluffs, IA 51501

Area XIV Agency on Aging
315 N. Elm
Creston, IA 50801

Area IX Agency on Aging
105 S. Main St.
Davenport, IA 52800

Iowa Department of Social Services
POLK County Office
Box 756
Des Moines, IA 50303

N.E. Iowa Area Agency on Aging
Dubuque Building
Dubuque, IA 52001

Northern Central Iowa Area Agency on Aging
North Iowa Area Community College
500 College Drive
Mason City, IA 50401

Area XV Agency on Aging
Indian Hills Community College
Ottumwa, IA 52501

Area IV Agency on Aging
SIMPCO
626 Insurance Exchange Building
Sioux City, IA 51102

Hawkeye Valley Area Agency on Aging
2530 University Ave.
Waterloo, IA 50704

KANSAS

South Central Kansas Area Agency on Aging
P.O. Box 1122
Arkansas City, KS 67005

Southwest Kansas Area Agency on Aging
Greater Southwest Regional Planning Commission
1802 Jones
Garden City, KS 67846

Northwest Kansas Area Agency on Aging
High Plains Comprehensive Mental Health Center
208 E. Seventh St.
Hays, KS 67601

Northeast Kansas Area Agency on Aging
200 S. Sixth St.
Hiawatha, KS 66434

Southeast Kansas Area Agency on Aging
201 S. Ninth St.
Humboldt, KS 66748

Wyandotte-Leavenworth County Area Agency on Aging
Civic Center 1
701 N. Seventh St.
Kansas City, KS 66101

Northern Central/Flint Hills Area Agency on Aging
425 Pierre
Manhattan, KS 66502

Mid-American Council on Aging
5311 Johnson Drive
Mission, KS 66205

State Services for Aging
State Office Building
Topeka, KS 66612

Central Plains Area Agency on Aging
Metropolitan Area Planning Dept.
455 N. Main
Wichita, KS 67202

KENTUCKY

Barren River Area Development
  District
P.O. Box 154
Bowling Green, KY 42101

Fivco Area Development District
P.O. Box 636
Cattlettsburg, KY 41129

Lincoln Trail Area Development
  District
305 First Federal Building
Elizabethtown, KY 42701

Northern Kentucky Area Development District
106 Eiseden Building
Tanners Lane
Florence, KY 41042

Kentucky River Area Development
  District
P.O. Box 986
Hazard, KY 41701

Pennyrile Area Development District
128 N. Main St.
Hopkinsville, KY 42240

Lake Cumberland Area Development
  District
P.O. Box 986
Jamestown, KY 48629

Bluegrass Area Development District
120 E. Reynolds Road
Lexington, KY 40503

Cumberland Valley
Moberly Building
London, KY 40741

Kentuckiana Regional Planning &
  Development Agency
505 W. Ormsby St.
Louisville, KY 40202

Purchase Area Development District
U.S. Highway 45 North
P.O. Drawer "N"
Mayfield, KY 42066

Buffalo Trace
State National Bank Building
Maysville, KY 41056

Green River Area Development District
P.O. Box 628
Owensboro, KY 42301

Gateway Area Development District
P.O. Box 107
Owingsville, KY 40360

Big Sandy Area Development District
Tourist Information Building
Prestonburg, KY 41653

LOUISIANA

Capitol Area Agency on Aging
P.O. Box 66638
Baton Rouge, LA 70806

Acadiana Area Agency on Aging
Acadiana Health Planning Council
College Inn
Rex St.
LaFayette, LA 70521

Area Agency on Aging
North Delta Regional Planning &
  Development, Inc.
2212 Justice St.
Monroe, LA 71301

Area Agency on Aging, District 1
333 St. Charles Ave.
New Orleans, LA 70130

Area Agency on Aging, District 7
Ricou-Brewster Building
425 Milam
Shreveport, LA 71101

MAINE

Central Maine Task Force on Aging
P.O. Box 484
Augusta, ME 04330

Eastern Task Force on Aging
153 Illinois Ave.
Bangor, ME 04401

Cumberland York Senior Citizens
  Council
142 High St.
Portland, ME 04101

Aroostook Regional Task Force of
  Older Citizens
457 Maine St.
Presque Isle, ME 04769

Western Maine Task Force on Aging
8 High St.
Wilton, ME 04294

MARYLAND

Baltimore City Area Agency
Waxter Center
861 Park Ave.
Baltimore, MD 21201

Central Maryland Area Agency on
  Aging
701 St. Paul St.
Baltimore, MD 21202

Division of Programs for the Elderly
9171 Central Ave.
Capitol Heights, MD 20027

Western Maryland Area Agency
Algonquin Motor Lodge
Cumberland, MD 21502

Montgomery County Area Agency
301 E. Jefferson St.
Rockville, MD 20850

MAC, Inc.
c/o Pine Bluff State Hospital
Riverside Drive – Route 1
Salisbury, MD 21801

MASSACHUSETTS

Commission of Affairs of the Elderly
One City Hall Square
Boston, MA 01520

Old Colony Elder Services Inc.
170 Main St.
Brockton, MA 02041

Bristol County Home Care for Elderly,
  Inc.
178 Pine St.
Fall River, MA 02720

Region II Area Agency on Aging, Inc.
697 Main St.
Holden, MA 01520

Holyoke-Chicopee Home Care Corp.
364-66 Maple St.
Holyoke, MA 01040

Cape-Islands Home Care Corp.
146 Main St.
Hyannis, MA 02601

Highland Valley Elder Service Center
58 Pleasant St.
Northampton, MA 01040

Berkshire County Home Care Corp.
246 North St.
Pittsfield, MA 01201

Region IV Area Agency on Aging, Inc.
P.O. Box 207
Raynham, MA 01520

Home Care Corporation of Springfield,
  Inc.
1414 State St.
Springfield, MA 01109

Franklin County Home Care Corp.
Central St.
Turners Falls, MA 01376

Region III Area Agency on Aging, Inc.
Lakeside Office Park
North Ave.
Wakefield, MA 01880

MICHIGAN

Region II Commission on Aging
3217 N. Adrian
Adrian, MI 49221

Northeast Michigan Community
  Action Agency
275 Bagley St.
Alpena, MI 49707

Southeast Area Agency on Aging
Oakland Div. – United Community
  Service
3900 W. 12-Mile Road
Berkley, MI 48072

16 THE OLDER AMERICAN'S HANDBOOK

Detroit-Wayne Area Agency on Aging
1900 David Scott Building
1150 Griswold
Detroit, MI 48226

Area Agency on Aging (Region XI)
118 N. 22nd St.
Escanaba, MI 49829

Valley Area Agency on Aging
708 Route 3
Old Sears Building
Flint, MI 48503

Region VIII Area Agency on Aging, Inc.
60 Monroe, NW
Grand Rapids, MI 49502

Tri County Office on Aging
206 E. Michigan Ave.
Lansing, MI 48933

Region XIV Council on Aging
315 Webster Ave.
Muskegon, MI 49440

South Central Michigan Commission on Aging
Nazareth College
Nazareth, MI 49074

Region VII Area Agency on Aging
971 Midland Rd.
Sadignay, MI 48603

Southwestern Michigan Regional Commission on Aging, Inc.
Peoples State Bank Building
St. Joseph, MI 49085

Northwest Michigan Planning & Development Services, Inc.
2334 Aeio Park Court
Traverse City, MI 49684

MINNESOTA

Headwaters Regional Development Commission, Headwaters Planning on Aging
P.O. Box 582
Bemidji, MN 56601

Arrowhead Regional Development Commission
200 Arrowhead Place
Duluth, MN 55802

Region IV Area Agency on Aging
West Central Regional Development Commission
Fergus Falls Community College
Fergus Falls, MN 56537

Area Agency on Aging
Region IX Regional Development Commission
709 N. Front St.
Mankat, MN 56001

Twin Cities Council Area Agency on Aging
Metro Square
Minneapolis, MN 55101

Southeastern Regional Development Commission
S. Broadway & Second St. SE
Rochester, MN 55901

Metropolitan Council's Plan for the Aging
Seventh & Robert Sts.
St. Paul, MN 55101

Area Agency on Aging
Region V Regional Development Commission
102 N. Sixth St.
Staples, MN 56479

MISSISSIPPI

Northeast PDD
Aging Division
P.O. Drawer 6D
Booneville, MS 38829

North Delta Area Agency on Aging
P.O. Box 1244
Clarksdale, MS 38614

South Delta Planning & Development District
Route 1
Greenville, MS 38701

Southern Mississippi Area Agency on Aging
1020 32nd Ave.
Gulfport, MS 39653

Central District PDD
Aging Division
2675 River Ridge Road
Jackson, MS 39216

S.W. Mississippi Area Agency on Aging
P.O. Box 429
Meadville, MS 39653

Golden Triangle PDD
Aging Division
P.O. Drawer DN
Mississippi State, MS 39762

East Central Area on Aging
Aging Division
410 Decatur St.
Newton, MS 39345

North Central PDD
Aging Division
P.O. Box 668
Winona, MS 38967

MISSOURI

Northwest Missouri Area Agency on Aging
County Court House
Albany, MO 64402

Southeast Missouri Area Agency on Aging
51 Plaza Way
Cape Girardeau, MO 63701

Mid-East Missouri Area Agency on Aging
555 S. Brentwood Blvd.
Clayton, MO 63105

Central Missouri Area Agency on Aging
909 University Ave.
Columbia, MO 65201

Mid American Regional Council
913 E. 63rd St.
Kansas City, MO 64105

Northeast Missouri Area Agency of Aging
400 N. Baltimore
P.O. Box 186
Kirksville, MO 63501

Mayor's Office for Senior Citizens
560 Delmar Blvd.
St. Louis, MO 63101

Southwest Missouri Area Agency on Aging
1824 S. Stewart St.
Springfield, MO 65804

District III Area Agency on Aging
604 N. McGuire
Warrensburg, MO 64093

MONTANA

Area V Agency on Aging
103 Main
Anaconda, MT 59711

Reservation Area Agency Seven
1500 N. 30th St.
Box 549
Billings, MT 59103

North Central Area Agency on Aging
9 Fourth Ave. SW
Concord, MT 59425

Action for Eastern Montana
Dilworth & Ames
Glendive, MT 59330

Area IV Agency on Aging
Rocky Mountain Development Council
201 S. Last Chance Gulch
Helena, MT 59601

Western Montana Agency on Aging
102-B First Ave., E.
Kalispell, MT 59901

Agency on Aging
201½ Main
Roundup, MT 59072

NEBRASKA

Blue Rivers Area Agency on Aging
Gage County Court House
Beatrice, NB 68310

Midland Area Agency on Aging
P.O. Box 905
Hastings, NB 68901

South Central Nebraska Area Agency on Aging
2022 Avenue A
Kerney, NB 68847

Lincoln-Lancaster Commission on Aging
411 S. 13th St.
Lincoln, NB 65808

AREA AGENCIES ON AGING

Eastern Nebraska Office on Aging
885 S. 72nd St.
Omaha, NB 68114

Western Nebraska Area Agency on Aging
P.O. Box 54
Scottsbluff, NB 69361

NEVADA

Department of Human Resources
Division for Aging Services
Administration Office
505 E. King St.
Capitol Complex
Carson City, NV 89710

NEW HAMPSHIRE

New Hampshire State Council on Aging
14 Depot St.
P.O. Box 786
Concord, NH 03301

NEW JERSEY

Camden County Office on Aging
129 White Horse Pike
Audubon, NJ 08106

Atlantic County Office on Aging
1607 Atlantic Ave.
Atlantic City, NJ 08401

Essex County Office on Aging
520 Belleville Ave.
Belleville, NJ 07109

Warren County Office on Aging
Court House Annex
Oxford St. and Hardwick
Belvedere, NJ 07823

Cumberland County Office on Aging
29 Fayette St.
Bridgeton, NJ 08302

Union County Office on Aging
208 Commerce Place
Elizabeth, NJ 07201

Hunterdon County Office on Aging
Community Building Flemington
Route 31 North
Flemington, NJ 08822

Monmouth County Office on Aging
10 Lafayette Place
Freehold, NJ 08302

Bergen County Office on Aging
355 Main St.
Hackensack, NJ 07601

Passaic County Office on Aging
675 Goffle Road
Hawthorne, NJ 07506

Hudson County Office on Aging
Murdock Hall
114 Clifton Place
Jersey City, NJ 07304

Morris County Office on Aging
Court House
Morristown, NJ 07960

Burlington County Office on Aging
42 Grant St.
Mount Holly, NJ 08060

Sussex County Office on Aging
16 Church St.
Newton, NJ 07860

Middlesex County Office on Aging
Middlesex County Office Annex
841 Georges Road
North Brunswick, NJ 08902

Cape May County Office on Aging
Social Services Building
Rio Grande, NJ 08242

Salem County Office on Aging
94 Market St.
Salem, NJ 08079

Somerset County Office on Aging
36 Grove St.
Somerville, NJ 08876

Ocean County Office on Aging
Court House
Toms River, NJ 08753

Mercer County Office on Aging
640 S. Broad St.
Trenton, NJ 08611

Gloucester County Office on Aging
44 Delaware St.
Woodbury, NJ 08096

NEW MEXICO

Metropolitan Areawide Aging Agency
City of Albuquerque
122 Amherst NE
Albuquerque, NM 87106

Eastern Plains Area Agency on Aging
Eastern Plains Council of Governments
Curry County Court House
Clovis, NM 88101

McKinley Area Agency on Aging
McKinley Area Council of Governments
300 W. Hill
Gallup, NM 87301

Southeastern New Mexico Area Agency on Aging
Southeastern New Mexico Economic Development District
P.O. Box 6639 RIAC
Roswell, NM 88201

North Central New Mexico Area Agency on Aging
North Central New Mexico Economic Development District
P.O. Box 4248
Sante Fe, NM 87501

Southern Rio Grande Area Agency on Aging
Southern Rio Grande Council of Governments
P.O. Box 216
Socorro, NM 87801

NEW YORK

Albany County Department for the Aging
90 State St.
Albany, NY 12207

Orleans County Office for the Aging
151 Pearl St.
Albion, NY 14411

Montgomery Countywide Office for the Aging
23 New St.
Amsterdam, NY 12010

Cayuga County Office for the Aging
160 Genesee St.
Auburn, NY 13021

Saratoga County Office for the Aging
40 Church Ave.
Ballston, NY 12020

Genesee County Office for the Aging
3837 W. Main St. Road
Batavia, NY 14020

Broome County Office for the Aging
Government Plaza
Binghampton, NY 13902

Erie County Office for the Aging
95 Franklin St.
Buffalo, NY 14202

Ontario County Office for the Aging
120 N. Main St.
Canandaigua, NY 14424

St. Lawrence County Office for the Aging
County Office Building
Canton, NY 13617

Nassau County Department of Senior Citizen Affairs
One Old County Road
Carle Place, NY 11514

Putnam County Office for the Aging
County Office Building
Carmel, NY 10512

Green County Office for the Aging
County Court House
Main St.
Catskill, NY 12412

Schoharie County Office for the Aging
One Lark St.
Cobleskill, NY 12043

Otsego County Office for the Aging
County Office Building
Cooperstown, NY 13326

Cortland County Office for the Aging
Court House
Cortland, NY 13045

Delaware County Office for the Aging
County House Square
72 Main St.
Delhi, NY 13753

Essex County Office for the Aging
Maple St.
Elizabethtown, NY 12932

Chemung County Office for the Aging
214 W. Grey St.
Elmira, NY 14901

Office of Suffolk County Executive
Senior Citizens Programs
County Center
Veterans Memorial Highway
Hauppauge, NY 11787

Herkimer County Office for the Aging
County Office Building
Mary St.
Herkimer, NY 13350

Columbia County Office for the Aging
127 Warren St.
Hudson, NY 12534

Tompkins County Office for the Aging
225 S. Fulton St.
Ithaca, NY 14850

Ulster County Office for the Aging
17 Pearl St.
Kingston, NY 12401

Warren/Hamilton Counties for the Aging
Warren County
Municipal Center
Lake George, NY 12845

Niagara County Office for the Aging
Civil Defense Building
Lockport, NY 14094

Lewis County for the Aging
Lewis County Court House
Lowville, NY 13367

Wayne County Office for the Aging
County Office Building
Lyons, NY 14489

Franklin County Office for the Aging
8 E. Main St.
Malone, NY 12953

Chautauqua County Office for the Aging
County Office Building
Mayville, NY 14757

Orange County Office for the Aging
R.D. No. 1
Route 416
Montgomery, NY 12549

Sullivan County Office for the Aging
New County Government Center
Monticello, NY 12701

New York City Department for the Aging
250 Broadway
New York, NY 10007

Chenango County Office for the Aging
6 Turner St.
Norwich, NY 13815

Cattaraugus County Office for the Aging
2245 W. State St.
Olean, NY 14760

Tioga County Office for the Aging
68 North Ave.
Owego, NY 13827

Rockland County
Office for the Aging
Health & Social Services Complex
Pamona, NY 10970

Yates County AAA
202 Main St.
Penn Yan, NY 14527

Clinton County Office for the Aging
79 Cornelia St.
Plattsburgh, NY 12901

Dutchess County Office for the Aging
236 Main St.
Poughkeepsie, NY 12601

Monroe County Office for the Aging
375 Westfall Road
Rochester, NY 14620

Schenectady County Office for the Aging
101 Nott Terrace
Schenectady, NY 12308

Department for the Aging
Staten Island Office
Ferry Terminal
Staten Island, NY 10301

Metropolitan Commission on Aging (Onondaga)
Civic Center
421 Montgomery St.
Syracuse, NY 13202

Rensselaer County Department for the Aging
8 Winter St.
Troy, NY 12180

Oneida County Office for the Aging
800 Park Ave.
Utica, NY 13501

Wyoming County Office for the Aging
76 N. Main St.
Warsaw, NY 14569

Seneca County Office for the Aging
County Court House Building
Waterloo, NY 13165

Jefferson County Office for the Aging
175 Arsenal St.
Watertown, NY 13601

Allegany County Office for the Aging
Alfred Agriculture & Technical College
Wellsville Campus
Wellsville, NY 14895

Washington County Office for the Aging
P.O. Box 56
Whitehall, NY 12887

Westchester County Office for the Aging
County Office Building
White Plains, NY 10601

NORTH DAKOTA

Aging Services
Social Services Board of North Dakota
Route No. 1
Bismarck, ND 58501

OHIO

Area Agency on Aging
P.O. Box 3377
Akron, OH 44307

Area Agency on Aging — PSA 9
127 S. Tenth St.
Cambridge, OH 43725

Stark-Wayne Area Agency on Aging
218 Cleveland Ave. SW
Canton, OH 44702

Council on Aging for the Cincinnati Area
Seventh and Vine
Cincinnati, OH 45202

Cuyahoga County Office on Aging
1276 W. Third St.
Cleveland, OH 44113

Mayors Commission on Aging
601 Lakeside Ave.
Cleveland, OH 44114

Central Ohio Area Agency on Aging
906 E. Broad St.
Columbus, OH 43204

Miami Valley Council on Aging
184 Salem Ave.
Dayton, OH 45406

Agency on Aging, Inc. — PSA 3
205 W. Market St.
First Lima Building
Lima, OH 45801

District Five Area Agency on Aging
50 Blymer Ave.
Mansfield, OH 44903

Buckeye Hills — Hocking Valley Regional Development
Dime Bank Building
Marietta, OH 45750

Rio Grande Areawide Project on Aging
Rio Grande College
Rio Grande, OH 45674

Area Agency on Aging
Community Planning Council of N.W. Ohio
One Stranahan Square
Toledo, OH 43604

District 11 Area Agency
976 W. Federal St.
Youngstown, OH 44510

OKLAHOMA

Southern Oklahoma Development Association
Area Agency on Aging
Industrial Park
Ardmore, OK 73401

Eastern Oklahoma Unit on Aging
Eastern Oklahoma Development
   District
P.O. Box 1367
Muskogee, OK 74401

Areawide Aging Agency, Inc.
125 NW Fifth St.
Oklahoma City, OK 73102

Tulsa Area Agency on Aging
200 Civic Center
Tulsa, OK 74103

KEDDO Area Agency on Aging
Vo-Tech Administration
Highway No. 2 — North of Wilburton
Wilburton, OK 74578

PENNSYLVANIA

Lehigh County Area Agency on Aging
523 Hamilton St.
Allentown, PA 18101

Blair County Offices of Services for
   the Aging
1512 13th Ave.
Altoona, PA 16601

Beaver/Butler Area Agency on Aging
841 Corporation St.
Beaver, PA 15009

Bedford/Fulton/Huntington Area
   Agency on Aging, Inc.
P.O. Box 46
Bedford, PA 15522

Centre County Area Agency on Aging
Centre Community Hospital
Willow Bank Unit
Bellafonte, PA 16823

Columbia-Montour Area Agency on
   Aging
587 E. Fifth St.
Bloomsburg, PA 17815

Cumberland County Office on Aging
35 East High St.
Carlisle, PA 17013

Franklin County Office for the Aging
Franklin Farm Lane
Chambersburg, PA 17201

Clearfield County Office of Aging
P.O. Box 627
Clearfield, PA 16830

Bucks County Adult Services
Neshaminy Manor Center
Doylestown, PA 18901

Northampton County Area Agency on
   Aging
15 N. Second St.
Easton, PA 18042

Cambria County Area Agency on Aging
Cambria County Court House
Ebensburg, PA 15931

Greater Erie Community Action
   Committee
2911 State St.
Erie, PA 16508

Venango Human Services Center
P.O. Box 231
Franklin, PA 16323

Adams County Area Agency on Aging
110 York St.
Gettysburg, PA 17325

Westmoreland County Office of Aging
524 E. Pittsburgh St.
Greensburg, PA 15601

Dauphin County Area Agency on Aging
128 Walnut St.
Harrisburg, PA 17101

Pike, Monroe & Wayne Area Agency
   on Aging
314 Tenth St.
Honesdale, PA 18431

Armstrong/Indiana Area Agency on
   Aging
Human Services Management Dept.
826 Philadelphia St.
Indiana, PA 15701

Carbon County Area Agency on Aging
P.O. Box 251
Jim Thorpe, PA 18229

Armstrong County Area on Aging
280 S. McKean St.
Kittanniny, PA 16201

Lancaster County Office for the Aging
50 S. Duke St.
Lancaster, PA 17602

Lebanon County Office for Aging
County Municipal Building
Lebanon, PA 17042

Mifflin-Juniata Area Agency on Aging
Buena Vista Circle
Lewiston, PA 17044

Lycoming-Clinton Bi-County Office
   on Aging
P.O. Box 770
Lock Haven, PA 17745

Crawford County Office of Aging
903 Chancery Lane
Meadville, PA 16335

Delaware County Services for the
   Aging
P.O. Box 166
Media, PA 19063

Mercer County Office for Aging
Court House
Mercer, PA 16137

Union/Snyder County Office of Aging
P.O. Box 245
Middleburg, PA 17842

Mon Valley H & W Council, Inc.
Mon Valley Community Health Center
Eastgate 8
Monessen, PA 15062

Perry County Office for Aging
North Carlisle St.
New Bloomfield, PA 17068

Catholic Social Services of Lawrence
   County
23 E. North St.
New Castle, PA 16101

Office on Older Adults
Court House
Norristown, PA 19401

Philadelphia Corporation for Aging
1317 Filbert St.
Philadelphia, PA 19107

Alleghany County Area on Aging
429 Forbes Ave.
Pittsburgh, PA 15219

Schuylkill County Area Agency on
   Aging
County Court House
Pottsville, PA 17901

Jefferson/Clarion Economic Oppor-
   tunity Association
P.O. Box 242
Punxsutawney, PA 15767

Berks County
Area Agency on Aging
756 Penn St.
Reading, PA 19602

North Central Pennsylvania Office of
   Human Services
208 Main St.
Ridgway, PA 15853

Lackawanna County Area Agency on
   Aging
200 Adams St.
Scranton, PA 18503

Northumberland County Area Agency
   on Aging
235 W. Spruce St.
Shamokin, PA 17872

Somerset County Offices for the Aging
147 E. Union St.
Somerset, PA 15501

Northern Tier Regional Planning &
   Development Commission
507 Main St.
Towanda, PA 18848

Experience, Inc.
900 Fourth Ave.
Warren, PA 16365

Chester County Services for Senior
   Citizens
14 E. Biddle St.
West Chester, PA 19380

United Service Agency
85 E. Union St.
Wilkes-Barre, PA 18701

York County Area Agency on Aging
125 E. Market St.
York, PA 17401

RHODE ISLAND

Rhode Island Division on Aging
150 Washington St.
Providence, RI 02903

SOUTH CAROLINA

Lower Savannah Areawide Services
  Planning for the Aging
Highway 215
Aiken, SC 29801

Trident Area Program for Aging
1069 King St.
Charleston, SC 29403

Pee Dee Regional Planning &
  Development Program
P.O. Box 5719
Florence, SC 29501

Appalachian Action Plan for Aging
211 Century Drive
Greenville, SC 29606

Upper Savannah Regional Aging
  Program
Textile Building
Greenwood, SC 29646

Catawba Regional Aging Program
107 Hampton St.
Rock Hill, SC 29730

SOUTH DAKOTA

Office on Aging Department of
  Social Services
State Office Building
Illinois St.
Pierre, SD 57501

TENNESSEE

Southeast Tennessee Development
  District
735 Broad St.
Chattanooga, TN 37402

South Central Tennessee Development
  District
805 Nashville Highway
Columbia, TN 38237

Upper Cumberland Development
  District
700 Burgess Falls Road
Cookeville, TN 38501

Southwest Tennessee Development
  District
P.O. Box 2385
Jackson, TN 38301

First Tennessee-Virginia Development
  District
207 N. Boone
Johnson City, TN 37601

East Tennessee Development District
1810 Lake Ave.
Knoxville, TN 37916

Northwest Tennessee Development
  District
P.O. Box 63
Martin, TN 38237

Memphis-Delta Development District
First Presbyterian Church
166-A Poplar
Memphis, TN 38105

Mid-Cumberland Development District
501 Union Building
Fifth Ave. & Union St.
Nashville, TN 37219

TEXAS

West Central Texas Area Agency on
  Aging
West Central Texas Council of
  Governments
3349 N. 12th St.
Abilene, TX 79604

North Central Texas Area Agency on
  Aging
North Central Texas Council of
  Governments
P.O. Drawer COG
Arlington, TX 76011

Capital Area Agency on Aging
Capital Area Planning Council
611 S. Congress
Austin, TX 78704

Brazos Valley Area Agency on Aging
Brazos Valley Development Council
3006 E. 29th St.
Bryan, TX 77801

Coastal Bend Area Agency on Aging
Coastal Bend Council of Government
P.O. Box 6609
Corpus Christi, TX 78411

Dallas Area Agency on Aging
Community Council of Greater Dallas
212 N. St. Paul
Dallas, TX 75201

El Paso Area Agency on Aging
West Texas Council of Governments
1200 N. Mesa
El Paso, TX 79902

Fort Worth Area Agency on Aging
Planning & Research Council
210 E. Ninth St.
Fort Worth, TX 76102

Houston-Galveston Area Agency on
  Aging
Houston-Galveston Area Council
P.O. Box 22777
Houston, TX 77027

Deep East Texas Area Agency on Aging
Deep East Texas Council of
  Governments
272 E. Lamar St.
Jasper, TX 75951

East Texas Area Agency on Aging
East Texas Council of Governments
Citizens Bank Building
Kilgore, TX 75662

South Texas Area Agency on Aging
South Texas Development Council
1104 Victoria
Laredo, TX 78040

Lower Rio Grande Valley Area
  Agency on Aging
Lower Rio Grande Valley Development
  Council
First National Bank Building
McAllen, TX 78501

South East Texas Area Agency on
  Aging
South East Texas Regional Planning
  Commission
P.O. Drawer 1387
Nederland, TX 77627

San Antonio Area Agency on Aging
Alamo Area Council of Governments
Three Americans Building
San Antonio, TX 78205

Ark-Tex Area Agency on Aging
Ark-Tex Council of Governments
P.O. Box 5307
Texarkana, TX 75501

Area Agency on Aging
Golden Crescent Council of
  Governments
P.O. Box 2028
Victoria, TX 77901

Heart of Texas Area Agency on Aging
Heart of Texas Council of Governments
110 S. 12th St.
Waco, TX 76701

UTAH

Box Elder County Area Agency on
  Aging
Box Elder County Court House
Brigham City, UT 84302

Emery County Area Agency on Aging
P.O. Box 484
Castle Dale, UT 84513

Five-County Multi-Association of
  Governments
P.O. Box 309
Cedar City, UT 84720

Davis County Area Agency on Aging
Davis County Court House
Farmington, UT 84025

Area Agency on Aging
P.O. Box 67
Fort Duchesne, UT 84026

District IV
Courthouse
Junction, UT 84740

Cache County Area Agency on Aging
236 N. First, E.
Logan, UT 84321

Weber County Area Agency on Aging
350 Healy st.
Ogden, UT 84401

Carbon County Area Agency on Aging
30 E. Second, S.
Price, UT 84501

Utah County Council on Aging
Utah County Area Agency on Aging
455 N. University Ave.
Provo, UT 84601

VERMONT

Central Vermont Area Agency on Aging
289 N. Main St.
Barre, VT 05641

East Central Area Agency on Aging
Box 327-A
Bradford, VT 05033

Southeastern Vermont Area Agency on Aging
139 Main St.
Brattleboro, VT 05301

Bennington Area on Aging
Box 364
North Bennington, VT 05257

Rutland Area on Aging
41 Washington St.
Rutland, VT 05701

Area Agency on Aging for Northeastern Vermont
Main St.
St. Johnsbury, VT 05819

Champlain Valley AAA
100 Dorset St.
South Burlington, VT 05401

VIRGINIA

Eastern Shore Community Development Group, Inc.
P.O. Box 316
Accomac, VA 23301

Piedmont Senior Resources
Area Agency on Aging
P.O. Box 55
Burkeville, VA 23922

Jefferson Area Board for Aging
c/o Thomas Jefferson Planning District Commission
701 E. High St.
Charlottesville, VA 22901

Rappahannock-Ratidan Community Mental Health & Mental Retardation Services Board
138 S. Main St.
Culpeper, VA 22701

Northern Virginia Area Agency on Aging
7309 Arlington Blvd.
Falls Church, VA 22042

Piedmont Area Community Mental Health & Mental Retardation Services Board
c/o Piedmont Planning District Commission
205 N. Virginia St.
Farmville, VA 23901

Shenandoah Area Agency on Aging, Inc.
28 N. Royal Ave.
Front Royal, VA 22630

Southside Gerontology Assn., Inc.
228 Main St.
Lawrenceville, VA 23868

Central Virginia Commission on Aging
1010 Miller Park Square
Lynchburg, VA 24501

Mount Rogers Governmental Cooperative
c/o Mount Rogers Planning District Commission
1021 Terrace Drive
Marion, VA 24354

Peninsula Area Agency on Aging
Patrick Henry Hospital
Denbigh Blvd.
Newport News, VA 23602

SEVAMO for Seniors
No. 9 Koger Executive Center
Norfolk, VA 23502

Mountain Empire Older Citizens
c/o Dilenowisco Education Cooperative
1032 Virginia Ave.
Norton, VA 24273

Crater District Senior's Agency
c/o Crater Planning District Commission
2825 S. Crater Road
Petersburg, VA 23803

New River Valley
Council on Aging
143 Third St., NW
Pulaski, VA 24301

Appalachian Agency for Senior Citizens
Box SVCC
Richlands, VA 24621

Capital Area Agency on Aging
6 N. Sixth St.
Richmond, VA 23219

League of Older Americans, Inc.
401 Campbell Ave. SW
Roanoke, VA 24016

Area Agency on Aging
Rappahannock Community College
North Campus
Warsaw, VA 22572

Valley Program for Aging Services, Inc.
P.O. Box 817
Waynesboro, VA 22980

WEST VIRGINIA

Southern West Virginia Area Agency on Aging
Concord College
Athens, WV 24712

Region VII Planning & Development Council
Upshur County Courthouse
Buckhannon, WV 26101

Regional Intergovernmental Council
410 Kanawha Blvd. E.
Charleston, WV 25301

Region VI Planning & Development Council
201 Deveny Building
Fairmont, WV 26554

Region IX Planning & Development Council
121 W. King St.
Martinsburg, WV 25401

Mid Ohio Valley Regional Council
217 Fourth St.
Parkersburg, WV 26101

Region VIII Planning & Development Council
One Virginia Ave.
Petersburg, WV 26847

Brooke-Hancock Region XI Planning & Development Council
3550 Main St.
Weirton, WV 26062

Bel-O-Mar Interstate Planning Commission
2177 National Road
Wheeling, WV 26003

WISCONSIN

Area Agency on Aging District III
Lake Winnebago
314 W. Wisconsin Ave.
Appleton, WI 54911

Comprehensive Planning for the Elderly (District IV)
220 South Clay St.
DePere, WI 54115

West Central Wisconsin District VI Comprehensive Planning
1810 Hoover Ave.
Eau Claire, WI 54843

Area Agency District IV Lake Michigan
1221 Bellevires
Green Bay, WI 54301

District VIII Area Agency on Aging
Box 526
Hayward, WI 54843

District V Area Agency on Aging
c/o La Crosse County Court House
La Crosse, WI 54601

District I Area Agency on Aging
1245 E. Washington Ave.
Madison, WI 53703

Area Agency on Aging District VII
Lincoln County Court House
Merrill, WI 54452

Milwaukee County Office on Aging
901 N. Ninth St.
Milwaukee, WI 53233

Southeastern Wisconsin Area Agency on Aging, Inc.
District 2-B
500 Riverview Ave.
Waukesha, WI 53186

WYOMING

Wyoming Eastern Area Agency on Aging
866 Cy Ave.
Casper, WY 82601

Wyoming Western Area Agency on Aging
609 E. Madison
Riverton, WY 82501

4
Associations and Organizations

In addition to being excellent sources of information, associations and organizations can provide guidance, literature, films, equipment, and, in some cases, even financial assistance.

If you need help, read over the list of associations and organizations that follows and select the one that seems to concentrate, either specifically or indirectly, in the area that interests you. If you're not sure which organization you need, a phone call to almost any one of them will put you on the right path.

Action
800 Connecticut Ave.
Washington, DC 20525
(202) 254-6886
Contact: Michael P. Balzano

Action for Independent Maturity
1909 K St., NW
Washington, DC 20006
(202) 872-4700
Contact: Cliff Fichtner

Administration on Aging
Dept. of Health, Education & Welfare
Washington, DC 20201
(202) 245-0213
Contact: Arthur S. Flemming

Adult Education Association of the U.S.A.
810 18th St., NW
Washington, DC 20006
(202) 347-9574
Contact: Charles Wood

Altrusa International, Inc.
332 S. Michigan Ave.
Chicago, IL 60604
(312) 341-0818
Contact: Dorothy Kuelhorn

Amalgamated Clothing Workers of America
15 Union Square
New York, NY 10003
(212) 255-7800
Contact: Joyce Miller

American Association of Emeriti
P.O. Box 24451
Los Angeles, CA 90024
(213) 825-1621
Contact: Albert Gordon

American Association of Homes for the Aging
1050 17th St., NW
Washington, DC 20036
(202) 347-2000
Contact: Constance Beaumont

American Association of Retired Persons
1909 K St., NW
Washington, DC 20049
(202) 872-4700
Contact: Harriet Miller

American Association of University Women
2401 Virginia Ave., NW
Washington, DC 20037
(202) 785-7700
Contact: Mary-Averett Seelye

American Association of Workers for the Blind, Inc.
1511 K St., NW
Washington, DC 20005
(202) 347-1559
Contact: Bruce Blasch

American Baptist Board of National Ministries
Valley Forge, PA 19481
(215) 768-2284
Contact: Lois Blankenship

American Baptist Women
Valley Forge, PA 19481
(215) 768-2284
Contact: Laura Hughes

American Bar Association
1155 E. 60th St.
Chicago, IL 60637
(312) 493-0533
Contact: L. E. Walsh

American Bar Foundation
1155 E. 60th St.
Chicago, IL 60637
(312) 667-4700
Contact: Spencer L. Kimball

American Cancer Society, Inc.
777 Third Ave.
New York, NY 10017
(212) 371-2900
Contact: Douglas Bethione

American College of Nursing Home Administrators
8641 Colesville Rd.
Silver Springs, MD 20910
(301) 652-8384
Contact: J. Albin Yokie

American Dental Association
211 E. Chicago Ave.
Chicago, IL 60611
(312) 944-6730
Contact: C. Gordon Watson

American Dietetic Association
430 N. Michigan Ave.
Chicago, IL 60611
(312) 822-0330
Contact: Isabelle Hallahan, R.D.

ASSOCIATIONS AND ORGANIZATIONS

American Federation of Labor and Congress of Industrial Organizations
815 16th St., NW
Washington, DC 20006
(202) 637-5000
Contact: John McManus

American Federation of Teachers
11 DuPont Plaza
Washington, DC 20036
(202) 797-4400
Contact: Carl Megel

American Foundation for the Blind, Inc.
15 W. 16th St.
New York, NY 10011
(212) 924-0420
Contact: Dorothy Demby

American Freedom from Hunger Foundation, Inc.
1625 Eye St., NW
Washington, DC 20006
(202) 254-3487
Contact: Gerald Connally

American Geriatrics Society, Inc.
10 Columbus Circle
New York, NY 10019
(212) 582-1333
Contact: Dr. William Reichel

American Heart Association
44 E. 23rd St.
New York, NY 10010
(212) 533-1100
Contact: William W. Moore

American Health Care Association
1200 15th St., NW
Washington, DC 20005
(202) 833-2050
Contact: Annette Brown

American Home Economics Association
2010 Massachusetts Ave., NW
Washington, DC 20036
(202) 833-3100
Contact: Irene H. Wolgamot

American Hospital Association
840 N. Lake Shore Drive
Chicago, IL 60611
(312) 645-9400
Contact: Meryl S. Dann

American Institute of Architects
1735 New York Ave., NW
Washington, DC 20006
(202) 638-3105
Contact: Jessie Weinstein

American Library Association
50 E. Huron St.,
Chicago, IL
(312) 944-6780
Contact: Emily Reed

American Medical Association
535 N. Dearborn St.
Chicago, IL 60610
(312) 751-6013
Contact: Herman W. Gruber

American Medical Association Auxiliary, Inc.
535 N. Dearborn St.
Chicago, IL 60610
(312) 751-6013
Contact: Muriel Bergnes

American Medical Women's Association, Inc.
1740 Broadway
New York, NY 10019
(212) 586-8683
Contact: Dr. Elizabeth Kahler

American Mental Health Foundation
2 E. 86th St.
New York, NY 10028
(212) 737-9027
Contact: Harvey J. Ross

American Mothers Committee, Inc.
The Waldorf-Astoria
301 Park Ave
New York, NY 10022
(212) 765-2755
Contact: Dorothy Lewis

American National Red Cross
17th & D Streets, NW
Washington, DC 20006
(202) 737-8300
Contact: Mrs. John W. Brynes

American Nurse's Association, Inc.
2420 Pershing Road
Kansas City, MO 64108
(816) 474-5720
Contact: Erika Bunke

American Occupational Therapy Association, Inc.
6000 Executive Boulevard
Rockville, MD 20852
(301) 770-2200
Contact: James J. Garibaldi

American Optometric Association
7000 Chippewa St.
St. Louis, MO 63119
(314) 832-5770
Contact: Dr. Hoyt Purvis

American Osteopathic Association
212 E. Ohio St.
Chicago, IL 60611
(312) 944-2713
Contact: Dr. F. L. Reed

American Podiatry Association
20 Chevy Chase Circle, NW
Washington, DC 20015
(202) 362-2700
Contact: John Couric

American Protestant Hospital Association
840 N. Lake Shore Drive
Chicago, IL 60611
(312) 944-2814
Contact: Martha Bennett

American Public Welfare Association
1155 16 St., NW
Washington, DC 20036
(202) 833-9350
Contact: David Racine

American Society for Geriatric Dentistry
431 Oaksdale Ave.
Chicago, IL 60657
(312) 477-2729
Contact: Arthur Elfenbaum

American Society for Personnel Administration
19 Church St.
Berea, OH 44017
(216) 234-2500
Contact: L. R. Brice

American Society of Internal Medicine
525 The Hearst Building
Third at Market
San Francisco, CA 94103
(415) 777-1000
Contact: Dr. David H. Feinburg

American Speech and Hearing Association
9030 Old Georgetown Road, NW
Washington, DC 20014
(301) 530-3400
Contact: Dr. Norman Barnes

Arrow, Inc.
1000 Connecticut Ave., NW
Suite 501
Washington, DC 20036
(202) 296-0685
Contact: E. Thomas Colosimo

Arthritis Foundation
221 Park Ave. South
New York, NY 10003
(212) 757-7600
Contact: Daniel E. Button

Association of Jewish Center Workers
15 East 26th St.
New York, NY 10010
(212) 532-4949
Contact: Ed Rosin

Association of Junior Leagues, Inc.
825 Third Ave.
New York, NY 10022
(212) 355-4380
Contact: Virginia V. De Margitay

Association of State & Territorial Health Officials
1555 Connecticut Ave.
Washington, DC 20002
(202) 265-4350
Contact: Maurice S. Reizen, M.D.

Black Caucus of Health Workers
c/o School of Business & Public Administration,
Howard University
Washington, DC 20059
(202) 638-4477
Contact: Ruth Adams

B'Nai B'Rith
1640 Rhode Island Ave. NW
Washington, DC 20036
(202) 393-5284
Contact: Dorothy Glazer

B'Nai B'Rith Women
1640 Rhode Island Ave., NW
Washington, DC 20036
(202) 393-5284
Contact: Amy Lynn

Boston Society of Gerontological Psychiatry, Inc.
International Universities Press, Inc.
315 Fifth Ave.
New York, NY 10003
(212) 684-7900
Contact: Martin Azarian

Catholic Daughters of America
10 W. 71st St.
New York, NY 10023
(212) 877-3041
Contact: Mae Burns

Catholic Hospital Association
1438 S. Grand Blvd.
St. Louis, MO 63104
(314) 773-0646
Contact: Sr. Mary Marita Sengelaub

Central Bureau for the Jewish Aged
225 Park Ave. South
New York, NY 10009
(212) 677-2100
Contact: John Karpeles

Central Conference of American Rabbis
790 Madison Ave.
New York, NY 10021
(212) 249-2811
Contact: Rabbi Albert Lewis

Christian Church Department of Church in Society
222 S. Downey Ave.
Indianapolis, IN
(317) 353-1491
Contact: Loisanne Buchanan

Christian Church (Disciples of Christ)
The National Benevolent Association
115 N. Jefferson
St. Louis, MO 63103
(314) 531-1470
Contact: Donald F. Clingan

Christian Reformed Church
3636 Stilesgate Court, SE
Grand Rapids, MI 49508
(616) 241-1691
Contact: Jack W. Stoepker

Church Women United
475 Riverside Drive
New York, NY 10027
(212) 870-2347
Contact: Sr. Mary Luke Tobin

Cooperative League of the U.S.A.
59 E. Van Buren St.
Chicago, IL 60605
(312) 872-0550
Contact: Eugene R. Clifford

Council of Jewish Federations & Welfare Funds, Inc.
315 Park Ave. South
New York, NY 10010
(212) 673-8200
Contact: Sophie B. Engel

CUNA International, Inc.
1617 Sherman Ave.
Madison, WI 53701
(608) 241-1211
Contact: DeMelt E. Walker

Daughters of Isabella
375 Whitney Ave.
New Haven, CT 06514
(203) 865-2570
Contact: Marie Heyer

Division of Vocational & Technical Education
Bureau of Adult, Vocational & Library Programs
Office of Education
Seventh & D Sts., SW
Washington, DC 20202
(202) 245-5740
Contact: Terrel H. Bell

Elder Craftsmen, Inc.
850 Lexington Ave.
New York, NY 10021
(212) LE5-8030
Contact: Samuel L. Kuhn

Euthanasia Educational Council
250 W. 57th St.
New York, NY 10017
(212) 246-6962
Contact: Mrs. A. J. Levinson

Evangelical Covenant Church of America, Board of Benevolence
5245 N. California Ave.
Chicago, IL 60625
(312) 561-9424
Contact: Nils Axelson

Evangelical Lutheran Good Samaritan Society
1000 West Ave., N.
Sioux Falls, SD 57104
(605) 336-2998
Contact: Ed Kilen

Family Service Association of America
44 E. 23 St.
New York, NY 10010
(212) 674-6100
Contact: W. Keith Daugherty

Fraternal Order of Eagles
3030 Sullivant Ave.
Columbus, OH 43201
(614) 274-1194
Contact: Philip Bigles

Future Homemakers of America
2010 Massachusetts Ave., NW
Washington, DC 20036
(202) 833-1925
Contact: Louisa Liddell

General Federation of Women's Clubs
1734 N St., NW
Washington, DC 20036
(202) 347-3168
Contact: Mrs. Carroll E. Miller

Gerontological Society
One DuPont Circle
Washington, DC 20036
(202) 659-4698
Contact: Edwin Kaskowitz

Girl Scouts of the United States of America
830 Third Ave.
New York, NY 10032
(212) 751-6900
Contact: Sara Ann Bermont

Golden Ring Council of Senior Citizens Clubs
22 W. 38th St.
New York, NY 10018
(212) 947-2019
Contact: Zalman J. Lichtenstein

Grand Circle Travel, Inc.
555 Madison Ave.
New York, NY 10022
(212) 688-5900
Contact: Eilene Pie

Greek Orthodox Archdiocese of North and South America
Ladies Philoptochos Society
10 E. 79th St.
New York, NY 10021
(212) 288-6820
Contact: Stella Coumantaros

Green Thumb, Inc.,
1012 14th St., NW
Washington, DC 20005
(202) 628-9774
Contact: Barbra Hall

Health Insurance Association of America
1701 K St., NW
Washington, DC 20006
(202) 331-1336
Contact: Donald D. Jones

Information Office, U.S. Administration on Aging
Department of Health, Education & Welfare
Washington, DC 20201
(202) 245-0727
Contact: Donald F. Reilly

Institute of Industrial Gerontology
c/o National Council on Aging
1828 L St., NW
Washington, DC 20036
(202) 223-6250
Contact: Albert J. Abrams

Institute of Life Insurance
277 Park Ave.
New York, NY 10017
(212) 922-3000
Contact: Joseph M. McCarthy

Intermedic
777 Third Ave.
New York, NY 10017
(212) 486-8974
Contact: Stanley Bell

ASSOCIATIONS AND ORGANIZATIONS

International Brotherhood of
  Electrical Workers
1125 15th St., NW
Washington, DC 20005
(202) 833-7000
Contact: H. G. Tate

International Executive Service Corps.
545 Madison Ave.
New York, NY 10011
(212) 490-6800
Contact: William L. Finger

International Federation of Aging
1909 K St., NW
Washington, DC 20006
(202) 872-4700
Contact: Harriet Miller

International Senior Citizens Assn., Inc.
11753 Wilshire Blvd.
Los Angeles, CA 90025
(213) 472-4704
Contact: Ruth Smith

Kiwanis International
101 E. Erie St.,
Chicago, IL 60611
(312) 943-2300
Contact: A. G. Terry Shaffer

Leadership Conference of Women
  Religious
1325 Massachusetts Ave., NW
Washington, DC 20005
(202) 737-5733
Contact: Sr. Rosemary Strain

League of United Latin American
  Citizens
2218 S. Birch St.
Santa Ana, California 92707
(714) 545-2816
Contact: Julia S. Zozoya

Legislative Council for Older
  Americans, Inc.
110 Arlington St.
Boston, MA 02116
(617) 426-0804
Contact: Frank J. Manning

Library of Congress
Division for the Blind and Physically
  Handicapped
Washington, DC 20540
(202) 426-5000
Contact: John G. Lorenz

Little Sisters of the Poor
601 Maiden Choice Lane
Baltimore, MD 21228
(617) 744-9367
Contact: Mother James

Loyal Order of Moose
Mooseheart, IL 60539
(312) 859-2000
Contact: Earle W. Horton

Lutheran Church in America
231 Madison Ave.
New York, NY 10016
(212) 481-9600
Contact: Dr. Cedric W. Tilberg

Lutheran Church — Missouri Synod
500 N. Broadway
St. Louis, MO 63102
(314) 231-6969
Contact: Rev. Eugene Gunther

Lutheran Resources Commission
1346 Connecticut Ave., NW
Washington, DC 20036
(202) 872-0110
Contact: Dr. Henry Endress

Mature Temps
Exxon Building
1251 Ave. of the Americas
New York, NY 10020
(212) 730-7020
Contact: Richard Ross

Mennonite Board of Missions
1711 Prairie St.,
Elkhart, IN 46514
(219) 294-7523
Contact: Luke Birky

National Alliance for Senior Citizens,
  Inc.
P.O. Box 40031
Washington, DC 20036
(202) 338-5632
Contact: Director

National Assembly of National
  Voluntary Health & Social
  Welfare Organizations, Inc.
345 E. 46 St.
New York, NY 10017
(212) 490-2900
Contact: Hobart A. Burch

National Association for Hearing &
  Speech Action
814 Thayer Ave.
Silver Spring, MD 20901
(301) 588-5242
Contact: Betsy G. Cunningham

National Association for Mental Health
1800 N. Kent St.
Arlington, VA 22209
(703) 528-6405
Contact: Brian O'Connell

National Association for Practical
  Nurse Education and Service, Inc.
122 E. 42nd St.
New York, NY 10017
(212) 682-3400
Contact: Lucille Etheridge

National Association for Public
  Continuing & Adult Education
1201 16th St., NW
Washington, DC 20036
(202) 833-5486
Contact: Dr. Monroe C. Neff

National Association for Statewide
  Health & Welfare
22 W. Gay St.
Columbus, OH 43218
(614) 221-4469
Contact: Theresa MacMillan

National Association of Building
  Manufacturers
1619 Massachusetts Ave., NW
Washington, DC 20036
(202) 234-1374
Contact: Don L. Gilchrist

National Association of Counties
1735 New York Ave., NW
Washington, DC 20006
(202) 785-9577
Contact: Mary Brugger Murphy

National Association of Investment
  Clubs
Box 22
Royal Oak, MI 48068
(313) 543-0612
Contact: Thomas E. O'Hara

National Association of Jewish Homes
  for the Aged
2525 Centerville Road
Dallas, Texas 75228
(214) 327-4503
Contact: Dr. Herbert Shore

National Association of Life
  Underwriters
1922 F St., NW
Washington, DC 20006
(202) ME8-3122
Contact: Marvin A. Kobel

National Association of Mutual
  Savings Banks
200 Park Ave.
New York, NY 10017
(212) 973-5432
Contact: Grover W. Ensley

National Association of Negro Business
  and Professional Women's Clubs,
  Inc.
2225 Lloyd Ave.
Pittsburgh, PA 15218
(301) 466-6675
Contact: Ruth Tucker

National Association of Retired
  Federal Employees
1533 New Hampshire Ave., NW
Washington, DC 20036
(202) 234-0832
Contact: John E. Worden

National Association of Retired
  Teachers
(see American Association of Retired
  Persons)

National Association of Social Workers
1425 H St., NW
Washington, DC 20035
(202) 628-6800
Contact: R. Cohen

National Association of State Units
  on Aging
West Virginia Commission on Aging
State Capitol
Charleston, WV 25305
(304) 348-3317
Contact: Dr. Louise Gerrard

The National Caucus on the Black Aged, Inc.
1730 M St., NW
Suite 811
Washington, DC 20036
(202) 785-8766
Contact: Director

National Center for Voluntary Action
1785 Massachusetts Ave., NW
Washington, DC 20036
(202) 797-7800
Contact: Maureen S. Aspin

National Clearing House on Aging
Dept. of Health, Education and Welfare
400 Sixth St., SW
Washington, DC 20201
(202) 245-0724
Contact: Director

National Climatic Center
Federal Building
Asheville, NC 28801
(704) 258-2850
Contact: Daniel Mitchell

National Conference of Catholic Charities
1346 Connecticut Ave., NW
Washington, DC 20036
(202) 785-2757
Contact: Brother Joseph Berg

National Council for Homemaker Home Health Aide Services, Inc.
67 Irving Place
New York, NY 10003
(212) 674-4990
Contact: Director

National Council of Catholic Women
1312 Massachusetts Ave., NW
Washington, DC 20005
(202) 659-5777
Contact: Ruth Wehle

National Council of Churches of Christ in the U.S.A.
475 Riverside Drive
New York, NY 10027
(212) 870-2200
Contact: Hulbert James

National Council of Jewish Women
One W. 47th St.
New York, NY 10036
(212) 674-8010
Contact: Adrienne Picard

National Council of Senior Citizens
1511 K St., NW
Washington, DC 20036
(202) 783-6850
Contact: William R. Hutton

National Council of the Young Men's Christian Association of the U.S.A.
291 Broadway
New York, NY 10007
(212) 374-2000
Contact: Charles C. Kujawa

National Council on the Aging
1828 L St., NW
Washington, DC 20036
(202) 223-6250
Contact: Jack Ossofsky

National Credit Union Administration
2025 M St., NW
Washington, DC 20456
(202) 254-9800
Contact: Herman Nickerson

National Federation of Settlements & Neighborhood Centers
232 Madison Ave.
New York, NY 10016
(212) 679-6110
Contact: Mrs. John Wasserman

National Federation of Temple Sisterhoods
832 Fifth Ave.
New York, NY 10021
(212) 249-0100
Contact: Mrs. Seymour Sims

National Geriatrics Society, Inc.
212 W. Wisconsin Ave.
Milwaukee, WI 53202
(414) 272-4130
Contact: Thomas J. Bergen

National Health Council, Inc.
1740 Broadway
New York, NY 10019
(212) 582-6040
Contact: Barney Sellers

National Hearing & Society
20361 Middlebelt Rd.
Livonia, MI 48152
(313) 478-2610
Contact: Richard Fralick

National Home Study Council
1601 18th St., NW
Washington, DC 20009
(202) 234-5100
Contact: William A. Fowler

National Institute of Senior Centers
c/o National Council on Aging
1828 L St., NW
Washington, DC 20036
(202) 223-6250
Contact: William R. Pothier

National Jewish Welfare Board
15 E. 26th St.
New York, NY 10010
(212) 532-4949
Contact: Seymour Kornblum

National League for Nursing, Inc.
10 Columbus Circle
New York, NY 10019
(212) 582-1022
Contact: Nancy Tigar

National Legal Aid & Defenders Association
2100 M St., NW
Washington, DC 20037
(202) 452-0620
Contact: Frank Jones

National Medical Association Foundation, Inc.
1150 17th St., NW
Washington, DC 20036
(202) 833-3560
Contact: E. Leon Cooper

National Park Service
U.S. Department of the Interior
Washington, DC 20240
(202) 343-8067
Contact: Gary E. Everhardt

National Recreation and Park Association
1601 N. Kent St.
Arlington, VA 22203
(703) 525-0606
Contact: Constance McAdam

National Retired Teachers Association
1909 K St., NW
Washington, DC 20049
(202) 872-4700
Contact: Harriet Miller

National Safety Council
425 N. Michigan Ave.
Chicago, IL 60611
(312) 527-4800
Contact: Harry Ecklund

National Society for the Prevention of Blindness, Inc.
79 Madison Ave.
New York, NY 10016
(212) 684-3505
Contact: John L. Wallace

National Sorority of Phi Delta Kappa
8333 S. Landey Ave.
Chicago, IL 60619
(312) 873-5503
Contact: Mable S. Bouldin

National University Extension Association
One Dupont Circle, NW
Washington, DC 20036
(202) 659-3130
Contact: D.W. Holbrook

National Urban League
500 E. 62nd St.
New York, NY 10021
(212) 644-6500
Contact: Barbara Cowan

National Voluntary Organization for Independent Living of the Aged
c/o National Council on Aging
1828 L Street, NW
Washington, DC 20036
(202) 223-6250
Contact: Albert J. Abrams

No-Load Mutual Fund Association
475 Park Ave. South
New York, NY 10022
(212) 532-8811
Contact: Irving L. Straus

ASSOCIATIONS AND ORGANIZATIONS 27

Office of Consumer Affairs
Executive Office of the President
New Executive Office Building
Washington, DC 20506
(202) 245-6158
Contact: Director

Pilot Club International
244 College St.
Macon, GA 31208
(912) 743-7403
Contact: Edith Upchurch

Presbyterian Church in the U.S.A.
Division of National Missions
342 Ponce De Leon Ave., NE
Atlanta, GA 30303
(404) 873-1531
Contact: Bruce W. Berry

Public Affairs Pamphlets
381 Park Ave. South
New York, NY 10016
(212) 683-4331
Contact: Adelle Broady

Retired Officers Association
1626 I Street, NW
Washington, DC 20006
(202) 331-1111
Contact: General John Carpenter III

Retirement Housing Foundation
555 E. Ocean Blvd.
Long Beach, CA 90802
(415) 432-0471
Contact: Director

Salvation Army
120 W. 14th St.
New York, NY 10011
(212) 243-8700
Contact: Lt. Col. Mary Verner

Serbian Eastern Orthodox Diocese
Monastery of the Most Holy Mother
 of God
Shadeland
Springboro, PA 16435
(814) 587-6032
Contact: Rev. Zivko Popovich

Service Corps of Retired Executives
1030 15th St., NW
Washington, DC 20005
(202) 382-3345
Contact: Lincoln A. Simon

Small Business Administration
1441 L St., NW
Washington, DC 20549
(202) 393-3111
Contact: Thomas S. Kleppe

Social Security Administration
6401 Security Blvd.
Baltimore, MD 21235
(301) 594-1234
Contact: James B. Cardwell

Society of St. Vincent De Paul
Superior Council of the U.S.
4140 Lindell Boulevard
St. Louis, MO 63108
(314) 371-4980

Soroptimist International of the
 Americas, Inc.
1616 Walnut St.
Suite 700
Philadelphia, PA 19103
(215) 732-0512
Contact: Valerie Levitan

Southern Baptist Convention
Christian Life Commission
460 James Robertson Parkway
Nashville, TN 37210
(615) 244-2495
Contact: Dr. W. L. Howse III

Special Committee on Aging
U.S. Senate Room G-225
Dirksen Senate Office Building
Washington, DC 20510
(202) 224-3121
Contact: Senator Frank Church

Synagogue Council of America
432 Park Ave. South
New York, NY 10016
(212) MU6-8670
Contact: Jess Gersky

Townsend Plan National Lobby
5500 Quincy St.
Hyattsville, MD 20784
(301) 864-1988
Contact: John Doyle Elliott

Travelers Aid International
 Social Service of America
345 E. 46th St.
New York, NY 10017
(212) 687-2747
Contact: Samuel Mopsik

Unitarian Universalist Association
Committee on Aging
25 Beacon St.
Boston, MA 02108
(202) 547-0254
Contact: Dr. Matilda Moore

United Cerebral Palsy Association, Inc.
66 E. 34th St.
New York, NY 02108
(212) 889-6655
Contact: Harold A. Benson, Jr.

United Methodist Church, Board of
 Discipleship
1908 Grand Ave.
Nashville, TN 37202
(615) 327-2700
Contact: None

United Methodist Church, Board of
 Global Ministries
475 Riverside Drive
New York, NY 10027
(212) 678-6161
Contact: Betty J. Letzig

United Methodist Church, Board of
 Health & Welfare Ministries
1200 Davis St.
Evanston, IL 60201
(312) 869-9600
Contact: John A. Murdock

United Mine Workers of America
900 15th St. NW
Washington, DC 20005
(202) 658-0530
Contact: Dr. Lorin E. Kerr

United Presbyterian Health, Education
 & Welfare Association
475 Riverside Drive
New York, NY 10027
(212) 870-2515
Contact: Priscilla Armstrong

United Nations
New York, NY 10017
(212) 296-5370
Contact: Marcial Tamayo

United States Catholic Conference
1312 Massachusetts Ave., NW
Washington, DC 20005
(202) 659-6600
Contact: Michael Bennett

United States Jaycees
4 W. 21st St.
Tulsa, OK 74102
(918) 584-2481
Contact: Ray Roper

U.S. Postal Service
Chief Postal Inspection
475 L Enfant Plaza West St.
Washington, DC 20260
(202) 245-4000
Contact: Benjamin F. Bailar

United Synagogue of America
National Women's League
48 E. 74th St.
New York, NY 10021
(212) 628-1600
Contact: Mrs. Herbert Quint

United Way of America
801 N. Fairfax
Alexandria, VA 22314
(703) 836-7100
Contact: Hamp Coley

University of Kentucky Writing
Work-Shop for People over Fifty-Seven
Council on Aging
University of Kentucky
Lexington, KY 40506
(606) 258-9000
Contact: C. R. Hager

Vacation Exchange Club
350 Broadway
New York, NY 10013
(212) 475-5861
Contact: Mary DeBaldo

Veterans of World War I of the U.S.A.,
 Inc.
916 Prince St.
Alexandria, VA 22314
(703) 836-3060
Contact: John McIntyre

Volunteers of America
340 W. 85th St.
New York, NY 10024
(212) 873-2600
Contact: John F. McMahon

5
Audio Visual Material

If you belong to a group or if you are a group leader in any of the areas of interest to the elderly, the Andrus Gerontology Center's book, *About Aging: A Catalog of Films,* will be of special interest to you. This book, now in its third edition, is the largest and most comprehensive catalog of films on topics of aging ever compiled. Each film listing includes a brief annotation, the purchase price, and the name of the distributor with instructions on purchase or rental procedures.

The categories of film include:

Aging: The Problems	Fiction/Fantasy	Nursing (Geriatric)
Aging: The Realities	Foreign Language Films	Nutrition
Aging: Some Solutions	Health Maintenance	People/Place
Aging in Other Countries	Home Care	Physical Health
Animated Films	Housing	Recreation/Leisure
Bibliography/Documentary	Humor/Satire	Rehabilitation Programs
Community Services and Programs	Income	Retirement
Crime/Consumer Protection	Institutionalized Aged	Rural Aged
Death/Dying	Life Styles: Options/Choices	Sexuality
Employment	Mental Health	Urban Aged
Ethnicity — Tradition/Heritage	Middle Age	Welfare
Federal/State Programs		

The book costs $3.50 plus 25¢ for postage and handling for orders under $5.00. For orders over $5.00, add 50¢ for postage and handling. California residents, add 6% sales tax. Send your order to:

Publications Office
Andrus Gerontology Center
University of Southern California
3715 McClintock Avenue
Los Angeles, CA 90007
(213) 746-6060

6
Books for the Blind and Physically Handicapped

The Library of Congress, Division for the Blind & Physically Handicapped,
1291 Taylor Street, NW, Washington, DC 20542
(202) 882-5500

In cooperation with a network of regional and subregional libraries, the Library of Congress provides a free library service to persons who are unable to read or use standard printed materials because of visual or physical impairment. Books and magazines in recorded form (talking books) or in braille are delivered to eligible readers by postage-free mail and are returned in the same manner. Specially designed phonographs and cassette players are also loaned free to persons borrowing talking books.

The following list contains the addresses, telephone numbers, and names of librarians in charge of each of the regional and subregional libraries in the network. The regional library or libraries listed under each state provide a full range of library services to handicapped readers. In many states, readers receive talking books through subregional libraries, which are local public libraries having collections of current materials and direct access to the resources of their regional libraries. In addition, they offer their handicapped readers reference and reader's advisory services.

Any residents of the United States or American citizens temporarily living abroad who wish to receive this free library service should send a statement describing their disability to the library serving their area. In cases of blindness, visual disability, or physical limitations, the statement must be signed by a doctor of medicine, optometrist, nurse, therapist, or professional staff member of a hospital, institution, or public agency. In the absence of any of these, a professional librarian may certify eligibility. A reading disability from organic dysfunction must be certified by a doctor of medicine.

ALABAMA

Regional Library

Library for the Blind and Physically
   Handicapped
525 N. Court St.
Talladega, AL 35160
(205) 362-1790
Contact: Charles Delong

Subregional Libraries

Library for the Blind and Handicapped
Public Library of Anniston and
   Calhoun County
P.O. Box 308
Anniston, AL 36201
(205) 237-8501
Contact: Deenie M. Culver

Service to the Blind and Physically
   Handicapped
North Birmingham Branch
Birmingham Public Library
3200 N. 27th St.
Birmingham, AL 35207
(205) 254-2529
Contact: Ron Countryman

Department for the Blind and
   Physically Handicapped
George S. Houston Memorial Library
P.O. Box 1369
Dothan, AL 36301
(205) 792-3164
Contact: Lynda Deal

Huntsville Subregional Library for the
   Blind and Physically Handicapped
P.O. Box 443
Huntsville, AL 35804
(205) 536-0022
Contact: Joyce L. Smith

Department for the Blind and
   Physically Handicapped
Mobile Public Library
Building S206
Avenue C
Mobile Aerospace Industrial Complex
Mobile, AL 36615
(205) 433-0483
Contact: Joyce Sowell

Department for the Blind and
   Physically Handicapped
Montgomery Public Library
Cleveland Avenue Branch
1276 Cleveland Avenue
Montgomery, AL 36108
(205) 264-3324
Contact: Gloria Norman

Friedman Public Library
Division for the Blind and Handicapped
1305 24th Ave.
Tuscaloosa, AL 35401
(205) 759-5141
Contact: Anne M. Sepe

ALASKA

Regional Library

Alaska State Library
Services for the Blind and Physically
   Handicapped
650 International Airport Road
Anchorage, AK 99502
(907) 274-6625
Contact: Mary Jennings

ARIZONA

Regional Library

Arizona Regional Library for the Blind
and Physically Handicapped
3120 E. Roosevelt St.
Phoenix, AZ 85008
(602) 271-5578
Contact: Arlene Bansal

Subregional Libraries

Special Services Branch
Flagstaff City-Coconino County Public
Library
324 W. Aspen
Flagstaff, AZ 86001
(602) 774-0270
Contact: Kathy Winel

Prescott Talking Book Library
215 E. Goodwin
Prescott, AZ 86301
(602) 445-8110
Contact: Joyce J. Segner

ARKANSAS

Regional Library

Arkansas Library Commission
Library for the Blind and Handicapped
311 W. Capitol
Little Rock, AR 72201
(501) 371-1155
Contact: Cleotta Mullen

Subregional Libraries

Library for the Blind and Handicapped
Ozarks Regional Library
217 E. Dickson St.
Fayetteville, AR 72701
(501) 442-6253
Contact: Joann Foley

Fort Smith Public Library for the
Blind and Handicapped
61 S. Eighth
Fort Smith, AR 72901
(501) 783-0229
Contact: Alice White

Library for the Blind and Handicapped,
Northeast
Crowley Ridge Regional Library
315 W. Oak
Jonesboro, AR 72401
(501) 935-5133
Contact: Teresa Wilson

Library for the Blind and Handicapped,
Southwest
CLOC Regional Library
P.O. Box 668
Magnolia, AR 71753
(501) 234-1991
Contact: Debra Purcell

CALIFORNIA

Regional Library (Southern)

Braille Institute of America, Inc.
Library
741 N. Vermont Ave.
Los Angeles, CA 90029
(213) 663-1111
Contact: Phyllis Cairns

Regional Library (Northern)

Books for the Blind and Physically
Handicapped
California State Library
600 Broadway
Sacramento, CA 95818
(916) 322-4090
Contact: Marion Bourke

Subregional Libraries

Fresno County Free Library
Special Services Department
2420 Mariposa Street
Fresno, CA 93721
(209) 488-3217
Contact: Julie J. Kindrick

San Francisco Public Library
Civic Center
San Francisco, CA 94102
(415) 558-3985
Contact: Leslie Eldridge

COLORADO

Regional Library

Colorado State Library — Services for the
Blind and Physically Handicapped
2030 Champa Street
Denver, CO 80205
(303) 892-2081
Contact: James M. Schubert

CONNECTICUT

Regional Library

Connecticut State Library
Library for the Blind and Physically
Handicapped
90 Washington St.
Hartford, CT 06106
(203) 566-3028
Contact: Mary E. Tincovich

DELAWARE

Regional Library

Handicapped Services
Division of Libraries
215 Dover St.
Dover, DE 19901
(302) 678-4523
Contact: Billie Jean Ouellette

DISTRICT OF COLUMBIA

Regional Library

District of Columbia Regional Library
for the Blind and Physically
Handicapped
901 G St., NW
Washington, DC 20001
(202) 727-2142
Contact: Grace J. Lyons

FLORIDA

Regional Library (Multistate Center)

Florida Regional Library for the Blind
and Physically Handicapped
P.O. Box 2299
Daytona Beach, FL 32015
(904) 252-7616
Contact: Donald J. Weber

Subregional Libraries

Department of Community Services
Division of Libraries
Broward County Library
P.O. Box 5463
Fort Lauderdale, FL 33310
(305) 765-1100
Contact: Head Librarian

Talking Book Library
Jacksonville Public Library
2809 Commonwealth Ave.
Jacksonville, FL 32205
(904) 633-6135
Contact: Gloria E. Zittrauer

Dade County Talking Book Library
Miami-Dade Public Library System
150 NE 79th St.
Miami, FL 33138
(305) 638-6937
Contact: Michael Sweeney

Orlando Public Library
Talking Book Section
453 N. Orange Ave.
Orlando, FL 32801
(305) 425-4694
Contact: J. Brock McNally

Talking Book Library
Palmetto Public Library
923 Sixth St.
Palmetto, FL 33561
(813) 722-3333
Contact: Mary Peach

Talking Book Library
Tampa-Hillsborough County Public
Library System
900 N. Ashley
Tampa, FL 33602
(813) 223-8349
Contact: Suzanne Hanselmann

Talking Books — Palm Beach County
Public Library System
3650 Summit Blvd.
West Palm Beach, FL 33406
(305) 686-0895
Contact: Arthur Weeks

GEORGIA

Regional Library

Library for the Blind and Physically
Handicapped
1050 Murphy Ave., SW
Atlanta, GA 30310
(404) 656-2465
Contact: Jim DeJarnatt

Subregional Libraries

Albany Talking Book Center
2040 Newton Road
Albany, GA 31701
(912) 435-2145
Contact: Jon McDaniel

Talking Book Center
Athens Regional Library
120 W. Dougherty St.
Athens, GA 30601
(404) 543-0134
Contact: Pat Salas

Talking Book Center
Augusta-Richmond County Public
    Library
902 Greene St.
Augusta, GA 30902
(404) 724-1871
Contact: Gary Swint

Talking Book Center
Southwest Georgia Regional Library
Shotwell & Monroe Streets
Bainbridge, GA 31717
(912) 246-3895
Contact: Rebecca De Shazo

Talking Book Center
Brunswick-Glynn County Regional
    Library
208 Gloucester St.
Brunswick, GA 31520
(912) 265-6232
Contact: Ruby Newton

Talking Book Center
Chattahoochee Valley Regional
    Library
Bradley Drive
Columbus, GA 31906
(404) 327-0211
Contact: Crawford Pike

Talking Book Center
Oconee Regional Library
801 Bellevue Ave.
Dublin, GA 31021
(912) 272-5710
Contact: Louise Cross

Talking Book Center
Chestatee Regional Library
127 N. Main St.
Gainesville, GA 30501
(404) 532-3311
Contact: Sadie Jenkins

Talking Book Center
Cherokee Regional Library
305 S. Duke Street
Lafayette, GA 30728
(404) 638-2992
Contact: Suzanne Gregory

Talking Book Center
Shurling Library
Shurlington Plaza
Macon, GA 31201
(912) 745-5813
Contact: Rebecca M. Sherrill

Tri-County Regional Library
Talking Book Center
609 Broad St.
Rome, GA 30161
(404) 235-5561
Contact: June M. Crider

Talking Book Center
Savannah Public Library
2002 Bull Street
Savannah, GA 31401
(912) 234-5127
Contact: Janet Wright Silver

Talking Book Center
South Georgia Regional Library
300 Woodrow Wilson Dr.
Valdosta, GA 31601
(912) 244-0202
Contact: Margaret Montgomery

HAWAII
Regional Library

Library for the Blind and Physically
    Handicapped
402 Kapahulu Avenue
Honolulu, HI 96815
(808) 732-7767
Contact: Lydia S. Ranger

IDAHO
Regional Library

Idaho State Library
325 W. State St.
Boise, ID 83702
(208) 384-2150
Contact: Flo Chriswisser

ILLINOIS
Regional Library

Department for the Blind and
    Physically Handicapped
Chicago Public Library
4544 N. Lincoln Ave.
Chicago, IL 60625
(312) 561-3971
Contact: Jerry Obrochta

Subregional Libraries

Shawnee Library System
R. R. No. 2
Carterville, IL 62918
(618) 985-3711
Contact: Ronald D. Reed

Books for the Blind and Physically
    Handicapped
River Bend Library System
P.O. Box 125
Coal Valley, IL 61240
(309) 799-3131
Contact: Louise Stoelting

Rolling Prarie Library System
345 W. Eldorado St.
Decatur, IL 62522
(217) 429-2586
Contact: Clara E. Castelo

Lewis and Clark Library System
P.O. Box 368
Edwardsville, IL 62025
(618) 656-3216
Contact: Nicholas Niederlander

Corn Belt and Lincoln Rail Library
    System
Service to the Blind and Physically
    Handicapped
Dominy Memorial Library
Fairbury, IL 61739
(815) 692-1985
Contact: Debbie Wheelock

Cumberland Trail Library System
12th & McCawley
Flora, IL 62839
(618) 662-2679
Contact: Vincent P. Schmidt

DuPage Library System
Talking Books Subregional Library
P.O. Box 268
Geneva, IL 60134
(312) 232-8457
Contact: Richard L. Shurman

The Suburban Library System
125 Tower Dr.
Burr Ridge
Hinsdale, IL 60521
(312) 325-6640
Contact: Carol Egan

Services for the Blind and Physically
    Handicapped
Bur Oak Library System
150 N. Ottawa St.
Joliet, IL 60431
(815) 726-5394
Contact: Karen Crites

Western Illinois Library System
58 W. Side Square
Monmouth, IL 61462
(309) 734-7141
Contact: Ellen Keip

Illinois Valley Library System
107 NE Monroe St.
Peoria, IL 61602
(309) 672-8887
Contact: Dena Wilson

Physically Handicapped Subregional
Starved Rock Library System
c/o Matson Public Library
15 Park Ave. W.
Princeton, IL 61356
(815) 879-8551
Contact: Carol Bird

Talking Book Library
Great River Library System
515 York St.
Quincy, IL 62301
(217) 223-2560
Contact: Karen Gray

Northern Illinois Library System
c/o Rockford Public Library
215 N. Wyman St.
Rockford, IL 61101
(815) 965-6731
Contact: Karen L. Odean

Kaskaskia Library System
306 N. Main St.
Smithton, IL 62285
(618) 235-4220
Contact: Hammon Harris

North Suburban Library System
200 W. Dundee Rd.
Wheeling, IL 60090
(312) 459-1300
Contact: James Denier

INDIANA

Regional Library

Indiana State Library
Physically Handicapped Division
140 N. Senate Ave.
Indianapolis, IN 46204
(317) 633-5404
Contact: Barney McEwen

Subregional Libraries

Bartholomew County Library
536 Fifth St.
Columbus, IN 47201
(812) 372-8801
Contact: Elizabeth Ann Booth

Talking Book Service
Elkhart Public Library
300 S. Second St.
Elkhart, IN 46514
(219) 523-0878
Contact: Helen Cooke

Talking Books Department
Fort Wayne Public Library
900 Webster St.
Fort Wayne, IN 46802
(219) 742-7241
Contact: Jeanne Cox

Talking Book Service
Lake County Public Library Central
1919 West Lincoln Highway
Merrillville, IN 46410
(219) 769-3541
Contact: Piper Smith

New Albany-Floyd County Public
  Library
180 W. Spring St.
New Albany, IN 47150
(812) 944-8464
Contact: Ann Wunderlich

Peru Public Library
102 E. Main St.
Peru, IN 46970
(317) 473-3069
Contact: Lucille Knight

Talking Book Department
Vincennes Public Library
502 N. Seventh St.
Vincennes, IN 47591
(812) 882-6007
Contact: Linda K. Namminga

IOWA

Regional Library

Library
Iowa Commission for the Blind
Fourth & Keosauqua
Des Moines, IA 50309
(515) 283-2601
Contact: Duane Gerstenberger

KANSAS

Regional Library

Kansas State Library
Division for the Blind and Physically
  Handicapped
529 Kansas Avenue
Topeka, KS 66603
(913) 296-3642
Contact: Sheila Merrell

Subregional Libraries

Talking Books
Southwest Kansas Library System
606 First Ave.
Dodge City, KS 67801
(316) 255-1231
Contact: Dannetta Harmon

Talking Book Service
CKLS Headquarters
1409 Williams
Great Bend, KS 67530
(316) 792-2409
Contact: Ruth Leek

Hutchinson Public Library
Talking Book Subregional
901 N. Main
Hutchinson, KS 67501
(316) 663-5441
Contact: Judy A. Roepka

Kansas City
Kansas Public Library
625 Minnesota Ave.
Kansas City, KS 66101
(913) 621-3073
Contact: Rose Mary Calovich

North Central Kansas Library System
Blind and Physically Handicapped
Juliette and Poyntz
Manhattan, KS 66502
(913) 776-4741
Contact: Frank Carroll

Talking Books
Topeka Public Library
1515 W. Tenth St.
Topeka, KS 66604
(913) 233-2040
Contact: Marlene Hendrick

Wichita Public Library
Talking Book Department
223 S. Main
Wichita, KS 67202
(316) 265-5281
Contact: Betty C. Spriggs

KENTUCKY

Regional Library

Kentucky Library for the Blind and
  Physically Handicapped
Twilight Trail
P.O. Box 818
Frankfort, KY 40601
(502) 564-5532
Contact: Head Librarian

Subregional Library

Louisville Subregional Library of the
  Kentucky Regional Library for
  the Blind and Physically
  Handicapped
Fourth & York Streets
Louisville, KY 40202
(502) 584-4154
Contact: Susan Murrell

LOUISIANA

Regional Library

Louisiana State Library
Department for the Blind and
  Physically Handicapped
P.O. Box 131
Baton Rouge, LA 70821
(504) 389-6651
Contact: Blanca J. Lastrapes

MAINE

Regional Library

Library Services for the Blind and
  Physically Handicapped
Maine State Library
Cultural Building
Augusta, ME 04333
(207) 289-3950
Contact: Cynthia A. Arnold

Subregional Libraries

Bangor Public Library
145 Harlow St.
Bangor, ME 04401
(207) 947-8336
Contact: Benita D. Davis

Cary Library
Maine St.
Houlton, ME 04730
(207) 532-3967
Contact: Norma Watson

Lewiston Public Library
118 Park St.
Lewiston, ME 04240
(207) 783-2331
Contact: Muriel Landry

Portland Public Library
Talking Books Department
615 Congress St., Suite 301
Portland, ME 04101
(207) 773-4761
Contact: Robert P. Britton

Waterville Public Library
73 Elm St.
Waterville, ME 04901
(207) 872-5433
Contact: Dorothy Parker

MARYLAND

Regional Library

Maryland State Library for the
  Physically Handicapped
1715 N. Charles St.
Baltimore, MD 21201
(301) 383-3111
Contact: James Murray

BOOKS FOR THE BLIND AND PHYSICALLY HANDICAPPED 33

Subregional Library

Service for the Physically Handicapped
Montgomery County Department of
  Public Libraries
99 Maryland Ave.
Rockville, MD 20850
(301) 279-1679
Contact: Caryl B. Emens

MASSACHUSETTS

Regional Library

Regional Library for the Blind and
  Physically Handicapped
Perkins School for the Blind
175 N. Beacon St.
Watertown, MA 02172
(617) 924-3434
Contact: Gisela M. Titman

Subregional Library

Talking Book Library
Worcester Public Library
Salem Square
Worcester, MA 01608
(617) 752-3751
Contact: Fritz Maiser

MICHIGAN

Regional Library (Wayne County only)

Wayne County Library for the Blind
  and Physically Handicapped
33030 Van Born Road
Wayne, MI 48184
(313) 722-8000
Contact: Head Librarian

*Regional Library
(Except Wayne County)*

Blind and Physically Handicapped
  Library
Michigan Department of Education
State Library Services
735 E. Michigan Ave.
Lansing, MI 48913
(517) 373-1590
Contact: Julie A. Nicol

Subregional Libraries

Washtenaw County Library for the
  Blind and Physically Handicapped
4133 Washtenaw Ave.
Ann Arbor, MI 48104
(313) 971-6059
Contact: Ruthe L. Marshall

Willard Library System
7 W. Van Buren
Battle Creek, MI 49016
(616) 968-8166
Contact: Margaret E. Ritz

Upper Peninsula Blind and Physically
  Handicapped Library
413 Ludington St.
Escanaba, MI 49829
(906) 786-5602
Contact: Charles M. Harper

Oakland County Library for the Blind
  and Physically Handicapped
Farmington Community Library
32737 W. Twelve Mile Road
Farmington Hills, MI 48024
(313) 477-1313
Contact: Beverly Daffern

Mideastern Michigan Library Co-op
Home Services Library
G-4195 W. Pasadena Ave.
Flint, MI 48504
(313) 732-1120
Contact: Joyce Wheat

Blind and Physically Handicapped
  Library
Kent County Library System
775 Ball, NE
Grand Rapids, MI 49503
(616) 774-3262
Contact: Jill Newhouse

Grand Traverse Area Library
  Federation
322 Sixth St.
Traverse City, MI 49684
(616) 947-3850
Contact: Carol Hubbell

MINNESOTA

Regional Library

Library for the Blind and Physically
  Handicapped
Braille and Sight Saving School
Faribault, MN 55021
(507) 334-6411
Contact: Myrna Wright

MISSISSIPPI

Regional Library

Mississippi Library Commission
Service for the Handicapped
P.O. Box 3260
Jackson, MS 39207
(601) 354-7208
Contact: Ted Thaxton Campbell

MISSOURI

Regional Library

Wolfner Memorial Library for the Blind
  and Physically Handicapped
1808 Washington Ave.
St. Louis, MO 63103
(314) 241-4227
Contact: Pennie D. Peterson

MONTANA

Regional Library

Montana State Library
Division for the Blind and Physically
  Handicapped
930 E. Lyndale Ave.
Helena, MT 59601
(406) 449-3004
Contact: Darlene Tiensvold

NEBRASKA

Regional Library

Nebraska Library Commission
Library for the Blind and Physically
  Handicapped
1420 P Street
Lincoln, NE 68508
(402) 471-2661
Contact: Frances Warnsholz

Subregional Libraries

Hastings Public Library
P.O. Box 849
Hastings, NE 68901
(402) 463-9855
Contact: Brenda Bostock

Kimball Public Library
208 S. Walnut
Kimball, NE 69145
(308) 235-4523
Contact: Patsy J. Stonehouse

North Platte Public Library
Blind and Physically Handicapped
  Program
120 W. Fourth
North Platte, NE 69101
(308) 532-6560
Contact: Ardenia Tupper

NEVADA

Regional Library

Nevada State Library
Special Services Division
Capitol Complex
Carson City, NV 89710
(702) 885-5155
Contact: Oscar Ford

NEW HAMPSHIRE

Regional Library

New Hampshire Library Service for
  the Handicapped
12 Hills Avenue
Concord, NH 03301
(603) 271-3429
Contact: Eileen Keim

NEW JERSEY

Regional Library

New Jersey Library for the Blind
  and Handicapped
1676 N. Olden Ave. Extension
Trenton, NJ 08638
(609) 292-6450
Contact: Marya Hunsicker

NEW MEXICO

Regional Library

New Mexico State Library for the Blind
  and Physically Handicapped
Box 1629
Santa Fe, NM 87501
(505) 827-2033
Contact: Susan Lilley

NEW YORK

Regional Library (Except New York City and Long Island)

New York State Library for the Blind and Visually Handicapped
226 Elm St.
Albany, NY 12202
(518) 474-5935
Contact: Adamae P. Henderson

Regional Library (New York City and Long Island)

Library for the Blind and Physically Handicapped
The New York Public Library
166 Avenue of the Americas
New York, NY 10013
(212) 925-1011
Contact: Alar Kruus

Subregional Libraries

Reading for the Handicapped
Suffolk Cooperative Library System
P.O. Box 187
Bellport, NY 11713
(516) 286-1600
Contact: Pamela K. Barr

Talking Books
Age Level Services
Nassau Library System
Roosevelt Field
Garden City, NY 11530
(516) 741-0060
Contact: Julia G. Russell

NORTH CAROLINA

Regional Library

North Carolina Library for the Blind and Physically Handicapped
1314 Dale St.
Raleigh, NC 27635
(919) 829-4379
Contact: Charles H. Fox

NORTH DAKOTA

Regional Library (served by South Dakota)

South Dakota State Library for the Blind and Physically Handicapped
701 E. Sioux Avenue
Pierre, SD 57501
(605) 224-3514
Contact: John J. Vincent

OHIO

Regional Library (Southern Ohio)

Public Library of Cincinnati and Hamilton County
Library for the Blind and Physically Handicapped
Cincinnati, OH 45202
(513) 369-6074
Contact: Rosemary Gaiser

Regional Library (Northern Ohio)

Braille and Talking Book Department
Cleveland Public Library
325 Superior Ave.
Cleveland, OH 44114
(216) 623-2911
Contact: Katherine Prescott

OKLAHOMA

Regional Library

Oklahoma Library for the Blind and Physically Handicapped
1108 NE 36
Oklahoma City, OK 73111
(405) 521-3514
Contact: Bill McIlvain

Subregional Library

Tulsa City-County Library
Special Service for Blind and Physically Handicapped
400 Civic Center
Tulsa, OK 74103
(918) 581-5125
Contact: Kathy Chapman

OREGON

Regional Library

Oregon State Library
Services for the Blind and Physically Handicapped
555 13th St., NE
Salem, OR 97301
(503) 378-3849
Contact: Duane A. Enck

PENNSYLVANIA

Regional Library (Eastern Pennsylvania)

Library for the Blind and Physically Handicapped
Free Library of Philadelphia
919 Walnut St.
Philadelphia, PA 19107
(215) 925-3213
Contact: Michael P. Coyle

Regional Library (Western Pennsylvania)

Library for the Blind and Physically Handicapped
Carnegie Library of Pittsburg
4724 Baum Blvd.
Pittsburgh, PA 15213
(412) 687-2440
Contact: Sue O. Murdock

PUERTO RICO

Regional Library

Puerto Rico Regional Library for the Blind and Physically Handicapped
Center for Occupational Training Building
Ponce de Leon Ave., Stop 8½
Puerta de Tierra, San Juan, PR 00901
(809) 723-2519
Contact: Leida Torres

RHODE ISLAND

Regional Library

Regional Library for the Blind and Physically Handicapped
Rhode Island Department of State Library Services
95 Davis St.
Providence, RI 02908
(401) 277-2726
Contact: Karen Gagnon

SOUTH CAROLINA

Regional Library

South Carolina State Library
Division for the Blind and Physically Handicapped
718 S. Edisto Ave.
Columbia, SC 29205
(803) 758-2726
Contact: James B. Johnson

SOUTH DAKOTA

Regional Library

South Dakota State Library for the Handicapped
State Library Building
Pierre, SD 57501
(605) 224-3514
Contact: John J. Vincent

TENNESSEE

Regional Library

Tennessee Regional Library for the Blind and Physically Handicapped
5200 Centennial Blvd.
Nashville, TN 37209
(615) 741-3915
Contact: Francis H. Ezell

TEXAS

Regional Library

Division for the Blind and Physically Handicapped
Texas State Library
P.O. Box 12927, Capitol Station
Austin, TX 78711
(512) 475-4758
Contact: Donald K. Bailey

UTAH

Regional Library (Multistate Center)

Utah State Library Commission
Division for the Blind and Physically Handicapped
2150 S. 300 West, Suite No. 16
Salt Lake City, UT 84115
(801) 533-5855
Contact: Gerald A. Buttars

VERMONT

Regional Library

Vermont Library for the Blind and Physically Handicapped
State of Vermont Department of Libraries
Montpelier, VT 05602
(802) 828-3273
Contact: Dorothy Allen

VIRGINIA

Regional Library

Virginia State Library for the Visually and the Physically Handicapped
611 W. Home St.
Richmond, VA 23222
(804) 786-8016
Contact: Judith B. Dunham

Subregional Libraries

Alexandria Library
Ellen Coolidge Burke Branch
4701 Seminary Road
Alexandria, VA 22304
(804) 768-8016
Contact: Anne Schmidt

Talking Book Service
Arlington County Department of Libraries
1015 N. Quincy St.
Arlington, VA 22201
(703) 527-4777
Contact: Mary M. Bergin

C. Bascom Slemp Memorial Library
Proctor St.
Big Stone Gap, VA 24219
(703) 523-1334
Contact: Sarah D. Collier

Fairfax County Public Library
Kings Park Branch
9000 Burke Lake Road
Burke, VA 22015
(703) 978-5600
Contact: Mary L. Williams

Brunswick-Greenville Regional Library
234 Main St.
Lawrenceville, VA 23868
(804) 848-4494
Contact: Sharon Pond

Newport News Public Library System
Library for the Blind and Physically Handicapped
112 Main St.
Newport News, VA 23601
(804) 247-8640
Contact: Joyce Lewis

Roanoke Public Library
706 South Jefferson St.
Roanoke, VA 24011
(703) 981-2471
Contact: Irene Anderson

Special Services Department
Bayside Branch
Virginia Beach Public Library
936 Independence Blvd.
Virginia Beach, VA 23455
(804) 464-9175
Contact: Marilyn W. Mortensen

WASHINGTON

Regional Library

Washington Regional Library for the Blind and Physically Handicapped
811 Harrison St.
Seattle, WA 98129
(206) 464-6930
Contact: Sharon Hammer

WEST VIRGINIA

Regional Library

West Virginia Library Commission
Services for the Blind and Physically Handicapped
Science and Culture Center
Capitol Complex
Charleston, WV 25305
(304) 348-4061
Contact: Hortenzia Rapking

Subregional Libraries

Services for the Blind and Physically Handicapped
Kanawha County Public Library
123 Capitol St.
Charleston, WV 25301
(304) 343-4646
Contact: Marilyn Long

Services for the Blind and Physically Handicapped
Cabell County Public Library
900 Fifth Ave.
Huntington, WV 25701
(304) 523-9451
Contact: Gerry E. Waller

Morgantown Public Library
373 Spruce St.
Morgantown, WV 26505
(304) 292-6066
Contact: Kathy Leemaster

Parkersburg & Wood County Public Library, Services for the Blind and Physically Handicapped
3100 Emerson Ave.
Parkersburg, WV 26101
(304) 485-6564
Contact: Loralee J. Hillyard

West Virginia School for the Blind
Romney, WV 26757
(304) 822-3521
Contact: Linda J. Blake

WISCONSIN

Regional Library

Wisconsin Regional Library for the Blind and Physically Handicapped
814 W. Wisconsin Ave.
Milwaukee, WI 53233
(414) 278-3045
Contact: Mary Leon Miller

Subregional Library

Special Services Division
Brown County Library
515 Pine Street
Green Bay, WI 54301
(414) 432-0311 ext. 58
Contact: Margaret Jaeger

WYOMING

Regional Library
(served by Utah)

Utah State Library Commission
Division for the Blind and Physically Handicapped
2150 S. 300 West, Suite No. 16
Salt Lake City, UT 84115
(801) 533-5855
Contact: Gerald A. Buttars

American citizens residing in foreign countries receive library service from:

Division for the Blind and Physically Handicapped
Library of Congress
1291 Taylor St., NW
Washington, DC 20542
(202) 882-5500

7 Employment Paid Employment Volunteer Work

Skills and experience, valuable to a community, are often ignored because of myths about aging. Although many older people need to be provided with services, hundreds of thousands of others need an opportunity to give service. In job after job across the country, wherever they have been hired or accepted as volunteers, older people have shown themselves to be dependable, capable, and willing workers. Yet, discrimination because of age bars many from both volunteer and paid employment programs.

Public Service

Many agencies of federal, state, and local government sponsor or assist in funding programs using the services of older people as volunteers and paid workers. Many of these are "demonstration" programs, federally funded for a limited time; programs that prove of value are continued on a more permanent basis with local funding.

In the landmark Foster Grandparent Program initiated by the Administration on Aging (AOA) older people with low incomes work with children in institutions such as schools for retarded or disturbed children, infant homes, temporary care centers, and convalescent hospitals. "Grandparents" do not replace regular staff, but establish a person-to-person relationship with a child, giving him or her the kind of love often missed in group-care settings. In return, "grandparents" receive an hourly stipend plus the affection and trust of a child.

The Green Thumb program employs low-income men and women in rural sections to beautify public areas such as parks and roadsides, and to help local government and community services by serving as aides in schools and libraries. Some provide outreach and homemaker services, make friendly visits, and provide transportation. This project is sponsored by the Farmers Union under a grant from the U.S. Department of Labor.

Under another Department of Labor contract, the American Association of Retired Persons and the National Retired Teachers Association have trained many older people in new skills and helped others brush up on unused skills. In most cases, training was given by community service agencies such as the Red Cross or the United Fund, with real work constituting the training mechanism. Trainees serve others while they learn.

Some Model Cities Areas have effectively employed older residents in day-care centers. Thus, parents of small children can go to work secure in the knowledge that their children are well cared for during their absence. The children, the parents, and the older residents all benefit.

In the Seattle Model Cities Neighborhood, older men and women are employed to give direct service as homemakers and handymen to other Model Neighborhood residents, serving both older persons and children. In Seattle, as in all Model Cities, older residents comprise a high proportion of the population.

The National Council of Senior Citizens employs older men and women as senior AIDES (Alert, Industrious, Dedicated, Energetic Service) in 21 projects from coast to coast under a Department of Labor contract. These senior citizens, who work 20 hours a week, perform a wide variety of community services, including low-cost meal preparation and outreach activities. Many have found full-time jobs as a direct result of this project. The National Council on the Aging, Inc. operates a similar program with Department of Labor funding.

Help in Schools

Schools in many parts of the country are using older volunteers as a major community resource to provide children with educational enrichment.

In Winnetka, Illinois, older members of the Project for Academic Motivation (PAM) meet children in a one-to-one relationship to discuss and experiment, work with small groups, or lecture before whole classes. They work with all school ages from elementary to senior grades and with children from a wide range of income and social backgrounds. A major contribution is the revelation to many children of the link between classroom work and its future use in the "real world" outside. With the help of the AOA demonstration fund, the program has spread throughout the state of Illinois and beyond through consultative help from PAM volunteers.

In public schools in Dade County, Florida, teacher aides were paid to perform a wide variety of noninstructional tasks, which support the teacher, pupil, and school in improving educational programs. Originally an AOA federally funded research and demonstration project, the teacher aides proved so valuable that Dade County hired them as regular employees after federal funding was discontinued.

Fill Community Needs

In Vermont, senior library aides are making it possible for public libraries, particularly in the rural areas, to remain open longer, on more days. Book circulation has zoomed upward, and students, among others, are making increased use of library facilities. Interestingly, there is no absentee problem, even during the severest of Vermont winters.

SERVE (Serve and Enrichment Retirement by Volunteer Experience) of New York uses groups of older volunteers in state hospitals and schools for the mentally retarded. Some work with patients or in the office, and some help with other hospital duties. The group idea, both in recruitment and actual service, is a major factor in the success of SERVE because the group experience itself brings benefits to older people. They make new friendships while riding together on the bus provided for them, and they gain a sense of belonging and *esprit de corps* by sharing their experiences in group discussions.

SERVE began on Staten Island, New York, as an AOA demonstration project. It has been so successful that the State of New York has continued to fund the project and has expanded it to include other locations throughout the state.

Senior citizens in two Michigan counties work as tourist guides during the summer, showing approximately 30,000 visitors the counties' scenic views and the good fishing and camping sites off the main roads. Many visitors stay on an extra day or two and promise to vacation on the Michigan peninsula again because the guides make their vacations so pleasant.

Private Industry

John Deere Tractor Co. hired 50 of its former employees as tour guides in its Waterloo, Iowa, plant. These retirees escort 14,000 tourists a year. When the company holds a meeting in Waterloo for its international sales representatives, the guides help give the salespeople their orientation. They are naturals as guides because they not only know about the plant and tractor-building processes, but they also care deeply about the company's "image."

Some companies, however, fear that hiring older workers will create problems with established retirement plans or health insurance. Since many older people prefer to work only part-time, ways to meet these situations have been devised by special employment and referral services for older people. Some are private profit-making firms, others are volunteer and community agencies.

Obstacles Overcome

The hiring, payroll, and paperwork for the John Deere guides are handled by Manpower, Inc., the national "temporaries' agency." Because the guides are actually employed by Manpower, which contracts their services to John Deere, no retirement benefits are affected.

One of the private firms specializing in older employees is Mature Temps, Inc. With offices in at least 13 major cities, it places older people in temporary jobs on a contract basis, and pays their salary, Social Security, and insurance. These programs have been so successful that some Mature Temps offices have had difficulty in hiring enough people to fill all their potential contracts. Mature Temps reports that many companies are so pleased with their employees that they are asking to hire them permanently. One New York firm employs 50 Mature Temps every month!

Retirement Jobs, Inc. of San Jose, California, has placed more than 5,000 older men and women in jobs since its beginning in 1963. "RJ" now has five offices serving Santa Clara, San Mateo, and San Francisco Counties. It estimates its members earn between $150,000 and $200,000 in a year and put several times that amount in purchasing power back into the community. No fees are charged.

With AOA help, a group of retirees in Norwalk, Connecticut organized the Senior Personnel Placement Bureau in 1966. They have placed persons in jobs paying up to $10,000 a year. Like other senior employment agencies, the bureau will pay a worker directly under a contract arrangement.

A Comprehensive Countywide Program

Under the sponsorship of the Montgomery County Federation of Women's Clubs, Senior Home Craftsmen and Good Neighbor Family Aides in Montgomery County, Maryland, work in their own neighborhoods. In a sprawling suburban area such as this county, where extensive travel time could prohibit part-time work, this is important.

Senior Home Craftsmen do home repairs such as replacing faucet washers, fixing locks, painting, wallpaper hanging, and other jobs that are too small for commercial firms. Potential conflict with commercial businesses has been resolved by the Over-60 Counseling, representing union members, and the Suburban Maryland Home Builders Association, representing commercial contractors.

Both agreed that the senior craftsmen could reasonably charge about half the going hourly rate because they would not necessarily work as fast as union members and because they might be unwilling to do everything required of a union worker, such as heavy lifting or working high above the ground. It was also agreed that the senior craftsmen would limit themselves to small home-repair jobs that would not be profitable to commercial contractors.

There is no absolute time or dollar maximum on jobs because a homeowner might want several small jobs done, such as repairing screens, painting a room, or replacing stairs, which would amount to considerable time and money but would still be unprofitable to a contractor. The rule of reasonableness and a common understanding of the position of both the senior craftsmen and the commercial contractors and unions govern. There have been no difficulties with this gentlemen's agreement.

Most of the men can do these jobs because they have had a lifetime of keeping their own homes in good repair. A few have had careers as professional carpenters or bricklayers but no longer can or want to work full-time at such strenuous jobs. One handyman teaches a home-repair course at the local YWCA to county residents who want to learn to do minor repair themselves. The adult education department of the public schools also offers a class for those who want to be senior craftsmen yet need instruction.

The Good Neighbor Family Aides are women who have been homemakers most of their lives and who can offer aid to other older persons or families who need help in caring for a home. The women receive training at no cost to them in the local Red Cross chapter house. A Red Cross nurse teaches home nursing skills, the state university extension agent teaches home economics, and a local psychiatrist who specializes in geriatrics volunteers time to give insight on care of elderly persons.

Members of the Montgomery County Federation provide transportation within the county to the Red Cross chapter house for the training. People from adjoining Maryland counties and the adjoining State of Virginia and the District of Columbia have also taken this training and now work in their own communities.

The aides have had enthusiastic acceptance by the community, with the Over-60 Counseling Service receiving about 12 requests for every one it is able to fill. The service frequently receives letters of gratitude from families who have benefited. Mothers of small children or adults who care for an elderly person in their homes are able to take short vacations knowing that their family responsibilities are in capable hands.

Although income, educational level, and social position of the Aides vary widely, a study of the aides done by a graduate student shows need for additional income as most of the aides' primary reason for working. A high percentage, however, also indicated the desire to be involved in the community, to fill a real need, and to have freedom to schedule their own working hours as reasons for being aides.

Over-60 also fills requests for all other kinds of jobs.

PAID EMPLOYMENT

Mature Temps is an employment service specializing in temporary job placements for people with mature work attitudes. A recommended service of the American Association of Retired Persons and National Retired Teachers Association, with offices in many major cities across the country, Mature Temps is ready to help you — whether you are skilled or unskilled — if you are seeking temporary work on a part-time or full-time basis.

There are many job opportunities for retired people and others with mature work attitudes. With the help of Mature Temps, getting back to work can be much easier than you may think — and there is no fee or charge of any kind to you.

Although people who are placed by Mature Temps work in the offices of various companies, they are employees of Mature Temps. It is Mature Temps who pays them, keeps their work records, makes the necessary employer's contributions for Social Security, and withholds for taxes. As the employer, Mature Temps pays its employees promptly each week, and makes sure that they have the best working conditions and assignments possible.

To get work for as many of its people as possible, Mature Temps actively seeks jobs in the business community. The success of its job hunting depends on such factors as business conditions, the state of the economy, and the local labor market.

How you can register

To register, go to your local Mature Temps office for an interview, explain your needs, and find out what jobs are available in your area. If you have office, clerical, and other skills that are in demand, in many instances you can decide just how many hours — and where — you want to work.

If you are interested in working again, Mature Temps makes it possible for you to:

- demonstrate your independence
- make use of your know-how and experience
- channel your energies productively
- add new excitement to your life
- develop new acquaintances
- earn extra money for a vacation trip
- buy a special gift for a loved one
- break up your daily routine.

But whether you want to come back to work to earn money, or simply because you feel like it, you will receive a warm welcome at Mature Temps. Their people are friendly, helpful, and especially sensitive to the needs of retirees. You may contact them either by phone or by mail.

Interested Professionals: At Mature Temps, your maturity is an asset. Mature Temps specializes in serving mature people and people with mature work attitudes, and the interviewers and placement specialists are aware of your needs and the problems faced by all retirees.

Kinds of Skills: The basic clerical skills such as typing, shorthand, and filing, and other administrative skills are most in demand. However, some retirees have found such jobs as messengers and mailroom clerks as meeting their requirements. There are also requests for managerial and professional people such as accountants, sales representatives, underwriters, etc.

Kinds of Firms: Both large and small organizations in such fields as banking, insurance, brokerage, advertising, pharmaceutics, data processing, retail, wholesale, architecture, manufacturing, publishing, and others use temporary help.

Age Limit: None at all. If you have a mature work attitude, and can do the job, you qualify.

Pay Scale: You get an individual rate based on your skills and the experience required for each specific job assignment.

Updating Skills: If you feel that your skills are not suited to the requirements of modern business, Mature Temps counselors would be glad to discuss the matter with you. On certain jobs, your experience and skills may be a definite asset. You may perhaps be qualified for related work, and can bring your skill up-to-date with just a few hours of practice. When work conditions permit, Mature Temps will make available to you some of its equipment and office space for practicing.

Registration: Call your local office for an appointment. You'll be invited to the office for an interview. Once you are registered, Mature Temps will contact you by phone when an available job comes up.

Work Schedule: The number of assignments available to a person depends on his or her skills, availability, and flexibility for work assignments.

When There's No Local Office: As representatives of Mature Temps must personally contact companies near you about job openings, the firm can serve you only if there is a Mature Temps office in your locality. However, they are planning for future expansion, and, if an office opens in your area, you will read about it in your Association's publications and in the local newspapers.

BRANCH OFFICES

CALIFORNIA
3660 Wilshire Blvd.
Los Angeles, CA 90010
(213) 380-6515

44 Montgomery St.
San Francisco, CA 94104
(415) 986-7787

DISTRICT OF COLUMBIA
1750 K Street, NW
Washington, DC 20006
(202) 833-8888

ILLINOIS
17 N. State St.
Chicago, IL 60602
(312) 368-0266

MARYLAND
10 E. Baltimore St.
Baltimore, MD 21202
(301) 837-2444

MASSACHUSETTS
47 Winter St.
Boston, MA 02108
(617) 482-7628

NEW YORK
1114 Avenue of the Americas
(43 W. 42nd St.)
New York, NY 10036
(212) 869-0740

PENNSYLVANIA
1700 Market St.
Philadelphia, PA 19103
(215) 665-1150

1 Plymouth Meeting Mall
Plymouth Meeting, PA 19462
(215) 825-4400

TEXAS
One Main Place
Dallas, TX 75250
(214) 651-9321

1100 Milam Building
Houston, TX 77002
(713) 237-8552

VOLUNTEER WORK

ACTION is the central focus in the federal government for volunteer programs. It administers a number of programs especially for older volunteers and others in which older volunteers may participate. These programs are the Retired Senior Volunteer Program (RSVP), the Foster Grandparent Program, the Service Corps of Retired Executives (SCORE), the Peace Corps, the Volunteers in Service to America (VISTA), and the Senior Companion Program (modeled after Foster Grandparent Program).

If any of these programs interests you, a complete description can be found under ACTION in Chapter 11, Government Programs.

Green Thumb, sponsored by the National Farmers Union in 24 states, provides part-time work in conservation, beautification, and community improvement in rural areas or in existing community-service agencies. Applicants should have a rural or farming background and must take a physical examination. For more information, contact

Green Thumb, Inc.
1012 14th St., NW
Washington, DC 20005

Senior Aides, administered by the National Council of Senior Citizens in 33 urban and rural areas, offers part-time work in community-service agencies in activities ranging from child care and adult education to home health and homemaker services. Contact

>National Council of Senior Citizens
>1511 K St., NW
>Washington, DC 20005

Senior Community Service Aides, sponsored by the National Council on the Aging in 18 urban and rural areas, provides part-time work in Social Security and state employment service offices, public housing, libraries, hospitals, schools, and food and nutrition programs. Aides also help provide escort services, homemaker and home-repair services, and outreach for information and referral. Write to

>National Council on the Aging
>1828 L St., NW
>Washington, DC 20036

Senior Community Aides, sponsored by the National Retired Teachers Association and the American Association of Retired Persons in 31 cities, recruits, trains, and finds part-time work for aides in public or private service programs, assisting in child-care centers, vocational education classes, or in clerical positions and buildings security. For information, write to

>NRTA/AARP
>1909 K St., NW
>Washington, DC 20049

Operation Mainstream Program, administered by the Forest Service of the U.S. Department of Agriculture in about 20 states under an agreement with the Department of Labor, offers employment to older persons on an average of 3 days a week in conservation and beautification projects. Contact

>USDA Forest Service
>12th St. and Independence Ave., SW
>Washington, DC 20250

Nearly all chapters of the *Junior Chamber of Commerce* have programs aimed at aiding the elderly in the local community. Contact your local chapter, which is listed in the white pages of your telephone directory; or contact the national headquarters,

>U.S. Jaycees
>4 West 21st St.
>Tulsa, OK 74102
>(918) 584-2481

There are so many opportunities for volunteering your services that it is impossible to list them all here. Therefore, we suggest you decide on the kind of work you wish to do and where, and then make the contact. You'll be amazed how receptive people will be to the idea, especially when the cost factor is minimal. We do think, however, that you should ask for and get expenses money.

(Also see Chapter 20, National Alliance of Businessmen.)

8 Foundations

Many foundations give money to projects for the elderly. The most comprehensive list of foundations is compiled by:

    The Foundation Center
    888 Seventh Avenue
    New York, NY 10024
    (212) 489-8610

If you have any questions about foundations, or if you would like a copy of The Foundation Directory, write or call the Foundation Center. The directory costs $30.

9 Friendly Visiting

Friendly visiting has been called organized neighborliness because, in this program, volunteers visit isolated homebound older persons on a regular schedule once, or more, a week. They do such things as play chess and cards, write letters, provide an arm to lean on during a shopping trip, or just sit and chat. The essential element is to provide continuing companionship for an elderly person who has no relative or friend able to do it.

This kind of visiting relieves loneliness of older people in a very real way. Older people themselves say such things as, "She has made my life over," "It makes me feel like I am still somebody worth talking to," "It gives me a chance to speak of things which are in my heart," and "Her visit is something to look forward to."

Professional staff workers have observed that clients look better and take more interest in things outside themselves after receiving friendly visiting. Frequently there is improvement in actual physical condition or, at least, less absorption in illness.

Although the visitor need not be a social worker or other professionally trained person, she should receive some orientation from the sponsoring agency and some continuing supervision or consultation. Visitors come from a variety of backgrounds. Qualities that seem to mark good friendly visitors are the ability to accept people as they are, and genuine friendliness plus commitment and reliability in visiting on a regular schedule. Older people themselves often prove to be the most effective visitors. The ideal friendly visitor is born, not made.

Pioneer Services

Friendly Visiting is an organized service began in Chicago in 1946. Social workers observed how extremely lonely many older clients were. Already swamped by case loads, they did not have the time to stay and chat with clients after their regular business was completed. The idea of asking volunteers to visit these isolated people grew out of this need.

The Volunteer Bureau of the Council for Community Services in Chicago coordinates the program of recruitment, training, and referral of visitors. Public and private agencies requesting Friendly Visitors draw up job descriptions, acquaint visitors with agency purposes and programs, and establish time and place for consultation of volunteers with a professional member of the staff.

A Great Need

Friendly Visiting is a service desired by many people in both rural and urban areas. It helps them to remain in their own homes, a goal shared by the great majority of older persons. In a recent survey of older people in the Portland, Oregon, Model Cities Area, home visits to shut-ins and persons living alone topped the list of needs. They were even placed ahead of need for higher income and low-cost transportation. ("Home visits" by Portland's definition included performance of some home chore and handyman services as well as Friendly Visiting.)

Although many Friendly Visiting programs assign a volunteer to only one or two clients, a school-bus driver in Yampa Valley, Colorado, visits several older people every day. After delivering the children to school, he parks his bus and makes "rounds," dropping in to say hello to people until it is time to start the bus for the children's return trip.

In the Youth Elderly Service (YES) program of Fall River, Massachusetts, 100 high-school students visit elderly residents in nine nursing homes.

In West Hartford, Connecticut, and San Francisco, California, high-school students take part in Adopt-a-Grandparent programs. They write letters, do errands, play cards, and mostly talk with their "grandparents."

Texas "Roadrunner" Volunteers, Inc. of Austin visits residents of 43 nursing homes, provides transportation to the nursing homes for visitors who cannot provide their own and takes groups of patients and visitors on outings.

For information on Friendly Visiting programs, contact your state or area Agency on Aging.

10
Fund-Raising for Nonprofit Organizations

The fund-raisers listed in this chapter are members of the American Association of Fund-Raising Counsel, Inc. These firms, which only raise money for nonprofit projects, may be very helpful to your group if you have a nonprofit project that needs subsidization.

American Association of Fund-Raising Counsel, Inc.
500 Fifth Avenue
New York, NY 10036
(212) 354-5799
Contact: John J. Schwartz, President

FUND-RAISING ORGANIZATIONS

American City Bureau/Beaver Associates
O'Hare East Plaza
9501 W. Devon Ave.
Rosemont, IL 60018
(312) 696-1450

G. A. Brakeley & Co. Inc.
3960 Wilshire Blvd.
Los Angeles, CA 90010
(213) 388-3426

John Price Jones Brakeley Inc.
6 E. 43rd St.
New York, NY 10017
(212) 697-7120

Community Counselling Service, Inc.
Empire State Building
New York, NY 10001
(212) OX5-1175

Branch Offices

International Tower
8550 W. Bryn Mawr
Chicago, IL 60631
(312) 332-7009

351 California St.
San Francisco, CA 94104
(415) 392-5395

Community Service Bureau, Inc.
505 N. Ervay St., Suite 806
Dallas, TX 75201
(214) 747-2581

Branch Offices

230 Peachtree St., NW
Suite 1800
Atlanta, GA 30303
(404) 622-5040

3939 Glenwood Ave.
Suite 608
Raleigh, NC 27612
(919) 787-7457

1971 Peabody Ave.
Memphis, TN 38104
(901) 274-6521

4615 Southwest Freeway
Suite 475-E
Houston, TX 77027
(713) 622-5040

Owen C. Coogan, Inc.
61 Pine View Ave.
Worcester, MA 01603
(617) 754-8440

Branch Office

12 Spruce Road
Larchmont, NY 10538
(914) 834-6043

Cosgriff Company
Woodmen Tower
Omaha, NE 68102
(402) 344-7220

Branch Offices

One Embarcadero Center
San Francisco, CA 94111
(415) 788-3066

Board of Trade Building
Chicago, IL 60604
(312) 922-0364

The Cumerford Corporation
2501 E. Commercial Blvd.
Ft. Lauderdale, FL 33308
(305) 772-9944

Branch Offices

105 Montgomery St.
San Francisco, CA 94104
(415) 788-8884

912 Baltimore Ave.
Kansas City, MO 64105
(816) 444-7777

106 Bradford Ave.
East Providence, RI 02914
(401) 434-0838

Donahue/Cooke, Inc.
104 South Michigan Ave.
Chicago, IL 60603
(312) 236-4848

Charles R. Feldstein & Co., Inc.
221 N. LaSalle St.
Chicago, IL 60601
(312) 332-7480

John Grenzebach & Associates, Inc.
211 E. Chicago Ave.
Chicago, IL 60611
(312) 787-6690

The Gurin Group, Inc.
366 Madison Ave.
New York, NY 10017
(212) 661-5124

Hanley Associates, Inc.
2284 Main St.
Concord, MA 01742
(617) 369-7300

Branch Offices

1900 Point West Way
Sacramento, CA 95815
(916) 929-6560

Branch Offices (cont.)

25 S. Sixth St.
Amelia Island, FL 32034
(904) 261-9165

7939 State Line
Kansas City, MO 64114
(816) 523-6700

502 Mears Building
Scranton, PA 18503
(717) 346-2939

314 Lloyd Building
Seattle, WA 98101
(206) 622-2558

Havey Fund-Raising Management, Inc.
8777 West Forest Home Ave.
Milwaukee, WI 53228
(414) 425-6200

The Hockenburg System, Inc.
400 Payne-Shoemaker Building
Harrisburgh, PA 17101
(717) 238-1625

Holland Estell & Company, Inc.
261 Madison Ave.
Suite 1100
New York, NY 10016
(212) 697-0080

Kersting, Brown & Co. Inc.
61 Broadway
New York, NY 10006
(212) 422-2250

Kersting, Holding & Street, Inc.
61 Broadway
New York, NY 10006
(212) 422-2254

Ketchum, Inc.
314 Chatham Center
Pittsburgh, PA 15219
(412) 281-1481

Branch Offices

2411 Prudential Plaza
Chicago, IL 60601
(312) 321-1166

500 Fifth Ave.
Suite 2628
New York, NY 10036
(212) 244-6807

808 American Building
Charlotte, NC 28202
(704) 376-5616

914 One Main Place
Dallas, TX 75250
(214) 741-4591

The Martin J. Moran Company, Inc.
Two Penn Plaza
New York, NY 10001
(212) PE6-9550

Marts & Lundy, Inc.
521 Fifth Ave.
New York, NY 10017
(212) 687-1340

The Oram Group, Inc.
Harold L. Oram, Inc.
95 Madison Ave.
New York, NY 10016
(212) 889-2244

Branch Offices

3235 Berry Drive
Studio City, CA 91604
(213) 654-0540

1712 N St., NW
Washington, DC 20036
(202) 659-8536

Philanthropic Fund-Raising Service, Inc.
5 Kenmore Road
Valley Stream, NY 11581
(516) 825-3062

Richard Pontz and Associates
526 N. President Ave.
Lancaster, PA 17603
(717) 393-0118

John F. Rich Company
5 Penn Center Plaza
Philadelphia, PA 19103
(215) 567-0526

Rusk and Oram, Inc.
95 Madison Ave.
New York, NY 10016
(212) 889-5220

Smith, Hazlett, & Darcy, Inc.
110 Allen's Creek Road
Rochester, NY 14618
(716) 275-9340

Tamblyn & Brown, Inc.
Empire State Building
New York, NY 10001
(212) 524-3200

Branch Offices

1717 Massachusetts Ave., NW
Washington, DC 20036
(202) 797-8100

959 Kenmoore Ave.
Buffalo, NY 14223
(716) 875-6319

Ward, Dreshman & Reinhardt, Inc.
6660 North High St.
Worthington, OH 43085
(614) 888-5376

Milton Hood Ward & Co., Inc.
Hotel Plaza
New York, NY 10019
(212) PL3-7680

Will, Folsom and Smith, Inc.
19 W. 44th St.
New York, NY 10036
(212) 490-2660

11
Government Programs

Elderly Americans who are having difficulties making ends meet in these times of inflation and recession may not be fully informed about federal programs that already exist to help them meet their most basic needs — income supplements, jobs, food, and medical care. This chapter details these programs, and specifies where to apply, who is qualified, and so on.

In all cases, the federal agencies in Washington will be glad to reply to inquiries, but it is quicker and more direct to ask for information on the state or community level. To speed up the process, we have listed herein all the regional offices for each department and agency immediately following its particular group of programs.

Income Supplements

Persons who have been employed long enough in jobs covered by Social Security are eligible, of course, for monthly cash benefits. Also, under a new Supplemental Security Income (SSI) program, persons aged 65 and older, as well as blind and disabled people with limited income and resources, may receive federal payments. SSI benefits, when combined with other income (if any), will usually give to an individual a minimum monthly income of $457.70 and to a couple, $236.60 each. SSI takes the place of the previous Old-Age Assistance program, which was administered through state and county departments of public welfare or social services. Some states that were paying higher benefits than those provided under SSI are supplementing the federal payments to maintain their previous benefit level. Application for both Social Security benefits and SSI assistance are made at the local Social Security office, (listed in the telephone book under U.S. Government).

Jobs

Older persons seeking employment may be able to participate in one of several federally sponsored job programs recently established. Jobs are available for older workers under Title III of the Comprehensive Employment and Training Act of 1973 (CETA). According to the type of project, older persons may be hired to work in conservation, community beautification, social services, libraries, hospitals, or nutrition programs. Also, on December 31, 1974, the Emergency Job Program (an amendment to CETA) was signed into law, making additional federal funds available to state and local governmental units for public service jobs. Age discrimination is prohibited and some jobs, including part-time employment, are set aside for middle-aged or older persons. Not all types of jobs are available in all states; also, the level of unemployment in a community may determine how many jobs are opened.

Information on these programs can be obtained from the U.S. Department of Labor, Washington, DC 20210, or from its regional offices. Another excellent general source of information about these and other jobs for the elderly is the state employment service, which serves everyone, free and without obligation. The local telephone directory will provide the address of the nearest office.

Food and Nutrition

Through the national Nutrition Program for the Elderly, low-cost meals and related social services are being provided to many people aged 60 and over and their spouses. Most meals are provided in group settings, such as schools, community centers, churches, and public housing. Under some circumstances, meals can be home-delivered. Information about such programs is available from the Administration on Aging, Washington, DC 20201, or the state or area agency on aging.

Also, many low-income, elderly persons can stretch their incomes with food stamps, which are coupons that are used like money at the grocery store and are obtained from the government for less than their face value. An individual need not be receiving assistance payments to qualify for food stamps. Information about the program is available from the state or area agency on aging or local departments of social services, human resources, or welfare.

Medical Services

Medicare and Medicaid are two programs that help older persons with medical bills. All persons 65 years and older are eligible for Medicare, whereas needy, low-income elderly persons may also be eligible for Medicaid. Medicare, a federal program, is the same all over the country. Medicaid is a federal-state partnership under which benefits vary from state to state. Anyone 65 or older and entitled to Social Security or Railroad Retirement is automatically covered under Medicare's basic hospital insurance plan (Part A). The supplemental medical insurance plan (Part B) of Medicare is voluntary; to participate, the eligible persons must enroll in the plan. Information on Medicare is available from the local Social Security office.

For low-income elderly persons, Medicaid often pays for services not covered by Medicare, such as eyeglasses, dental care, and prescribed drugs. In the majority of states, a person need not be receiving SSI assistance to be eligible for Medicaid. Application should be made to the local social services or welfare office.

How to Find Help

Older Americans have an advocate agency headquartered in Washington, DC, which operates across the country. This is the Administration on Aging (AOA), which was set up by Congress under the Older Americans Act of 1965 to foster and coordinate programs, services, and research to help the elderly. It is part of the Department of Health, Education, and Welfare. Now, official area agencies on aging have been set up in every state and in many communities, especially where there are large numbers of elderly. (See Chapter 3, Area Agencies on Aging.) These agencies also serve as advocates for older Americans and coordinate activities on their behalf.

The area agencies on aging can supply information about the programs described in this chapter — Social Security, SSI, food stamps, meals, Medicare, Medicaid, and jobs — and can help older persons to interpret requirements for eligibility and to approach the proper agency. The agencies also advise and inform the elderly about housing, transportation, counseling, homemaker-home health aid, and other important services. A special goal of the AOA and the agencies throughout the country is to help older Americans remain independent in their homes, in comfort and safety, as long as possible, by means of appropriate services.

An individual can inquire at the state agency for help and also to find out how to contact the nearest area Agency on Aging.

Of course, not all elderly persons have critical problems. Many just want to volunteer to serve their communities or simply wish to participate in recreational, social, and educational activities. The state and area Agency on Aging can assist these persons also.

Information and Referral Services

Information and Referral services have been established in many communities. Their purpose is to guide people with specific problems or needs to appropriate facilities where assistance can be obtained. The Older Americans Act requires that all elderly persons in the country be provided reasonably convenient access to an information and referral (I&R) service. All state and area agencies on aging are now striving to meet this requirement. In some cases, a separate I&R service has been set up. The name, address, and telephone number of the nearest I&R service for the elderly can usually be obtained from the telephone directory, or the state or area agency on aging.

ACTION
806 Connecticut Ave., NW
Washington, DC 20525
(202) 393-3111
Contact: Chairman

ACTION Cooperative Volunteer Program

OBJECTIVE: To strengthen and supplement efforts to meet a broad range of human, social, and environmental needs, particularly those related to poverty by encouraging and enabling persons from all walks of life and from all age groups to perform meaningful and constructive volunteer service in agencies, institutions, and situations where the application of human talents and dedication may help to meet such needs.

PROGRAM: To provide specialized services, advisory services, and counseling.

RESTRICTIONS: Provides full-time volunteers who are willing to live in and work with disadvantaged communities. The volunteers live on allowances at the level of those people whom they serve. Volunteers do not displace employed workers or impair existing contracts for work, nor does an agency supervising any volunteer program receive compensation for services of volunteers. Volunteers are not to be involved in religious, labor, antilabor, or political activities. Discrimination against any person on grounds of race, creed, color, age, sex, or national origin is not allowed.

REQUIREMENTS: Sponsors applying for ACTION Cooperative Volunteers (ACV) must be nonprofit organizations; they may be public or private. The project in which they propose to use the volunteers must serve human, social, and environmental needs, especially those related to poverty. The sponsoring organization in an ACV agreement pays to ACTION the direct cost of volunteer support in the ACTION region in which the volunteers will serve. These direct costs are approximately commensurate with the actual standard of living of the low-income community that is served.

APPLICATION: Prospective sponsors apply through the ACV developers in ACTION regional offices. The final contract is a memorandum of agreement, which is signed by the regional director, by ACTION headquarters in Washington, DC, and by the sponsoring organization.

APPROVAL: None.

PUBLICATIONS: "ACTION Cooperative Volunteer Program (ACV) Handbook for Sponsors."

RELATED PROGRAMS: The Foster Grandparents Program, Retired Senior Volunteer Program, and Volunteers in Service to America.

The Foster Grandparents Program

OBJECTIVE: To provide part-time volunteer opportunities for low-income persons age 60 and over and to render supportive person-to-person services in health, education, welfare, and related residential settings to children with special needs.

PROGRAM: To provide project grants.

RESTRICTIONS: The grants may be used for: staff salaries, foster grandparent stipends, staff fringe benefits, foster grandparent fringe benefits, staff travel, foster grandparent transportation, meals, physical examinations, uniforms/smocks, laundry, supplies, consultant and contract services, equipment, space costs, etc. Assignment of foster grandparents to children with special needs may occur in residential and nonresidential facilities, including day-care or preschool establishments, and to children living in their own homes. Funds are not available for construction.

REQUIREMENTS: Any public or nonprofit private agency or organization may apply. A community action agency (established under Title II Economic Opportunity Act) is the preferred applicant if a project is to be undertaken entirely in the community served by this agency. The state agency on aging is the preferred applicant if the area to be served is broader than one community. An agency or institution that provides a program setting should not also serve as grantee.

APPLICATION: Application materials may be obtained from ACTION headquarters or the regional office. The original and four copies are submitted by the applicant agency to the ACTION regional office.

APPROVAL: The ACTION regional director makes all grant awards.

PUBLICATIONS: "The Foster Grandparents Program Information Statement," "Foster Grandparents Program Policies," "Cost Benefit Profile of the Foster Grandparents Program," "Foster Grandparents Program – One Part of ACTION" (ACTION Pamphlet 4400-2), and "The Foster Grandparents Program" (ACTION Flyer 4400-1).

RELATED PROGRAM: Retired Senior Volunteer Program and the Senior Companion Program.

Retired Senior Volunteer Program

OBJECTIVE: To establish a recognized role in the community and a meaningful life in retirement by developing a wide variety of community volunteer-service opportunities for persons 60 years of age or over.

PROGRAM: To provide project grants.

RESTRICTIONS: Grants may be made to establish community-service organizations (public or private nonprofit) to assist in the development or operation, or both, of locally organized senior volunteer programs directed by competent staff. This local community-service organization develops a wide variety of volunteer-service opportunities throughout the community, in hospitals, schools, courts, day-care centers, libraries, and so on. A local program also arranges for transportation and a meal for the senior volunteer as needed.

REQUIREMENTS: Grants are made to public and private nonprofit organizations.

APPLICATION: RSVP application forms are issued to applicants who have established their eligibility through the preliminary inquiry procedure. Applications are submitted to ACTION, with a copy to the state office on aging.

APPROVAL: Grant awards are made by the director of ACTION.

PUBLICATION: *Federal Register* Vol. 36, No. 125, and "RSVP Program Information Statement."

RELATED PROGRAMS: The Foster Grandparent Program.

Service Corps of Retired Executives and Active Corps of Executives

OBJECTIVE: To utilize the management experience of retired and semiretired (SCORE) and active (ACE) business executives for the benefit of new and existing small businesses as well as nonprofit community organizations.

PROGRAM: To provide advisory services and counseling.

RESTRICTIONS: Working closely with the Small Business Administration, which has responsibility for direction and administration of SCORE and ACE, ACTION helps strengthen the SCORE and ACE programs through recruitment of cases, new volunteers, publicity, and providing new opportunities for volunteer service. A small business or nonprofit community organization seeking business management counseling may apply to the nearest Small Business Administration or ACTION field office. SCORE and ACE volunteers are remunerated for any out-of-pocket expenses, but do not accept compensation or fees for services rendered.

REQUIREMENTS: Existing and potential small-business people and not-for-profit community organizations requiring management counseling are eligible. A small business is one that is independently owned and operated and not dominant in its field. More specific criteria defining small businesses are established by Small Business Administration.

APPLICATION: Personal or written application (SBA Form or ACTION Form request for SCORE/ACE counseling) to Small Business Administration or ACTION field offices.

APPROVAL: None.

PUBLICATIONS: SCORE and ACE ("One Part of ACTION") brochures.

Volunteers in Service to America

OBJECTIVE: To supplement efforts of community organizations to eliminate poverty by enabling persons from all walks of life and all age groups to perform meaningful and constructive service as volunteers in situations where the application may help the poor to overcome the handicaps of poverty and poverty-related problems and secure opportunities for self-advancement.

PROGRAM: To provide specialized services, training, advisory services, and counsel.

RESTRICTIONS: Provides full-time volunteers at the request of community groups to provide service not exceeding 2 years, but for not less than 1 year, except as the director determines, in clearly defined jobs that lead to mobilization of the community's resources. The volunteers live among, and on allowances at the level of, the people they serve. Many volunteers such as lawyers, health-personnel teachers, architects, businesspeople, and craftspeople, contribute specific skills, and all volunteers work to improve the community's ability to solve its own problems. Members of the poor community must actively participate in the development and implementation of the program. Volunteers do not displace employed workers nor does an agency supervising any volunteer program receive compensation for services of volunteers. Volunteers are not to be involved in religious, labor, antilabor, or political activities.

REQUIREMENTS: Sponsors applying for VISTA volunteers must be a nonprofit organization; they may be public or private. The project in which they propose to use the volunteers must be poverty-related.

APPLICATION: Prospective sponsors apply through VISTA program officers in ACTION regional offices.

APPROVAL: None.

PUBLICATION: "Guidelines for Prospective Sponsoring Organizations."

RELATED PROGRAMS: Teacher Corps Operations and Training, Management Assistance to Small Businesses, the Foster Grandparents Program, Retired Senior Volunteer Program, and University Year for Action (UYA).

The Senior Companion Program

OBJECTIVE: To provide part-time volunteer opportunities for low-income persons age 60 and over and to provide supportive person-to-person services to persons (other than children) with special needs, especially older persons living in their own homes, and in nursing homes and other institutions.

PROGRAM: To provide project grants.

RESTRICTIONS: The grants may be used for: staff salaries, senior companion stipends, staff fringe benefits, senior companion fringe benefits, staff travel, senior companion transportation, meals, physical examinations, uniforms/smocks, laundry, supplies, consultant and contract services, equipment, space costs, and so forth. Assignment of senior companions to older persons with special needs may occur in residential and nonresidential facilities including day-care or preschool establishments and to older persons in their own homes. Funds are not available for construction.

REQUIREMENTS: Any public or nonprofit private agency or organization may apply. A community-action agency (established under Title II Economic Opportunity Act) is the preferred applicant if a project is to be undertaken entirely in the community served by this agency. The state agency on aging is the preferred applicant if the area to be served is broader than one community. An agency or institution that provides a program setting should not also serve as grantee.

APPLICATION: Application materials may be obtained from ACTION headquarters or the regional office. The original and four copies are submitted by the applicant agency to the ACTION regional office.

APPROVAL: The ACTION regional director will make all grant awards.

PUBLICATIONS: "ACTION: Meeting Community Needs through Voluntarism."

RELATED PROGRAMS: The Foster Grandparents Program and Retired Senior Volunteer Program.

GOVERNMENT PROGRAMS 49

REGIONAL OFFICES

1333 Westwood Blvd.
Los Angeles, CA 90024
(213) 824-7742

1068 16th St.
San Diego, CA 92101
(714) 293-5083

100 McAllister St.
San Francisco, CA 94102
(415) 556-2080

1050 17th St.
Denver, CO 80202
(303) 837-4173

812 Connecticut Ave., NW
Washington, DC
(202) 382-2841

730 Peachtree St., NE
Atlanta, GA 30308
(404) 526-6825

1001 S. Wright
Champaign, IL 61820
(217) 356-1159

Federal Building
Indianapolis, IN 46204
(317) 633-7500

Federal Building
Des Moines, IA 50309
(515) 284-4087

Fifth & State
Kansas City, KS 66101
(816) 374-4556

John W. McCormack Federal Building
Boston, MA 02109
(617) 223-7366

Federal Building
Detroit, MI 48226
(313) 226-7928

Old Federal Building
Minneapolis, MN 55401
(612) 725-2593

90 Church St.
New York, NY 10007
(212) 264-7123

Federal Building
Rochester, NY 14614
(716) 546-4900

214 Pittsboro St.
Chapel Hill, NC 27514
(919) 967-1421

U.S. Post Office & Courthouse
Cincinnati, OH 45202
(513) 684-3136

Federal Building
Toledo, OH 43604
(419) 259-7442

Federal Building
Portland, OR 97201
(503) 221-2411

1405 Locust St.
Philadelphia, PA 19102
(215) 597-0744

212 N. St. Paul St.
Dallas, TX 75201
(214) 749-1855

1601 Second Ave.
Seattle, WA 98101
(206) 442-5490

306 N. Brooks St.
Madison, WI 53715
(608) 252-5279

APPALACHIAN REGIONAL COMMISSION

1666 Connecticut Ave., NW
Washington, DC 20235
(202) 967-5728

Contact: Chairman

Appalachian Housing Fund

OBJECTIVE: To stimulate the construction of low and moderate income housing in growth areas of the Appalachian Region and to meet the objectives stated under the program entitled Appalachian Regional Development.

PROGRAM: To provide direct loans.

RESTRICTIONS: Used for costs of planning projects and obtaining mortgage insurance. Included may be preliminary surveys of market needs, preliminary site engineering and architectural fees, site options, Federal Housing Administration (FHA) and Federal National Mortgage Association (FNMA) fees, construction loan fees, and discounts. Use restrictions are low- and moderate-income mortgage insurance as provided by the National Housing Act.

REQUIREMENTS: Nonprofit, limited dividend, cooperative, or public corporation or bodies.

APPLICATION: After a preliminary conference with FHA, the sponsor submits an application to FHA for the loan. This is followed by application for assistance under the National Housing Act. An executed FHA form No. 2200 is required with the submission.

APPROVAL: The Appalachian Regional Commission (ARC) has delegated authority to the federal cochairman and the state's regional representative to approve individual projects. The federal cochairman determines that the project satisfies all federal requirements. The Department of Housing and Urban Development is then notified and administers the grants and disburses funds. The ARC notifies congressional offices and the governor's office of the grant approval. Notification of grant award to the State Central Information Reception Agency (SCIRA) and Department of Treasury is required.

PUBLICATIONS: "The Appalachian Regional Commission Code," "Guidelines for Funding Appalachian Projects, Development Districts, and Research," and *Appalachia*, a journal devoted to the special problems of regional development.

RELATED PROGRAMS: Appalachian Housing Technical Assistance, Appalachian Supplements to Federal Grant-in-Aid, Interest Subsidy Homes for Lower Income Families, Mortgage Insurance Homes, and Public Housing Acquisition (with or without Rehabilitation) and Construction.

Appalachian Housing Site Development

OBJECTIVE: To assist in developing site and offsite improvements for low- and moderate-income families in the Appalachian Region.

PROGRAM: To provide project grants.

RESTRICTIONS: Funds are to be used only for reasonable site development costs and necessary offsite improvement costs. The grants must be essential to the economic feasibility of housing constructed or rehabilitated for low- and moderate-income families.

REQUIREMENTS: Nonprofit organizations and public bodies.

APPLICATION: Application must comply with all current FHA underwriting requirements. Upon notification that grant funds have been reserved, the applicant submits a contract encompassing the terms and conditions of the project.

APPROVAL: The ARC federal cochairman and regional representatives approve individual projects. The federal cochairman determines that the project satisfies all federal requirements. The Department of Housing and Urban Development is notified and administers the grant, disburses funds, and makes notification of grant award to the designated SCIRA and the Department of Treasury. The ARC notifies congressional offices and the office of the governor of grant approval.

PUBLICATIONS: "The Appalachian Regional Commission Code," "Guidelines for Funding Appalachian Projects, Development Districts, and Research," *Appalachia*, a journal devoted to special problems of regional development.

RELATED PROGRAMS: Appalachian Regional Development, Appalachian Housing Fund, Appalachian Housing Technical Assistance, and Rural Housing Site Loans.

Appalachian Housing Technical Assistance

OBJECTIVE: To support state housing programs designed to help the region overcome its housing deficit and generate more properly conceived and executed housing projects.

PROGRAM: To provide advisory services and counseling and dissemination of technical information; also project grants.

RESTRICTIONS: The ARC or the Secretary of Housing and Urban Development with the approval of the commission, may provide, or contract to provide, technical assistance concerning construction, rehabilitation, and operation of housing with monies available from the Appalachian Housing Fund. The technical assistance must be for the benefit of nonprofit housing organizations.

REGIONAL OFFICES

State Office Building
Montgomery, AL 36104
(205) 269-7171, Ext. 12

270 Washington St., SW
Atlanta, GA 30334
(404) 656-3820

Rm. 142
The Capitol
Frankfort, KY 40601
(502) 564-3605

2525 Riva Rd.
Annapolis, MD 21404
(301) 267-5501

City-County Building
P.O. Box 1606
Tupelo, MS 38801
(601) 844-1184

Rm. 249, State Capitol
Albany, NY 12224
(518) 474-7955

116 W. Jones St.
Raleigh, NC 27602
(919) 829-7232

65 S. Front St.
P.O. Box 1001
Columbus, OH 43215
(614) 466-3379

503 Finance Building
Box 1323
Harrisburg, PA 17120
(717) 787-2086

P.O. Box 11450
Columbia, SC 29211
(803) 758-3261

1222 Andrew Jackson State
Nashville, TN 37219
(615) 741-2549

Richmond, VA 23219
(804) 770-2211

Charleston, WV 26305
(304) 348-2000

DEPARTMENT OF AGRICULTURE
14th St. and Independence Ave., SW
Washington, DC 20250
(202) 655-4000
Contact: Secretary

Community Facilities Loans

OBJECTIVE: To construct, enlarge, extend, or otherwise improve community facilities providing essential service to rural residents.

PROGRAM: To provide guaranteed and insured loans.

RESTRICTIONS: Community facilities are included, but are not limited to those providing or supporting overall community development such as fire and rescue services, transportation, traffic control, community, social, cultural, health and recreational benefits, and industrial and business development. Loans shall not be made for community electric or telephone systems. All facilities financed in whole or in part with FHA funds shall be for public use.

REQUIREMENTS: Public and quasipublic bodies and associations including corporations, Indian tribes on federal and state reservations, and other federally recognized Indian tribes and existing private corporations, which (1) are operated on a not-for-profit basis; (2) have or will have the legal authority necessary for constructing, operating, and maintaining the proposed facility or service and for obtaining, giving security for, and repaying the loan, and (3) are unable to finance the proposed project from its own resources or through commercial credit at reasonable rates and terms.

APPLICATION: Application is made at the local FHA county office.

APPROVAL: The state director approves all loans.

RELATED PROGRAMS: Cooperative Extension Service.

Food and Nutrition Service
Contact: Administration

Food Distribution:

OBJECTIVE: To improve the diets of schoolchildren and needy persons in households and charitable institutions, and other individuals in need of food assistance, and to increase the market for domestically produced foods acquired under surplus removal or price-support operations.

PROGRAM: To provide formula grants, and the sale, exchange, or donation of property and goods.

RESTRICTIONS: Food is made available for distribution to qualifying households, charitable institutions, and summer camps.

REQUIREMENTS: Those state and federal agencies who are designated as distributing agencies by the governor, legislature, or other authority, may receive and distribute donated foods.

APPLICATION: All states now have distributing agencies — no application is necessary. Local governments, schools, summer camps, and institutions must apply to the state distributing agency on its forms. Requests for programs for individuals and federal agencies must be forwarded to the Department of Agriculture for approval. Individuals apply to approved health facilities. Heads of households apply to local welfare authorities on forms supplied by state or local office.

APPROVAL: Funds are offered by the Department of Agriculture to the state agency (for use in household program improvement). Agency need only accept or reject.

PUBLICATIONS: "USDA Food Donation Program," "How to Plan a Self-Service Food Donation Center," "You Can Help Fight Hunger in America — Donated Foods Handbook for Volunteers," "Guide for Warehousing USDA Donated Foods," "Drive to Serve, A Public Service for Senior Citizens," "Food for the Elderly," "Food for Emergencies and Disasters," and "Donated Foods for Disasters."

RELATED PROGRAMS: Food Stamps, Special Food Service Program for Children, School Breakfast Program, National School Lunch Program, Special Milk Program for Children, Follow Through, and Child Development — Head Start.

Food Stamps:

OBJECTIVE: To improve diets of low-income households and expand the market for domestically produced foods.

PROGRAM: To provide direct payments for specified use. Families buy stamps or coupons worth more than the purchase amount, which varies according to income and family size. The coupons are used for food in retail stores.

RESTRICTIONS: Certain elderly persons and their spouses who cannot prepare their own meals may also use their food coupons to pay for meals delivered to their homes by authorized nonprofit meal-delivery services.

REQUIREMENTS: The state agency responsible for federally aided public assistance programs submits requests for the program to USDA's Food and Nutrition Service on behalf of local political subdivisions that want to participate. Families apply for assistance at their local welfare office.

APPLICATION: Individuals and families apply through their local welfare offices in those areas where the program is in operation.

APPROVAL: Approval is given by the Foods and Nutrition Service.

PUBLICATIONS: "Food Stamp Regulations," "Food Stamp Fact Sheets" (English and Spanish), "Food Stamp Changes," "Food Stamp Handbook for Volunteers," "You and Food Stamps," "You're in Good Company," "Food Stamp Program — More Food, Better Diets for Low-Income Families," "Food Stamps Make the Difference," "Reaching People," and "Food Makes the Difference — Ideas for Economy-Minded Families."

RELATED PROGRAMS: Food Distribution. Public Assistance — Social Services.

Low- to Moderate-Income Housing Loans
(Rural Housing Loans)

OBJECTIVE: To assist rural families in obtaining decent, safe, and sanitary dwellings and related facilities.

PROGRAM: To provide guaranteed and insured loans.

RESTRICTIONS: The loans may be used for: construction; repair or purchase of housing; provide necessary and adequate sewage-disposal facilities for the applicant and his or her family; purchase or install essential equipment, which, upon installation, becomes part of the real estate; buy a site on which to place a dwelling for applicant's own use. Housing debts may under certain circumstances be refinanced. Restrictions on the use of the loans are: a dwelling financed for a family with a low or moderate income must be modest in size, design, and cost. An applicant must be without sufficient resources to provide on his or her own account the necessary housing, or related facilities, and be unable to secure the necessary credit from other sources upon terms and conditions which he reasonably could be expected to fulfill.

REQUIREMENTS: Be an owner or, when the loan is closed, become the owner of a farm or nonfarm tract in a rural area. Be a citizen of the United States or reside in the United States after having been legally admitted for permanent residence. Have adequate and dependably available income to meet operating and family living expenses, including taxes, insurance, and maintenance, and repayments on debts including the proposed loan. Interest credits may, under certain conditions, be granted to lower-income families, which will reduce the effective interest rate paid to as low as 1 percent, depending on the size and income of the applicant family. Also, the applicant should be able to submit evidence of inability to obtain credit elsewhere, verification of income and debts, plans, specifications, and cost estimates.

APPLICATION: File an application with the county office of the Farmers Home Administration serving the county where the dwelling is or will be located.

APPROVAL: Made by county supervisor.

PUBLICATIONS: "Home Ownership," and "Rural Housing."

RELATED PROGRAMS: Rural Housing Site Loans, Very Low-Income Housing Repair Loans, Rural Self-Help Housing Technical Assistance, Interest Subsidy-Homes for Lower Income Families, and Mortgage Insurance — Homes in Outlying Areas.

Rural Rental Housing Loans

OBJECTIVE: To provide economically designed and constructed rental and cooperative housing and related facilities suited for independent living for rural residents.

PROGRAM: To provide guaranteed and insured loans.

RESTRICTIONS: Loans can be used to construct, purchase, improve, or repair rental or cooperative housing.

REQUIREMENTS: Applicants may be individuals, cooperatives, nonprofit organizations, or corporations unable to finance the housing either with their own resources or with credit obtained from private sources. However, applicants must be able to assume the obligations of the loan, furnish adequate security, and have sufficient income for repayment.

APPLICATION: The application will be in the form of a letter to the FHA county supervisor in the county where the housing will be located.

APPROVAL: Award is made by the state director or county supervisor.

PUBLICATIONS: "Rental Housing Units."

RELATED PROGRAMS: Rural Housing Site Loans, Mortgage Insurance — Rental Housing for Low or Moderate Income Families, Market Interest Rate, and Mortgage Insurance — Rental Housing.

Rural Housing Site Loans

OBJECTIVE: To assist public or private nonprofit organizations interested in providing sites for housing.

PROGRAM: To provide direct loans, and guaranteed and insured loans.

RESTRICTIONS: For the purchase and development of adequate sites, including necessary equipment, which becomes a permanent part of the development; loan limitation of $1 million without national office approval.

REQUIREMENTS: A nonprofit organization that will provide the developed sites to qualified borrowers on a nonprofit basis.

APPLICATION: The application will be in the form of a letter to the county supervisor of the Farmers Home Administration. Supporting information and costs should be included as needed.

APPROVAL: After application has been approved by the county supervisor and the county committee, it is given final approval by the state director.

PUBLICATIONS: "Rural Housing Site Loans" and "Farmers' Home Administration Fact Sheet."

RELATED PROGRAMS: Low to Moderate Income Housing Loans, Rural Renting Housing Loans, Mortgage Insurance — Land Development and New Communities, and Nonprofit Housing Sponsor Loans — Planning Projects for Low and Moderate Income Families.

Very-Low-Income Housing Repair Loans

OBJECTIVE: To give very-low-income rural homeowners an opportunity to make essential minor repairs to their homes, to make them safe and to remove health hazards to the family or the community.

PROGRAM: To provide guaranteed and insured loans.

RESTRICTIONS: To assist owner-occupants in rural areas who do not qualify for section 502 loans to repair or improve their dwelling in order to make such dwelling safe and sanitary and remove hazards to the family or the community.

REQUIREMENTS: Applicant must own and occupy a farm or rural nonfarm tract, and be without sufficient income to qualify for a section 502 loan.

APPLICATION: Application form obtainable in the local FHA office.

RELATED PROGRAMS: Low to Moderate Income Housing Loans, Major Home Improvement Loan Insurance — Housing Outside Urban Renewal Areas, and Property Improvement Loan Insurance — All Existing Structures.

REGIONAL OFFICES

General

Clemson University
Sirrine Textile Building
Clemson, SC 29631
(803) 654-2631 or 2659

4841 Summer Ave.
Memphis, TN 38117
(901) 682-1601

Texas A&M University
USDA Building
College Station, TX 77814
(713) 846-8821

Mills Building
303 N. Oregon St.
El Paso, TX 79901
(915) 533-5485

Food and Nutrition Service

550 Kearny St.
San Francisco, CA 94108
(415) 556-4951

1100 Spring St., NW
Atlanta, GA 30309
(404) 526-5131

536 South Clark St.
Chicago, IL 60605
(312) 353-6664

729 Alexander Road
Princeton, NJ 08540
(609) 452-1712

1100 Commerce St.
Dallas, TX 75202
(214) 749-2877

DEPARTMENT OF DEFENSE

The Pentagon
Washington, DC 20301
(202) 545-6700
Contact: Secretary

Military Retirement

The military retirement program provides protection against loss of income to members of the armed forces and their families due to the retirement of the member.

Eligibility. Eligibility for retirement benefits is possible under three criteria: (1) age or length of service, (2) disability incurred during active service, or (3) eligibility for annuity payments (survivors of retired armed forces members).

Nondisability Retirement Eligibility Requirements: Any regular or reserve commissioned officer or warrant officer may be retired after 20 years of active service, at least 10 of which are commissioned service for commissioned officers. Enlisted members may retire after 20 years of service either active or inactive. Retirement for age varies according to rank, with 60 years of age generally being the minimum age at which servicemen and women may retire. Regular officers are also mandatorily retired if they are passed over for promotion. This provision varies by amount of service and rank.

Disability Retirement Eligibility Conditions: Members who have a service-incurred disability of at least 30 percent (as determined by the Veterans Administration rating) may be retired for permanent disability if they are physically incapable of performing the duties of their grade.

If disability is not permanent, the member is placed on the temporary disability list. After 5 years, the member must be either retired for permanent disability or removed from the disability list. Any member found unfit for further service but ineligible for disability retired pay may receive disability severance pay.

Annuities to Dependents upon Death of Service Member in Retired Status: Members who retired before September 21, 1972, could elect to participate in the Retired Serviceman's Family Protection Plan (RSFPP) by voluntarily accepting a reduced monthly retirement benefit in order to provide for a continuation of a portion of retired pay for their survivors. Members already retired on September 21, 1972, who were participating in the RSFPP could elect to: (1) continue in the RSFPP and not join the new Survivor Benefit Plan (SBP), (2) drop RSFPP and join SBP, or (3) continue in RSFPP and join SBP provided that combined coverage does not exceed 100 percent of retired pay.

Members who retired after September 20, 1972, may not participate in RSFPP. Those members with spouse or children will automatically be covered under SBP unless they choose to decline coverage prior to their retirement.

The cost to the service member of providing a survivor benefit is 2½ percent of the first $300 of the base amount, plus 10 percent of the remaining base amount. (The base amount chosen by the member may range from $300 to total retirement pay.) This cost continues for the lifetime of the member. Cost for an annuity for children only is based on an actuarial charge dependent upon the age of the member and the youngest child.

Members may elect to provide annuities for surviving spouses, surviving children, surviving spouse and children, or, under the new plan only, for other natural persons with an insurable interest.

Other Eligibility Requirements: None. Noncitizens are entitled to benefits except that any retiree who becomes a citizen of a country other than the United States *after* retirement loses retirement benefits.

Benefits based on years of service.

Nondisability Benefits: The retired pay is equal to 2½ percent of the basic pay multiplied by the number of years of service, with the maximum benefit equal to 75 percent of basic pay.

Credited service for enlisted members is active service only. Officers may be credited with active and inactive service depending upon branch of service and whether retirement was voluntary or mandatory. The retired grade is generally the grade whether temporary or permanent in which the member is serving on the date of retirement.

Disability Benefits: Benefits are determined by multiplying the basic pay of the member's retired grade by the percentage of disability or 2½ percent multiplied by years of active service, whichever provides the larger benefit. Maximum benefits amount to 75 percent of basic pay; the minimum benefit is 30 percent of basic pay.

Members have the option of receiving disability compensation from the Veterans Administration rather than disability retired pay. Disability severance pay is equal to 2 months' basic pay for each year of service, not to exceed 2 years of basic pay.

Survivor Benefits: Under RSFPP, a member could elect to receive actuarially reduced benefits for his or her lifetime in order to provide benefits to the survivors upon the member's death. Payments to surviving spouse terminate upon the spouse's death or remarriage. Payments to an eligible child stop upon attainment of age 18, or age 23 if the child is attending school. Election of this plan had to have been made prior to the member completing 19 years of service or, if after 19 years of service, at least 2 years before receiving retirement pay.

Under the SBP, the benefit paid to the survivor is 55 percent of the base amount, where the base amount is that portion of the full amount of retired pay specified by the retiree at the time of retirement. This benefit is reduced by the Social Security survivor benefit attributable to military service after the spouse attains age 62. Payments to a surviving spouse cease upon death or upon remarriage prior to age 60. Payments to eligible children cease at 18 or at age 22 if the child is attending school.

Under the new SBP, payment to a surviving spouse of a member who dies on active duty after 20 years of service, is equal to the difference between the Dependency and Indemnity Compensation paid to the spouse and 55 percent of the retired pay to which the member would have been entitled had he retired on the date of death.

Relationship of Benefit Amount to Cost-of-Living Changes: Retirement and survivor annuities are automatically increased whenever the consumer price index (CPI) rises at least 3 percent over the last adjustment period and remains above this for 3 consecutive months. The increase is equal to the percentage rise in the CPI plus an additional 1 percent.

Other Benefits/Related Programs: Most benefits available to active-duty members, such as medical care, commissary and exchange privileges, and space available for air travel, are available to retirees.

Interactions with Other Programs:

Program Eligibility: Automatically entitled to Veterans Outpatient Care, Veterans Hospitalization, Prescription Service, and Domiciliary Care.

Program Income: No taxation of income from any other program except that persons receiving benefits under the SBP program may not also receive Social Security benefits based on credits earned while in military service.

U.S. Soldiers' and Airmen's Home

OBJECTIVE: To provide a self-supporting permanent residence for the relief and support of certain elderly, invalid, or disabled soldiers of the regular army and airmen of the air force.

PROGRAM: Provision of specialized services for this program.

RESTRICTIONS: Complete domiciliary and medical care.

REQUIREMENTS: Former warrant officers and enlisted personnel of the regular army and air force with the following qualifications: honest and faithful service for 20 years or more; or service-connected disability rendering them unable to earn a livelihood; or non-service-connected disability rendering them unable to earn a livelihood, provided they had service during a war.

APPLICATION: Letter to Secretary, Board of Commissioners.

PUBLICATIONS: Informational pamphlet available from U.S. Soldier's and Airmen's Home.

RELATED PROGRAMS: Veterans State Hospital Care. Veterans Information and Assistance.

CONTACT: Secretary.

REGIONAL OFFICES

P.O. Box 7287
Santa Rosa, CA 95401
(707) 544-1330

Denver Federal Center
Building 710
Denver, CO 80225
(303) 234-2553

Thomasville, GA 31792
(912) 226-1761

Olney, MD 20832
(301) 926-5110

Maynard, MA 01754
(617) 897-9381

Battle Creek, MI 49016
(616) 968-8142

Federal Regional Center
Denton, TX 76201
(817) 387-5811

Federal Regional Center
Bothell, WA 98011
(206) 486-0721

DEPARTMENT OF HEALTH, EDUCATION AND WELFARE (HEW)

330 Independence Ave., SW
Washington, DC 20201
(202) 962-2246
Contact: Secretary

OFFICE OF EDUCATION (OE)
Contact: Commissioner

Adult Education — Grants to States

OBJECTIVE: To expand educational opportunity and encourage the establishment of programs of adult public education to the level of completion of secondary school and make available the means to secure training that will enable them to become more productive and responsible citizens.

PROGRAM: To provide formula grants.

RESTRICTIONS: First priority is given to instructions in speaking, reading, or writing the English language for adults functioning at the eighth-grade level or below; second priority is for programs serving adults above the eighth grade and through the twelfth-grade level, but only if it can be shown that needs for adult basic education have been met in the school district or other areas to be served by such programs. In addition, state grant funds may be used for special projects, teacher training, and research programs related to the activities authorized under this title.

REQUIREMENTS: Designated state educational agencies for adults 16 years of age and over with less than a twelfth-grade level of competence or who do not have a secondary school certificate. A state plan is required under Part III of the Office of Management and Budget circular No. A-95. The state plan shall include a certification from the state attorney general that all plan provisions and amendments thereto are consistent with state law.

APPLICATION: State plans and amendments must be submitted to the governor for his review and comments before they are forwarded (prior to the beginning of each fiscal year) to the Office of Education Regional Director of Adult, Vocational, and Technical Education in the DHEW regional office. The regional director will provide guidance on specific problems and technical assistance in the preparation of state plan. Each state agency must submit to (or have available at a designated location for review by) the regional director in the DHEW regional office a state plan or amendment that sets forth the manner and procedures under which the state will carry out the state plan.

PUBLICATIONS: "Rules and Regulations," "Guide for Preparing a State Plan for Adult Basic Education Programs Under the Adult Education Act of 1966."

RELATED PROGRAMS: Adult Education — Special Projects, Adult Education — Teacher Education.

Adult Education — Special Projects

OBJECTIVE: To strengthen the ongoing state grant adult basic education program through experimentation with new teaching methods, programs, techniques, and with new operational and administrative systems.

PROGRAM: To provide project grants.

RESTRICTIONS: Projects must involve the use of innovations of national significance or special value to the adult education program and must involve cooperative arrangements with other programs in a way that has unusual promise in promoting a comprehensive or coordinated approach to the problems of persons with basic educational deficiencies. Grants cannot be made to divinity schools or departments of divinity.

REQUIREMENTS: Local educational agencies or other public or private nonprofit agencies, including educational television stations. Adults 16 years of age and over with less than a twelfth-grade level of competency or who do not have a secondary school certificate.

APPLICATION: The standard application forms as furnished by the federal agency and required by the Office of Management and Budget (OMB) circular No. A-102 must be used for this program. The Division of Adult Education Programs, Bureau of Occupational and Adult Education, will provide the required preapplication and application forms. Each applicant seeking support for a Special Experimental Demonstration Project must submit a preapplication and/or application form in accordance with procedures established by Attachment M of OMB circular A-102. Preapplication and application forms are submitted to:

Division of Adult Education Programs
Bureau of Occupational and Adult Education
Office of Education
Washington, DC 20202

APPROVAL: The Associate Commissioner of the Bureau of Adult, Vocational, and Technical Education approves a proposal for support, and a procurement cover sheet (OE form 5291) is issued. After negotiation is completed, the OE grants officer sends the notification of grant award (OE form 5232) to the grantee. A notification of grant-in-aid action SF 240 is also sent to the designated State Central Information Reception Agency and Office of Management and Budget.

PUBLICATIONS: "Guidelines — Adult Education Programs under Title III, Section 309 of the Adult Education Act," "General Provisions Regulations for Office of Education Programs," "Office of Management and Budget Circular No. A-102."

RELATED PROGRAMS: Adult Education — Grants to States, Adult Education — Teacher Education.

Civil Rights Compliance Activities

OBJECTIVE: To enforce Title VI of the Civil Rights Act of 1964, which prohibits federal funds for programs that discriminate as to race, color, or national origin. Responsible for implementing an Executive Order that prohibits discrimination in federally supported employment because of race, color, religion, age, sex, or national origin.

PROGRAM: To insure investigation of complaints.

RESTRICTIONS: HEW is responsible for assuring that beneficiaries of major programs receive services without discrimination or segregation. This assistance is provided through state agencies, school districts, nursing homes, extended care facilities, medical laboratories, hospitals, colleges and universities, vocational broadcasting facilities, day-care centers, and social-service agencies. Any person who believes that he or she has been discriminated against in the provision of these services as to race, color, or national origin may file a complaint or grievance with the HEW Office for Civil Rights. The office will investigate and take corrective steps to assure equal opportunity. Individuals may also file complaints of sex discrimination concerning all education programs or activities receiving federal financial assistance. The office investigates patterns of discrimination and practices affecting classes of employees to ensure that federal contractors and subcontractors do not practice discrimination in employment on the basis of race, color, religion, sex, or national origin, and that they take affirmative action to ensure that employees are treated without regard to such factors. Individual complaints about employment discrimination should be made to the Equal Employment Opportunity Commission.

REQUIREMENTS: Anyone who feels discriminated against in the manner previously outlined.

APPLICATIONS: Formal complaint to the Office for Civil Rights.

APPROVAL: None.

PUBLICATIONS: "U.S. Department of Health, Education and Welfare Regulation under Title VI of the Civil Rights Act of 1962;" "HEW and Civil Rights," a booklet in English or Spanish; "Executive Order 11246," as amended; "Higher Education Guidelines, Executive Order 11246"; statistical and descriptive material on school desegregation, equal employment opportunity, and equal opportunity in general.

RELATED PROGRAMS: Desegregation of Public Education, Equal Employment Opportunity, Equal Enjoyment of Public Accommodations, Fair Housing, Protection of Voting Rights, Desegregation of Public Facilities, Community Relations Service, Clearinghouse Services and Civil Rights Complaints, Job Discrimination – Investigation and Conciliation of Complaints, Job Discrimination – Special Project Grants, and Job Discrimination – Technical Assistance to Employers, Unions, and Employment Agencies.

Comprehensive Health Planning – Grants to States (314a Public Health Service Act)

OBJECTIVE: To provide financial support for state programs in comprehensive health planning.

PROGRAM: To provide formula grants.

RESTRICTIONS: The state formula-grant funds may be used only to administer or supervise the administration of the state's comprehensive health-planning functions. No more than 50 percent of the grant funds for any state may be expended for contract services. Money may not be used to provide or administer health services.

REQUIREMENTS: A single agency in each state designated by the governor to administer or supervise the administration of the state's health-planning functions is eligible to apply.

APPLICATION: New state plans and amendments thereto must be submitted to the governor for review and comments 45 days before they are sent to the regional office, unless the agency preparing the plans is located in the governor's office. The standard application forms as furnished by the federal agency and required by OMB circular No. A-102 must be used for this program. Designated state agencies must submit a state program and budget for comprehensive health planning for approval by the regional health director. The regional health director has approval authority for the program.

APPROVAL: After approval by the regional health director, the regional grants management office prepares a notice of award, secures necessary clearances and approval signatures, issues the award, and enters the approved award in the grant payment process. Provides notification of the grant approval to the public as well as the designated State Central Information Reception Agency and the Department of the Treasury on SF 240.

PUBLICATIONS: "42 CFR Part 51, Subpart A," "Directory of State and Areawide Comprehensive Health Planning Agencies under Section 314, Public Health Service Act as of July 1, 1973," "The Review and Comment Responsibilities of State and Areawide CHP Agencies."

RELATED PROGRAMS: Comprehensive Health Planning – Areawide Grants, Comprehensive Public Health Services – Formula Grants, Health Facilities Construction – Grants, Health Services Development – Project Grants.

Comprehensive Public Health Services – Formula Grants (314d Partnership for Health)

OBJECTIVE: To assist states in establishing and maintaining adequate community, mental, and environmental public health services, including training of personnel for state and local public-health work.

PROGRAM: To provide formula grants.

RESTRICTIONS: Assist states in making significant contributions toward providing and strengthening public health services in various political subdivisions. Restrictions are that 70 percent of federal funds allotted to the state health and mental-health agencies must be available to support services in communities of the state; 15 percent of a state's allotment must be allocated to the state mental-health authority. The state plan must provide for services for prevention and treatment of drug and alcohol abuse commensurate with the extent of the problem. The state plan must contain or be supported by satisfactory assurances that public health services are furnished in accordance with the planning recommendations of the state comprehensive health planning agency supported by the Public Health Service Act.

REQUIREMENTS: Only state health and mental-health authorities are eligible for formula grants for public health services. United States territories are also eligible. Compliance with standards for a merit system for personnel administration, 45 CFR Part 70, new state plans and amendments thereto must be submitted to the Governor for review and comments 45 days before they are sent to the regional office as required under Part III of OMB circular No. A-95 (revised).

APPLICATION: States are required to submit a state plan and budget for provision of public health and mental-health services to be supported in part by funds provided under section 314d and which contain the information and meet the requirements specified in subsection 314d (2) of the Public Health Service Act and in the regulations.

APPROVAL: The regional health director has approval authority for the program. After approval, the regional grants management office prepares a notice of award, secures necessary clearances and approval signatures, issues the award, and enters the approved award in the grant-payment process. Provides notification of the grant approval to the public as well as the designated SCIRA and the OMB on SF 240.

PUBLICATIONS: "Comprehensive Public Health Services Grants to States — Regulations."

RELATED PROGRAMS: Maternal and Child Health Services, Medical Assistance Programs, Comprehensive Planning Assistance, Health Services Development Projects Grants, Alcohol Community Service Programs, Alcohol Formula Grants, Drug Abuse Community Service Programs.

Health Facilities Construction Grants (Hill-Burton Program)

OBJECTIVE: To assist the states in planning for and providing hospitals, public health centers, state health laboratories, outpatient facilities, emergency rooms, neighborhood health centers, long-term-care facilities, rehabilitation facilities, and other related health facilities.

PROGRAM: To provide formula grants.

RESTRICTIONS: The grants, combined with local funds, may be used for the new construction or replacement of facilities, the expansion or remodeling of existing facilities or buildings, and equipment necessary for a construction project or for the provision of a new service in a community. Federal assistance is not available for the purchase of land except for public health centers.

REQUIREMENTS: State and local governments, hospitals, districts, or authorities, and private nonprofit organizations. Private-for-profit corporations are not eligible.

APPLICATION: Coordination with Model Cities planning and notification of state, regional, and metropolitan clearinghouses under OMB circular No. A-95, Part I (revised), are required. An environmental impact statement is required to accompany the application. If there is an areawide health-planning agency (314b), it must have an opportunity to comment on the project. If there is no areawide agency, then the state comprehensive health-planning agency (314b) must comment on the project. An informal preapplication conference with the state Hill-Burton agency is recommended; this agency will assist in the preparation of the application. Application forms may be obtained from the state Hill-Burton agency.

APPROVAL: The award is made by the approval of the application by the regional health director. Notification of grant award must be made to the designated SCIRA and the OMB on SF 240.

PUBLICATIONS: "42 CFR Part 53. Hill-Burton Aid for Building and Modernizing Community Health Facilities," "Minimum Requirements of Construction and Equipment for Hospitals and Medical Facilities," "Publications of the Health Care Facilities Services."

RELATED PROGRAMS: Health Facilities Construction —Technical Assistance, Health Facilities Construction — Loans and Loan Guarantees, Health Professions Teaching Facilities — Construction Grants, Mortgage Insurance — Group Practice Facilities, Mortgage Insurance — Hospitals, Mortgage Insurance — Nursing Homes and Related Care Facilities, Grants to States for Construction of State Nursing Home Care Facilities, Grants to States for Remodeling of State Home Hospital/Domiciliary Facilities.

Health Facilities Construction — Technical Assistance (Hill-Burton Program)

OBJECTIVE: To elevate the quality of design, construction, and operation of facilities through the provision of consultation services, which include development of guide materials.

PROGRAM: To provide advisory services and counseling and the dissemination of technical information.

RESTRICTIONS: This program provides consultation services and technical assistance for planning, designing, and construction of health facilities. Functional programming of the various service departments of a hospital or health center, such as the surgical suite, and consultation on nursing training and organization, fire safety standards, dietary practice and equipment, and environmental problems are examples of technical services rendered.

REQUIREMENTS: Hill-Burton state agencies, project sponsors, and other representatives of the health-delivery community are eligible to apply.

APPLICATION: Applicant may contact state Hill-Burton agencies, HEW regional offices, or HEW headquarters office with a request.

APPROVAL: None.

PUBLICATIONS: "Publications of the Health Care Facilities Service," "Consultative Assistance in Specialized Clinical Areas of Health Facilities," "Hill-Burton Hi-Lites."

RELATED PROGRAMS: Health Facilities Construction — Grants, Health Facilities Construction — Loans and Loan Guarantees, Grants to States for Construction of State Nursing Home Care Facilities, Grants to States for Remodeling of State Home Hospital/Domiciliary Facilities.

Health Services Development — Project Grants (Partnership for Health)

OBJECTIVE: To support a full range of public health services to meet special needs at the community level, especially health problems of regional or national significance; develop and support, for an initial period, new programs of health services, including related training; and development of comprehensive health centers. Priorities will be focused on the maintenance of existing centers, expansion of population and service coverage in existing centers, and development of third party reimbursement capabilities.

PROGRAM: To provide project grants.

RESTRICTIONS: Project grants must involve one or more of the following: The measures to be employed have not been applied beyond a successful development state and demonstration; have not been applied in the location identified by the application; or will be extended to serve a population not being served. Services must be provided in accordance with plans of the state comprehensive health-planning agency. Proposals designed to improve the accessibility of health care to the poor within their communities, and projects for attacking primary causes of sickness and mortality, especially through model comprehensive health-service centers, will receive highest priority.

REQUIREMENTS: Any public or nonprofit private agency, institution, or organization. Profit-making organizations are not eligible.

APPLICATION: Necessary coordination varies; however, applicants must secure a Certification of HEW Model Cities Relatedness (OMB form 85-RO145) from the local city demonstration agency director for projects with a significant impact in the Model Neighborhood Areas of Model Cities. Contact the HEW regional offices for details.

APPROVAL: After approval by the regional health director, the regional grants management office prepares a notice of award, secures necessary clearances and approval signatures, issues the award, and enters the approved award in the grant payment process. Provides notification of the grant approval to the public as well as the designated SCIRA and the OMB on SF 240.

PUBLICATIONS: "Fact Sheet on Partnership for Health," "Health Services Development Project Grants — Policy Statement."

RELATED PROGRAMS: Comprehensive Public Health Services — Formula Grants, Health Services Research and Development — Grants and Contracts, Maternal and Child Health Services, Migrant Health Grants, Health Maintenance Organization Services.

Indian Education — Adult Indian Education (Indian Education — Part C)

OBJECTIVE: To plan, develop, and implement programs for Indian adults.

PROGRAM: To provide project grants.

RESTRICTIONS: Grants are used for the establishment and operation of programs designed to stimulate the provision of basic literacy opportunities for nonliterate Indian adults and high-school equivalency opportunities in the shortest period of time feasible. Funds may be used to encourage dissemination of information and materials relating to, and evaluation of the effectiveness of, programs that may offer educational opportunities to Indian adults.

REQUIREMENTS: Indian tribes, institutions, and organizations may apply for grants.

APPLICATION: Proposals for developing programs in adult indian education are submitted by Indian organizations or other organizations in accordance with the rules and regulations for funding under Part C.

APPROVAL: Final funding decisions are made by the commissioner of education upon recommendations made by the deputy commissioner of Indian education.

PUBLICATIONS: *Federal Register,* Vol. 38, No. 141, July 24, 1973 (Title 45 CFR, Part 188).

RELATED PROGRAMS: Indian Education — Special Programs and Projects. Information and materials relating to, and evaluation of other information and materials relating to, and evaluation of the effectiveness of, programs that may offer educational opportunities to Indian adults.

Indian Health Services (Indian Health)

OBJECTIVE: To improve the health of approximately 488,000 American Indians and Alaska Natives by providing a full range of curative, preventive, and rehabilitative services that include public health nursing, maternal and child health care, dental and nutrition services, psychiatric care, and health education.

PROGRAM: To provide specialized services and advisory services and counseling.

RESTRICTIONS: Inpatient and outpatient medical care is provided through a system that includes 50 U.S. Public

Health Service Indian hospitals, 84 health centers and school health centers, over 300 other health stations and locations, and contracted arrangements with private and community hospitals, private physicians, dentists, and other professionals, and state and local agencies. Funds are spent to provide direct and contractual medical care and a full range of field health services for about 488,000 Indian and Alaska natives who meet eligibility requirements.

REQUIREMENTS: Generally, Indians qualify who live on or near a reservation and are recognized as members of a tribe with whom the federal government has a special relationship, or are recognized as Indians by the communities in which they live.

APPLICATION: Direct health services are provided through federal facilities or under contract with community facilities and private physicians and dentists.

APPROVAL: None.

PUBLICATIONS: "The Indian Health Program of the U.S. Public Health Service"; "To the First Americans," an annual report on the Indian health program; "Indian Health Trends and Services," A Statistical Report; "Sanitation Facilities for Indians."

RELATED PROGRAMS: Water and Waste Disposal Systems for Rural Communities, Public Housing — Homeownership for Low-Income Families, Indian Housing — Development, Indian Housing — Improvement, Public Housing Homeownership for Low-Income Families.

Indian Sanitation Facilities

OBJECTIVE: To alleviate gross unsanitary conditions, lack of safe water supplies, and inadequate waste-disposal facilities, which contribute to the high rate of infectious and gastroenteric diseases among Indians and Alaska natives, the Indian Health Service engages in environmental health activities, including construction of sanitation facilities for individual homes and communities.

PROGRAM: To provide specialized services.

RESTRICTIONS: Funds restricted to sanitation facilities, construction, and environmental health activities among Indians and Alaska natives.

REQUIREMENTS: Generally, Indians qualify who live on or near a reservation and are recognized as members of a tribe with whom the federal government has a special relationship or are recognized as Indians by the communities in which they live.

APPLICATION: Upon request of tribal or community organizations and with their active participation, Indian and Alaska native communities and homes — including homes being constructed under federal housing programs — may be provided with modern sanitation facilities by the Indian Health Service. Application is made by submitting a project proposal form (Public Health Service 3256) to the service unit director.

APPROVAL: The proposal is reviewed by program staff and approval is made by the area director. All applicants will be advised by letter from the area office of the disposition of their application.

PUBLICATIONS: "The Indian Health Program of the U.S. Public Health Service"; "To the First Americans," an annual report on the Indian health program; "Indian Health Trends and Services," a statistical report; "Sanitation Facilities for Indians."

RELATED PROGRAMS: Water and Waste Disposal Systems for Rural Communities, Public Housing — Homeownership for Low-Income Families, Indian Housing — Development, Indian Housing — Improvement, Public Housing Homeownership for Low-Income Families.

Library Services — Grants for Public Libraries (LSCA — Title I)

OBJECTIVE: To assist in (1) extending public library services to areas without service or with inadequate service, (2) establishing and expanding state institutional library services and library services to the physically handicapped, (3) establishing and expanding library services to the disadvantaged in urban and rural areas, and (4) strengthening the metropolitan public libraries, which serve as national or regional resource centers.

PROGRAM: To provide formula grants.

RESTRICTIONS: Funds may be used for books and other library materials, library equipment, salaries, and other operating expenses, for administration of state plans and for strengthening the capacity of state library administrative agencies for meeting the needs of the people of the states. Funds may not be used for libraries such as law, medical, school, and academic libraries, which are organized to serve a special clientele; or for construction purposes.

REQUIREMENTS: State library extension agencies, which have authority to administer federal funds, supervise public library service within a state and, together with participating libraries, have financial resources sufficient to match federal funds on a percentage basis according to *per capita* wealth.

APPLICATION: To qualify for a grant, states must submit for approval of the U.S. Commissioner of Education a basic state plan (state-federal agreement) as defined in Section 3 (11) of the act. This will include the state's assurance of its capabilities for administering the program, specific policies, criteria, and priorities for implementing programs as defined in the act, a certificate of maintenance of effort, and a listing of the state-wide Advisory Council on Libraries. By July 1, 1976, a long-range program (5 years) must be submitted. Annually, thereafter, the state must (1) review and amend where necessary the approved basic state plan, (2) review and revise its long-range program, and (3) submit an annual program consisting of projects (OE form 3114-1). All programs must be developed with the advice of the State Advisory Council and in consultation with the appropriate regional representative of the U.S. Commissioner of Education.

APPROVAL: The appropriate regional commissioner is responsible for providing notification of the grant approval to the state, designated SCIRA, and Department of the Treasury on SF 240.

PUBLICATIONS: Title 45 CFR, Chapter I, Part 130, Section 1 130.0 to 130.55 of the proposed regulations.

RELATED PROGRAMS: Library Services — Interlibrary Cooperation, Construction of Public Libraries, Depository Libraries for Government Publications, Distribution of Library of Congress Catalog Cards, and Reference and Consultation Services in Preservation, Restoration, and Protection of Library Materials.

Library Services — Interlibrary Cooperation (LSCA — Title III)

OBJECTIVE: To provide for the systematic and effective coordination of the resources of school, public, academic, and special libraries and special information centers for improved services of a supplementary nature to the special clientele served by each type of library center.

PROGRAM: To provide formula grants.

RESTRICTIONS: Funds may be used for services and equipment necessary for the establishment and operation of systems or networks of libraries and information centers working together to achieve maximum service to all users. Neither library materials nor construction are eligible expenditures.

APPLICATION: To qualify for a grant, states must submit for approval of the U.S. Commissioner of Education, a basic state plan (state-federal agreement) as defined in Section 3 (11) of the act. This will include the state's assurance of its capabilities for administering the program; specific policies, criteria, and priorities for implementing programs as defined in the act; a certificate of maintenance of effort; and a listing of the statewide Advisory Council on Libraries. By July 1, 1976, a long-range program (5 years) should have been submitted. Annually thereafter, the state must (1) review and amend where necessary the approved basic state plan, (2) review and revise its long-range program, and (3) submit an annual program consisting of projects (OE form 3114-1). All programs must be developed with the advice of the State Advisory Council and in consultation with the appropriate regional representative (listed in the appendix) representing the U.S. Commissioner of Education.

APPROVAL: The appropriate regional commissioner is responsible for providing notification of the grant approval to the state, designated SCIRA, and Department of the Treasury on SF 240.

PUBLICATIONS: Title 45 CFR Chapter 1, Part 130, Section 130.1 to 130.55 of the proposed regulations.

RELATED PROGRAMS: Library Services — Grants for Public Libraries, Distribution of Library of Congress Catalog Cards, and Reference and Consultation Services in Preservation, Restoration, and Protection of Library Materials.

Medical Assistance Program — Medicaid (Title XIX)

OBJECTIVE: To provide financial assistance to states for payments of medical assistance on behalf of cash assistance recipients and, in certain states, on behalf of other medically needy, who except for income and resources, are categorically eligible.

PROGRAM: To provide formula grants.

RESTRICTIONS: States must provide for the categorically needy, inpatient and outpatient hospital services; other laboratory and X-ray services; skilled nursing home services; home health services for persons over 21; family-planning services; physicians' services; and early periodic screening, diagnosis, and treatment for individuals under 21. For the medically needy, states are required to provide any seven of the services for which federal financial participation is available.

REQUIREMENTS: State and local welfare agencies must operate under a HEW-approved (Medicaid) state plan and comply with all federal regulations governing aid and medical assistance to the needy. The state plan, coordinated with the governor's office, is required under Part III of OMB circular No. A-95. Federal funds must go to a certified state welfare agency. Individuals must meet state requirements.

APPLICATION: States should contact the HEW regional office for assistance with developing state plans for the Medicaid program. State governors review state plans, amendments, quarterly estimates, and any other federally required reports prior to submission to HEW. Individuals needing medical assistance should apply directly to the state or local welfare agency. States should contact the SRS regional commissioner.

APPROVAL: Regional commissioners have authority to approve or disapprove state plans. Once a state plan is approved, states are awarded funds quarterly based on their estimates of funds needed to provide medical assistance to the needy. Awards are made quarterly on a fiscal-year basis as follows: June 1, September 1, December 1, and March 1. Notification of grant awards is made to the State Central Information Reception Agency and the OMB on SF 240. Individuals receive medical care as specified under the state plan from providers of medical care who are participating in the Medicaid program.

PUBLICATIONS: "Questions and Answers, Medical Assistance," "Medicaid," "Medicaid, Medicare, Which is Which," "What's Medicaid to an M.D.?," "What's Medicaid to a Dentist," "What's Medicaid to a Pharmacist?"

RELATED PROGRAMS: Comprehensive Public Health Services — Formula Grants, Health Services Development — Project Grants, Migrant Health Grants, Medicare — Hospital Insurance, Medicare — Supplementary Medical Insurance.

GOVERNMENT PROGRAMS

SOCIAL SECURITY ADMINISTRATION
Contact: Commissioner

Medicare — Hospital Insurance

OBJECTIVE: To provide hospital insurance protection for covered services to any person 65 or above and to certain disabled persons.

PROGRAM: To provide insurance in this program.

RESTRICTIONS: Hospital insurance benefits are paid to participating hospitals, extended-care facilities (skilled nursing homes), and related providers of health care to cover the reasonable cost of medically necessary services furnished to individuals entitled under this program.

REQUIREMENTS: Persons 65 or over, and certain disabled persons, are eligible for hospital insurance protection. Nearly everyone who reached 65 before 1968 is eligible for hospital insurance, including people not eligible for cash Social Security benefits. A person who reached 65 in 1968 or after, who is not eligible for cash benefits, needs some work credit to qualify for hospital insurance benefits. The amount needed depends on his or her age. Disabled persons who have been entitled to Social Security or railroad retirement disability benefits for at least 24 months will be eligible for hospital insurance benefits effective July 1973. Also, proof of age or disability is needed.

APPLICATION: Telephone or visit the local Social Security office. Individuals entitled to Social Security or railroad retirement are enrolled without application.

APPROVAL: The individual will be notified by mail of enrollment, whether automatic or applied for.

PUBLICATIONS: "Code of Federal Regulations, Title 20, Parts 401, 405, 422," "Your Medicare Handbook," "SSI-50" and other publications are available from any Social Security office.

RELATED PROGRAMS: Medicare — Supplementary Medical Insurance, Medical Assistance Program, Social Security — Disability Insurance.

Medicare — Supplementary Medical Insurance (Medicare)

OBJECTIVE: To provide insurance protection against most of the costs of health care to persons 65 or over and to certain disabled persons who elect this coverage.

PROGRAM: To provide insurance in this program.

RESTRICTIONS: Benefits are paid for covered services on the basis of reasonable charges for medically necessary services furnished aged or disabled enrollees, by physicians and other suppliers of medical services, and on the basis of reasonable costs for necessary services furnished by providers such as hospitals and extended-care facilities.

REQUIREMENTS: Persons age 65 or above and certain disabled persons who are eligible for hospital insurance benefits were automatically enrolled under medical insurance effective July 1973. Disabled persons who had been entitled to Social Security or railroad retirement disability benefits for at least 24 months became eligible for medical insurance benefits effective July 1976. Medical insurance is voluntary; it may be declined. The enrollee pays a monthly premium (increased to $6.30 effective July 1973). Some states pay the premium on behalf of qualifying individuals. Proof of age or disability is needed.

APPLICATION: Telephone or visit the local Social Security office.

APPROVAL: After review of the application is completed, the applicant will be notified by mail.

PUBLICATIONS: "Your Medicare Handbook," "SSI-50," and other publications are available from any Social Security office.

RELATED PROGRAMS: Medicare — Hospital Insurance, Medical Assistance Program, Social Security — Disability Insurance.

Mental Health — Community Mental Health Centers

OBJECTIVE: To provide funds to finance building of public and other nonprofit community mental-health centers; to improve organization and allocation of mental-health services; and to provide modern treatment and care within the geographical community of the consumer. To meet a portion of compensation costs of professional and technical personnel in initial operation of the center; to develop community programs by obtaining local support and community involvement in comprehensive mental-health services.

PROGRAM: To provide project grants.

RESTRICTIONS: Funds may be used for construction of new facilities or for acquisition, remodeling, alteration, or expansion of existing facilities that fulfill requirements of the law as a community mental-health center; staffing grants provide funds on a matching basis for salaries of professional and technical personnel providing new services within a community mental-health center; initiation and development grants cover costs of assessing local needs, designing service programs, obtaining local financial and professional support, and fostering community involvement in developing mental-health-service programs in urban or rural poverty areas designated by the HEW secretary. Initiation and development funds may not be used for direct treatment services to patients, foreign travel, or alterations and renovations. An applicant for an initiation and development grant must not have previously received a community mental-health center construction or staffing grant, or an initiation and development grant for comprehensive community mental-health services; applicant must be located in the area to be served or have designated responsibility for planning and developing mental-health services in that area, and the area must be designated by the HEW secretary as a rural or urban poverty area. For construction grant, individual community projects must be part of the state plan for community mental-health centers, be approved by the appropriate state authority, and be cleared with state/regional/metropolitan clearinghouse as required by OMB circular No. A-95, Part I. Applicants must secure a Certification of Department of HEW Model Cities Relatedness from the local city demonstration agency director for projects with a significant impact in the Model Neighborhood area of Model Cities.

REQUIREMENTS: Construction grants are available to a state, political subdivision, and public or private nonprofit agency to operate an approvable community mental-health center program under the state plan. To be eligible for a staffing grant, applicant must furnish at least five essential services to prescribed geographic areas; inpatient, outpatient, 24-hour emergency care; partial hospitalization; consultation; and education.

APPLICATION: The standard application forms as furnished by the federal agency and required by OMB circular A-102 must be used when the applicant is a state or local government. Environmental impact statement applicable to construction projects. The state agency will advise applicant of eligibility of proposed project, the possibility of receiving a grant, and, if in line for consideration, will furnish application forms and other materials. All application documents, including plans and specifications, must be reviewed and approved by state agency, which will transmit documents and its recommendations to appropriate HEW regional office; staffing applicants use form MH-23, and initiation and development applicants use form Public Health Service-398, both of which can be obtained from the appropriate HEW regional office. Completed applications are forwarded to the regional office for review.

APPROVAL: The regional health director makes final decision to approve or defer individual projects. That office is also responsible for providing notification of grant approval to the state agency as well as the designated SCIRA and Office of Management and Budget on SF 240.

PUBLICATIONS: 42 CFR 54.201-54.215, available in kit from HEW regional office center; "The Comprehensive Community Mental Health Center"; Public Health Service publication No. 2136.

RELATED PROGRAMS: Drug Abuse Community Service Programs, Alcohol Community Service Programs, and Alcohol, Drug Abuse, and Mental Health Administration Scientific Communications and Public Education.

Mental Health – Hospital Improvement Grants

OBJECTIVE: The objective of this program is to provide funds to state mental hospitals for projects that will improve the quality of care, treatment, and rehabilitation of patients; encourage transition to open institutions; and develop relationships with community programs for mental health.

PROGRAM: To provide project grants.

RESTRICTIONS: Grant funds may be used for expenses directly related to projects that are carried on within the program of a state mental hospital and are focused on use of current knowledge for immediate improvement of the care, treatment, and rehabilitation of the mentally ill.

REQUIREMENTS: An application may be submitted by a state hospital for the mentally ill, which is directly administered by the state agency responsible for mental hospitals, or by any installation not directly administered by the state agency but which is a part of the state's formal system for institutional care of the mentally ill. Each application must be endorsed by the administrator of the state agency responsible for the mental hospital and must be accompanied by a statement indicating how the project relates to overall state needs and to the state's comprehensive plan for mental health.

APPLICATION: Application is submitted on form HSM-550-1. Application kits containing necessary form and instructions may be obtained from the appropriate HEW regional office. Applications are reviewed by federal and nonfederal consultants recruited nationwide from the mental-health field. The amount and period of support of the award are determined on the basis of merit of the project.

APPROVAL: An HEW regional office awards grants to support approved applications on the basis of merit. The regional office also transmits notification of the award to the designated SCIRA and the Office of Management and Budget on SF 240.

PUBLICATIONS: Pamphlet describing program is included in each application kit and may be obtained from the mental health section of the HEW regional office. "National Institute of Mental Health Support Programs."

RELATED PROGRAMS: Mental Health Hospital Staff Development Grants; Alcohol, Drug Abuse, and Mental Health Administration Scientific Communications and Public Education; Mental Health – Community Mental Health Centers Mental Health Research Grants.

National Health Service Corps

OBJECTIVE: To improve the delivery of health care and services to residents in areas critically short of health personnel.

PROGRAM: To provide specialized services.

RESTRICTIONS: Health personnel – including, but not limited to, physicians, dentists, nurses, pharmacists, psychologists, paramedical personnel, medical services administrators or planners, and medical and psychiatric technicians may be assigned by the HEW secretary to areas of the nation designated as having critical shortages of such personnel. Assigned personnel can be federal employees under either the civil service system or the Commissioned Corps of the U.S. Public Health Service. These services may be provided entirely by the federal government or in conjunction with local providers and organizations. Services provided by corps assignees will be available to anyone who wishes them. Persons receiving services shall be charged at a rate established by the HEW secretary to recover reasonable costs of providing these services. No charge or a reduced charge may be made for a person who is determined unable to pay the regular charge. Scope of services provided by the corps will depend on the nature of shortages in that area; not all corps field projects will offer all services. Communities may apply for designation as having a critical health manpower shortage and assignment of corps personnel. Designation and assignment, however, are at the discretion of the secretary, and will be based in part on availability of service personnel to provide requested services.

REQUIREMENTS: Applications for designation of an area as having a critical shortage of health manpower and for assignment of corps personnel may be made by state or local health agencies or any other public or nonprofit private health or health-related organization. Although intermediate-level applicants may apply for local-level services, the potential beneficiary community must be closely involved with such an application. State and district medical societies, or other appropriate health societies must certify the need for health personnel in the area proposed, as must the local government. Recommendations should be sought from state and areawide comprehensive health-planning agencies and from the regional medical program as well as from other medical personnel in the area concerned. Application is not complete until such certifications are obtained. If the HEW secretary determines a society has withheld that certification in an arbitrary or capricious manner, he or she may then override and assign personnel. Before applications are submitted to the National Health Service Corps, all parties to the application — including professional societies and local governments whose certifications are required, provider groups, consumer groups, and any other parties — should coordinate the application. Cooperation from recommending agencies, such as comprehensive health-planning agencies and regional medical programs, should also be obtained. The corps will assist in preparation of applications, but there is no substitute for close, local-level cooperation and participation before a formal inquiry is made regarding application. Applicants are encouraged to secure a Certificate of HEW Model Cities Relatedness from the local city demonstration agency director for projects with a significant impact in the Model Neighborhood area of Model Cities.

APPLICATION: At present, there is no standard application form. Applications may be may be made in whatever format seems appropriate and forwarded to the appropriate regional health director. The corps interim guidelines outline the types of information necessary to an application. Applications will differ depending on nature of problem and proposed solutions discussed. (An application form is under development.)

APPROVAL: Decisions to assign personnel will be made by the HEW secretary depending on applications and personnel availability. Applicant agencies or groups will be notified directly by the corps if the applicant will be retained for further consideration.

PUBLICATIONS: "CFR Title 42, Chapter I, Subchapter B, Part 23," "Interim Guide for Applicant Communities (National Health Services)," "Some Questions and Answers."

RELATED PROGRAMS: Comprehensive Health Planning — Areawide Grants, Comprehensive Public Health Services — Formula Grants, Family Health Centers.

Native American Programs

OBJECTIVE: To provide direct support for self-determination programs aimed at improving the health, education, and welfare of native Americans both on and off reservations.

PROGRAM: To provide project grants.

RESTRICTIONS: Grants may be used for such purposes as, but not limited to: projects aimed at increasing the capabilities of Indian tribes to take over services now provided by non-Indian-controlled organizations; projects designed to meet the nutritional and emergency medical needs of native Americans and to provide other needed services to promote individual and family self-sufficiency; provide for the establishment and operation of urban centers serving Indian people living off-reservation; provide for self-help and community economic development efforts. Office of Native American Programs funds may not be used to support legal service projects.

REQUIREMENTS: Indian tribe councils or other public or private nonprofit agencies.

APPLICATION: The Office of Native American Programs (ONAP), HEW headquarters, will provide each applicant agency with the appropriate forms for the preapplication and application for federal assistance and instructions on applying for a Native American Program Grant. Applications for urban Indian programs should be submitted to the HEW regional offices. All other applications should be submitted to ONAP headquarters.

APPROVAL: All funds are awarded directly to the grantees. Funds are awarded to urban Indian programs through HEW regional offices. Funds to all other grantees are awarded by ONAP headquarters.

PUBLICATIONS: Regulations and guidelines are in the process of revision; they will be available upon request from ONAP headquarters. Literature: "Self-Determination."

RELATED PROGRAMS: None.

Office for the Handicapped

OBJECTIVE: To serve as the focal point within the Office of Human Development (OHD) for review, coordination, information, and planning related to department-wide policies, programs, procedures, and activities relevant to the physically and mentally handicapped. The Office for the Handicapped (OFH) implements the provisions of section 405 of Public Law 93-112.

PROGRAM: To provide advisory services and counseling and to disseminate technical information.

RESTRICTIONS: None.

REQUIREMENTS: The services of OFH are available to all interested persons and organizations upon request.

APPLICATION: By verbal or written request.

APPROVAL: None.

PUBLICATIONS: Numerous publications in the area of the handicapped, published by HEW agencies, will be made available to the public upon request.

RELATED PROGRAMS: Medical Assistance Program, Rehabilitation Services and Facilities — Basic Support, Books for the Blind and Physically Handicapped, Handicapped Employment Promotion.

Physical-Fitness Clinics (President's Council Fitness Clinics)

OBJECTIVE: To convey innovative fitness ideas and improved methodologies for achieving physical fitness to physical-fitness educators, teachers, school administrators, recreation professionals, and so forth, so that they can adapt them to their own programs.

PROGRAM: To provide for training and the dissemination of technical information.

RESTRICTIONS: Six to eight physical-fitness clinics per year are conducted by the council. Although aimed at professional personnel, they are open to the public. The council staff and its professional clinicians present new fitness routines, new fitness scheduling, innovative approaches to the use of standard equipment, and so on, for possible adaptation by clinic attendees to their own local situation. Clinic publications describing and illustrating both material presented at the clinics as well as material beyond just the clinic scope are made available to clinic attendees. Frequently, the clinic is joined by local educational and recreational organizations in the presentation of a clinic program.

REQUIREMENTS: Any person with an interest in physical-fitness and physical-education programs.

APPLICATION: Organizations or individuals interested in having a council physical-fitness clinic conducted in their geographic area should make this interest known to the council.

APPROVAL: Applications are considered by the council staff and are approved on the basis of regional coverage and staff resources.

PUBLICATIONS: The council does not have program literature devoted only to the clinics programs. Interested persons should write to the council stating the nature of their interest, to which the council will respond in substantial detail.

RELATED PROGRAMS: Physical Fitness and Sports Information, Physical Fitness Demonstration Center Schools, Physical Fitness Program Development, Presidential Physical Fitness Award, Health-Exercise Symposia.

Public Assistance — Maintenance Assistance (State Aid)

OBJECTIVE: To provide financial aid to states for aid to the aged, blind, permanently and totally disabled, families with dependent children, emergency welfare assistance, assistance to repatriated United States Nationals, and administration of these welfare programs.

PROGRAM: To provide formula grants.

RESTRICTIONS: Money payments — made directly to eligible needy aged, blind, disabled, and families with dependent children — are to cover costs for food, shelter, clothing, and other necessary items of daily living. Payments in the form of money or vendor payments assist needy families in emergency or crisis situations, such as imminent eviction or exhaustion of food supplies. Under the program, payments are made for care of specified children in foster homes or institutions. Federal funds up to $250 per home may be available for home repairs. Under the repatriation program, money is provided for food, shelter, clothing, medical care (including hospitalization and treatment of mentally ill persons), and transportation to persons who have been returned to the United States because of destitution and who are not eligible for other financial assistance programs. Funds for state and local administration of programs are for costs of interviewing public assistance applicants for eligibility determination and validation of eligibility; costs of state and local personnel engaged in program direction and management; and other ongoing costs and activities related to administering the program.

REQUIREMENTS: State and local welfare agencies must operate under an approved HEW state plan and must comply with all federal regulations governing aid and subsistence to aged, blind, permanently and totally disabled, families with dependent children, and so forth.

APPLICATION: Applications are available from HEW/SRS (Social and Rehabilitation Service) regional offices. States should contact these offices for developing state plans for various activities within the maintenance-assistance program. State governors review state plans, amendments, quarterly estimates, and any other federally required reports prior to submission to SRS. Eligible individuals — the aged, blind, disabled, needy families with dependent children, and the destitute — should apply directly to the state or local welfare agency. States should contact SRS regional commissioners for application forms. Regional commissioners have authority to approve or disapprove state plans and amendments. States contact HEW regional offices for applications for administrative funds.

APPROVAL: Once a state plan is approved, states are awarded funds quarterly based on their estimates needed to provide maintenance assistance and administrative costs. Notification of awards must be made through the designated

SCIRA and the OMB on SF 240. Individuals receive monthly subsistence checks from state or local welfare agencies.

PUBLICATIONS: A copy of the state plan must be available in the local agency office. SRS regulations are published in the *Federal Register,* 45 CFR 200 et seq. Also, "Temporary Assistance for Repatriates," "Old Age Assistance," "When You Need Help," "Aid to Blind or Disabled People," "Aid to Families with Dependent Children," "When the Needy Ask for Help," "Public Assistance."

RELATED PROGRAMS: Medical Assistance Programs, Rehabilitation Services and Facilities — Basic Support, Public Assistance — Social Services, Social Security — Disability Insurance, Supplemental Security Income.

Public Assistance Research (SRS Research)

OBJECTIVE: To discover, test, demonstrate, and promote utilization of new social service concepts that will provide service to dependent and vulnerable populations such as the poor, the aged, children, and youth.

PROGRAM: To provide project grants and research contracts.

RESTRICTIONS: Grants and contracts are awarded for innovative research and demonstrations of regional and national significance that are responsive to SRS program priorities in public assistance, child welfare, and for coordination, administration, and provision of services to these target populations. Funds authorized by section 1115 of the Social Security Act are limited to state public assistance agencies. All applications must meet standards of excellence in research or evaluation design. A portion of the funds under this program are used by the Social Security Administration for research into all aspects of current Social Security programs, their economic and social impact, alternative methods of providing services to the population groups covered or potentially covered by these programs.

REQUIREMENTS: Grants may be made to states and nonprofit organizations. Contracts may be executed with nonprofit or profit organizations. Grants cannot be made directly to individuals.

APPLICATION: Application forms are submitted to:

Director
Division of Project Grants Administration
SRS, Department of HEW
330 C Street, SW
Washington, DC 20201

or to:

Office of Research and Statistics
Social Security Administration
P.O. Box 2361
Baltimore, MD 21203

PUBLICATIONS: SRS Research 1971, and Grants Administration policies may be obtained from:

Division of Project Grants Administration
Social and Rehabilitation Service
330 C Street, SW — Room 1427
Washington, DC 20201

The pamphlet, "Research Grants in Social Security," and SSA grants administration policies may be obtained from:

Office of Research and Statistics
Social Security Administration
P.O. Box 2361
Baltimore, MD 21203

RELATED PROGRAMS: Child Welfare Services, Educationally Deprived Children in State Administered Institutions Serving Neglected or Delinquent Children, Child Development — Technical Assistance, Child Development — Child Welfare Research and Demonstration Grants, Public Assistance — Social Services.

Public Assistance — Social Services (Social Services)

OBJECTIVE: To provide social services to needy individuals such as the blind, aged, the permanently and totally disabled, and families with dependent children. Services are directed toward assisting individuals to attain or retain self-support and self-sufficiency, and to maintain and strengthen family life.

PROGRAM: To provide formula grants.

RESTRICTIONS: Federal funds may be used for the proper and efficient operation of social-service programs to enable individuals to attain or retain the capability of self-support and self-sufficiency; provide legal services, family planning, home and money management, housing improvement, child care, or protective services. Funds must be spent on the basis of a federally approved state plan.

REQUIREMENTS: A state plan, coordinated with the governor's office, is required under Part III of OMB circular No. A-95. Federal funds must go to a certified state social-service agency. All states, the District of Columbia, Puerto Rico, Virgin Islands, and Guam are eligible. It covers any needy person, who is or may become a recipient of welfare funds for the blind, aged, permanently and totally disabled, or a dependent child, who meets state requirements.

APPLICATION: State governors review state plans, amendments, quarterly estimates, and any other federally required reports. Regional office staff are available to assist with technical development of state plans, amendments, revisions, and so forth. Applications are made in the form of a state plan, prepared in the format prescribed by the Social and Rehabilitation Service.

APPROVAL: States are awarded funds quarterly based on their estimates of funds needed to provide social services to individuals eligible under an approved state plan. Notification of grant award must be made to the designated SCIRA and the OMB on SF 240.

PUBLICATIONS: "Federal Interagency Day Care Requirements," "States Can Help," "Many Children."

RELATED PROGRAMS: Child Welfare Services, Public Assistance — Maintenance Assistance (State Aid), Public Assistance Research, Supplemental Security Income.

Rehabilitation Services and Facilities — Special Projects (Rehabilitation Service Projects)

OBJECTIVE: To provide funds to state vocational rehabilitation agencies and related institutions for the expansion and improvement of services for the mentally and physically handicapped over and above those provided by the basic support program administered by states.

PROGRAM: To provide project grants and contracts.

RESTRICTIONS: Expansion grants, projects with industry, new career opportunities for the handicapped. Grants and contracts must substantially contribute to solution of vocational rehabilitation problems common to the total physically and mentally handicapped population. For example: projects to prepare handicapped individuals for gainful employment in the competitive labor market; payment to cover cost of planning, preparing, and initiating services for the handicapped; cost of recruiting and training individuals for new career opportunities for the handicapped in the fields of rehabilitation, health, welfare, safety, and law enforcement; technical assistance to states in developing programs to fit these criteria. *Staffing of facilities.* Grants must assure that the facility constructed will be used as a public nonprofit rehabilitation facility for at least 20 years; meets the standards of safety for rehabilitation facilities and specifications established by HEW and the state, and that labor costs, etc., meet HEW and state regulations. *Facility improvement.* Funds may be awarded when HEW is assured that the purpose of the project is to prepare the handicapped for gainful employment. Contract funds may be used to analyze, improve, and increase professional services staff, and to provide technical assistance to rehabilitation facilities through the purchase of services of experts, and others including *per diem,* travel expenses, etc.

REQUIREMENTS: Submit proof of nonprofit status and certification of compliance with all federal and state employment practices such as Title VI, Civil Rights Act of 1964, building and safety regulations, and wage and hour standards. Nonprofit institution or organization or state agency for the physically, mentally, or emotionally handicapped.

APPLICATION: Applications must be approved by the state vocational rehabilitation agency before submission to HEW regional office. Applicants are encouraged to secure a Certification of HEW Model Cities Relatedness from the local city demonstration agency director for projects with a significant impact in the Model Neighborhood area of Model Cities. The standard application forms as furnished by the federal agency and required by OMB circular A-102 must be used for this program when applicant is a state or local government agency. Applications approved by the state vocational rehabilitation agency should be submitted to the SRS regional office for project grants.

APPROVAL: Awards are made on approval of the SRS regional commissioner. Notification of grant award must be made to the designated SCIRA and the OMB on SF 240.

PUBLICATIONS: Specific guidelines and literature may be obtained from SRS regional offices.

RELATED PROGRAMS: Rehabilitation Services and Facilities — Basic Support, Vocational Rehabilitation Services for Social Security Disability Beneficiaries, Supplemental Security Income.

Social Security — Disability Insurance

OBJECTIVE: To replace part of the income lost because of a physical or mental impairment severe enough to prevent a person from working.

PROGRAM: To provide direct payments with unrestricted use.

RESTRICTIONS: Monthly cost benefits are paid to eligible disabled persons and their eligible dependents throughout the period of disability. Costs of vocational rehabilitation are also paid for certain beneficiaries. Disability benefits are not payable for the first 5 months of disability. There are no restrictions on the use of benefits received by beneficiaries.

REQUIREMENTS: A disabled worker under age 65 is eligible for Social Security disability benefits if he has worked for a sufficient period of time under Social Security to be insured. The insured status requirements depend upon the age of the applicant and the date he became disabled. Also, a person continuously disabled since childhood (before 22) is entitled if one of the parents covered by Social Security retires, becomes disabled, or dies. A disabled widow 50 or over is entitled if her deceased husband was covered by Social Security; applies also to disabled widowers and certain disabled surviving divorced wives. Dependents of disabled workers also eligible for benefits: (1) unmarried children under 18, (2) children 18 through 21 if unmarried and full-time students, (3) unmarried disabled children of any age if disabled before 22, (4) wife at any age if child in her care is receiving benefits on worker's Social Security record, (5) wife or dependent husband 62 or over.

APPLICATION: Telephone or visit the local Social Security office.

APPROVAL: After review of the application is completed, the applicant will be notified by mail.

PUBLICATIONS: "If You Become Disabled," SSI-29, and other publications are available from any Social Security office.

RELATED PROGRAMS: Special Benefits for Disabled Coal Miners, Vocational Rehabilitation Services for Social Security Disability Beneficiaries, Social Insurance for Railroad Workers, Medicare — Hospital Insurance, Medicare — Supplementary Medical Insurance, Supplemental Security Income.

Social Security — Retirement Insurance

OBJECTIVE: To replace income lost because of retirement.

PROGRAM: To provide direct payments with unrestricted use.

RESTRICTIONS: Monthly cash benefits are paid to eligible retired workers and their eligible dependents. There are no restrictions on use of benefits by a beneficiary.

REQUIREMENTS: Retired workers age 62 and over who have worked the required number of years under Social Security are eligible for monthly benefits. If an eligible worker applies before age 65, he will receive permanently reduced benefits. Certain dependents can receive benefits, too. They include a wife or a dependent husband 62 or over; a wife of any age with a dependent child in her care if the child is entitled to payment based on the worker's record; unmarried children under 18 (22, if in school); unmarried disabled children if disabled before age 22. Proof of age is also needed. If applying for benefits for dependents, additional proofs of age, relationship to the retired worker, or school attendance may be required.

APPLICATION: Telephone or visit the local Social Security office.

APPROVAL: After review of the application is completed, the applicant will be notified by mail.

PUBLICATIONS: "Your Social Security," SSI-35, and many other publications are available from any Social Security office.

RELATED PROGRAMS: Social Security — Special Benefits for Persons Aged 72 and Over, Social Security — Survivors Insurance, Special Benefits for Disabled Coal Miners, Social Insurance for Railroad Workers.

Social Security — Special Benefits for Persons Aged 72 and Over

OBJECTIVE: To assure regular income to persons age 72 and over who had little or no opportunity to earn Social Security protection during their working years.

PROGRAM: To provide direct payments with unrestricted use.

RESTRICTIONS: Special monthly benefits are paid to eligible beneficiaries age 72 and over.

REQUIREMENTS: Individuals who attained age 72 before 1968 need no work credits under Social Security to be eligible for special payments. Those who reach age 72 in 1968 or later need some work credits to be eligible. The amount of work credit needed increases each year for people reaching age 72 after 1968, until it is the same as for Social Security retirement benefits. Special payments can also be made to an eligible wife aged 72 or over.

APPLICATION: Telephone or visit the local Social Security office.

APPROVAL: After review of the application is completed, the applicant will be notified by mail.

PUBLICATIONS: "Your Social Security," "SSI-35."

RELATED PROGRAMS: Social Security — Retirement Insurance, Social Security — Survivors Insurance.

Social Security — Survivors' Insurance

OBJECTIVE: To replace income lost to dependents because of worker's death.

PROGRAM: To provide direct payments with unrestricted use.

RESTRICTIONS: Monthly case benefits are paid to eligible dependents of deceased workers.

REQUIREMENTS: Benefits are payable only if the deceased had enough wage credits. Dependents eligible for monthly cash benefits are the following: any widow, or dependent widower age 60 or older; a widow of any age if she is caring for a child who is under 18 or disabled, and who gets payments; unmarried children under 18 (22, if in school); unmarried disabled children if disabled before 22; a widow or widower 50 or older who becomes disabled not later than 7 years after death of the worker; and dependent parents 62 or older.

APPLICATION: Visit the Social Security office.

APPROVAL: After review, the applicant will be notified by mail.

PUBLICATIONS: "Your Social Security," "SSI-35."

RELATED PROGRAMS: Special Benefits for Disabled Coal Miners, Social Insurance for Railroad Workers, Pension to Veterans' Widows and Children.

Special Benefits for Disabled Coal Miners

OBJECTIVES: To replace income lost to coal miners because they have become totally disabled due to pneumoconiosis (black-lung disease), and replace income lost to widows of miners who were receiving black-lung benefits when they died, totally disabled by this disease at the time of death, or who died because of this disease.

RESTRICTIONS: Monthly cash benefits are paid to entitled coal miners; widows of coal miners.

REQUIREMENTS: In order to become entitled, the miner must have become "totally disabled" from black-lung disease. Widows of coal miners whose deaths resulted from black-lung diseases are also eligible for benefits.

APPLICATION: Telephone or visit the local Social Security office.

APPROVAL: Applicant will be notified by mail after review.

PUBLICATIONS: Code of Federal Regulations, "The New Coal Miners' Black Lung Benefits."

RELATED PROGRAMS: Social Security — Disability Insurance, Social Security — Survivors Insurance, Supplemental Security Income.

Special Programs for the Aging (Aging Programs)

OBJECTIVE: To provide assistance to states and substate or organizations for support of programs for the aged and aging, via statewide planning, area planning and social services, model projects, research and development, manpower programs, and a national nutrition program.

PROGRAM: To provide formula grants and project grants.

RESTRICTIONS: Funds must be used to assist the aged and aging. For example: setting up and maintaining area agencies on aging; planning and coordinating special programs for the aging; training of personnel to work on behalf of the elderly; demonstration of successful research programs; and model projects for the aging in high-priority areas of states; and nutrition projects.

REQUIREMENTS: All states and territories with approved plans.

APPLICATION: State plans are submitted on the state-plan format; application forms for project grants are available from state agencies or regional offices.

APPROVAL: Notification of award must be made to the designated SCIRA and to Department of Treasury on SF 240.

PUBLICATIONS: "45 CFR 903 and the Guidelines for Implementing Title III of the Older Americans Act of 1965," as amended, and "45 CFR 909 – Nutrition."

RELATED PROGRAMS: Employment Service, Operation Mainstream, The Foster Grandparents Program, Retired Senior Volunteer Program.

Supplemental Security Income

OBJECTIVES: To provide supplemental income to persons aged 65 and over and to persons blind or disabled.

PROGRAM: To direct payments with unrestricted use.

RESTRICTIONS: Payments are made to persons age 65 or over, or who are blind or disabled.

REQUIREMENTS: The eligibility of an individual who is at least 65 or who is blind or disabled.

APPLICATION: Visit Social Security Office.

APPROVAL: The individual will be notified by mail.

RELATED PROGRAMS: Social Security – Disability Insurance, Social Security – Retirement Insurance, Social Security – Special Benefits for Persons Aged 72 and Over, Social Security – Survivors Insurance, Special Benefits for Disabled Coal Miners, Medical Assistance Program.

REGIONAL OFFICES

Federal Office Building
50 Fulton St.
San Francisco, CA 94102
(415) 556-6746

Federal Office Building
1961 Stout St.
Denver, CO 80202
(303) 837-3373

50 Seventh St., NE
Atlanta, GA 30323
(404) 526-5817

300 Wacker Dr.
Chicago, IL 60606
(312) 353-5160

John F. Kennedy Federal Building
Government Center
Boston, MA 02203
(617) 223-6831

601 E. 12th St.
Kansas City, MO 64106

26 Federal Plaza
New York, NY 10007
(212) 264-4600

P.O. Box 13716
3535 Market St.
Philadelphia, PA 19101
(215) 597-6492

1114 Commerce St.
Dallas, TX 75202
(214) 749-3396

Arcade Plaza
1321 Second Ave.
Seattle, WA 98101
(206) 442-0420

DEPARTMENT OF HOUSING AND URBAN DEVELOPMENT (HUD)

451 Seventh St., SW
Washington, DC 20410
(202) 655-4000
Contact: Secretary

Interest Subsidy-Acquisition and Rehabilitation of Homes for Resale to Lower-Income Families

OBJECTIVE: To make it possible for a nonprofit organization or public body to finance the acquisition and the rehabilitation of housing that will be sold to lower-income families.

PROGRAM: To provide insured loans. To provide direct payment for specified use.

RESTRICTIONS: The Federal Housing Administration (FHA) insures lenders against loss on mortgage loans. These loans may be used to finance the purchase and rehabilitation of housing for subsequent resale to lower-income families. Nonprofit sponsors as well as the home purchasers can receive the benefits of interest-reduction payments. The project must consist of four or more single- or two-family dwellings, or dwelling units in a multifamily structure for which a plan of family unit ownership is approved. The maximum insurable loan per unit is $18,000, or up to $21,000 in high-cost areas. For duplex units, the maximum insurable loan ranges from $24,000 to $30,000. An additional amount up to $3,000 is available to large families when the property contains four or more bedrooms and cost levels so require.

REQUIREMENTS: Eligible sponsors are private nonprofit organizations and public bodies that have been approved by HUD. Sponsors must have capacity to purchase, accomplish the rehabilitation, sell the finished properties to low-income purchasers, and provide counseling to the new homeowner.

APPLICATION: The sponsor submits a formal application (FHA form 2013 RS-J) through an FHA-approved mortgagee to local HUD insuring office or area office.

APPROVAL: (Award approved by local HUD area or insuring office.) Interest assistance payments will be paid to the mortgagee on behalf of the nonprofit sponsor/mortgager or the outstanding loan balance, starting with the final endorsement of the project mortgage.

PUBLICATIONS: "Homeownership Assistance for Purchase and Resale of Housing to Low Income Families under Section 235(j)," and HUD handbook 4515.1.

RELATED PROGRAMS: Interest Subsidy – Homes for Lower Income Families, Interest Subsidy – Purchase of Rehabilitated Homes by Lower Income Families, Nonprofit Housing Sponsor Loans – Planning Projects for Low and Moderate Income Families.

Interest Subsidy – Homes for Lower Income Families

OBJECTIVE: To make homeownership more readily available to lower-income families by providing monthly payments to lenders of FHA-insured mortgage loans on behalf of the lower-income families.

PROGRAM: To provide guaranteed insured loans.

RESTRICTIONS: FHA insures lenders against losses on mortgage loans. These loans may be used to finance the purchase of a single-family dwelling, a two-family, or a unit in a multifamily structure that has been constructed or substantially rehabilitated under FHA within 2 years prior to applying for Section 235 assistance. Maximum insurable loans for an occupant mortgagor are: three-bedroom home, $18,000, or up to $21,000 in high-cost areas; two-family home, $24,000, or up to $30,000 in high-cost areas. For a large family, the limit for a four-bedroom home is $21,000, or up to $24,000 in high-cost areas.

REQUIREMENTS: Families, handicapped persons, or single persons 62 years old or older are eligible to receive the benefits of the subsidies and the mortgage insurance if they fall within certain income and asset limits as explained in program literature.

APPLICATION: Application, along with necessary exhibits, is submitted to local HUD area or insuring office through the approved mortgage lender.

APPROVAL: The HUD office informs the mortgage lender of approval or disapproval.

PUBLICATIONS: Regulations are contained in FHA 3000, Part 235. Guidelines are contained in HUD Handbook, FHA 4210.1. "Homeownership for Lower Income Families."

RELATED PROGRAMS: Interest Subsidy – Acquisition and Rehabilitation of Homes for Resale to Lower Income Families, Interest Subsidy – Purchase of Rehabilitated Homes by Lower Income Families, Public Housing – Home Ownership for Low Income Families.

Interest Subsidy – Purchase of Rehabilitated Homes by Lower Income Families

OBJECTIVE: To assist lower-income families to purchase rehabilitated homes from nonprofit sponsors at prices they can afford.

PROGRAM: To provide guaranteed insured loans.

RESTRICTIONS: FHA insures lenders against loss on mortgage loans. These loans may be used to finance the purchase of a single-family dwelling, a two-family dwelling, or a unit in a multifamily structure that has been rehabilitated by a nonprofit sponsor. Maximum insurable loans for an occupant mortgagor are: One-family home, $18,000, or up to $21,000 in high-cost areas; two-family home, $24,000, or up to $30,000 in high-cost areas. For a large family, the limit for a single home is $21,000, or up to $24,000 in high-cost areas.

REQUIREMENTS: Families eligible to apply for mortgage insurance and receive the benefits of the subsidies must fall within certain income limits and other criteria (as determined by locality on a case-by-case basis) as explained in program literature.

APPLICATION: Application is submitted to local HUD insuring or area office through an FHA-approved mortgagee.

APPROVAL: Application approved through local HUD insuring or area office.

PUBLICATIONS: "Homeownership Assistance for Purchase and Resale of Housing to Lower Income Families under Section 235 (j)," and HUD Handbook 4515.1.

RELATED PROGRAMS: Interest Subsidy – Homes for Lower Income Families, Mortgage Insurance – Homes in Urban Renewal Areas, Public Housing – Home Ownership for Low Income Families, Interest Subsidy – Acquisition and Rehabilitation of Homes for Resale to Lower Income Families.

Major Home Improve Loan Insurance – Housing Outside Urban Renewal Areas

OBJECTIVE: To help families repair or improve existing residential structures outside urban-renewal areas.

PROGRAM: To provide guaranteed insured loans.

RESTRICTIONS: HUD insures lenders against loss of loans. These loans may be used to finance the alteration, repair, or improvement of existing one- to four-family housing not within urban-renewal areas. The housing must be at least 10 years old, unless the loan is primarily to make major structural improvements. The maximum insurable loan on a single-family structure is $12,000 or $17,400 in areas where cost levels so require.

REQUIREMENTS: All families are eligible to apply.

APPLICATION: Application is submitted to a local HUD insuring or area office through an FHA-approved mortgagee.

APPROVAL: Application approved or disapproved by local HUD insuring or area office.

PUBLICATIONS: "HUD Residential Rehabilitation Program," "Fact Sheet: Major Home Improvements (Loan Insurance)."

RELATED PROGRAMS: Mortgage Insurance — Housing in Older, Declining Areas, Property Improvement Loan Insurance — All Existing Structures, Property Improvement Loan Insurance — Existing Multifamily Dwellings, Housing Rehabilitation Loans.

Mortgage Insurance — Homes for Low- and Moderate-Income Families

OBJECTIVE: To make homeownership more readily available to families displaced by urban-renewal or other government actions as well as other low-income and moderate-income families.

PROGRAM: To provide guaranteed insured loans.

RESTRICTIONS: HUD insures lenders against loss on mortgage loans. These loans may be used to finance the purchase of proposed or existing low-cost, one- to four-family housing, or rehabilitation of such housing. Maximum insurable loans for an occupant mortgagor are $18,000 for a single-family home, or up to $21,000 for a single-family home in high-cost areas. For a large family (five or more persons), the limits are $21,000 for a single-family home, or up to $24,000 for a single-family home in high-cost areas. Higher mortgage limits are available for two- to four-family housing.

REQUIREMENTS: All families are eligible to apply. Displaced families qualify for special terms. Certification of eligibility as a displaced family is made by the appropriate local government agency.

APPLICATION AND APPROVAL: Application is submitted for review and approval or disapproval to the local HUD insuring or area office through an FHA-approved mortgagee.

PUBLICATION: "Fact Sheet: Homes for Low and Moderate Income Families (Mortgage Insurance)."

RELATED PROGRAMS: Interest Subsidy — Homes for Lower Income Families, Interest Subsidy — Purchase of Rehabilitated Homes by Lower Income Families, Mortgage Insurance — Homes, Mortgage Insurance — Housing in Older, Declining Areas.

Mortgage Insurance — Homes in Outlying Areas

OBJECTIVE: To help families purchase homes in outlying areas.

PROGRAM: To provide guaranteed insured loans.

RESTRICTIONS: HUD insures lenders against loss on mortgage loans. These loans may be used to finance the purchase of proposed, under-construction, or existing one-family nonfarm housing, or new farm housing on 5 or more acres adjacent to a highway. The maximum insurable loan for an occupant mortgagor on a one-family home is $16,200.

REQUIREMENTS: All families are eligible to apply.

APPLICATION AND APPROVAL: Application is submitted for review and approval or disapproval to the local HUD insuring or area office through an FHA-approved mortgagee.

PUBLICATIONS: "Home Mortgage Insurance."

RELATED PROGRAMS: Low to Moderate Income Housing Loans, Mortgage Insurance — Homes.

Mortgage Insurance — Housing in Older, Declining Areas

OBJECTIVE: To help families purchase or rehabilitate housing in older, declining urban areas.

PROGRAM: To provide guaranteed insured loans.

RESTRICTIONS: HUD insures lenders against loss on mortgage loans. These loans may be used to finance the purchase, repair, rehabilitation, and construction of housing in older, declining urban areas where conditions are such that certain normal eligibility requirements for mortgage insurance under a particular program cannot be met. The property must be an acceptable risk giving consideration to the need for providing adequate housing for low- and moderate-income families.

REQUIREMENTS: All families are eligible to apply.

APPLICATION AND APPROVAL: Application is submitted for review and approval or disapproval to the local HUD insuring or area office through an FHA-approved mortgagee.

PUBLICATIONS: HUD handbook 4260.1, "Miscellaneous Type Home Mortgage Insurance."

RELATED PROGRAMS: Mortgage Insurance — Homes, Housing Rehabilitation Grants.

Mortgage Insurance — Nursing Homes and Related Care Facilities

OBJECTIVE: To make possible financing for construction or rehabilitation of nursing homes and other long-term care facilities.

PROGRAM: To provide guaranteed insured loans.

RESTRICTIONS: HUD insures lenders against loss on mortgages. Insured mortgages may be used to finance construction or renovation of facilities to accommodate 20 or more patients requiring skilled nursing care and related medical services, or those who, while not in need of nursing-home care, are in need of minimum but continuous care provided by licensed or trained personnel. Nursing-home and intermediate-care services may be combined in the same facility covered by an insured mortgage or may be in separate facilities. Major equipment for operation may be included in the mortgage.

REQUIREMENTS: Eligible mortgagors include investors, builders, developers, and private nonprofit corporations or associations licensed or regulated by the state for the accommodation of convalescents and persons requiring skilled nursing care or intermediate care.

APPLICATION: The sponsor submits a formal application through a HUD-approved mortgagee to the local HUD area or insuring office.

APPROVAL: The local insuring or area office makes the final decision to approve, hold, or reject individual projects.

PUBLICATION: "Fact Sheet: Nursing Homes (Mortgage Insurance)," "Minimum Property Standards for Nursing Homes," "FHA Regulations," "Regulatory Agreement," "Handbook for Nursing Homes and Intermediate Care Facilities," "Sponsor's Guide," "Nursing Homes and Related Facilities."

RELATED PROGRAMS: Mortgage Insurance – Hospitals, Supplemental Loan Insurance – Multi-Family Rental Housing, Health Facilities Construction – Grants, Grants to States for Construction of State Nursing Home Care Facilities.

Mortgage Insurance – Rental Housing for the Elderly

OBJECTIVE: To provide good quality rental housing for the elderly.

PROGRAM: To provide guaranteed insured loans.

RESTRICTIONS: HUD insures lenders against loss on mortgages. Insured mortgages may be used to finance construction or rehabilitation of detached, semidetached, walk-up, or elevator-type rental housing designed for occupancy by elderly or handicapped individuals and consisting of eight or more units. The unit mortgage limits for non-elevator apartments are: efficiency, $8,800; one bedroom, $12,375; two bedroom, $14,850; three bedroom, $18,700; four or more bedrooms, $21,175. Limits per family unit are somewhat higher for elevator apartments. In areas where cost levels so require, limits per family unit may be increased up to 45 percent.

REQUIREMENTS: Eligible mortgagors include investors, builder developers, public bodies, and nonprofit sponsors. Nonprofit sponsors and public bodies can obtain rent-supplement contract.

APPLICATION: The sponsor submits a formal application through an FHA-approved mortgagee to the local HUD area or insuring office.

APPROVAL: If the project meets program requirements, the area or insuring office issues a commitment to insure the mortgage to the lender.

PUBLICATIONS: "Programs of Interest to Senior Citizens," "Fact Sheet: Senior Citizens Housing," "Section 231 Housing for the Elderly for Project Mortgage Insurance."

Mortgage Insurance – Rental Housing for Moderate-Income Families

OBJECTIVE: To provide good quality rental housing within the price range of moderate-income families.

PROGRAM: To provide guaranteed insured loans.

RESTRICTIONS: HUD insures lenders against loss on mortgages. Insured mortgages may be used to finance construction or rehabilitation of detached, semidetached, row, walk-up, or elevator-type rental housing containing 5 or more units. The unit mortgages for nonelevator apartments are: efficiency, $9,200; one bedroom, $12,937; two bedroom, $15,525; three bedroom, $19,550; four or more bedroom, $22,137. Unit-mortgage limits are somewhat higher for elevator-type structures. In areas where cost levels so require, limits per family unit may be increased up to 45 percent. Rental rates must permit occupancy by moderate-income families.

REQUIREMENTS: To provide profit-motivated sponsors.

APPLICATION: The sponsor submits a formal application through an FHA-approved mortgagee to the local HUD insuring or area office.

APPROVAL: If the project meets program requirements, the insuring or area office issues a commitment to insure the mortgage to the lender.

PUBLICATIONS: "Fact Sheet: Rental Housing for Moderate Income Families," "HUD Handbook 4560.2," "Mortgage Insurance for Moderate-Income Housing Projects, Section 221."

RELATED PROGRAMS: Mortgage Insurance – Rental Housing, Mortgage Insurance – Rental Housing for Low and Moderate Income Families, Market Interest Rate.

Nonprofit Housing Sponsor Loans – Planning Projects for Low- and Moderate-Income Families

OBJECTIVE: To assist and stimulate prospective nonprofit sponsors of FHA-insured low- and moderate-income housing to develop sound housing projects.

PROGRAM: To provide direct loans and project grants.

RESTRICTIONS: FHA may make interest-free loans to nonprofit sponsors to cover 80 percent of preconstruction expenses for planning low- and moderate-income housing projects to be developed under Sections 236, 221 (d) (3), mortgage-interest-rate rent-supplement housing, and 235 (1). Eligible expenses include organization expenses, legal fees, consultant fees, architect fees, preliminary site engineering fees, land options, FHA and FNMA (Federal National Mortgage Association) application fees, and construction loan fees. If the repayment of the loan is not recoverable from mortgage proceeds, the loan may be converted to a grant.

REQUIREMENTS: Nonprofit organizations wishing to sponsor low- and moderate-income housing projects.

APPLICATION: The sponsor submits a formal application form 2290, directly to the appropriate local HUD area or insuring office.

APPROVAL: The local office will receive and process applications for approval subject to the availability of planning funds.

PUBLICATIONS: "Financial Assistance for Nonprofit Sponsors of Low and Moderate Income Housing."

RELATED PROGRAMS: Interest Reduction Payments — Rental and Cooperative Housing for Lower Income Families, Interest Subsidy — Acquisition and Rehabilitation of Homes for Resale to Lower Income Families, Rent Supplements — Rental Housing for Lower Income Families.

Public Housing — Leased

OBJECTIVE: To assist local public agencies to provide decent, safe, and sanitary low-rent housing and related facilities for families of low income through the leasing of existing or newly constructed housing from private owners.

PROGRAM: To provide project grants.

RESTRICTIONS: Provides annual contributions that permit local public agencies to provide decent, safe, and sanitary housing for low-income families at rents they can afford. The annual contributions are used to make up the difference between (a) the rents paid to owners, plus local public agency operating expense, by the local public agency, and (b) the rents the low-income tenants can afford to pay based upon the tenant income, but not in excess of 25 percent of such income as adjusted. The annual contributions cannot exceed the amount that would be paid for a newly constructed project by the local public agency designed to accommodate a comparable number, sizes, and kinds of families. Additional contributions are available for operating subsidies and for elderly, displaced, extremely low income, and large families.

REQUIREMENTS: Local housing authorities established by a local government in accordance with state law, authorized public agencies, or Indian tribal organizations are eligible.

APPLICATION: Submission of Application for Low-Rent Housing Program (forms HUD 52470, 52470A, 52470B, and sometimes 52470C) to the HUD area or insuring office director. HUD handbook RHA 7430.1 covers application procedures.

APPROVAL: HUD area or insuring office director makes final decision to authorize approval or individual applications.

PUBLICATIONS: "Low-Rent Housing," "Leased Housing Handbook."

Public Housing — Modernization of Projects

OBJECTIVE: To provide loans and annual contributions to bring existing public housing projects up to present day-physical standards, and to involve tenants in management, including planning and implementing modernization programs, developing management policies and practices, expanding services and facilities, and providing employment opportunities.

PROGRAM: To provide direct loans.

RESTRICTIONS: The loans may be used for upgrading those low-rent housing projects that, for reasons of physical condition, location, and outmoded management policies, adversely affect the quality of living of the tenants. Loans are limited to the amount that can be amortized within the remaining years of the annual contributions contract. The program must provide for the involvement of tenants in the plans for the rehabilitation of projects, changes in management policies and practices, and expansion of community-service programs and community facilities where needed to meet the requirements of the program.

REQUIREMENTS: Local housing authorities operating federally assisted public housing projects under an existing annual contributions contract.

APPLICATION: The initial submission should be in the form of a letter to the HUD area office indicating the authority's interest in the program and a preliminary cost estimate of the physical improvements needed. The final submission involves submission of a modernization program budget following procedures outlined in the "Low-Rent Housing Modernization Program Handbook."

APPROVAL: Subsequent to the approval of modernization programs and related modernization program budgets by HUD area offices, funds to finance the program are approved by the area director. The area office is responsible for providing notification to the central office of the approval of funds.

PUBLICATIONS: "Low-Rent Housing Modernization Handbook," "Fact Sheet: Modernization of Public Housing Projects."

RELATED PROGRAMS: Interest Reduction Payments — Rental and Cooperative Housing for Lower Income Families, Interest Subsidy — Acquisition and Rehabilitation of Homes for Resale to Lower Income Families, Mortgage Insurance — Experimental Rental Housing, Model Cities Supplemental Grants, Neighborhood Facilities Grants, Neighborhood Development.

Rent Supplements — Rental Housing for Lower-Income Families

OBJECTIVE: To make good quality rental housing available to low-income families at a cost they can afford.

PROGRAM: To provide direct payments for specified use.

RESTRICTIONS: HUD makes payments to owners of approved multifamily rental housing projects to supplement the partial rental payments of eligible tenants. Rental projects must be part of an approved workable program for community improvement or be approved by local government officials. Assistance covers the difference between the tenant's payment and the market rental, but may not exceed 70 percent of the market rental. The Rent Supplement Program can be used to further supplement the rental charges for tenants. Appalachian Housing Assistance grants are available to nonprofit sponsors of rent supplement projects to help defray planning and development costs.

REQUIREMENTS: Eligible sponsors include nonprofit, cooperative builder-seller, investor-sponsor, and limited distribution mortgagors.

APPLICATION: Sponsor submits FHA form No. 2013, Application for Project Mortgage Insurance, to local HUD area or insuring office.

APPROVAL: The local office reviews the application to determine the eligibility and feasibility of the proposal; market need, correct zoning, architectural merits, and availability of community resources are considered. The local office grants a reservation of contract authority upon determination of eligibility and feasibility, and the sponsor is invited to apply for mortgage commitment through an approved mortgagee.

PUBLICATIONS: "Fact Sheet: Rent Supplements."

RELATED PROGRAMS: Interest Reduction Payments — Rental and Cooperative Housing for Lower Income Families; Mortgage Insurance — Rental Housing; Mortgage Insurance — Rental Housing for Low and Moderate Income Families, Market Interest Rate; Mortgage Insurance — Rental Housing in Urban Renewal Areas; Nonprofit Housing Sponsor Loans — Planning Projects Low and Moderate Income Families; Public Housing — Leased; Appalachian Housing Technical Assistance.

REGIONAL OFFICES

15 S. 20th St.
Birmingham, AL 35233
(205) 325-3264

334 W. Fifth Ave.
Anchorage, AK 99501
(907) 272-5561

244 W. Osborn Rd.
P.O. Box 13468
Phoenix, AZ 85002
(602) 261-4441

Union National Bank Building
One Union National Plaza
Little Rock, AR 72201
(501) 378-5401

2500 Wilshire Blvd.
Los Angeles, CA 90057
(213) 688-5973

801 I St.
P.O. Box 1978
Sacramento, CA 95809
(916) 449-3471

110 West C St.
P.O. Box 2648
San Diego, CA 92112
(714) 293-5310

450 Golden Gate Ave.
P.O. Box 36003
San Francisco, CA 94102
(415) 556-4752

1 Embarcadero Center
San Francisco, CA 94111
(415) 556-2238

1440 E. First St.
Santa Ana, CA 92701
(714) 836-2451

1961 Stout St.
Denver, CO 80202
(303) 837-4881

909 17th St.
Denver, CO 80202
(303) 837-2441

999 Asylum Ave.
Hartford, CT 06105
(203) 244-3638

Farmers Bank Building
919 Market St.
Wilmington, DE 19801
(302) 658-6911

Universal North Building
1875 Connecticut Ave., NW
Washington, DC 20009
(202) 382-4855

3001 Ponce deLeon Blvd.
Coral Gables, FL 33134
(305) 445-2561

661 Riverside Ave.
Jacksonville, FL 33204
(904) 791-2626

4224-28 Henderson Blvd.
Tampa, FL 33609
(813) 228-2501

50 Seventh St., NE
Atlanta, GA 30323
(404) 526-5585

230 Peachtree St., NW
Atlanta, GA 30303
(404) 526-4576

Bishop St.
Honolulu, HI 96813
(808) 546-2136

331 Idaho St.
Boise, ID 83707
(208) 342-2711

17 N. Dearborn St.
Chicago, IL 60602
(312) 353-7660

300 South Wacker Dr.
Chicago, IL 60606
(312) 353-7660

542 S. Second St.
Springfield, IL 62704
(217) 525-4414

4720 Kingsway Dr.
Indianapolis, IN 46205
(317) 633-7188

210 Walnut St.
Des Moines, IA 50309
(515) 284-4512

Fourth & State Sts.
P.O. Box 1339
Kansas City, KS 66101
(816) 374-4355

Kansas Ave.
Topeka, KS 66603
(913) 234-8241

Children's Hospital Foundation
   Building
601 S. Floyd St.
Louisville, KY 40201
(502) 582-5251

1001 Howard Ave.
New Orleans, LA 70113
(405) 231-4181

425 Milam St.
Shreveport, LA 71101
(318) 425-1241

202 Harlow St.
Bangor, ME 04401
(207) 942-8271

Two Hopkins Plaza
Baltimore, MD 21201
(301) 962-2121

800 John F. Kennedy Federal Building
Boston, MA 02203
(617) 223-4066

15 New Chardon St.
Boston, MA 02114
(617) 223-4111

660 Woodward Ave.
Detroit, MI 48226
(313) 226-7900

2922 Fuller Ave., NE
Grand Rapids, MI 49505
(616) 456-2225

1821 University Ave.
St. Paul, MN 55104
(612) 725-4701

300 Woodrow Wilson Ave., W.
Jackson, MS 39213
(601) 366-2634

911 Walnut St.
Kansas City, MO 64106
(816) 374-2661

210 N. 12th St.
St. Louis, MO 63101
(314) 622-4760

616 Helena Ave.
Helena, MT 59601
(406) 442-3237

7100 West Center
Omaha, NB 68106
(402) 221-9301

1050 Bible Way
Reno, NV 89505
(702) 784-5356

1230 Elm St.
Manchester, NH 03101
(603) 669-7681

519 Federal St.
Camden, NJ 08103
(609) 963-2541

Gateway 1 Building
Raymond Plaza
Newark, NJ 07102
(201) 645-3010

625 Truman St., NE
Albuquerque, NM 87110
(505) 766-3251

30 Russell Rd.
Albany, NY 12206
(518) 472-3567

560 Main St.
Buffalo, NY 14202
(716) 842-3510

175 Fulton Ave.
Hempstead, NY 11550
(516) 485-5000

120 Church St.
New York, NY 10007
(212) 264-2870

26 Federal Plaza
New York, NY 10007
(212) 264-8068

2309 W. Cone Blvd.
Greensboro, NC 27408
(919) 275-9111

653 Second Ave.
Fargo, ND 58102
(701) 237-5136

550 Main St.
Cincinnati, OH 45202
(513) 684-2884

1240 E. Ninth St.
Cleveland, OH 44199
(216) 522-4065

60 E. Main St.
Columbus, OH 43215
(614) 469-7345

301 N. Hudson St.
Oklahoma City, OK 73102
(405) 231-5511

1708 Utica Square
Tulsa, OK 74152

520 Southwest Sixth Ave.
Portland, OR 97204
(503) 221-2558

624 Walnut St.
Philadelphia, PA 19106
(215) 597-2560

Two Allegheny Center
Pittsburgh, PA 15212
(412) 644-2802

New Pan Am Building
255 Ponce deLeon Ave.
San Juan, PR 00936
(809) 765-0404

330 Post Office Annex
Providence, RI 02903
(401) 528-4351

1801 Main St.
Columbia, SC 29202
(803) 765-5591

400 S. Phillips Ave.
Sioux Falls, SD 57102
(605) 336-2980

1111 Northside Dr.
Knoxville, TN 37909
(615) 584-8527

100 N. Main St.
Memphis, TN 38103
(901) 534-3141

1717 West End Building
Nashville, TN 37203
(615) 749-5521

New Dallas Federal Building
Dallas, TX 75202
(214) 749-7401

2001 Bryan Tower
Dallas, TX 75202
(214) 749-1601

819 Tower
Fort Worth, TX 76102
(817) 334-3233

Two Greenway Plaza, E.
Houston, TX 77046
(713) 226-4335

1205 Texas Ave.
Lubbock, TX 79408
(806) 747-3711

410 S. Main
San Antonio, TX 78285
(512) 225-3251

125 S. State St.
Salt Lake City, UT 84111
(801) 524-5237

Elmwood Ave.
Burlington, VT 05401
(802) 862-6501

701 E. Franklin St.
Richmond VA 23219
(804) 782-2721

1321 Second Ave.
Seattle WA 98101
(206) 442-7456

Riverside Ave., W.
Spokane, WA 99201
(509) 456-4571

500 Quarter St.
Charleston, WV 25330
(304) 343-6181

744 North Fourth St.
Milwaukee, WI 53203
(414) 224-3223

100 East B St.
Casper, WY 82601
(307) 265-5550

DEPARTMENT OF THE INTERIOR

C St., between 18th & 19th Sts.
Washington, DC 20240
(202) 343-1100
Contact: Secretary

BUREAU OF INDIAN AFFAIRS (BIA)

Indian Education — Adults

OBJECTIVE: To provide general instruction for Indian adults in literacy and high-school equivalency.

PROGRAM: To provide training.

RESTRICTIONS: This program provides basic adult education through direct training by the BIA employees or teachers contracted by the BIA. Adult basic education includes reading, English, and mathematics, as well as a broader range of such subject matters as citizenship and consumer protection. Generally, courses are restricted to those not otherwise provided by other federal, state, or local agencies.

REQUIREMENTS: The program generally is limited to persons 18 years or older residing on trust land who are one-quarter Indian or more.

APPLICATION: Verbal or written request to the agency superintendent.

APPROVAL: Agency superintendent makes the necessary arrangements.

PUBLICATIONS: None.

RELATED PROGRAMS: Indian Education — Federal Schools, Indian Education — Colleges and Universities, Adult Education — Grants to States, Citizenship Education and Training.

Indian Housing — Development

OBJECTIVE: To eliminate substandard Indian housing in the 1970s in accordance with the joint plans of the Departments of HEW, HUD, and the Interior, in conjunction with the Indian-Housing Improvement Program.

PROGRAM: To provide training, advisory services, and counseling, and dissemination of technical information.

RESTRICTIONS: Assistance is provided to Indian tribes in establishing housing authorities to obtain benefits of HUD housing programs; in carrying out construction of the projects and in managing them. Assistance is restricted to Indian tribes that are able to establish housing authorities and carry out programs under the U.S. Housing Act of 1937, as amended, the U.S. Housing Act of 1949, as amended, and the rules and regulations of HUD.

REQUIREMENTS: Indians and other persons who meet the income criteria and other rules and regulations of the legally established local Indian housing authorities.

APPLICATION: Verbal or written request from tribe, local Indian housing authority, or other interested groups of Indians to agency superintendent.

APPROVAL: Not applicable.

PUBLICATIONS: HUD publications, pamphlets, and informational materials, "Public Housing Program for Indians," and "Indian Housing Program."

RELATED PROGRAMS: Indian Housing — Improvement, Low- to Moderate-Income Housing Loans, Indian Sanitation Facilities, Interest Reduction Payments — Rental and Cooperative Housing for Lower Income Families, Interest Subsidy — Homes for Lower Income Families, Public Housing Acquisition (With or Without Rehabilitation) and Construction, Public Housing — Home Ownership for Low Income Families, Public Housing — Leased, Rent Supplements — Rental Housing for Lower Income Families.

Indian Housing — Improvement

OBJECTIVE: To eliminate substandard Indian housing in the 1970s in conjunction with other federal housing programs.

PROGRAM: To provide project grants.

RESTRICTIONS: The program is mainly devoted to housing improvement. The Bureau does, however, build an entire house in special situations where no other program will meet the need, i.e., extremely isolated areas or reservations where only a very small number of homes are needed.

REQUIREMENTS: Indians in need of financial assistance to help repair or renovate existing homes, or who need a new house and cannot be helped by any other federal program. Indians who have the financial ability to provide their own housing are not eligible to participate.

APPLICATION: Verbal or written request from Indians to the local Indian housing organization.

APPROVAL: Grants are approved by the Indian tribe, and they may be concurred by the agency superintendent or made under a standing agreement previously approved.

PUBLICATIONS: "Housing Improvement Program Administration."

RELATED PROGRAMS: Indian Housing — Development, Indian Sanitation Facilities.

Indian Loans — Economic and Social Development

OBJECTIVE: Assistance is provided to Indians, Eskimos, and Aleuts to obtain financing from private and governmental sources that serve other citizens. When otherwise unavailable, financial assistance through the BIA is provided to eligible applicants for any purpose that will promote their economic or social development.

PROGRAM: To provide direct loans and specialized services.

RESTRICTIONS: Loans may be used for business, industry, agriculture, rehabilitation, housing, education, and for relending to members of Indian organizations. Funds must be unavailable from other sources at reasonable rates of interest. Funds may not be used for speculation. Except for educational purposes, BIA financial assistance must be used on or near Indian reservations.

REQUIREMENTS: Indians, Eskimos, and Aleuts. Individual applicants must be at least one-quarter degree of Indian blood and not members of an Indian organization that conducts its own credit program. Organizational applicants must have a form of organization recognized by the commissioner of Indian affairs.

APPLICATION: Applications must be initiated at the local, or usually the agency level, and submitted on forms approved by the commissioner of Indian affairs.

APPROVAL: Action approving or disapproving loans is taken at various levels pursuant to delegated authority. Local office notifies applicants of action taken on applications.

PUBLICATIONS: None.

RELATED PROGRAMS: Farm Operating Loans, Farm Ownership Loans, Soil and Water Loans, Economic Opportunity Loans for Small Businesses, Small Business Loans, Veterans Business Loans – Guaranteed and Insured Loans, Veterans Farm Loans, Veterans Housing – Direct Loans and Advances, Veterans Housing – Guaranteed and Insured Loans.

Indian Social Services – General Assistance

OBJECTIVE: To provide assistance for living needs to needy Indians on reservations, including those Indians living in jurisdictions under the BIA in Alaska and Oklahoma, when such assistance is not available from state or local public agencies.

PROGRAM: To provide direct payments with unrestricted use.

RESTRICTIONS: Provides cash payments to meet daily living needs (e.g., food, clothing, shelter).

REQUIREMENTS: Needy Indians living on Indian reservations or in jurisdictions under the BIA in Alaska and Oklahoma.

APPLICATION: A request for assistance, using an application for assistance form No. 5-1200, to the Indian Agency superintendent.

APPROVAL: Assistance is provided by the Indian Agency.

RELATED PROGRAMS: Indian Social Services – Child Welfare Assistance, Indian Social Services Counseling.

Indian Social Services – Counseling

OBJECTIVE: To help Indians cope with family problems or other serious social problems. To determine eligibility for general assistance and child-welfare assistance. To develop tribal welfare programs. To provide information and liaison assistance enabling Indians to secure welfare services and assistance from state and local agencies.

PROGRAM: To provide advisory services and counseling.

RESTRICTIONS: Counseling and advice are available to Indians regarding problems of family or social welfare nature. This is a counseling service only, and no financial aid is available under this program.

REQUIREMENTS: Indians living on reservations, including Indians in Alaska or Oklahoma. Other Indians who come to BIA agency offices, where services can be provided at the office.

APPLICATION: Verbal request at agency office or letter to office.

APPROVAL: Not applicable.

RELATED PROGRAMS: Child Welfare Services; Indian Social Services – Child Welfare Assistance, Indian Social Services – General Assistance, Indian Advice and Special Services.

REGIONAL OFFICES

555 Cordova Ave.
Anchorage, AK 99501
(907) 277-1561

Federal Building
Phoenix, AR 85025
(602) 261-3873

Federal Office Building
2800 Cottage Way
Sacramento, CA 95825
(916) 484-4676

Room 700
Colorado State Bank Building
1600 Broadway
Denver, CO 80202
(303) 837-4325

Federal Building
550 W. Fort St.
Boise, ID 83724
(208) 342-2401

7981 Eastern Ave.
Silver Spring, MD 20910
(301) 427-7500

Federal Building
316 N. 26th St.
Billings, MT 59101
(406) 245-6711

Federal Building
300 Booth St.
Reno, NV 89502
(702) 784-5451

U.S. Post Office Building &
Federal Building
South Federal Place
Santa Fe, NM 87501
(505) 988-6217

729 N.E. Oregon St.
Portland, OR 97208
(503) 234-3361

Federal Building
125 S. State
Salt Lake City, UT 84111
(801) 524-5311

Joseph C. O'Mahoney Federal Center
2120 Capitol Ave.
Cheyenne, WY 82001
(307) 778-2326

DEPARTMENT OF LABOR

Constitution Ave and 14th St., NW
Washington, DC 20210
(202) 393-2420
Contact: Secretary

EMPLOYMENT STANDARDS ADMINISTRATION
Contact: Assistant Secretary

Age Discrimination in Employment

OBJECTIVE: To prohibit arbitrary age discrimination in hiring and other employment practices, promote the employment of older workers based on ability rather than age, and help employers and employees find ways to meet problems arising from the impact of age on employment.

PROGRAM: To provide advisory services and counseling, and to investigate complaints.

RESTRICTIONS: Individuals 40 to 65 years of age are protected from age discrimination by employers engaged in an industry affecting commerce who have 20 or more employees, by employment agencies serving such employers, and by labor organizations with 25 or more members in an industry affecting commerce. It is unlawful for employers, employment agencies, or labor organizations to use advertisements indicating any preference, limitation, specification, or discrimination based on age. Exceptions are provided where age is a *bona fide* occupational qualification; the differentiation is based on reasonable factors other than age or in observance of the terms of a *bona fide* seniority system or employee benefit plan. The secretary of labor may establish such reasonable exemptions as he or she may find necessary and proper in the public interest.

REQUIREMENTS: Persons who believe that they have been discriminated against because of age or who believe that such discrimination is occurring against others.

APPLICATION: Requests for assistance may be made either orally or in writing to the appropriate local office of the Employment Standards Administration, Department of Labor. (The names of persons making inquiries are held in confidence.)

APPROVAL: None.

PUBLICATION: "The Age Discrimination in Employment Act, 29 CFR."

RELATED PROGRAMS: Job Discrimination — Investigation and Conciliation of Complaints.

Comprehensive Employment and Training Programs
(Comprehensive Employment and Training Act of 1973)

OBJECTIVE: To provide funds to state and local prime sponsors to plan and operate manpower programs that meet local needs.

PROGRAM: To provide project grants.

RESTRICTIONS: Title I — Assistance to provide training or employment opportunities for low-income, unemployed, or underemployed persons; Title II — grants for areas of high employment.

REQUIREMENTS: Units of state and local general government that have a population of 100,000 or more persons; consortia consisting of general local government, at least one of which has a population of 100,000 or more; and Indian eligible prime sponsors.

APPLICATION: Comprehensive Employment and Training Act (CETA) replaces the following programs previously listed separately: Public Service Careers; and Job Opportunities in the Business Sector Optional Programs. Also part of Operation Mainstream: see entry for residual program. Note: at local option, the program no longer available through application to the federal government may continue to retain the federal name and format. Despite similarity of name, these programs are local responsibility. The prime sponsor may provide any type of activity consistent with the act. Job Corps, previously authorized under the Economic Opportunity Act of 1964, is retained under CETA; all requests for information should go to the nearest regional Office of the Manpower Administration.

APPROVAL: The award is made by the assistant regional director for Manpower. Notification of grant award must be made to the designated SCIRA and the Department of the Treasury on SF 240.

PUBLICATIONS: *Federal Register,* February 15, 1974, Programs under Title II of the Comprehensive Employment and Training Act. *Federal Register,* March 19, 1974, Comprehensive Manpower Program and Grants to Areas of High Unemployment.

RELATED PROGRAMS: Vocational Education — Basic Grants to States, Bilingual Education, Educationally Deprived Children — Migrants, Dropout Prevention, Work Incentives Program and Incentives.

Employment Service

OBJECTIVE: To place persons in employment by providing services to individuals in need of preparation and placement and to employers seeking qualified individuals to fill job openings.

PROGRAM: To provide project grants, advisory services, counseling, and specialized services.

RESTRICTIONS: The United States Employment Service (ES) and affiliated state agencies operate over 2,400 local offices to serve those seeking or needing employment and those providing it. General services include outreach, interviewing, testing, counseling, and referral to placement, appropriate training or other services involved in readying individuals for employment. Specialized services include:

1. *Services to veterans.* By law and regulations, state employment service local offices provide priority in counseling and placement services to veterans seeking employment assistance, with preferential treatment of disabled. Each state is assigned a federal veterans' employment representative, and the local employment service office assigns a staff member with the responsibility for functional supervision of services to veterans and insuring that the intent of laws covering veterans' priority and preferential treatment in services is effectively carried out. In addition, visits are made to military bases and veterans' hospitals to explain the services available to provide assistance to veterans and servicemen. Special efforts are presently being made to accommodate the large number of Vietnam-era veterans – including disabled veterans – seeking employment and training under the President's Veterans Program, through coordinated action by federal agencies and organizations such as the National Alliance of Businessmen (NAB).

2. *Services to the disadvantaged.* The ES emphasizes services to the poor, and unemployed or underemployed persons handicapped by race, age, lack of education, and physical or mental disabilities, and assists them through such services as testing, counseling, referral to training for which ES is the subcontractor for selection; and other supportive services, i.e., job search and development, and job placement and follow-up.

3. *Services to youth.* The ES maintains a year-round program of services to youth, including counseling, testing, referral to training and other agencies, job development, and placement. Services are provided through local ES offices and, in some metropolitan areas, through Youth Opportunity Centers. The program is designed to provide employment services to youth between 14 and 22, who are either recent high-school dropouts or other youth entering the labor market. Among the significant components or activities included in the ES youth program are: (a) the Summer Employment Program designed to give priority of service to disadvantaged youth to enable them to return to school, (b) the Cooperative ES – School Program, which reaches out to new job market entrants to assist them in the crucial period of transition from school to work, and (c) recruitment, screening, and referral of young people for manpower training programs.

4. *Services to older workers.* Services to older workers, those 45 years of age and over, include specialized job counseling, job development, referral to training or necessary health and social services and job placement. A limited number of local offices have older worker service units to intensify, individualize, and personalize services to this group.

5. *Services to the handicapped.* These services in cooperation with other community agencies include special employment counseling and placement assistance to physically and mentally handicapped persons seeking work. Counselors use special placement techniques to help match the physical demands of a job to the capabilities of a worker. Highly personalized job development is provided the worker through contact with employers. Information, promotional, and educational activities are directed toward employers and labor organizations to improve employment opportunities for the handicapped.

6. *Rural services.* Special services are provided in rural and farm area to meet the needs of the particular areas. The state employment services receive guidance in providing these services from the Rural Manpower Service (RMS) of the Manpower Administration. These services provided by the employment service are: year-round recruitment and placement of workers in farm and woods occupations, assistance to farmers in meeting critical, seasonal labor needs by "day-haul" of workers, recruitment and arrangement of the movement of migratory farmworkers from supply to demand areas, and determination of the needs for training in farm- and woods-related industry skills. Ottumwa, or area concept expansion, is an experimental approach to providing manpower services to rural areas. Employment security agencies in 12 states have organized their local office structure in certain rural areas to better provide manpower services to a functional economic area, rather than to a limited geographical area, as was formerly the case. Specialized services are now centered in an area office, usually in the "hub" city of the area, and other offices serve as "satellite offices," calling on the area office for specialized services. An area manager is responsible for all ES activities in the designated area, and tie-ins with job banks are being initiated. The Smaller Communities Program consists of mobile employment service teams sent by the state employment services to provide rural areas with manpower and supportive services. To attract new industry to an area, the mobile team compiles and publishes a comprehensive manpower resource report on each area served, profiling its available and potential skills, detailed information on the area's economy and its institutional components. The Hitchhike Program is a method of overlaying manpower programs on existing compatible institutions successfully functioning in rural areas. Cooperative Extension Service county offices, community colleges, farmer groups, and state and/or local welfare agencies are examples of facilities with potential delivery capability. State employment security agency subcontracts with the delivery agency (such as the State Cooperative Extension Service) to provide a broad spectrum of manpower services to residents of remote rural areas.

7. *Services to inmates of correctional institutions and others in the criminal justice system.* Special services are provided to inmates and former inmates of correctional institutions in cooperation with federal, state, and local correctional institutions and probation officers by making available placement, employment counseling, and testing services to assist in the placement and job adjustment of inmates who are currently being released from correctional institutions. Local office assistance can be arranged to include group orientation, testing, and counseling before, during, and after incarceration, as well as job-market information, job development, and placement assistance.

Correctional authorities are also given technical assistance in planning training programs. Bonding assistance is provided to those denied employment for reasons other than ability to perform, including difficulty in securing bonds.

8. *Services to Selective Service rejectees.* Interviews of young men rejected for the military service are conducted by state employment service representatives at some of the larger armed forces examining and entrance stations to provide assistance in finding suitable employment. After identifying the assistance needed by the young men, interviewers refer them to the local office of the state employment service for special employment services or to cooperating agencies for remedial education, skills development, medical, welfare, rehabilitation, or other needed services.

9. *Services to employers.* ES employer services activities involve contacts with employers and employer groups, assistance to employers in recruitment, help to fill job openings with special skill or other requirements, identification of training and assistance in developing training programs and industrial services that include assistance or information for use in job restructuring, in dealing with turnover and absenteeism, and in developing personnel-management tools or techniques and upgrading systems.

10. *Job information service.* The Department of Labor and the state employment agencies collect and disseminate labor-market information. Information is collected, analyzed, and distributed on job opportunities, labor supply, labor-market trends, the job-market situation in particular industries, and the employability of unemployed workers and programs aimed at resolving these problems. Occupational projections are made, and occupational releases are developed for selected occupations showing nature of work, working conditions, entry requirements, outlook, and method of entry.

11. *Early warning of mass layoff.* Local offices, acting on evidence or information of pending mass layoffs of substantial numbers of workers in an area, try to determine the number and skills of those to be laid off. Assessments are made of reemployment prospects; interviews of those who will be affected by layoffs are arranged; and plans are developed for placement and related services. The ES participates in community action aimed at interesting new industries in relocation in the area. "Mass layoffs" may be defined as ranging from 100 layoffs in areas of under 20,000 in population to 500 layoffs in larger areas. Mass layoff reporting is also used to alert the national office to layoffs attributable to foreign import competition so that determinations of benefits to laid-off workers under the Trade Expansion Act may be made.

12. *Defense Manpower Policy No. 4.* Through this activity, employers in areas of concentrated, persistent, and substantial unemployment may be certified for special consideration in the award of contracts to supply goods to the federal government.

13. *Apprenticeship information.* Apprenticeship Information Centers (AIC) are located in selected state employment-service local offices for the purpose of providing central and easily accessible sources of information, guidance, counseling, referral, and placement in apprenticeship opportunities.

14. *Computerized job placement.* The ES establishes and operates a computerized listing of employer openings against which applicant characteristics can be matched.

REQUIREMENTS: State employment security agencies.

APPLICATION: Contact the nearest local office of the state employment service.

APPROVAL: Notification of grant award must be made to the designated SCIRA and the Department of the Treasury on SF 240.

PUBLICATIONS: "Veterans Try the Employment Service," "Manpower Programs in Rural Areas," "Area Trends in Employment and Unemployment," "State and Labor Area Newsletters Directory of Important Labor Areas," "Industry Manpower Surveys," "Occupational Guides to Local Office Occupations," "Directory of Occupational Titles," "Job Guide for Young Workers 1969-70 Edition," "Interviewing Guides for Specific Disabilities."

RELATED PROGRAMS: Federal Civil Service Employment, Federal Employment Assistance for Veterans, Federal Employment of Disadvantaged Youth – Part Time, Federal Employment for Disadvantaged Youth – Summer, Federal Employment for the Handicapped, Handicapped Employment Promotion, Migrant Workers.

Manpower Research Small Grant Projects

OBJECTIVE: To broaden and strengthen national and local manpower research and operating program capability through grants to public and private nonprofit academic institutions and research organizations.

PROGRAM: To provide project grants.

RESTRICTIONS: Research project grants support innovative or exploratory research projects or research-related activities in the manpower field.

REQUIREMENTS: Academic institutions and other public and private nonprofit organizations may apply.

APPLICATION: Made in the form of a proposal completed in accordance with guidelines obtainable from the Manpower Administration.

APPROVAL: Described in guidelines and under conditions published in Manpower Research and Development Projects.

PUBLICATIONS: "Manpower Research and Development Projects."

RELATED PROGRAMS: Manpower Research – Doctoral Dissertation Grants, Manpower Institutional Grants.

Minimum Wage and Hour Standards
(Federal Wage-Hour Law)

OBJECTIVE: To provide standards protecting wages of working persons by requiring a minimum hourly wage rate, overtime pay, and equal pay for men and women performing the same or substantially equal work. Additional standards apply to child labor.

PROGRAM: To provide advisory services and counseling, and to investigate complaints.

RESTRICTIONS: Federal wage and hour standards apply generally to employers engaged in interstate or foreign commerce or in the production of goods for such commerce. For most nonfarm-covered employment, the current minimum hourly wage, which was effective January 1, 1976, is $2.30. For nonfarm employment covered by the law as a result of the 1966 amendments or the 1974 amendments, the minimum hourly wage became $2.30 an hour as of January 1, 1977. To the extent necessary to prevent curtailment of employment opportunity, certificates authorizing special minimum-wage rates are issued for learners, handicapped workers, full-time students, student workers, and apprentices. Employees of contractors performing on federal or federally financed construction projects, or services to federal agencies, are subject to special standards. These special standards require that employees receive no less than the wages and fringe benefits prevailing in the locality as determined by the Secretary of Labor, and that daily and weekly overtime be paid. The standards apply to performance on direct federal contracts and also the other construction projects financed in whole or in part by the federal government (e.g., projects under the Revenue Sharing Act of 1972 and National Housing Act). For federally assisted construction subject to prevailing wage requirements, contracting agencies must request a wage determination.

REQUIREMENTS: Any covered employee, unless specifically exempt, is entitled to be paid in accordance with applicable monetary standards.

APPLICATION: Persons having knowledge of wage and employment practices that are not in compliance with the minimum standards of these acts, and persons requesting additional information concerning these standards, are encouraged to write, telephone, or visit the nearest Employment Standards Administration Office. Information should be provided describing the type of business and the nature of the work performed. The names of persons making inquiries are treated in complete confidence. For federally assisted construction subject to prevailing wage requirements, the contracting agency (sponsor of the project) — which may include a state, county, or municipality — must request a wage determination from the nearest regional office of the Employment Standards Administration. The wage determination must be furnished to bidders and is made a part of the contract.

APPROVAL: None.

PUBLICATIONS: "Handy Reference Guide to the Fair Labor Standards Act," "Handy Guide to the Walsh-Healey Public Contracts Act," "Guide to the McNamara O'Hara Service Contract Act of 1965," "Your Rights as an Employee on a Federal or Federally-Financed Construction Job," "Information on the Equal Pay Act of 1963."

RELATED PROGRAMS: Equal Employment Opportunity, Apprenticeship Training, Certification of Foreign Workers for Agricultural and Logging Employment, Certification of Immigrant Nonagricultural Workers Farm Labor Contractor Registration, Women's Special Employment Assistance.

Operation Mainstream

OBJECTIVE: To provide work-training and employment activities, with necessary supportive services, for chronically unemployed poor older workers who have poor employment prospects and are unable, because of age, lack of employment opportunity, or otherwise, to secure appropriate employment or training assistance under other programs.

PROGRAM: To provide project grants.

RESTRICTIONS: Job opportunities may involve the management, development, and conservation of parks, highways, and recreational areas of federal, state and local governments; the improvement and rehabilitation of other community facilities; and the provision of social, health, and educational services to the poor. No enrollees may be employed on projects involving construction, operation, or maintenance of any facility used or intended for use in sectarian instruction or religious worship. No enrollees may displace any employed workers nor impair existing contracts for service. No enrollee will be employed on projects involving political parties.

REQUIREMENTS: Private nonprofit national organizations may sponsor projects under this program. Emphasis is placed on establishing projects in rural areas or towns.

APPLICATION: Applications are made to the Office of National Projects Administration of the Manpower Administration in the form of contract proposals.

APPROVAL: Awards are made at the national level in accordance with the program guidelines.

PUBLICATIONS: "Pamphlets: Older Workers," "Operation Mainstream Can Help," "Green Thumb, Inc.," "Senior Community Service Project."

RELATED PROGRAMS: None.

National On-the-Job Training

OBJECTIVE: To provide occupational training for unemployed and underemployed persons who cannot reasonably be expected to otherwise obtain appropriate full-time employment.

PROGRAM: To provide project grants.

RESTRICTIONS: National on-the-job-training contracts cross regional boundaries and/or are national in scope. Funds may be expended for reimbursement of instructors, administrative costs, supplies, supplementary classroom education, trainee allowances (when coupled with classroom instruction), and supportive services.

REQUIREMENTS: National organizations possessing the capacity, the ability, and desire to carry out the objectives of the program.

APPLICATION: Made in the form of a proposal to conduct a training program to the Office of National Programs.

APPROVAL: The contract is awarded by the director of the office of National Projects Administration.

PUBLICATION: On-the-Job Training program description booklet.

RELATED PROGRAMS: None.

Unemployment Insurance Grants to States

OBJECTIVE: To provide unemployment-insurance coverage to eligible workers through federal and state cooperation.

PROGRAM: To provide project grants.

RESTRICTIONS: The states have the direct responsibility for establishing and operating their own unemployment-insurance programs. While the federal government finances the cost of administration, state unemployment-insurance tax collections are used solely for the payment of benefits. Federal unemployment-insurance tax collections are used to finance expenses deemed necessary for proper and efficient administration of the state unemployment-insurance programs.

REQUIREMENTS: State unemployment-insurance agencies. All workers whose employers contribute to state unemployment-insurance programs, federal civilian employees, and ex-servicemen are eligible if they are involuntarily unemployed, registered for work, ready for work, and meet the earnings requirements of the state law. Individual state information and eligibility requirements are available from local employment offices.

APPLICATION: State applies for grants to the regional office of the Manpower Administration.

APPROVAL: Notification of award is made to the designated SCIRA and to the Department of the Treasury on SF 240.

PUBLICATIONS: "Unemployment Insurance in the United States," "Attention Federal Employees — Facts About Your Unemployment Compensation," "Attention Ex-servicemen," "Facts About Your Unemployment Compensation," "Questions and Answers on Employment Security Amendments of 1970," "Significant Provisions of State Unemployment Insurance Laws," "Your Unemployment Tax Dollar," "Comparison of State Unemployment Insurance Laws."

RELATED PROGRAMS: Social Insurance for Railroad Workers.

Welfare and Pension Plan Reports

OBJECTIVE: To provide for registration, reporting, and disclosure of employee welfare and pension benefit plans, to provide for bonding of persons responsible for plan assets; and to make public disclosure, upon request, of reports filed under the act.

PROGRAM: To provide advisory services and counseling; investigation of complaints; and technical information.

RESTRICTIONS: Enables participants of employee health, welfare, pension, and profit-sharing plans, to obtain information about plan provisions and financial operations, so that they may protect their interests in such plans; safeguards assets of plans through bonding of plan personnel handling or controlling such assets and by making plan information available to participants, beneficiaries, and the public; obtains reports on plan provisions and financial operations from plan administrators; assists participants and beneficiaries in obtaining copies of required reports.

REQUIREMENTS: Plan administrators, or others involved in the administration of plans, may obtain assistance in preparing reports or otherwise complying with the act. Plan participants or their beneficiaries, may request assistance to investigate alleged failures by plan administrators to meet requirements of the act. All reports filed are available for disclosure to the general public.

APPLICATION: Contact the nearest regional office of the Labor-Management Services Administration.

PUBLICATIONS: "The Welfare and Pension Plans Disclosure Act, WPPDA Guide," for plan administrators and insurance carriers with responsibilities under the WPPDA; "Rights of Pension Plan Participants"; "Your Employee Benefit Plans."

RELATED PROGRAMS: Labor Organization Reports.

APPROVAL: None.

REGIONAL OFFICES

Federal Building
300 N. Los Angeles St.
Los Angeles, CA 90012
(213) 688-4975

450 Golden Gate Ave.
San Francisco, CA 94102
(415) 556-3178

1020 15th St.
Denver, CO 80202
(303) 837-3203

Vanguard Building
1111 20th St., NW
Washington, DC 20036
(202) 961-4471

18350 N.W. Second Ave.
Miami, FL 33169
(305) 350-5011

1371 Peachtree St., NE
Atlanta, GA 30309
(404) 526-5416

1833 Kalakaua Ave.
Honolulu, HI 96815
(808) 955-0259

Federal Office Building
219 S. Dearborn St.
Chicago, IL 60604
(312) 353-1920

300 S. Wacker Dr.
Chicago, IL 60606
(312) 353-7226

Federal Office Building
600 South St.
New Orleans, LA 70130
(504) 527-6173

New Studio Building
110 Tremont St.
Boston, MA 02108
(617) 223-6736

234 State St.
Detroit, MI 48226
(313) 226-6200

Federal Courts Building
110 S. Fourth St.
Minneapolis, MN 55401
(612) 725-2691

Federal Office Building
911 Walnut St.
Kansas City, MO 64106
(816) 374-5941

210 N. 12th Blvd.
St. Louis, MO 63101
(314) 622-4691

9 Clinton St.
Newark, NJ 07102
(201) 645-3712

Federal Building
111 West Huron St.
Buffalo, NY 14202
(716) 842-3260

1515 Broadway
New York, NY 10036
(212) 971-5401

Federal Office Building
1240 E. Ninth St.
Cleveland, OH 44199
(216) 522-3855

3535 Market St.
Philadelphia, PA 19107
(215) 597-7816

Federal Office Building
1000 Liberty Ave.
Pittsburgh, PA 15222
(412) 644-2925

1808 West End Building
Nashville, TN 37203
(615) 749-5906

Bryan and Ervay Sts.
Dallas, TX 75221
(214) 749-2886

1100 Commerce St.
Dallas, TX 75202
(214) 749-3641

Smith Tower Building
506 Second Ave.
Seattle, WA 98104
(206) 442-5216

LIBRARY OF CONGRESS
10 First St., SE
Washington, DC 20540
(202) 426-5000
Contact: Deputy Librarian

Books for the Blind and Physically Handicapped

OBJECTIVE: To provide library service to the blind and physically handicapped residents of the United States and its territories.

PROGRAM: To provide for use of property, facilities, and equipment.

RESTRICTIONS: The program provides talking books, books in braille, and talking-book machines. There are 53 regional libraries in the United States with a collection of approximately 28,500 titles in recorded and braille form and 27,000 music scores in braille.

REQUIREMENTS: An applicant must provide a certificate of his or her inability to read or manipulate conventional printed material — defined in cases of blindness, visual disability, or physical limitations — from a competent authority such as a doctor of medicine, an ophthalmologist, or an optometrist. Other acceptable certifying authorities include registered nurses, professional staffs of hospitals, rehabilitation centers, and health and welfare agencies. In the case of reading disability from organic disfunction, competent authority is defined as a doctor of medicine.

APPLICATION: Applications can be made to the Division for the Blind and Physically Handicapped in Washington, D.C., or through one of the 53 regional libraries.

APPROVAL: None.

PUBLICATIONS: "Reading Is for Everyone."

RELATED PROGRAMS: Handicapped Innovative Programs — Deaf-Blind Centers.

RAILROAD RETIREMENT BOARD
844 Rush St.
Chicago, IL 60611
(312) 944-5500
Contact: Chairman

Social Insurance for Railroad Workers

OBJECTIVE: To provide partial protection against loss of income for the nation's railroad workers and their families, resulting from retirement, death, unemployment, or sickness of the wage earner.

PROGRAM: To provide direct payments with unrestricted use.

RESTRICTIONS: Under the provision of the Railroad Retirement Act and the Railroad Unemployment Insurance Act, benefits are provided for: (1) workers who retire because of age or disability, including supplemental annuities for long-service employees, (2) eligible spouses of retired employees, (3) surviving widows, widowers, children, and parents of deceased employees, (4) unemployed workers, and (5) workers who are sick or injured. In addition, the Railroad Retirement Board participates in the administration of the federal health-insurance program for the aged and the disabled. This program, established by the Social Security Amendments of 1965, covers railroad retirement beneficiaries and aged railroad employees on the same basis as other aged persons.

REQUIREMENTS: Under the Railroad Retirement Act, an employee must have 10 or more years of railroad service for himself and his wife to be eligible, and must have been insured at death for his survivors to be eligible for benefits. Under the Railroad Unemployment Insurance Act, an employee must have earned at least $1,000 in railroad wages and, if a new employee, must have worked for a railroad in at least 7 months in a calendar (base) year to be a qualified employee in the applicable benefit year.

APPLICATION: Application for retirement, disability, survivor, or sickness benefits should be made to any office of the Railroad Retirement Board. Application for unemployment benefits should be made to a railroad unemployment claims agent, generally at a railroad office or other facility.

APPROVAL: The bureau of retirement claims makes awards under the Railroad Retirement Act and the bureau of unemployment and sickness insurance makes awards under the Railroad Unemployment Insurance Act.

PUBLICATIONS: "Benefits for Railroad Workers and Their Families." A series of free leaflets is available from Information Service, Railroad Retirement Board.

RELATED PROGRAMS: Medicare – Hospital Insurance, Medicare – Supplementary Medical Insurance, Social Security – Retirement Insurance, Social Security – Special Benefits for Persons Aged 72 and Over, Social Security – Survivors Insurance.

VETERANS ADMINISTRATION (VA)
Vermont Ave., between H and I Sts., NW
Washington, DC 20420
(202) 393-4120
Contact: Administrator

Automobiles and Adaptive Equipment for Certain Veterans and Members of the Armed Forces

OBJECTIVE: To provide financial assistance to certain disabled veterans toward the purchase price of an automobile or other conveyance, not to exceed $2,800, and for additional adaptive equipment deemed necessary to insure the eligible person will be able to operate the automobile or other conveyance.

PROGRAM: To provide direct payments for specified use.

RESTRICTIONS: This is a one-time payment only and must be used toward the purchase of an automobile or other conveyance, including special appliances thereon. Necessary adaptive equipment may be repaired, replaced, or reinstalled on the one conveyance that may be purchased with assistance, or any other conveyance subsequently acquired, but not for more than one conveyance at one time.

REQUIREMENTS: Veterans of World War II and the Korean conflict with honorable service having a service-connected disability due to loss or permanent loss of use of one or both feet, one or both hands, or a permanent impairment of vision of both eyes to a prescribed degree. Servicemen on active duty also qualify under the same criteria as World War II and Korean-conflict veterans. Veterans who serve after January 31, 1955, with the preceding disabilities incurred on or after February 1, 1955, are also eligible if they meet the foregoing and if the disability was incurred in the line of duty as a direct result of the performance of military duty.

APPLICATION: An application (VA form 21-4502) may be obtained from any VA office or regional office and submitted to the regional office.

APPROVAL: Awards are authorized at the regional office.

PUBLICATIONS: "Federal Benefits for Veterans and Dependents."

RELATED PROGRAMS: Veterans Prosthetic Appliances.

DEPARTMENT OF MEDICINE AND SURGERY
Contact: Administrator

Biomedical Research

OBJECTIVE: To provide the best available medical care for the veteran patient.

PROGRAM: To provide for use of property, facilities, and equipment.

RESTRICTIONS: Medical research is an intramural activity conducted in VA hospitals and medical clinics. This is not an assistance program in the sense of providing grants or direct service to individual applicants. Assistance is provided in the larger context through staffing in the operation of veterans hospitals and clinics with physicians or scientists at hospitals affiliated with medical schools, and research institutes.

REQUIREMENTS: Non-VA physicians and other biomedical investigators with the appropriate level of education and training who are affiliated institutionally or otherwise with the VA.

APPLICATION: Approval by local VA research and education committee.

APPROVAL: Not applicable.

PUBLICATIONS: "Annual Report, Medical Research in the VA" (fiscal year 1973).

RELATED PROGRAMS: Education and Training of Health Service Personnel, Exchange of Medical Information.

Blind Veterans Rehabilitation Centers

OBJECTIVE: To provide personal and social-adjustment programs and medical or health-related services for blinded veterans at selected VA hospitals maintaining blind rehabilitation centers.

PROGRAM: To provide specialized services.

RESTRICTIONS: To assist in the rehabilitation of blinded veterans.

REQUIREMENTS: Any blind veteran who meets one of the following requirements for admission to a VA hospital: (1) requires treatment for a service-connected disability or disease incurred or aggravated in military service, (2) has a service-connected, compensable disability or is in receipt of retirement pay for a service-incurred disability when in need of hospital care for a non-service-connected condition, (3) has been discharged under other than dishonorable conditions: (a) from wartime service, (b) after January 31, 1955, or (c) was awarded the Medal of Honor in peacetime, and is unable to pay the cost of necessary care and so states under oath, or (4) regardless of ability to defray the expenses of hospital care, is: (a) in receipt of a VA pension or (b) 65 years of age or older and has had either wartime or peacetime active military service. Active-duty personnel of the armed forces may be transferred to a center.

APPLICATION: Application may be made through any VA hospital or outpatient clinic, by completing VA form 10-10. Also transfer of active-duty personnel of armed forces.

APPROVAL: VA ward physician determines, with recourse to hospital director.

PUBLICATIONS: "Federal Benefits for Veterans and Dependents," "When Vision Fails," "Blind Rehabilitation in the Veterans Administration."

RELATED PROGRAMS: Veterans Outpatient Care, Rehabilitation Services and Facilities — Basic Support.

Burial Allowance for Veterans

OBJECTIVE: To provide a monetary allowance not to exceed $250 toward the funeral and burial expenses, plus $150 for plot or interment expenses if not buried in a National Cemetery. If death is service-connected, $800 is payable for funeral and burial expenses. In addition to the $250 and $800, the cost of transporting the remains from place of death to site of burial is paid by VA, if death occurs in a VA hospital. Also to provide flag for the burial of a deceased veteran.

PROGRAM: To provide direct payments for specified use.

RESTRICTIONS: No restrictions.

REQUIREMENTS: The person who bore the veteran's burial expense or the undertaker, if unpaid, is eligible for reimbursement of the burial expense. The next of kin, friend, or associate of the deceased veteran is eligible for the flag.

APPLICATION: An application (VA form 21-530) may be obtained from any VA office or regional office and submitted to the regional office.

APPROVAL: Awards are authorized at the regional office.

PUBLICATIONS: "Federal Benefits for Veterans and Dependents," "VA Fact Sheet IS-1."

RELATED PROGRAMS: Pension to Veterans Widows and Children, Memorial Plots and Markers in National Cemeteries, National Cemeteries, Procurement of Headstones and Markers.

Community Nursing-Home Care (Community Contract)

OBJECTIVE: To provide service-connected veterans with nursing-home care and to aid the veteran, his family, and the community in making the transition from a hospital to a community care facility. It provides time at VA expense to marshal resources for the veteran's continued care.

PROGRAM: To provide direct payments for specified use.

RESTRICTIONS: Limited to veterans: (a) requiring nursing-home care for a service-connected condition, (b) hospitalization in VA hospitals, (c) hospitalized in non-VA hospitals in Alaska and Hawaii, (d) hospitalized in an armed forces hospital and who on discharge will become a veteran, or (e) who have been furnished hospital care at VA expense in the Republic of the Philippines. Such nursing home care may not exceed VA prescribed *per diem* rates.

REQUIREMENTS: Applicants are nursing homes, which (1) must be inspected by VA personnel for compliance with VA standards established for skilled nursing homes, or (2) accredited by the Joint Commission on Accreditation of Hospitals.

APPLICATION: For veterans under care at VA expense, a medical determination as to need for nursing-home care will be made by designated physician; veterans have recourse to hospital director. Veterans not under care at VA expense should submit application for medical benefits, VA form 10-10, to nearest VA medical facility.

APPROVAL: None.

RELATED PROGRAMS: Veterans Nursing Home Care, Veterans State Nursing Home Care, Medical Assistance Program, Medicare — Hospital Insurance.

Grants to States for Construction of State Nursing-Home-Care Facilities

OBJECTIVE: To assist states in the construction of state home facilities furnishing nursing care to war veterans.

PROGRAM: To provide project grants.

RESTRICTIONS: Grant funds must be used to construct nursing-home care projects that have VA approval; VA participation is limited to not more than 65 percent of actual project cost.

REQUIREMENTS: Any state may apply after assuring that the assisted facility will be operated by the state; and will furnish nursing-home care primarily to war veterans.

APPLICATION: VA form 10-1161, State Nursing Home Project Construction Application, should be submitted to the VA headquarters office.

APPROVAL: Formal approval of the award to the state is made by the administrator of veterans' affairs, with program administered by Extended Care Service. When a specific award of funds is granted, increased, or decreased, notification must be made to the designated SCIRA and to the Department of the Treasury on SF 240.

PUBLICATION: "VA Regulations 6170-6176 State Home Facilities for Furnishing Nursing Home Care."

RELATED PROGRAMS: Grant to States for Remodeling of State Home Hospital/Domiciliary Facilities, Health Facilities Construction — Grants, Health Facilities Construction — Technical Assistance.

Grants to States for Remodeling of State Home Hospital/Domiciliary Facilities

OBJECTIVE: To assist states in remodeling existing hospital/domiciliary facilities in state homes providing care and treatment to war veterans.

PROGRAM: To provide project grants.

RESTRICTIONS: Grant funds must be used to remodel existing state home hospital/domiciliary facilities. Grants are not for new construction. Projects must have VA approval and prior funding.

REQUIREMENTS: Any state may apply after assuring that the facility will be operated by the state as a state home and will furnish hospital/domiciliary care principally to war veterans.

APPLICATION: VA form 10-1369, "State Home Hospital/Domiciliary Project Construction Application."

APPROVAL: Formal approval of the award of the assistance grant to the state is made by the administrator of veterans affairs with program administered by Extended Care Service. Where a specific award of funds is granted, increased, or decreased, notification of grant award must be made to the designated SCIRA and to Department of the Treasury on SF 240.

PUBLICATION: "VA Regulations 6180-6184, Grants for Assistance in Remodeling, Modification or Alteration of Existing State Home Hospital and Domiciliary Facilities."

RELATED PROGRAMS: Grants to States for Construction of State Nursing Home Care Facilities, Health Facilities Construction — Grants, Health Facilities Construction — Technical Assistance.

Sharing Specialized Medical Resources

OBJECTIVE: To secure the use of specialized medical resources that otherwise might not be feasibly available by the VA and to provide services to the community through specialized medical resources that are not being utilized to their maximum effectiveness within the VA hospital.

PROGRAM: To provide specialized services.

RESTRICTIONS: To provide for the exchange of or mutual use of specialized medical resources when such an agreement will obviate the need for a similar resource to be provided in a VA hospital, or for the mutual use, or exchange of use, of specialized medical resources in a VA hospital that have been justified on the basis of veterans' care, but which are not utilized to their maximum effective capacity. Agreements must be made with hospitals, medical installations with hospital facilities, medical schools, or clinics.

REQUIREMENTS: Medical schools, medical installations having hospital facilities, hospitals, or clinics.

APPLICATION: Negotiated contracts must be approved by the Chief Medical Director, VA Central Office, Washington, DC.

APPROVAL: None.

PUBLICATION: "VA Regulation 6210."

RELATED PROGRAMS: Exchange of Medical Information, Laboratory Animal Sciences and Primate Research, Clinical Research Centers, Medical Library Assistance — Regional Medical Libraries, Biotechnology Resources.

Specially Adapted Housing for Disabled Veterans

OBJECTIVE: To assist certain totally disabled veterans in acquiring suitable housing units, with special fixtures and facilities made necessary by the nature of the veterans' disabilities.

PROGRAM: To provide direct payments for specified use.

RESTRICTIONS: The program provides 50 percent of the cost to the veteran of the housing unit, land, fixtures, and allowable expenses, not to exceed $17,500. The money may be used for assistance in: (a) construction of a suitable home on land to be acquired by the veteran, or (b) construction of a home on suitable land owned by the veteran, or (c) remodeling an existing home if it can be suitably adapted, or (d) for application against an outstanding mortgage on a specially adapted home owned by the veteran. In computing the amount of the grant payable to a veteran, the housing unit cost may include incidental expenses, such as connections or extensions to public facilities, and customary attorney's, architect's loan-closing, and other service fees. Restrictions on the use of a grant are that if a loan is necessary to supplement the grant, monthly payments on and the cost of maintaining the housing unit must bear a proper relation to the veteran's present and prospective income; the housing unit must be suitable for the veteran's special dwelling needs; the veteran's acquired interest in or title to the property must meet standards generally acceptable to informed real-estate-market participants in the locality of property.

REQUIREMENTS: Veterans with permanent, total, and compensable disabilities based on service after April 20, 1898, due to (a) loss or loss of use of both lower extremities to an extent precluding locomotion without braces, canes, crutches, or wheelchairs, or (b) blindness in both eyes, having only light perception, plus loss or loss of use of one lower extremity, or (c) due to loss or loss of use of one lower extremity with residuals or organic disease or injury affecting balance or propulsion so as to preclude locomotion without resort to wheelchairs. It must be medically feasible for the veteran to reside in the proposed or existing housing unit, and in the locality.

APPLICATION: Initial application for determination of basic eligibility may be made on VA form 21-4555 to the VA regional office holding veteran's claim folder. After eligibility determination, a VA employee will personally assist the veteran throughout subsequent processing, including advice on a suitable house plan and lot, location of a qualified builder and architect, and preparation of the supplemental application necessary for final grant approval.

APPROVAL: VA regional office will send the supplemental application to Director, Veterans Benefits Office, Washington, DC 20421, which returns the grant proceeds to the regional office with authority for payout to the veteran or for his account after conditions of the proposal and contract are fulfilled.

PUBLICATIONS: "Questions and Answers on Specially Adapted Housing for Veterans," "VA Pamphlet 26-69-1, Federal Benefits for Veterans and Dependents," "VA Fact Sheet IS-1."

RELATED PROGRAMS: Veterans Housing – Guaranteed and Insured Loans, Veterans Housing – Direct Loans for Disabled Veterans, Mortgage Insurance – Homes for Certified Veterans, Life Insurance for Veterans.

Veterans Hospitalization

OBJECTIVE: To provide inpatient, medical, surgical, and neuropsychiatric care and related medical and dental services to veterans.

PROGRAM: To provide specialized services.

RESTRICTIONS: Hospital care includes (1) medical services (rendered during the course of hospitalization), transportation, and incidental expenses for a veteran who is in need of treatment for a service-connected disability or who is unable to defray the expense of transportation, and (2) such mental-health services, counseling, and training of the members of the immediate family as may be necessary to the effective treatment or rehabilitating of the veteran.

REQUIREMENTS: Any veteran who: (1) requires treatment for a service-connected disability or disease incurred or aggravated in military service; or (2) has a service-connected, compensable disability or is in receipt of retirement pay for a service-incurred disability when in need of hospital care for a non-service-connected condition; or (3) has been discharged under other than dishonorable conditions and is unable to pay the cost of necessary care and so states under oath; or (4) regardless of ability to defray the expenses of hospital care, is: (a) in receipt of a VA pension or (b) 65 years of age or older. A spouse or child of a veteran who has a total disability, and the widow or child of a veteran who had died as a result of a service-connected disability, under special circumstances outlined in VA regulations and guidelines.

APPLICATION: Application may be made: (1) personally at a VA hospital, outpatient clinic, or regional office, (2) through any veterans' service organization representative, or (3) by mailing VA form 10-10, Application for Medical Benefits, to nearest VA hospital.

APPROVAL: None.

PUBLICATION: "Federal Benefits for Veterans and Dependents."

RELATED PROGRAMS: Community Nursing Home Care, Blind Veterans Rehabilitation Centers, Veterans Domiciliary Care, Veterans Nursing Home Care, Veterans Outpatient Care, Veterans Prosthetic Appliances.

Veterans Nursing Home Care

OBJECTIVE: To accommodate individuals who are not acutely ill and not in need of hospital care, but who require skilled nursing care, related medical services, supportive personal care, and individual adjustment services (including social, diversional, recreational, and spiritual activities and opportunities) in a homelike atmosphere.

PROGRAM: To provide specialized services.

RESTRICTIONS: All veterans may be admitted directly to VA nursing-home-care units. For non-service-connected care conditions, priority will be given to veterans being transferred from inpatient or member status in a VA facility or non-VA facility at VA expense.

REQUIREMENTS: The veterans must require skilled nursing care and the related medical services for a protracted period of time. Medical determination as to need for nursing-home care will be made by designated physician.

APPLICATION: Medical determination as to need for nursing-home care will be made by VA ward physician, with recourse to hospital director. Veterans not under care at VA expense should submit Application for Medical Benefits, VA form 10-10, to nearest VA medical facility.

APPROVAL: Not applicable.

PUBLICATIONS: "VA Fact Sheet IS-1."

RELATED PROGRAMS: Veterans Outpatient Care, Veterans State Nursing Home Care.

Veterans Outpatient Care

OBJECTIVE: To provide medical and dental services, medicines, and medical supplies to eligible veterans on an outpatient basis.

PROGRAM: To provide specialized service.

RESTRICTIONS: Outpatient medical and dental services are available to eligible veterans in VA facilities or under fee-basis hometown care program when properly authorized. The outpatient care includes the availability of all professional and paramedical services, use of private physicians, the issuance of drugs and medicines, prosthetic appliances, and transportation.

REQUIREMENTS: The following veterans are eligible for medical outpatient services: (1) veterans suffering from a non-service-connected illness that has aggravated an existing service-connected illness, (2) veterans with established eligibility for pre- and post-hospital care, (3) Spanish-American war veterans, (4) veterans entitled to vocational rehabilitation, (5) military retirees, (6) veterans who have a disability, rated at 80 percent or more resulting from a service-connected disability, (7) veterans in receipt of increased pension or additional compensation based on the need for regular aid and attendance by reason of being permanently housebound, (8) veterans who require outpatient treatment to obviate the need for hospitalization, (9) the wife or child of a veteran who has a total disability, permanent in nature, resulting from a service-connected disability. The widow, widower, or child of a veteran who has died as the result of a service-connected disability, may be provided care through the Civilian Health and Medical Program, Veterans Administration (CHAMPVA). Additionally, outpatient dental care may be provided for those veterans who: (1) have a service-connected compensable dental disability or condition, (2) have a service-connected, noncompensable dental condition or disability and were former prisoners of war, (3) have a service-connected, noncompensable condition or disability resulting from combat wounds or service trauma, (4) have been found in need of training authorized under 38 U.S.C. Chapter 31, (5) had served in the active military or naval forces during the Spanish-American War, the Indian wars, the Philippine Insurrection, or the Boxer Rebellion, and (6) have a service-connected, noncompensable disability and who apply for treatment of such condition within 1 year following discharge or release from active duty. Treatment under this latter authority is limited to a one-time correction of the service-connected dental condition.

APPLICATION: File VA form 10-10, Application for Medical Benefits.

APPROVAL: Not applicable.

PUBLICATIONS: VA Regulation 6060, 6033, 6045, 6123, 6060(h), (i), and 6060.4, "Federal Benefits for Veterans and Dependents," and VA pamphlet IS-1.

RELATED PROGRAMS: Veterans Prescription Service, Veterans Prosthetic Appliances.

Veterans Prescription Service

OBJECTIVE: To provide veterans and certain dependents and survivors of veterans in need of regular aid and attendance with prescription drugs and expendable prosthetic medical supplies from VA pharmacies upon presentation of prescription(s) from a licensed physician.

PROGRAM: To provide for the sale, exchange, or donation of property and goods.

RESTRICTIONS: Drugs or medicines and expendable medical supplies prescribed by a licensed physician as specific therapy in treatment of an illness or injury suffered by the veteran will be dispensed by VA pharmacists directly to veterans or dispatched to them by mail through VA pharmacies. Prescription refill service is available on physicians' authorization. In Alaska or U.S. Territories, where there are no VA pharmacies, payment for prescribed drugs is provided on a reimbursable basis. *Use restrictions:* Limited to drugs prescribed by physician(s). Prescriptions are not filled for alcoholic beverages or dietary supplements used for weight control. Veterans living abroad are ineligible for program benefits.

REQUIREMENTS: Eligible veterans, dependents, or survivors of eligible veterans are those in receipt of increased compensation or pension based on need of regular aid and attendance, or by reason of being permanently housebound. Veterans, whose pension payments have been discontinued because their annual income exceeds the applicable maximum limitation, continue their eligibility for drugs, medicines, and expendable prosthetics medical supplies until their income exceeds the maximum limitation by more than $500.

APPLICATION: VA form 10-1151, Application to Receive Drugs, Medicines, and Expandable Prosthetic Medical Supplies, is furnished to each eligible veteran dependent or survivor of eligible veteran by the VA. Signed applications received from veterans constitute application for their benefit. These prescriptions, in most cases, should be taken to the nearest VA pharmacy.

APPROVAL: Not applicable.

PUBLICATIONS: "Federal Benefits for Veterans and Dependents," and VA Fact Sheet IS-1.

RELATED PROGRAMS: Veterans Outpatient Care, Medical Assistance Program, Medicare – Supplementary Medical Insurance.

Veterans State Domiciliary Care

OBJECTIVE: To provide financial assistance to states furnishing domiciliary care to war veterans in state veterans' homes.

PROGRAM: To provide formula grants.

RESTRICTIONS: The assistance provided is for domiciliary care; the provision of shelter, sustenance; continued medical care on an ambulatory self-care basis to assist eligible veterans, disabled by age or disease to attain physical, mental, and social well-being through rehabilitative programs.

REQUIREMENTS: Applicant in any state that operates a designated facility to furnish domiciliary care primarily for war veterans.

APPLICATION: Letter of application from state addressed to Chief Medical Director (126), Veterans Administration, 810 Vermont Avenue, NW, Washington, DC 20420.

APPROVAL: Grant awards must be processed through the SCIRA on SF 240 in compliance with Department of the Treasury circular No. 1082.

PUBLICATION: "Payment of VA Aid for State Soldiers' Home."

RELATED PROGRAMS: Veterans State Nursing Home Care, Veterans State Hospital Care.

Veterans State Hospital Care

OBJECTIVE: To provide financial assistance to states furnishing hospital care to war veterans in state veterans' homes.

PROGRAM: To provide formula grants.

RESTRICTIONS: This assistance provides for hospital care. The provision of diagnosis and treatment for inpatients with medical, surgical, or psychiatric conditions, who generally require the services of a physician on a daily basis with attendant diagnostic, therapeutic, and rehabilitative services.

REQUIREMENTS: Applicant is any state that operates a designated facility to furnish hospital care primarily for war veterans.

APPLICATION: Letter of application from state addressed to Chief Medical Director (136), Veterans Administration, 810 Vermont Avenue, NW, Washington, DC 20420.

APPROVAL: Grant awards must be processed through the SCIRA on SF 240 in compliance with Department of the Treasury circular No. 1082.

PUBLICATIONS: "Payment of VA Aid for State Soldiers' Home."

RELATED PROGRAMS: Veterans State Domiciliary Care, Veterans State Nursing Home Care.

Veterans State Nursing-Home Care

OBJECTIVE: To provide financial assistance to states furnishing nursing-home care to war veterans in state veterans homes.

PROGRAM: To provide formula grants.

RESTRICTIONS: The assistance provided is for nursing-home care. The accommodation of convalescents or other persons who are not acutely ill and not in need of hospital care or domiciliary care but who require skilled nursing care and related medical services.

REQUIREMENTS: Applicant is any state that operates a designated facility to furnish domiciliary or nursing-home care primarily for war veterans.

APPLICATION: Letter of application from state addressed to Chief Medical Director (136), Veterans Administration, 810 Vermont Avenue, NW, Washington, DC 20420.

APPROVAL: Grant awards must be processed through the state Central Information Reception Agency on SF 240 in compliance with Department of the Treasury circular No. 1082.

PUBLICATIONS: "Payment of VA Aid for State Soldiers Home."

RELATED PROGRAMS: Veterans State Domiciliary Care, Veterans State Hospital Care.

REGIONAL OFFICES

474 S. Court St.
Montgomery, AL 36104
(205) 265-5611

429 D St.
Anchorage, AK 99501
(907) 279-3561

230 N. First Ave.
Phoenix, AZ 85025
(602) 261-4771

700 W. Capitol Ave.
Little Rock, AR 72201
(501) 378-4517

101 S. Willowbrook Ave.
Compton, CA 90220
(213) 537-3203

1250 Sixth Ave.
San Diego, CA 92101
(714) 293-5730

11000 Wilshire Blvd.
Los Angeles, CA 90024
(213) 824-7237

211 Main St.
San Francisco, CA 94105
(415) 556-3300

Denver Federal Center
Denver, CO 80225
(303) 234-4089

450 Main St.
Hartford, CT 06103
(203) 244-3740

1601 Kirkwood Hwy.
Wilmington, DE 19805
(302) 994-2511

2033 M St., NW
Washington, DC 20421
(202) 872-1151

GOVERNMENT PROGRAMS

25 K St., NE
Washington, DC 20002
(202) 638-2966

311 W. Monroe St.
Jacksonville, FL 32201
(904) 791-2756

51 SW First Ave.
Miami, FL 33130
(305) 350-4176

144 First Ave., S.
St. Petersburg, FL 33371
(813) 983-2121

730 Peachtree St., NE
Atlanta, GA 30308
(404) 875-7601

680 Ala Mona Blvd.
Honolulu, HI 96801
(808) 546-5991

550 W. Fort St.
Boise, ID 83724
(205) 342-6581

2030 W. Taylor St.
Chicago, IL 60680
(312) 353-4400

36 S. Pennsylvania St.
Indianapolis, IN 46204
(317) 633-7000

210 Walnut St.
Des Moines, IA 50309
(515) 284-4370

5500 E. Kellogg
Wichita, KS 67218
(316) 685-2221

600 Federal Place
Louisville, KY 40202
(502) 582-5801, 5811

701 Loyola Ave.
New Orleans, LA 70113
(504) 527-6401

510 E. Stoner Ave.
Shreveport, LA 71101
(318) 423-8249

76 Pearl St.
Portland, ME 04111
(207) 775-3223

31 Hopkins Plaza
Baltimore, MD 21201
(301) 962-4686

John F. Kennedy Federal Building
Boston, MA 02203
(617) 223-3080

1200 Main St.
Springfield, MA 01103
(413) 781-2301

801 W. Baltimore and Third St.
Detroit, MI 48232
(313) 874-5190

Federal Building, Fort Snelling
St. Paul, MN 55111
(612) 725-4242

1500 E. Woodrow Wilson Dr.
Jackson, MS 39216
(601) 362-4471

601 E. 12th St.
Kansas City, MO 64106
(816) 374-5761

1520 Market St.
St. Louis, MO 63103
(314) 622-8100

VA Center
Fort Harrison, MT 59636
(406) 442-6410

220 S. 17th St.
Lincoln, NB 68508
(402) 475-3416

1201 Terminal Way
Reno, NV 89502
(702) 784-8330

497 Silver St.
Manchester, NH 03103
(603) 669-7011

20 Washington Place
Newark, NJ 07102
(201) 645-2150

500 Gold Ave., SW
Albuquerque, NM 87101

Executive Park North
Stuyvesant Plaza
Albany, NY 12201
(518) 472-4206

111 W. Huron St.
Buffalo, NY 14202
(716) 842-2285

252 Seventh Ave.
New York, NY 10001
(212) 620-6901

100 State St.
Rochester, NY 14614
(716) 263-5740

301 N. Main St.
Winston-Salem, NC 27102
(919) 723-9211

21st Ave. and Elm St.
Fargo, ND 58102
(701) 232-3241

550 Main St.
Cincinnati, OH 45202
(513) 684-2624

1240 E. Ninth St.
Cleveland, OH 44199
(216) 522-3131

360 S. Third St.
Columbus, OH 43206
(614) 469-7336

Second and Court Sts.
Muskogee, OK 74401
(918) 683-3111

200 NW Fourth St.
Oklahoma City, OK 73102
(405) 231-4145

426 SW Stark St.
Portland, OR 97204
(503) 221-3361

5000 Wissahickon Ave.
Philadelphia, PA 19101
(215) 438-5200

1000 Liberty Ave.
Pittsburgh, PA 15222
(412) 281-4233

19-27 N. Main St.
Wilkes-Barre, PA 18701
(717) 825-6811

Kennedy Plaza
Providence, RI 02903
(401) 528-4431

1801 Assembly St.
Columbia, SC 29201
(803) 765-5861

2501 W. 22nd St.
Sioux Falls, SD 57101
(605) 336-3230

801 Broadway
Nashville, TN 37203
(615) 749-5251

1100 Commerce St.
Dallas, TX 75202
(214) 749-3201

515 Rusk Ave.
Houston, TX 77061
(713) 226-4132

1205 Texas Ave.
Lubbock, TX 79401
(806) 747-3248

410 S. Main St.
San Antonio, TX 78285
(512) 255-5511, Ext. 4420

1400 N. Valley Mills Dr.
Waco, TX 76710
(817) 756-7622

125 S. State St.
Salt Lake City, UT 84138
(801) 524-5500

White River Junction
VT 05001
(802) 295-3131

211 W. Campbell Ave.
Roanoke, VA 24011
(703) 343-1581

Sixth & Lenora Building
Seattle, WA 98121
(206) 682-9100

502 Eighth St.
Huntington, WV 25701
(304) 529-2311

342 N. Water St.
Milwaukee, WI 53202
(414) 224-1101

2360 E. Pershing Blvd.
Cheyenne, WY 82001
(307) 778-7550

12 Health

If you have a question in the area of health, contact either the HEW regional health administrator or your *local* health systems agency. The local agency will probably be in closer touch with your specific needs and more familiar with your community.

REGIONAL HEALTH ADMINISTRATION
DEPARTMENT OF HEALTH, EDUCATION AND WELFARE

REGION I (Connecticut, Maine, Massachusetts, New Hampshire, Rhode Island, Vermont)
John F. Kennedy Federal Building
Boston, MA 02203
(617) 223-6827
Contact: Gertrude T. Hunter, M.D.

REGION II (New York, New Jersey, Puerto Rico, Virgin Islands)
Regional Health Administrator
26 Federal Plaza
New York, NY 10007
(212) 264-2562
Contact: Nicholas J. Galluzzi, M.D.

REGION III (Delaware, Maryland, Pennsylvania, Virginia, West Virginia, District of Columbia)
Regional Health Administrator
P.O. Box 13176
Philadelphia, PA 19108
(215) 596-6637
Contact: George C. Gardiner, M.D.

REGION IV (Alabama, Florida, Georgia, Kentucky, Mississippi, North Carolina, South Carolina, Tennessee)
Regional Health Administrator
50 Seventh St., NE
Atlanta, GA 30323
(404) 526-5007
Contact: A. Reich, M.D.

REGION V (Illinois, Indiana, Michigan, Minnesota, Ohio, Wisconsin)
Regional Health Administrator
300 S. Wacker Drive
Chicago, IL 60606
(312) 353-1385
Contact: E. Frank Ellis, M.D.

REGION VI (Arkansas, Louisiana, New Mexico, Oklahoma, Texas)
Regional Health Administrator
1200 Main Towers Building
Dallas, TX 75202
(214) 655-3879
Contact: Floyd A. Norman, M.D.

REGION VII (Iowa, Kansas, Missouri, Nebraska)
Regional Health Administrator
601 E. 12th St.
Kansas City, MO 64106
(816) 374-3291
Contact: Holman R. Wherritt, M.D.

REGION VIII (Colorado, Montana, North Dakota, South Dakota, Utah, Wyoming)
Regional Health Administrator
9017 Federal Office Building
Denver, CO 80202
(303) 837-4461
Contact: Hilary H. Connor, M.D.

REGION IX (Arizona, California, Hawaii, Nevada, Guam, Trust Territory of Pacific Islands, American Samoa)
Regional Health Administrator
50 Fulton St.
San Francisco, CA 94102
(415) 556-5810
Contact: Sheridan L. Winstein, M.D.

REGION X (Alaska, Idaho, Oregon, Washington)
Regional Health Administrator
Arcade Plaza
1321 Second Ave.
Seattle, WA 98101
(206) 442-0430
Contact: David W. Johnson, M.D.

HEALTH SYSTEMS AGENCY

Note: "CD" indicates congressional district.

ALABAMA

Health Service Area 1
North Alabama Health Systems Agency
Huntsville-Madison County Jetport
P.O. Box 6145
Huntsville, AL 35806
(205) 772-3492
Serves CD 4, 5

Area 2
West Alabama Health Council, Inc.
P.O. Box 1488
Tuscaloosa, AL 35401
(205) 345-4916
Serves CD 4, 7

Area 3
Birmingham Regional Health Systems Agency, Inc.
1612 Tenth Ave., South
Birmingham, AL 35205
(205) 933-1403
Serves CD 4, 6, 7

Area 4
Health Systems Agency
P.O. Box 264
Gadsden, AL 35902
(205) 543-9451
Serves CD 3, 4

Area 5
Southeast Alabama Health System Agency
P.O. Box 11292
Montgomery, AL 36111
(205) 264-1049
Serves CD 2, 3

Area 6
Southwest Alabama Health Planning Council
812 Downtowner Blvd., Suite E
Mobile, AL 36609
(205) 343-3320
Serves CD 1, 2, 7

Area 7
See Georgia Area 5

ALASKA

Health Service Area 1
Southeast Alaska Health Systems Agency
433 Jackson St.
Ketchikan, AK 99909
(907) 225-2620
Serves CD at large

Area 2
South Central Health Planning & Development, Inc.
1135 W. Eighth Ave.
Anchorage, AK 99502
(907) 278-3631
Serves CD at large

Area 3
Northern Alaska Health Resources Association, Inc.
Doyon Building
First and Hall Sts.
Fairbanks, AK 99701
(907) 456-2553
Serves CD at large

ARIZONA

Health Service Area 1
Central Arizona Health Systems Agency
124 W. Thomas
Phoenix, AZ 85013
(602) 263-5277
Serves CD 1-4

Area 2
Health Systems Agency of Southeastern Arizona
405 Transamerica Building
117 N. Church St.
Tucson, AZ 85701
(602) 792-1093
Serves CD 2, 4

Area 4
Navajo Health Systems Agency
P.O. Box 643
Navajo Nation
Window Rock, AZ 86515
(602) 871-4831
Serves CD 3, 4 (AZ), 2 (NM), 1 (UT)

ARKANSAS

Health Service Area 1
West Arkansas Health Systems Agency
P.O. Box Drawer H
Russellville, AR 72801
(501) 785-2651
Serves CD 2-4

Area 2
Delta Hills Health Systems Agency
P.O. Box 701
Newport, AR 72112
(501) 793-2339
Serves CD 1, 2

Area 3
Central Arkansas Health Systems Agency
1 Riverfront Place
North Little Rock, AR 72116
(501) 372-6273
Serves CD 1, 2

Area 4
South Arkansas Health Systems Agency
P.O. Box 1917
El Dorado, AR 71730
(501) 536-1971
Serves CD 2, 4

CALIFORNIA

Health Service Area 1
Norcoa-Superior Health Systems Agency
P.O. Box 126
Eureka, CA 95501
(707) 443-8469
Serves CD 1, 2, 4

Area 2
Golden Empire Health Systems Agency
1401 21st St.
Sacramento, CA 95814
(916) 440-5841
Serves CD 1, 3, 4, 14

Area 3
North Bay Health Systems Agency
730 Randolph St.
Napa, CA 94558
(707) 544-7565
Serves CD 2, 4, 5

Area 6
North San Joaquin Valley Health Systems Agency
P.O. Box 1020
Stockton, CA 95201
(209) 982-1800
Serves CD 14, 15

Area 7
Santa Clara County Health Systems Agency
County Board of Supervisors
County Health Department
2220 Moorpark Ave.
San Jose, CA 95128
(408) 297-1636
Serves CD 10, 12, 13

Area 8
Mid-Coast Health Systems Agency
344 Salinas St.
P.O. Box 1068
Salinas, CA 93901
(408) 757-2044
Serves CD 16, 19

Area 9
Central California Health Systems Agency
208 W. Main St.
Visalia, CA 93277
(209) 733-8678
Serves CD 15, 17, 18

Area 10
Ventura-Santa Barbara Health Systems Agency
226 E. Canon Perdido
P.O. Box 644
Santa Barbara, CA 93102
(805) 962-8158
Serves CD 19

92 THE OLDER AMERICAN'S HANDBOOK

Area 11
Health Systems Agency for Los Angeles County
1930 Wilshire Blvd.
Los Angeles, CA 90057
(213) 380-1450
Serves CD 18, 20-35

Area 12
Inland Counties Health Systems Agency
2039 North D St.
San Bernardino, CA 92405
(714) 882-1787
Serves CD 14, 18, 36, 37, 43

Area 13
Orange County Health Planning Council
202 Fashion Lane
Tustin, CA 92680
(714) 832-1841
Serves CD 38-40

Area 14
Health Systems Agency of San Diego & Imperial Counties
Health Care Agency
1600 Pacific Highway
San Diego, CA 92101
(714) 236-2881
Serves CD 40-43

COLORADO

Health Service Area 1
Central Northeast Colorado Health Systems Area
7290 Samuel Drive
Denver, CO 80221
(303) 861-2432
Serves CD 1, 2, 4, 5

Area 2
Southeast Colorado Health Systems Agency, Inc.
Pikes Peak Center
1715 Monterey Rd.
Colorado Springs, CO 80910
(303) 486-0230
Serves CD 3, 5

Area 3
West Colorado Health Systems Agency, Inc.
2525 N. Seventh St.
Grand Junction (Mesa), CO 81501
(303) 858-3643
Serves CD 3, 4

CONNECTICUT

Health Service Area 1
Southwest Connecticut Health Systems Agency
20 N. Main St.
Norwalk, CT 06854
(203) 853-1501
Serves CD 3-5

Area 2
Health Systems Agency of South Central Connecticut
125 Bradley Rd.
Woodbridge, CT 06525
(203) 562-5154
Serves CD 3, 5

Area 3
Health Systems Agency of Eastern Connecticut, Inc.
Pinebrook Apts.
2 Sheraton Lane
Norwich, CT 06360
(203) 886-1996
Serves CD 1, 2

Area 4
Health Systems Agency North Central Connecticut
999 Asylum Ave.
Hartford, CT 06105
(203) 249-7581
Serves CD 1, 2, 6

Area 5
Northwest Connecticut Health Systems Agency
20 E. Main St.
Waterbury, CT 06702
(203) 757-9601
Serves CD 5, 6

FLORIDA

Health Service Area 1
Florida Panhandle Health Systems Agency, Inc.
812 W. 11th St.
Panama City, FL 32401
(904) 769-1406
Serves CD 1, 2

Area 2
North Central Florida Health Planning Council, Inc.
232 SW Fourth Ave.
Gainesville, FL 32601
(904) 377-4404
Serves CD 2, 4, 5

Area 3
Health Systems Agency of Northeastern Florida Area III, Inc.
1045 Riverside Ave.
Jacksonville, FL 32204
(904) 356-9731
Serves CD 2-4

Area 4
Florida Gulf Health Systems Agency, Inc.
The Bullard Executive Center
10051 Fifth St.
St. Petersburg, FL 33702
(813) 576-7772/229-2082
Serves CD 5-8

Area 5
Health Systems Agency of East Central Florida, Inc.
303 Park Lane Circle
Orlando, FL 32803
(305) 425-0261
Serves CD 4, 9, 10

Area 6
South Central Florida Health Systems Council, Inc.
1390 Main St.
Sarasota, FL 33578
(813) 366-9755
Serves CD 8, 10

Area 7
Health Planning Council, Inc.
324 Datura St.
West Palm Beach, FL 33401
(305) 655-9330
Serves CD 10, 11

Area 8
Health Planning & Development Council for Broward County
416 SW First Ave.
Ft. Lauderdale, FL 33301
(305) 763-8778
Serves CD 11-13

Area 9
Health Systems Agency of South Florida
3050 Biscayne Blvd.
Miami, FL 33137
(305) 573-0220
Serves CD 13-15

GEORGIA

Health Service Area 1
See Tennessee Area 3

Area 2
Appalachian Georgia Health Systems Agency
P.O. Box 829
Cartersville, GA 30120
(404) 386-2431
Serves CD 6, 7, 9

Area 3
North Central Georgia Health Systems Agency, Inc.
Kennesaw Life Building
1447 Peachtree St., NE
Atlanta, GA 30309
(404) 892-5952
Serves CD 3-7, 9, 10

Area 4
East Central Georgia Health Systems Agency, Inc.
Georgia Railroad Bank Building
Suite 1114
Augusta, GA 30902
(404) 724-9927
Serves CD 1, 9, 10 (GA), 3 (SC)

Area 5
Health Systems Agency of Central Georgia, Inc.
P.O. Box 2305
1000 Executive Park, E.
Warner Robins, GA 31093
(912) 922-2215
Serves CD 1-3, 6, 8, 10 (GA), 3 (AL)

Area 6
Southwest Georgia Health Systems Agency, Inc.
P.O. Box 4229
Albany, GA 31706
(912) 883-5070
Serves CD 2, 3, 8

Area 7
Southeast Georgia Health Systems Agency, Inc.
P.O. Box 1455
Brunswick, GA 31520
(912) 254-6960
Serves CD 1, 8

IDAHO

Health Service Area 1
Idaho Health Systems Agency, Inc.
703 S. Eighth St.
Boise, ID 83707
(208) 366-1660
Serves CD 1, 2

ILLINOIS

Health Service Area 1
Comprehensive Health Planning Northwestern Illinois, Inc.
304 N. Main St.
Rockford, IL 61101
(815) 968-0720
Serves CD 15, 16, 19

Area 2
Illinois Central Health Systems Agency
P.O. Box 2200
East Peoria, IL 61611
(309) 694-6451
Serves CD 15, 18, 19

Area 3
West Central Illinois Health Systems Agency, Inc.
504 E. Monroe
Springfield, IL 62701
(217) 544-3412
Serves CD 18-22

Area 4
East Central Illinois Health Systems Agency
302 E. John St.
Champaign, IL 61820
(217) 333-3987
Serves CD 15, 17, 21, 22

Area 5
Comprehensive Health Planning in Southern Illinois, Inc.
903 S. Elizabeth St.
Carbondale, IL 62901
(618) 549-2161
Serves CD 22, 24

Area 6
Commission for Health Planning & Resources Development
180 N. LaSalle St.
Chicago, IL
(312) 744-5877
Serves CD 1, 2, 5, 7-9, 11

Area 7
Suburban Cook/Dupage Health Systems Agency, Inc.
421 N. County Farm Rd.
Wheaton, IL 60187
(312) 682-7326
Serves CD 2-4, 6, 10, 12, 14, 17

Area 8
Health Systems Agency Planning Group for Kane Lake & McHenry Counties
400 S. Old Rand Rd.
Lake Zurich, IL 60047
(815) 438-7373
Serves CD 12, 13, 15, 16

Area 9
Region 9 Health Systems Agency, Inc.
1255 Eagle St.
Joliet, IL 60047
(815) 722-9151
Serves CD 15, 17

Area 10
Illowa Health Systems Agency
215 Insurance Exchange Building
Davenport, IA 52801
(319) 326-6244
Serves CD 19 (IL), 1 (IA)

Area 11
See Missouri Area 3

INDIANA

Health Service Area 1
N. Indiana Health Systems Agency, Inc.
900 E. Colfax Ave.
South Bend, IN 46601
(219) 233-5149
Serves CD 1-5, 10

Area 2
Central Indiana Health Systems Agency, Inc.
3901 W. 86th St.
Indianapolis, IN 46268
(317) 297-3990
Serves CD 1, 2, 5-7, 9-11

Area 3
Southern Indiana Health Systems Agency, Inc.
1602 I St.
Bedford, IN 47421
(812) 275-5984
Serves CD 7-9

IOWA

Health Service Area 1
Iowa Health Systems Agency
218 Sixth Ave.
Des Moines, IA 50309
(515) 247-8711
Serves CD 1-6 (IA); 1, 2 (NB)

Area 2
See Nebraska Area 3

Area 3
See Illinois Area 10

KANSAS

Health Service Area 1
Health Planning Association of Western Kansas, Inc.
2705 Vine – Unit No. 7
Hays, KS 67601
(913) 628-2868
Serves CD 1

Area 2
Northeast Kansas Health System Agency
1275 Topeka Ave.
Topeka, KS 66612
(913) 235-6550
Serves CD 1-5

Area 3
Health Systems Agency of Southeast Kansas, Inc.
212 N. Market
Wichita, KS 67202
(316) 264-2861
Serves CD 1, 4, 5

Area 4
See Missouri Area 1

KENTUCKY

Health Service Area 1
Kentucky Health Systems Agency, West, Inc.
1941 Bishop Lane
Louisville, KY 40218
(502) 456-6400
Serves CD 1-6

Area 2
East Kentucky Health Systems Agency, Inc.
P.O. Box 531
Winchester, KY 40391
(606) 272-4581
Serves CD 2, 4-7

Area 3
See Ohio Area 1

LOUISIANA

Health Service Area 1
New Orleans Area Health Planning Council
333 St. Charles Ave.
New Orleans, LA 70130
(504) 581-6821
Serves CD 1-3, 8

Area 2
Mid-Louisiana Health Systems Agency
2726 Continental Drive
Baton Rouge, LA 70808
(504) 937-9740
Serves CD 3, 6-8

Area 3
Northeast Louisiana Area Health Planning Council
1204 Stubbs Ave.
Monroe, LA 71201
(318) 255-3780
Serves CD 4, 5, 8

MAINE

Health Service Area 1
Maine Health Systems Agency, Inc.
Two Central Plaza
Augusta, ME 04330
(207) 623-1182
Serves CD 1, 2

MARYLAND

Health Service Area 1
Western Maryland Health Systems Agency
134 N. Mechanic St.
Cumberland, MD 21502
(301) 724-1616
Serves CD 6

Area 2
Department of Health Systems Planning
Montgomery County Government
611 Rockville Pike
Rockville, MD 20805
(301) 340-2773
Serves CD 5, 6, 8

Area 3
Southern Maryland Health Systems Agency
P.O. Box 301
Waldorf, MD 20601
(301) 645-2693
Serves CD 1, 4, 5

Area 4
Central Maryland Health Systems Agency
501 St. Paul Place
Baltimore, MD 21202
(301) 752-3500
Serves CD 1-4, 6, 7

Area 5
Health Planning Council of the Eastern Shore, Inc.
P.O. Box 776
Cambridge, MD 21613
(301) 228-8911
Serves CD 1-4

MASSACHUSETTS

Health Service Area 1
Western Massachusetts Health Planning Council
380 Union St.
West Springfield, MA 01089
(413) 781-2845
Serves CD 1, 2

Area 2
Central Massachusetts Health Systems Agency
415 Boston Turnpike
Shrewsbury, MA 01545
(617) 798-8667
Serves CD 2-4

Area 3
Merrimack Valley Health Planning Council, Inc.
One Elm Square
Andover, MA 01810
(617) 475-1184
Serves CD 5, 6

Area 4
Health Planning Council for Greater Boston
46 Leo M. Birmingham Parkway
Brighton, MA 02135
(617) 787-5800
Serves CD 3-5, 7-11

Area 5
Southeastern Massachusetts Health & Planning & Development, Inc.
Route 28 Office Building
Middleboro, MA 02346
(617) 947-6300
Serves CD 10-12

Area 6
North Shore Health Planning Council
10 First Ave.
Peabody, MA 01960
(617) 531-7006
Serves CD 7, 8, 10-12

MICHIGAN

Health Service Area 1
Comprehensive Health Planning Council of Southeast Michigan
1300 Book Building
Detroit, MI 48226
(313) 964-6950
Serves CD 1, 2, 6, 12-19

Area 2
Michigan Mid-South Health Systems Agency, Inc.
411 N. Cedar Rd.
Mason, MI 48854
(517) 676-4046
Serves CD 3-6

Area 3
Southwest Michigan Health Systems Agency, Inc.
6126 Lovers Lane
Kalamazoo, MI 49002
(616) 323-3410
Serves CD 3-5

Area 4
West Michigan Health Systems Agency
300 Peoples Building
Grand Rapids, MI 49503
(616) 459-1323
Serves CD 3, 5, 9, 10

Area 5
GLS Health Systems Agency
432 N. Saginaw St.
Flint, MI 48502
(313) 235-3506
Serves CD 7, 8, 10

Area 6
East Central Michigan CHP Council
Plaza North
Saginaw, MI 48604
(517) 799-9650
Serves CD 7, 8, 10-12

Area 7
Northern Michigan Health System Agency
325 E. Lake St.
Petoskey, MI 49770
(616) 347-7772
Serves CD 9-11

Area 8
Upper Peninsula Health Systems Agency
1500 W. Washington St.
Marquette, MI 49855
(906) 228-7733
Serves CD 11

MINNESOTA

Health Service Area 1
See North Dakota Area 2

Area 2
Health Systems Agency of Western Lake Superior, Inc.
424 W. Superior St.
Duluth, MN 55802
(218) 727-8371
Serves CD 3, 5, 6, 8, 13, 14 (MN), 9 (WI)

HEALTH

Area 3
See North Dakota area 3

Area 4
Central Minnesota Health System Agency
1528 N. Sixth Ave.
St. Cloud, MN 56301
(612) 253-2930
Serves CD 6-8

Area 5
Metropolitan Council
Seventh & Robert St.
St. Paul, MN 55101
(612) 291-6351
Serves CD 1-6, 8

Area 6
Minnesota Health Systems Agency
P.O. Box 156
Redwood Falls, MN 56283
(507) 637-3575
Serves CD 2, 6, 7

Area 7
Southeastern Minnesota Health Service Agency
S. Broadway & Second St., SE
Rochester, MN 55901
(507) 285-2570
Serves CD 1, 2

MISSISSIPPI

Health Service Area 1
Mississippi Health Systems Agency, Inc.
P.O. Box 16471
Jackson, MS 39206
(601) 956-5441
Serves CD 1-5

MISSOURI

Health Service Area 1
Mid-America Health Systems Agency
20 Ninth St.
Kansas City, MO 64105
(816) 421-2710
Serves CD 4-6 (MO), 2, 3 (KS)

Area 2
Area II Health Systems Agency of Missouri, Inc.
405 W. Jackson
Albany, MO 64402
(816) 726-5665
Serves CD 4, 6-9

Area 3
Greater St. Louis Health Systems Agency, Inc.
607 N. Grand Blvd.
St. Louis, MO 63103
(314) 241-5810
Serves CD 20, 23, 24 (IL), 1-3, 8-10 (MO)

Area 4
Southwest Missouri Health System Agency
2835 'B' East Division
Springfield, MO 65803
(417) 866-2727
Serves CD 4, 7, 8

Area 5
Missouri Area Five Health Systems Agency Council
Malden Industrial Park
P.O. Box 397
Malden, MO 63863
(314) 376-2242
Serves CD 8, 10

MONTANA

Health Service Area 1
Montana Health Service Agency
P.O. Box 302
Roundup, MT 59072
(406) 323-2547
Serves CD 1, 2

NEBRASKA

Health Service Area 1
Greater Nebraska Health Systems Agency, Inc.
2201 N. Wheeler
Grand Island, NB 68801
(308) 384-2368
Serves CD 1-3

Area 2
Southeast Nebraska Health System Agency
215 Centennial Mall South
Lincoln, NB 68508
(402) 432-4402
Serves CD 1, 2, 3

Area 3
Health Planning Council of the Midlands, Inc.
7202 Jones St.
Omaha, NB 68114
(402) 393-6404
Serves CD 1, 2, (NB), 5 (IA)

Area 4
See Iowa area 1

NEVADA

Health Service Area 1
Greater Nevada Health Systems Agency
c/o St. Mary's Hospital
Reno, NV 89503
(702) 323-2041
Serves CD at large

Area 2
Health Systems Agency of Clark County
625 Shadow Lane
P.O. Box 4426
Las Vegas, NV 89106
(702) 385-1291
Serves CD at large

NEW HAMPSHIRE

Health Service Area 1
United Health Systems Agency, Inc.
P.O. Box 1078
Concord, NH 03301
(603) 228-1506

NEW JERSEY

Health Service Area 1
Bergen-Passaic Health Systems Agency
365 W. Passaic St.
Rochelle Park, NJ 07662
(201) 368-0240
Serves CD 7-9, 11

Area 2
Hospital & Health Council of Metro New Jersey
2 Park Place
Newark, NJ 07102
(210) 622-3240
Serves CD 5, 11-13, 15

Area 3
Hudson Health Systems Agency
871 Bergen Ave.
Jersey City, NJ 07306
(201) 451-5024
Serves CD 9, 10, 14

Area 4
Central New Jersey Health Planning Council
Twin Rivers Mall
Route 33
Hightstown, NJ 08520
(609) 443-4232
Serves CD 2-6, 13, 15

Area 5
Southern New Jersey Health Systems Agency
Interstate Industrial Park
Bellmawr, NJ 08030
(609) 933-0641
Serves CD 1, 2, 4, 6

NEW MEXICO

Health Service Area 1
New Mexico Health Systems Agency
P.O. Box 1296
Sante Fe, NM 87501
(474) 988-8079
Serves CD 1, 2

Area 2
See Arizona Area 4

NEW YORK

Health Service Area 1
Health Systems Agency of Western New York
Genesee Building
Buffalo, NY 14202
(716) 854-4812
Serves CD 35-39

Area 2
Fingerlakes Health Systems Agency
360 East Ave.
Rochester, NY 14604
(716) 325-2270
Serves CD 27, 33-36, 39

Area 3
Central New York Health Systems Agency
1010 James St.
Syracuse, NY 13203
(315) 472-6353
Serves CD 27, 29, 30, 32, 33

Area 4
NY-Penn Health Systems Agency
504 Press Building
Binghamton, NY 13902
(607) 722-3445
Serves CD 27, 32 (NY), 10, 11 (PA)

Area 5
Health Systems Agency of Northeastern New York, Inc.
75 New Scotland Ave.
Albany, NY 12208
(518) 445-0511
Serves CD 27-32

Area 6
Hudson Valley Health Systems Agency
Westchester County Medical Center
Valhalla, NY 10595
(914) 592-8500
Serves CD 23-27

Area 7
Health Systems Agency of New York City
111 Broadway
New York, NY 10007
(212) 577-0554
Serves CD 6-23

Area 8
Nassau-Suffolk Health Systems Agency
P.O. Box 35
Huntington Station, NY 11746
(516) 420-1187
Serves CD 1-7

NORTH CAROLINA

Health Service Area 1
Western North Carolina Health Systems Agency
306 S. King St.
Morganton, NC 28655
(704) 433-1636
Serves CD 5, 10, 11

Area 2
Piedmont Health Systems Agency, Inc.
2120 Pinecroft Rd.
Greensboro, NC 27407
(919) 294-4950
Serves CD 2, 4-6, 8

Area 3
Southern Piedmont Health Systems Agency
1229 Greenwood Cliff
P.O. Box 4588
Charlotte, NC 28204
(704) 372-8494
Serves CD 8-10

Area 4
Capital Health Systems Agency, Inc.
501 Willard St.
Durham, NC 27701
(919) 682-3640
Serves CD 2-4

Area 5
Cardinal Health Systems Agency Inc.
2775 N. Elm St.
Lumberton, NC 28358
(919) 738-9316
Serves CD 3, 7, 8

Area 6
Eastern Carolina Health Systems Agency
223 W. Tenth St.
Greenville, NC 27834
(919) 758-1372
Serves CD 1-3

NORTH DAKOTA

Health Service Area 1
Western North Dakota Health Systems Agency, Inc.
209 N. Seventh St.
Bismarck, ND 58501
(701) 223-8085
Serves CD 1

Area 2
Agassiz Health Planning Council, Inc.
123 Demers Ave.
East Grand Forks, MN 56721
(218) 773-2471
Serves CD 1 (ND), 7 (MN)

Area 3
Min-Kak Areawide Chapter Council
Box 915
Moorhead, MN 56560
(218) 236-2746
Serves CD 1 (ND), 7 (MN)

OHIO

Health Service Area 1
Health Planning & Resources Development Association of Central Ohio River Valley
222 E. Central Parkway
Cincinnati, OH 45202
(313) 621-2434
Serves CD 4, 6 (KY), 1, 2, 6, 8 (OH)

Area 2
Miami Valley Health Systems Agency
32 N. Main St.
Dayton, OH 45402
(513) 461-5495
Serves CD 4-6

Area 3
West Central Ohio Health System Agency
616 S. Collett
Lima, OH 45805
(419) 227-8361
Serves CD 4, 5, 7

Area 4
Health Planning Association of Northwest Ohio
225 Allen at W. Wayne St.
Maumee, OH 43537
(419) 983-0287
Serves CD 5, 9, 13

Area 5
Mid-Ohio Health Planning Federation
2015 W. Fifth Ave.
Columbus, OH 43216
(614) 461-4230
Serves CD 4, 6, 7, 10, 12, 15, 17

Area 6
Health Planning & Development Council
201 E. Liberty St.
Wooster, OH 44691
(216) 264-9939
Serves CD 16-18

Area 7
Health Systems Agency for Summit Portage County
411 Woldledges Park
Akron, OH 44311
(216) 762-9417
Serves CD 13, 14, 16

Area 8
Metropolitan Health Planning Corp.
903 Standard Building
Cleveland, OH 44113
(216) 771-6814
Serves CD 11, 13, 20-23

Area 9
Mahoning Valley Health Planning Association
15 Colonial Drive
Youngstown, OH 44505
(216) 759-2794
Serves CD 11, 18, 19

OKLAHOMA

Health Service Area 1
Oklahoma Health Systems Agency
800 NE 15th St.
Oklahoma City, OK 73105
(405) 271-2434
Serves CD 1-6

OREGON

Health Service Area 1

Comprehensive Health Planning Association for the Metropolitan Portland Area
5301 SW Westgate Drive
Portland, OR 97221
(503) 297-2241
Serves CD 1-3

Area 2

Western Oregon Health Systems Agency, Inc.
4399 Coast Highway
North Bend, OR 97459
(503) 756-6382
Serves CD 1, 2, 4

Area 3

Eastern Oregon Health Systems Agency
Formation Steering Committee
P.O. Box 575
Redmond, OR 97756
(503) 548-5185
Serves CD 2

PENNSYLVANIA

Health Service Area 1

Health Systems Council of Eastern Pennsylvania, Inc.
1401 Cedar Crest Blvd.
Allentown, PA 18104
(215) 432-2575
Serves CD 6, 10, 11, 15

Area 2

Health Systems Agency of Northeastern Pennsylvania, Inc.
Warm Building
Avoca, PA 18641
(717) 655-3703
Serves CD 6, 10, 11

Area 3

Health Resources Planning & Development, Inc.
1104 Fernwood Ave.
Camp Hill, PA 17011
(717) 761-3252
Serves CD 6, 9, 16, 17, 19

Area 4

Central Pennsylvania Health Systems Agency
400 Market St.
Lewisburg, PA 17837
(717) 524-2266
Serves CD 9, 11, 12, 17, 23

Area 5

Health Systems Agency of Southwestern Pennsylvania, Inc.
P.O. Box 1588
Pittsburgh, PA 15222
(412) 562-1811
Serves CD 12, 14, 18, 20-22, 25

Area 6

Health Systems, Inc. of Northwestern Pennsylvania
1545 W. 38th St.
Erie, PA 16508
(814) 868-4671
Serves CD 12, 23, 24

Area 7

See New York Area 4

Area 8

Keystone Health Systems Agency
615 Howard Ave.
Altoona, PA 16601
(814) 946-3641
Serves CD 9, 12

SOUTH CAROLINA

Health Service Area 1

South Carolina Appalachian Health Council
211 Century Drive
Greenville, SC 29606
(803) 242-1895
Serves CD 3-5

Area 2

Three Rivers Health Systems Agency, Inc.
3325 Medical Park Rd.
Columbia, SC 29203
(803) 779-6790
Serves CD 2, 3, 5

Area 3

Pee Dee Regional Health Systems Agency, Inc.
P.O. Box 5959
Florence, SC 29502
(803) 669-1347
Serves CD 5, 6

Area 4

Palmetto-Lowcountry Health Systems Agency, Inc.
107 W. Sixth North St.
Summerville, SC 29483
(803) 536-7013
Serves CD 1, 2

Area 5

See Georgia area 4

SOUTH DAKOTA

Health Service Area 1

South Dakota Health Systems Agency, Inc.
216 E. Clark St.
Vermillion, SD 57069
(605) 624-4446
Serves CD 1, 2

TENNESSEE

Health Service Area 1

East Tennessee Health Improvement Council, Inc.
10901-½ Lake Ridge Rd.
Knoxville, TN 37922
(615) 966-9737
Serves CD 1-3

Area 2

Georgia-Tennessee Regional Health Commission
James Building
Chattanooga, TN 37402
(615) 266-2151
Serves CD 2-4 (TN), 7, 9 (GA)

Area 3

Middle Tennessee Health System Agency, Inc.
2 International Plaza Drive
Nashville, TN 37217
(615) 361-8100
Serves CD 4-7

Area 4

West Tennessee Health Improvement Association, Inc.
1804 Highway 45 Bypass
Watkins Towers
Jackson, TN 38301
(901) 668-8236
Serves CD 6, 7

Area 5

Mid-South Medical Center Council
969 Madison Ave.
Memphis, TN 38104
(901) 726-1581
Serves CD 6-8

TEXAS

Health Service Area 1

Panhandle Regional Planning Commission
P.O. Box 9257
Amarillo, TX 79103
(806) 372-3381
Serves CD 9, 13

Area 2

South Plains Health Systems, Inc.
1217 Ave. K
Lubbock, TX 79401
(806) 747-0181
Serves CD 13, 17, 19

Area 3

Health Systems Agency of the West Texas Council of Governments
1200 N. Mesa St.
El Paso, TX 79902
(915) 544-3827
Serves CD 16

Area 4

Tri-Region Health Systems Agency
c/o Hendricks Memorial Hospital
Abilene, TX 79601
(915) 677-3551
Serves CD 11, 13, 17, 21

Area 5

Texas Area 5 Health Systems Agency, Inc.
3704 MacArthur Blvd.
Irving, TX 75060
(817) 640-3300
Serves CD 1, 3-6, 11, 12, 17, 24

98 THE OLDER AMERICAN'S HANDBOOK

Area 6
Central Texas Health Systems Agency, Inc.
P.O. Box 15027
Austin, TX 78761
(512) 472-2431
Serves CD 2, 6, 10, 11, 23

Area 7
Northeast Texas Health Systems Agency, Inc.
P.O. Box 2044
Texarkana, TX 75501
(214) 794-2711
Serves CD 1, 2, 4

Area 8
South Texas Health Systems Agency
Texas A&I University
Station I
Kingsville, TX 78363
(512) 855-9708
Serves CD 10, 14, 15, 23

Area 9
Camino Real Health Systems Agency, Inc.
118 Broadway
San Antonio, TX 78205
(512) 225-4426
Serves CD 15, 20, 21, 23

Area 10
Greater East Texas Health Systems Agency
P.O. Drawer 1387
Nederland, TX 77627
(713) 727-2384
Serves CD 1, 2, 9

Area 11
Houston-Galveston Area Council
Area Health Commission
3701 West Alabama
Houston, TX 77027
(713) 627-3200
Serves CD 2, 7-10, 14, 18, 22

Area 12
Permian Basin Regional Planning Commission
P.O. Box 6391
Midland, TX 79701
(915) 563-1061
Serves CD 16, 17, 19, 21

UTAH
Health Service Area 1
Utah Health Systems Agency
State Capitol
Salt Lake City, UT 84114
(801) 581-7927
Serves CD 1, 2

Area 2
See Arizona area 4

VIRGINIA
Health Service Area 1
Northwestern Virginia Health Systems Agency, Inc.
P.O. Box 550
Culpeper, VA 22701
(703) 825-2600
Serves CD 1, 6, 7

Area 2
Health Systems Agency for Northern Virginia, Inc.
7245 Arlington Blvd.
Falls Church, VA 22042
(703) 573-3100
Serves CD 8, 10

Area 3
Southwest Virginia Health Systems Agency, Inc.
200 South Country Club Drive
Blacksburg, VA 24060
(703) 951-0170
Serves CD 5, 6, 9

Area 4
Central Virginia Health Systems Agency
2015 Stapels Mill Rd.
Richmond, VA 23230
(804) 355-5723
Serves CD 1, 3-5, 7

Area 5
Eastern Virginia Health Systems Agency
11 Koger Executive Center
Norfolk, VA 23502
(804) 461-1236
Serves CD 1, 2, 4

WASHINGTON
Health Service Area 1
Puget Sound Health Planning Council
601 Valley St.
Seattle, WA 98107
(206) 464-6143
Serves CD 1-3, 6, 7

Area 2
Southwest Washington Health Systems Agency
320 W. Bay Drive
Olympia, WA 98502
(206) 753-8135
Serves CD 3, 4

Area 3
Central Washington Health Systems Agency
P.O. Box 1131
Moses Lake, WA 98837
(509) 762-5366
Serves CD 4, 5

Area 4
Eastern Washington Health Systems Agency
N. 1728 Jackson Ave.
Spokane, WA 99205
(509) 456-3178
Serves CD 5

WEST VIRGINIA
Health Service Area 1
West Virginia Health Systems Agency
815 Quarrier St.
Charleston, WV 25301
(304) 346-0656
Serves CD 1-4

WISCONSIN
Health Service Area 1
Health Planning Council, Inc.
310 Price Place
Madison, WI 53705
(608) 238-2641
Serves CD 1-3, 9

Area 2
Southeastern Wisconsin Health Systems Agency
735 N. Fifth St.
Milwaukee, WI 53203
(414) 271-9788
Serves CD 1, 4, 5, 9

Area 3
Lake Winnebago Areawide Health Systems Agency
404 N. Main
Oshkosh, WI 54901
(414) 231-2907
Serves CD 2, 6, 8

Area 4
New Health Planning Council, Inc.
828 Cherry St.
Green Bay, WI 54301
(414) 432-5234
Serves CD 6, 8

Area 5
Western Wisconsin Health Planning Organization
1707 Main St.
Lacrosse, WI 54601
(608) 782-4310
Serves CD 3, 6, 7

Area 6
North Central Area Health Planning Association
811 N. First Ave.
Wausau, WI 54401
(715) 845-3107
Serves CD 6-8

Area 7
See Minnesota Area 2

WYOMING
Health Service Area 1
Wyoming Health Systems Agency, Inc.
P.O. Box 106
Cheyenne, WY 82001
(307) 635-2426
Serves CD at large

13
Home Health Agencies

Home Health Aides are paraprofessionals who meet a variety of out-of-hospital health needs. Over 2,000 home health agencies have qualified to participate in the Medicare program. Home Health Aides are usually called in a time of crisis, and frequently they will substitute their judgment for that of the older person in their care. In other words, they will help out in every way possible.

The following list of home health agencies is Medicare-approved. If you are in trouble, call one of them. Their services are available to everyone without regard to income, social status, or other arbitrary limitations.

HOME HEALTH AGENCIES

ALABAMA

Henry County Health Dept.
Nursing Division
Doswell St.
Abbeville, AL 36310

Covington County Health Dept.
Nursing Division
300 Watson St.
Andalusia, AL 36420

Calhoun County Health Dept.
309 E. Eighth St.
Anniston, AL 36201

Clay County Health Dept.
Nursing Division
P.O. Box 325
Ashland, AL 36251

St. Clair County Health Dept.
Nursing Division
205 19th St., N.
Ashville, AL 35953

Baldwin County Health Dept.
Hand Ave.
Bay Minette, AL 36502

Jefferson County Dept. of Health
1912 Eighth Ave., S.
Birmingham, AL 35202

Visiting Nurse Assn. & Home Health
  Aide Service
3600 Eighth Ave., S.
Birmingham, AL 35233

Escambia County Health Dept.
Belleville Ave.
Brewton, AL 36426

Choctaw County Home Health Agency
214 W. Church St.
Butler, AL 36904

Cherokee County Home Health Agency
Cedarbluff Rd.
Centre, AL 35918

Washington County Health Dept.
P.O. Box 417
Chatom, AL 36518

Chilton County Health Dept.
Home Health Agency
Fifth St. & First Ave.
Clanton, AL 35045

Barbour County Health Dept.
Nursing Division
201 S. Conecuh St.
Clayton, AL 36016

Shelby County Health Dept.
Nursing Division
P.O. Box 967
Columbiana, AL 35051

Tallapoosa County Home Health
  Agency
202 Lafayette St.
Dadeville, AL 36853

Tri-County District Health Service
302 Davis St., N.E.
Decatur, AL 35601

Houston County Health Dept.
Nursing Division
Dothan, AL 36302

Winston County Health Dept.
Nursing Division
Double Springs, AL 35553

Coffee County Health Dept.
Nursing Division
Enterprise, AL 36331

Conecuh County Health Dept.
Highway 31
Evergreen, AL 36401

Fayette County Health Dept.
Nursing Division
P.O. Box 976
Fayette, AL 35555

Lauderdale Home Health Agency
200 W. Tennessee St.
Florence, AL 35630

Gulf Coast Home Health Agency
224 W. Laurel
Foley, AL 36535

Dekalb County Health Dept.
Nursing Division
500 Grand Ave.
Ft. Payne, AL 35967

Etowah County Health Dept.
Nursing Division
109 S. Eighth St.
Gadsden, AL 35902

Geneva County Health Dept.
Nursing Division
606 S. Academy St.
Geneva, AL 36340

Hale County Health Dept.
Nursing Division
1102 Centreville St.
Greensboro, AL 36744

Butler County Health Dept.
Nursing Division
201 S. Conecuh St.
Greenville, AL 36037

Clarke County Health Dept.
P.O. Box 475
Grove Hill, AL 36451

Marshall County Health Dept.
275 Broad St.
Gunterville, AL 35976

Marion County Health Dept.
Nursing Division
P.O. Box 103
Hamilton, AL 35570

Lowndes County Health Dept.
Tuskenna St.
Hayneville, AL 36040

Cleburne County Home Health Agency
P.O. Box 36
Heflin, AL 36264

Madison County Health Dept.
Nursing Division
304 Eustis Ave.
Huntsville, AL 35804

Walker County Health Dept.
Nursing Division
17th St. & Fifth Ave.
Jasper, AL 35501

Chambers County Home Health
Agency
Lafayette, AL 36862

Marengo County Health Dept.
P.O. Box 454
Linden, AL 36748

Sumter County Health Dept.
P.O. Box 340
Livingston, AL 35470

Crenshaw County Health Dept.
Nursing Division
Glenwood Ave.
Luverne, AL 36049

Gulf Coast Home Health Agency
160 A Louiselle
Mobile, AL 36607

Mobile County Board of Health
248 Cox St.
Mobile, AL 36604

Mobile Visiting Nurse Association
800 Saint Anthony St.
Mobile, AL 36603

South Alabama Home Health Care
1710-C Center St.
Mobile, AL 36604

Monroe County Health Dept.
Mt. Pleasant Ave.
Monroeville, AL 36460

Bureau of Public Health Nursing
Home Health Division
State Office Building
Montgomery, AL 36104

Central Alabama Home Health Service
1758 Holly St.
Montgomery, AL 36106

Health Services
1000 Adams Ave.
Montgomery, AL 36104

Montgomery County Health Dept.
Nursing Division
P.O. Box 4008
Montgomery, AL 36104

Alabama Home Health Care
Building 15
Office Park Circle
Suite 205
Mountain Brook, AL 35223

Blount County Health Dept.
Nursing Division
P.O. Box 96
Oneonta, AL 35121

Lee County Health Dept.
P.O. Box 2207
Opelika, AL 36801

Dale County Health Dept.
207 S. Merrick Ave.
Ozark, AL 36360

Russell County Home Health Agency
1320 Broad St.
Phenix City, AL 36867

Autauga County Health Dept.
Nursing Division
P.O. Box 450
Prattville, AL 36067

Coosa County Home Health Agency
Rockford, AL 35136

Franklin County Health Dept.
Nursing Division
E. Limestone St.
Russellville, AL 35653

Jackson County Health Dept.
Nursing Division
609 S. Broad
Scottsboro, AL 35768

Dallas County Home Health Agency
108 Church St.
Selma, AL 36701

Talladega County Health Dept.
Nursing Division
109 S. Anniston Ave.
Sylacauga, AL 35150

Pike County Health Dept.
Nursing Division
P.O. Box 425
Troy, AL 36081

Tuscaloosa County Health Dept.
Nursing Division
607 Tenth St.
Tuscaloosa, AL 35401

Colbert County Health Dept.
Nursing Division
108 Water St.
Tuscumbia, AL 35674

Macon County Health Dept.
Nursing Division
N. Main St.
Tuskegee, AL 36083

Bullock County Health Dept.
P.O. Drawer 430
Union Springs, AL 36089

Randolph County Health Dept.
Nursing Division
Court House
Wedowee, AL 36278

Elmore County Home Health Agency
P.O. Box 316
Wetumpka, AL 36092

ALASKA

Greater Anchorage Health Dept.
327 Eagle St.
Anchorage, AK 99501

ARIZONA

Cochise County Health Dept.
P.O. Box 1858
Bisbee, AZ 85603

Coconino Home Health Services
2500 Ft. Valley Rd.
Flagstaff, AZ 86001

Mohave County Home Health Agency
305 W. Beale St.
Kingman, AZ 86401

Good Samaritan Hospital
Home Care Program
1033 E. McDowell Rd.
Phoenix, AZ 85006

Visiting Nurse Service
1515 E. Osborn Rd.
Phoenix, AZ 85014

Yavapai County Health Dept.
106 N. Cortez
Box 2111
Prescott, AZ 86301

Boswell Memorial Hospital
Home Care Program
10401 Thunderbird Blvd.
Sun City, AZ 85351

Pima County Health Dept.
151 W. Congress St.
Tucson, AZ 85701

Tucson Visiting Nurse Assn.
268 W. Adams St.
Tucson, AZ 85705

Yuma County Health Dept.
201 Second Ave.
Yuma, AZ 85364

ARKANSAS

Clark County Health Unit
Arkadelphia, AR 71923

Little River County Health Unit
Ashdown, AR 71822

Woodruff County Health Unit
Augusta, AR 72006

Independence County Health Unit
Batesville, AR 72501

Saline County Health Unit
Benton, AR 72015

Benton County Health Unit
Bentonville, AR 72712

Carroll County Health Unit
103 Old Courthouse
Berryville, AR 72616

Mississippi County Health Unit
Blytheville, AR 72315

Monroe County Health Unit
Brinkley, AR 72021

Quachita County Health Unit
Camden, AR 71701

Johnson County Health Unit
Clarksville, AR 72830

Van Buren County Health Unit
Clinton, AR 72031

Faulkner County Health Unit
Conway, AR 72032

Yell County Health Unit
Danville, AR 72833

Sevier County Health Unit
P.O. Box 406
DeQueen, AR 71832

Prairie County Health Unit
Des Arc, AR 72040

Arkansas County Health Unit
De Witt, AR 72042

Union County Health Unit
El Dorado, AR 71730

Sharp County Health Unit
Evening Shade, AR 72532

Arkansas Home Health Services
1665 N. College
Fayetteville, AR 72764

Washington County Health Unit
Fayetteville, AR 72701

Dallas County Health Unit
Fordyce, AR 71742

St. Francis County Health Unit
Forrest City, AR 72335

Home Health Services
321 N. Greenwood
Fort Smith, AR 72901

Sebastian County Health Unit
Fort Smith, AR 72901

Ashley County Health Unit
Hamburg, AR 71646

Poinsett County Health Unit
Harrisburg, AR 72432

Boone County Health Unit
Harrison, AR 72601

Cleburne County Health Unit
Heber Springs, AR 72543

Phillips County Health Unit
Helena, AR 72342

Hempstead County Health Unit
Hope, AR 71801

Garland County Health Unit
Hot Springs, AR 71901

Madison County Health Unit
Huntsville, AR 72740

Newton County Health Department
P.O. Box 34
Jasper, AR 72641

Craighead County Health Unit
Jonesboro, AR 72401

Chicot County Health Unit
Lake Village, AR 71653

Lafayette County Health Unit
Lewisville, AR 71845

Arkansas State Dept. of Health
4815 W. Markham St.
Little Rock, AR 72201

Pulaski County Visiting Nurse Assn.
9911 W. Markham
Little Rock, AR 72201

Lonoke County Health Unit
Lonoke, AR 72086

Columbia County Health Unit
Magnolia, AR 71753

Hot Spring County Health Unit
Malvern, AR 72104

Lee County Health Unit
Marianna, AR 72360

Crittenden County Health Unit
Marion, AR 72364

Searcy County Health Unit
Marshall, AR 72650

Desha County Health Unit
McGehee, AR 71654

Izard County Health Unit
Melbourne, AR 72556

Arkansas Home Health Service Agency
602 De Queen St.
Box 1285
Mena, AR 71953

Polk County Health Unit
Mena, AR 71953

Drew County Health Unit
Monticello, AR 71655

Conway County Health Unit
Morrilton, AR 72110

Montgomery County Health Unit
Mount Ida, AR 71957

Stone County Health Unit
Mount View, AR 72560

Baxter County Health Unit
Mountain Home, AR 72560

Pike County Health Unit
Murfreesboro, AR 71958

Howard County Health Unit
Nashville, AR 71852

Jackson County Health Unit
Newport, AR 72112

Franklin County Health Unit
Ozark, AR 72949

Community Methodist Hospital
Home Health Agency
900 W. Kings Highway
Paragould, AR 72450

Greene County Health Unit
Paragould, AR 72450

Logan County Health Unit
Paris, AR 72855

Perry County Health Unit
Perryville, AR 72126

Clay County Health Unit
P.O. Box 206
Piggott, AR 72454

Jefferson County Health Unit
Pine Bluff, AR 71601

Randolph County Health Unit
Pocahontas, AR 72455

Nevada County Health Unit
Federal Building
Prescott, AR 71857

Cleveland County Health Unit
P.O. Box 446
Rison, AR 71665

Pope County Health Unit
Russellville, AR 72801

Fulton County Health Unit
Salem, AR 72576

White County Health Unit
Searcy, AR 72143

Grant County Health Unit
Sheridan, AR 72150

Lincoln County Health Unit
Star City, AR 71667

Miller County Health Unit
Texarkana, AR 75501

Crawford County Health Unit
Van Buren, AR 72956

Scott County Health Unit
Waldron, AR 72958

Lawrence County Health Unit
Walnut Ridge, AR 72476

Bradley County Health Unit
Warren, AR 71671

Cross County Health Unit
Wynne, AR 72396

Mid-South Comprehensive Home
  Health Agency
509 N. Falls Blvd.
Wynne, AR 72396

Marion County Health Unit
Yellville, AR 72687

CALIFORNIA

Santa Cruz County Visiting Nurse
  Assn.
7000 Soquel Ave.
Aptos, CA 95003

Alta Bates Hospital
Home Care Program
Webster & Colby
Berkeley, CA 94705

Berkeley Visiting Nurse Assn.
2121 McKinley Ave.
Berkeley, CA 94703

Century Home Health Agency
2080 Century Park E.
Beverly Hills, CA 90212

Clinica de Salubridad de Campesinos
1166 K St.
Brawley, CA 92227

Home Kare
256 E. Hamilton Ave.
Campbell, CA 95150

Community Home Health Services
556 Cohasset Rd.
Chico, CA 95926

Restorative Home Care
3100 Susana Rd.
Compton, CA 90221

Clarke Home Nursing Service
1601 Second St.
Corte Madera, CA 94925

East San Gabriel Valley Visiting Nurse
  Assn.
230 W. Orange
Covina, CA 91722

St. Helena Hospital
Home Health Services
Deer Park, CA 94576

Home Care
11411 Brookshire Ave.
Downey, CA 90241

Rancho Los Amigos Hospital
Home Care Program
8601 E. Imperial Highway
Downey, CA 90242

City of Hope Medical Center
Home Care Program
1500 E. Duarte Rd.
Duarte, CA 91010

Humboldt County Home Health
  Agency
529 I St.
Eureka, CA 95501

Mediserv Home Health Agency
38235 Logan Dr.
Freemont, CA 94536

Fresno County Home Health Agency
515 S. Cedar St.
Fresno, CA 93702

St. Agnes Hospital
Home Care Agency
1303 E. Herndon Ave.
Fresno, CA 93728

Town & County Home Nursing Service
9872 Chapman Ave.
Garden Grove, CA 92641

Verdugo Hills Visiting Nurse Assn.
135 S. Maryland Ave.
Glendale, CA 91205

Inyo County Health Dept.
Home Health Agency
Market & Jackson Sts.
Independence, CA 93526

Laguna Hills Medical Center
Home Health Agency
23561 Paseo De Valencia
Laguna Hills, CA 92653

Homemakers of Lake County
339 N. Main St.
Lakeport, CA 95453

Loma Linda University Hospital
Home Health Agency
11234 Anderson St.
Loma Linda, CA 92354

Long Beach Visiting Nurse Service
3295 Pacific Ave.
Long Beach, CA 90806

Advanced Home Health Assn.
211 W. Vernon Ave.
Los Angeles, CA 90037

Continuity of Care Home Health
  Agency
6124 Whittier Blvd.
Los Angeles, CA 90022

Inter-City Home Health Assn.
601 N. Vermont Ave.
Los Angeles, CA 90004

Los Angeles County Health Dept.
313 N. Figueroa St.
Los Angeles, CA 90012

Los Angeles Visiting Nurse Assn.
2850 Artesia Blvd.
Los Angeles, CA 90057

Medical Outreach Foundation
2707 S. Central Ave.
Los Angeles, CA 90011

Residential Health Services
9206 S. Vermont St.
Los Angeles, CA 90014

Southern California Home Health
  Assn.
2010 Wilshire Blvd.
Los Angeles, CA 90057

University of Southern California
  Medical Center
Home Care Program
1200 N. State St.
Los Angeles, CA 90033

Watts Home Health Agency
2051 E. 103rd St.
Los Angeles, CA 90002

Contra Costa County Home Health
  Agency
1111 Ward St.
Martinez, CA 94553

Merced County Home Health Agency
240 E. 15th St.
Merced, CA 95340

Stanislaus County Visiting Nurse Assn.
346 Burney St.
Modesto, CA 95354

Visiting Nurse Assn. of Pomona
West End
5156 Holt Blvd.
Montclair, CA 91763

Monterey Peninsula Visiting Nurse
  Assn.
187 El Dorado
Monterey, CA 93940

Paradise Valley Hospital
Home Care Program
2400 E. Fourth St.
National City, CA 92050

Alameda County Home Health Care
  Service
499 Fifth St.
Oakland, CA 94607

Oakland Visiting Nurse Assn., Inc.
5232 Claremont Ave.
Oakland, CA 94618

Theramedics Home Health Agency
1500 E. Katella
Orange, CA 92667

Pasadena Visiting Nurse Assn.
2500 E. Colorado Blvd.
Pasadena, CA 91107

Home Health & Counseling Services
408 E. Ninth Ave.
Pittsburg, CA 94565

Town & Country Home Nursing Service
238½ S. Main St.
Red Bluff, CA 96080

Community Home Health Service
1045 Tehama St.
Redding, CA 96001

Sequoia Hospital
Home Care Program
Whipple & Alameda
Redwood City, CA 94062

Palm Terrace In-Home Health Services
8595 Philbin Ave.
Riverside, CA 92503

Riverside Visiting Nurse Assn.
3615 Main St.
Riverside, CA 92501

Easter Seal Society of Sacramento
3205 Hurley Way
Sacramento, CA 95825

Home Care Program Sacramento
  Medical Center
2315 Stockton Blvd.
Sacramento, CA 95817

HOME HEALTH AGENCIES

Home Kare
2115 J St.
Sacramento, CA 95816

Sacramento Visiting Nurse Assn.
2206 29th St.
Sacramento, CA 95817

Salinas Valley Visiting Nurse Assn.
51 E. Romie Lane
Salinas, CA 93901

San Bernardino County Health Dept.
351 Mt. View Ave.
San Bernardino, CA 92404

Allied Home Health Assn.
6154 Mission Gorge Rd.
San Diego, CA 92115

Alvarado Home Health Service
6655 Alvarado Rd.
San Diego, CA 92120

Home Health Services
4526 54th St.
San Diego, CA 92115

Visiting Nurse Assn. of San Diego County
8123 Engineer Rd.
San Diego, CA 92111

Southern California Permanente Medical Group
328 Maple St.
San Diego, CA 92103

Health Conservation Inc.
278 Post St.
San Francisco, CA 94108

Mt. Zion Hospital
Home Care Program
1600 Divisadero St.
San Francisco, CA 94115

San Francisco Home Health Agency
2940 16th St.
Suite 301
San Francisco, CA 94103

University of California
Home Health Agency
Third & Parnassus
San Francisco, CA 94122

Visiting Nurse Assn. of San Francisco
401 Duboce Ave.
San Francisco, CA 94117

Medi-Health Comprehensive Home Care
2505 Samaritan Dr.
San Jose, CA 95124

San Luis Obispo County Health Dept.
2191 Johnson Ave.
San Luis Obispo, CA 93401

San Mateo County Visiting Nurse Assn.
225 37th Ave.
San Mateo, CA 94403

Marin Home Care
2144 Fourth St.
San Rafael, CA 94901

Santa Barbara Visiting Nurse Assn.
133 E. Haley St.
Santa Barbara, CA 93101

Santa Clara County Visiting Nurse Assn.
2216 The Alameda
Santa Clara, CA 95050

North Santa Barbara County Visiting Nurse Assn.
1035 W. Main St.
Santa Maria, CA 93554

Sonoma County Coordinated Home Care
3313 Chanate Rd.
Santa Rosa, CA 95405

Visiting Nursing Service for Sonoma County
2765 Fourth St.
Santa Rosa, CA 95405

Coordinated Home Care Services
306 Spruce Ave.
South San Francisco, CA 94080

San Joaquin County Home Health Service
Visiting Nurse Assn.
1111 W. Robinhood Dr.
Stockton, CA 95207

San Joaquin Local Health District
Home Health Agency
1601 E. Hazelton Ave.
Stockton, CA 95201

Hospital Home Health Care Agency
23228 Hawthorne Blvd.
Torrance, CA 90505

Orange County Visiting Nurse Assn.
17921-D Sky Park Blvd.
Tustin, CA 92680

Homemaker Services
162 W. Smith St.
Ukiah, CA 95482

Solano County Home Health Agency
355 Tuolumne St.
Vallejo, CA 94591

National In-Home Health Services
14411 Van Owen St.
Van Nuys, CA 91405

Ventura County Visiting Nurse Assn.
3451 Foothill Rd.
Ventura, CA 93003

Tulare County Home Health Agency
County Civic Center
Visalia, CA 93277

Golden Rain Foundation
1006 Stanley Dollar Dr.
Walnut Creek, CA 94529

Whittier Visiting Nurse Assn.
13012 E. Philadelphia St.
Whittier, CA 90601

Sutter County General Hospital
Home Health Agency
1965 Live Oak Blvd.
Yuba City, CA 95991

COLORADO

Alamosa County Nursing Service
610 State St.
Alamosa, CO 81101

Aspen Valley Visiting Nurses Assn.
Smuggler Grove
Aspen, CO 81611

Boulder County Visiting Nurses Assn.
3450 Broadway
Boulder, CO 80302

Fremont County Nursing Service
Courthouse
Canon City, CO 81212

Colorado Springs Visiting Nurses Assn.
501 N. Foote Ave.
Colorado Springs, CO 80909

Montezuma County Nursing Service
Courthouse
Cortez, CO 81321

Delta County Nursing Service
Fifth & Palmer
Delta, CO 81416

Denver Visiting Nurses Assn.
659 Cherokee St.
Denver, CO 80204

Dominican Sisters of the Poor
2501 Gaylord
Denver, CO 80205

Home Health Services of Metropolitan Denver
3456 W. 23rd Ave.
Denver, CO 80211

San Juan Basin Health Unit
1905 E. Third Ave.
Durango, CO 81301

Mesa County Dept. of Public Health
515 Patterson Ave.
Grand Junction, CO 81501

Weld County Health Dept.
16th & 17th Ave.
Greeley, CO 80631

Gunnison County Nursing Service
County Courthouse
Gunnison, CO 81230

Elbert County Nursing Service
P.O. Box 51
Kiowa, CO 80107

Otero County Health Dept. Nursing Service
Courthouse
La Junta, CO 81050

Nursing Division
Jefferson County Health Dept.
260 S. Kipling St.
Lakewood, CO 80226

Bent County Nursing Service
Community Services Building
Las Animas, CO 81054

Larimer County Visiting Nurse Assn.
201 E. Fourth St.
Loveland, CO 80537

Montrose Public Health Nursing Service
P.O. Box 783
Montrose, CO 81401

Pueblo City County Health Dept.
151 Central Main
Pueblo, CO 81003

Clagett Memorial
Home Health Program
Fifth & Ute Sts.
Rifle, CO 81650

Chaffee County Nursing Service
202 North F St.
Salida, CO 81201

Tri-State Area Health Service
373 E. Tenth Ave.
Springfield, CO 81073

Northwest Colorado Visiting Nurse Assn.
P.O. Box 417
Steamboat Springs, CO 80477

Northeast Colorado Health Dept.
Visiting Nurse Service
700 Columbine St.
Sterling, CO 80751

Las Animas Huerfano District Public Health Dept.
723 Arizona St.
Trinidad, CO 81082

Custer County Nursing Service
Box 293
Westcliffe, CO 81252

CONNECTICUT

Public Health Nursing & Homemaker Services
75 Liberty St.
Ansonia, CT 06401

Avon Public Health Nurse Assn.
Simsbury Rd.
Avon, CT 06001

Sprague Public Health Nurse Assn.
Baltic Town Hall
Baltic, CT 06330

Berlin Public Nursing Service
983 Worthington Bridge
Berlin, CT 06037

Bethel Visiting Nurse Assn.
Bethel Town Hall
Library Place
Bethel, CT 06801

Branford Visiting Nurse Assn.
40 Kirkham St.
Branford, CT 06405

The Visiting Nurse Assn. of Bridgeport
87 Washington Ave.
Bridgeport, CT 06604

Bristol Visiting Nurse Assn.
88 Goodwin St.
Bristol, CT 06010

North Canaan Visiting Nurse Assn.
Town Hall
Canaan, CT 06018

Essex Public Health Assn.
Main St.
Centerbrook, CT 06409

Chaplin-Hampton-Scotland Public Health Nurse Assn.
P.O. Box 122
Route 97
Chaplin, CT 06235

Public Health Nursing Service
Town Hall, 845 Main St.
Cheshire, CT 06410

Chester Public Health Nursing Service
Ridge Rd.
Chester, CT 06412

Clinton Public Health Nursing Assn.
15 Commerce
Clinton, CT 06413

Canton Public Health Nursing Assn.
4 Market St.
Collinsville, CT 06022

Columbia-Hebron-Andover Public Health Nursing Agency
Route 6A
Columbia, CT 06237

Coventry Public Health Nursing Assn.
P.O. Box 203
Route 31
Coventry, CT 06238

Cromwell Public Health Nursing Service
Town Hall
5 West St.
Cromwell, CT 06416

Danbury Visiting Nurse Assn., Inc.
21 Montgomery St.
Danbury, CT 06810

Killingly-Brooklyn Nurse and Health Service
127 Main St.
Danielson, CT 06239

Public Health Nursing Assn. of Darien, Inc.
719 Post Rd.
Darien, CT 06820

Deep River Public Health Nursing Service
6 Elm St.
Deep River, CT 06417

East Haddam Public Health Nursing & Community Health Service
Town Office
East Haddam, CT 06423

East Hartford Combined Public Health Nursing Service
11 Wells Ave.
East Hartford, CT 06108

Public Health Nursing Assn. of Easton, Inc.
Center Rd.
Easton, CT 06425

Fairfield Visiting Nurse Assn.
413 S. Beason Rd.
Fairfield, CT 06430

Farmington Visiting Nurse Assn.
8 Garden St.
Farmington, CT 06032

Glastonbury Visiting Nurse Assn.
2210-12 Main St.
Glastonbury, CT 06033

Granby Public Health Nursing Assn.
15 N. Granby Rd.
Granby, CT 06035

Greenwich Hospital
Home Care Program
Perryridge Rd.
Greenwich, CT 06830

Groton Public Health Nursing Service
53 Cottage St.
Groton, CT 06340

Guilford Public Health Nurse Assn.
35 State St.
Guilford, CT 06437

Regional Visiting Nurse Assn
2372 Whitney Ave.
Hamden, CT 06518

Hartford Visiting Nurse Assn.
40 Woodland St.
Hartford, CT 06105

Haddam Public Health Nursing Assn.
Haddam Elementary School
Higganum, CT 06441

Griswold Public Health Nursing Service
Town Hall, School St.
Jewett City, CT 06351

Salisbury Public Health Nursing Assn.
P.O. Box 176
Depot Place
Lakeville, CT 06039

Ledyard Public Health Nursing Service
Colonel Ledyard Highway
Ledyard, CT 06339

Madison Public Health Nursing Assn.
8 Meeting House
Madison, CT 06443

Manchester Public Health Nursing Assn.
55 E. Center St.
Manchester, CT 06040

Meriden Public Health Visiting Nurse Assn.
212 Colony St.
Meriden, CT 06450

Middletown District Nursing Assn.
51 Broad St.
Middletown, CT 06457

Stonington Visiting Nurse Assn.
20 Holmes St.
Mystic, CT 06355

Community Health Service of Central Connecticut
205 W. Main St.
New Britain, CT 06052

New Canaan Visiting Nurse Assn.
102 South Ave.
New Canaan, CT 06840

Yale-New Haven Hospital
Discharge Planning & Home Care Dept.
789 Howard Ave.
New Haven, CT 06504

New Haven Visiting Nurse Assn.
1 State St.
New Haven, CT 06511

New London Visiting Nurse Assn.
12 Hempstead St.
New London, CT 06320

New Milford Visiting Nurse Assn.
68 Park Lane
New Milford, CT 06776

East Lyme Nursing Assn.
P.O. Box 213
Niantic, CT 06357

North Branford Public Health Nursing Assn.
Caputo Rd.
North Branford, CT 06471

Thompson Public Health Assn.
Thatcher Rd.
North Grosvenordale, CT 06255

North Stonington Public Health Nursing Service
North Stonington School
North Stonington, CT 06359

United Workers of Norwich
Public Health Nursing Service
P.O. Box 428
Norwich, CT 06360

Old Saybrook Public Health Nursing Service
80 Old Boston Post Rd.
Old Saybrook, CT 06475

Orange Public Health Nursing Service
637 Orange Center Rd.
Orange, CT 06477

Plainfield-Sterling Public Health Nursing Assn.
Community Ave.
Plainfield, CT 06374

Portland Community Health Service Assn., Inc.
376 Main St.
Portland, CT 06480

Putnam Visiting Nurse Assn.
32 S. Main St.
Putnam, CT 06260

Ridgefield District Nursing Assn.
7 Catoonah St.
Ridgefield, CT 06877

Rockville Public Health Nursing Assn.
62 Park St.
Rockville, CT 06066

Simsbury Visiting Nurse Assn.
8 Old Mill Lane
Simsbury, CT 06070

Norwalk Dept. of Health
137-139 East Ave.
South Norwalk, CT 06854

South Windsor Public Health Nurse Assn.
1540 Sullivan Ave.
South Windsor, CT 06074

Visting Nurse Assn. of Southbury & Roxbury
Peter Rd. & Main St.
Southbury, CT 06488

Southington Public Health Assn.
81 Meriden Ave.
Southington, CT 06489

Visiting Nurse Assn. of Stamford, Connecticut, Inc.
60 Guernsey St.
Stamford, CT 06903

Mansfield Public Health Nursing Assn.
Route 3
Storrs, CT 06268

Stratford Visiting Nurse Assn.
Town Hall
2725 Main St.
Stratford, CT 06497

Suffield Emergency Aid Assn.
450 South St.
Suffield, CT 06078

Plymouth Public Health Service
Town Hall
Main St.
Terryville, CT 06786

Enfield Visiting Nurse Assn.
1077 Enfield St.
Thompsonville, CT 06082

Maria Seymour Brooker Memorial Visiting Nurse Assn.
157 Litchfield St.
Torrington, CT 06790

Trumbull Public Health Nursing Assn.
571 Church Hill Rd.
Trumbull, CT 06611

Montville Visiting Nurse Assn.
RFD 2
Uncasville, CT 06382

Wallingford Visiting Nurse Assn.
51 S. Whittlesey Ave.
Wallingford, CT 06492

Waterford Public Health Nursing Service
722 Broad St. Ext.
Waterford, CT 06385

Watertown Public Health Nursing Assn.
10 De Forest St.
Watertown, CT 06795

Westbrook Public Health Nursing Service
McVeagh Rd.
Westbrook, CT 06498

W. Bradford Walker Community Health Assn., Inc.
West Cornwall, CT 06796

Aspetuck Valley Health District
Public Health Nursing Service
180 Bayberry Lane
Westport, CT 06880

Windham Visiting Nurse Assn.
71 Church St.
Willimantic, CT 06226

Wilton Public Health Nursing Assn.
P.O. Box 43
Wilton, CT 06897

Windsor Locks Public Health Nurse Assn.
Church St. Town Building
Windsor Locks, CT 06096

Winsted Visiting Nurse Assn.
71 Spencer St.
Winsted, CT 06098

Woodstock Public Health Assn.
P.O. Box 148
Woodstock, CT 06281

DELAWARE

Delaware State Board of Health
Federal St.
Dover, DE 19901

Kent County Health Unit
Federal St.
Dover, DE 19901

Sussex County Health Unit
South Bedford St. E
Georgetown, DE 19947

Delaware Curative Workshop
Home Care
16th & Washington Sts.
Wilmington, DE 19802

New Castle County Health Unit
800 West St.
Wilmington, DE 19801

Visiting Nurse Assn.
104 Greenhill Ave.
Wilmington, DE 19805

Wilmington Medical Center
Home Care Program
501 W. 14th St.
Wilmington, DE 19801

DISTRICT OF COLUMBIA

Community Group Health Foundation
Home Health Agency
3308 14th St., NW
Washington, DC 20010

District of Columbia Public Health
Home Care Services Division
1875 Connecticut Ave., NW
Washington, DC 20009

Visiting Nurse Assn. of Washington, DC
1842 Mintwood Place, NW
Washington, DC 20009

FLORIDA

Holmes County Health Dept.
Iowa Ave.
Box 337
Bonifay, FL 32452

Manatee County Health Dept.
202 Sixth Ave., E
Bradenton, FL 33505

Florida Health Related & Professional
   Services
1539 San Remo Ave.
Coral Gables, FL 33146

Okaloosa County Health Dept.
Nursing Section
Brackin & First St.
Crestview, FL 32536

Volusia County Health Dept.
440 S. Beach St.
Daytona Beach, FL 32015

Public Health Nursing Section
Route 3
De Funiak Springs, FL 32433

Associated Home Health Agency
2370 W. Oakland Park Blvd.
Ft. Lauderdale, FL 33311

Broward County Visiting Nurse Assn.
1300 S. Andrews Ave.
Ft. Lauderdale, FL 33316

Unicare
2500 W. Oakland Park Blvd.
Ft. Lauderdale, FL 33310

Lee County Public Health Nursing
   Advisory Council
2115 Second St.
Ft. Myers, FL 33902

Clay County Public Health Nursing
   Advisory Council
1575 Idlewild Ave.
Green Cove Springs, FL 32043

Holywood Home Health Agency
2100 E. Hallandale Beach Blvd.
Hallandale, FL 33009

Home Health Services of the U.S., Inc.
2500 E. Hallandale Beach Blvd.
Hallandale, FL 33009

Duval County Visiting Nurse Assn.
2105 Jefferson St.
Jacksonville, FL 32206

St. Vincent's Hospital
Home Care Program
Barrs & St. Johns Ave.
Jacksonville, FL 32203

Jackson County Health Dept.
Fourth St.
Marianna, FL 32446

Dade County Visiting Nurse Assn.
203 SW 13th St.
Miami, FL 33130

Jackson Memorial Hospital
Home Care Program
1700 NW Tenth Ave.
Miami, FL 33136

Total Care Home Health Agency
137 Golden Isles Dr.
Miami, FL 33137

Unicare
1150 NW St.
Miami, FL 33136

Santa Rosa County Health Dept.
1177 N. Stewart St.
Milton, FL 32570

Collier County Health Dept.
P.O. Box 477
Naples, FL 33940

Dade County Home Health Services
1720 79th St. Causeway
North Bay Village, FL 33141

Marion County Health Dept.
1117 S. Orange St.
Ocala, FL 32670

Orange County Visiting Nurse Assn.
1213 N. Orange Ave.
Orlando, FL 32804

Visiting Nurses Assn. of Pensacola
2251 N. Palafox St.
Pensacola, FL 32505

American Home Health Care
7751 W. Broward Blvd.
Plantation, FL 33314

Gold Coast Home Health Services
2027 NE 49th St.
Pompano Beach, FL 33064

Charlotte County Health Dept.
County Courthouse
Punta Gorda, FL 33950

Brevard County Health Dept.
1744 S. Cedar St.
Rockledge, FL 32955

St. Johns County Health Dept.
49 Orange St.
St. Augustine, FL 32084

Alaris Home Health Care Agency
715-49th St., N.
St. Petersburg, FL 33710

Bay Area Home Health Services
8081 38th Ave., N.
St. Petersburg, FL 33710

Community Nursing Service
500 Seventh Ave., S.
St. Petersburg, FL 33701

Gulf Coast Home Health Services
411 Pasadena Ave., S.
St. Petersburg, FL 33707

Public Health Nursing Section
900 French Ave.
Sanford, FL 32771

Public Health Nursing Section
1938 Laurel St.
Sarasota, FL 33579

Bradford Public Health Advisory
   Council
329 N. Church St.
Starke, FL 32091

Leon County Health Dept.
2965 Municipal Way
Tallahassee, FL 32302

Tampa Gulf Coast Home Health
   Services
4023 N. Armenia Ave.
Tampa, FL 33607

Visiting Nurse Assn. of Hillsborough
   County
901-A Swann Ave.
Tampa, FL 33606

Palm Beach County Visiting Nurse
   Assn.
3222 S. Dixie Highway
West Palm Beach, FL 33405

Polk County Assn. of Nursing Councils
229 Ave. D., NW
Winter Haven, FL 33880

GEORGIA

St. Mary's Hospital
Home Health Care Dept.
1230 Baxter St.
Athens, GA 30601

Atlanta East Seal Rehabilitation
   Center
Home Health Agency
1362 W. Peachtree St., NW
Atlanta, GA 30309

Metropolitan Atlanta Visiting Nurse
   Assn.
1859 Cheshire Bridge Rd., NE
Atlanta, GA 30324

Southside Comprehensive Health
   Center
Home Health Agency
1039 Ridge Ave., SW
Atlanta, GA 30315

Glynn County Board of Health
501 Mansfield St.
Brunswick, GA 31520

Medical Center
Home Care Program
710 Center St.
Columbus, GA 31902

Dalton-Whitfield County Health
   District 16
P.O. Box 278
Dalton, GA 30720

South Central Home Health Agency
2121 Bellevue Rd.
Dublin, GA 31021

North District 2
Home Health Agency
315 S. Enota Dr., NE
Gainesville, GA 30501

Wayne County Home Health Agency
262 W. Plum St.
Jesup, GA 31545

Central Georgia Home Health Agency
963 Washington Ave.
Macon, GA 31209

Macon-Bibb County Health Dept.
770 Hemlock St.
Macon, GA 31201

HOME HEALTH AGENCIES

Floyd County Board of Health Home
  Health Agency
P.O. Box 446
Rome, GA 30161

Mary MacLean Visiting Nurse Service
P.O. Box 6148
Savannah, GA 31405

Archbold Memorial
Home Care Program
Gordon Ave.
Thomasville, GA 31792

Ware County Health Dept.
215 Oak St.
Waycross, GA 31501

HAWAII

Hilo Hospital
Home Health Service
1190 Waianuenue Ave.
Hilo, HI 96720

Honolulu Home Care Programs
St. Francis Hospital
2260 Liliha St.
Honolulu, HI 96817

Straub Clinic
Home Health Agency
888 S. King St.
Honolulu, HI 96813

Hale Makua Home Health Services
1540 E. Main St.
Wailuku, HI 96793

IDAHO

Ada County Visiting Nurse Assn.
1455 N. Orchard
Boise, ID 83704

Caldwell Memorial Hospital
Home Care Program
300 E. Logan St.
Caldwell, ID 83605

Panhandle District Health Unit
Government Way & Garden Ave.
Coeur d Alene, ID 83814

City-County Public Health Dept.
Home Health Agency
520 Legion Dr.
Idaho Falls, ID 83401

St. Benedict's Hospital
Home Care Program
709 N. Lincoln
Jerome, ID 83338

North Central District Health Dept.
1221 F St.
Lewiston, ID 83501

Latah Home Health Agency
710 S. Main St.
Moscow, ID 83843

Mercy Medical Center
Home Health Agency
1512 12 Ave. Rd.
Nampa, ID 83651

Southeastern District Health Dept.
115 N. Sixth Ave.
Pocatello, ID 83201

ILLINOIS

Alton Woodriver Family Service &
  Visiting Nurse Assn.
211 E. Broadway
Alton, IL 62002

St. Anthony's Hospital
Home Care Program
2120 Central Ave.
Alton, IL 62002

Northwest Community Hospital
Home Care Dept.
800 W. Central Rd.
Arlington Heights, IL 60005

Visiting Nurse Assn. of Aurora
57 E. Downer Pl.
Aurora, IL 60504

Proviso Township Community Nursing
  Home
330 Eastern Ave.
Bellwood, IL 60104

Mennonite Hospital
Home Care Program
807 N. Main St.
Bloomington, IL 61701

Henry County Health Dept.
Courthouse Annex
Cambridge, IL 61238

Greene County Health Dept.
229 N. Fifth St.
Carrollton, IL 62016

B.C.M.W. Combined Health Services
P.O. Box 845
Centralia, IL 62801

Champaign-Urbana Public Health
  District
505 S. Fifth St.
Champaign, IL 61820

Charleston Community Hospital
Home Care Program
825 18th St.
Charleston, IL 61920

Babette & Emanuel Mandel Clinic
2839 S. Ellis Ave.
Chicago, IL 60616

Chicago Visiting Nurse Assn.
232 E. Ohio St.
Chicago, IL 60611

Cook County Dept. of Public Health
600 W. Jackson Blvd.
Chicago, IL 60606

Home Aid Nursing Service
6354 N. Broadway
Chicago, IL 60626

Home Health Service of Chicago North
233 E. Erie St.
Chicago, IL 60611

Home Health Service of Chicago South
1 IBM Plaza
Chicago, IL 60611

Mile Square Health Center
Home Care Program
2040 W. Washington Blvd.
Chicago, IL 60612

Mt. Sinai Hospital
Home Care Program
2755 W. 15th St.
Chicago, IL 60608

Vermilion County Health Dept.
Community Nursing Service
808 N. Logan Ave.
Danville, IL 61832

Macon County Visiting Nurse Assn.
1567 N. Water St.
Decatur, IL 62530

De Kalb County Board of Health
1731 Sycamore Rd.
De Kalb, IL 60115

Des Plaines Health Dept.
1426 Miner St.
Des Plaines, IL 60018

Suburban Home Health Service
2250 E. Devon Ave.
Des Plaines, IL 60018

Visiting Nurse Assn. of St. Clair
  County
1269 N. 89th St.
East St. Louis, IL 62203

Egyptian Health Dept.
1333 Locust St.
Eldorado, IL 62930

Visiting Nurse Service of Elgin
222 Cooper Ave.
Elgin, IL 60120

Visiting Nurse Assn.
828 Davis St.
Evanston, IL 60201

Fairfield Memorial Hospital
N.W. 11th St.
Fairfield, IL 62837

Clay County Health Dept.
104½ W. Second St.
Flora, IL 62839

Amity Society Visiting Nurse Assn.
7 N. State St.
Freeport, IL 61032

Stephenson County Health Dept.
Courthouse
Freeport, IL 61032

Galesburg Visiting Nurse Assn.
674 N. Seminary
Galesburg, IL 61401

Community Hospital
Home Health Service
416 S. Second St.
Geneva, IL 60134

Quadri-County Health Dept.
P.O. Box 437
Golconda, IL 62938

Bond County Health Dept.
107 W. College St.
Greenville, IL 62246

Calhoun County Health Dept.
Sweeney Professional Building
Hardin, IL 62047

Home Health Services of Highland
1515 Main St.
Highland, IL 62249

Morgan County Health Dept.
234½ W. State St.
Jacksonville, IL 62650

Visiting Nurses Assn. of Morgan County
102 N. West St.
Jacksonville, IL 62650

Jersey County Health Dept.
Courthouse
Jerseyville, IL 62052

Franklin Williamson Bi-County Health Dept.
217 E. Broadway
Johnston City, IL 62951

Public Health Council
102½ Van Buren St.
Joliet, IL 60432

St. Mary's Hospital
Home Care Program
150 S. Fifth Ave.
Kankakee, IL 60901

North Shore Visiting Nurse Assn.
509 Park Dr.
Kenilworth, IL 60043

Lake Forest Hospital
Home Health Care
660 N. Westmoreland Rd.
Lake Forest, IL 60045

Hygienic Institute
151 Fifth St.
La Salle, IL 61301

Lawrence County Health Dept.
Courthouse
Lawrenceville, IL 62439

West Towns Community Nursing Service
7915 Ogden Ave.
Lyons, IL 60534

Visiting Nurse Assn. of Mattoon
P.O. Box 825
Mattoon, IL 61938

Community Nursing Services of Moline
1409 Seventh Ave.
Moline, IL 61265

Grundy County Health Dept.
1340 Edwards St.
Morris, IL 60450

Wabash County Health Dept.
Courthouse
Mt. Carmel, IL 62863

Good Samaritan Hospital
Home Care Program
605 N. 12th St.
Mt. Vernon, IL 62864

Jackson County Health Dept.
1015½ Chestnut St.
Murphysboro, IL 62966

Oak Park & River Forest Community Nursing Service
124 S. Marion St.
Oak Park, IL 60302

Home Health Agency of Olympia Fields
2555 W. Lincoln Hwy.
Olympia Fields, IL 60461

Ottawa Public Health Nursing Assn.
417 W. Madison St.
Ottawa, IL 61350

Park Forest Public Health Dept.
200 Forest Blvd.
Park Forest, IL 60466

Lutheran General Hospital
Home Care Program
1775 Dempster St.
Park Ridge, IL 60068

Pekin Memorial Hospital
Home Care Program
Court & 14th Sts.
Pekin, IL 61554

Peoria County Health Dept.
2114 N. Sheridan Rd.
Peoria, IL 61606

Peoria Visiting Nurse Assn. & Home Care Plan
510 W. High St.
Peoria, IL 61606

Menard County Health Dept.
County Courthouse
Petersburg, IL 62675

Pike County Health Dept.
Courthouse
Pittsfield, IL 62363

Livingston County Health Dept.
419 Bank of Pontiac Building
Pontiac, IL 61764

Home Health Agency of Adams County
333 N. Sixth St.
Quincy, IL 62301

Whiteside County Health Dept.
201 W. First St.
Rock Falls, IL 61071

Visiting Nurse Assn.
703 Grove St.
Rockford, IL 61108

Rock Island County Board of Health
2116 25th Ave.
Rock Island, IL 61201

Visiting Nurse Assn.
1019 27th Ave.
Rock Island, IL 61201

Shelby County Health Dept.
123 N. Broadway
Shelbyville, IL 62565

Skokie Health Dept.
5127 Oakton St.
Skokie, IL 60076

Randolph County Health Dept.
Home Health Agency
112 W. Jackson St.
Sparta, IL 62286

Sangamon County Visiting Nurse Assn.
730 E. Vine St.
Springfield, IL 62703

Christian County Dept. of Public Health
106 E. Main St.
Taylorville, IL 62568

Iroquois County Health Dept.
Home Health Agency
Courthouse
Watseka, IL 60970

Lake County Home Health Service
3010 Grand Ave.
Waukegan, IL 60085

Dupage County Health Dept & Community Nursing Service
222 E. Willow Ave.
Wheaton, IL 60187

Wilmette Visiting Nurse Association & Health center
905 Ridge Rd.
Wilmette, IL 60091

McHenry County Health Dept.
2200 N. Seminary Ave.
Woodstock, IL 60098

Kendall County Health Dept.
County Courthouse
Yorkville, IL 60560

INDIANA

Bloomington Public Health Nursing Assn.
315 W. Dodds St.
Bloomington, IN 47401

Bartholomew County Health Dept
Home Health Service
2400 E. 17th St.
Columbus, IN 47201

Lake County Health Dept.
Courthouse
Crown Point, IN 46307

Elkhart County Health Unit
220 W. Franklin St.
Elkhart, IN 46514

Visiting Nurse Assn. of Southwestern Indiana, Inc.
120 SE First St.
Evansville, IN 47708

Ft. Wayne Visiting Nurse Service
227 E. Washington Blvd.
Ft. Wayne, IN 46802

Indiana Homemakers
2250 Lake Ave.
Ft. Wayne, IN 46805

Johnson County Nurse Service
Boehne Hospital Rd.
Franklin, IN 46131

Home Health Service
Visiting Nurse Assn.
3442 170th St.
Hammond, IN 46323

Home Nursing Service United
  Health Program
111 Sibley St.
Hammond, IN 46320

East Side Home Care
120 S. Ridgeview Dr.
Indianapolis, IN 46219

Indiana Homemakers
6214 N. Carrollton
Indianapolis, IN 46208

Indianapolis Home Care Agency
2902 N. Meridian St.
Indianapolis, IN 46208

Visiting Nurse Assn.
615 N. Alabama St.
Indianapolis, IN 46204

Lafayette Visiting Nursing Service
1114 State St.
Lafayette, IN 47904

Visiting Nurse Assn. of La Porte
  County
903 Indiana Ave.
La Porte, IN 46350

Memorial Hospital Home Care
  Program
1101 Michigan Ave.
Logansport, IN 46947

Jefferson County Health Dept.
608 Broadway
Madison, IN 47250

Grant County Visiting Nurse Assn.
116 Cherry St.
Marion, IN 46952

Visiting Nurse Assn. of Muncie,
  Indiana
2500 Bethel Ave.
Muncie, IN 47304

Wayne County Health Dept
Nursing Division
Rm. 113, Courthouse
Richmond, IN 47374

Rush County Public Health Dept.
Courthouse
Rushville, IN 46173

Scott County Health Dept.
Home Care Division
RR 2
Scottsburg, IN 47170

Jackson County Dept. of Health
Poplar & Bruce Sts.
Seymour, IN 47274

Indiana Homemakers
120 W. LaSalle
South Bend, IN 46601

St. Josephs County Visiting Nurse
  Assn.
321 Lincolnway W.
South Bend, IN 46601

Mary Sherman Hospital
Home Care Agency
320 N. Section St.
Sullivan, IN 47882

Terre Haute Visiting Nurse Assn.
328 S. Fifth St.
Terre Haute, IN 47807

Porter County Visiting Nurse Assn.
2304 N. Calumet Ave.
Valparaiso, IN 46383

IOWA

Dallas County Public Health Nursing Service
Courthouse
Adel, IA 50003

Monroe County Public Health
  Nursing Service
Courthouse
Albia, IA 52531

Ames Visiting Nurse Service
121 12th St.
Ames, IA 50010

Cass County Memorial Hospital
Home Health Care Dept.
1501 E. Tenth St.
Atlantic, IA 50022

Boone County Public Health Nursing Service
County Courthouse
Boone, IA 50036

Burlington Visiting Nurse Assn.
522 N. Third St.
Burlington, IA 52601

Des Moines County Public Health
  Nursing Service
522 N. Third St.
Burlington, IA 52601

Carroll County Home Health
  Agency
Courthouse
Carroll, IA 51401

Public Health Nursing Assn. of
  Linn County
400 Third Ave., SE
Cedar Rapids, IA 52401

St. Luke's Methodist Hospital
Home Health Agency
1026 A Ave., NE
Cedar Rapids, IA 52402

Appanoose County Board of Health
Home Care Program
Courthouse
Centerville, IA 52544

Lucas County Public Health
  Nursing Service
City Hall
Chariton, IA 50049

Floyd County Memorial Hospital
Home Care Program
11th St. & S. Main
Charles City, IA 50616

Cherokee County Public Health
  Nursing Service
Courthouse
Cherokee, IA 51012

Clinton-Camanche Visiting Nurse Assn.
309 N. Fourth St.
Clinton, IA 52732

Wayne County Public Health Nursing
  Service
Legion Building
Corydon, IA 50060

Visiting Nurse Assn.
303 City Hall
Council Bluffs, IA 51501

Union County Public Health Nursing
  Service
208 E. Montgomery St.
Creston, IA 50801

Davenport Visiting Nurse Assn.
1202 W. Third St.
Davenport, IA 52802

Winneshiek County Public Health
  Nursing Service
Courthouse
Decorah, IA 52101

Crawford County Home Health
  Agency
Courthouse
Denison, IA 51442

Polk County Public Health Nursing
  Assn.
E. First & Des Moines Sts.
Des Moines, IA 50316

Clinton County Nursing Service
818 Sixth Ave.
Deke Building
De Witt, IA 52742

Dubuque Visiting Nurse Assn.
412 Loras Blvd.
Dubuque, IA 52001

Earlham Care Program
Earlham, IA 50072

Hardin County Public Health Nursing
  Service
County Office Building
Eldora, IA 50627

Clayton County Public Health Nursing
  Service
Theatre Building
Elkader, IA 52043

Apalo Alto County Public Health
  Nursing Service
Henely Hall
Emmetsburg, IA 50536

Winnebago County Public Health
  Nursing Service
Courthouse
Forest City, IA 50436

Lee County Public Health Nursing
  Service
631 Ave. H
Ft. Madison, IA 52627

Hancock County Nursing Service
110 E. Eighth St.
Garner, IA 50438

Grundy County Nursing Service
Courthouse
Grundy Center, IA 50638

Shelby County Home Health Agency
Courthouse
Harlan, IA 51537

Buchanan County Home Health Agency
County Courthouse
Independence, IA 50644

Warren County Public Health Nursing Service
Courthouse
Indianola, IA 50125

Iowa City Visiting Nurse Assn.
1115 S. Gilbert St.
Iowa City, IA 52240

Visiting Nurse Assn.
Masonic Building
Keokuk, IA 52632

Marion County Board of Health
Public Health Nursing Service
Courthouse
Knoxville, IA 50138

Harrison County Home Health Service
110½ N. Second Ave.
Logan, IA 51546

Poweshiek County Health Service
Box E
Malcom, IA 50157

Mills County Public Health Nursing Service
108 W. Fourth
Malvern, IA 51551

Jackson County Home Health Agency
201 W. Platt St.
Maquoketa, IA 52060

Marshaltown Community Nursing Service
709 Center St., S.
Marshaltown, IA 50158

Cerro Gordo County Public Health Nursing Service
200 N. Washington
Mason City, IA 50401

Mason City Public Health Nursing Assn.
19 W. State St.
Mason City, IA 50401

Ringgold County Public Health Nursing Service
211 Shellway Dr.
Mount Ayr, IA 50854

Public Health Nursing Assn.
415 Cedar St.
Muscatine, IA 52761

Story County Public Health Nursing Service
Courthouse
Nevada, IA 50201

Jasper County Public Health Nursing Service
County Courthouse
Newton, IA 50208

Worth County Public Health Nursing Service
93 Eighth St., S.
Northwood, IA 50459

Monona County Home Health Agency
902 Tenth St.
Onawa, IA 51040

Mitchell County Homemaker Health Aide Service
616 N. Eighth St.
Osage, IA 50461

Mahaska County Public Health Nursing Service
1229 C Ave., E.
Oskaloosa, IA 52577

Ottumwa Public Health Nursing Service
City Hall
Ottumwa, IA 52501

Wapello County Public Health Nursing Service
Courthouse
Ottumwa, IA 52501

Sioux City-Woodbury County Health Dept.
Sixth & Douglas Sts.
Sioux City, IA 51101

St. Joseph Mercy Hospital
Home Care Program
2101 Court St.
Sioux City, IA 51104

Clay County Public Health Nursing Service
Box 975
Spencer, IA 51301

Cedar County Public Health Nursing Service
400 Cedar St.
Tipton, IA 52772

Tama County Health Service
125 W. High St.
Toledo, IA 52342

Benton Health Service
Courthouse
Vinton, IA 52349

Louisa County Public Health Nursing Service
Courthouse
Wapello, IA 52653

Black Hawk County Dept. of Health
316 E. Fifth St.
Waterloo, IA 50703

Waterloo Visiting Nurse Assn.
1028 Headford Ave.
Waterloo, IA 50703

KANSAS

Harper County Home Health Agency
Courthouse
Anthony, KS 67003

Republic County Health Dept.
Courthouse
Belleville, KS 66935

Coffey County Home Health Agency
Courthouse
Burlington, KS 66839

Clay County Home Health Agency
427 Court St.
Clay Center, KS 67432

Far Northwest Home Health Agency
210 S. Range
Colby, KS 67701

Cloud County Health Dept.
P.O. Box 142
Concordia, KS 66901

Morris County Health Dept.
Courthouse
Council Grove, KS 66846

Ellsworth County Health Dept.
Courthouse
122 N. Douglas St.
Ellsworth, KS 67439

Mercy Hospital
Home Care Program
816 Burke St.
Fort Scott, KS 66701

Barton County Home Health Agency
Courthouse
Great Bend, KS 67530

Ellis County Home Health Agency
307 W. 13th St.
Hays, KS 67601

Northeast Kansas Multi-County Home Health Agency
611 Utah
Hiawatha, KS 66434

Graham County Hospital
Home Care Program
304 W. Prout St.
Hill City, KS 67642

Sheridan County Home Health Agency
Courthouse
Hoxie, KS 67740

Reno County Home Health Agency
103 S. Walnut
Hutchinson, KS 67501

Southeast Kansas Multi-County Home Health Agency
221 S. Jefferson
Iola, KS 66749

Junction City-Geary County Home Health Agency
119 E. Ninth
Junction City, KS 66441

Clinicare
Family Health Services
510 SW Boulevard
Kansas City, KS 66103

Visiting Nurse Assn.
750 Armstrong St.
Kansas City, KS 66101

HOME HEALTH AGENCIES

Kingman County Health Dept.
Courthouse
Kingman, KS 67068

Douglas County Visiting Nurse Assn.
342 Missouri St.
Lawrence, KS 66044

Leavenworth City-County Health Dept.
Home Health Agency
422 Walnut St.
Leavenworth, KS 66048

Riley County Health Dept.
616 Poyntz St.
Manhattan, KS 66502

McPherson County Health Dept.
119 N. Maple St.
McPherson, KS 67460

Ottawa County Health Dept.
County Courthouse
Minneapolis, KS 67467

Harvey County Home Health Agency
Courthouse
Newton, KS 67114

Jefferson County Home Health Agency
County Courthouse
Oskaloosa, KS 66066

Franklin County Home Health Dept.
112 W. Tecumseh
Ottawa, KS 66067

Labette County Health Dept.
P.O. Box 786
Parsons, KS 67357

Russell County Home Health Agency
County Courthouse
Russell, KS 67665

Salina-Saline County Health Dept.
415 E. Mulberry St.
Salina, KS 67401

Topeka-Shawnee County Health Dept.
1615 W. Eighth St.
Topeka, KS 66606

Washington County Nursing Services
115 W. Third St.
Washington, KS 66968

Wichita Sedgwick County Dept. of Public Health
E. Ninth St.
Wichita, KS 67214

KENTUCKY

King's Daughters Hospital
Home Care Program
2201 Lexington Ave.
Ashland, KY 41101

Knox County Home Health Agency
Liberty St.
Barbourville, KY 40906

Lee County Health Dept.
Home Health Agency
P.O. Box 398
Beattyville, KY 41311

Owsley County Health Dept.
P.O. Box 24
Booneville, KY 41314

Warren County Hospital
Home Care Program
Reservoir Hill
Bowling Green, KY 42101

St. Elizabeth Hospital
Home Care Program
21 St. & Eastern Ave.
Covington, KY 41014

Harrison County Health Dept.
416 E. Pleasant St.
Cynthiana, KY 41031

McDowell Home Health Agency
141 N. Third St.
Danville, KY 40422

Lyon County Health Dept.
Home Health Agency
Fairview Ave. & Hillwood St.
Eddyville, KY 42038

Appalachian Regional Hospital
Home Health Service
Martins Fork Rd.
Harlan, KY 40831

Hazard Appalachian Regional Hospital
Home Health Agency
P.O. Box 928
Hazard, KY 41701

Kentucky River District Health Dept.
523 High St.
Hazard, KY 41701

Knott County Health Agency
Hindman, KY 41822

Leslie County Health Dept.
Box 113
Hyden, KY 41749

Breathitt County Home Health Agency
1133 Main St.
Jackson, KY 41339

Rough River Home Health Agency
124 E. White Oak St.
Leitchfield, KY 42754

Lexington-Fayette County Health Dept.
330 Waller Ave.
Lexington, KY 40504

Seton Home Health Services
East Sixth St.
London, KY 40741

Visiting Nurse Assn.
207 W. Market St.
Louisville, KY 40202

Hopkins County Hospital
Home Care Program
P.O. Box 466
Madisonville, KY 42431

Clay County Health Dept.
Home Health Agency
Manchester, KY 40962

Cumberland Valley District Health Dept.
Home Health Agency
P.O. Box 126
Manchester, KY 40962

Hayswood Hospital
Home Care Program
8 W. Fourth St.
Maysville, KY 41056

McDowell Home Health Service
P.O. Box 46
McDowell, KY 41647

Jackson County Health Dept.
Home Health Agency
McKee, KY 40447

Middlesboro Appalachian Hospital
Home Health Agency
36th St. & W. Cumberland Ave.
Middlesboro, KY 40965

St. Claire Medical Center
Home Health Services
222 Fleming Ave.
Morehead, KY 40351

Sisters of Nazareth Community Health Services
Nazareth, KY 40048

Green River District Home Health Agency
3520 New Hartford Pike
Owensboro, KY 42301

Paducah-McCracken County Health Dept.
916 Kentucky Ave.
Paducah, KY 42001

Johnson-Magoffin County Health Dept.
Second St.
Paintsville, KY 41240

Wedco District Home Health Agency
269 E. Main St.
Paris, KY 40361

Martin County Home Health Agency
General Delivery
Pilgrim, KY 41250

Pineville Community Hospital
Riverview Ave.
Pineville, KY 40977

Logan County Hospital
Home Care Program
E. Fourth St. & Bowling Green Rd.
Russellville, KY 42276

Somerset City Hospital
Home Health Agency
Bourne Ave.
Somerset, KY 42501

Lend-A-Hand Center
Walker, KY 40997

Frontier Nursing Service
Wendover, KY 41775

Whitesburg Appalachian Region Hospital
Home Health Agency
Whitesburg, KY 41858

Whitley County Health Dept.
S. Second St.
Williamsburg, KY 40769

Clark County Health Dept.
Home Health Agency
East Lexington Ave.
Winchester, KY 40391

LOUISIANA

Vermilion Home Health Agency
304C N. Hospital Dr.
Abbeville, LA 70510

Vermilion Parish Health Unit
401 S. St. Charles
Abbeville, LA 70510

Professional Home Health Services
4102 Parliament Drive
Alexandria, LA 71301

Rapides General Hospital
Home Care Program
400 Fourth St.
Alexandria, LA 71301

Rapides Parish Health Unit
1200 Texas Ave.
Alexandria, LA 71303

Tangipahoa Parish Health Unit
E. Oak St.
Amite, LA 70422

Bienville Parish Health Unit
Chestnut & Beech Sts.
Arcadia, LA 71001

Capitol Home Health Services
4163 North Blvd.
Baton Rouge, LA 70806

East Baton Rouge Parish Health Unit
353 N. 12th St.
Baton Rouge, LA 70812

Home Health Services of Louisiana
723 Main St.
Baton Rouge, LA 70802

Homemakers International
251 Florida
Baton Rouge, LA 70801

Professional Home Health Services
4545 North Blvd.
Baton Rouge, LA 70806

Washington-Tangipahoa Area Home Health Agency
112 Georgia St.
Bogalusa, LA 70427

Professional Home Health Services
1301 Delhi
Bossier City, LA 71010

St. Bernard Parish Health Unit
2712 Palmisano Blvd.
Chalmette, LA 70043

East Felciana Parish Health Unit
Spring & St. Helena Sts.
Clinton, LA 70722

Grant Parish Health Unit
P.O. Box 572
Colfax, LA 71417

Caldwell Parish Health Unit
224 Pearl St.
Columbia, LA 71418

St. Tammany Area Home Health Agency
312 S. Jefferson Ave.
Covington, LA 70433

St. Tammany Parish Health Unit
639 N. Theard St.
Covington, LA 70433

Acadia Parish Health Unit
West Mill St.
Crowley, LA 70526

Crowley Home Health Services
1817 N. Parkerson Ave.
Crowley, LA 70526

Beauregard Parish Health Unit
201 Third St., Box 327
DeRidder, LA 70634

Ascension Parish Health Unit
201 Opelousas St.
Donaldsonville, LA 70346

Eunice Home Health Services
2011 W. Laurel St.
Eunice, LA 70535

Union Parish Health Unit
P.O. Box 516
Farmerville, LA 71241

Washington Parish Health Unit
902 Pearl St.
Franklinton, LA 70438

St. Helena Parish Health Unit
P.O. Box 216
Greensburg, LA 70441

St. Charles Parish Health Unit
P.O. Box 456
Hahnville, LA 70057

Catahoula Parish Health Unit
P.O. Box 240
Harrisonburg, LA 71340

Jefferson Parish Health Unit
1901 Eighth St.
Harvey, LA 70058

Terrebonne Parish Health Unit
P.O. Box 309
Houma, LA 70361

Jefferson Davis Parish Health Unit
Church St., Box 92
Jennings, LA 70546

Jackson Parish Health Unit
326 Eighth St.
Jonesboro, LA 71251

Acadian Home Health Agency
410 Heymann Blvd.
Lafayette, LA 70501

Lafayette Parish Health Unit
P.O. Box 5186
Lafayette, LA 70501

Calcasieu-Lake Charles Health Unit
P.O. Box 3169
Lake Charles, LA 70601

Home Health Services
707 S. Ryan St.
Lake Charles, LA 70601

Southwest Louisiana Visiting Nurse Assn.
3727 Ryan St.
Lake Charles, LA 70601

East Carroll Parish Health Unit
407 Second St.
Lake Providence, LA 71254

Vernon Parish Health Unit
361 S. Magnolia St.
Livingston, LA 70754

St. James Parish Health Unit
P.O. Box 387
Lutcher, LA 70071

Avoyelles Parish Health Unit
112 S. Lee St.
Marksville, LA 71351

Golden Age Home Care
4300 Houma Blvd.
Metairie, LA 70002

Minden Home Health Services
201 Dennis St.
Minden, LA 71055

Quachita Parish Health Unit
2913 de Siard St.
Monroe, LA 71201

Professional Home Health Services
1205 N. 18th St.
Monroe, LA 71201

St. Mary Area Home Care Agency
3025 Helen Dr.
Morgan City, LA 70380

Assumption Parish Health Unit
P.O. Drawer 9
Napoleonville, LA 70390

Professional Home Health Services
415 Bienville St.
Natchitoches, LA 71457

Professional Home Health
911B Torrido Village
New Iberia, LA 70560

Teche Home Health Agency
137½ Duperier St.
New Iberia, LA 70560

City of New Orleans Health Dept.
1420 S. Jefferson Davis Pkwy.
New Orleans, LA 70125

Health-Tex
1713 Dryades St.
New Orleans, LA 70113

Home Health Services of Louisiana, Inc.
2001 Canal St.
New Orleans, LA 70130

Hotel Dieu Hospital
Home Care Program
2004 Tulane Ave.
New Orleans, LA 70112

HOME HEALTH AGENCIES 113

Louisiana Health & Social & Rehabilitative Services Administration
325 Loyola Ave.
New Orleans, LA 70160

Pointe Coupee Parish Health Unit
Main St.
New Roads, LA 70760

Professional Home Health Services of Allen
E. Fifth St.
Oakdale, LA 71463

Allen Parish Health Unit
601 Fifth St.
Oberlin, LA 70665

St. Londry Parish Health Unit
P.O. Box 552
Opelousas, LA 70570

Iberville Parish Health Unit
1100 Meriam St.
Plaquemine, LA 70764

Tangipahoa Area Home Health Agency
187 Kemp St.
Ponchatoula, LA 70454

Richland Parish Health Unit
P.O. Box 666
Rayville, LA 71269

St. John Parish Health Unit
P.O. Box 326
Reserve, LA 70084

West Feliciana Parish Health Unit
P.O. Box 271
St. Francisville, LA 70775

Caddo-Shreveport Health Unit
1966 Kings Hwy.
Shreveport, LA 71104

Homemakers International
1600 Fairfield Ave.
Shreveport, LA 71101

Professional Home Health Services
2710 Line Ave.
Shreveport, LA 71104

Shreveport Home Care Agency
2600 Greenwood Rd.
Shreveport, LA 71103

Madison Parish Health Unit
400 E. Green St.
Tallulah, LA 71282

Lafourche Parish Health Unit
805 E. Seventh St.
Thibodaux, LA 70301

Concordia Parish Health Unit
P.O. Box 657
Vidalia, LA 71373

Evangeline Council on Aging
Home Health Agency
P.O. Box 312
Ville Platte, LA 70586

Evangeline Parish Health Unit
P.O. Box 367
Ville Platte, LA 70586

MAINE

Androscoggin Home Health Services, Inc.
59 Mill St.
Auburn, ME 04210

Bangor District Nursing Assn.
Bangor Municipal Building
Bangor, ME 04401

Counseling Center
Home Health Service Agency
43 Illinois Ave.
Bangor, ME 04401

Bar Harbor Public Health Nursing Assn.
39 Cottage St.
Bar Harbor, ME 04609

Bath Public Health Nursing Assn.
4 Park St.
Bath, ME 04530

Biddeford Public Health Nurse Assn.
205 Main St.
Biddeford, ME 04005

Four Town Nursing Service
Main St.
Blue Hill, ME 04614

Aroostook Home Care Agency
3 Jefferson St.
Caribou, ME 04736

Kennebunk Public Health Assn.
10 Storer St.
Kennebunk, ME 04043

Old Orchard Beach Public Health Nursing Service
Old Orchard St.
Old Orchard, ME 04064

Community Health Services
681 Congress St.
Portland, ME 04102

Coordinated Home Health Care Program
144 State St.
Portland, ME 04101

Mid-Coast Home Health Agency
22 White St.
Rockland, ME 04841

Saco Public Health Nurse Assn.
5 Cutts Ave.
Saco, ME 04072

Sanford Community Health Assn.
263 Main St.
Sanford, ME 04073

Public Health Nursing Assn.
109 Ocean St.
South Portland, ME 04106

Community Health Services
151 Silver St.
Waterville, ME 04901

Wells Town Home Helath Agency
P.O. Box 398
Wells, ME 04090

York Hospital
Home Care Program
15 Hospital Dr.
York, ME 03909

MARYLAND

Anne Arundel County Health Dept.
3 Broadcreek Pkwy.
Annapolis, MD 21401

Instructive Visiting Nurse Assn.
5 E. Read St.
Baltimore, MD 21202

Provident Comprehensive Health Center
907 Edmondson Ave.
Baltimore, MD 21223

Sinai Hospital
Home Care Program
Belvedere & Greenspring Aves.
Baltimore, MD 21215

West Baltimore Community Health Corp.
1850 W. Baltimore St.
Baltimore, MD 21223

Harford County Health Dept.
119 Hays St.
Bel Air, MD 21014

Dorchester County Home Health
P.O. Box 319
Cambridge, MD 21613

Kent County Health Dept.
College Ave., Extended
Chestertown, MD 21620

Prince Georges County Health Dept.
Cheverly, MD 20785

Allegany County Health Dept.
111 Union St.
Cumberland, MD 21502

Memorial Hospital
Home Care Program
Memorial Ave.
Cumberland, MD 21502

Talbot County Health Dept.
100 S. Hanson St.
Easton, MD 21601

Cecil County Health Dept.
201 Courthouse Building
Elkton, MD 21921

Howard County Health Dept.
199 Courthouse Dr.
Ellicott City, MD 21043

Frederick County Health Dept.
12 E. Church St.
Frederick, MD 21701

Frederick Memorial Hospital
Home Health Agency
W. Seventh St.
Frederick, MD 21701

Washington County Health Dept.
1302 Pennsylvania Ave.
Hagerstown, MD 21740

Adventist Home Health Service
4807 42nd Place
Hyattsville, MD 20781

St. Marys County Health Dept.
Tudor Hall Dr.
Leonardtown, MD 20650

Garrett County Health Dept.
251 N. Fourth St.
Oakland, MD 21550

Somerset County Health Dept.
56 Prince William St.
Princess Anne, MD 21853

Wicomico County Health Dept.
W. Locust St.
Salisbury, MD 21801

Holy Cross Hospital Home Health
Agency
1500 Forest Glen Rd.
Silver Spring, MD 20910

Leisure World Foundation Medical
Center
Home Health Agency
3701 Rossmoor Blvd.
Silver Spring, MD 20906

Baltimore County Dept. of Health
105 W. Chesapeake Ave.
Towson, MD 21204

Carroll County Health Dept.
Memorial Ave.
Westminster, MD 21157

MASSACHUSETTS

Abington Visiting Nurse Assn.
10 Railroad St.
Abington, MA 02351

Acton Public Health Nursing Service
69 Hayward Rd.
Acton, MA 01720

Acushnet Board of Health
122 Main St.
Acushnet, MA 02743

Adams Board of Health
65 Park St.
Adams, MA 01220

Amesbury Board of Health
11 School St.
Amesbury, MA 01913

Amherst Board of Health
Town Hall
Amherst, MA 01002

Andover Visiting Nurse Assn.
4 Punchard Ave.
Andover, MA 01810

Arlington Visiting Nurse Assn.
1026 Massachusetts Ave.
Arlington, MA 02174

Home Health Service Board of Health
Main St.
Ashland, MA 01721

Athol-Orange Community Health
Service Agency
2033 Main St.
Athol, MA 01331

Community Health Agency
150 Bank St.
Attleboro, MA 02703

Auburn District Nursing Assn.
104 Central St.
Auburn, MA 01501

Nashoba Nursing Service
Central Ave.
Ayer, MA 01432

Bedford Public Nursing Assn.
16 South Rd.
Bedford, MA 01730

Belmont-Watertown Community
Health Assn.
455 Concord Ave.
Belmont, MA 02178

Beverly Hospital
Home Care Program
Herrick St.
Beverly, MA 01915

Beverly Visiting Nurse Assn.
19 Broadway
Beverly, MA 01915

Beth Israel Hospital
Home Care Program
330 Brookline Ave.
Boston, MA 02115

Boston Visiting Nurse Assn.
14 Somerset St.
Boston, MA 02108

South End Community Health Center
65 W. Brookline St.
Boston, MA 02118

Tufts-Columbia Point Health Center
300 Mt. Vernon St.
Boston, MA 02125

Braintree Visiting Nurse Assn.
648 Washington St.
Braintree, MA 02184

Bridgewater Visiting Nurse Assn.
39 Central Square
Bridgewater, MA 02324

Brockton Visiting Nurse Assn.
300 Battle St.
Brockton, MA 02401

Brookline Visiting Nurse Service
11 Pierce St.
Brookline, MA 02146

Board of Health
Town Hall
Burlington, MA 01803

Cambridge Visiting Nurse Assn.
35 Bigelow St.
Cambridge, MA 02139

Canton Nursing Assn.
742 Washington St.
Canton, MA 02021

Carver Public Health Nursing
Committee
Carver, MA 02330

Chatham Visiting Nurse Assn.
Shattuck Place
Chatham, MA 02633

Chicopee Visiting Nurse Assn.
10 Center St.
Chicopee, MA 01013

Cohasset Social Service League
76 S. Main St.
Cohasset, MA 02025

Emerson Hospital
Home Care Program
Old Rd. & Nine Acre Corner
Concord, MA 01742

Dalton Board of Health Nursing
Service
Town Hall
Dalton, MA 01226

Danvers Visiting Nurse Assn.
Town Hall
Danvers, MA 01923

Dartmouth Board of Health Nursing
Service
Town Office Building
Dartmouth, MA 02714

Dedham Visiting Nurse Assn.
82 Court St.
Dedham, MA 02026

East Bridgewater Home Health Agency
137 Central St.
East Bridgewater, MA 02333

Douglas Board of Health
Main St.
East Douglas, MA 01516

Eastham Town Nursing Service
Route 6
Eastham, MA 02642

Easthampton Visiting Nurse Assn.
216 Main St.
Easthampton, MA 01027

Easton Nursing Assn., Inc.
Barrows St.
Easton, MA 02356

Whidden Memorial Hospital
Home Care Program
103 Garland St.
Everett, MA 02149

Fairhaven Community Nurse Assn.
Town Hall
Fairhaven, MA 02719

Fall River District Nursing Assn.
101 Rock St.
Fall River, MA 02720

Falmouth Nursing Assn.
19 Locust St.
Falmouth, MA 02540

Burbank Hospital
Home Care Program
Nichols Rd.
Fitchburg, MA 10420

HOME HEALTH AGENCIES

Fitchburg Visiting Nurse Assn.
54 Grove St.
Fitchburg, MA 10420

Community Health Service
24 Melrose St.
Framington, MA 01701

Franklin Board of Health
Nursing Service
70 W. Central St.
Franklin, MA 02038

Gardner Visiting Nurse Assn.
City Hall
Gardner, MA 01440

Gloucester District Nursing Assn.
8 Angle St.
Gloucester, MA 01930

Grafton Community Nursing Service
District Assn.
1 Central Square
Town Hall
Grafton, MA 10519

Southern Berkshire Visiting Nurse
Assn.
54 Castle St.
Great Barrington, MA 01230

Franklin County Home Health Care
39 Federal St.
Greenfield, MA 01301

Greenfield Visiting Nurse Assn.
52 Beacon St.
Greenfield, MA 01301

Hanover Visiting Nurse Assn.
Town Hall
Hanover, MA 02339

Hanson Visiting Nurse Assn.
High St.
Hanson, MA 02341

Harwich Town Nursing Service
Main St.
Harwich, MA 02645

Visiting Nurse Assn.
68 Buttonwoods Ave.
Haverhill, MA 01830

Hingham Visiting Nurse & Community
Service
178 North St.
Hingham, MA 02043

Holbrook Visiting Nurse Assn.
Town Hall
Holbrook, MA 02343

Wachusett Home Health Care Agency
Holden, MA 01520

Holyoke Visiting Nurse Assn.
25 Hospital Dr.
Holyoke, MA 01040

Hudson Community Health Assn.
34 Pope St.
Hudson, MA 01749

Hull Board of Health
253 Atlantic Ave.
Hull, MA 02045

Central Cape Cod Visiting Nurse Assn.
429 South St.
Hyannis, MA 02601

Cable-Coburn Regional Home Health
Service
County Rd.
Ipswich, MA 01938

Lawrence General Hospital
Home Care Program
1 Garden St.
Lawrence, MA 01842

Lee Visiting Nurse Assn. Center
17 Main St.
Lee, MA 01238

Leominster Visiting Nurse Assn.,
Inc.
13 Chandler St.
Leominster, MA 01453

Lexington Visiting Nurse Assn.
38 Woburn St.
Lexington, MA 02173

Lowell Visiting Nurse Assn.
150 Middlesex St.
Lowell, MA 01854

Lunenburg Board of Health
P.O. Box 255
Lunenburg, MA 01462

Greater Lynn Visiting Nurse Assn.
196 Ocean St.
Lynn, MA 01902

Pernet Family Health Service
55 Lynn Shore Dr.
Lynn, MA 01902

Malden Community Nursing Assn.
15 Ferry St.
Malden, MA 02148

Manchester Nursing Service
P.O. Box 6
Manchester, MA 01944

Marblehead Visiting Nurse Assn.
1 Taft St.
Marblehead, MA 01945

Marion Visiting Nurse Assn.
Converse Rd.
Marion, MA 02738

Marlboro Visiting Nurse Assn.
Oak Crest Ave.
Marlborough, MA 01752

Mattapoisett District Nurse Service
P.O. Box 414
Mattapoisett, MA 02739

Maynard Health Dept.
244 Main St.
Maynard, MA 01754

Medfield, Dover & Norfolk Visiting
Nurse Assn.
5041 Main St.
Medfield, MA 02052

Medford Visiting Nurse Assn.
15 Hadley Pl.
Medford, MA 02155

Melrose Red Cross District Nursing
Service
786 Main St.
Melrose, MA 02176

Melrose-Wakefield Hospital
Home Care Program
585 Lebanon St.
Melrose, MA 02176

Middleton Community Services
P.O. Box 357
Central St.
Middleton, MA 01923

Milford Nursing Assn.
219 Main St.
Milford, MA 01757

Millbury Society for District Nursing
128A Elm St.
Millbury, MA 01527

Millis Visiting Nurse Assn.
Millis Jr.-Sr. High School
Millis, MA 02054

Visiting Nurse & Social Service League
92 Highland St.
Milton, MA 02186

Monson Visiting Nurse Assn.
91 Main St.
Monson, MA 01057

Natick Visiting Nurse Assn.
33 W. Central St.
Natick, MA 01760

Needham Visiting Nurse Assn.
51 Lincoln St.
Needham, MA 02192

St. Luke's Hospital
Home Care Program
37 Taber St.
New Bedford, MA 02740

Newburyport Health Center
2 Harris St.
Newburyport, MA 01950

Visiting Nurse Assn. of North Adams
85 Main St.
North Adams, MA 01247

Northamptom Visiting Nurse Assn.
240 Main St.
Northampton, MA 01060

Northboro District Nurse Assn.
11 South St.
Northboro, MA 01532

Northfield Board of Health
Main St.
Northfield, MA 01360

Norwood Visiting Nurse Assn.
50 Walnut Ave.
Norwood, MA 02062

Orleans Town Nursing Service
P.O. Box 87
Orleans, MA 02653

Palmer Visiting Nurse Assn.
King St.
Palmer, MA 01069

Peabody Visiting Nurse Assn.
Main St.
Peabody, MA 01960

J.B. Thomas Hospital
Home Care Program
15 King St.
Peabody, MA 01960

Pembroke Public Health Nursing Assn.
Center St.
Pembroke, MA 02359

Pittsfield Visiting Nurse Assn.
54 Wendell Ave.
Pittsfield, MA 01201

Plymouth Community Nurse Assn.
22 Summer St.
Plymouth, MA 02360

Health Dept. Visiting Nurse Assn.
26 Alden St.
Provincetown, MA 02657

Quincy Visiting Nurse Assn.
1116 Hancock St.
Quincy, MA 02169

Randolph Health Center
19 N. Main St.
Randolph, MA 02368

Richmond Community Health Assn.
State Rd.
Richmond, MA 01254

Rockland Visiting Nurse Assn.
40 Butternut Lane
Rockland, MA 02370

Rockport Public Health Nursing Service
Town Hall
Rockport, MA 01966

Salem District Nursing Committee
5 Broad St.
Salem, MA 01970

Town of Sandwich Nursing Agency
Summer St.
Sandwich, MA 02563

Scituate Home Health Agency
Town Hall
Scituate, MA 02066

Sharon Health Dept.
100 Maple Ave.
Sharon, MA 02067

Somerset Board of Health
Town Hall
Somerset, MA 02721

Somerville Visiting Nurse Assn.
131 Highland Ave.
Somerville, MA 02143

Laboure Center Visiting Nurse Service
371 W. 4th St.
South Boston, MA 02127

Home Care Program
Harrington Memorial Hospital
100 South St.
Southbridge, MA 01550

Hamilton-Wenham Visiting Nurse Assn.
P.O. Box 265
South Hamilton, MA 01982

Spencer Good Samaritan District Nurse Assn.
Main St.
Spencer, MA 01562

Springfield Visiting Nurse Assn.
837 State St.
Springfield, MA 01109

New England Memorial Hospital
Home Care Program
5 Woodland Rd.
Stoneham, MA 02180

Stoughton Health Dept.
Town Hall
Stoughton, MA 02072

Sudbury Public Health Nursing Assn.
278 Old Sudbury Rd.
Sudbury, MA 01776

Ashfield-Conway-Sunderland-Whately Home Health Agency
Town Hall
Sunderland, MA 01375

Sutton Board of Health
Town Hall
Sutton, MA 01527

Swansea Board of Health
Town Hall
Swansea, MA 02777

Taunton Visiting Nurse Assn.
14 Church Green
Taunton, MA 02780

Topsfield-Boxford Community Club Home Health Agency
7 School St.
Topsfield, MA 01983

Town of Montague Nursing Dept.
1 Ave. A
Turners Falls, MA 01376

Upton Board of Health
Milford St.
Upton, MA 01568

Uxbridge Board of Health
Town Hall
Uxbridge, MA 01569

Martha's Vineyard Visiting Nurse & Homemakers Service
Main St.
Vineyard Haven, MA 02568

Newton Visiting Nurse Assn.
1589 Beacon St.
Waban, MA 02168

Walpole Visiting Nurse Assn.
Town Hall
Walpole, MA 02081

Waltham Hospital Home Health Agency
Hope Ave.
Waltham, MA 02154

Waltham Visiting Nurse Assn.
764 Main St.
Waltham, MA 02154

Mary Lane Hospital
Home Care Program
85 South St.
Ware, MA 01082

Wareham Visiting Nurse Assn.
Marion Rd.
Wareham, MA 02571

Parmenter Health Center
Cochituate Rd.
Wayland, MA 10778

Webster Samaritan Assn.
Main St.
Webster, MA 01570

Wellfleet Home Health Agency
Cove Rd.
Wellfleet, MA 02667

Westboro District Nursing Assn.
8 Charles St.
Westboro, MA 01581

Weston Public Health Nursing Assn.
75 School St.
Weston, MA 02193

Westport Board of Health
Town Hall
Westport, MA 02790

Westwood Community Health Assn.
Town Hall
580 High St.
Westwood, MA 02090

Weymouth Visiting Nurse Assn.
402 Essex St.
Weymouth, MA 02188

Northbridge Nursing Assn.
Elm Place
Whitinsville, MA 01588

Whitman Visiting Nurse Assn.
74 Stetson St.
Whitman, MA 02382

Williamstown Visiting Nurse Assn.
131 Cole St.
Williamstown, MA 01267

Winchester Visiting Nurse Assn.
20 Fairmount St.
Winchester, MA 01890

Woburn Visiting Nurse Assn.
244 Main St.
Woburn, MA 01867

Pernet Family Health Center
18 Claremont St.
Worcester, MA 01610

Worcester Visiting Nurse Assn.
50 Elm St.
Worcester, MA 01609

MICHIGAN

Lenawee County Health Dept.
113 W. Front St.
Adrian, MI 49221

Gratiot Community Home Care Service
300 S. Warwick Dr.
Alma, MI 48801

HOME HEALTH AGENCIES 117

Washtenew County Health Dept.
313 County Building
Ann Arbor, MI 48108

Huron County Health Dept.
Huron County Building
Bad Axe, MI 48413

Calhoun County Visiting Nurse
   Service
183 West St.
Battle Creek, MI 49017

Bay County Health Dept.
County Building
Bay City, MI 48706

Mecosta County Health Dept
220 S. Stewart St.
Big Rapids, MI 49307

Thumb District Health Dept.
2266 W. Caro Rd.
Caro, MI 48723

Cass County Health Dept.
130 N. Broadway
Cassopolis, MI 49031

District Dept. of Health 3
203 Antrim St.
Charlevoix, MI 49720

Barry-Eaton District Health Dept.
528 Beech St.
Charlotte, MI 48813

Branch-Hillsdale-St. Joseph Health
   Dept.
274 E. Chicago St.
Coldwater, MI 49036

Shiawassee County Health Dept.
120 Mack St.
Corunna, MI 48817

Detroit Visiting Nurse Assn.
4421 Woodward Ave.
Detroit, MI 48201

Delta-Menominee District Health Dept.
Delta County Building
Escanaba, MI 49829

Flint Visiting Nurse Assn.
202 E. Blvd. Dr.
Flint, MI 48503

Ottawa County Health Dept.
Washington St.
Grand Haven, MI 49417

Community Health Service
1619 Walker Ave., NW
Grand Rapids, MI 49504

McPherson Community Health Center
   Home Care
620 Byron Rd.
Howell, MI 48843

Ionia County Health Dept.
111 N. Kidd St.
Ionia, MI 48846

Home Health Services of Jackson
111 Third St.
Jackson, MI 49201

Jackson County Health Dept.
410 Erie
Jackson, MI 49202

Kalamazoo Visiting Nurse Assn.
610 S. Burdick Ave.
Kalamazoo, MI 49006

District Health Dept. 1
1680 W. Sanborn Rd.
Lake City, MI 49651

Greater Lansing Visiting Nurse Assn.
211 W. Saginaw
Lansing, MI 48933

Western Upper Peninsula District
   Health Dept.
301 Hecla St.
Laurium, MI 49913

Manistee-Mason District Health Dept.
Courthouse
Manistee, MI 49660

Midland Visiting Nurse Assn.
301 W. Main St.
Midland, MI 48640

Monroe County Health Dept.
650 Stewart Rd.
Monroe, MI 48161

Macomb County Health Dept.
42525 Elizabeth Rd.
Mt. Clemens, MI 48043

Central Michigan District Health Dept.
1222 North Dr.
Mt. Pleasant, MI 48858

Muskegon County Visiting Nurse Assn.
1415 Leahy St.
Muskegon, MI 49442

Marquette County Health Dept.
Route 1
Negaunee, MI 49866

Mackinac-Schoolcraft District Health
   Dept.
405 Newberry Ave.
Newberry, MI 49868

Van Buren County Health Dept.
P.O. Box 307
Paw Paw, MI 49079

Pontiac Visiting Nurse Assn.
132 Franklin Blvd.
Pontiac, MI 48053

St. Clair County Health Dept.
108 McMorran Blvd.
Port Huron, MI 48060

St. Clair County Visiting Nurse Assn.
1021 Kearney St.
Port Huron, MI 48060

District Health Dept. 4
1400 Larke Ave.
Rogers City, MI 49779

District Health Dept. 2
126 E. Main St.
Rose City, MI 48654

Saginaw Visiting Nurse Assn.
3037 Davenport
Saginaw, MI 48602

Berrien County Health Dept.
Courthouse
St. Joseph, MI 49085

Sanilac County Health Dept.
114 N. Elk St.
Sandusky, MI 48471

Chippewa County Health Dept.
139 Arlington St.
Sault Ste. Marie, MI 49783

Dickinson-Iron District Health Dept.
130 Third St.
Stambaugh, MI 49964

Mid-Michigan District Health Dept.
Courthouse
Stanton, MI 48888

Munson Medical Center
Home Care Program
Sixth & Madison Sts.
Traverse City, MI 49684

District Health Dept. 5
Courthouse
White Cloud, MI 49349

MINNESOTA

Aitkin County Public Health Nursing
   Service
209 Second St., NW
Aitkin, MN 56431

Freeborn County Public Health
   Nursing Service
South Broadway
Albert Lee, MN 56007

Douglas County Public Health Nursing
   Service
Courthouse Annex
Alexandria, MN 56308

Anoka County Comprehensive Health
   Dept.
325 E. Main St.
Anoka, MN 55303

Mower County Public Health Nursing
   Service
Courthouse Building
Austin, MN 55912

Inter-County Nursing Service
Clearwater County Courthouse
Bagley, MN 56621

Beltrami County Public Health
   Nursing Service
Third St. & Bemidji Ave.
Bemidji, MN 56601

Countryside Nursing Service
301 14th St., N.
Benson, MN 56215

Bloomington Health Dept.
1900 W. Old Shakopee Rd.
Bloomington, MN 55431

118 THE OLDER AMERICAN'S HANDBOOK

Crow Wing County Public Health
 Nursing Service
Federal Center
Brainerd, MN 56401

Wilkin County Public Health Nursing
 Service
Courthouse Building
Breckenridge, MN 56520

Wright County Public Health Nursing
 Service
Courthouse Building
Buffalo, MN 55313

Isanti County Public Health Nursing
 Service
Courthouse
Cambridge, MN 55008

Carlton County Nursing Service
Carlton, MN 55718

Chisago County Public Health Nursing
 Service
Center City, MN 55012

Carver County Public Health Nursing
 Service
Courthouse
Chaska, MN 55318

Polk County Nursing Service
N. Main St.
Crookston, MN 56716

Multi-County Nursing Service
227 W. Front St.
Detroit Lakes, MN 56501

St. Louis County Health Dept
512 Courthouse
Duluth, MN 55802

Sherburne County Public Health
 Nursing Service
Elk River, MN 55330

Rice County Public Health Nursing
 Service
Courthouse Building
Faribault, MN 55021

Otter Tail County Public Health
 Nursing Service
Courthouse Building
Fergus Falls, MN 56537

Benton County Public Health Nursing
 Service
421 Dewey St.
Foley, MN 56329

McLeod County Public Health Nursing
 Society
830 Franklin
Glencoe, MN 55336

Itasca County Public Health Nursing
 Society
Courthouse Building
Grand Rapids, MN 55744

Le Sueur County Public Health
 Nursing Service
Courthouse
Le Center, MN 56057

Meeker County Public Health Nursing
 Service
Courthouse Building
Litchfield, MN 55355

Morrison County Public Health
 Service
Courthouse Building
Little Falls, MN 56345

St. Gabriel's Hospital
Home Care Program
Eighth Ave. & Second St., SE
Little Falls, MN 56345

Todd County Public Health Nursing
 Service
119 Third St., S.
Long Prairie, MN 56347

Blue Earth County Nursing Service
204 S. Fifth St.
Mankato, MN 56001

Immanuel St. Joseph's Home Care
 Services
325 Garden Blvd.
Mankato, MN 56001

Dodge County Nursing Service
County Courthouse
Mantorville, MN 55955

Lyon County Public Health Nursing
 Service
Courthouse
Marshall, MN 56258

Mille Lacs County Public Health
 Nursing Service
635 Second St., SE
Milaca, MN 56353

Minnesota University Hospital
Home Care Program
412 Union St., SE
Minneapolis, MN 55455

North Memorial Hospital
Home Care Program
3220 Lowry Ave.
Minneapolis, MN 55422

Visiting Nurse Service
Combined Nursing Service of
 Minneapolis
250 S. Fourth St.
Minneapolis, MN 55401

Clay County Public Health Nursing
 Service
807 N. 11th St.
Moorhead, MN 56560

Stevens County Public Health Nursing
 Service
Home Health Agency
500 Colorado Ave.
Morris, MN 56267

Brown County Nursing Service
2 S. State St.
New Ulm, MN 56073

Big Stone County Public Health
 Nursing Service
Courthouse Building
Ortonville, MN 56278

Steele County Nursing Service
Courthouse Building
Owatonna, MN 55060

Pine County Public Health Nursing
 Service
Courthouse Building
Pine City, MN 55063

Pipestone County Hospital
Home Care Dept.
911 Fifth Ave., SW
Pipestone, MN 56164

Fillmore County Nursing Service
P.O. Box 84
Preston, MN 55965

Goodhue County Public Health
 Nursing Service
Courthouse Building
Red Wing, MN 55066

Rochester-Olmsted County Health
 Unit
415 Fourth St., SE
Rochester, MN 55901

Stearns County Public Health Nursing
 Service
P.O. Box 153
St. Cloud, MN 56301

Hennepin County Public Health
 Nursing Service
6490 Excelsior Blvd.
St. Louis Park, MN 55426

Ramsey County Nursing Service
319 Eagle St.
St. Paul, MN 55102

St. John's Hospital
Home Care Program
403 Maria Ave.
St. Paul, MN 55106

Nicollet County Public Health Nursing
 Service
Courthouse
St. Peter, MN 56082

Scott County Public Health Nursing
 Service
135 E. First Ave.
Shakopee, MN 55379

Dakota County Public Health Nursing
 Service
744 19th Ave., N.
South St. Paul, MN 55075

Washington County Public Health
 Nursing Service
939 W. Anderson St.
Stillwater, MN 55082

Lake-Cook Home Health Service
Fourth St. at 11th Ave.
Two Harbors, MN 55616

Wadena County Public Health Nursing
 Service
Courthouse
Wadena, MN 56482

Cass County Public Health Nursing
  Service
P.O. Box 179
Walker, MN 56482

Marshall County Public Health Nursing
  Service
208 E. Calvin Ave.
Warren, MN 56762

Kandiyohi County Public Health
  Nursing Service
P.O. Box 592
Willmar, MN 56201

Winona County Public Health Nursing
  Service
175 Washington St.
Winona, MN 55987

MISSISSIPPI

Monroe County Health Dept.
Jefferson St.
Aberdeen, MS 39730

Choctaw County Health Dept.
123 Chester St.
Ackerman, MS 39735

Benton County Health Dept.
Ashland, MS 38603

Panola County Health Dept
206 Pamela St.
Batesville, MS 38606

Hancock County Health Dept.
Dunbar Ave.
Bay St. Louis, MS 39520

Jasper County Health Dept.
Bay Springs, MS 39422

Humphreys County Health Dept.
Castleman St.
Belzoni, MS 39038

Prentiss County Health Dept.
First St.
Booneville, MS 38829

Rankin County Health Dept.
North St.
Brandon, MS 39042

Lincoln County Health Dept.
Second St.
Brookhaven, MS 39601

Calhoun County Health Dept.
Calhoun City, MS 38916

Madison County Health Dept.
317 N. Union
Canton, MS 39046

Leake County Health Dept.
302 Ellis
Carthage, MS 39051

Tallahatchie County Health Dept.
Charleston, MS 38921

Coahoma County Health Dept.
P.O. Box 128
Clarksdale, MS 38614

Bolivar County Health Dept.
Court & Pearman
Cleveland, MS 38732

Yalobusha County Health Dept.
Coffeeville, MS 38922

Covington County Health Dept.
P.O. Box 321
Collins, MS 39428

Covington Hospital
Home Health Agency
P.O. Box 321
Collins, MS 39428

Marion County Health Dept.
600 Broad St.
Columbia, MS 39429

Marion County Hospital
Home Health Agency
Sumrall Rd.
Columbia, MS 39429

Lowndes County Health Dept.
1112 Military Rd.
Columbus, MS 39701

Alcorn County Health Dept.
125 S. Franklin
Corinth, MS 38834

Newton County Health Dept.
P.O. Box 210
Decatur, MS 39327

Kemper County Health Dept.
P.O. Box 96
De Kalb, MS 39328

Webster County Health Dept.
9 South
Eupora, MS 39744

Jefferson County Health Dept.
P.O. Box 446
Fayette, MS 39069

Scott County Health Dept.
Third St.
Forest, MS 39074

Itawamba County Health Dept.
504 W. Main St.
Fulton, MS 38843

Southern Home Health Agency, Inc.
Hallmark Plaza
Gautier, MS 39553

Washington County Health Dept.
Home Health Agency
P.O. Box 1219
Greenville, MS 38701

Leflore County Health Dept.
305 W. Market St.
Greenwood, MS 38930

Grenada County Health Dept.
30 Govan St.
Grenada, MS 38901

Harrison County Health Dept.
Broad & 15th Sts.
Gulfport, MS 39501

Forrest County Health Dept.
322 Forrest St.
Hattiesburg, MS 39401

South Mississippi Home Health Agency
2707 Camp St.
Hattiesburg, MS 39401

Copiah County Health Dept.
121 W. Frost St.
Hazlehurst, MS 39401

De Soto County Health Dept.
107 Highway S.
Hernando, MS 38632

Marshall County Health Dept.
Randolph at Falconer
Holy Springs, MS 38635

Chickasaw County Health Dept.
334 N. Jackson
Houston, MS 38851

Sunflower County Health Dept.
200 Baker St.
Indianola, MS 38751

Tishomingo County Health Dept.
Home Health Agency
1505 Bethdale
Iuka, MS 38852

Central Mississippi Home Health
  Agency
4654 McWillie Dr.
Jackson, MS 39206

Hinds County Health Dept.
420 E. Woodrow Wilson
Jackson, MS 39205

Mississippi State Board of Health
Home Health Agency
P.O. Box 1700
Jackson, MS 39205

Attala County Health Dept.
Kosciusko, MS 39090

Jones County Health Dept.
735 S. Magnolia
Laurel, MS 39440

Green County Health Dept
Leakesville, MS 39451

Holmes County Health Dept.
115 China St.
Lexington, MS 39005

Amite County Health Dept.
P.O. Box 209
Liberty, MS 39645

Winston County Health Dept
South Court St.
Louisville, MS 39339

George County Health Dept.
P.O. Box 106
Lucedale, MS 39452

Noxubee County Health Dept.
South Jefferson St.
Macon, MS 39341

Quitman County Health Dept.
Pecan St.
Marks, MS 38646

Pike County Health Dept.
South Broadway
McComb, MS 39648

Franklin County Health Dept.
Meadville, MS 39653

Simpson County Health Dept.
P.O. Box 385
Mendenhall, MS 39114

Lauderdale County Health Dept.
23rd & 14th St.
Meridian, MS 39301

Lawrence County Health Dept.
P.O. Box 246
Monticello, MS 39654

Delta Community Home Health
  Agency
P.O. Drawer 209
Mound Bayou, MS 38762

Adams County Health Dept.
409 N. Union
Natchez, MS 39120

Union County Health Dept.
Main St.
New Albany, MS 38652

Perry County Health Dept.
P.O. Box 126
New Augusta, MS 39462

Carroll County Health Dept.
P.O. Box 87
North Carrollton, MS 38947

Lafayette County Health Dept.
1219 Monroe Ave.
Oxford, MS 38655

Jackson County Health Dept.
P.O. Box 429
Pascagoula, MS 39567

Neswoba County Health Dept.
Myrtle St.
Philadelphia, MS 39350

Pontotoc County Health Dept.
222 E. Marion St.
Pontotoc, MS 38863

Pearl River County Health Dept.
P.O. Box 101
Poplarville, MS 39470

Claiborne County Health Dept.
Port Gibson, MS 39150

Jefferson Davis County Health Dept.
247 Leo St.
Prentiss, MS 39474

Lamar County Health Dept.
Courthouse Square
Purvis, MS 39475

Smith County Health Dept.
P.O. Box 305
Raleigh, MS 39153

Tippah County Health Dept.
West 1st St.
Ripley, MS 38663

Issawuena-Sharkey County Health
  Dept.
416 Race St.
Rolling Fork, MS 39159

North Sunflower County Hospital
Home Care Program
840 N. Oak Ave.
Ruleville, MS 38771

Tate County Health Dept.
102 McKie
Senatobia, MS 38668

Clark County Health Dept.
P.O. Box 477
Shubuta, MS 39360

Oktibbeha County Health Dept.
P.O. Box 108
Starkville, MS 39759

Tunica County Health Dept.
P.O. Box 55
Tunica, MS 38676

Lee County Health Dept.
P.O. Box 408
Tupelo, MS 38801

North Mississippi Medical Center
Home Health Agency
830 S. Gloster St.
Tupelo, MS 38801

Waithall County Health Dept.
P.O. Box 21
Tylertown, MS 39667

Warren County Health Dept.
New Courthouse Building
Vicksburg, MS 39180

Wayne County Health Dept.
812 Chickasawhay
Waynesboro, MS 39367

Clay County Health Dept.
206 Highway 45 N.
West Point, MS 39773

Stone County Health Dept.
Critz St.
Wiggins, MS 39577

Montgomery County Health Dept.
Liberty St.
Winona, MS 38967

Wilkinson County Health Dept.
308½ First St., W.
Woodville, MS 39669

Yazoo County Health Dept.
222 E. Broadway St.
Yazoo City, MS 39194

MISSOURI

Pike County Home Health Agency
Courthouse
Bowling Green, MO 63334

Columbia Visiting Nurse Assn.
Parkade Plaza
Columbia, MO 65201

Lake Ozark Home Health Agency
P.O. Box 498
Crocker, MO 65452

Shannon County Home Health Agency
P.O. Box 278
Eminence, MO 65466

Howard County Home Health Agency
116 N. College Ave.
Fredericktown, MO 63645

Marion County Home Health Agency
906 Broadway
Hannibal, MO 63401

SEMO Regional Home Health Agency
East Reed St.
Hayti, MO 63851

City of Independence Home Health
  Agency
210 S. Pleasant St.
Independence, MO 64050

St. John's Medical Center
Home Health Agency
2727 McClelland Blvd.
Joplin, MO 64801

Clark-Scotland County Home Health
  Agency
510 N. Johnson St.
Kahoka, MO 63445

Catholic Family & Community Services
527 W. 39th St.
Kansas City, MO 64111

Kansas City Visiting Nurse Assn.
4128 Broadway
Kansas City, MO 64111

Kirksville Osteo Hospital
Home Care Program
800 W. Jefferson St.
Kirksville, MO 63501

John Knox Home Health Agency
1702 W. O'Brien
Lee's Summit, MO 64063

Audrain City-County Health Unit
620 E. Monroe St.
Mexico, MO 65265

Nevada City Hospital
Home Care Program
815 S. Ash
Nevada, MO 64772

Professional Home Health Services, Inc.
Arizona & Maupin
New Haven, MO 63068

Ralls County Home Health Agency
Courthouse
New London, MO 63459

Monroe County Home Health Agency
Courthouse
Paris, MO 65275

McDonald County Home Health
  Agency
Pineville, MO 64856

Ozark Foothills Home Health Agency
1618 N. Main St.
Poplar Bluff, MO 63901

Washington County Home Health
  Agency
104 E. Hickory St.
Potosi, MO 63664

Meramec Home Health Agency
Courthouse
Rolla, MO 65401

St. Joseph-Buchanan County Health
  Dept.
11th & Frederick Sts.
St. Joseph, MO 64501

Cardinal Ritter Institute
Home Care Program
4532 Lindell Blvd.
St. Louis, MO 63108

Greater St. Louis Visiting Nurse Assn.
1129 MacKlind St.
St. Louis, MO 63110

Jewish Hospital
Home Care Program
216 S. Kings Hwy.
St. Louis, MO 63110

Lutheran Hospital
Home Care Program
3535 S. Jefferson
St. Louis, MO 63118

Neighborhood Health Center
2500 Hadley St.
St. Louis, MO 63106

St. Louis City Hospital
Home Care Dept.
1625 S. 14th St.
St. Louis, MO 63104

Andrew County Home Health Agency
Box 206
County Courthouse
Savannah, MO 64485

Spelman Memorial Hospital
Home Care Program
Smithville, MO 64089

Green County Visiting Nurse Assn.
2003 S. Stewart
Springfield, MO 65804

Trenton Home Health Agency
608 E. Ninth St.
Trenton, MO 64683

MONTANA

Yellowstone County Home Health
  Agency
Room 202
E. Courthouse
Billings, MT 59101

City-County Home Health Services
Continental Dr.
Butte, MT 59701

Columbus Hospital
Home Care Program
1601 Second Ave., N.
Great Falls, MT 59401

Montana Deaconess Hospital
Home Care Program
1101 26th St., S.
Great Falls, MT 59401

Ravalli County Public Health Nursing
  Service
311 S. Second
Hamilton, MT 59840

West-Mont Home Health Care
530 N. Ewing
Helena, MT 59601

Flathead County Health Dept.
Box 919
Courthouse
Kalispell, MT 59901

Park County Home Health Agency
130 S. Fifth
Livingston, MT 59047

Missoula City-County Health Dept.
Courthouse
Missoula, MT 59801

Richland County Health Dept.
P.O. Box 868
Sidney, MT 59270

NEBRASKA

Menonite Hospital
Home Care Program
1110 N. Tenth St.
Beatrice, NB 68310

Jennie M. Melham Memorial Medical
  Center
Broken Bow, NB 68822

Cozad Community Hospital
Home Care Program
300 E. 12th St.
Cozad, NB 69130

St. Francis Hospital
Home Care Program
1405 W. Koenig St.
Grand Island, NB 68801

Mary Lanning Memorial Hospital
Home Care Program
715 N. St. Joseph Ave.
Hastings, NB 68901

Phelps County Memorial Hospital
Home Health Care Unit
1220 Miller St.
Holdrege, NB 68949

Good Samaritan Hospital
Home Care Program
31st Central Ave.
Kearney, NB 68847

Tabitha Home Health Care
4730 Randolph St.
Lincoln, NB 68510

Lutheran Community Hospital
Home Care Program
2700 Norfolk Ave.
Norfolk, NB 68701

Omaha-Douglas County Health Dept.
Visiting Nurse Assn.
1201 S. 42nd St.
Omaha, NB 68105

West Nebraska General Hospital
Home Care Program
4021 Ave. B.
Scottsbluff, NB 69361

York Home Health Care Agency
2222 Lincoln Ave.
York, NB 68467

NEVADA

Nevada Home Health Services
487 Railroad St.
Room 215
Elko, NV 89801

Clark County Visiting Nurse Assn.
625 Shadow Lane
Las Vegas, NV 89106

Washoe County District Health Dept.
Visiting Nurse Service
10 Kirman Ave.
Reno, NV 89502

NEW HAMPSHIRE

City Health Dept.
City Hall
Berlin, NH 03570

Newfound Area Nursing Assn.
Lake St.
Bristol, NH 03222

Charlestown Visiting Nurse Assn.
P.O. Box 15
Charlestown, NH 03603

Claremont Visiting Nurse Assn.
Police Court
Claremont, NH 03743

Convalesce
Hospital Rd.
Colebrook, NH 03576

Visiting Nurse Assn. of Concord
1 Thompson St.
Concord, NH 03301

Derry Visiting Nurse Assn.
20 E. Broadway
Derry, NH 03038

Dover District Nursing Assn.
789 Central Ave.
Dover, NH 03820

Oyster River Home Health Assn.
13 Newmarket Rd.
Durham, NH 03824

Mascoma Area Health Council
P.O. Box 378
Enfield, NH 03748

Exeter Visiting Nurse Assn.
10 Front St.
Exeter, NH 03833

Rural District Health Council, Inc.
6 S. Main St.
Farmington, NH 03835

The Visiting Nurse Assn.
Goss Wing
Franklin Regional Hospital
Franklin, NH 03235

North Cheshire County
Home Health Service
P.O. Box 36
Gilsum, NH 03448

Seacoast Home Health Assn.
Professional Building
Park Ave.
Hampton, NH 03842

Visiting Nurse Service
43 S. Main St.
Hanover, NH 03755

Hinsdale Public Health Nursing Assn.
Main St.
Hinsdale, NH 03451

Keene Visiting Nurse Assn.
40 Mechanic St.
Keene, NH 03431

Central New Hampshire Home Care
653 Main St.
Laconia, NH 03246

Lancaster Public Health Nursing Assn.
B.D. Weeks Memorial Hospital
Lancaster, NH 03584

Dept. of Public Health Nursing Assn.
North Park St.
Lebanon, NH 03766

North Country Home Health Agency
60 High St.
Littleton, NH 03561

Lyme Home Health Agency
Box 111
Lyme, NH 03561

Manchester Visiting Nurse Assn.
194 Concord St.
Manchester, NH 03104

Marlborough Community Nursing Assn.
Box 66
Marlborough, NH 03455

Public Health Nursing Assn.
Main St.
Meredith, NH 03253

Merrimack Valley Home Health Care Assn.
Daniel Webster Highway
Merrimack, NH 03054

Souhegan Community Nursing Assn.
Union St.
Milford, NH 03055

Kearsarge Visiting Nurse Assn.
County Rd.
New London, NH 03257

Newport Area Home Health Agency
167 Summer St.
Newport, NH 03773

Home Health Agency of the Memorial Hospital
North Conway, NH 03860

Monadnock Community Visiting Nurse Assn.
70 Main St.
Peterborough, NH 03264

Pemi-Baker Home Health Agency
47 Main St.
Plymouth, NH 03264

Portsmouth Community Health Services
Junkins Ave.
Portsmouth, NH 03801

Rochester Visiting Nurse Assn.
Whitehall Rd.
Rochester, NH 03867

Salem District Nurse Assn.
Geremont Dr.
Salem, NH 03079

Tri-Area Visiting Nurses Assn.
Main St.
Somersworth, NH 03878

Troy Visiting Nursing Assn.
Troy, NH 03465

Winchester District Nursing Assn.
8 S. Main St.
Winchester, NH 03470

Wolfeboro Public Health Nurse Assn.
Wolfeboro, NH 03894

NEW JERSEY

Bayonne Visiting Nurse Assn.
899 Ave. C
Bayonne, NJ 07002

Warren County Public Health Nursing Agency
Courthouse
Belvidere, NJ 07823

Somerset Hills Visiting Nurse Assn.
12 Olcott Ave.
Bernardsville, NJ 07924

Cumberland County Health Dept.
800 E. Commerce St.
Bridgeton, NJ 08302

Somerset Valley Visiting Nurse Assn.
586 E. Main St.
Bridgewater, NJ 08807

Visiting Nurse & Health Assn. of Camden County
608 Broadway
Camden, NJ 08103

Cape May County Dept. of Health
Crest Haven
Garden State Pkwy.
Cape May Court House, NJ 08210

Community Health & Nursing Services of Greater Camden County
28 W. Collins Ave.
Collingswood, NJ 08108

Community Nursing Service of Essex & West Hudson
25 S. Harrison St.
East Orange, NJ 07018

East Orange Health Dept.
143 New St.
East Orange, NJ 07017

Visiting Nurse & Health Services
354 Union Ave.
Elizabeth, NJ 07208

Public Health Nursing Service
350 Engle St.
Englewood, NJ 07631

Hunterdon County Public Health Assn.
Route 69
Flemington, NJ 08822

Hackensack Hospital
Home Care Program
22 Hospital Place
Hackensack, NJ 07601

Hoboken Public Health Nursing Service
916 Garden St.
Hoboken, NJ 07030

Public Health Nursing Service
Medical Center Surgical Building
Jersey City, NJ 07304

Visiting Health Services of Passaic Valley
101 E. Main St.
Little Falls, NJ 07424

Long Branch Public Health Assn.
111 Union Ave.
Long Branch, NJ 07740

Atlantic County Health Dept.
1200 Harding Hwy.
Mays Landing, NJ 08330

Neighborhood Assn. of Milburn Township
12 Taylor St.
Millburn, NJ 07041

Montclair Community Nursing Service
65 Chestnut St.
Montclair, NJ 07042

Moorestown Visiting Nurse Assn.
16 E. Main St.
Moorestown, NJ 08057

Visiting Nurse Assn. of Morris County
38 Elm St.
Morristown, NJ 07960

Burlington Public Health Nursing Assn.
160 Madison Ave.
Mt. Holly, NJ 08060

Middlesex General Hospital
Home Care Program
180 Somerset St.
New Brunswick, NJ 08901

Sussex County Dept. of Social & Health Service
18 Church St.
Newton, NJ 07860

Visiting Nurse Assn. in Middlesex County
1915 Old George Rd.
North Brunswick, NJ 08902

HOME HEALTH AGENCIES

Nutley Dept. of Health
Kennedy Dr.
Nutley, NJ 07110

Passaic Tri-Hospital Home Care
 Program
70 Parker Ave.
Passaic, NJ 07055

Public Health Nursing Dept.
25 Mill St.
Paterson, NJ 07501

Plainfield & N. Plainfield Visiting
 Nurse Assn.
212 E. Seventh St.
Plainfield, NJ 07061

Princeton Medical Center
Dept. of Community Health Services
253 Witherspoon St.
Princeton, NJ 08540

Northern Bergen County Visiting
 Nurse Assn.
5 S. Island Ave.
Ramsey, NJ 07446

Monmouth County Family Health &
 Nursing Service
141 Bodman Place
Red Bank, NJ 07701

Nursing Service
74 Godwin Ave.
Ridgewood, NJ 07750

Visiting Nurse Assn. Home Care Service
193 Morris Ave.
Summit, NJ 07901

Ocean County Health Dept.
119 Hooper Ave.
Toms River, NJ 08753

Visiting Nurse Assn.
1112 Riverside Ave.
Trenton, NJ 08618

Union City Public Health Nursing
 Service
710 31st St.
Union City, NJ 07087

Vineland Dept. of Health
111 N. Sixth St.
Vineland, NJ 08360

West Essex Nursing Service
1059 Bloomfield Ave.
West Caldwell, NJ 07006

Woodbridge Township Division of
 Health
Nursing Program
800 St. George Ave.
Woodbridge, NJ 07095

Gloucester County Visiting Nurse Assn.
Carpenter St. & Allens Lane
Woodbury, NJ 08096

Salem County Dept. of Health
Woodstown Rd.
Woodstown, NJ 08098

NEW MEXICO

St. Joseph Presbyterian Hospital
Home Health Agency
400 Walter, NE
Albuquerque, NM 87102

Visiting Nurse Service
815 Vassar Dr., NE
Albuquerque, NM 87100

Associated Home Health Services
900 N. Main St.
Las Cruces, NM 88001

San Miguel County Health Dept.
1800 New Mexico Ave.
Las Vegas, NM 87701

Los Alamos Visiting Nurse Service,
 Inc.
P.O. Box 692
Los Alamos, NM 87544

Chaves County Home Health Service
P.O. Box 1435
Roswell, NM 88201

Visiting Nurse Service
223 Cathedral Place
Santa Fe, NM 87501

NEW YORK

Albany County Health Dept.
Div. of Nursing
South Ferry & Green Sts.
Albany, NY 12201

Albany Visiting Nurse Assn.
245 Lark St.
Albany, NY 12210

St. Peter's Hospital Home Health
 Program
316 S. Manning Blvd.
Albany, NY 12208

Orleans County Health Dept.
151 Platt St.
Albion, NY 14411

Allegany County Dept. of Health
Div. of Nursing
R.D. 1
Angelica, NY 14709

Cayuga County Dept. of Health
160 Genesee St.
Auburn, NY 13021

Genesee County Health Dept.
3837 W. Main St., Rd.
Batavia, NY 14020

Steuben County Home Health Agency
Rumsey St.
Bath, NY 14810

Broome County Health Dept.
20 Wall St.
Binghamton, NY 13901

Bronx Municipal Hospital Center
Home Care Program
Pelham Pkwy. & Eastchester Rd.
Bronx, NY 10461

Fordham Hospital
Home Care Program
Southern Blvd. & Crotona Ave.
Bronx, NY 10458

Lincoln Hospital
Home Care Program
Concord Ave. & E. 141st St.
Bronx, NY 10454

Misericordia Hospital
Home Care Program
600 E. 233rd St.
Bronx, NY 10467

Montefiore Hospital
Home Care Program
111 E. 210th St.
Bronx, NY 10467

Morrisania City Hospital
Home Care Program
E. 168th St. & Gerard Ave.
Bronx, NY 10452

Brookdale Hospital Center
Home Care Program
Linden Blvd & Rockaway Pkwy.
Brooklyn, NY 11212

Brooklyn Hospital
Home Care Program
121 DeKalb Ave.
Brooklyn, NY 11201

Brooklyn Visiting Nurse Assn.
138 S. Oxford St.
Brooklyn, NY 11217

Coney Island Hospital
Home Care Program
Ocean & Shore Parkways
Brooklyn, NY 11235

Cumberland Hospital
Home Care Program
39 Auburn Place
Brooklyn, NY 11205

Greenpoint Hospital
Home Care Program
300 Skillman Ave.
Brooklyn, NY 11211

Jewish Hospital
Home Care Program
555 Prospect Place
Brooklyn, NY 11238

Kingsbrook Jewish Home Care Medical
 Center
86 E. 49th St.
Brooklyn, NY 11203

Kings County Hospital Center
Home Care Program
451 Clarkson Ave.
Brooklyn, NY 11203

Long Island College Hospital
Home Care Program
340 Henry St.
Brooklyn, NY 11201

Maimonides Medical Center
Home Care Program
4802 Tenth Ave.
Brooklyn, NY 11219

Methodist Hospital
Home Care Program
506 Sixth St.
Brooklyn, NY 11215

Nursing Sisters Home Visiting Service
310 Prospect Park W.
Brooklyn, NY 11215

St. Mary's Hospital
Home Care Program
1298 St. Mark's Ave.
Brooklyn, NY 11213

Buffalo Visiting Nurse Assn.
1255 Delaware Ave.
Buffalo, NY 14209

Erie County Health Dept.
Home Health Services Program
95 Franklin St.
Buffalo, NY 14202

Greene County Public Health Nursing Service
P.O. Box G
Cairo, NY 12413

Ontario County Home Health Agency
120 N. Main St.
Canadaigua, NY 14424

Putnam County Dept. of Health
Nursing Service
40 Gleneida Ave.
Carmel, NY 10512

Otsego County Public Health Nursing Service
197 Main St.
Cooperstown, NY 13326

Cortland County Health Dept.
County Courthouse
Cortland, NY 13045

Essex County Nursing Service
Courthouse
Elizabethtown, NY 12932

Elmhurst City Hospital
Home Care Program
79-01 Broadway
Elmhurst, Queens, NY 11373

Chemung County Health Dept.
Home Health Agency
Heritage Park, John St.
Elmira, NY 14901

Booth Memorial Hospital
Home Health Agency
56-45 Main St.
Flushing, NY 11355

Flushing Hospital
Home Care Program
44-14 Parsons Blvd.
Flushing, NY 11355

Montgomery County Nursing Service
County Office Building
Fonda, NY 12068

Orange County Public Health Nursing Service
124 Main St.
Goshen, NY 10924

St. Lawrence County Public Health Nursing Service
223 E. Main St.
Gouverneur, NY 13642

Suffolk County Health Dept.
Dennison Office Building
Vets Memorial Highway
Hauppauge, NY 11787

Herkimer County Public Health Nursing Service
Courthouse
Main St.
Herkimer, NY 13350

Washington County Public Health Nursing Service
Lower Main St.
Hudson Falls, NY 12839

Visiting Nurse Service of Huntington Township, Inc.
52 Elm St.
Huntington, NY 11743

Tompkins County Dept. of Health
Division of Nursing
1287 Trumansburg Rd.
Ithaca, NY 14850

Mary Immaculate Hospital
Home Care Program
152-11 89th Ave.
Jamaica, Queens, NY 11432

Queens Hospital Center
Home Care Program
82-68 164th St.
Jamaica, Queens, NY 11432

Jamestown Visiting Nurse Assn., Inc.
Jones Hill
Jamestown, NY 14701

Fulton County Nursing Service
W. Main St.
Johnstown, NY 12095

Ulster County Health Dept.
244 Fair St.
Kingston, NY 12401

Warren County Public Health Nursing Service
Municipal Center
Lake George, NY 12845

Sullivan County Public Health Nursing Service
Infirmary Rd.
Liberty, NY 12754

Niagara County Health Dept.
Main & Market Sts.
Lockport, NY 14094

Lewis County Public Health Nurse Service
7660 State St.
Lowville, NY 13367

Wayne County Home Health Agency
P.O. Box 107
Lyons, NY 14489

Franklin County Nursing Service
Courthouse
Malone, NY 12953

North Shore Hospital
Home Care Program
300 Community Dr.
Manhasset, NY 11030

North Shore Visiting Nurse Service
400 Community Dr.
Manhasset, NY 11030

Chautauqua County Health Dept.
County Courthouse Annex
Mayville, NY 14757

Nassau County Health Dept.
Office of Home Care
240 Old Country Rd.
Mineola, NY 11501

District Nursing Assn. of Northern Westchester County
25 Moore Ave.
Mt. Kisco, NY 10549

Livingston County Health Dept.
Home Health Agency
Murray Hill Campus
Mt. Morris, NY 14510

Long Island Jewish-Hillside Medical Center
Home Care Program
270-05 76th Ave.
New Hyde Park, Queens, NY 11040

New Rochelle Hospital
Home Care Program
16 Guion Place
New Rochelle, NY 10801

Bellevue Hospital Center
Home Care Program
First Ave. & 27th St.
New York, NY 10016

Cabrini Health Care Center
227 E. 19th St.
New York, NY 10003

Gouverneur Hospital
Home Care Program
227 Madison Ave.
New York, NY 10002

Harlem Hospital Center
Home Care Program
136th St. & Lenox Ave.
New York, NY 10037

Lenox Hill Hospital
Home Care Program
100 E. 77th St.
New York, NY 10021

Metropolitan Hospital
Home Care Program
1901 First Ave.
New York, NY 10029

Mt. Sinai Hospital
Home Care Program
11 E. 100th St.
New York, NY 10029

HOME HEALTH AGENCIES

New York Hospital
Home Care Program
525 E. 68th St.
New York, NY 10021

New York Infirmary
Home Care Program
321 E. 15th St.
New York, NY 10003

Roosevelt Hospital
Home Care Program
428 W. 59th St.
New York, NY 10019

St. Clare's Hospital Center
Home Care Program
415 W. 51st St.
New York, NY 10019

St. Luke's Hospital Center
Home Care Program
Amsterdam Ave. & 114th St.
New York, NY 10025

St. Vincent's Hospital
Home Care Program
153 W. 11th St.
New York, NY 10011

Visiting Nurse Service of New York
107 E. 70th St.
New York, NY 10021

Phelps Memorial Hospital
Home Care Program
North Broadway
North Tarrytown, NY 10591

Chenango County Public Health
Nursing Service
County Building
Court St.
Norwich, NY 13815

Nyack Hospital
Home Care Program
North Midland Ave.
Nyack, NY 10960

Cattaraugus County Health Dept.
302 Laurens St.
Olean, NY 14760

Madison County Public Health Nursing
Service
225 Broad St.
Oneida, NY 13421

Dominican Sisters Family Health
Service Inc.
Mariandale
Ossining, NY 10562

Oswego County Dept. of Health
Division of Nursing
28 W. Bridge St.
Oswego, NY 13126

Tioga County Public Health Nursing
Service
56 Main St.
Owego, NY 13827

Brookhaven Memorial Hospital
Home Care Program
101 Hospital Rd.
Patchogue, NY 11772

Yates County Home Health Agency
418 Main St.
Penn Yan, NY 14527

Clinton County Health Dept.
6 Healy Ave.
Plattsburgh, NY 12901

United Hospital
Home Care Program
Boston Post Rd.
Port Chester, NY 10573

Dutchess County Health Dept.
22 Market St.
Poughkeepsie, NY 12601

Poughkeepsie City & Town Visiting
Nurse Service
75 Market St.
Poughkeepsie, NY 12601

Genesee Region Home Care Assn.
311 Alexander St.
Rochester, NY 14604

Monroe County Health Dept.
Home Care Program
111 Westfall Rd.
Rochester, NY 14602

Rochester & Monroe County Visiting
Nurse Assn.
500 East Ave.
Rochester, NY 14607

Saratoga County Public Health
Nursing Service
31 Woodlawn Ave.
Saratoga Springs, NY 12866

Schenectady County Visiting Nurse
Assn.
205 Union St.
Schenectady, NY 12307

Schoharie County Health Dept.
Main St.
Schoharie, NY 12157

Staten Island Hospital
Home Care Dept.
101 Castleton Ave.
Staten Island, NY 10301

Staten Island Visiting Nurse Assn.
61 Stuyvesant Place
Staten Island, NY 10301

Good Samaritan Hospital
Home Care Program
Nyack Turnpike
Suffern, NY 10901

Onondaga County Health Dept.
300 S. Geddes St.
Syracuse, NY 13204

Visiting Nurse Assn. of Central
New York, Inc.
113 E. Onondaga St.
Syracuse, NY 13202

Leonard Hospital Home Care Program
74 New Turnpike Rd.
Troy, NY 12182

Rensselaer County Health Dept.
Seventh & State St.
Troy, NY 12180

Visiting Nurse Assn. of Troy, Inc.
2212 Burdett Ave.
Troy, NY 12180

Public Health Nursing Organization
of Eastchester, Inc.
69 Main St., W.
Tuckahoe, NY 10707

Oneida County Health Dept.
Division of Nursing
800 Park Ave.
Utica, NY 13501

Utica Visiting Nurse Assn.
316 Elizabeth St.
Utica, NY 13501

Wyoming County Health Dept.
400 N. Main St.
Warsaw, NY 14569

Seneca County Health Dept.
E. Main St.
Waterloo, NY 13165

Jefferson County Public Health
Nursing Service
135 Park Pl.
Watertown, NY 13601

Schuyler County Home Health Agency
105 Ninth St.
Watkins Glen, NY 14891

Rockland County Health Dept.
50 Samsondale Plaza
West Haverstraw, NY 10993

Associated Visiting Nurse Services
111 Church St.
White Plains, NY 10601

St. Agnes Hospital
Home Care Program
305 North St.
White Plains, NY 10605

Westchester County Health Dept.
County Office Building
White Plains, NY 10601

White Plains Hospital
Home Care Program
41 E. Post Rd.
White Plains, NY 10601

NORTH CAROLINA

Randolph County Health Dept.
139 N. Cox St.
Asheboro, NC 27203

Buncombe County Health Dept.
P.O. Box 7606
Asheville, NC 28807

Carteret County Home Health Agency
P.O. Box 239
Beaufort, NC 28516

Royster Memorial Hospital
Home Health Agency
W. College Ave.
Boiling Springs, NC 28017

Alleghany-Ashe-Watauga District
  Health Dept.
P.O. Box 233
Boone, NC 28607

Transylvania Community Hospital
Home Care Program
P.O. Box 1116
Brevard, NC 28712

Pender County Home Health Agency
P.O. Box 455
Burgaw, NC 28425

Alamance County Health Dept.
Graham-Hopedale Rd.
Burlington, NC 27215

Chapel Hill Home Health Agency
210 N. Columbia St.
Chapel Hill, NC 27514

Orange-Chatham Comprehensive
  Health Service
157 E. Rosemary St.
Chapel Hill, NC 27514

Charlotte Family Health Service
1029 Arosa Ave.
Charlotte, NC 28203

Sampson County Home Health
  Agency
Cooper Dr.
Clinton, NC 28328

Martin-Tyrell-Washington District
Home Health Agency
Washington St.
Columbia, NC 27925

Cabarrus County Home Health Agency
P.O. Box 1149
Concord, NC 28025

Durham County Visiting Nurse Service
300 E. Main St.
Durham, NC 27701

Rockingham County Home Health
  Agency
205 Boone Rd.
Eden, NC 27288

District Health Dept.
Home Health Service
Harney & Cedar Sts.
Elizabeth, NC 27909

Cumberland County Home Health
  Services
907 Hay St.
Fayetteville, NC 28305

Angel Community Hospital
Home Health
Riverview & Whiteoak Sts.
Franklin, NC 28734

Gaston County Health Dept.
615 N. Highland St.
Gastonia, NC 28052

Guilford County Health Dept.
300 E. Northwood St.
Greensboro, NC 27401

Halifax County Health Dept.
P.O. Box 178
Halifax, NC 27839

Glenmary Sisters Home Nursing
  Service
P.O. Box 232
Hayesville, NC 28904

Mountain Home Nursing Service
P.O. Box 306
Hayesville, NC 28904

Henderson County Home Health
  Agency
P.O. Box 925
Hendersonville, NC 28739

Catawba County Home Health Agency
Highway 64-70 SE
Hickory, NC 28601

Orange County Home Health Agency
144 E. Margaret Lane
Hillsborough, NC 27278

Hot Springs Home Health Services
Box 68
Hot Springs, NC 28743

Onslow County Health Dept.
Home Health Agency
P.O. Box 460
Jacksonville, NC 28540

Duplin County Home Health Agency
P.O. Box 449
Kenansville, NC 28349

Scotland County Home Health Agency
County Health Dept.
S. Main St.
Laurinburg, NC 28352

Franklin County Home Health Agency
Blickett Blvd.
Louisburg, NC 27549

McDowell County Home Health Care
  Program
State St.
Marion, NC 28752

Multi-County Home Care Program
201 S. Green St.
Morganton, NC 28655

Surry County Health Dept.
113 S. Gilmer St.
Mt. Airy, NC 27030

Nash County Home Health Agency
Barnes St.
Nashville, NC 27856

Craven County Health Dept.
Home Health Agency
403 George St.
New Bern, NC 28560

Avery County Health Dept.
Home Health Agency
P.O. Box 235
Newland, NC 28657

Granville-Vance District Home Health
  Agency
P.O. Box 367
Oxford, NC 27565

Chatham County Home Health Agency
Route 1, Box 5
Pittsboro, NC 27312

Wake County Health Dept.
3010 New Bern Ave.
Raleigh, NC 27602

Richmond County Home Health
  Agency
Long Drive, Box 300
Rockingham, NC 28379

Person County Home Health Agency
Madison Blvd.
Roxboro, NC 27573

Cleveland County Home Health
  Agency
806 N. Washington St.
Shelby, NC 28150

Johnston County Home Health
  Agency
1102 Massey St.
Smithfield, NC 27577

Home Health Care Joint Venture
P.O. Box 38
Soul City, NC 27553

Moore County Home Health Agency
P.O. Box 780
Southern Pines, NC 28387

Brunswick County Health Dept.
127 E. Moore St.
Southport, NC 28461

Iredell County Home Health Agency
735 Hartness Rd.
Statesville, NC 28677

Home Health Agency
59 Hospital Rd.
Sylva, NC 28779

Edgecombe County Health Dept.
Home Health Service
2909 Main St.
Tarboro, NC 27886

Montgomery County Home Health
  Agency
S. Main St.
Troy, NC 27371

Eastern Carolina Home Health Services
400 E. Main St.
Washington, NC 27889

Haywood County Hospital
Home Health Agency
1615 N. Main St.
Waynesville, NC 28786

Wilkes County Health Dept.
Home Health Agency
P.O. Box 794
Wilkesboro, NC 28697

Consolidated Board of Health
Nursing Division
21 N. Fourth St.
Wilmington, NC 28401

Wilson County Health Dept.
Route 2
Wilson, NC 27893

Bertie County Home Health Agency
Sterlingworth St.
Windsor, NC 27983

Forsyth County Health Dept.
720 Ridge Ave.
Winston-Salem, NC 27102

Hertford-Gates District Health Dept.
P.O. Box 246
Winton, NC 27986

Davie-Yadkin Home Health Agency
P.O. Box 457
Yadkinville, NC 27055

NORTH DAKOTA

Ashley Hospital
Home Health Agency
612 Center Ave., N.
Ashley, ND 58413

Bismarck Home Health Agency
405 E. Broadway
Bismarck, ND 58501

Southwest District Home Health
  Agency
216 First Ave., W.
Dickinson, ND 58601

City of Fargo
Community Health Care
401 Third Ave., N.
Fargo, ND 58102

Grand Forks Home Health Agency
402 Second Ave., N.
Grand Forks, ND 58201

Jamestown Hospital
Home Health Agency
419 Fifth St., NE
Jamestown, ND 58401

First District Home Health Agency
215 Fifth Ave., NW
Minot, ND 58701

Richland County Home Health Agency
P.O. Box 226
Wahpeton, ND 58075

Williston Home Health Agency
309 Washington Ave.
Williston, ND 58801

OHIO

Lower River Nursing Assn.
235 Main St.
Addyston, OH 45001

Summit County Visiting Nurse Assn.
1659 W. Market St.
Akron, OH 43313

Alliance Visiting Nurse Assn.
145 S. Linden
Alliance, OH 44601

Ashland County-City Health Dept.
206 Claremont Ave.
Ashland, OH 44805

Ashtabula Home Health Service
P.O. Drawer 920
Ashtabula, OH 44004

Barnesville Home Health Care Agency
639 W. Main St.
Barnesville, OH 43713

Bellaire Medical Foundation
Home Care Dept.
3000 Guernsey St.
Bellaire, OH 43906

Logan County Health Dept.
Memorial Hall
Bellefontaine, OH 43311

Wood County Health Dept.
541 W. Wooster St.
Bowling Green, OH 43402

Bucyrus City Health Dept.
821 Kaler St.
Bucyrus, OH 43907

Harrison County Health Dept.
Route 1
Cadiz, OH 43907

Noble County Health Dept
Courthouse
Caldwell, OH 43724

Guernsey County General Health
  District
Steubenville Ave.
Cambridge, OH 43725

Central Stark County Visiting Nurse
  Assn.
618 Second St., NW
Canton, OH 44703

Mercer County Health Dept.
Courthouse
Celina, OH 45822

Health Center
University
50 Pohlman Rd.
Chillicothe, OH 45601

Cincinnati Area Visiting Nurse Assn.
2400 Reading Rd.
Cincinnati, OH 45202

Cincinnati City Health Dept.
3101 Burnet Ave.
Cincinnati, OH 45229

Providence Hospital Home Care
  Program
2446 Kipling Ave.
Cincinnati, OH 45239

Cleveland City Visiting Nurse Assn.
3300 Chester Ave.
Cleveland, OH 44114

Cuyahoga County Health Dept.
210 St. Clair, NW
Cleveland, OH 44113

Deaconess Home Care
4229 Pearl Rd.
Cleveland, OH 44109

Home Health Care of Cleveland
10605 Carnegie Ave.
Cleveland, OH 44106

Community Health & Nursing Services
181 Washington Blvd.
Columbus, OH 43215

Community Home Care Services
181 Washington Blvd.
Columbus, OH 43215

Dominican Sisters of the Poor
168 E. Lincoln St.
Columbus, OH 43215

Franklin County Health Dept.
Mound & High St.
Columbus, OH 43215

Coshocton City Health Dept.
538½ Main St.
Coshocton, OH 43812

Coshocton County Health Dept.
Route 5
Coshocton, OH 43812

Montgomery County Combined
  General Health District
451 W. 3rd St.
Dayton, OH 45402

Defiance County Health Dept.
113 Biede Ave.
Defiance, OH 43512

Delaware County Health Dept.
115 N. Sandusky St.
Delaware, OH 43015

Tuscarawas County Health Dept.
818 Blvd.
Dover, OH 44622

Preble County Health Dept.
107 E. Main St.
Eaton, OH 45320

Lorain County Health Dept.
9880 S. Murray Ridge Rd.
Elyria, OH 44035

Hancock County Home Health
  Nursing Agency
222 Broadway
Findlay, OH 45840

Sandusky County-Fremont City
  General Health Dept.
Courthouse
Fremont, OH 43420

Galion City Health Dept.
740 Grove Ave.
Galion, OH 44833

Gallipolis City Health Dept.
518 Second Ave.
Gallipolis, OH 45631

Holzer Medical Center
Home Health Services Program
385 Jackson Pike
Gallipolis, OH 45631

Brown County General Hospital
Home Care Program
Home St.
Georgetown, OH 45121

Darke County Health Dept.
Courthouse
Greenville, OH 45331

Butler County Home Health Service
Courthouse
Hamilton, OH 45011

Hamilton City Public Health Nurse Service
Municipal Building
Hamilton, OH 45011

Highland County Health Dept.
135½ High St.
Hillsboro, OH 45133

Lawrence County General Hospital
Home Care Program
724 Scott Ave.
Ironton, OH 45638

Jackson County Health Dept.
Main St.
Jackson, OH 45640

Kent Social Service & Visiting Nurse Service
143 Gougler Ave.
Kent, OH 44240

Hardin County-Kenton City Health Dept.
Courthouse
Kenton, OH 43326

Warren County General Health District
416 S. East St.
Lebanon, OH 45036

Lima-Allen County General Health District
405 E. Market St.
Lima, OH 45801

Lima Visiting Nurse Assn.
226 S. West St.
Lima, OH 45801

Home Health Care
210 N. Main St.
London, OH 43140

Lorain City Health Dept.
205 W. 14th St.
Lorain, OH 44052

Mansfield-Richland County Health Dept.
Visiting Nurse Assn.
600 W. Third St.
Mansfield, OH 44906

Washington County Home Nursing Service
304 Putnam St.
Marietta, OH 45750

Marion County Health Dept.
McKinley Park Dr.
Marion, OH 43302

Martins Ferry City Health Dept.
City Building
Martins Ferry, OH 43935

Visiting Nurse Society
876 Amherst Rd., NE
Massillon, OH 44646

Vinton County Health District
112 N. Market
McArthur, OH 45651

Morgan Home Nursing Service
65 W. Union Ave.
McConnelsville, OH 43756

Medina County Health Dept.
220 E. Liberty St.
Medina, OH 44256

Bureau of Public Health Nursing
101 N. Broad St.
Middletown, OH 45042

Holmes County General Health District
Courthouse
Millersburg, OH 44654

Morrow County Health Dept.
Courthouse
Mt. Gilead, OH 43338

Knox County Health Dept.
112 E. Chestnut St.
Mt. Vernon, OH 43050

Mt. Vernon City Health Dept.
40 Public Square
Mt. Vernon, OH 43050

Mt. St. Mary Hospital
Home Care Program
West Franklin St.
Nelsonville, OH 45764

Licking County Health Dept.
Route 3
Newark, OH 43055

Newark City Health Dept.
40 W. Main St. Building
Newark, OH 43055

New Philadelphia City Health Dept.
166 E. High Ave.
New Philadelphia, OH 44663

Huron County Dept. of Health
Courthouse
Norwalk, OH 44857

Putnam County Health Dept.
Courthouse
Ottawa, OH 45875

Lake County Health Dept.
121 Liberty St.
Painesville, OH 44077

Paulding County Health Dept.
102-A S. Williams St.
Paulding, OH 45879

Piqua Memorial Hospital
Home Care Program
624 Park Ave.
Piqua, OH 45356

Home Health Service
Mulberry Heights
Pomeroy, OH 45769

Scioto Memorial Hospital
Home Care Program
1805 27th St.
Portsmouth, OH 45562

Portage County Health Dept.
225 S. Chestnut
Ravenna, OH 44266

Visiting Nurse Assn.
209 S. Chestnut
Ravenna, OH 44266

Salem Area Visiting Nurse Assn.
180 Penn St.
Salem, OH 44460

Sandusky City-Erie County Health Dept.
Meigs St.
Sandusky, OH 44870

Shelby Public Health League
23 W. Main St.
Shelby, OH 44875

Community Hospital
Home Care Program
2615 E. High St.
Springfield, OH 45501

Dominican Sisters of the Sick Poor
641 E. High St.
Springfield, OH 45505

Steubenville City Health Dept.
205 City Annex Building
Steubenville, OH 43952

Seneca County General Health District
Home Health Agency
Municipal Building
Tiffin, OH 44883

Lucas County Health Dept.
416 N. Erie St.
Toledo, OH 43624

Toledo District Nurse Assn.
635 N. Erie St.
Toledo, OH 43612

Wyandot County Health Dept.
111 W. Walker St.
Upper Sandusky, OH 43351

Van Wert Visiting Nurses' Assn.
704 E. Central Ave.
Van Wert, OH 45895

Auglaize County Health Dept.
15 Willipie St.
Wapakoneta, OH 45895

Warren Visiting Nurse Assn.
636 N. Park
Warren, OH 44483

Fayette County Health Dept.
129 N. Hinde St.
Washington, OH 43160

Pike County Health Dept.
103 E. Third St.
Waverly, OH 45690

Adams County Health Dept.
508 E. Main St.
West Union, OH 45693

Clinton County Health Dept.
P.O. Box 629
Wilmington, OH 45177

HOME HEALTH AGENCIES

Wayne County Home Health Agency
1761 Beall Ave.
Wooster, OH 44691

Greene County Health Dept.
1157 Monroe Dr.
Xenia, OH 45385

Youngstown Visiting Nurse Assn.
518 E. Indianola Ave.
Youngstown, OH 44502

Zanesville-Muskingum County General
   Health District
932 Maple Ave.
Zanesville, OH 43701

OKLAHOMA

Pontotoc County Nursing Service
106 E. 13th St.
Ada, OK 74820

Jackson County Health Dept.
201 S. Lee
Altus, OK 73521

Woods County Nursing Service
324 Seventh St.
Alva, OK 73717

Caddo County Health Dept.
City Hall
Anadarko, OK 73005

Pushmataha County Health Dept.
117 W. Main St.
Antlers, OK 74523

Carter County Health Dept.
107 First Ave., SW
Ardmore, OK 73401

Grady County Health Dept.
Westminister & 22nd St.
Chickasha, OK 73018

Rogers County Nursing Service
108 W. Blue Starr Dr.
Claremore, OK 74017

Nursing Service of Coal County
   Health Dept.
210 N. Main
Coalgate, OK 74538

Bryan County Health Dept.
303 Waco
Durant, OK 74701

Nursing Service of Garfield County
   Health Dept.
2111 Lahoma Rd.
Enid, OK 73701

Nursing Service of McIntosh County
   Health Dept.
215 N. Sixth St.
Eufaula, OK 74432

Logan County Nursing Service
123 N. Broad St.
Guthrie, OK 73044

Texas County Health Dept.
1410 N. East St.
Guymon, OK 73942

Kiowa County Nursing Service
Courthouse Annex
Hobart, OK 73651

Hughes County Health Dept.
300 N. Broadway
Holdenville, OK 73105

Choctaw County Nursing Service
City Hall
Hugo, OK 74743

Delaware County Health Dept.
Jay, OK 74346

Kingfisher County Nursing Service
Courthouse
Kingfisher, OK 73750

Comanche County Health Dept.
1010 S. Sheridan Rd.
Lawton, OK 73501

Marshall County Nursing Service
Second & Overton Sts.
Madill, OK 73446

Love County Nursing Service
101 SW Fourth St.
Marietta, OK 73448

Pittsburg County Nursing Service
Third & Chadick Park
McAlester, OK 74501

Ottawa County Nursing Service
Courthouse
Miami, OK 74354

Muskogee County Nursing Service
519 S. Third St.
Muskogee, OK 74401

Cleveland County Health Dept.
641 E. Robinson, Box 787
Norman, OK 73069

Okfuskee County Health Dept.
112 S. Third St.
Okemah, OK 74859

Oklahoma State Dept. of Health
3400 N. Eastern Ave.
Oklahoma City, OK 73105

Visiting Nurse Assn.
2021 N. Portland
Oklahoma City, OK 73102

Okmulgee County Nursing Service
918 N. Seminole
Okmulgee, OK 74447

Garvin County Health Dept.
220 N. Chickasaw
Pauls Valley, OK 73075

Kay County Nursing Service
1201 E. Hartford
Ponca City, OK 74601

Leflore County Nursing Service
Courthouse Annex
Poteau, OK 74953

Mayes County Nursing Service
102 N. Adair
Pryor, OK 74361

McClain County Nursing Service
City Hall
Purcell, OK 73080

Sequoyah County Nursing Service
109 E. Choctaw St.
Sallisaw, OK 74955

Bartlett Memorial Hospital
Home Health Agency
519 S. Division St.
Sapulpa, OK 74066

Creek County Health Dept.
1020 E. Bryan St.
Sapulpa, OK 74066

Pottawatomie County Nursing Service
Beard & Mission Hills Blvd.
Shawnee, OK 74801

Mary Mahoney Memorial Health
   Center
12500 NE 42nd St.
Spencer, OK 73084

Nursing Service of Haskell County
   Health Dept.
403 NW H St.
Stigler, OK 74462

Payne County Nursing Service
Seventh & Walnut Sts.
Stillwater, OK 74074

Adair County Health Dept.
P.O. Box 223
Stilwell, OK 74960

Murray County Nursing Service
Arbuckle Memorial Hospital
Sulphur, OK 73086

Cherokee County Health Dept.
302 S. College
Tahlequah, OK 74464

Neighborhood Comprehensive Health
   Service
603 E. Pine St.
Tulsa, OK 74106

Tulsa County Public Health Nursing
   Service
4616 E. 15th St.
Tulsa, OK 74101

Craig County Health Dept.
115 E. Delaware Ave.
Vinita, OK 74301

Wagoner County Nursing Service
203 W. Cherokee St.
Wagoner, OK 74467

Cotton County Health Center Nursing
   Service
122 E. Colorado St.
Walters, OK 73572

Seminole County Nursing Service
110-120 W. Fourth St.
Wewoka, OK 74884

Nursing Service of Latimer County
   Health Dept.
P.O. Box 488
Wilburton, OK 74578

OREGON

Linn County Health Dept.
Courthouse Building
Albany, OR 97321

Clatsop County Health Dept.
857 Commercial St.
Astoria, OR 97103

St. Elizabeth Community Hospital
Home Care Program
3325 Pocahontas Rd.
Baker, OR 97814

Tri-County Home Health Agency
Courthouse Building
Bend, OR 97701

Harney County Health Agency
P.O. Box 551
Burns, OR 97720

Benton County Health Dept.
126 N. Fifth St.
Corvallis, OR 97330

Polk County Health Dept.
Courthouse Building
Dallas, OR 97338

Health Services
2815 Potter St.
Eugene, OR 97405

Lane County Home Health Service
740 E. 13th St.
Eugene, OR 97401

Curry County Health Dept.
P.O. Box 696
Gold Beach, OR 97444

Josephine County Health Dept.
P.O. Box 1091
Grants Pass, OR 97526

Washington County Home Health Care Center
323 NE Lincoln St.
Hillsboro, OR 97123

Klamath County Health Dept.
3300 Vandenberg Rd.
Klamath Falls, OR 97601

Lake District Hospital
Home Health Service
700 S. J St.
Lakeview, OR 97630

Yamhill County Health Dept.
Visiting Nurse Service
Fifth & Evans Sts.
McMinnville, OR 97128

Jackson County Health Dept.
1313 Maple Grove Dr.
Medford, OR 97501

Lincoln County Health Dept.
225 W. Olive St.
Newport, OR 97365

Clackamas County Health Dept.
1425 S. Kaen Rd.
Oregon City, OR 97045

St. Anthony Hospital
Home Care Program
1606 SE Court St.
Pendleton, OR 97801

Associated Home Health Service
1715 E. Burnside St.
Portland, OR 97214

Kaiser Foundation Hospital Home Care Program
5055 N. Greeley Ave.
Portland, OR 97217

Visiting Nurse Assn.
621 NE 49th Ave.
Portland, OR 97213

Douglas County Health Dept.
P.O. Box 1146
Roseburg, OR 97470

Columbia District Hospital
Home Care Program
500 N. Columbia River Hwy.
St. Helens, OR 97051

Marion County Health Dept.
2455 Franzen St., NE
Salem, OR 97308

Malheur County Health Dept.
Courthouse Building
Vale, OR 97918

PENNSYLVANIA

Eastern Montgomery County Visiting Nurse Assn.
1421 Highland Ave.
Abington, PA 19001

Aliquippa Hospital
Home Health Program
2500 Hospital Dr.
Aliquippa, PA 15001

Allentown Hospital
Home Care Program
17th & Chew Sts.
Allentown, PA 18102

Lehigh County Public Health Nursing Service
1620 Highland St.
Allentown, PA 18102

North Pennsylvania Visiting Nurse Assn.
219 Race St.
Ambler, PA 18102

Community Health & Civic Assn.
25 E. Athens Ave.
Ardmore, PA 19003

Medical Center of Beaver County
Home Health Agency
900 Third Ave.
Beaver Falls, PA 15010

Bethlehem Visiting Nurse Assn.
520 E. Broad St.
Bethlehem, PA 18018

Columbia Montour Home Health Service
38 W. Main St.
Bloomsburg, PA 17815

North Pennsylvania Home Health Agency
520 Ruah St.
Blossburg, PA 16912

Lower Bucks County Hospital
Home Care Program
Bath Rd. & Orchard Ave.
Bristol, PA 19007

Bryn Mawr Hospital
Home Care Program
Bryn Mawr Ave.
Bryn Mawr, PA 19010

Butler County Visiting Nurses Assn.
921 E. Brady St.
Butler, PA 16001

Carlisle Hospital
Home Care Program
224 Park St.
Carlisle, PA 17013

Franklin County Health Center
518 Cleveland Ave.
Chambersburg, PA 17201

Community Nursing Service & Child Health Center
152 W. Fifth St.
Chester, PA 19013

Crozer-Chester Medical Center
Home Care Program
15th & Upland Ave.
Chester, PA 19013

Clearfield Hospital
Home Health Service Dept.
809 Turnpike Ave.
Clearfield, PA 16830

Coatesville Visiting Nurse Assn.
City Hall Building
Coatesville, PA 19320

Mercy Catholic Medical Center
Home Care Program
Lansdowne Ave. & Baily Rd.
Darby, PA 19023

Bucks County Public Health Visiting Nurse Assn.
Neshaminy Manor Center
Doylestown, PA 18901

Doylestown Hospital
Home Care Program
Belmont Ave. & Spruce St.
Doylestown, PA 18901

Sullivan County Health Center
110 German St.
Dushore, PA 18614

Easton Visiting Nurse Assn.
S Third & Riverside
Easton, PA 18042

Home Health Services of Greater Philadelphia
333 Township Line Rd.
Elkins Park, PA 19117

Visiting Nurse Assn.
319 W. Eighth St.
Erie, PA 16502

HOME HEALTH AGENCIES

Lock Haven Community Service Assn.
100 High St.
Flemington, PA 17745

Venango County Visiting Nurse Assn.
P.O. Box 231
Franklin, PA 16323

Centerville Clinics
Home Health Service
Route 1
Fredericktown, PA 15333

Adams County Visiting Nurse Assn.
453 S. Washington St.
Gettysburg, PA 17325

Westmoreland County Health Center
115 W. Otterman St.
Greensburg, PA 15601

Greenville Hospital
Home Care Program
110 N. Main St.
Greenville, PA 16125

Hanover Visiting Nurse Assn.
217 Broadway
Hanover, PA 17331

Harrisburg Visiting Nurse Assn.
2705 N. Front St.
Harrisburg, PA 17110

Pennsylvania Public Health Nurse
  Service
Commonwealth Ave. & Forster St.
Harrisburg, PA 17108

Home Nursing Agency of Blair County
509 Walnut St.
Hollidaysburg, PA 16648

Holy Redeemer Visiting Nurse Assn.
521 Moredon Rd.
Huntingdon Valley, PA 19006

Indiana County Visiting Nurse Assn.
Indiana Hospital
Indiana, PA 15701

Community Nursing Service
Municipal Building
Jeannette, PA 15644

Johnstown Community Nursing Service
600 Swank Building
Johnstown, PA 15901

McKean County Health Center
2 Thompson Park
Kane, PA 16735

Visiting Nurse Home Care Assn. of
  Lancaster County
630 Janet Ave.
Lancaster, PA 17601

Penn Valley Visiting Nurse Assn.
220 S. Broad St.
Lansdale, PA 19446

Delaware County Community Nursing
  Service
60 S. Lansdowne Ave.
Lansdowne, PA 19050

Carbon County Health Center
209 E. Bertsch St.
Lansford, PA 18232

Latrobe Area Hospital
Home Care Services
Second Ave.
Latrobe, PA 15650

Lebanon County Visiting Nurse Assn.
900 Hauck St.
Lebanon, PA 17042

Community Nursing Service
1034 Grove St.
Meadville, PA 16335

Mechanicsburg Visiting Nurse Assn.
Exchange Place
Mechanicsburg, PA 17055

Mon Valley United Health Services
Visiting Nurse Service
Eastgate 8
Monessen, PA 15062

Susquehanna County Health Center
P.O. Box 92
Montrose, PA 18801

Lawrence County Visiting Nurse Assn.
19 E. Washington St.
New Castle, PA 16101

Home Health Service Miners Clinic
1260 Martin Ave.
New Kensington, PA 15068

Western Westmoreland County
  Visiting Nurse Assn.
2200 Leishman Ave.
New Kensington, PA 15068

Norristown Visiting Nurse Assn.
1109 Dekala St.
Norristown, PA 19401

North East Home Health Agency
58 E. Main St.
North East, PA 16428

Paoli Memorial Hospital Home Care
  Program
W. Lancaster Ave.
Paoli, PA 19301

Upper Perkiomen Valley Nursing
  Agency
Sixth & Dotts Sts.
Pennsburg, PA 18073

Albert Einstein Medical Center Home
  Care Program
York & Tabor Rds.
Philadelphia, PA 19141

Homemaker Service
Home Health Division
1015 Chestnut St.
Philadelphia, PA 19107

Lankenau Hospital
Home Care Program
705 E. Taylor
Philadelphia, PA 19151

Pernet Family Health Service
1001 S. 47th St.
Philadelphia, PA 19143

Philadelphia Community Nursing
  Service
500 Broad St., S.
Philadelphia, PA 19146

Philadelphia General Hospital
Home Care Program
34th St. & Civic Center Blvd.
Philadelphia, PA 19104

University of Pennsylvania Home
  Care Program
19th & Lombard Sts.
Philadelphia, PA 19146

Northern Chester County Community
  Nurse Service
301 Gay St.
Phoenixville, PA 19460

Allegheny County Visiting Nurse
  Assn.
815 Union Place
Pittsburgh, PA 15219

Allegheny General Hospital
Home Care Program
320 E. North Ave.
Pittsburgh, PA 15212

Homewood-Brushton Home Health
  Agency
7227 Hamilton Ave.
Pittsburgh, PA 15208

Montefiore Hospital
Home Care Program
3459 Fifth Ave.
Pittsburgh, PA 15213

St. Francis General Hospital
Home Health Program
Penn Ave. & 45th St.
Pittsburgh, PA 15201

South Hills Health System Home
  Health Agency
1800 West St.
Pittsburgh, PA 15120

Western Pennsylvania Hospital
Home Health Agency
4800 Friendship Ave.
Pittsburgh, PA 15224

Pottstown Visiting Nurse Assn.
1035 High St.
Pottstown, PA 19464

Schuylkill County Health Center
433 S. Centre St.
Pottsville, PA 17901

Adrian Hospital Home Health Care
  Service
Jenks & Park Aves.
Punxsutawney, PA 15767

Reading & Berks County Visiting
  Nurse Assn.
220 N. Fifth St.
Reading, PA 19601

Red Lion Visiting Nurse Assn.
19 W. Broadway
Red Lion, PA 17356

Community Nurse Service
159 Main St.
Ridgway, PA 15853

Elk County Health Center
222 Race St.
Ridgway, PA 15853

St. Marys Visiting Nurse Assn.
319 Erie Ave.
St. Marys, PA 15857

Visiting Nurse Assn. & Home Health
    Maintenance Organization
615 Jefferson Ave.
Scranton, PA 18510

Sewickley Valley Hospital
Home Care Program
Exchange Place
Sewickley, PA 15143

Shamokin Visiting Nurse Assn.
618 W. Walnut St.
Shamokin, PA 17872

Sun Home Nursing Services
P.O. Box 206
Shamokin Dam, PA 17876

Sharon General Hospital
Home Care Program
740 E. State St.
Sharon, PA 16146

Visiting Nurse Assn. of Monroe County
7 N. Eighth St.
Shroudsburg, PA 18360

Visiting Nurse Assn.
86 S. Main St.
Spring Grove, PA 17363

Crawford County Health Center
123 E. Main St.
Titusville, PA 16354

Bradford County Health Center
387 York Ave., Extended
Towanda, PA 18848

Fayette County Health Center
50 W. Main St.
Uniontown, PA 15401

Kiski Valley Visiting Nurse Assn.
200 N. Warren Ave.
Vandergrift, PA 15690

Warren General Hospital Visiting
    Nurse Service
2-12 Crescent Park
Warren, PA 16365

Central Washington County Visiting
    Nurse Assn.
850 Beech Ave.
Washington, PA 15301

Washington County Health Center
83 E. Maiden Ave.
Washington, PA 15301

Neighborhood League Visiting Nurse
    Service
119 W. Wayne Ave.
Wayne, PA 19087

Greene County Health Center
Democrat Messenger Building
Waynesburg, PA 15370

Central Chester County Visiting
    Nurse Assn.
121 W. Union St.
West Chester, PA 19380

Chester County Health Dept.
Home Health Agency
326 N. Walnut St.
West Chester, PA 19380

Home Health Services of Lucerne
    County
71 N. Franklin St.
Wilkes-Barre, PA 18701

Lycoming County Visiting Nurse
    Assn.
912 W. Fourth St.
Williamsport, PA 17701

York County Visiting Nurse Assn.
218 E. Market St.
York, PA 17403

PUERTO RICO

Aibonito Home Care Program
Rius Rivera 102
Aibonito, PR 00609

St. Luke's Episcopal Hospital
Home Care Program
Rd. 63, Hectometer 1
Arecibo, PR 00612

St. Luke's Episcopal Hospital
Home Care Program
Lomas Verdes Ave.
Bayamon, PR 00619

Castaner Home Care Program
Castaner, PR 00631

Coamo Home Care Program
5 Carrion Madero St.
Coamo, PR 00640

Guayama Home Care Program
Calle Vicente Pales 23 Oeste
Guayama, PR 00654

Assn. for Comprehensive Visiting
    Nurse Service
Ave. Manuel V. Domenech 255
Hato Rey, PR 00918

Ryder Memorial Hospital
Home Care Program
46 Font Martelo St.
Humacao, PR 00661

Juana Diaz Home Care Program
Calle Munoz Rivera 70
Juana Diaz, PR 00655

St. Luke's Episcopal Hospital
Home Care Program
200 Guadalupe St.
Ponce, PR 00731

Visiting Health Care Service Program
P.O. Box 1910
Ponce, PR 00731

Salinas Home Care Program
Guayama St., No. 6
Salinas, PR 00751

Yauco Home Care Program
Edificio Gerardino 65, Infanteria
Yauco, PR 00678

RHODE ISLAND

Washington County Public Health
    Nursing Assn.
P.O. Box 24
Alton, RI 02803

Little Compton Public Health Nursing
    Assn.
The Commons
Little Compton, RI 02837

Narrangansett Public Health Nursing
    Assn.
Fifth Ave.
Narragansett, RI 02882

Newport Visiting Nurse Service
21 Chapel St.
Newport, RI 02840

Northwest Community Nursing &
    Health Service
Bridgeway
Pascoag, RI 02859

Memorial Hospital
Home Care Dept.
Prospect St.
Pawtucket, RI 02860

Pawtucket Visiting Nurse Service
226 Cottage St.
Pawtucket, RI 02863

Home Care Assn. of Greater
    Providence, Inc.
157 Waterman St.
Providence, RI 02906

Metropolitan Nursing & Health
    Services Assn.
157 Waterman St.
Providence, RI 02906

East Shore District Nursing Assn.
624 Main St.
Warren, RI 02885

Kent County Memorial Hospital
Home Care Program
455 Toll Gate Rd.
Warwick, RI 02886

Kent County Visiting Nurses Assn.
2977 W. Shore Rd.
Warwick, RI 02886

Westerly Hospital
Home Care Program
Wells St.
Westerly, RI 02891

Greater Woonsocket Visiting Nurse
    Service
383 Arnold St.
Woonsocket, RI 02895

SOUTH CAROLINA

Hitchcock Rehabilitation Center
721 Richland Ave., W.
Aiken, SC 29801

Lower Savannah District I
736 Richland Ave.
Aiken, SC 29801

Appalachia I Home Health Services
P.O. Box 1906
Anderson, SC 29621

Trident Home Health Services
334 Calhoun St.
Charleston, SC 29401

Central Midlands Home Health Service
J. Marion Sims Building
Columbia, SC 29201

South Carolina State Board of Health
2600 Bull St.
Columbia, SC 29201

Pee Dee Home Health Service
306 S. Graham St.
Florence, SC 29501

Home Health Services Section,
  Waccamaw District
Hazard St., Box 397
Georgetown, SC 29440

Appalachia II Home Health Service
200 University Ridge
Greenville, SC 29602

Upper Savannah Home Health Services
P.O. Box 797
Greenwood, SC 29646

Hampton County Health Dept.
Home Health Service
Highway 278
Hampton, SC 29924

Catawba District Home Health Service
Catawba & Dunlap Sts.
Lancaster, SC 29720

Appalachia III
Home Health Services
151 E. Wood St.
Spartanburg, SC 29303

Lower Savannah II
Home Health Services
151 E. Wood St.
Spartanburg, SC 29115

Wateree Home Health Services
P.O. Box 1628
Sumter, SC 29150

Union County Health Dept.
Thompson Blvd.
Union, SC 29379

Colleton County Health Dept.
115 Benson St.
Walterboro, SC 29488

York County Health Dept.
Main St.
York, SC 29745

SOUTH DAKOTA

Brown County Home Health Agency
Municipal Building
Aberdeen, SD 57401

Brookings County Home Health
  Agency
County Courthouse
Brookings, SD 57006

Lincoln County Home Health Agency
County Courthouse
Canton, SD 57013

Union County Home Health Agency
County Courthouse
Elk Point, SD 57025

Moody County Home Health Agency
Flandreau, SD 57028

Hamlin County Home Health Agency
County Courthouse
Hayti, SD 57241

Hyde County Home Health Agency
County Courthouse
Highmore, SD 57345

St. John Regional Medical Center
Fourth & Iowa
Huron, SD 57350

Lake County Home Health Agency
County Courthouse
Madison, SD 57042

Grant County Home Health Agency
County Courthouse
Milbank, SD 57252

Davison County Home Health Agency
County Courthouse
Mitchell, SD 57301

Turner County Home Health Agency
County Courthouse
Parker, SD 57053

Division Public Health Nursing
Home Health Agency Unit III
State Capitol
Pierre, SD 57501

Division of Nursing
Home Health Agency
615 Kansas City St.
Rapid City, SD 57701

Minnehaha County Visiting Nurses
  Assn.
2116 S. Minnesota Ave.
Sioux Falls, SD 57105

Meade County Home Health Agency
County Courthouse
Sturgis, SD 57785

Clay County Home Health Agency
County Courthouse
Vermillion, SD 57069

Dakota Hospital
Home Care Program
801 E. Main St.
Vermillion, SD 57069

Codington County Home Health
  Agency
Watertown, SD 57201

Day County Home Health Agency
County Courthouse
Webster, SD 57274

Sacred Heart Hospital
Home Care Program
W. Fourth St.
Yankton, SD 57078

Yankton County Home Health Agency
County Courthouse
Yankton, SD 57078

TENNESSEE

Crockett County Health Dept.
308 E. Church St.
Alamo, TN 38001

Grundy County Health Dept.
Box 65
Altamount, TN 373701

Cheatham County Health Dept.
Main St.
Ashland City, TN 37015

McMinn County Health Dept.
107 College St., NW
Athens, TN 37303

Polk County Health Dept.
P.O. Drawer 269
Benton, TN 37307

Sullivan County Health Dept.
Blountville, TN 37617

Hardeman County Health Dept.
Nursing Division
301 E. Jackson St.
Bolivar, TN 38008

Haywood County Health Dept.
110 Wilson St.
Brownsville, TN 38012

Pickett County Health Dept.
Byrdstown, TN 38549

Benton County Home Health Agency
113 Maple St.
Camden, TN 38320

Smith County Health Dept.
High St.
Carthage, TN 37030

Clay County Health Dept.
Brown St.
Celina, TN 38551

Hickman County Health Dept.
College Ave.
Centerville, TN 37033

Alton Park Family Health Center
200 E. 37th St.
Chattanooga, TN 37410

Chattanooga-Hamilton County
  Health Dept.
Chattanooga, TN 37403

134 THE OLDER AMERICAN'S HANDBOOK

Montgomery County Health Dept.
Division of Public Health Nursing
1606 Haynes St.
Clarksville, TN 37040

Bradley County Health Dept.
Cleveland, TN 37311

Anderson County Health Dept.
141 E. Broad St.
Clinton, TN 37716

Maury County Health Dept.
P.O. Box 790
Columbia, TN 38401

Putnam County Home Health Agency
121 S. Dixie
Cookeville, TN 38501

Tipton County Health Dept.
Church St.
Covington, TN 38019

Cumberland County Health Dept.
Hayes & Webb St.
Crossville, TN 38555

Jefferson County Health Dept.
Dandridge, TN 37725

Rhea County Health Dept.
Walnut Grove Rd.
Dayton, TN 37321

Meigs County Health Dept.
Watts Bar Rd.
Decatur, TN 37322

Dickson County Health Dept.
117 Academy St.
Dickson, TN 37055

Stewart County Health Dept.
Dover, TN 37058

Sequatchie County Health Dept.
Dunlap, TN 37327

Dyer County Health Dept.
Dyersburg, TN 38024

Carter County Health Dept.
Elizabethton, TN 37643

Houston County Health Dept.
Division of Public Health Nursing
County Courthouse
Erin, TN 37061

Unicoi County Health Dept.
P.O. Box 339
Erwin, TN 37650

Lincoln County Health Dept.
Fayetteville, TN 37334

Williamson County Health Dept.
Franklin, TN 37064

Jackson County Health Dept.
Gainesboro, TN 38562

Sumner County Health Dept.
411 S. Water St.
Gallatin, TN 37066

Greene County Health Dept.
Greeneville, TN 37743

Chester County Health Dept.
159 E. Main St.
Henderson, TN 38340

Lewis County Health Dept.
P.O. Box 112
Hohenwald, TN 38462

Carroll County Health Dept.
West Paris St.
Huntingdon, TN 38344

Scott County Health Dept.
Huntsville, TN 37756

Campbell County Health Dept.
Jackson, TN 37757

Home Health Services of Madison
County
131 Tucker St.
Jackson, TN 38301

Jackson-Madison County Health Dept.
745 W. Forest
Jackson, TN 38301

Fentress County Health Dept.
P.O. Box 636
Jamestown, TN 38556

Marion County Health Dept.
Gamble Lane
Jasper, TN 37347

Washington County Health Dept.
P.O. Box 67
Jonesboro, TN 37659

Roane County Health Dept.
Kingston, TN 37763

Home Health Care Services
605 Walnut St.
Knoxville, TN 37902

Knox County Health Dept.
Knoxville, TN 37901

Your Home Visiting Nurse Service
703 Cherry St.
Knoxville, TN 37914

Macon County Health Dept.
Lafayette, TN 37083

Lawrence County General Hospital
Home Care Program
374 Brink St.
Lawrenceburg, TN 38464

Wilson County Health Dept.
East Spring St.
Lebanon, TN 37087

Marshall County Health Dept.
206 Legion St.
Lewisburg, TN 37091

Perry County Health Dept.
Mill St.
Linden, TN 37096

Overton County Health Dept.
Livingston, TN 38570

Loudon County Health Dept.
501 Mulberry St.
Loudon, TN 37774

Moore County Health Dept.
Lynchburg, TN 37352

Monroe County Health Dept.
Madisonville, TN 37354

Coffee County Health Dept.
Manchester, TN 37355

Blount County Health Dept.
Maryville, TN 37801

Union County Health Dept.
P.O. Box 9
Maynardville, TN 37807

Warren County Health Dept.
McMinnville, TN 37130

Home Health Services of Memphis
3100 Walnut Grove Rd.
Memphis, TN 38111

Memphis-Shelby County Health Dept.
814 Jefferson Ave.
Memphis, TN 38105

Memphis Visiting Nurse Assn.
283 N. Bellevue
Memphis, TN 38105

Mid-South Comprehensive Home
Health Service
43 N. Cleveland
Memphis, TN 38104

Hamblen County Health Dept.
Morristown, TN 37814

Johnson County Health Dept.
College St.
Mountain City, TN 37683

Rutherford County Health Dept.
Murfreesboro, TN 37130

Metropolitan Health Dept.
311 23rd Ave., N.
Nashville, TN 37203

Cocke County Health Dept.
Newport, TN 37821

Public Health & Welfare Dept.
Tulane Ave.
Oak Ridge, TN 37830

Henry County Health Dept.
614 N. Poplar St.
Paris, TN 38242

Decatur County Home Health Agency
1001 Tennessee Ave., S.
Parsons, TN 38363

Bledsoe County Health Dept.
Pikeville, TN 37367

Giles County Health Dept.
Pulaski, TN 38478

Lauderdale County Health Dept.
Courthouse Building
Ripley, TN 38063

Hawkins County Health Dept.
Rogersville, TN 37857

Grainger County Health Dept.
P.O. Box 27
Rutledge, TN 37861

HOME HEALTH AGENCIES

Hardin County Health Dept.
1916 Davis St.
Savannah, TN 38372

McNairy County Health Dept.
Courthouse Building
Selmer, TN 38375

Sevier County Health Dept.
Sevierville, TN 37862

Bedford County Health Dept.
Union St.
Shelbyville, TN 37160

De Kalb County Health Dept.
Smithville, TN 37166

Hancock County Home Health Agency
P.O. Box 102
Sneedville, TN 37869

Fayette County Health Dept.
P.O. Box 188
Somerville, TN 38068

White County Health Dept.
Walker St.
Sparta, TN 38583

Van Buren County Health Dept.
Spencer, TN 38585

Robertson County Health Dept.
Springfield, TN 37172

Clairborne County Health Dept.
Irish Cemetery Rd.
Tazewell, TN 37819

Gibson County Health Dept.
200 E. Eaton St.
Trenton, TN 38382

Obion County Health Dept.
1402 Church St.
Union City, TN 38261

Morgan County Health Dept.
Wartburg, TN 37887

Humphreys County Health Dept.
208 Wyly St.
Waverly, TN 37185

Wayne County Health Dept.
Waynesboro, TN 38485

Franklin County Health Dept.
1007 First Ave., NE
Winchester, TN 37398

Cannon County Health Dept.
Woodbury, TN 37190

TEXAS

Abilene-Taylor County Health Dept.
2241 S. 19th St.
Abilene, TX 79605

Visiting Nurse Assn. of Brazoria County
810 W. Lang St.
Alvin, TX 77511

Amarillo Bi-County City Health Unit
411 Austin St.
Amarillo, TX 79105

Schlesinger Home Health Service Agency
502 Richardson
Athens, TX 75751

Austin-Travis County Health Unit
1313 Sabine St.
Austin, TX 78726

Girling & Associates Home Health Service
4205 Marathon
Austin, TX 78756

Schlesinger Home Health Service Agency
600 W. 28th St.
Austin, TX 78705

Mainland Home Nursing Services
4728 Second St.
Bacliff, TX 77518

Beaumont Home Health Service
3155 Stagg Dr.
Beaumont, TX 77704

Schlesinger Home Health Service Agency
2870 Laurel
Beaumont, TX 77702

Texas Home Health Agency Visiting Nurse Service
127 N. San Jacinto
Cleveland, TX 77327

Cen-Tex Home Care Service
218 N. Ave. D
Clifton, TX 76634

Visiting Nurse Assn. of Montgomery County, Inc.
310 S. First
Conroe, TX 77301

Schlesinger Home Health Service Agency
3166 Reid Dr.
Corpus Christi, TX 78404

Dallas Visiting Nurse Assn.
4606 Greenville Ave.
Dallas, TX 75206

Home Care of Dallas
2707 Gaston Ave.
Dallas, TX 75203

Home Health Services of Dallas, Inc.
2639 Walnut Hill Lane
Dallas, TX 75229

Maverick County Hospital District Home Care Program
Ft. Duncan Area
Eagle Pass, TX 78852

Hidalgo County Home Health Services
1425 S. Ninth St.
Edinburg, TX 78539

El Paso Visiting Nurse Assn.
5732-B Trowbridge Dr.
El Paso, TX 79925

North Central Texas Home Health Agency
6601 Wrigley Way
Ft. Worth, TX 76133

Tarrant County Home Care Program
1500 S. Main St.
Ft. Worth, TX 76104

Home Health Service Dept.
1115 N. MacGregor
Houston, TX 77025

Houston Visiting Nurse Assn.
3410 Montrose Blvd.
Houston, TX 77006

Schlesinger Home Health Service Agency
Huntsville-Conroe Branch
1520 Eleventh St.
Huntsville, TX 77340

Cherokee Home Health Care Center
Route 3 & Antioch Rd.
Jacksonville, TX 75766

Schlesinger Home Health Service Agency
804 W. Larissa St.
Jacksonville, TX 75766

Schlesinger Home Health Service Agency
P.O. Box 976
Liberty, TX 77575

West Texas Home Health Agency
2161 50th St.
Lubbock, TX 79412

Madison County Hospital Home Care Program
100 W. Cross St.
Madisonville, TX 77864

Schlesinger Home Health Service Agency
312 W. Fourth St.
Odessa, TX 79761

Jones Home Health Agency
3000 Cardinal
Orange, TX 77630

Schlesinger Home Health Service Agency
1406 W. Park St.
Orange, TX 77630

Home Health
Home Care
3409 Spencer Hwy.
Pasadena, TX 77587

Port Arthur Home Health Service
3039 39th St.
Port Arthur, TX 77640

Schlesinger Home Health Service Agency
3649 Professional Dr.
Port Arthur, TX 77640

Valley Home Health Agency
1525 Sixth St.
Raymondville, TX 78580

Schlesinger Home Health Service
  Agency
22 S. Magdalen
San Angelo, TX 76901

San Antonio Metropolitan Health
  District Nursing Service
131 W. Nueva St.
San Antonio, TX 78204

Visiting Nurse Assn. of San Antonio
214 Dwyer Ave.
San Antonio, TX 78205

West Texas Home Health Agency
Seymour Branch
Stadium Dr.
Seymour, TX 76380

Denison-Sherman-Grayson County
  Health Dept.
P.O. Box 1295
Sherman, TX 75090

Texas Home Health of Silsbee
1180 Railroad
Silsbee, TX 77656

Greater Texarkana Visiting Nurse
  Assn.
708 W. Ninth St.
Texarkana, TX 75501

Schlesinger Home Health Service
  Agency
780 S. Beckman
Tyler, TX 75701

Victoria Home Health Agency
107 W. River
Victoria, TX 77901

Victoria Home Health Care Service
305 E. Santa Rosa
Victoria, TX 77901

Waco-McClennan County Home
  Health Care Service
225 W. Waco Dr.
Waco, TX 76707

Wichita Home Health Service
1500 Eighth St.
Wichita Falls, TX 76301

UTAH

Iron County Home Health Agency
595 S. 75 E.
Cedar City, UT 84720

Davis County Health Dept.
County Courthouse
Farmington, UT 84025

Piute County Home Health Agency
Junction, UT 84740

Bear River Home Health Agency
160 N. Main St.
Logan, UT 84321

McKay-Dee Home Care Program
2440 Harrison Blvd.
Ogden, UT 84403

Southeastern Utah Home Health
  Agency
6 E. Main St.
Price, UT 84501

Utah County Home Health Services
107 City & County Building
Provo, UT 84601

Community Nursing Service
1370 SW Temple St.
Salt Lake City, UT 84105

VERMONT

Central Vermont Home Health
18 S. Main St.
Barre, VT 05641

Bennington Home Health Agency
310 Main St.
Bennington, VT 05201

Brattleboro Public Health Nursing
  Service
15 Western Ave.
Brattleboro, VT 05301

Visiting Nurse Assn. of Burlington,
  Inc.
260 College St.
Burlington, VT 05401

Ellsworth Nursing Service
Main St.
Chester, VT 05143

Dorset Nursing Assn.
P.O. Box 52
Dorset, VT 05251

Manchester Welfare & Nursing Assn.
Main St.
Manchester Center, VT 05255

Addison County Home Health Agency
Porter Medical Center
Middlebury, VT 05753

Lamoille Home Health Agency
Washington Hwy.
Morrisville, VT 05661

Orleans & Northern Essex Home
  Health Agency, Inc.
103 Main St.
Newport, VT 05855

Rutland Area Visiting Nurse Assn.
15 E. Washington St.
Rutland, VT 05701

Franklin County Home Health Agency
St. Albans Hospital
St. Albans, VT 05478

Caledonia Home Health Care Agency
8 Summer St.
St. Johnsbury, VT 05819

Springfield Visiting Nurse Service
2 Summer St.
Springfield, VT 05156

Waterbury Public Health Assn., Inc.
87 S. Main St.
Waterbury, VT 05676

Community Health Services, Inc.
Box 411
White River Junction, VT 05001

Woodstock Visiting Nurse & Public
  Health Society, Inc.
32 Pleasant St.
Woodstock, VT 05091

VIRGINIA

Washington County Health Dept.
234 W. Valley St.
Abingdon, VA 24210

Alexandria City Health Dept.
517 N. St. Asaph St.
Alexandria, VA 22314

Arlington County Dept. of Human
  Resources
1800 N. Edison St.
Arlington, VA 22207

Northern Virginia Visiting Nurse Assn.
5055 S. Chesterfield Rd.
Arlington, VA 22206

Mecklenburg County Health Dept.
P.O. Box 97
Boydton, VA 23917

Bristol City Health Dept.
North St.
Bristol, VA 24201

Charlottesville City Health Dept.
1138 Rose Hill Dr.
Charlottesville, VA 22902

Chesapeake City Health Dept.
300 Cedar Rd.
Chesapeake, VA 23320

Chesterfield County Health Dept.
Chesterfield, VA 23832

Montgomery County Health Dept.
P.O. Box 449
Christiansburg, VA 24073

Danville City Health Dept.
1057 Main St.
Danville, VA 24541

Greensville County Health Dept.
P.O. Box 306
Emporia, VA 23847

Fairfax County Health Dept.
3750 Old Lee Hwy.
Fairfax, VA 22030

Visiting Nurse Assn.
P.O. Box 477
Fairfax, VA 22030

Prince Edward County Health Dept.
P.O. Box 347
Farmville, VA 23901

Fredericksburg City Health Dept.
435 Hunter St.
Fredericksburg, VA 22401

Scott County Health Dept.
Route 1
Gate City, VA 24251

HOME HEALTH AGENCIES 137

Hampton City Health Dept.
3130 Victoria Blvd.
Hampton, VA 23361

Hanover County Health Dept.
116 N. Center St.
Hanover, VA 23069

King & Queen County Health Dept.
King & Queen Court House, VA 23085

Loudoun County Health Dept.
18 N. King St.
Leesburg, VA 22075

Louisa County Health Dept.
McDonald St.
Louisa, VA 23093

Lynchburg City Health Dept.
701 Hollins St.
Lynchburg, VA 24504

Prince William County Health Dept.
500 Lee Ave.
Manassas, VA 22110

Martinsville City Health Dept.
P.O. Box 1028
Martinsville, VA 24112

Northampton County Health Dept.
Cross St.
Nassawadox, VA 23413

Newport News City Health Dept.
210 26th St.
Newport News, VA 23607

Norfolk City Health Dept.
401 Colley Ave.
Norfolk, VA 23507

Orange County Health Dept.
350 Madison Rd.
Orange, VA 22960

Petersburg City Health Dept.
35 W. Fillmore St.
Petersburg, VA 23803

Portsmouth City Health Dept.
439 Green St.
Portsmouth, VA 23705

Instructive Visiting Nurse Assn.
City Nursing Service
223 S. Cherry St.
Richmond, VA 23220

Richmond City Health Dept.
500 N. Tenth St.
Richmond, VA 23219

Virginia Dept. of Health
109 Governor St.
Richmond, VA 23219

Roanoke City Health Dept.
516 Eighth St., SW
Roanoke, VA 24016

Salem City Health Dept.
510 S. College Ave.
Salem, VA 24153

Middlesex County Health Dept.
Saluda, VA 23149

Staunton City Health Dept.
1410 N. Augusta St.
Staunton, VA 24401

Suffolk City Health Dept.
P.O. Box 1587
Suffolk, VA 23434

Tazewell County Health Dept.
P.O. Box 561
Tazewell, VA 24651

Virginia Beach City Health Dept.
16th St. & Arctic Ave.
Virginia Beach, VA 23451

Richmond County Health Dept.
110-12 Main St.
Warsaw, VA 22527

Williamsburg City Health Dept.
1216 Richmond Rd.
Williamsburg, VA 23185

Winchester City Health Dept.
150 Commercial St.
Winchester, VA 22601

Wythe County Health Dept.
140 S. First St.
Wytheville, VA 24382

WASHINGTON

Grays Harbor-Pacific Health District
223 Finch Building
Aberdeen, WA 98520

Bellingham Visiting Nurse Assn.
210 Lottie St.
Bellingham, WA 98225

Kitsap Bremerton County Health
  District
109 Austin Dr.
Bremerton, WA 98310

St. Helen Hospital
Home Care Program
1332 Washington
Chehalis, WA 98532

Island County Health Dept.
P.O. Box 218
Coupeville, WA 98239

Kittitas County Health Dept.
507 Nanum
Ellensburg, WA 98926

Snohomish County Visiting Nurse
  Assn.
2202 Colby Ave.
Everett, WA 98201

Cowlitz-Wahkiakum Counties District
Courthouse Building
Kelso, WA 98626

Skagit County Health Dept.
Courthouse Building
Mt. Vernon, WA 98273

Thurston-Mason Health District
Courthouse Building
Olympia, WA 98501

Benton-Franklin County Health District
1218 N. 4th
Pasco, WA 99301

Good Samaritan Hospital
Home Care Program
407 14th Ave., SE
Puyallup, WA 98371

Ballard Community Hospital
Home Care Program
5409 Barnes Ave., NW
Seattle, WA 98107

Home Health Services of King County
7109 Woodlawn Ave., NE
Seattle, WA 98115

Puget Sound Group Health Coop
Home Health Agency
200 15th Ave., E.
Seattle, WA 98102

Seattle-King County Visiting Nurse
  Service
1700 E. Cherry
Seattle, WA 98122

St. Luke's Memorial Hospital
Home Care Program
S. 711 Cowley St.
Spokane, WA 99202

Spokane County Health District
819 N. Jefferson St.
Spokane, WA 99201

Spokane Public Health Visiting Nurse
  Service
N. 812 Monroe St.
Spokane, WA 99208

Tacoma-Pierce County Public Health
  Dept.
930 Tacoma Ave., S.
Tacoma, WA 98402

Southwest Washington Health District
12th & Franklin Sts.
Vancouver, WA 98660

St. Mary's Community Hospital
Home Care Program
Fifth & Poplar
Walla Walla, WA 98362

Central Washington Deaconess Hospital
Home Health Agency
325 Okanogan Ave.
Wenatchee, WA 98801

Yakima County Health District
Home Health Agency
104 N. First St.
Yakima, WA 98901

WEST VIRGINIA

Mountaineer Family Health Plan
P.O. Box 1149
Beckley, WV 25801

Southern West Virginia Regional
Home Health Program
Route 2
Bluefield, WV 24701

Aupshur County Home Health Agency
26 N. Kanawha St.
Buckhannon, WV 26201

Kanawha-Charleston Health Dept. &
  Visiting Nurse Assn.
404 City Building
Charleston, WV 25301

Harrison-Clarksburg Health Dept.
301 W. Main St.
Clarksburg, WV 26301

Family Health Service
Fourth St.
Elkins, WV 26241

Marion County Health Dept.
300 Second St.
Fairmont, WV 26554

MVA Home Health Service
Fairmont Clinic Building
Fairmont, WV 26554

Tri-County Visiting Nurse Assn.
Home Health Agency
948 Main St.
Follansbee, WV 26037

Taylor County Health Dept.
1336 16th St.
Huntington, WV 25701

Man Appalachian Regional Hospital
Home Health Agency
600-800 E. McDonald Ave.
Man, WV 25635

Monongalia County Health Dept.
Van Voorhis Rd.
Morgantown, WV 26505

Wetzel-Tyler Home Health Agency
240 North St.
New Martinsville, WV 26155

Wood Parkersburg Health Dept.
314 Third St.
Parkersburg, WV 26101

Mountaintop Home Health Agency
P.O. Box 1
Thomas, WV 26292

Lewis County Home Health Agency
214 Bank St.
Weston, WV 26452

Ohio County Visiting Nurse Assn.
South Wheeling Bank Building
Wheeling, WV 26003

Williamson Appalachian Region
  Hospital
Home Health Agency
Mounted Route 2
Williamson, WV 25661

WISCONSIN

Buffalo County Home Health Agency
Courthouse
Alma, WI 54610

Langlade County Home Nursing Care
  Service
Courthouse
Antigo, WI 54409

Appleton Visiting Nurse Assn.
718 W. Fifth St.
Appleton, WI 54911

Ashland County Home Health Agency
201 Second St., W.
Ashland, WI 54806

Polk County Home Care Program
Courthouse Annex
Balsam Lake, WI 54810

Sauk County Home Nursing Care
  Program
P.O. Box 30
Baraboo, WI 53913

Barron County Home Care Program
Courthouse
Barron, WI 54812

Greater Beloit Home Nursing Service
220 W. Grand Ave.
Beloit, WI 53511

Jackson County Nursing Service Agency
221 Main St.
Black River Falls, WI 54615

Chippewa County Nursing Service
711 Bridge St.
Chippewa Falls, WI 54729

Trinity Memorial Hospital
Home Care Program
5900 S. Lake Dr.
Cudahy, WI 53110

Lafayette County Community Health
  Nursing Service
626 Main St.
Darlington, WI 53530

Pepin County Nursing Service
315 W. Main St.
Durand, WI 54736

Eau Clair City Health Dept.
414 E. Grand Ave.
Eau Claire, WI 54701

Eau Claire Visiting Nurse Assn.
1300 First Ave.
Eau Claire, WI 54701

Walworth County Home Nursing
  Care Program
Walworth St.
Elkhorn, WI 53121

Pierce County Home Care Program
Courthouse
Ellsworth, WI 54011

Fond du Lac County Home Health
  Service
190 S. Main St.
Fond du Lac, WI 54935

Green Bay Curative Workshop
342 S. Webster Ave.
Green Bay, WI 54303

Green Bay Visiting Nurse Assn.
1550 Dousman St.
Green Bay, WI 54303

Green Lake County Nursing Service
Courthouse
Green Lake, WI 54941

St. Croix County Home Nursing Care
  Program
Red Brick Building
Hammond, WI 54015

Sawyer County Home Health Agency
406 Iowa Ave.
Hayward, WI 54843

Iron County Home Nursing Care
  Program
Courthouse
Hurley, WI 54534

Visiting Nurse Assn.
City Hall
Janesville, WI 53545

Jefferson County Nursing Service
Courthouse Annex
Jefferson, WI 53549

Dodge County Home Nursing Care
  Service
Courthouse
Juneau, WI 53039

Kenosha Visiting Nurse Assn.
6036 Eighth Ave.
Kenosha, WI 53140

LaCrosse City Health Dept.
City Hall
LaCrosse, WI 54601

LaCrosse County Home Health
  Nursing Service
Courthouse
LaCrosse, WI 54601

Grant County Home Nursing Service
Courthouse
Lancaster, WI 53813

Dane County Health Dept.
210 Monona Ave.
Madison, WI 53709

Visiting Nurse Assn.
2059 Atwood Ave.
Madison, WI 53704

Manitowoc County Nursing Service
Courthouse
Manitowoc, WI 54220

Marinette County Public Health
  Nursing Service
1926 Hall Ave.
Marinette, WI 54143

Juneau County Nursing Service
Courthouse
Mauston, WI 53948

Dunn County Home Care Program
Menominie, WI 54751

Mequon Home Nursing Service
11333 N. Cedarburg Rd.
Mequon, WI 53092

Milwaukee Curative Workshop
750 N. 18th St.
Milwaukee, WI 53233

Mt. Sinai Hospital
Home Care Program
948 N. 12th St.
Milwaukee, WI 53233

Visiting Nurse Assn.
1540 N. Jefferson St.
Milwaukee, WI 53202

Green County Home Nursing Care
 Agency
Courthouse
Monroe, WI 53566

Marquette County Nursing Service
Courthouse
Montello, WI 53949

Neenah-Manasha Visiting Nurse Assn.
406 E. Wisconsin St.
Neenah, WI 54956

Clark County Home Care Agency
Courthouse
Neillsville, WI 54456

Oconto County Home Nursing Program
Courthouse
Oconto, WI 54153

Oshkosh Visiting Nurse Assn.
726 Cherry St.
Oshkosh, WI 54901

Winnebago County Home Nursing
 Service
415 Jackson St.
Oshkosh, WI 54901

Price County Home Nursing Agency
Phillips, WI 54555

Columbia County Public Health Service
DeWitt St.
Portage, WI 53901

Memorial Hospital Home Care Program
705 E. Taylor St.
Prairie du Chien, WI 53821

Racine Curative Workshop
2335 North Western Ave.
Racine, WI 53404

Oneida County Home Nursing Service
Courthouse
Rhinelander, WI 54501

Richland County Public Health
 Nursing Service
P.O. Box 404
Richland Center, WI 53581

Shawano County Nursing Service
Courthouse
Shawano, WI 54166

Visiting Nurse Assn.
1825 Erie Ave.
Sheboygan, WI 53081

Monroe County Home Health Nursing
 Service
Box 354, Courthouse
Sparta, WI 54656

Door County Nursing Service
Courthouse
Sturgeon Bay, WI 54235

Bayfield County Hone Nursing Service
117 E. Fifth St.
Washburn, WI 54891

Visiting Nurse Assn. of Greater
 Waukesha Area
500 Prospect Ave.
Waukesha, WI 53186

Waupaca County Home Nursing
 Service
Waupaca, WI 54981

Marathon County Nursing Service
Courthouse
Wausau, WI 54401

Wausau Visiting Nurse Assn.
1322 Grand Ave.
Wausau, WI 54401

Waushara County Home Health
 Agency
County Highway Building
Wautoma, WI 54982

Washington County Public Health
 Nursing Service
320 Fifth Ave.
West Bend, WI 53095

Trempealeau County Nursing Service
Courthouse
Whitehall, WI 54773

Wood County Home Nursing Service
Courthouse
Wisconsin Rapids, WI 54494

WYOMING

Casper-Natrona Health Dept.
241 S. Conwell
Casper, WY 82601

Cheyenne City-Laramie County Health
 Unit
315 W. 20th St.
Cheyenne, WY 82001

Division of Health Medical Services
State Office Building, West
Cheyenne, WY 82002

Park County Public Health Nursing
 Service
Courthouse
Cody, WY 82414

Fremont County Public Health
 Nursing Service
County Courthouse
Lander, WY 82520

Sheridan County Public Health
 Nursing Service
P.O. Box 508
Sheridan, WY 82801

Hot Springs County Public Health
 Nursing Service
P.O. Box 948
Thermopolis, WY 82443

Goshen Community Health Services
2017 East D St.
Torrington, WY 82240

Washakie County Public Health
 Nursing Service
116 S. 11th
Worland, WY 82401

14 Homemaker-Home Health Aide Service

A Homemaker-Home Health Aide is a mature, professionally trained and supervised woman who likes people. She is trained and supervised by a staff member of a health or welfare agency.

While in the home, a Homemaker-Home Health Aide's duties include:

Planning and preparing nutritious meals within the family budget
Marketing (food, etc.)
Personal care under professional supervision
Child care and care for the handicapped, ill, and elderly
Home safety and accident prevention
Home management

The parent organization, The National Council for Homemaker-Home Health Aide Services, Inc. (67 Irving Place, New York, NY 10003, telephone 212-674-4990), publishes numerous free booklets explaining its in-home services. They are: "Fact Sheet About Homemaker-Home Health Aide Service," "Publications and Visual Aid List," "Whereas... National Social Policy Statement," "Help at Home," "Directory of Approved Services," "Current Annual Report," "Focus on the Future – A Ten Year Report," and "Packet of Miniposters."

A list of Homemaker-Home Health Aide services follows. Contact them if you or your family need help in the home.

HOMEMAKER-HOME HEALTH AIDE SERVICES

ALABAMA

Huntsville Madison County Multi-Purpose Senior Center, Inc.
218 Randolph Ave., SE
Huntsville, AL 35801

ALASKA

Alaska Homemaker-Home Health Aide Service, Inc.
519 W. Eighth Ave.
Anchorage, AK 99501

Alaska Homemaker-Home Health Aide Service, Inc.
510 Second Ave.
Fairbanks, AK 99701

Alaska Homemaker-Home Health Aide Service, Inc.
325 Gold St.
Juneau, AK 99801

CALIFORNIA

Family Service of Long Beach
Homemaker Division
1041 Pine Ave.
Long Beach, CA 90813

Visiting Nurse Association of Pomona-West End, Inc.
Homemaker-Home Health Aide Service
5156 Holt Blvd.
Montclair, CA 91763

Homemaker Service of San Diego
8123 Engineer Rd.
San Diego, CA 92111

Health Conservation, Inc.
Homemaker-Home Health Aide Service
278 Post St.
San Francisco, CA 94108

San Francisco Home Health Service
2940 16th St.
San Francisco, CA 94103

Homemaker Service of Santa Clara County, Inc.
2908 Scott Blvd.
Santa Clara, CA 95050

COLORADO

Community Homemaker Service, Inc.
1375 Delaware St.
Denver, CO 80204

CONNECTICUT

Homemaker-Home Health Aide Service of the Branford Area, Inc.
40 Kirkham St.
Branford, CT 06405

Homemaker Service of the Bristol Area, Inc.
124 Main St.
Bristol, CT 06010

Homemaker Service, Inc.
41 Church Rd.
Clinton, CT 06413

Homemaker-Home Health Aide
    Services
Family and Children's Aid, Inc.
75 West St.
Danbury, CT 06810

Homemaker Service
Department of Social Services
    Town of Greenwich
P.O. Box 929
Greenwich, CT 06830

Homemaker-Home Health Aide Service
    of Guilford, Inc.
55 Park St.
Guilford, CT 06437

Homemaker-Home Health Aide Service
Family Service Society
36 Trumbull St.
Hartford, CT 06103

Greater Middletown Homemaker
    Service, Inc.
27 Washington St.
Middletown, CT 06457

Community Health Services of Central
    Connecticut, Inc.
205 W. Main St.
New Britain, CT 06052

Homemaker Services Bureau of Greater
    New Haven
1 State St.
New Haven, CT 06511

Homemaker-Home Health Aide Service
The Family Service Association of
    Southern New London County
11 Granite St.
New London, CT 06320

Homemaker-Home Health Aide
    Services
Family & Children's Aid, Inc.
156 East Ave.
Norwalk, CT 06851

The United Workers of Norwich, Inc.
Homemaker-Home Health Aide Service
34 E. Town St.
Norwich, CT 06360

Community Health and Home Care,
    Inc.
Homemaker Division
68 Main St.
Putnam, CT 06260

Homemaker-Home Health Aide Service
    of the District Nursing Service of
    Ridgefield
13 Catoonah St.
Ridgefield, CT 06877

Valley Homemaker Service, Inc.
8 Old Mill Lane
Simsbury, CT 06070

Homemaker-Home Health Aide Service
    of Stamford-Darien, Inc.
1845 Summer St.
Stamford, CT 06905

Maria Seymour Brooker Memorial, Inc.
157 Litchfield St.
Torrington, CT 06790

The Housatonic Homemaker-Health
    Aide Service, Inc.
P.O. Box 951
West Cornwall, CT 06796

Homemaker-Home Health Aide Service
    of Windham Area, Inc.
948 Main St.
Willimantic, CT 06226

Regional Health Services, Inc.
384 Main St.
Winsted, CT 06098

DISTRICT OF COLUMBIA

Homemaker Health Aide Service of
    the National Capital Area, Inc.
1825 Connecticut Ave., NW
Washington, DC 20009

FLORIDA

Visiting Homemaker-Home Health
    Aide Services, Inc.
1860 NW Second Ave.
Boca Raton, FL 33432

Family Counseling Center
Homemaker-Home Health Aide Service
2960 Roosevelt Blvd.
Clearwater, FL 33520

GEORGIA

Athens Community Council on Aging,
    Inc.
230 S. Hull St.
Athens, GA 30601

ILLINOIS

Child and Family Services
Homemaker Service Division
234 S. Wabash Ave.
Chicago, IL 60604

The Salvation Army
Family Service Division
Homemaker Service Unit
10 E. Pearson
Chicago, IL 60611

The Visiting Nurse Association of
    St. Clair County
Homemaker-Home Health Aide Service
1269 N. 89th St.
East St. Louis, IL 62203

INDIANA

Lake County Department of Public
    Welfare
Homemaker Service
800 Massachusetts St.
Gary, IN 46402

The Family Service Association
Homemaker Program
615 North Alabama
Indianapolis, IN 46204

IOWA

Family Service Agency
Homemaker Service
400 Third Ave., SE
Cedar Rapids, IA 52401

Homemaker Service of Scott County,
    Inc.
416 W. Fourth St.
Davenport, IA 52801

Home Care-Homemaker Service of
    Des Moines, Polk County
602 E. First St.
Des Moines, IA 50309

Harden County Homemaker-Home
    Health Aide Service, Inc.
County Office Building
Eldora, IA 50627

MAINE

Home Health Services Agency of the
    Counseling Center
43 Illinois Ave.
Bangor, ME 04401

Diocesan Human Relations Services,
    Inc.
York County Homemaker Service
41 Birch St.
Biddeford, ME 04005

Diocesan Human Relations Services,
    Inc.
Aroostook County Homemaker
    Service
15 Vaughan St.
Caribou, ME 04736

Diocesan Human Relations Services,
    Inc.
Homemaker-Home Health Aide Service
95 Main St.
Orono, ME 04473

Diocesan Human Relations Services,
    Inc.
Holy Innocents' Home Care Service
83 Sherman St.
Portland, ME 04104

Diocesan Human Relations Services,
    Inc.
Kennebec/Somerset Home Aide Service
224 Main St.
Waterville, ME 04901

MASSACHUSETTS

Homemaker Service
Family Service Association of Greater
    Boston
34½ Beacon St.
Boston, MA 02108

Homemaker-Home Health Aide Service
    of Greater Fall River, Inc.
101 Rock St.
Fall River, MA 02720

142 THE OLDER AMERICAN'S HANDBOOK

Holyoke Visiting Nurse Association, Inc.
Homemaker-Home Health Aide Service
359 Dwight St.
Holyoke, MA 01040

Intercommunity Homemaker Service, Inc.
1150 Walnut St.
Newton Highlands, MA 02161

Homemaker-Home Health Aide Service
Diocese of Worcester, Inc.
26 Vernon St.
Worcester, MA 01610

MICHIGAN

Visiting Nurse Association of Metropolitan Detroit
4421 Woodward Ave.
Detroit, MI 48201

MINNESOTA

Ebenezer Society
Home Service Program
2523 Portland Ave.
Minneapolis, MN 55404

Home Services Association, Inc.
1954 University Ave.
St. Paul, MN 55104

NEBRASKA

Madonna Homemakers, Inc.
5407 South St.
Lincoln, NB 68506

NEW JERSEY

Visiting Homemaker Service of Warren County, Inc.
Court House Annex
Belvidere, NJ 07823

Visiting Homemaker Service of Bergen County, Inc.
10 Grand St.
Englewood, NJ 07631

Visiting Homemaker Service of Hudson County, Inc.
857 Bergen Ave.
Jersey City, NJ 07306

Chr-Ill Service, Inc.
60 South Fullerton Ave.
Montclair, NJ 07042

Visiting Homemaker Service of Morris County
62 Elm St.
Morristown, NJ 07960

Visiting Homemaker Service of Ocean County, Inc.
57 E. Water St.
Toms River, NJ 08753

Visiting Homemaker Service of Greater Trenton-Mercer Street Friends Center
151 Mercer St.
Trenton, NJ 08611

Visiting Homemaker Service of Central Union County, Inc.
526 N. Avenue East
Westfield, NJ 07090

NEW YORK

Home Aide Service of Eastern New York, Inc.
179 N. Main Ave.
Albany, NY 12206

Visiting Homemaker Service of Suffolk County, Inc.
50 Elm St.
Huntington, NY 11743

Family and Children's Service of Ithaca
315 N. Tioga St.
Ithaca, NY 14850

Homemaker-Home Health Aide Service
Family and Children's Society of Broome County, Inc.
257 Main St.
Johnson City, NY 13905

The Children's Aid Society
Homemaker Service
150 E. 45th St.
New York, NY 10017

Home Health-Homemaker Services
326 W. 42nd St.
New York, NY 10036

Homemaker-Home Health Aides of Greater Rochester
Rochester Society for the Prevention of Cruelty to Children
156 Plymouth Ave., N.
Rochester, NY 14608

Home Aides of Central New York, Inc.
224 W. Onondaga St.
Syracuse, NY 13202

Westchester Jewish Community Services, Inc.
Panel Homemaker Services
172 S. Broadway
White Plains, NY 10605

Family Service Society of Yonkers
Homemaker Service
219 Palisade Ave.
Yonkers, NY 10703

NORTH CAROLINA

Mecklenburg County Department of Social Services — Homemaker Service
301 Billingsley Road
Charlotte, NC 28211

Wake County Council on Aging
Homemaker-Home Health Aide Service
616 Tucker St.
Raleigh, NC 27603

OHIO

Home Aid Service
2400 Reading Road
Cincinnati, OH 45202

Center for Human Services
Homemaker-Home Health Aide Service
1001 Huron Road
Cleveland, OH 44115

Family Service Agency of Springfield and Clark County, Inc.
Homemaker Service
Tecumseh Building
Springfield, OH 45502

OKLAHOMA

Mary Mahoney Memorial Health Center
Community Health Project
12716 NE 36th St.
Spencer, OK 73084

OREGON

Metropolitan Family Service
Homemaker Service
2281 NW Everett St.
Portland, OR 97210

Salem Area Family Counseling Service
Homemaker Service
990 Commercial St., SE
Salem, OR 97302

PENNSYLVANIA

Centre County Home Health Service
315 W. High St.
Bellefonte, PA 16823

Homemaker-Home Health Aide Service, Inc.
520 E. Broad St.
Bethlehem, PA 18018

Montgomery County Homemaker-Home Health Aide Service, Inc.
650 Blue Bell W.
Blue Bell, PA 19422

Homemaker Service of Erie County, Inc.
110 W. Tenth St.
Erie, PA 16501

Homemaker-Home Health Aide Service of Chester County, Inc.
222 N. Pottstown Pike
Exton, PA 19341

Homemaker-Home Health Aide Service, Inc.
2001 N. Front St.
Harrisburg, PA 17102

Home Nursing Agency of Blair County
Homemaker-Home Health Aide Service
509 Walnut St.
Hollidaysburg, PA 16648

Lebanon County Homemaker-Home Health Aide Service, Inc.
483 N. Fifth St.
Lebanon, PA 17042

Homemaker Service of Delaware County, Inc.
210 W. Baltimore Ave.
Media, PA 19063

Homemaker Service of the Metropolitan Area, Inc.
1015 Chestnut St.
Philadelphia, PA 19107

Homemaker Service
Jewish Family Service of Philadelphia
1610 Spruce St.
Philadelphia, PA 19103

Visiting Nurse Association of Allegheny County, Inc.
Homemaker-Home Health Aide Service
815 Union Place
Pittsburgh, PA 15212

Berks County Home Service
241 S. Fifth Street
Reading, PA 19602

Homemaker-Home Health Aide Services
Lutheran Social Services
750 Kelly Drive
York, PA 17404

RHODE ISLAND

Homemaker-Home Health Aide Services of Rhode Island
265 Melrose St.
Providence, RI 02907

SOUTH CAROLINA

Homemaker Service Division
Charleston County Department of Social Services
The Center
Charleston, SC 29403

TENNESSEE

Senior Citizens Services, Inc.
127 Madison Ave.
Memphis, TN 38103

TEXAS

Home Management Service
4606 Greenville Ave.
Dallas, TX 75206

Family Service Association of San Antonio, Inc.
Homemaker-Home Health Aide Service
109 Lexington
San Antonio, TX 78205

WISCONSIN

Visiting Homemaker-Home Health Aide Service
Manitowoc Family Service Association
701 Buffalo St.
Manitowoc, WI 54220

Family Service of Milwaukee
Homemaker Service
P.O. Box 08517
Milwaukee, WI 53208

Family Service of Racine, Inc.
Homemaker-Home Health Aide Service
420 Seventh St.
Racine, WI 53403

15 Housing

Many communities throughout the country have retirement housing developments designed especially to meet the requirements of older adults and aged persons. Some are for the great majority of older people who want and are fully able to live independently; others are designed for elderly persons who want a residence that provides meals, social activities, and housekeeping as well as readily available medical services.

Housing and congregate living facilities for older people range from apartments and retirement-home and mobile-home communities to residential hotels and personal-care homes. One of the most interesting developments in retirement housing is the multi-type facility, which includes a variety of living arrangements designed for those who are fully independent as well as for older persons who want meal and housekeeping services or who require medical care on a temporary or continuing basis. Such facilities may be in a campus-type setting with cottages, apartments, residential, and skilled-nursing-care facilities or with the different types of living accommodations housed in one building.

There are a number of directories, federal and state agencies, and private organizations that may be helpful in locating and choosing the housing or facility that is best suited to meeting an older adult's particular needs. However, before committing yourself to a move, it is good insurance to weigh all of the advantages and disadvantages of relocating in new housing or in a new community. Many factors should be considered in order to ensure your comfort, safety, financial security, and happiness. The initial and ongoing cost of the housing you choose, proximity to family and friends, and availability of shopping, transportation, recreation, and medical services are among the points to be taken into account in deciding if you should move from your present residence. Careful advance planning should include a consideration of your personal needs, desires, and resources, not only for the immediate future, but also as you envision them to be in a decade or two from now. It is wise, if not absolutely essential, to visit an area before settling there and to carefully inspect the housing or facility you wish to reside in before making a financial or legal commitment.

Directories of Retirement Housing

A list of several directories that provide information on retirement housing and facilities follows. Most of them should be available in local libraries or bookstores, or can be ordered directly from the publisher.

The National Directory of Retirement Residences: Best Place to Live When You Retire by Noverre Musson, 1973. Frederick Fell, Inc., 386 Park Avenue South, New York, NY 10016. Price: $9.95. This book contains brief but concise descriptions of 1,000 retirement residences, including villages of single dwellings, groups of apartments, group residences, and multi-type facilities, built or modernized since 1950. A short description of climatic and geographic conditions for each state is included. The listings include type of facility, number of units, fees, type of sponsorship, special features and services on the premises, type of locale, and proximity to needed facilities. The directory also includes detailed introductory chapters offering guidance on choosing a retirement residence; financial, legal, and health needs in retirement; and selling a house on surplus belongings when moving to a retirement home.

A National Directory of Housing for Older People, 1969-70 by the National Council on the Aging, 1969. National Council on the Aging, 1828 L Street, NW, Washington, DC 20049. Price: $5.50. This directory lists retirement housing including self-contained housekeeping units, residential club and hotel residences, and multi-type facilities available or under construction as of 1969.

Listings are arranged by state and provide information about sponsorship, type of facility and number of units, special features and services on the premises, eligibility requirements, admissions procedures, initial and ongoing costs, type of locale, and proximity to needed facilities. An introductory guide to selection surveys the advantages and disadvantages of remaining in one's present home or community, living with other family members, or moving to special retirement housing. The guide also surveys and defines the various types of living arrangements available — their advantages, disadvantages, and relative costs, and what to look for when visiting retirement housing.

Guide to Retirement Housing by Paul Holter, 1972. Rand McNally & Company, P.O. Box 7600, Chicago, IL 60680. Price: $3.95. Lists over 1,000 retirement facilities including apartments, condominiums, mobile-home communities, homes for the aged, and multi-type facilities. Housing is listed by state and provides information about sponsorship, type of housing, number of units, and special features and services on the premises. The guide also contains an introductory section on advantages and disadvantages of retirement housing, definitions of various types of housing, and gives points on selling one's home, moving, how to handle finances in the retirement years, and residing in other countries.

Woodall's Mobile Home and Park Directory, published annually. Woodall's Publishing Co., 500 Hyacinth Place, Highland Park, IL 60036. Price: $6.95. This directory lists over 13,000 mobile-home and trailer-park communities and rates them on a 1-to-5 scale. Communities must meet certain standards to be included. Provides information on proximity to nearest business district, residence requirements, special features on premises, and lists mobile-home park associations. Includes feature articles of interest to mobile-home owners.

General Publications on Retirement Housing

In addition, a general survey called *Your Home... and Your Retirement,* which provides an outline of living, availability of housing, and climatic conditions by state, is available from *Retirement Living,* 150 E. 58th Street, New York, NY 10022 for $1.25. The American Association of Retired Persons publishes a "Better Retirement" series, which includes three booklets on the subject of retirement housing including *"Your Retirement Home Guide," "Your Retirement Moving Guide,"* and *"Your Retirement Home Repair Guide."* These booklets offer useful suggestions that will help in making decisions regarding housing in the retirement years. Individual copies of these booklets are free upon request from the AARP, which is located at 1909 K Street, NW, Washington, DC 20046.

Agencies that Can Assist in Locating Retirement Housing

Information about publicly sponsored low-cost and moderate-income housing for older people is available from local housing authorities, located in most major cities. The Department of Housing and Urban Development, which is the federal agency principally involved in housing for the elderly, can also provide information about the nearest local HUD office, which can direct older people to housing sponsored under programs supported by HUD. The address is 451 Seventh Street, SW, Washington, DC 20410.

Some 30 states now have Public Housing Agencies, which may be helpful in locating housing to meet your needs. The addresses of these agencies are listed in this chapter. If your state, or the state in which you intend to live, does not have a state housing agency, the state agency on aging may be able to direct you to housing in the area in which you would like to reside.

The Farmers Home Administration of the U.S. Department of Agriculture also sponsors programs for the construction of rural housing including rental housing units for older people with low and moderate incomes. Information about the location of projects sponsored under these programs is available from the Farmers Home Administration county office, listed in this chapter.

The following housing organizations are listed in this chapter:

Farmers Home Administration (State Directors) (USDA)
Field Office Jurisdictions (HUD)
Housing Finance and Development Agencies (HEW)
Public Housing Agencies (HUD)
U.S. Housing Developments for the Elderly (HUD)

FARMERS HOME ADMINISTRATION
14th St. and Independence Ave., SW
Washington, DC 20250
(202) 655-4000

STATE DIRECTORS

ALABAMA

John A. Garrett
P.O. Box 1165
Montgomery, AL 36102

ALASKA

Kenneth Keith Keudell
Room 1590
Federal Building
1220 S.W. Third Ave.
Portland, OR 97204

ARIZONA

Andrew B. Mayberry
Room 6095
Federal Building
230 N. First Ave.
Phoenix, AZ 85025

ARKANSAS
Robert L. Hankins
P.O. Box 2778
Little Rock, AR 72203

CALIFORNIA
Douglas W. Young
459 Cleveland Street
Woodland, CA 95695

COLORADO
G. Leo French
Room 231 No. 1 Diamond Plaza
2490 W. 26th Ave.
Denver, CO 80211

CONNECTICUT
Sherman K. Sprague
141 Main St.
P.O. Box 588
Montpelier, VT 05602

DELAWARE
Morris Monesson
Suite 2
Robscott Building
151 E. Chestnut Hill Road
Newark, DE 19713

DISTRICT OF COLUMBIA
Morris Monesson
Suite 2
Robscott Building
151 E. Chestnut Hill Road
Newark, DE 19713

FLORIDA
Claude L. Greene, Jr.
P.O. Box 1088
Gainesville, FL 32602

GEORGIA
John Paul Homes, Jr.
355 E. Hancock St.
Athens, GA 30601

HAWAII
Douglas W. Young
459 Cleveland St.
Woodland, CA 95695

IDAHO
Willard D. Stevenson
Room 429
Federal Building
304 N. Eighth St.
Boise, ID 83702

ILLINOIS
Charles W. Shuman
2106 W. Springfield Ave.
Champaign, IL 61820

INDIANA
J.D. Thompson
Suite 1700
5610 Crawfordsville Rd.
Indianapolis, IN 46224

IOWA
Robert R. Pim
Room 873
Federal Building
210 Walnut
Des Moines, IA 50309

KANSAS
E. Morgan Williams
536 Jefferson St.
Topeka, KS 66607

KENTUCKY
John H. Burris
333 Waller Ave.
Lexington, KY 40504

LOUISIANA
Thomas Julius Dewey, Jr.
3727 Government St.
Alexandria, LA 71301

MAINE
Mahlon M. Delong
USDA Office Building
Orono, ME 04473

MARYLAND
Morris Monesson
Suite 2
Robscott Building
151 E. Chestnut Hill Rd.
Newark, DE 19713

MASSACHUSETTS
Sherman K. Sprague
141 Main St.
P.O. Box 588
Montpelier, VT 05602

MICHIGAN
Calvin C. Lutz
Room 209
1405 S. Harrison Rd.
East Lansing, MI 48823

MINNESOTA
Gordon F. Klenk
252 Federal Office Building &
    U.S. Courthouse
St. Paul, MN 55101

MISSISSIPPI
Jeptha F. Barbour III
Room 528
Milner Building
Jackson, MS 39201

MISSOURI
John O. Foster
Parkade Plaza, Terrace Level
Columbia, MO 65201

MONTANA
Merle Peterson (Acting)
Federal Building
P.O. Box 850
Bozeman, MT 59715

NEBRASKA
Kenneth L. Bowen
Room 308
Federal Building
100 Centennial Mall N.
Lincoln, NB 68508

NEW HAMPSHIRE
Sherman K. Sprague
141 Main St.
P.O. Box 588
Montpelier, VT 05602

NEW JERSEY
Morris Monesson
Suite 2
Robscott Building
151 E. Chestnut Hill Rd.
Newark, DE 19713

NEW MEXICO
Carroll D. Hunton
Room 3414
Federal Building
517 Gold Ave., SW
Albuquerque, NM 87102

NEW YORK
David J. Nolan
Room 871
U.S. Courthouse & Federal Building
100 S. Clinton St.
Syracuse, NY 13202

NORTH CAROLINA
James T. Johnson
Room 514
310 New Bern Ave.
Raleigh, NC 27601

NORTH DAKOTA
Joseph J. Schneider
P.O. Box 1737
Bismarck, ND 58501

OHIO
Lester M. Stone
Room 448
U.S. Post Office (Old)
121 E. State St.
Columbus, OH 43215

HOUSING

OKLAHOMA
Ludwig W. "Bud" Johnson
Agricultural Center Office Building
Stillwater, OK 74074

PENNSYLVANIA
Penrose Hallowell, Sr.
Federal Building, Room 728
228 Walnut St.
P.O. Box 905
Harrisburg, PA 17108

PUERTO RICO
Frank A. Beososa
GPO Box 6106 G
San Juan, PR 00936

RHODE ISLAND
Sherman K. Sprague
141 Main St.
P.O. Box 588
Montpelier, VT 05602

SOUTH CAROLINA
E. Whitson Brooks
P.O. Box 21607
Columbia, SC 29221

SOUTH DAKOTA
Archie Gubbrud
P.O. Box 821
Huron, SD 57350

TENNESSEE
Paul M. Koger
538 U.S. Court House Building
801 Broadway
Nashville, TN 37203

TEXAS
J. Lynn Futch
3910 S. General Bruce Drive
Temple, TX 76501

UTAH
Clarence A. Anderson
Room 5311
Federal Building
125 S. State St.
Salt Lake City, UT 84138

VERMONT
Sherman K. Sprague
141 Main St.
P.O. Box 588
Montpelier, VT 05602

VIRGIN ISLANDS
Frank A. Besosa
GPO Box 6106 G
San Juan, PR 00936

WASHINGTON
Michael C. Horan
Room 319
Federal Office Building
301 Yakima St.
Wenatchee, WA 98801

WEST VIRGINIA
J. Kenton Lambert
P.O. Box 678
Morgantown, WV 26505

WISCONSIN
Willis W. Capps
Suite 209
First Financial Plaza
1305 Main St.
Stevens Point, WI 54481

WYOMING
Glenn J. Hertzler, Jr.
P.O. Box 820
Casper, WY 82601

FIELD OFFICE JURISDICTIONS
U.S. DEPARTMENT OF HOUSING AND URBAN DEVELOPMENT
HUD Building
451 Seventh Street, SW
Washington, DC 20410
(202) 655-4000

REGION I
U.S. Dept. HUD
John F. Kennedy Federal Building
Boston, MA 02203
(617) 223-4066

Area Offices

U.S. Dept. HUD
999 Asylum Ave.
Hartford, CT 06105
(203) 244-3638

U.S. Dept. HUD
Bulfinch Building
15 New Chardon St.
Boston, MA 02114
(617) 223-4111

U.S. Dept. HUD
Davison Building
1230 Elm St.
Manchester, NH 03101
(603) 669-7011, Ext. 7681

Insuring Offices

U.S. Dept. HUD
Federal Building
202 Harlow St.
P.O. Box 1357
Bangor, ME 04401
(207) 942-8271, Ext. 7341

U.S. Dept. HUD
330 Post Office Annex
Providence, RI 02903
(401) 528-4351

U.S. Dept. HUD
Federal Building
Elmwood Ave.
P.O. Box 989
Burlington, VT 05401
(802) 862-6501, Ext. 6274

REGION II
U.S. Dept. HUD
26 Federal Plaza
New York, NY 10007
(212) 264-8068

Area Offices

U.S. Dept. HUD
The Parkade Building
519 Federal St.
Camden, NJ 08103
(609) 757-5081

U.S. Dept. HUD
Gateway 1 Building
Raymond Plaza
Newark, NJ 07102
(201) 645-3010

U.S. Dept. HUD
Grant Building
560 Main St.
Buffalo, NY 14202
(716) 842-3510

U.S. Dept. HUD
666 Fifth Ave.
New York, NY 10019
(212) 399-5290

Caribbean Area Office

U.S. Dept. HUD
New Federal Building & Courthouse
Ave. Carlos Chardon
Hato Rey, PR 00917
(809) 765-0538

Insuring Offices

U.S. Dept. HUD
Leo W. O'Brien Federal Building
North Pearl St., & Clinton Ave.
Albany, NY 12207
(518) 472-3567

REGION III

U.S. Dept. HUD
Curtis Building
Sixth & Walnut Sts.
Philadelphia, PA 19106
(215) 597-2560

Area Offices

U.S. Dept. HUD
Universal North Building
1875 Connecticut Ave., NW
Washington, DC 20009
(202) 382-4855

U.S. Dept. HUD
Two Hopkins Plaza
Mercantile Bank & Trust Building
Baltimore, MD 21201
(301) 962-2121

U.S. Dept. HUD
Curtis Building
625 Walnut St.
Philadelphia, PA 19106
(215) 597-2645

U.S. Dept. HUD
Two Allegheny Center
Pittsburgh, PA 15212
(412) 644-2802

U.S. Dept. HUD
701 E. Franklin St.
Richmond, VA 23219
(804) 782-2721

Insuring Offices

U.S. Dept. HUD
Farmers Bank Building
919 Market St.
Wilmington, DE 19801
(302) 571-6330

U.S. Dept. HUD
New Federal Building
500 Quarrier St.
P.O. Box 2948
Charleston, WV 25330
(304) 343-6181

Special Recovery Office

U.S. Dept. HUD
Lackawanna County Building
Spruce & Adams Ave.
Scranton, PA 18503
(717) 961-5351

REGION IV

U.S. Dept. HUD
Pershing Point Plaza
1371 Peachtree St., NE
Atlanta, GA 30309
(404) 526-5585

Area Offices

U.S. Dept. HUD
Daniel Building
15 S. 20th St.
Birmingham, AL 35233
(205) 254-1617

U.S. Dept. HUD
Peninsular Plaza
661 Riverside Ave.
Jacksonville, FL 32204
(904) 791-2626

U.S. Dept. HUD
Peachtree Center Building
230 Peachtree St., NW
Atlanta, GA 30303
(404) 526-4576

U.S. Dept. HUD
Children's Hospital Foundation Building
601 S. Floyd St.
P.O. Box 1044
Louisville, KY 40201
(502) 582-5251

U.S. Dept. HUD
300 Woodrow Wilson Ave., W.
Jackson, MS 39213
(601) 969-4703

U.S. Dept. HUD
415 N. Edgeworth St.
Greensboro, NC 27401
(919) 378-5361

U.S. Dept. HUD
1801 Main St.
Columbia, SC 29202
(803) 765-5591

U.S. Dept. HUD
One Northshore Building
1111 Northshore Drive
Knoxville, TN 37919
(615) 637-9300, Ext. 1222

Insuring Offices

U.S. Dept. HUD
3001 Ponce de Leon Blvd.
Coral Gables, FL 33134

U.S. Dept. HUD
4224-28 Henderson Blvd.
Tampa, FL 33679
(813) 228-2501

U.S. Dept. HUD
100 N. Main St.
Memphis, TN 38103
(901) 534-3141

U.S. Dept. HUD
Federal Building
801 Broadway
Nashville, TN 37203
(615) 749-5521

REGION V

U.S. Dept. HUD
300 S. Wacker Drive
Chicago, IL 60606
(312) 353-5680

Area Offices

U.S. Dept. HUD
1 N. Dearborn St.
Chicago, IL 60602
(312) 353-7660

U.S. Dept. HUD
Willowbrook 5 Building
4720 Kingsway Drive
Indianapolis, IN 46205
(317) 269-6303

U.S. Dept. HUD
Patrick V. McNamara Federal Building
477 Michigan Ave.
Detroit, MI 48226
(313) 226-7900

U.S. Dept. HUD
Griggs-Midway Building
1821 University Ave.
St. Paul, MN 55104
(612) 725-4701

U.S. Dept. HUD
60 E. Main St.
Columbus, OH 43215
(614) 469-7345

U.S. Dept. HUD
744 N. Fourth St.
Milwaukee, WI 53203
(414) 224-1493

Insuring Offices

U.S. Dept. HUD
Lincoln Tower Plaza
524 S. Second St.
Springfield, IL 62701
(217) 525-4414

U.S. Dept. HUD
Northbrook Building
2922 Fuller Ave., NE
Grand Rapids, MI 49505
(616) 456-2225

U.S. Dept. HUD
Federal Office Building
550 Main St.
Cincinnati, OH 45202
(513) 684-2884

U.S. Dept. HUD
777 Rockwell
Cleveland, OH 44114

REGION VI

U.S. Dept. HUD
Earle Cabell Federal Building
U.S. Courthouse
1100 Commerce St.
Dallas, TX 75242
(214) 749-7401

Area Offices

U.S. Dept. HUD
One Union National Plaza
Little Rock, AK 72201
(501) 378-5401

U.S. Dept. HUD
Plaza Tower
1001 Howard Ave.
New Orleans, LA 70113
(504) 589-2063

U.S. Dept. HUD
301 N. Hudson St.
Oklahoma City, OK 73102
(405) 231-4891

U.S. Dept. HUD
2001 Bryan Tower
Dallas, TX 75201
(214) 749-1601

U.S. Dept. HUD
Kallison Building
410 S. Main Ave.
P.O. Box 9163
San Antonio, TX 78285
(512) 229-6800

Insuring Offices

U.S. Dept. HUD
New Federal Building
500 Fannin
Shreveport, LA 71120
(318) 226-5385

U.S. Dept. HUD
625 Truman St., NE
Albuquerque, NM 87110
(505) 766-3251

U.S. Dept. HUD
1708 Utica Square
Tulsa, OK 74152
(918) 581-7435

U.S. Dept. HUD
819 Taylor St.
Fort Worth, TX 76102
(817) 334-3233

U.S. Dept. HUD
Two Greenway Plaza E.
Houston, TX 77046
(713) 226-4335

U.S. Dept. HUD
Courthouse & Federal Office Building
1205 Texas Ave.
Lubbock, TX 79408
(806) 762-7265

REGION VII

U.S. Dept. HUD
Federal Office Building
911 Walnut St.
Kansas City, MO 64106
(816) 374-2661

Area Offices

U.S. Dept. HUD
Two Gateway Center
Fourth & State Sts.
Kansas City, KS 66101
(816) 374-4355

U.S. Dept. HUD
210 N. 12th St.
St. Louis, MO 63101
(314) 425-4761

U.S. Dept. HUD
Univac Building
7100 W. Center Rd.
Omaha, NB 68106
(402) 221-9301

Insuring Offices

U.S. Dept. HUD
210 Walnut St.
Des Moines, IA 50309
(515) 284-4512

U.S. Dept. HUD
700 Kansas Ave.
Topeka, KS 66603
(913) 234-8241

REGION VIII

U.S. Dept. HUD
Executive Tower
1405 Curtis St.
Denver, CO 80202
(303) 837-4513

Insuring Offices

U.S. Dept. HUD
909 17th St.
Denver, CO 80202
(303) 837-2441

U.S. Dept. HUD
616 Helena Ave.
Helena, MT 59601
(406) 449-5237

U.S. Dept. HUD
653 Second Ave., N.
P.O. Box 2483
Fargo, ND 58102
(701) 237-5771

U.S. Dept. HUD
400 S. Phillips Ave.
Sioux Falls, SD 57102
(605) 336-2980

U.S. Dept. HUD
125 S. State St.
Salt Lake City, UT 84147
(801) 524-5237

U.S. Dept. HUD
Federal Office Building
100 East B St.
Casper, WY 82601
(307) 265-5550

REGION IX

U.S. Dept. HUD
450 Golden Gate Ave.
San Francisco, CA 94102
(415) 556-4752

Area Offices

U.S. Dept. HUD
2500 Wilshire Blvd.
Los Angeles, CA 90057
(213) 688-5973

U.S. Dept. HUD
1 Embarcadero Center
San Francisco, CA 94111
(415) 556-2238

U.S. Dept. HUD
1000 Bishop St.
P.O. Box 3377
Honolulu, HI 96813
(808) 546-2136

Insuring Offices

U.S. Dept. HUD
244 W. Osborn Rd.
Phoenix, AZ 85002
(602) 261-4434

U.S. Dept. HUD
801 I St.
Sacramento, CA 95809
(916) 440-3471

U.S. Dept. HUD
110 West C St.
San Diego, CA 92112
(714) 293-5310

U.S. Dept. HUD
34 Civic Center Plaza
Santa Ana, CA 92701
(714) 836-2451

U.S. Dept. HUD
1050 Bible Way
Reno, NV 89505
(702) 784-5356

REGION X

U.S. Dept. HUD
Arcade Plaza Building
1321 Second Ave.
Seattle, WA 98101
(206) 442-5414

Area Offices

U.S. Dept. HUD
520 S.W. 6th Ave.
Portland, OR 97204
(503) 221-2561

U.S. Dept. HUD
Arcade Plaza Building
1321 Second Ave.
Seattle, WA 98101
(206) 442-7456

Insuring Offices

U.S. Dept. HUD
334 W. Fifth Ave.
Anchorage, AK 99501
(907) 272-5561, Ext. 871

U.S. Dept. HUD
419 N. Curtis Rd.
Boise, ID 83707
(208) 342-2711

U.S. Dept. HUD
W. 920 Riverside Ave.
Spokane, WA 99201
(509) 456-4571

HOUSING FINANCE AND DEVELOPMENT AGENCIES

U.S. Department of Health, Education and Welfare
Office of Human Development
330 Independence Ave., SW
Washington, DC 20201
(202) 962-2246

ALABAMA

Alabama Development Office
State Office Building
501 Dexter Avenue
Montgomery, AL 36104
(205) 269-7171

ALASKA

Alaska Housing Finance Corporation
P.O. Box 80
Anchorage, AK 99510
(907) 279-7643

CALIFORNIA

Senate Select Committee on Housing
 and Urban Affairs
California State Senate
116 Ninth St.
Sacramento, CA 95814
(916) 445-8740

COLORADO

Colorado Housing Division
State Capitol
Denver, CO 80203
(303) 892-2748

CONNECTICUT

Connecticut Department of
 Community Affairs
1179 Main St.
Hartford, CT 06101
(203) 525-9311

Connecticut Housing Finance
 Authority
1179 Main St.
Hartford, CT 06101
(203) 525-9311

DELAWARE

Division of Housing
Department of Community Affairs
 and Economic Development
State of Delaware
55 The Green
Dover, DE 19901
(302) 678-4264

DISTRICT OF COLUMBIA

Office of Housing and Community
 Development
1350 E St., NW
Washington, DC 20004
(202) 724-8721

FLORIDA

Executive Office of the Governor
State of Florida
Tallahassee, FL 32304
(904) 222-7344

Florida Department of Community
 Affairs
309 Office Plaza
Tallahassee, FL 32301
(904) 488-8466

Governor's Task Force on Housing
 and Community Development
614-B Bellamy Building
Florida State University
Tallahassee, FL 32306
(904) 644-2230

GEORGIA

Committee on State Planning and
 Community Affairs
House of Representatives
State of Georgia
Atlanta, GA 30303
(404) 656-5105

State Office of Housing
Georgia Department of Human
 Resources
47 Trinity Ave.
Atlanta, GA 30303
(404) 656-4650

HAWAII

Hawaii Housing Authority
Department of Social Services and
 Housing
1002 N. School St.
Honolulu, HI 96817
(808) 845-6491

IDAHO

Idaho State Housing Agency
The State House
Boise, ID 83707
(208) 336-0161

State Planning and Community Affairs
State of Idaho
State Capitol
Boise, ID 83707
(208) 336-0161

ILLINOIS

Illinois Housing Development
 Authority
201 N. Wells St.
Chicago, IL 60606
(312) 793-2060

IOWA

Planning and Program Division of
 Municipal Affairs
Iowa State Planning Agency
523 12th St.
Des Moines, IA 50319
(515) 281-3832

KENTUCKY

Kentucky Housing Corporation
New Capitol Annex
Frankfort, KY 40601
(502) 564-6620

LOUISIANA

Kisatchie-Delta Regional Planning
 District, Inc.
1254 Dorchester Drive
Alexandria, LA 71301
(318) 448-3271

MAINE

Maine State Housing Authority
128 Sewall St.
State House Complex
Augusta, ME 04330
(207) 622-3126

MARYLAND

Community Development
 Administration
2525 Riva Road
Annapolis, MD 21401
(301) 267-5831

MASSACHUSETTS

Massachusetts Housing Finance Agency
45 School St.
Boston, MA 02108
(617) 723-9770

MICHIGAN

Michigan State Housing Development
 Authority
300 S. Capitol Ave.
Lansing, MI 48926
(515) 373-1385

MINNESOTA

Minnesota Housing Finance Agency
Hanover Building
580 Cedar St.
St. Paul, MN 55101
(612) 296-6959

MISSISSIPPI

State of Mississippi
Watkins Building
510 George St.
Jackson, MS 39101
(601) 354-7570

MISSOURI

Missouri Housing Development
Commission
583 Missouri State Office Building
615 E. 13th St.
Kansas City, MO 64106
(816) 274-6751

MONTANA

Planning and Economic Development
Division
1424 Ninth Ave.
Helena, MT 59601
(406) 449-3757

NEW JERSEY

New Jersey Housing Finance Agency
101 Oakland St.
Trenton, NJ 08618
(609) 292-6617

NEW MEXICO

Natural Resources Division - Housing
Section
State Planning Office
Executive/Legislative Building
Santa Fe, NM 87503
(505) 827-2315

NEW YORK

New York City Housing and Development Administration
100 Gold St.
New York, NY 10038
(212) 566-4440

New York City Housing Development
Corporation
110 William St.
New York, NY 10038
(212) 566-4446

New York State Housing Finance
Agency
1250 Broadway
New York, NY 10001
(212) 736-4949

New York State Urban Development
Corporation
1345 Avenue of the Americas
New York, NY 10019
(212) 974-8086

State of New York Mortgage Agency
55 Liberty St.
New York, NY 10005
(212) 488-3178

NORTH CAROLINA

North Carolina Housing Corporation
Albemarle Building
State Treasurer Department
325 N. Salisbury St.
Raleigh, NC 27611
(919) 829-3064

OHIO

Ohio Department of Urban Affairs
30 E. Broad St.
Columbus, OH 43215
(614) 466-2480

OREGON

Housing Division
Oregon Department of Commerce
308 State Library Building
Salem, OR 97310
(503) 378-4343

PENNSYLVANIA

Pennsylvania Housing Finance Agency
3211 N. Front St.
Harrisburg, PA 17110
(717) 787-1450

RHODE ISLAND

Housing Assistance Section
Department of Community Affairs
State of Rhode Island
150 Washington St.
Providence, RI 02903
(401) 277-2892

SOUTH CAROLINA

South Carolina State Housing
Authority
1122 Lady St.
Columbia, SC 29201
(803) 758-2844

SOUTH DAKOTA

State Technical Assistance Program
Housing Specialist
State Economic Opportunity Office
State Capitol
Pierre, SD 57501
(605) 224-3663

TENNESSEE

Executive Office of the Governor
State of Tennessee
1025 Andrew Jackson State Office
Building
Nashville, TN 37219
(615) 741-3621

TEXAS

Housing Division
Texas Department of Community
Affairs
611 S. Congress
Austin, TX 70704
(512) 475-2431

UTAH

State Planning Coordinator
State Capitol
Salt Lake City, UT 84114
(801) 328-5246

Utah Housing Development Division
110 State Capitol
Salt Lake City, UT 84114
(801) 328-5141

VERMONT

Vermont State Housing Authority
101 Main St.
Montpelier, VT 05602
(802) 828-3295

VIRGINIA

Virginia Housing Development
Authority
Fifth & Franklin Sts.
Richmond, VA 23219
(804) 770-7588

Virginia Housing Development
Authority
901 Chamberlain Ave.
Richmond, VA 23220
(804) 644-9881

WEST VIRGINIA

West Virginia Housing Development
Fund
900 Charleston National Plaza
Charleston, WV 25301
(304) 348-3732

WISCONSIN

Wisconsin Housing Finance Authority
14 N. Carole St.
Madison, WI 53702
(608) 266-7884

WYOMING

Planning Division
Department of Economic Planning
and Development
720 W. 18 St.
Cheyenne, WY 82002
(307) 777-7284

PUBLIC HOUSING AGENCIES

U.S. Department of Housing and Urban Development
451 Seventh St., SW
Washington, DC 20410
(202) 655-4000

ALABAMA

Abbeville Housing Authority
P.O. Box 69
Abbeville, AL 36310

Albertville Housing Authority
South Broad Street
Albertville, AL 35950

Alexander City Housing Authority
P.O. Drawer 788
Alexander City, AL 36201

Aliceville Housing Authority
P.O. Box 485
Aliceville, AL 35442

Andalusia Housing Authority
P.O. Box 927
Andalusia, AL 36420

Anniston Housing Authority
P.O. Box 841
Anniston, AL 36201

Arab Housing Authority
P.O. Box 452
Arab, AL 35016

Ashford Housing Authority
P.O. Box 1
Ashford, AL 36312

Ashland Housing Authority
Box 25 Route 3
Ashland, AL 36251

Athens Housing Authority
P.O. Box 853
Athens, AL 35611

Atmore Housing Authority
P.O. Drawer AD
Atmore, AL 36502

Attalla Housing Authority
904 Ninth St., SW
Attalla, AL 35954

Auburn Housing Authority
P.O. Box 1912
Auburn, AL 36830

Bay Minette Housing Authority
P.O. Box 937
Bay Minette, AL 36507

Bayou Labatre Housing Authority
P.O. Box 517
Bayou Labatre, AL 36509

Berry Housing Authority
c/o Executive Director
Berry, AL 35546

Bessemer Housing Authority
1100 Fifth Ave., N.
Bessemer, AL 35020

Birmingham District HSG Authority
600 N. 24th St.
Birmingham, AL 35203

Blountsville Housing Authority
P.O. Box 8
Blountsville, AL 35031

Altoona Housing Authority
P.O. Drawer B
Boaz, AL 35957

Boaz Housing Authority
P.O. Drawer B
Boaz, AL 35957

Centre Housing Authority
P.O. Drawer B
Boaz, AL 35957

Collinsville Housing Authority
P.O. Drawer B
Boaz, AL 35957

Crossville Housing Authority
P.O. Drawer B
Boaz, AL 35957

Rainsville Housing Authority
P.O. Drawer B
Boaz, AL 35957

Brantley Housing Authority
P.O. Box 44
Brantly, AL 36009

Brent Housing Authority
c/o Executive Director
Brent, AL 35034

Brewton Housing Authority
P.O. Box 387
Brewton, AL 36426

Bridgeport Housing Authority
c/o Executive Director
Bridgeport, AL 35740

Boston Housing Authority
c/o Executive Director
Brilliant, AL 35548

Brundidge Housing Authority
P.O. Box 11
Brundidge, AL 36010

Calera Housing Authority
P.O. Box 136
Calera, AL 35040

Carbon Hill Housing Authority
P.O. Box 70
Carbon Hill, AL 35549

Carrollton Housing Authority
P.O. Drawer 400
Carrollton, AL 35447

Washington County Housing Authority
P.O. Box 186
Chatom, AL 36518

Chickasaw Housing Authority
604 Dumont St.
Chickasaw, AL 36611

Childersburg Housing Authority
P.O. Box 396
Childersburg, AL 35044

Clanton Housing Authority
Box 408
Clanton, AL 35045

Clayton Housing Authority
P.O. Box 127
Clayton, AL 36016

Columbia Housing Authority
P.O. Box F
Columbia, AL 36319

Columbiana Housing Authority
P.O. Box 498
Columbiana, AL 35051

Cordova Housing Authority
Cook Boulevard
Route 2
Cordova, AL 35550

Cottonwood Housing Authority
P.O. Box 356
Cottonwood, AL 36320

Cullman Housing Authority
P.O. Box 460
Cullman, AL 35055

Dadeville Housing Authority
P.O. Box 292
Dadeville, AL 36853

Daleville Housing Authority
101 Donnell Circle
Daleville, AL 36322

Decatur Housing Authority
P.O. Box 878
Decatur, AL 35601

Lawrence Housing Authority
P.O. Box 1069
Decatur, AL 35601

Demopolis Housing Authority
P.O. Drawer 730
Demopolis, AL 36732

Walker County Housing Authority
P.O. Box Q
Dora, AL 35062

Dothan Housing Authority
P.O. Box 1727
Dothan, AL 36301

Elba Housing Authority
P.O. Box 338
Elba, AL 36323

Enterprise Housing
P.O. Box 192
Enterprise, AL 36330

Eufaula Housing Authority
P.O. Box 36
Eufaula, AL 36027

Eutaw Housing Authority
221 Main St.
Eutaw, AL 35462

Greene County Housing Authority
P.O. Box 187
Eutaw, AL 35462

Evergreen Housing Authority
P.O. Box 187
Evergreen, AL 36401

Fairfield Housing Authority
P.O. Box 352
Fairfield, AL 35064

Fayette Housing Authority
P.O. Box 266
Fayette, AL 35555

Flomaton Housing Authority
P.O. Box 638
Flomaton, AL 36441

Florala Housing Authority
c/o Executive Director
Florala, AL 36442

Florence Housing Authority
303 N. Pine St.
Florence, AL 35630

Foley Housing Authority
302 Fourth Ave.
Foley, AL 36535

Fort Payne Housing Authority
203 13th St., NW
Fort Payne, AL 35967

Valley Head Housing Authority
P.O. Box 212
Fort Payne, AL 35967

Jefferson County Housing Authority
2100 Walker Chapel Road
Fultondale, AL 35068

Greater Gadsden Housing Authority
400 N. Sixth St.
Gadsden, AL 35801

Georgiana Housing Authority
P.O. Box 249
Georgiana, AL 36033

Goodwater Housing Authority
c/o Executive Director
Goodwater, AL 35072

Gordo Housing Authority
P.O. Drawer I
Gordo, AL 35466

Greensboro Housing Authority
c/o Executive Director
Greensboro, AL 36744

Greenville Housing Authority
P.O. Box 521
Greenville, AL 36037

Guntersville Housing Authority
P.O. Box 4
Guntersville, AL 35976

Haleyville Housing Authority
2523 Newburg Road
Haleyville, AL 35565

Hamilton Housing Authority
2523 Newbury Rd.
Haleyville, AL 35565

Bear Creek Housing Authority
P.O. Box 190
Hamilton, AL 35570

Guin Housing Authority
P.O. Box 190
Hamilton, AL 35570

Hackleburg Housing Authority
P.O. Box 190
Hamilton, AL 35570

Phil Campbell Housing Authority
P.O. Box 190
Hamilton, AL 35570

Hanceville Housing Authority
P.O. Box 330
Hanceville, AL 35077

Hartford Housing Authority
RFD Number 2
Hartford, AL 36344

Hartselle Housing Authority
P.O. Box 550
Hartselle, AL 35640

Headland Housing Authority
P.O. Box 248
Headland, AL 36345

Heflin Housing Authority
P.O. Box 515
Heflin, AL 36264

Hobson City Housing Authority
601 Park Ave.
Hobson City, AL 36201

Homewood Housing Authority
1903 29th Ave. South
Homewood, AL 35209

Huntsville Housing Authority
P.O. Box 486
Huntsville, AL 35804

Top of Alabama Reg. Authority
P.O. Box 2144
Huntsville, AL 35804

Jacksonville Housing Authority
P.O. Box 497
Jacksonville, AL 36265

Jasper Housing Authority
P.O. Box 582
Jasper, AL 35501

Lanett Housing Authority
P.O. Box 465
Lanett, AL 36863

Leeds Housing Authority
P.O. Box 513
Leeds, AL 35094

Linden Housing Authority
P.O. Box 572
Linden, AL 36748

Lineville Housing Authority
P.O. Box 455
Lineville, AL 36266

Livingston Housing Authority
P.O. Box 397
Livingston, AL 35470

Luverne Housing Authority
P.O. Box 311
Luverne, AL 36049

H A City of Triana
200 Stone St.
Madison, AL 35758

Marion Housing Authority
P.O. Box 428
Marion, AL 36756

Midland City Housing Authority
Route 1
Box 100
Midland City, AL 36350

Millport Housing Authority
P.O. Box 235
Millport, AL 35576

Mobile Housing Authority
P.O. Box 1345
Mobile, AL 36601

Monroeville Housing Authority
P.O. Box 732
Monroeville, AL 36460

Montevallo Housing Authority
P.O. Box 136
Montevallo, AL 35115

Montgomery Housing Authority
1020 Bell St.
Montgomery, AL 36104

Moulton Housing Authority
P.O. Box 566
Moulton, AL 35650

New Brockton Housing Authority
P.O. Box 159
New Brockton, AL 36351

Newton Housing Authority
P.O. Box 153
Newton, AL 36352

Northport Housing Authority
P.O. Drawer 349
Northport, AL 35476

Oneonta Housing Authority
P.O. Box 129
Oneonta, AL 35121

Lafayette Housing Authority
P.O. Box 786
Opelika, AL 36801

Opelika Housing Authority
P.O. Box 786
Opelika, AL 36801

Opp Housing Authority
P.O. Box 368
Opp, AL 36467

Ozark Housing Authority
P.O. Box 566
Ozark, AL 36360

Parrish Housing Authority
Box 8
Parrish, AL 35580

Pell City Housing Authority
P.O. Box 681
Pell City, AL 35125

Phenix City Housing Authority
P.O. Box 338
Phenix City, AL 36867

Piedmont Housing Authority
P.O. Box 420
Piedmont, AL 36272

Prattville Housing Authority
P.O. Box 6
Prattville, AL 36067

Prichard Housing Authority
P.O. Box 10307
Prichard, AL 36601

Ragland Housing Authority
P.O. Box 69
Ragland, AL 35131

Red Bay Housing Authority
P.O. Drawer L
Red Bay, AL 35882

Reform Housing Authority
P.O. Box 535
Reform, AL 35481

Roanoke Housing Authority
Administration Building
Roanoke, AL 36274

Roosevelt City Housing Authority
435 O'Neal Ave.
Roosevelt City, AL 35020

Russellville Housing Authority
100 Adams St.
Russellville, AL 35653

Samson Housing Authority
City Hall
Samson, AL 36477

Scottsboro City Housing Authority
102 Worthington St.
Scottsboro, AL 35678

Selma Housing Authority
P.O. Box S
Selma, AL 36701

Sheffield Housing Authority
P.O. Box 457
Sheffield, AL 35660

Stevenson Housing Authority
P.O. Drawer E
Stevenson, AL 35772

Sulligent Housing Authority
P.O. Box 656
Sulligent, AL 35586

Sumiton Housing Authority
P.O. Box 220
Sumiton, AL 35148

Sylacauga Housing Authority
P.O. Box 539
Sylacauga, AL 35150

Talladega Housing Authority
151 Curry Court
Talladega, AL 35160

Tallassee Housing Authority
904 Hickory St.
Tallassee, AL 36078

Tarrant Housing Authority
624 Bell Ave.
Tarrant, AL 35217

H A Town of Ft. Deposit
100 Spring Road
Troy, AL 36081

Troy Housing Authority
P.O. Box 321
Troy, AL 36081

Tuscaloosa Housing Authority
P.O. Box 2281
Tuscaloosa, AL 35401

Tuscumbia Housing Authority
P.O. Box 350
Tuscumbia, AL 35674

Tuskegee Housing Authority
201 Azalea St.
Tuskegee, AL 36083

Union Springs Housing Authority
P.O. Box 388
Union Springs, AL 36089

Uniontown Housing Authority
P.O. Box 633
Uniontown, AL 36786

Kennedy Housing Authority
P.O. Box 490
Vernon, AL 35592

Vernon Housing Authority
Route 2, Box 37
Vernon, AL 35592

Vincent Housing Authority
P.O. Box F
Vincent, AL 35178

Winfield Housing Authority
P.O. Box 609
Winfield, AL 35594

York Housing Authority
P.O. Box 267
York, AL 36925

ALASKA

Alaska State Housing Authority
P.O. Box 80
Anchorage, AK 99510

Tlinget-Haida Authority
P.O. Box 525
Juneau, AK 99801

Metlakatla Housing Authority
P.O. Box 18
Metlakatla, AK 99926

ARIZONA

Pinal County Housing Authority
Route 1
Box 191
Casa Grande, AZ 85222

Chandler Housing Authority
P.O. Box 336
Chandler, AZ 85224

Camp Verde Indian Housing Authority
P.O. Box 248
Cottonwood, AZ 86326

Eloy Housing Authority
P.O. Box 637
Eloy, AZ 85231

Flagstaff Housing Authority
P.O. Box 1387
Flagstaff, AZ 86002

Kaibab-Paiute Tribal Housing
Authority
P.O. Box 323
Fredonia, AZ 86022

Glendale Housing Authority
6842 N. 61st Ave.
Glendale, AZ 85301

Hopi Tribal Housing Authority
P.O. Box 158
Keams Canyon, AZ 86034

Mesa Housing Authority
415 N. Pasadena St.
Mesa, AZ 85202

Nogales Housing Authority
Box 777
Nogales, AZ 85621

Colorado River Indian HSG Authority
P.O. Box 1716
Parker, AZ 85344

Hualapai Housing Authority
Hualapai Tribal Office
Peach Springs, AZ 86434

Maricopa County Housing Authority
1510 S. 19th Drive
Phoenix, AZ 85009

Phoenix Housing Authority
251 W. Washington St.
Phoenix, AZ 85030

Gila River Housing Authority
P.O. Box 528
Sacaton, AZ 85247

San Carlos Housing Authority
P.O. Box 187
San Carlos, AZ 85550

Fort McDowell Apache HSG Authority
Route 1
Box 907
Scottsdale, AZ 85257

Salt River – Maricopa HSG Authority
Route 1
Box 120
Scottsdale, AZ 85256

Papago Tribal Housing Authority
P.O. Box 776
Sells, AZ 85634

Cocopah Housing Authority
Route No. 1
Box 77
Somerton, AZ 85350

HOUSING 155

South Tucson Housing Authority
P.O. Box 3666
South Tucson, AZ 85713

Tucson Housing AUthority
P.O. Box 5547
Tucson, AZ 85703

White Mountain Apache HSG
   Authority
Fort Apache Indian Reservation
Whiteriver, AZ 85941

Navajo Housing Authority
P.O. Box 387
Window Rock, AZ 86515

Winslow Housing Authority
P.O. Box 1391
Winslow, AZ 86047

Quechan Tribal Housing Authority
P.O. Box 1591
Yuma, AZ 85364

Yuma County Housing Authority
P.O. Box 969
Yuma, AZ 85364

ARKANSAS

Alma Housing Authority
Box 386
Alma, AR 72921

Amity Housing Authority
P.O. Box 6
Amity, AR 71921

Arkadelphia Housing Authority
670 S. Sixth St.
Arkadelphia, AR 71923

Atkins Housing Authority
P.O. Box 245
Atkins, AR 72823

Augusta Housing Authority
101 N. Second St.
Augusta, AR 72006

Bald Knob Housing Authority
Drawer Q
Bald Knob, AR 72010

Beebe Housing Authority
Drawer Q
Bald Knob, AR 72010

Heber Springs Housing Authority
Drawer Q
Bald Knob, AR 72010

Hoxie Housing Authority
Drawer Q
Bald Knob, AR 72010

Imboden Housing Authority
Drawer Q
Bald Knob, AR 72010

Judsonia Housing Authority
Drawer Q
Bald Knob, AR 72010

Batesville Housing Authority
P.O. Box 73
Batesville, AR 72501

Black Rock Housing Authority
c/o Executive Director
Black Rock, AR 72415

Blytheville Housing Authority
P.O. Box 387
Blytheville, AR 72315

Booneville Housing Authority
P.O. Box 476
Booneville, AR 72927

Brinkley Housing Authority
501 W. Cedar St.
Brinkley, AR 72021

Camden Housing Authority
Box 39
Camden, AR 71701

Caraway Housing Authority
c/o Executive Director
Caraway, AR 72419

Lonoke County Housing Authority
Box 74
Carlisle, AR 72024

Carthage Housing Authority
Box 157
Carthage, AR 71725

Clarendon Housing Authority
c/o Executive Director
Clarendon, AR 72029

Clarksville Housing Authority
P.O. Box 407
Clarksville, AR 72830

Coal Hill Housing Authority
P.O. Box 6
Coal Hill, AR 72832

Conway Housing Authority
Box 15
Conway, AR 72032

Cotton Plant Housing Authority
Box 25
Cotton Plant, AR 72036

Crossett Housing Authority
Box 488
Crossett, AR 71635

Dardanelle Housing Authority
402 S. 5th St.
Dardanelle, AR 72834

Decatur Housing Authority
Box 237
Decatur, AR 72722

Dell Housing Authority
Box 237
Dell, AR 72426

Housing Authority, County of Sevier
P.O. Box 807
DeQueen, AR 71832

Dermott Housing Authority
City Hall
Dermott, AR 71638

Des Arc Housing Authority
Box 309
Des Arc, AR 72040

Arkansas County Housing Authority
Box 477
Dewitt, AR 72042

Dewitt Housing Authority
Box 477
Dewitt, AR 72042

Dover Housing Authority
Box 106
Dover, AR 72837

Dumas Housing Authority
P.O. Box 115
Dumas, AR 71639

Earle Housing Authority
531 Second St.
Earle, AR 72331

Emmet Housing Authority
Box 324
Emmet, AR

England Housing Authority
P.O. Box 21
England, AR 72046

Fayetteville Housing Authority
1 N. School Ave.
Fayetteville, AR 72701

Fordyce Housing Authority
City Hall
Fordyce, AR 71742

Little River County Housing Authority
P.O. Box 278
Foreman, AR 71836

Sevier County Housing Authority
Box 278
Foreman, AR 71836

Forrest City Housing Authority
P.O. Box 997
Forrest City, AR 72335

Fort Smith Housing Authority
2100 N. 31st St.
Fort Smith, AR 72901

Gilmore Housing Authority
c/o Executive Director
Gilmore, AR 72339

Gould Housing Authority
Drawer P
Gould, AR 71643

Greenwood Housing Authority
Dr. Chase W Hall Homes
Greenwood, AR 72936

Gurdon Housing Authority
Box 36
Gurdon, AR 71743

Hamburg Housing Authority
City Hall
Hamburg, AR 71646

Hardy Housing Authority
c/o Locator
Hardy, AR

Harrison Housing Authority
City Hall
Harrison, AR 72601

Helena Housing Authority
1000 Holly St.
Helena, AR 72342

Hickory Ridge Housing Authority
Box 718
Hickory Ridge, AR 72347

Hope Housing Authority
720 Texas St.
Hope, AR 71801

Hot Springs Housing Authority
Box 1257
Hot Springs, AR 71901

Hughes Housing Authority
c/o Executive Director
Hughes, AR 72348

Huntsville Housing Authority
Box 549
Huntsville, AR 72740

Jonesboro Housing Authority
519 W. Washington
Jonesboro, AR 72401

Lake City Housing Authority
c/o Executive Director
Lake City, AR 72437

Leachville Housing Authority
P.O. Box 54
Leachville, AR 72438

Little Rock Housing Authority
1000 Wolfe St.
Little Rock, AR 72202

Luxora Housing Authority
Box 70
Luxora, AR 72358

Magnolia Housing Authority
Box 488
Magnolia, AR 71753

Malvern Housing Authority
P.O. Box 550
Malvern, AR 72104

Sparkman Housing Authority
P.O. Box 550
Malvern, AR 72104

Mammoth Spring Housing Authority
City Hall
Mammoth Spring, AR 72554

Manila Housing Authority
P.O. Box 376
Manila, AR 72442

Marianna Housing Authority
P.O. Box 756
Marianna, AR 72360

Poinsett County Housing Authority
Box 661
Marked Tree, AR 72365

Marmaduke Housing Authority
c/o Executive Director
Marmaduke, AR 72443

McGehee Housing Authority
Box 725
McGehee, AR 71654

McRae Housing Authority
Box 147
McRae, AR 72853

Melbourne Housing Authority
Box 436
Melbourne, AR 72556

Mena Housing Authority
Box 720
Mena, AR 71953

Polk County Housing Authority
Box 720
Mena, AR 71953

Monette Housing Authority
P.O. Box 76
Monette, AR 72447

Monticello Housing Authority
P.O. Box 505
Monticello, AR 71655

Conway County Housing Authority
P.O. Box 229
Morrilton, AR 72110

Morrilton Housing Authority
P.O. Box 229
Morrilton, AR 72110

Mount Ida Housing Authority
c/o Executive Director
Mount Ida, AR 71957

Cushman Housing Authority
c/o Executive Director
Mount Pleasant, AR 72561

Mount Pleasant Housing Authority
c/o Executive Director
Mount Pleasant, AR 72561

Pike County Housing Authority
Box 241
Murfreesboro, AR 71958

Howard County Housing Authority
P.O. Box 209
Nashville, AR 71852

Newark Housing Authority
P.O. Box 111
Newark, AR 72562

Newport Housing Authority
600 Garfield St.
Newport, AR 72112

North Little Rock Housing Authority
Box 516
North Little Rock, AR 72115

Ola Housing Authority
Box 277
Ola, AR 72853

Osceola Housing Authority
P.O. Box 585
Osceola, AR 72370

Ozark Housing Authority
Box 283
Ozark, AR 72949

Pangburn Housing Authority
P.O. Box 347
Pangburn, AR 72121

Paragould Housing Authority
P.O. Box 137
Paragould, AR 72450

Paris Housing Authority
1201 Logan Drive
Paris, AR 72855

Parkin Housing Authority
Box 324
Parkin, AR 72373

Piggott Housing Authority
City Hall
Piggott, AR 72454

Plainview Housing Authority
c/o Executive Director
Plainview, AR 72857

Pocahontas Housing Authority
P.O. Box 266
Pocahontas, AR 72455

Prescott Housing Authority
P.O. Box 702
Prescott, AR 71857

Quitman Housing Authority
City Hall
Quitman, AR 72131

Rector Housing Authority
147 N. Stewart St.
Rector, AR 72461

Rison Housing Authority
c/o Executive Director
Rison, AR 71665

Russellville Housing Authority
P.O. Box 825
Russellville, AR 72801

Saint Francis Housing Authority
c/o Executive Director
Saint Francis, AR 72200

Salem Housing Authority
c/o Executive Director
Salem, AR 72575

Kensett Housing Authority
104 W. Race St.
Searcy, AR 72143

McCrory Housing Authority
104 W. Race St.
Searcy, AR 72143

Pine Bluff Housing Authority
104 W. Race St.
Searcy, AR 72143

Searcy Housing Authority
501 S. Fir St.
Searcy, AR 72143

Springdale Housing Authority
Box 763
Springdale, AR 72764

Star City Housing Authority
Box 666
Star City, AR 71667

Stephens Housing Authority
Box 276
Stephens, AR 71764

Texarkana Housing Authority
P.O. Box 1259
Texarkana, AR 75501

Truman Housing Authority
Box J
Truman, AR 72472

Turrell Housing Authority
Box 297
Turrell, AR 72384

Van Buren Housing Authority
1701 Chestnut St.
Van Buren, AR 72956

Waldron Housing Authority
Box 39
Waldron, AR 72958

Walnut Ridge Housing Authority
Box 415
Walnut Ridge, AR 72476

Warren Housing Authority
Box 602
Warren, AR 71671

West Helena Housing Authority
P.O. Box 2667
West Helena, AR 72390

West Memphis Housing Authority
2911 Henry St.
West Memphis, AR 72301

Wheatley Housing Authority
c/o Executive Director
Wheatley, AR 72392

Marie Housing Authority
c/o Executive Director
Wilson, AR 72395

Wilson Housing Authority
c/o Executive Director
Wilson, AR 72395

Wynne Housing Authority
Box 552
Wynne, AR 72396

Yellville Housing Authority
c/o Executive Director
Yellville, AR 72687

CALIFORNIA

Alameda Housing Authority
737 Eagle Avenue
Alameda, CA 94501

Kern County Housing Authority
525 Roberts Lane
Bakersfield, CA 93308

Benicia Housing Authority
28 Riverhill Drive
Benicia, CA 94510

Berkeley Housing Authority
2000 Hearst Ave.
Berkeley, CA 94704

Brawley Housing Authority
1401 D St.
Brawley, CA 92227

Calipatria Housing Authority
c/o Ivcha - 1401 D St.
Brawley, CA 92227

El Centro Housing Authority
c/o Ivcha - 1401 D St.
Brawley, CA 92227

Holtville Housing Authority
c/o Ivcha - 1401 D St.
Brawley, CA 92227

Imperial Housing Authority
c/o Ivcha - 1401 D St.
Brawley, CA 92227

Imperial Valley Coord HSG Authority
c/o Ivcha - 1401 D St.
Brawley, CA 92227

Westmoreland Housing Authority
c/o Ivcha - 1401 D St.
Brawley, CA 92227

Calexico Housing Authority
c/o Executive Director
Calexico, CA 90000

Carlsbad Housing Authority
2777 Jefferson St.
Carlsbad, CA 92008

Modoc-Lassen Indian HSG-Authority
P.O. Box 187
Cedarville, CA 96104

Compton Housing Authority
136 East Palm
Compton, CA 90220

Crescent City Housing Authority
1020 Mason Mall
Crescent City, CA 95531

Eureka Housing Authority
735 W. Everding St.
Eureka, CA 95501

Humboldt County Housing Authority
735 W. Everding St.
Eureka, CA 95501

Fairfield Housing Authority
1000 Webster St.
Suite 111
Fairfield, CA 94533

Quechan Tribal Housing Authority
c/o Executive Director
Fort Yuma, CA 95800

Fresno City Housing Authority
c/o Executive Director
Fresno, CA 93723

Fresno County Housing Authority
P.O. Box 2388
Fresno, CA 93723

Butte County Housing Authority
P.O. Box 326
Gridley, CA 95948

Kings County Housing Authority
Box 355
Hanford, CA 93230

Inglewood Housing Authority
105 E. Queen St.
Inglewood, CA 90301

Livermore Housing Authority
P.O. Box 729
Livermore, CA 94550

Santa Barbara County HSG Authority
P.O. Box 397
Lompoc, CA 93436

Long Beach Housing Authority
944 Pacific Ave.
Long Beach, CA 90813

Los Angeles City Housing Authority
P.O. Box 17157, Foy Station
Los Angeles, CA 90017

Los Angeles County Housing Authority
430 N. Mednik Ave.
Los Angeles, CA 90022

Madera City Housing Authority
205 W. Fourth St.
Madera, CA 93637

Contra Costa County Housing Authority
P.O. Box 549
Martinez, CA 94553

Merced County Housing Authority
405 U St.
Merced, CA 95340

Stanislaus County Housing Authority
1701 Robertson Rd, P.O. Box 3958
Modesto, CA 95352

Napa City Housing Authority
1700 Second St., Suite 146
Napa, CA 94558

Needles Housing Authority
908 Sycamore Drive
Needles, CA 92363

Oakland Housing Authority
935 Union St.
Oakland, CA 94607

Oxnard Housing Authority
300 N. Marquita St.
Oxnard, CA 93030

All Mission Indian Housing Authority
Box D-7
Pala Indian Reservation
Pala, CA 92059

Pasadena Housing Authority
100 N. Garfield Ave.
Pasadena, CA 91109

Paso Robles Housing Authority
P.O. Box 817
Paso Robles, CA 93466

Pittsburg Housing Authority
65 Civic Ave.
Pittsburg, CA 94565

Pleasanton Housing Authority
P.O. Box 395
Pleasanton, CA 94566

Port Hueneme Housing Authority
250 N. Ventura Rd.
Port Hueneme, CA 93041

Plumas County Housing Authority
P.O. Box 480
Quincy, CA 95971

Richmond Housing Authority
P.O. Box 515 Station A
Richmond, CA 94808

Riverbank Housing Authority
P.O. Box 885
Riverbank, CA 95367

Riverside County Housing Authority
6850 Brockton Ave.
Room 212
Riverside, CA 92506

Sacramento City Housing Authority
P.O. Box 1834
Sacramento, CA 95819

Sacramento County Housing Authority
P.O. Box 1834
Sacramento, CA 95819

Monterey County Housing Authority
134 Carneros St.
Salinas, CA 93901

San Bernardino County Housing Authority
1053 North D St.
San Bernardino, CA 92410

San Diego Housing Authority
202 C St.
San Diego, CA 92101

San Francisco City & County Housing Authority
440 Turk St.
San Francisco, CA 94102

San Jose Housing Authority
999 W. Taylor St.
San Jose, CA 95126

San Luis Obispo Housing Authority
P.O. Box 638
San Luis Obispo, CA 93401

San Mateo County Housing Authority
456 Peninsula Ave.
San Mateo, CA 94401

San Pablo Housing Authority
2324 College Lane
San Pablo, CA 94806

Santa Ana Housing Authority
20 Civic Center Plaza
Santa Ana, CA 92701

Santa Barbara City Housing Authority
330 E. Cannon Perdido St.
Santa Barbara, CA 93101

Santa Clara County Housing Authority
Box 2250 Mission Station
Santa Clara, CA 95051

Santa Cruz County Housing Authority
1543 112 Pacific Ave.
Santa Cruz, CA 95060

Santa Paula Housing Authority
P.O. Box 404
Santa Paula, CA 93060

Ventura County Housing Authority
P.O. Box 404
Santa Paula, CA 93060

City of Santa Rosa HSG Authority
Box 1806
Santa Rosa, CA 95403

Marin County Housing Authority
P.O. Box 988
Sausalito, CA 94965

Soledad Housing Authority
P.O. Box 1136
Soledad, CA 93960

So. San Francisco Housing Authority
351 C St.
So. San Francisco, CA 94080

San Joaquin County Housing Authority
Box 6186
Stockton, CA 95206

Suisun City Housing Authority
710 Suisun St.
Suisun City, CA 94585

Mendocino County Housing Authority
166 W. Smith St.
Ukiah, CA 94582

Alameda County Housing Authority
33934 Alvarado-Niles Rd.
Union City, CA 94587

Upland Housing Authority
1248 N. Campus Ave.
Upland, CA 91786

Vallejo Housing Authority
P.O. Box 1432
Vallejo, CA 94590

San Buenaventura Housing Authority
P.O. Box 99
Ventura, CA 93003

Tulare County Housing Authority
P.O. Box 791
Visalia, CA 93277

Wasco Housing Authority
617 Sixth St.
Wasco, CA 93280

Yolo County Housing Authority
P.O. Box 57
Woodland, CA 95695

Sutter County Housing Authority
P.O. Box 631
Yuba City, CA 95991

COLORADO

Aguilar Housing Authority
P.O. Box 477
Aguilar, CO 81020

Alamosa Housing Authority
Box 145
Alamosa, CO 81101

Antonito Housing Authority
Box 25
Antonito, CO 81120

Boulder Housing Authority
Municipal Building
Broadway & Canyon
Boulder, CO 80302

Brighton Housing Authority
105 A Bridge St.
Brighton, CO 80601

Burlington Housing Authority
509 Tenth St.
Burlington, CO 80807

Center Housing Authority
P.O. Box P
Center, CO 81125

Cheyenne Wells Housing Authority
Town Hall
Cheyenne Wells, CO 80810

Colorado Springs Housing
105 E. Vermijo, Room 336
Colorado Springs, CO 80903

Conejos County Housing Authority
Conejos County Courthouse
Conejos, CO 81129

Denver City & County HSG Authority
P.O. Box 4226, Santa Fe Station
Denver, CO 80204

Fort Lupton Housing Authority
330 Park Ave.
Fort Lupton, CO 80621

Fort Morgan Housing Authority
P.O. Box 100
Fort Morgan, CO 80701

Greeley Housing Authority
923 16th St.
Greeley, CO 80631

Haxtun Housing Authority
Town Hall
Haxtun, CO 80731

Holly Housing Authority
209 S. Main St.
Holly, CO 81047

Holyoke Housing Authority
City Hall
Holyoke, CO 80734

Southern Ute Housing Authority
P.O. Box 447
Ignacio, CO 81137

Keenesburg Housing Authority
Town Hall
Keenesburg, CO 80643

Kersey Housing Authority
P.O. Box 117
Kersey, CO 80644

Lajunta Housing Authority
City Hall
Lajunta, CO 81050

Limon Housing Authority
1880 Circle Lane
Limon, CO 80828

Littleton Housing Authority
2450 W. Main St.
City Hall
Littleton, CO 80102

Pueblo Housing Authority
2601 Crawford St.
Pueblo, CO 81004

Salida Housing Authority
Box 887
Salida, CO 81201

Sterling Housing Authority
P.O. Box 528
Sterling, CO 80751

Trinidad Housing Authority
Box 36
Trinidad, CO 81082

Walsenburg Housing Authority
Box 312
Walsenburg, CO 81089

Wellington Housing Authority
214 Cleveland Ave.
Wellington, CO 80549

Custer County Housing Authority
Court House Building, Box 1
Westcliffe, CO 81252

Wray Housing Authority
Box 5
Wray, CO 80758

Yuma Housing Authority
Box 66
Yuma, CO 80759

CONNECTICUT

Ansonia Housing Authority
15 Maple St.
Ansonia, CT 06401

Bridgeport Housing Authority
376 E. Washington Ave.
Bridgeport, CT 06608

Bristol Housing Authority
P.O. Box 918
Bristol, CT 06012

Danbury Housing Authority
2 Mill Ridge Rd.
Danbury, CT 06813

Derby Housing Authority
c/o Executive Director
Derby, CT 06418

East Hartford Housing Authority
62 Columbus St.
East Hartford, CT 06108

East Haven Housing Authority
Town Hall
East Haven, CT 06512

Enfield Housing Authority
17 Enfield Terrace
Enfield, CT 06082

Greenwich Housing Authority
P.O. Box 141
Greenwich, CT 06831

Hartford Housing Authority
475 Flatbush Ave.
Hartford, CT 06106

Manchester Housing Authority
24 Bluefield Drive
Manchester, CT 06040

Meriden Housing Authority
46 Broadvale Rd.
Meriden, CT 06451

Middletown Housing Authority
1000 Silver St.
Middletown, CT 06457

Milford Housing Authority
100 Viscount Drive
Milford, CT 06460

New Britain Housing Authority
34 Marimac Rd.
New Britain, CT 06053

New Haven Housing Authority
230 Ashmun St.
New Haven, CT 06511

New London Housing Authority
186 Colman St.
New London, CT 06320

South Norwalk Housing Authority
26 Monroe St.
Norwalk, CT 06854

Norwich Housing Authority
10 Westwood Park
Norwich, CT 06360

Portland Housing Authority
29 Main St.
Portland, CT 06480

Putman Housing Authority
123 Laconia Ave.
Putman, CT 06260

Seymour Housing Authority
Lock Drawer 191
Seymour, CT 06483

Stamford Housing Authority
100 Ayano Lane
Stamford, CT 06920

Stratford Housing Authority
Box 344
Stratford, CT 06497

Torrington Housing Authority
c/o Torrington Towers
Torrington, CT 06790

Rockville Housing Authority
114 Franklin Park West
Vernon Town, CT 06066

Wallingford Housing Authority
P.O. Box 415
Wallingford, CT 06492

Waterbury Housing Authority
70 Lakewood Rd.
Waterbury, CT 06704

West Haven Housing Authority
413 Main St.
West Haven, CT 06516

Willimantic Housing Authority
49 West Ave.
Willimantic, CT 06226

Winchester Housing Authority
P.O. Box 797
Winchester, CT 06098

Windsor Locks Housing Authority
Town Hall
Windsor Locks, CT 06096

DELAWARE

Dover Housing Authority
375 Simon Circle
Dover, DE 19901

Newark Housing Authority
P.O. Box 1067
Newark, DE 19711

Delaware State Housing Authority
601 Delaware Ave.
Wilmington, DE 19801

Wilmington Slum Clearing &
 Redevelopment
Public Building
Wilmington, DE 19899

DISTRICT OF COLUMBIA

National Capital Housing Authority
1170 12th St., NW
Washington, DC 20430

FLORIDA

Apalachicola Housing Authority
P.O. Box 730
Apalachicola, FL 32320

Arcadia Housing Authority
P.O. Box 948
Arcadia, FL 33821

Avon Park Housing Authority
P.O. Box 1327
Avon Park, FL 33825

Bartow Housing Authority
P.O. Box 1413
Bartow, FL 33830

Bradenton Housing Authority
13th Ave. & Fifth St. W.
Bradenton, FL 33508

Suwannee County Housing Authority
c/o Executive Director
Branford, FL 32008

Levy County Housing Authority
P.O. Box 38
Bronson, FL 32621

Brooksville Housing Authority
26 S. Brooksville Ave.
Brooksville, FL 33512

Flagler County Housing Authority
P.O. Box 188
Bunnell, FL 32010

Chipley Housing Authority
P.O. Box 218
Chipley, FL 32428

Clearwater Housing Authority
1100 E. Druid Rd.
Clearwater, FL 33518

Pinellas County Housing Authority
418 S. Ft. Harrison Ave.
Clearwater, FL 33516

Cocoa Housing Authority
Five Point Station P.O. Box 3128
Cocoa, FL 32922

Eau Gallie Housing Authority
P.O. Box 3128 Five Point Station
Cocoa, FL 32922

Crestview Housing Authority
P.O. Box 218
Crestview, FL 32536

Dade City Housing Authority
P.O. Box 1355
Dade City, FL 33525

Daytona Beach Housing Authority
118 Cedar St.
Daytona Beach, FL 32014

De Funiak Springs Housing Authority
121 Oerting Drive
De Funiak Springs, FL 32433

Deland Housing Authority
P.O. Box 2071
Deland, FL 32720

Delray Beach Housing Authority
P.O. Box 1581
Delray Beach, FL 33444

Dunedin Housing Authority
750 Milwaukee Ave.
Dunedin, FL 33528

Eustis Housing Authority
P.O. Box AT
Eustis, FL 32736

Fernandina Beach Housing Authority
1300 Hickory St.
Fernandina Beach, FL 32034

Broward County Housing Authority
305 South Andrews Ave.
Ft. Lauderdale, FL 33301

Ft. Lauderdale Housing Authority
437 SW Fourth Ave.
Ft. Lauderdale, FL 33318

Fort Myers Housing Authority
1406 Dean St.
Fort Myers, FL 33901

Fort Pierce Housing Authority
601 Ave. B
Fort Pierce, FL 33450

Fort Walton Beach Housing Authority
27 Robinwood Drive SE
Fort Walton Beach, FL 32548

Alachua County Housing Authority
103 SE First St.
Gainesville, FL 32601

Gainesville Housing Authority
P.O. Box 1468
Gainesville, FL 32601

H A Town of Slocomb
P.O. Drawer 218
Graceville, FL 32440

NW Florida Regional Housing Authority
P.O. Box 218
Graceville, FL 32440

Hialeah Housing Authority
70 E. Seventh St.
Hialeah, FL 33010

Seminole Tribal Housing Authority
P.O. Box 6787
Holywood, FL 33024

Homestead Housing Authority
P.O. Box 278
Homestead, FL 33030

Collier County Housing Authority
106 S. Third St.
Inmokalee, FL 33931

Jacksonville Housing Authority
124 W. Ashley St.
Jacksonville, FL 32202

Key West Housing Authority
P.O. Box 9
Key West, FL 33040

Union County Housing Authority
P.O. Box 3.7
Lake Butler, FL 32054

Lakeland Housing Authority
P.O. Box 1009
Lakeland, FL 33802

Lake Wales Housing Authority
P.O. Box 426
Lake Wales, FL 33853

Live Oak Housing Authority
205 Houston Ave. SW
Live Oak, FL 32060

Macclenny Housing Authority
P.O. Box 977
Macclenny, FL 32063

Marianna Housing Authority
337 Albert St.
Marianna, FL 32446

Melbourne Housing Authority
1279 Houston St.
Melbourne, FL 32901

Brevard County Housing Authority
Box 338
Merritt Island, FL 32952

Dade County Dept. of Housing &
Urban Development
Box 250
Miami, FL 33135

Miami Beach Housing Authority
150 Alton Rd.
Miami Beach, FL 33139

Milton Housing Authority
1498 Byrom St.
Milton, FL 32570

Mount Dora Housing Authority
P.O. Box 598
Mount Dora, FL 32757

New Smyrna Beach Housing Authority
P.O. Box 688
New Smyrna Beach, FL 32069

Niceville Housing Authority
312 Niceville Ave.
Niceville, FL 32578

Ocala Housing Authority
1415 NE 32nd Terrace
Ocala, FL 32670

Orlando Housing Authority
P.O. Box 3746
Orlando, FL 32802

Pahokee Housing Authority
465 Friend Terrace
Pahokee, FL 33476

Palatka Housing Authority
P.O. Box 1277
Palatka, FL 32077

Panama City Housing Authority
P.O. Box 897
Panama City, FL 32401

Springfield Housing Authority
P.O. Box 3656
Panama City, FL 32401

Pensacola Housing Authority
P.O. Box 1325
Pensacola, FL 32506

Mulberry Housing Authority
1306 Larrick Lane
Plant City, FL 33566

Plant City Housing Authority
P.O. Box HHH
Plant City, FL 33566

Pompano Beach Housing Authority
P.O. Box 2006
Pompano Beach, FL 33061

Punta Gorda Housing Authority
P.O. Box 1146
Punta Gorda, FL 33950

Riviera Beach Housing Authority
1340 W. Eighth St.
Riviera Beach, FL 33403

St. Petersburg Housing Authority
325 Ninth St., S.
St. Petersburg, FL 33705

Sanford Housing Authority
Castle Brewer Court
Sanford, FL 32771

Seminole County Housing Authority
Administration Building
Castle Brewer Court
Sanford, FL 32771

Sarasota Housing Authority
1300 Sixth St.
Sarasota, FL 33577

Stuart Housing Authority
P.O. Box 1787
Stuart, FL 33494

Tallahassee Housing Authority
P.O. Box 1713
Tallahassee, FL 32302

Tampa Housing Authority
P.O. Box 4766
Tampa, FL 33135

Tarpon Springs Housing Authority
P.O. Box 282
Tarpon Springs, FL 33589

Titusville Housing Authority
Box 6416
Titusville, FL 32780

Gilchrist County Housing Authority
P.O. Box 241
Trenton, FL 32693

Venice Housing Authority
Box 835
Venice, FL 33595

Palm Beach County Housing Authority
301 N. Olive Ave.
West Palm Beach, FL 33401

West Palm Beach Housing Authority
P.O. Box 6247
West Palm Beach, FL 33405

Winter Park Housing Authority
718 Margaret Square
Winter Park, FL 32789

GEORGIA

Abbeville Housing Authority
c/o Executive Director
Abbeville, GA 31001

Acworth Housing Authority
P.O. Box 347
Acworth, GA 30101

Adairsville Housing Authority
P.O. Box 381
Adairsville, GA 30103

Alamo Housing Authority
P.O. Box 334
Alamo, GA 30411

Albany Housing Authority
P.O. Box 485
Albany, GA 31702

Alma Housing Authority
801 12th St.
Alma, GA 31510

Americus Housing Authority
P.O. Box 1226
Americus, GA 31709

Buena Vista Housing Authority
P.O. Box 1226
Americus, GA 31709

Ellaville Housing Authority
P.O. Box 1226
Americus, GA 31709

Lee County Housing Authority
P.O. Box 1226
Americus, GA 31709

Arlington Housing Authority
P.O. Box 217
Arlington, GA 31713

Ashburn Housing Authority
P.O. Box 55
Ashburn, GA 31714

Athens Housing Authority
P.O. Box 1469
Athens, GA 30601

Atlanta Housing Authority
801 Hurt Building
Atlanta, GA 30303

Augusta Housing Authority
P.O. Box 3206, Hill Station
Augusta, GA 30904

Bainbridge Housing Authority
P.O. Box 304
Bainbridge, GA 31717

Barnesville Housing Authority
City Hall Building
Barnesville, GA 30204

Jackson City Housing Authority
City Hall
Barnesville, GA 30204

Baxley Housing Authority
P.O. Box 56
Baxley, GA 31516

Blackshear Housing Authority
P.O. Box 678
Blackshear, GA 31516

Blakely Housing Authority
M & M Office, Cedar Hill Homes
Blakely, GA 31723

Blue Ridge Housing Authority
706 Willingham Dr.
Blue Ridge, GA 30513

Bremen Housing Authority
City Hall
Bremen, GA 30110

Brunswick Housing Authority
P.O. Box 1118
Brunswick, GA 31520

Buford Housing Authority
110 Park St.
Buford, GA 30518

Butler Housing Authority
P.O. Box 311
Butler, GA 31006

Byron City Housing Authority
P.O. Box 11
Byron, GA 31008

Cairo Housing Authority
P.O. Box 512
Cairo, GA 31728

Calhoun Housing Authority
111-F Fair St.
Calhoun, GA 30701

Camilla Housing Authority
P.O. Box 247
Camilla, GA 31730

Newton Housing Authority
P.O. Box 247
Camilla, GA 31730

Canton Housing Authority
1 Shipp St.
Canton, GA 30114

Housing Authority City of Bowdon
1 Roop St.
Carrollton, GA 30117

Carrollton Housing Authority
P.O. Box 627
Carrollton, GA 30117

Cartersville Housing Authority
c/o Executive Director
Cartersville, GA 30120

Cave Spring Housing Authority
P.O. Box 206
Cave Spring, GA 30124

Cedartown Housing Authority
P.O. Box 211
Cedartown, GA 30125

Chatsworth Housing Authority
415 Ross Ave
Chatsworth, GA 30705

Claxton Housing Authority
P.O. Box 7
Claxton, GA 30417

Cochran Housing Authority
P.O. Box 32
Cochran, GA 31014

College Park Housing Authority
1908 W. Princeton
College Park, GA 30337

Colquitt Housing Authority
c/o Executive Director
Colquitt, GA 31737

Columbus Housing Authority
P.O. Box 630
Columbus, GA 31902

Comer Housing Authority
P.O. Box 157
Comer, GA 30629

Commerce Housing Authority
c/o Executive Director
Commerce, GA 30529

Conyers Housing Authority
P.O. Box 435
Conyers, GA 30207

Cordele Housing Authority
401 Tenth St., South
Cordele, GA 31015

Covington Housing Authority
P.O. Box 632
Covington, GA 30209

Crawfordville Housing Authority
c/o Executive Director
Crawfordville, GA 30631

Cumming Housing Authority
P.O. Box 36
Cumming, GA 30130

Cuthbert Housing Authority
P.O. Box 36
Cuthbert, GA 31740

Dahlonega Housing Authority
P.O. Box 703
Dahlonega, GA 30533

Dallas Housing Authority
P.O. Box 74
Dallas, GA 30132

Dalton Housing Authority
Underwood Circle
Dalton, GA 30720

Danielsville Housing Authority
P.O. Box 5
Danielsville, GA 30633

Dawson Housing Authority
Lemon St.
Dawson, GA 31742

Decatur Housing Authority
P.O. Box 1627
Decatur, GA 30031

Dekalb County Housing Authority
P.O. Box 1627
Decatur, GA 30031

Douglas City Housing Authority
P.O. Box 917
Douglas, GA 31533

Douglas County Housing Authority
W. Strickland St.
Douglasville, GA 30134

Dublin Housing Authority
P.O. Box 36
Dublin, GA 31021

Eastman Housing Authority
P.O. Box 69
Eastman, GA 31023

Housing Authority, City of East Point
1600 Connally Drive
East Point, GA 30344

Eatonton Housing Authority
P.O. Box 72
Eatonton, GA 31024

Edison Housing Authority
c/o Executive Director
Edison, GA 31746

Elberton Housing Authority
109 Heard St.
Elberton, GA 30635

Ellijay Housing Authority
P.O. Box 426
Ellijay, GA 30540

Fairburn Housing Authority
c/o R.M. Gaddy Route 2
Box 244
Fairburn, GA 30213

Union City Housing Authority
Route 3, Box 244
Fairburn, GA 30213

Fayetteville Housing Authority
P.O. Box 36
Fayetteville, GA 30214

Fitzgerald Housing Authority
P.O. Box 547
Fitzgerald, GA 31750

Folkston Housing Authority
P.O. Box 546
Folkston, GA 31537

Forest Park Housing Authority
785 Central Ave.
Forest Park, GA 30050

Fort Gaines Housing Authority
c/o Executive Director
Fort Gaines, GA 31751

Fort Oglethorpe Housing Authority
Memorial Drive
Fort Oglethorpe, GA 30741

Fort Valley Housing Authority
P.O. Box 10
Fort Valley, GA 31030

Franklin Housing Authority
c/o Executive Director
Franklin, GA 30217

Gainesville Housing Authority
P.O. Box 653
Gainesville, GA 30501

Gibson Housing Authority
P.O. Box 653
Gibson, GA 30510

Glennville Housing Authority
Mack Kennedy Homes
Glennville, GA 30427

Glenwood Housing Authority
P.O. Box 396
Glenwood, GA 30428

Greensboro Housing Authority
c/o Executive Director
Greensboro, GA 30642

Greenville Housing Authority
P.O. Box 252
Greenville, GA 30222

Griffin Housing Authority
110 N. Sixth St.
Griffin, GA 30223

Harris County Housing Authority
P.O. Box 327
Hamilton, GA 31811

Hampton Housing Authority
c/o Executive Director
Hampton, GA 30228

Harlem Housing Authority
P.O. Box 36
Harlem, GA 30814

Hartwell Housing Authority
c/o Executive Director
Hartwell, GA 30643

Hawkinsville Housing Authority
P.O. Box 52
Hawkinsville, GA 31036

Hazlehurst Housing Authority
c/o Executive Director
Hazlehurst, GA 31539

Lumber City Housing Authority
P.O. Box 36
Hazlehurst, GA 31539

Hinesville Housing Authority
301 Olive St.
Hinesville, GA 31313

Hogansville Housing Authority
c/o Executive Director
Hogansville, GA 30230

Jasper Housing Authority
147 Landrum Circle
Jasper, GA 30143

Jefferson Housing Authority
c/o Executive Director
Jefferson, GA 30549

Jesup Housing Authority
P.O. Box 396
Jesup, GA 31545

Jonesboro Housing Authority
P.O. Box 458
Jonesboro, GA 30236

Kingsland Housing Authority
c/o Executive Director
Kingsland, GA 31548

LaFayette Housing Authority
P.O. Box 567
LaFayette, GA 30728

Menlo Housing Authority
P.O. Box 567
LaFayette, GA 30728

LaGrange Housing Authority
P.O. Box 626
LaGrange, GA 30240

Lavonia Housing Authority
P.O. Box 4
Lavonia, GA 30553

Lawrenceville Housing Authority
c/o Executive Director
Lawrenceville, GA 30245

Lincolnton Housing Authority
c/o Executive Director
Lincolnton, GA 30817

Lithonia Housing Authority
6878 E. Church St.
Lithonia, GA 30058

Stewart County Housing Authority
P.O. Box 145
Lumpkin, GA 31815

Lyons Housing Authority
315 N. Lanier St.
Lyons, GA 30436

Macon Housing Authority
P.O. Box 4928
Macon, GA 31208

Manchester Housing Authority
P.O. Box 26
Manchester, GA 31816

Marietta Housing Authority
P.O. Drawer K
Marietta, GA 30060

McCaysville Housing Authority
P.O. Box 247
McCaysville, GA 30555

McDonough Housing Authority
P.O. Box 73
McDonough, GA 30253

McRae Housing Authority
P.O. Box 181
McRae, GA 31055

HOUSING 163

Metter Housing Authority
P.O. Box 207
Metter, GA 30439

Milledgeville Housing Authority
P.O. Box 112
Milledgeville, GA 31061

Loganville Housing Authority
P.O. Box 550
Monroe, GA 30655

Madison Housing Authority
P.O. Box 550
Monroe, GA 30655

Monroe Housing Authority
P.O. Box 550
Monroe, GA 30655

Social Circle Housing Authority
P.O. Box 550
Monroe, GA 30655

Winder Housing Authority
P.O. Box 550
Monroe, GA 30655

Montezuma Housing Authority
P.O. Box 67
Montezuma, GA 31063

Monticello Housing Authority
P.O. Box 391
Monticello, GA 31064

Doerun Housing Authority
P.O. Box 1048
Moultrie, GA 31768

Moultrie Housing Authority
P.O. Box 1048
Moultrie, GA 31768

Mount Vernon Housing Authority
c/o Executive Director
Mount Vernon, GA 30445

Adel Housing Authority
P.O. Box 278
Nashville, GA 31639

Atkinson County Housing Authority
P.O. Box 278
Nashville, GA 31639

Hahira Housing Authority
P.O. Box 278
Nashville, GA 31639

Homerville City Housing Authority
P.O. Box 278
Nashville, GA 31639

Lakeland City Housing Authority
P.O. Box 278
Nashville, GA 31639

Nashville Housing Authority
P.O. Box 278
Nashville, GA 31639

Ocilla Housing Authority
P.O. Box 278
Nashville, GA 31639

Pearson Housing Authority
P.O. Box 278
Nashville, GA 31639

Grantville Housing Authority
P.O. Box 881
Newman, GA 30263

Newman Housing Authority
P.O. Box 881
Newman, GA 30263

Palmetto Housing Authority
P.O. Box 881
Newman, GA 30263

Nicholls Housing Authority
P.O. Box 382
Nicholls, GA 31554

Norcross Housing Authority
22 Garner St.
Norcross, GA 30071

Pelham Housing Authority
P.O. Box 269
Pelham, GA 31779

Perry Housing Authority
909 Ball St.
Perry, GA 31069

Woodbury Housing Authority
P.O. Box 146
Pine Mt. Valley, GA 31823

Quitman City Housing Authority
P.O. Box 551
Quitman, GA 31643

Reidsville Housing Authority
213 Hill St.
Reidsville, GA 30453

Marshallville Housing Authority
P.O. Box 311
Reynolds, GA 31076

Reynolds Housing Authority
P.O. Box 311
Reynolds, GA 31076

Ringgold Housing Authority
P.O. Box 547
Ringgold, GA 30736

Roberta Housing Authority
c/o Executive Director
Roberta, GA 31708

Rochelle Housing Authority
P.O. Box 156
Rochelle, GA 31079

Rockmart Housing Authority
P.O. Box 312
Rockmart, GA 30153

Rome Housing Authority
P.O. Box 1428
Rome, GA 30161

Roswell Housing Authority
P.O. Box 387
Roswell, GA 30075

Royston Housing Authority
124 Royston Homes
Royston, GA 30662

Housing Authority City of Woodbine
P.O. Box 526
St. Marys, GA 31558

St. Mary's Housing Authority
P.O. Box 526
St. Marys, GA 31558

Sandersville Housing Authority
P.O. Box 711
Sandersville, GA 31082

Savannah Housing Authority
P.O. Box 1179
Savannah, GA 31402

Senoia Housing Authority
P.O. Box 98
Senoia, GA 30276

Shellman Housing Authority
c/o Executive Director
Shellman, GA 31786

Soperton Housing Authority
700 Eastman Rd.
Soperton, GA 30457

Hancock County Housing Authority
718 New St.
Sparta, GA 31087

Sparta Housing Authority
718 New St.
Sparta, GA 31087

Statesboro Housing Authority
P.O. Box 552
Statesboro, GA 30458

Summerville Housing Authority
P.O. Box 162
Summerville, GA 30747

Swainsboro Housing Authority
P.O. Box 265
Swainsboro, GA 30401

Sylvester Housing Authority
P.O. Box 386
Sylvester, GA 31791

Talbotton Housing Authority
P.O. Box 97
Talbotton, GA 31827

Buchanan City Housing Authority
100 W. View Apts.
Arbacoochee Rd.
Tallapoosa, GA 30176

Tallapoosa Housing Authority
Arbacoochee Rd.
Tallapoosa, GA 30176

Tennille Housing Authority
c/o Executive Director
Tennille, GA 31089

Thomaston Housing Authority
547 Trivne Ave.
Thomaston, GA 30286

Boston Housing Authority
125 Grant St.
Thomasville, GA 31792

Thomasville Housing Authority
P.O. Box 1057
Thomasville, GA 31792

Thomson Housing Authority
P.O. Box 627
Thomson, GA 30824

Tifton Housing Authority
P.O. Box 12
Tifton, GA 31794

Clarkesville Housing Authority
P.O. Drawer J
Toccoa, GA 30577

Clayton Housing Authority
P.O. Box 203
Toccoa, GA 30577

Cleveland Housing Authority
P.O. Drawer J
Toccoa, GA 30577

Cornelia Housing Authority
P.O. Box 203
Toccoa, GA 30577

Homer Housing Authority
P.O. Box 203
Toccoa, GA 30577

Toccoa Housing Authority
P.O. Drawer J
Toccoa, GA 30577

Unadilla Housing Authority
c/o Executive Director
Unadilla, GA 31901

Union Point Housing Authority
P.O. Box 206
Union Point, GA 30669

Valdosta Housing Authority
610 E. Ann St.
Valdosta, GA 31601

Vidalia Housing Authority
P.O. Box 508
Vidalia, GA 30474

Vienna Housing Authority
Drawer B
Vienna, GA 31902

Villa Rica Housing Authority
P.O. Box 665
Villa Rica, GA 30180

Warner Robins Housing Authority
Warner Robins, GA 31093

Warrenton Housing Authority
P.O. Box 389
Warrenton, GA 30828

Washington Housing Authority
P.O. Box 675
Washington, GA 30673

Waycross Housing Authority
P.O. Box 1407
Waycross, GA 31501

Housing Authority City of Millen
P.O. Box 597
Waynesboro, GA 30830

Housing Authority City of Sylvania
P.O. Box 597
Waynesboro, GA 30830

Louisville Housing Authority
P.O. Box 597
Waynesboro, GA 30830

Screven County Housing Authority
P.O. Box 597
Waynesboro, GA 30830

Waynesboro Housing Authority
P.O. Box 597
Waynesboro, GA 30830

West Point Housing Authority
P.O. Box 545
West Point, GA 31833

Woodland Housing Authority
P.O. Box 126
Woodland, GA 31836

Wrightsville Housing Authority
P.O. Box 107
Wrightsville, GA 31096

HAWAII

Hawaii Housing Authority
P.O. Box 17907
Honolulu, HI 96817

IDAHO

American Falls Housing Authority
P.O. Box 327
American Falls, ID 83211

Boise Housing Authority
700 Cunningham Place
Boise, ID 83702

Buhl Housing Authority
1310 Main St.
Buhl, ID 83316

Burley Housing Authority
1401 Overland Ave.
Burley, ID 83118

Fort Hall Housing Authority
Fort Hall Indian Agency
Fort Hall, ID 83201

Nez Perce Tribal Housing Authority
Northern Idaho Agency
Lapwai, ID 83540

Nampa Housing Authority
1703 Third St., N.
Nampa, ID 83651

Coeur D Alene Tribal Housing Authority
Coeur D Alene Tribal Sub-Agency
Plummer, ID 83851

Pocatello Housing Authority
P.O. Box 4161
Pocatello, ID 83201

Jerome Housing Authority
200 N. Elm St.
Twin Falls, ID 83301

Twin Falls Housing Authority
200 N. Elm St.
Twin Falls, ID 83301

ILLINOIS

Edwards County Housing Authority
125 W. Cherry St.
Albion, IL 62806

Alton Housing Authority
Belle and Mitchell Sts.
Alton, IL 62003

Union County Housing Authority
131 Hillside Terrace
Anna, IL 62906

Cass County Housing Authority
211 S. Illint St.
Ashland, IL 62612

Aurora Land Clearance Commission
1449 Westwood Drive
Aurora, IL 60538

Pike County Housing Authority
838 Mason
Barry, IL 62312

Bloomington Housing Authority
104 E. Wood St.
Bloomington, IL 61701

Alexander County Housing Authority
100 The River View
Cairo, IL 62914

Fulton County Housing Authority
414 N. First Ave.
Canton, IL 61520

Macouping County Housing Authority
P.O. Box 140
Carlinville, IL 62626

Marion County Housing Authority
719 E. Howard St.
Centralia, IL 62802

St. Clair County Housing Authority
500 Hinckley St.
Centreville, IL 62206

Randolph County Housing Authority
214 Opdyke St.
Chester, IL 62233

Chicago Housing Authority
22 W. Madison St.
Chicago, IL 60616

Cook County Housing Authority
407 S. Dearborn St.
Chicago, IL 60650

Dewitt County Housing Authority
700 N. Cain St.
Clinton, IL 61727

White County Housing Authority
P.O. Box 64
Crossville, IL 62827

Hancock County Housing Authority
P.O. Box 63
Dallas City, IL 62330

Danville Housing Authority
P.O. Box 312
Danville, IL 61832

Decatur Housing Authority
401 Longview Place
Decatur, IL 62521

De Kalb County Housing Authority
507 E. Taylor St.
De Kalb, IL 60115

Lee County Housing Authority
906 Washington Ave.
Dixon, IL 61021

HOUSING

Perry County Housing Authority
P.O. Box 255
Du Quoin, IL 62832

Rock Island County Housing Authority
2215 Seventh Ave. Administration Building
East Moline, IL 61244

East St. Louis Housing Authority
690 N. 20th St.
East St. Louis, IL 62205

Effingham County Housing Authority
Box 479
Effingham, IL 62401

Elgin Housing Authority
P.O. Box 784
Elgin, IL 60120

Hardin County Housing Authority
c/o Executive Director
Elizabethtown, IL 62931

Wayne County Housing Authority
303 N. First St.
Fairfield, IL 62837

Clay County Housing Authority
210 S. Locust St.
Flora, IL 62869

Freeport Housing Authority
600 N. Van Buren Ave.
Freeport, IL 61033

Jo Daviess County Housing Authority
341 Franklin St.
Galena, IL 61036

Knox County Housing Authority
255 W. Tompkins St.
Galesburg, IL 61401

Pope County Housing Authority
P.O. Drawer A
Golconda, IL 62938

Granite City Housing Authority
1800 Kirk Patrick Homes
Granite City, IL 62040

Bond County Housing Authority
220 E. Winter St.
Greenville, IL 62246

Calhoun County Housing Authority
c/o Executive Director
Hardin, IL 62047

Saline County Housing Authority
927 Barnett St.
Harrisburg, IL 62946

Mason County Housing Authority
200 E. Hurst Ave.
Havana, IL 62644

Williamson County Housing Authority
601 N. Sixth St.
Herrin, IL 62948

Montgomery County Housing Authority
P.O. Box 558
Hillsboro, IL 62049

Morgan County Housing Authority
301 W. Beecher St.
Jacksonville, IL 62650

Jersey County Housing Authority
505 Horn Drive
Jerseyville, IL 62052

Joliet Housing Authority
310 N. Joliet St.
Joliet, IL 60435

Kankakee County Housing Authority
1015 N. Washington Ave.
Kankakee, IL 60901

Henry County Housing Authority
Administration Building
Kewanee, IL 61443

Lawrence County Housing Authority
P.O. Box 346
Lawrenceville, IL 62439

Logan County Housing Authority
20 Centenniel Court
Lincoln, IL 62656

Mcdonough County Housing Authority
425 N. Prairie St.
Macomb, IL 61455

Madison County Housing Authority
Market & Washington Sts.
Madison, IL 62060

Clark County Housing Authority
P.O. Box 239
Marshall, IL 62441

Coles County Housing Authority
P.O. Box 866
Mattoon, IL 61938

Hamilton County Housing Authority
210 E. Main St.
Mcleansboro, IL 62859

Massac County Housing Authority
P.O. Box 528
Metropolis, IL 62960

Moline Housing Authority
41st St. & 11th Ave. A
Moline, IL 61465

Warren County Housing Authority
200 E. Harlem Ave.
Monmouth, IL 61462

Grundy County Housing Authority
1231 Gladys St.
Morris, IL 60450

Pulaski County Housing Authority
P.O. Box 246
Mounds, IL 62964

Wabash County Housing Authority
330 W. Tenth St.
Mt. Carmel, IL 62863

Brown County Housing Authority
P.O. Box 209
Mt. Sterling, IL 62353

Jefferson County Housing Authority
1000 S. Ninth St.
Mt. Vernon, IL 62864

Jackson County Housing Authority
300 N. Seventh St.
Murphysboro, IL 62966

Oak Park Housing Authority
1025 Pleasant Place
Oak Park, IL 60301

Richland County Housing Authority
114 Fair St.
Olney, IL 62450

La Salle County Housing Authority
526 E. Norris Dr.
Ottawa, IL 61350

Crawford County Housing Authority
100 S. Lincoln
Palestine, IL 62451

Christian County Housing Authority
P.O. Box 86
Pana, IL 62557

Ford County Housing Authority
140 N. Taft St.
Paxton, IL 60957

Pekin Housing Authority
1901 Broadway
Pekin, IL 61554

Peoria Housing Authority
814 W. Brotherson St.
Peoria, IL 61650

Peoria-Woodford-Fulton Housing Authority
814 W. Brotherson St.
Peoria, IL 61650

Menard County Housing Authority
100 E. Sheridan Rd.
Petersburg, IL 62675

Livingston County Housing Authority
903 W. North St.
Pontiac, IL 61764

Bureau County Housing Authority
444 S. Church St.
Princeton, IL 61356

Adams County Housing Authority
510 Vermont St.
Quincy, IL 62301

Quincy Housing Authority
540 Harrison St.
Quincy, IL 62301

Crawford County Housing Authority
401 W. Main St.
Robinson, IL 62451

Whiteside County Housing Authority
401 Coloma Court
Rock Falls, IL 61071

Rockford Housing Authority
330 15th Ave.
Rockford, IL 61108

Winnebago Housing Authority
330 15th Ave.
Rockford, IL 61108

Rock Island Housing Authority
111 20th St.
Rock Island, IL 61201

Vermillion County Housing Authority
116 S. Chicago St.
Rossville, IL 60963

Schuyler County Housing Authority
405 E. Adams St.
Rushville, IL 62681

Carroll County Housing Authority
41 S. Fifth St.
Savanna, IL 61074

Gallatin County Housing Authority
P.O. Box 377
Shawneetown, IL 62984

Shelby County Housing Authority
P.O. Box 362
Shelbyville, IL 62565

Springfield Housing Authority
1320 E. Reynolds St.
Springfield, IL 62702

Cumberland County Housing
 Authority
Box 428
Toledo, IL 62468

Champaign County Housing Authority
P.O. Box 183
Urbana, IL 61801

Fayette County Housing Authority
528 Washington St.
Vandalia, IL 62471

Johnson County Housing Authority
Box 188
Vienna, IL 62471

Waukegan Housing Authority
200 S. Utica St.
Waukegan, IL 60085

Franklin County Housing Authority
302 E. Elm St.
West Frankfort, IL 62896

Greene County Housing Authority
325 N. Carr St.
White Hall, IL 62092

Scott County Housing Authority
P.O. Box 126
Winchester, IL 62694

Lake County Housing Authority
1525 27th St.
Zion, IL 60099

INDIANA

Anderson Housing Authority
120 E. Eighth St.
Room 120
Anderson, IN 46015

Angola Housing Authority
617 N. Williams
Angola, IN 46703

Bedford Housing Authority
1305 K St.
Bedford, IN 47421

Bloomfield Housing Authority
P.O. Box 801
Bloomfield, IN 47424

Bloomington Housing Authority
1007 N. Summitt St.
Bloomington, IN 47401

Boonville Housing Authority
113 S. Second St.
Boonville, IN 47601

Brazil Housing Authority
120 W. Jackson
Brazil, IN 47834

Charlestown Housing Authority
214 McCampbell St.
Charlestown, IN 47111

Clinton Housing Authority
Clinton, IN 47842

Crawfordsville Housing Authority
Ben Hur Building
Crawfordsville, IN 47933

East Chicago Housing Authority
4920 Larkspur Dr.
East Chicago, IN 46312

Elkhart Housing Authority
501 W. Indiana Ave.
Elkhart, IN 46514

Evansville Housing Authority
411 SE Eighth St.
Evansville, IN 47713

Fort Wayne Housing Authority
1 Maine St.
Suite 800
Fort Wayne, IN 46802

Gary Housing Authority
504 Broadway
Suite 301
Gary, IN 46402

Hammond Housing Authority
7329 Columbia Circle W.
Hammond, IN 46324

Huntingburg Housing Authority
No. 2 Friendship Village
Huntingburg, IN 47542

Indianapolis Housing Authority
410 N. Meridian St.
Indianapolis, IN 46204

Jeffersonville Housing Authority
1701 Spring St.
Jeffersonville, IN 47130

Kendallville Housing Authority
Box 127
Kendallville, IN 46755

Kokomo Housing Authority
800 E. Hoffer St.
Kokomo, IN 46902

Marion Housing Authority
312 Iroquois Building
Marion, IN 46952

Michigan Housing Authority
621 E. Michigan Blvd.
Michigan City, IN 46360

Mishawaka Housing Authority
500 Lincoln Way East
Mishawaka, IN 46544

Delaware County Housing Authority
173 Middletown Gardens
Muncie, IN 47302

Muncie Housing Authority
402 E. Second St.
Muncie, IN 47301

New Albany Housing Authority
169-171 Woodland Drive
New Albany, IN 47150

New Castle Housing Authority
274 S. 14th St.
New Castle, IN 47362

Richmond Housing Authority
81 S. 14th St.
Richmond, IN 47374

Rockport Housing Authority
714 Sycamore St.
Rockport, IN 47635

Rockville Housing Authority
105 W. Hight St.
Rockville, IN 47842

South Bend Housing Authority
501 So. Scott St.
South Bend, IN 46624

Sullivan Housing Authority
P.O. Box 524
Sullivan, IN 47882

Tell City Housing Authority
1648 Tenth St.
P.O. Box 103
Tell City, IN 47586

Terre Haute Housing Authority
P.O. Box 3086
Terre Haute, IN 47807

Vincennes Housing Authority
501 Hart St.
Vincennes, IN 47591

Washington Housing Authority
520 SE Second St.
Washington, IN 47501

West Baden Springs Housing Authority
c/o Executive Director
West Baden Springs, IN 47469

IOWA

Afton Housing Authority
Box 365
Afton, IA 50830

Low Rent Housing Agency of Albia
c/o Executive Director
Albia, IA 52531

Low Rent Housing Authority of
 Atlantic
c/o Executive Director
Atlantic, IA 50022

HOUSING 167

Bancroft Housing Authority
Box 267
Bancroft, IA 50517

Burlington Low Rent Housing Agency
2820 Winegard Drive
Burlington, IA 52601

Cedar Falls Low Rent Housing Agency
220 Clay St.
Cedar Falls, IA 50613

Cedar Rapids Low Rent Housing
    Agency
City Hall
Cedar Rapids, IA 52401

Centerville Low Rent Housing Agency
Box 492
Centerville, IA 52544

Chariton Housing Authority
429 South Main St.
Chariton, IA 50049

Charles City Housing Commission
501 Court St.
Charles City, IA 50616

Clarinda Low Rent Housing Authority
City Hall
Clarinda, IA 51632

Low Rent Housing Agency of Clinton
611 So. Third St.
P.O. Box 337
Clinton, IA 52732

Corning Housing Commission
P.O. Box 22
Corning, IA 50841

Council Bluffs Housing Authority
505 S. Sixth St.
Council Bluffs, IA 51501

Davenport Housing Authority
City Hall
Davenport, IA 52801

Des Moines-Iowa Housing Agency
1101 Crocker St.
Des Moines, IA 50309

Essex Housing Agency
c/o Executive Director
Essex, IA 51638

Farragut Housing Agency
c/o Executive Director
Farragut, IA 51639

Low Rent Housing Agency of
    Fort Dodge
c/o Executive Director
Fort Dodge, IA 50501

Fort Madison Low Rent Housing
    Agency
713 Seventh St.
Fort Madison, IA 52627

Goldfield Low Rent Housing Agency
c/o Executive Director
Goldfield, IA 50542

Hamburg Housing Authority
P.O. Box 70
Hamburg, IA 51640

Low Rent Housing Agency of Harlan
c/o Executive Director
Harlan, IA 51537

Low Rent Housing Agency of
    Warren Co.
P.O. Box 372
Indianola, IA 50125

Iowa City Housing Authority
Civic Center
Iowa City, IA 52240

Keduck Housing Authority
111 S. Second St.
Keokuk, IA 52632

Low Rent Housing Agency, Lake City
c/o Executive Director
Lake City, IA 51449

Lenox Low Rent Housing Agency
404 W. Ohio
Lenox, IA 50851

Leon Housing Authority
c/o Exeuctive Director
Leon, IA 50144

Southern Iowa Regional Housing
    Authority
L Hullinger, Hospital Annex Building
Leon, IA 50144

Lone Tree Housing Commission
City Hall
Lone Tree, IA 52755

Malvern Housing Agency
c/o Executive Director
Malvern, IA 51551

Low Rent Housing Agency of Manila
c/o Hon. Lyle Grunn, Mayor
Manila, IA 51454

Manning Housing Agency
421 Center St.
Manning, IA 51455

Low Rent Housing Agency of Mason
    City
c/o Executive Director
Mason City, IA 50401

Missouri Valley Housing Authority
Culavin Heights
Missouri Valley, IA 51555

Mount Ayr Housing Authority
c/o Executive Director
Mount Ayr, IA 52854

Muscatine Housing Authority
City Hall
Muscatine, IA 52761

Low Rent Housing Agency
22 South Locust
New Hampton, IA 50659

Onawa Housing Agency
1019 Ninth St.
Onawa, IA 51040

Ottumwa Housing Agency
102 W. Finley Ave.
Ottumwa, IA 52501

Red Oak Low Rent Housing Authority
415 Coolvaugh St.
Red Oak, IA 51566

Low Rent Housing Agency of Sac
    City
c/o Executive Director
Sac City, IA 50583

Shenandoah Housing Agency
707 W. Summit Ave.
Shenandoah, IA 51601

Sidney Housing Agency
c/o Executive Director
Sidney, IA 51652

Sioux Center Housing Authority
510 N. Meadow Drive
Sioux Center, IA 51250

Sioux City Housing Authority
P.O. Box 447
Sioux City, IA 51102

Stanton Housing Commission
P.O. Box D
Stanton, IA 51573

Tabor Low Rent Housing Authority
Valley View Villa
Tabor, IA 51653

Sac and Fox Housing Authority
Sac and Fox Settlement
Tama, IA 52339

Dept. of Housing and Rehabilitation
715 Mulberry St.
Waterloo, IA 50705

Waverly Housing Authority
320 15th St. NW
Waverly, IA 50677

Winterset Housing Agency
Second and Filmore Sts.
Winterset, IA 50273

KANSAS

Agra Housing Authority
Office of City Clerk
Agra, KS 67621

Anthony Housing Authority
Box 247
Anthony, KS 67003

Atchison City Housing Authority
Mall Towers
Atchison, KS 66002

Atwood Housing Authority
509 Main St.
Atwood, KS 66730

Augusta Housing Authority
Box 516
Augusta, KS 67010

Beloit Housing Authority
c/o Executive Director
Beloit, KS 67420

Bird City Housing Authority
Box 46
Bird City, KS 67731

168 THE OLDER AMERICAN'S HANDBOOK

Blue Rapids Housing Authority
500 E. Fifth St.
Blue Rapids, KS 66411

Bonner Springs Housing Authority
Box 237
Bonner Springs, KS 66012

Burrton Housing Authority
Box 135
Burrton, KS 67020

Chanute Housing Authority
Box 311
Chanute, KS 66720

Clay Center Housing Authority
Box 224
Clay Center, KS 67432

Colby Housing Authority
Box 835
Colby, KS 67701

Dodge City Housing Authority
111 Gunsmoke
Dodge City, KS 67801

Fort Scott Housing Authority
Box 269
Fort Scott, KS 66701

Galena Housing Authority
P.O. Box 336
Galena, KS 66739

Garden City Housing Authority
Box 499
Garden City, KS 67846

Gaylord Housing Authority
City Hall
Gaylord, KS 67638

Girard Housing Authority
P.O. Box 325
Girard, KS 66743

Goodland Housing Authority
City Hall
Goodland, KS 67735

Great Bend Housing Authority
P.O. Box 625
Great Bend, KS 67530

Hanover Housing Authority
City Hall
Hanover, KS 66945

Hill City Housing Authority
304 W. Prout
Hill City, KS 67642

Holton Housing Authority
City Hall
Holton, KS 66436

Horton Housing Authority
City Hall
Room 202
Horton, KS 66439

Kickapoo Tribe Housing Authority
Horton Agency Kickapoo Reservation
Horton, KS 66439

Hoxie Housing Authority
821 Main St.
Hoxie, KS 67740

Humboldt Housing Authority
P.O. Box 66
Humboldt, KS 66748

Iola Housing Authority
Box 622
Iola, KS 66749

Jetmore Housing Authority
City Hall
Jetmore, KS 67854

Kansas City Housing Authority
1124 N. Ninth St.
Kansas City, KS 66101

Kinsley Housing Authority
City of Kinsley
Kinsley, KS 67547

Lawrence Housing Authority
City Hall
Lawrence, KS 66044

Leavenworth Housing Authority
City Hall
Leavenworth, KS 66048

Lindsborg Housing Authority
P.O. Box 427
Lindsborg, KS 67456

Linn Housing Authority
City Hall
Linn, KS 66953

Luray Housing Authority
City Hall
Luray, KS 67649

Lyons Housing Authority
City Hall
Lyons, KS 67554

Manhattan Housing Authority
P.O. Box 1024
Manhattan, KS 66502

Marion Housing Authority
City Clerk's Office
Marion, KS 66861

Marysville Housing Authority
c/o City Clerk
Marysville, KS 66508

Medicine Lodge Housing Authority
City Hall
Medicine Lodge, KS 67104

Minneapolis Housing Authority
Box 207
Minneapolis, KS 67467

Moundridge Housing Authority
P.O. Box 14
Moundridge, KS 67107

Neodesha Housing Authority
118 S. Sixth
P.O. Box 184
Neodesha, KS 66600

Newton Housing Authority
115 W. Ninth St.
Newton, KS 67114

North Newton Housing Authority
Science Hall
North Newton, KS 67117

Norton Housing Authority
City Hall
Norton, KS 67654

Oakley Housing Authority
Box 606
Oakley, KS 67748

Oberlin Housing Authority
City Offices
Oberlin, KS 67749

Olathe Housing Authority
P.O. Box 205
Olathe, KS 66061

Osborne Housing Authority
City Hall
Osborne, KS 67473

Paola Housing Authority
310 S. Iron
Paola, KS 66071

Parsons Housing Authority
Municipal Building
Parsons, KS 67357

Phillipsburg Housing Authority
P.O. Box 81
Phillipsburg, KS 67761

Pleasanton Housing Authority
Ninth and Broad Sts.
Pleasanton, KS 66075

Russell Housing Authority
City Hall
Russell, KS 67665

Sabetha Housing Authority
City Hall
805 Main St.
Sabetha, KS 66534

St. Francis City Housing Authority
City Office
St. Francis, KS 67756

Salina Housing Authority
P.O. Box 1202
Salina, KS 67401

Sedgwick City Housing Authority
City Hall
Sedgwick, KS 67135

Seneca Housing Authority
35 South Fifth St.
Seneca, KS 66538

South Hutchinson Housing Authority
441 N. Washington
South Hutchinson, KS 67501

Sterling Housing Authority
City Hall
Sterling, KS 67579

Strong City Housing Authority
P.O. Box H
Strong City, KS 66869

Topeka City Housing Authority
P.O. Box 1551
Topeka, KS 66601

Ulysses Housing Authority
City Hall
Ulysses, KS 67880

Valley Falls City Housing Authority
City Hall
Valley Falls, KS 66088

Wamego Housing Authority
1507 Morningside Drive
Wamego, KS 66547

Washington City Housing Authority
Box 287
Washington, KS 66968

Waterville Housing Authority
City Hall
Waterville, KS 66548

Wellington Housing Authority
400 South C St.
Wellington, KS 67152

Iowa Tribe Kansas and Nebraska
 Housing Authority
Box 73
White Cloud, KS 66094

Wichita Housing Authority
1631 E. 17th St.
Wichita, KS 67214

KENTUCKY

Albany Municipal Housing Comm.
900 Third St.
Albany, KY 42602

Ashland Housing Authority
3131 Winchester Ave.
Ashland, KY 41101

Barboursville Municipal Housing
 Commission
P.O. Box 69
Barboursville, KY 40906

Bardstown Municipal Housing
513 W. Broadway
Bardstown, KY 40004

Beattyville Municipal Housing
 Commission
Boone Ave.
Beattyville, KY 41311

Beaver Dam Housing Authority
City Hall
Beaver Dam, KY 42320

Benton Municipal Housing
 Commission
101 Walnut Court
Benton, KY 42025

Berea Municipal Housing Commission
c/o Executive Director
Berea, KY 40403

Bowling Green Municipal Housing
 Commission
P.O. Box 116
Bowling Green, KY 42010

Burkesville Municipal Housing
 Commission
155 Sunset Drive
Burkesville, KY 42717

Cadiz Municipal Housing Authority
c/o Executive Director
Cadiz, KY 42211

Campbellsville Municipal Housing
 Commission
Box 254
Campbellsville, KY 42718

Carrollton Municipal Housing
 Commission
P.O. Box 305
Carrollton, KY 41008

Catlettsburg Municipal Housing
 Commission
Grandview Manor
Catlettsburg, KY 41129

Central City Municipal Housing
 Commission
P.O. Box 348
Central City, KY 42330

Greenville Municipal Housing
 Authority
P.O. Box 348
Central City, KY 42330

Clinton Municipal Housing Authority
City Hall
Clinton, KY 42031

Columbia Municipal Housing
 Commission
P.O. Box 205
Columbia, KY 42728

Corbin Municipal Housing Commission
1336
Corbin, KY 40701

Covington Municipal Housing
 Commission
2940 Madison Ave.
Covington, KY 41015

Cumberland Municipal Housing
 Commission
5 Russell
Cumberland, KY 40823

Cynthiana Municipal Housing
 Commission
P.O. Box 119
Cynthiana, KY 41031

Danville Municipal Housing
 Commission
P.O. Box 666
Danville, KY 40422

Dawson Springs Municipal Housing
 Commission
P.O. Box 472
Dawson Springs, KY 42408

Earlington Municipal Housing
 Commission
309 Westside
Earlington, KY 42410

Lyon County Housing Commission
P.O. Box 190
Eddyville, KY 42038

Elizabethtown Municipal Housing
 Commission
P.O. Box 623
Elizabethtown, KY 42701

Housing Authority of Radcliff
P.O. Box 623
Elizabethtown, KY 42701

Eminence Municipal Housing
 Commission
100 Circle Drive
Eminence, KY 40019

Falmouth Municipal Housing
 Commission
412 Beech St.
Falmouth, KY 41040

Flemingsburg Municipal Housing
 Commission
107 Circle Drive
Flemingsburg, KY 41041

Frankfort Municipal Housing
 Commission
901 Leestown Rd.
Frankfort, KY 40601

Franklin Municipal Housing
 Commission
P.O. Box 361
Franklin, KY 42134

Fulton Municipal Housing Commission
200 N. Highland
Fulton, KY 42041

Georgetown Municipal Housing
 Commission
P.O. Box 496
Georgetown, KY 40324

Glasgow Municipal Housing
 Commission
201 St. Mary's Court
Glasgow, KY 42141

Greensburg Municipal Housing
 Commission
422 Depot St.
Greensburg, KY 42743

Harlan Municipal Housing Commission
P.O. Box 855
Harlan, KY 40831

Harrodsburg Municipal Housing
 Commission
P.O. Box 385
Harrodsburg, KY 40330

Hazard Municipal Housing Commission
P.O. Box 360
Hazard, KY 41701

Henderson Municipal Housing
 Commission
901 Dixon St.
Henderson, KY 42420

Hickman Municipal Housing
 Commission
P.O. Box 296
Hickman, KY 42050

Knott County Housing Commission
P.O. Box 225
Hindman, KY 41822

Hodgenville Municipal Housing
 Commission
501 Miami Court
Hodgenville, KY 42748

Hopkinsville Municipal Housing
 Commission
P.O. Box 437
Hopkinsville, KY 42240

Horse Cave Municipal Housing
 Commission
140 Vila Drive
Horse Cave, KY 42749

Irvine Municipal Housing Commission
200 Wallace Court
Irvine, KY 40336

Irvington Municipal Housing
 Commission
P.O. Box 158
Irvington, KY 40146

Jackson Municipal Housing
 Commission
1126 Main St.
Jackson, KY 41339

Lancaster Municipal Housing
 Commission
P.O. Box 207
Lancaster, KY 40444

Lebanon Municipal Housing
 Commission
P.O. Box 633
Lebanon, KY 40033

Lexington-Fayette Urban Co Housing
600 Blue Grass Park Drive
Lexington, KY 40508

Liberty Municipal Housing Commission
P.O. Box 267
Liberty, KY 42539

London Municipal Housing Commission
100 McFadden Lane
London, KY 40741

Lawrence County Housing Commission
P.O. Box 306
Louisa, KY 41230

Jefferson County Housing Authority
400 S. Sixth St.
Louisville, KY 40201

Louisville Municipal Housing Authority
P.O. Box 1674
Louisville, KY 40203

Madisonville Municipal Housing
 Commission
211 Pride
Madisonville, KY 42431

Manchester Housing Authority
AMC Office Building No. 306
Manchester, KY 40962

Martin Municipal Housing Commission
P.O. Box 804
Martin, KY 41649

Mayfield Municipal Housing
 Commission
P.O. Box 474
Mayfield, KY 42066

Maysville Municipal Housing
 Commission
P.O. Box 446
Maysville, KY 41056

Middlesborough Municipal Housing
 Commission
S. 38th St.
Middlesborough, KY 40965

Monticello Municipal Housing
 Commission
P.O. Box 347
Monticello, KY 42633

Morehead Municipal Housing
 Commission
200 Heritage Place
Morehead, KY 40351

Morganfield Municipal Housing
 Commission
703 Culver Drive
Morganfield, KY 42437

Morgantown Municipal Housing
 Commission
P.O. Box 187
Morgantown, KY 42261

Mount Sterling Housing Authority
P.O. Box 245
Mount Sterling, KY 40353

Stanton Municipal Housing
 Commission
P.O. Box 245
Mount Sterling, KY 40353

Mount Vernon Municipal Housing
 Commission
P.O. Box 456
Mount Vernon, KY 40456

Murray Municipal Housing
 Commission
716 Nash Drive
Murray, KY 42071

Newport Municipal Housing
 Commission
P.O. Box 459
Newport, KY 41072

Nicholasville Municipal Housing
 Authority
601 Broadway
P.O. Box 155
Nicholasville, KY 40356

Olive Hill Municipal Housing
P.O. Box 472
Olive Hill, KY 41164

Owensboro Housing Authority
316 Hale Ave.
Owensboro, KY 42301

Owenton Housing Authority
Owenton, KY 40359

Owingsville Municipal Housing
 Commission
P.O. Box 734
Owingsville, KY 40360

Puducah Municipal Housing
 Commission
P.O. Box 1317
Paducah, KY 42001

Paintsville Municipal Housing
 Commission
P.O. Box 880
Paintsville, KY 41240

Paris Municipal Housing Commission
P.O. Box 468
Paris, KY 40361

Pikeville Municipal Housing
 Commission
P.O. Box 327
Main St. Station
Pikeville, KY 41501

Housing Authority of Pineville
911 Alabama Ave.
Pineville, KY 40977

Prestonburg Municipal Housing
 Commission
P.O. Box 361
Prestonburg, KY 41653

Princeton Municipal Housing
 Commission
City Hall
Princeton, KY 42455

Providence Municipal Housing
 Authority
434 Center Ridge Drive
Providence, KY 42450

Richmond Municipal Housing
 Commission
P.O. Box 447
Richmond, KY 40475

Russellville Municipal Housing
 Commission
701 Day St.
Russellville, KY 42276

Scottsville Municipal Housing
 Commission
c/o Executive Director
Scottsville, KY 42164

Shelbyville Municipal Housing
 Commission
41 Cardinal Drive
Shelbyville, KY 40065

McCreary County Housing Commission
P.O. Box 449
Somerset, KY 42501

Somerset Municipal Housing
 Commission
P.O. Box 449
Somerset, KY 42501

Housing Authority of Springfield
1057 Melavin Court
Springfield, KY 40069

Stanford Municipal Housing
    Commission
P.O. Box 181
Stanford, KY 40484

Sturgis Municipal Housing Commission
Box 252
Sturgis, KY 42459

Tompkinsville Municipal Housing
    Commission
108 W. Third St.
Tompkinsville, KY 42167

Vanceburg Municipal Housing
    Commission
802 Fairland Drive
Vanceburg, KY 41179

Versailles Municipal Housing
    Commission
519 Poplar St.
Versailles, KY 40383

Whitesburg Municipal Housing
    Commission
101 Alaska Ave.
Whitesburg, KY 41858

Williamsburg Municipal Housing
    Commission
153 Mackey Ave.
Williamsburg, KY 40769

Williamstown Municipal Housing
    Commission
514 Helton Heights
Williamstown, KY 41097

Winchester Housing Authority
Box 56
Winchester, KY 40391

LOUISIANA

Abbeville Housing Authority
P.O. Box 435
Abbeville, LA 70501

Alexandria Housing Authority
P.O. Box 4196
Alexandria, LA 71301

Rapides Parish Housing Authority
P.O. Box 1150
Alexandria, LA 71301

Arcadia Housing Authority
Box 210
Arcadia, LA 71001

Basile Housing Authority
P.O. Box 355
Basile, LA 70515

East Baton Rouge Parish Housing
    Authority
P.O. Box 65038
Baton Rouge, LA 70821

Berwick Housing Authority
P.O. Box 231
Berwick, LA 70342

Bogalusa Housing Authority
Box 1113
Bogalusa, LA 70427

Bossier City Housing Authority
P.O. Box 5666
Bossier City, LA 71010

Saint Charles Parrish Housing Authority
P.O. Box 448
Boutte, LA 70039

Breaux Bridge Housing Authority
327 Washington St.
Breaux Bridge, LA 70517

Lafayette Parrish Housing Authority
c/o Executive Director
Broussard, LA 70808

Bunkie Housing Authority
P.O. Box 603
Bunkie, LA 71322

Church Point Housing Authority
P.O. Box 143
Church Point, LA 70525

Clarence Village Housing Authority
Town Hall
Clarence, LA 71414

Colfax Housing Authority
401 Eighth St.
Colfax, LA 71417

Caldwell Parish Housing Authority
Box 217
Columbia, LA 71418

Cottonport Housing Authority
Box 487
Cottonport, LA 71327

Cotton Valley Housing Authority
Box 266
Cotton Valley, LA 71018

Crowley Housing Authority
P.O. Box 1347
Crowley, LA 70526

Delcambre Housing Authority
P.O. Box 417
Delcambre, LA 70528

Delhi Housing Authority
106 Oak St.
Delhi, LA 71232

Denham Springs Housing Authority
P.O. Box 965
Denham Springs, LA 70726

Dequincy Housing Authority
P.O. Box 126
Dequincy, LA 70633

Deridder Housing Authority
P.O. Box 387
Deridder, LA 70634

Donaldsonville Housing Authority
P.O. Box 5
Donaldsonville, LA 70346

East Hodge Housing Authority
P.O. Box 237
East Hodge, LA 71247

Elton Housing Authority
Box 425-A
Elton, LA 70532

Erath Housing Authority
205 N. Mouton St.
Erath, LA 70533

Southwest Acadia Consol Housing
    Authority
Box 114
Esterwood, LA 70534

Eunice Housing Authority
P.O. Box 224
Eunice, LA 70535

Farmerville Housing Authority
Box 446
Farmerville, LA 71241

Ferriday Housing Authority
c/o Executive Director
Ferriday, LA 70800

Gibsland Housing Authority
P.O. Box 275
Gibsland, LA 71028

Grambling Housing Authority
Box 829
Grambling, LA 71245

South Landry Housing Authority
P.O. Drawer E
Grand Coteau, LA 70541

Gueydan Housing Authority
City Hall
Gueydan, LA 70542

Hammond Housing Authority
211 W. Thomas St.
Hammond, LA 70401

Haynesville Housing Authority
Drawer 751
Haynesville, LA 71038

Homer Housing Authority
329 S. Fourth St.
Homer, LA 71040

Houma Housing Authority
332 W. Park Ave.
Houma, LA 70360

Independence Housing Authority
P.O. Box 56
Independence, LA 70443

Jennings Housing Authority
Drawer 921
Jennings, LA 70546

Jonesboro Housing Authority
839 Harvey Place
Jonesboro, LA 71251

Kaplan Housing Authority
205 N. Cushing Ave.
Kaplan, LA 70548

Kenner Housing Authority
1013 31st St.
Kenner, LA 70062

Kinder Housing Authority
P.O. Box 808
Kinder, LA 70648

Lafayette Housing Authority
100 C O Circle
Lafayette, LA 70501

Lake Arthur Housing Authority
P.O. Box R
Lake Arthur, LA 70549

Lake Charles Housing Authority
Box 1206
Lake Charles, LA 70601

Lake Providence Housing Authority
Box 126
Lake Providence, LA 71254

St. John the Baptist Parish Housing Authority
Drawer S
LaPlace, LA 70068

Leesville Housing Authority
Drawer 648
Leesville, LA 71446

Logansport Housing Authority
Box Q
Logansport, LA 71049

Saint James Parish Housing Authority
Box 280
Lutcher, LA 70071

Mamou Housing Authority
1016 Maple St.
Mamou, LA 70554

Mansfield Housing Authority
P.O. Box 671
Mansfield, LA 71052

Sabine Parish Housing Authority
110 Esso Drive
Many, LA 71449

Marksville Housing Authority
102 Vettas St.
Marksville, LA 71351

Sabine Parish Housing Authority
102 Vettas St.
Marksville, LA 71351

Jefferson Parish Housing Authority
1718 Betty St.
Marrero, LA 70072

Merryville Housing Authority
P.O. Box L
Merryville, LA 70653

Minden Housing Authority
P.O. Box 628
Minden, LA 71055

Monroe Housing Authority
Box 1194
Monroe, LA 71201

Morgan City Housing Authority
P.O. Box 2393
Morgan City, LA 70380

Assumption Parish Housing Authority
P.O. Box 308
Napoleonville, LA 70390

Natchitoches Housing Authority
Box 754
Natchitoches, LA 71457

New Iberia Housing Authority
325 North St.
New Iberia, LA 70560

New Orleans Housing Authority
918 Carondelet St.
New Orleans, LA 70130

New Roads Housing Authority
P.O. Box 338
New Roads, LA 70760

Oakdale Housing Authority
Drawer BQ
Oakdale, LA 71463

Oberlin Housing Authority
Box 338
Oberlin, LA 70655

Oil City Housing Authority
Box 206
Oil City, LA 71061

Olla Housing Authority
Box 223
Olla, LA 71465

Opelousas Housing Authority
P.O. Box 689
Opelousas, LA 70570

Parks Housing Authority
Fire Station
Parks, LA 70582

Patterson Housing Authority
Box 329
Patterson, LA 70392

Pineville Housing Authority
P.O. Box 190
Pineville, LA 71360

Ponchatoula Housing Authority
P.O. Box 783
Ponchatoula, LA 70454

LaFourche Parish Housing Authority
P.O. Box 499
Raceland, LA 70394

Rayne Housing Authority
P.O. Box 164
Rayne, LA 70578

Rayville Housing Authority
Drawer 780
Rayville, LA 71269

Ruston Housing Authority
Drawer 1283
Ruston, LA 71270

Saint Martinville Housing Authority
431 Washington St.
Saint Martinville, LA 70582

Shreveport Housing Authority
2725 Southern Ave.
Shreveport, LA 71104

Simmesport Housing Authority
Laurel St.
Simmesport, LA 71369

Slidell Housing Authority
3700 Pontchartrain Drive
Slidell, LA 70458

Sulphur Housing Authority
211 Pinecrest Drive
Sulphur, LA 70663

Thibodaux Housing Authority
Box 775
Thibodaux, LA 70301

Ville Platte Housing Authority
P.O. Box 259
Ville Platte, LA 70586

Vinton Housing Authority
Box 687
Vinton, LA 70668

Vivian Housing Authority
609 Redbud Courts
Vivian, LA 71082

Saint Landry Parish Housing Authority
Box 276
Washington, LA 70589

Welsh Housing Authority
P.O. Box 356
Welsh, LA 70591

Westlake Housing Authority
522 Miller Ave.
Westlake, LA 70669

Westwego Housing Authority
P.O. Box 248
Westwego, LA 70094

White Castle Housing Authority
P.O. Box 58
White Castle, LA 70788

Winnfield Housing Authority
P.O. Box 190
Winnfield, LA 71483

Winnsboro Housing Authority
P.O. Box 267
Winnsboro, LA 71295

Youngsville Housing Authority
Box 367
Youngsville, LA 70592

MAINE

Auburn Housing Authority
74 Lake Auburn Ave.
Auburn, ME 04210

Maine State Housing Authority
State House
Augusta, ME 04330

Bangor Housing Authority
26 Down East Circle
Bangor, ME 04401

Bar Harbor Housing Authority
Municipal Building
Cottage St.
Bar Harbor, ME 04609

Mt. Desert Island Housing Authority
Box 174
Bar Harbor, ME 04609

Bath Housing Authority
55 Front St.
Bath, ME 04530

Brewer Housing Authority
80 N. Main St.
Brewer, ME 04412

Brunswick Housing Authority
51 N. Brunswick St.
Brunswick, ME 04011

Fort Fairfield Housing Authority
P.O. Box 252
Fort Fairfield, ME 04742

Lewiston Housing Authority
90 Blake St. Towers
Lewiston, ME 04240

Old Town Housing Authority
St. Mary's Church
Old Town, ME 04468

Penobscot Trial Reservation Housing Authority
Indian Island
Old Town, ME 04468

Pleasant Point Passamaquoddy Reservation Housing Authority
P.O. Box 282
Perry, ME 04667

Portland Housing Authority
211 Cumberland Ave.
Portland, ME 04102

Presque Isle Housing Authority
P.O. Drawer C
Presque Isle, ME 04769

Passamaquaddy Reservation
P.O. Box 127
Princeton, ME 04668

Sanford Housing Authority
c/o Executive Director
Sanford, ME 04073

South Portland Housing Authority
425 Broadway
South Portland, ME 04106

Southwest Harbor Housing Authority
c/o City Manager
Southwest Harbor, ME 04679

Van Buren Housing Authority
P.O. Box 96
Van Buren, ME 04785

Waterville Housing Authority
50 Main St.
Waterville, ME 04904

Westbrook Housing Authority
c/o Executive Director
Westbrook, ME 04092

MARYLAND

Annapolis Housing Authority
P.O. Box 1727
Annapolis, MD 21404

Department of Housing and Community Development
222 E. Saratoga St.
Baltimore, MD 21203

Maryland State Economic and Community Development Commission
c/o Locator
Baltimore, MD 21203

Cambridge Housing Authority
P.O. Box 443
Cambridge, MD 21613

Prince George's County Housing Authority
9171 Center Ave.
Capitol Heights, MD 20027

College Park Housing Authority
9014 Rhode Island Ave. (Exit)
College Park, MD 20074

Crisfield Housing Authority
P.O. Box 26
Crisfield, MD 21817

Cumberland Housing Authority
P.O. Box 506
Cumberland, MD 21502

Easton Housing Authority
P.O. Box 777
Easton, MD 21601

Elkton Housing Authority
P.O. Box 328
Elkton, MD 21921

Frederick Housing Authority
23 W. Sixth St.
Frederick, MD 21701

Frostburg Housing Authority
City Hall
Frostburg, MD 21532

Anne Arundel County Housing Authority
6652 Shelly Rd.
Glen Burnie, MD 21061

Hagerstown Housing Authority
11 W. Baltimore St.
Hagerstown, MD 21740

Havre De Grace Housing Authority
101 Stansbury Court
Havre De Grace, MD 21078

St. Mary's County Housing Authority
c/o Hartman Building
Hurley, MD 20637

Glenarden Housing Authority
8614 Fulton Ave.
Lanham, MD 20801

Rockville Housing Authority
14 Moore Drive
Rockville, MD 20850

St. Michaels Housing Authority
c/o Executive Director
St. Michaels, MD 21663

Wicomico County Housing Authority
911 Booth St.
Salisbury, MD 21801

Montgomery County Housing Authority
1400 Fenwick Lane
Silver Spring, MD 20910

MASSACHUSETTS

Arlington Housing Authority
4 Winslow St.
Arlington, MA 02174

Newton Housing Authority
2000 Commonwealth Ave.
Auburndale, MA 02166

Beverly Housing Authority
60 Herrick St.
Beverly, MA 01915

Boston Housing Authority
230 Congress St.
Boston, MA 02110

Brockton Housing Authority
45 Goddard Rd.
Brockton, MA 02401

Brookline Housing Authority
226 High St.
Brookline, MA 02146

Cambridge Housing Authority
678 Massachusetts Ave.
Cambridge, MA 02139

Chelsea Housing Authority
54 Lock St.
Chelsea, MA 02150

Chicopee Housing Authority
118 Meetinghouse Rd.
Chicopee, MA 01013

Clinton Housing Authority
58 Fitch Rd.
Clinton, MA 01510

Dedham Housing Authority
163 Dedham Blvd.
Dedham, MA 02026

Dracut Housing Authority
149 Pleasant St.
Dracut, MA 01826

Fall River Housing Authority
P.O. Box 989
Fall River, MA 02722

Falmouth Housing Authority
Choate Lane
Box 324
Falmouth, MA 02541

Fitchburg Housing Authority
13 Normandy Rd.
Fitchburg, MA 01420

Framingham Housing Authority
P.O. Box 165
Framingham, MA 01702

Gloucester Housing Authority
Maplewood Park
Gloucester, MA 01930

Holyoke Housing Authority
475 Maple
Holyoke, MA 01040

Barnstable Housing Authority
P.O. Box 452
Hyannis, MA 02601

Lawrence Housing Authority
353 Elm St.
Lawrence, MA 01841

Lowell Housing Authority
350 Moody St.
Lowell, MA 01854

Lynn Housing Authority
455 Garfield Ave.
Lynn, MA 01905

Malden Housing Authority
630 Salem St.
Malden, MA 02148

Medford Housing Authority
121 Riverside Ave.
Medford, MA 02155

New Bedford Housing Authority
P.O. Box A-2081
New Bedford, MA 02741

Newburyport Housing Authority
25 Temple St.
Newburyport, MA 01951

North Adams Housing Authority
150 Ashland St.
North Adams, MA 01247

Northampton Housing Authority
49 Old South St.
Northampton, MA 01061

Pittsfield Housing Authority
2 North St.
Pittsfield, MA 01201

Quincy Housing Authority
95 Martensen St.
Quincy, MA 02169

Revere Housing Authority
70 Cooledge St.
Revere, MA 02151

Shrewsbury Housing Authority
P.O. Box 203
Shrewsbury, MA 01545

Somerville Housing Authority
30 Memorial Rd.
Somerville, MA 02145

Springfield Housing Authority
82 Division St.
Springfield, MA 01101

Taunton Housing Authority
1 Dewert Ave.
Taunton, MA 02780

Waltham Housing Authority
110 Pond St.
Waltham, MA 02154

Weymouth Housing Authority
77 Memorial Drive
Weymouth, MA 02189

Winchendon Housing Authority
110 Front St.
Winchendon, MA 01475

Woburn Housing Authority
No. 4 Federal St.
Suite 110
Woburn, MA 01801

Worcester Housing Authority
40 Belmont St.
Worcester, MA 01605

MICHIGAN

Albion Housing Commission
507 W. Broadwell St.
Albion, MI 49224

Algonac Housing Commission
906 St. Clair River Drive
Algonac, MI 48001

Allen Park Housing Commission
City Hall
Allen Park, MI 48101

Alma Housing Commission
City Hall
Alma, MI 48801

Alpena Housing Authority
325 Fowler Drive
Alpena, MI 49707

Ann Arbor Housing Commission
727 Miller Ave.
Ann Arbor, MI 48103

Baldwin Housing Commission
Village Hall
Baldwin, MI 49304

Baraga Housing Commission
c/o Executive Director
Baraga, MI 49908

Battle Creek Housing Commission
380 Truth Drive
Battle Creek, MI 49017

Bay City Housing Commission
315 14th St.
Bay City, MI 48706

Belding Housing Committee
City Hall
Belding, MI 48809

Sumpter Township Housing Commission
23483 Sumpter Rd.
Belleville, MI 48111

Benton Harbor Housing Authority
1216 Blossom Lane
Benton Harbor, MI 49022

Benton Township Housing Authority
c/o Executive Director
Benton Harbor, MI 49022

Bessemer Housing Commission
c/o Executive Director
Bessemer, MI 49911

Big Rapids Housing Commission
9 Parkview Village
Big Rapids, MI 49307

Boyne City Housing Commission
City Hall
Boyne City, MI 49712

Bay Mills Indian Housing Commission
Rural Route No. 1
Box 175
Brimley, MI 49715

Bronson Housing Commission
119 S. Matteson St.
Bronson, MI 49028

Cadillac Housing Commission
111 S. Simons
Cadillac, MI 49601

Calumet Housing Commission
Village of Calumet
Calumet, MI 49913

Cheboygan Housing Commission
659 Cuyler St.
Cheboygan, MI 49721

Coldwater Housing Commission
5 South Monroe St.
Coldwater, MI 49036

Iron County Housing Authority
412 Crystal Ave.
Crystal Falls, MI 49920

Dearborn Housing Commission
13615 Michigan Ave.
Dearborn, MI 48126

Detroit Housing Commission
2211 Orleans T.
Detroit, MI 48207

East Detroit Housing Commission
15711 Nine Mile Rd.
East Detroit, MI 48021

Ecorse Housing Commission
266 Hyacinth St.
Ecorse, MI 48229

Elk Rapids Housing Commission
602 E. Third St.
Elk Rapids, MI 49627

Escanaba Housing Commission
116 S. Fifth St.
Escanaba, MI 49829

Evart Housing Commission
843 N. Main St.
Evart, MI 49631

Ferndale Housing Authority
300 E. Nine Mile Rd.
Ferndale, MI 48220

Royal Oak Housing Commission
21075 Wyoming Ave.
Ferndale, MI 48601

Flint Housing Commission
Room 302
Municipal Center
Flint, MI 48502

Gladstone Housing Commission
415 S. Fourth St.
Gladstone, MI 49837

Grand Rapids Housing Commission
Room G
Civic Auditorium
Grand Rapids, MI 49501

Grayling Housing Commission
103 James St.
Grayling, MI 49738

Greenville Housing Authority
Greenville, MI 48838

Hamtramck Housing Commission
12025 Dequindre Ave.
Hamtramck, MI 48212

HOUSING

Hancock Housing Commission
502 Quincy St.
Hancock, MI 49930

Hazel Park Housing Commission
22422 Stephenson Highway
Hazel Park, MI 48030

Highland Park Housing Authority
c/o Executive Director
Highland Park, MI 48000

Inkster Housing & Redevelopment
   Commission
30005 Pine St.
Inkster, MI 48141

Ionia Housing Authority
114 N. Kidd St.
Ionia, MI 48816

Iron Mountain Housing Commission
401 East D St.
Iron Mountain, MI 49801

Iron River Housing Commission
106 W. Genesee St.
Iron River, MI 49935

Ironwood Housing Commission
Municipal Memorial Building
Ironwood, MI 49938

Lac Vieux District Chippewa Housing
   Authority
P.O. Box 188
Ironwood, MI 49938

Ishpeming Housing Commission
100 E. Division St.
Ishpeming, MI 49849

Jackson Housing Commission
301 Steward Ave.
Jackson, MI 49203

Kingsford Housing Commission
1025 Woodward Ave.
Kingsford, MI 49801

Lake Linden Housing Authority
Lake Linden, MI 49945

Ojibwa Housing Authority
Box 226
L'Anse, MI 49946

Village of L'Anse
811 Lakeside Ave.
L'Anse, MI 49946

Lansing Housing Commission
310 Seymour St.
Lansing, MI 48933

Lapeer Housing Board
307 Clay St.
Lapeer, MI 48446

Laurium Housing Commission
310 Hecla St.
Laurium, MI 49914

Lincoln Park Housing Commission
1355 Southfield Rd.
Lincoln Park, MI 48146

Livonia Housing Commission
19500 Purlingbrook
Livonia, MI 48152

Luna Pier Housing Commission
Municipal Building
Luna Pier, MI 48157

Manistee Housing Commission
330 River St.
Manistee, MI 49660

Manistique Housing Commission
City Hall
Manistique, MI 49854

Marquette Housing Commission
City Hall
Marquette, MI 49855

Menominee Housing Commission
P.O. Box 64
Menominee, MI 49858

Monroe Housing Commission
20 N. Roessler St.
Monroe, MI 48161

Clinton Township Housing
   Commission
34947 Village Rd.
Mount Clemens, MI 48043

Mount Clemens Housing Commission
169 N. Walnut
Mount Clemens, MI 48043

Mount Pleasant Housing Commission
120 S. College
Mount Pleasant, MI 48858

Saginaw Chippewa Housing Authority
Route No. 6
2463 Nishnobe Rd.
Mount Pleasant, MI 48858

Munising Housing Commission
127 E. Chocolay St.
Munising, MI 49862

Muskegon Housing Authority
1080 Terrace
Muskegon, MI 49442

Muskegon Heights Housing Authority
615 E. Hovey Ave.
Muskegon Heights, MI 49444

Negaunee Housing Commission
98 Croix St.
Negaunee, MI 49866

Niles Housing Commission
508 E. Main St.
Niles, MI 49120

Ontonagon Village Housing
   Commission
311 N. Steel St.
Ontonagon, MI 49953

Paw Paw Housing Commission
Village Hall
Paw Paw, MI 49079

Plymouth Housing Commission
201 S. Main St.
Plymouth, MI 48170

Pontiac Housing Commission
255 Carriage Circle
Pontiac, MI 48058

Port Huron Housing Commission
905 Seventh St.
Port Huron, MI 48060

Reed City Housing Commission
802 Mill St.
Reed City, MI 49677

River Rouge Housing Commission
16 Haltiner St.
River Rouge, MI 48218

Rockford Housing Authority
c/o Executive Director
Rockford, MI 48000

Rockwood Housing Commission
c/o Executive Director
Rockwood, MI 49341

Rogers City Housing Commission
193 E. Michigan Ave.
Rogers City, MI 49779

Romulus Twp. Housing Commission
5907 Chamberlain
Romulus, MI 48184

Roseville Housing Commission
25524 Lawn Boulevard
Roseville, MI 48066

Saginaw Housing Commission
1803 Norman St.
Saginaw, MI 48601

St. Clair Housing Commission
411 Trumbull St.
St. Clair, MI 48079

St. Clair Shores Housing Commission
27600 E. Jefferson
St. Clair Shores, MI 48081

St. Joseph Housing Commission
620 Broad St.
St. Joseph, MI 49085

St. Louis Housing Commission
108 W. Saginaw St.
St. Louis, MI 48880

Saranac Housing Commission
c/o Executive Director
Saranac, MI 48881

Sault Sainte Marie Housing
   Commission
608 Pine St.
Sault Sainte Marie, MI 49783

South Haven Housing Commission
529 Phoenix St.
South Haven, MI 49090

South Lyon Housing Commission
432 Washington St.
South Lyon, MI 48178

Stambaugh Housing Commission
208 Third St.
Stambaugh, MI 49964

Sturgis Housing Commission
130 N. Nattawa St.
Sturgis, MI 49091

Taylor Township Housing Commission
23555 Goddard Rd.
Taylor, MI 48180

176 THE OLDER AMERICAN'S HANDBOOK

Traverse City Housing Commission
160 E. State St.
Traverse City, MI 49684

Trenton Housing Commission
2872 W. Jefferson Ave.
Trenton, MI 48183

Wakefield Housing Commission
200 Pierce St.
Wakefield, MI 49968

Wayne Housing Commission
34808 Sims Ave.
Wayne, MI 48184

Ypsilanti Housing Commission
601 Armstrong Drive
Ypsilanti, MI 48197

MINNESOTA

Aitkin County Housing & Redevelopment Authority
37 Second Ave. SE
Aitkin, MN 56431

Albert Lea Housing & Redevelopment Authority
City Center
221 E. Clark St.
Albert Lea, MN 56007

Alexandria Housing & Redevelopment Authority
P.O. Box 231
Alexandria, MN 56308

Austin Housing & Redevelopment Authority
200 First Ave. NE
Austin, MN 55912

Bagley Housing & Redevelopment Authority
c/o Village Offices
Bagley, MN 56621

Barnesville Housing & Redevelopment Authority
c/o Executive Director
Barnesville, MN 56514

Belgrade Housing Authority
c/o Executive Director
Belgrade, MN 56312

Bemidji Housing & Redevelopment Authority
600 America Ave.
Bemidji, MN 56601

Leech Lake Reservation Housing Authority
Federal Building
Bemidji, MN 56601

White Earth Reservation Housing Authority
c/o Bia
Federal Building
Bemidji, MN 56601

Benson Housing & Redevelopment Authority
City Office
Benson, MN 56215

Bertha Housing & Redevelopment Authority
c/o Executive Director
Bertha, MN 56437

Bloomington Housing & Redevelopment Authority
2215 W. Skaopee Rd.
Bloomington, MN 55431

Blue Earth Housing & Redevelopment Authority
220 E. Seventh St.
Blue Earth, MN 56013

Braham Housing & Redevelopment Authority
Box 457
Braham, MN 55006

Brainerd Housing Authority
Box 99
Brainerd, MN 56401

Breckenridge Housing & Redevelopment Authority
c/o Executive Director
Breckenridge, MN 56520

Cambridge Housing & Redevelopment Authority
114 N. Main St.
Cambridge, MN 55008

Carlton Housing & Redevelopment Authority
910 Cloquet Ave.
Carlton, MN 55400

Cass Lake Housing & Redevelopment Authority
c/o Executive Director
Cass Lake, MN 56633

Chisholm Housing & Redevelopment Authority
519 Sixth St. SW
Chisholm, MN 55719

Clarkfield Housing & Redevelopment Authority
c/o Executive Director
Clarkfield, MN 56223

Cloquet Housing & Redevelopment Authority
950 14th St.
Cloquet, MN 55720

Fond Du Lac Reservation Housing Authority
709 Larch St.
Cloquet, MN 55720

Columbia Heights Housing & Redevelopment Authority
c/o City Hall
Columbia Heights, MN 55421

Cook Housing & Redevelopment Authority
c/o Executive Director
Cook, MN 55723

Cottonwood Housing & Redevelopment Authority
c/o Executive Director
Cottonwood, MN 56229

Crookston Housing & Redevelopment Authority
114½ W. Robert St.
Crookston, MN 56716

Crosby Housing & Redevelopment Authority
c/o Executive Director
Crosby, MN 56441

Delano Housing & Redevelopment Authority
Box 94
Delano, MN 55328

Detroit Lakes Housing & Redevelopment Authority
P.O. Box 731
Detroit Lakes, MN 56501

Duluth Housing & Redevelopment Authority
301 E. Second Ave
Duluth, MN 55805

East Grand Forks Housing Authority
202 S. Second St.
East Grand Forks, MN 56721

Ely Housing & Redevelopment Authority
432 E. Camp St.
Ely, MN 55731

Eveleth Housing & Redevelopment Authority
902 Clay Court
Eveleth, MN 55734

Fairmont Housing & Redevelopment Authority
City Hall
Fairmont, MN 56031

Faribault Housing Authority
c/o Executive Director
Faribault, MN 55021

Fergus Falls Housing & Redevelopment Authority
P.O. Box 436
Fergus Falls, MN 56537

Forest Lake Housing & Redevelopment Authority
7 NE Fifth Ave.
Forest Lake, MN 55025

Sibley County Housing Authority
c/o Executive Director
Gaylord, MN 55334

Gilbert Housing & Redevelopment Authority
c/o Executive Director
Gilbert, MN 55741

Glencoe Housing & Redevelopment Authority
804 Franklin
Glencoe, MN 55336

Glenwood Housing & Redevelopment Authority
Lock Box E
Glenwood, MN 56334

Grand Rapids Housing & Redevelopment Authority
411 Seventh St. NW
Grand Rapids, MN 55744

Itasca County Housing & Redevelopment Authority
c/o Executive Director
Grand Rapids, MN 55744

Greenbush Housing & Redevelopment Authority
c/o Executive Director
Greenbush, MN 56726

Dakota County Housing & Redevelopment Authority
Court House
Hastings, MN 55033

Hennings Housing & Redevelopment Authority
First National Bank Building
Henning, MN 56551

Hibbing Housing & Redevelopment Authority
3112 Sixth Ave., E.
Hibbing, MN 55746

Hopkins Housing & Redevelopment Authority
1010 First St., S.
Hopkins, MN 55343

Hutchinson Housing & Redevelopment Authority
c/o Executive Director
Hutchinson, MN 55350

International Falls Housing Authority
1015 Second St.
International Falls, MN 56649

Koochiching County Housing Authority
c/o Executive Director
International Falls, MN 56649

Jackson Housing & Redevelopment Authority
501 E. First St.
Jackson, MN 56143

Lake Benton Housing & Redevelopment Authority
c/o Executive Director
Lake Benton, MN 56149

Filimore County Housing & Redevelopment Authority
c/o Executive Director
Lanesboro, MN 55949

Le Sueur Housing Authority
218 S. Main St.
Le Sueur, MN 56058

Lindstrom Housing & Redevelopment Authority
c/o Executive Director
Lindstrom, MN 55045

Litchfield Housing & Redevelopment Authority
122 W. Fourth St.
Litchfield, MN 55355

Little Falls Housing & Redevelopment Authority
901 S. First Ave.
Little Falls, MN

Long Prairie Housing & Redevelopment Authority
c/o Executive Director
Long Prairie, MN 56347

Luverne Housing & Redevelopment Authority
216 North McKenzie
Luverne, MN 56156

Madison Housing & Redevelopment Authority
404 Sixth Ave.
Madison, MN 56256

Mankato Housing & Redevelopment Authority
615 Nicolle Ave.
Mankato, MN 56001

Marshall Housing & Redevelopment Authority
202 N. First St.
Marshall, MN 56258

Melrose Housing & Redevelopment Authority
225 E. First St., S.
Melrose, MN 56352

Northwest Multi. County Housing & Redevelopment Authority
1522 Maple Lake
Mentor, MN 56736

Minneapolis Housing & Redevelopment Authority
217 S. Third St.
Minneapolis, MN 55401

Montevideo Housing & Redevelopment Authority
Box 8
City Hall
Montevideo, MN 56265

Montgomery Housing & Redevelopment Authority
c/o Executive Director
Montgomery, MN 56069

Moorhead Housing & Redevelopment Authority
P.O. Box 686
Moorhead, MN 56561

Moose Lake Housing & Redevelopment Authority
c/o Executive Director
Moose Lake, MN 55767

Mora Housing Authority
c/o Executive Director
Mora, MN 55051

Morris Housing & Redevelopment Authority
City Hall
Morris, MN 56267

Mound Housing & Redevelopment Authority
2020 Commerce Blvd.
Mound, MN 55364

Mountain Lake Housing & Redevelopment Authority
241 N. Tenth St.
Mountain Lake, MN 56159

Bois Forte Reservation Housing Authority
c/o Executive Director
Nett Lake, MN 55772

New Richland Housing Authority
c/o Executive Director
New Richland, MN 56072

New Ulm Housing & Redevelopment Authority
Box 355
New Ulm, MN 56073

North Mankato Housing & Redevelopment Authority
P.O. Box 2006
North Mankato, MN 56001

North St. Paul Housing Authority
c/o Executive Director
North St. Paul, MN 55109

Renville County Housing & Redevelopment Authority
c/o Executive Director
Olivia, MN 56277

Ortonville Housing & Redevelopment Authority
301 NW First St.
Ortonville, MN 56278

Park Rapids Housing & Redevelopment Authority
P.O. Box 33
Park Rapids, MN 56470

Pequot Lakes Housing & Redevelopment Authority
c/o Executive Director
Pequot Lakes, MN 56472

Perham Housing & Redevelopment Authority
Box 302
Perham, MN 56573

Pine City Housing & Redevelopment Authority
Village Hall
Pine City, MN 55063

Pine County Housing & Redevelopment Authority
c/o Executive Director
Pine City, MN 55063

Pine River Housing & Redevelopment Authority
c/o Executive Director
Pine River, MN 56474

Pipestone Housing & Redevelopment Authority
Box 12 A
Pipestone, MN 56164

Princeton Housing & Redevelopment Authority
801 Third St. N.
Princeton, MN 55371

Redlake Reservation Housing Authority
c/o Red Lake Council
Redlake, MN 56671

Red Lake Falls Housing & Redevelopment Authority
Box 448
Red Lake Falls, MN 56750

Red Wing Housing & Redevelopment Authority
c/o Executive Director
Red Wing, MN 55066

Redwood Falls Housing Authority
P.O. Box 396
Redwood Falls, MN 56283

Rochester Housing & Redevelopment Authority
Room 208
City Hall
Rochester, MN 55901

Saint Cloud Housing & Redevelopment Authority
Physician & Surgeon Building
Saint Cloud, MN 56301

Saint James Housing & Redevelopment Authority
City Hall
Saint James, MN 56081

St. Louis Park Housing & Redevelopment Authority
5005 Minnetonka Blvd.
St. Louis Park, MN 55416

St. Paul Housing Authority
55 E. Fifth St.
St. Paul, MN 55101

Saint Peter Housing & Redevelopment Authority
1010 S. Fourth St.
Saint Peter, MN 56082

Sauk Centre Housing & Redevelopment Authority
407 First St. N.
Sauk Centre, MN 56378

Wadena County Housing Authority
c/o Executive Director
Sebeka, MN 56477

Murray County Housing & Redevelopment Authority
c/o Executive Director
Slayton, MN 56172

Sleepy Eye Housing & Redevelopment Authority
313 Fourth Ave. SE
Sleepy Eye, MN 56085

South Saint Paul Housing Authority
Municipal Building
South Saint Paul, MN 55075

Staples Housing & Redevelopment Authority
Box 185
Staples, MN 56479

Thief River Falls Housing Authority
415 S. Arnold Ave.
Thief River Falls, MN 56701

Tracy Housing & Redevelopment Authority
760 Morgan St.
Tracy, MN 56175

Two Harbors Housing & Redevelopment Authority
807 12th Ave.
Two Harbors, MN 55616

Virginia Housing & Redevelopment Authority
Silver Lake Homes
Virginia, MN 55792

Wabasha Housing & Redevelopment Authority
257 Main St. W.
Wabasha, MN 55981

Waconia Housing & Redevelopment Authority
46 W. Main St.
Waconia, MN 44387

Wadena Housing & Redevelopment Authority
121 N. Jefferson
Wadena, MN 56482

Walker Housing & Redevelopment Authority
c/o Executive Director
Walker, MN 56484

Warren Housing & Redevelopment Authority
406 N. Minnesota
Warren, MN 56762

Warroad Housing & Redevelopment Authority
Village Hall
Warroad, MN 56763

Waseca Housing & Redevelopment Authority
c/o Executive Director
Waseca, MN 56093

Willmar Housing & Redevelopment Authority
414 W. Becker Ave.
Willmar, MN 56201

Windom Housing & Redevelopment Authority
P.O. Box 252
Windom, MN 56101

Winona Housing & Redevelopment Authority
165 E. Fourth St.
Winona, MN 55987

Worthington Housing Authority
819 Tenth St.
Worthington, MN 56187

MISSISSIPPI

Aberdeen Housing Authority
P.O. Box 69
Aberdeen, MS 39730

Amory Housing Authority
118 N. Main St.
Amory, MS 38821

Baldwyn Housing Authority
P.O. Box 442
Baldwyn, MS 38824

Bay St. Louis Housing Authority
601 Bienville St.
Bay St. Louis, MS 39520

Biloxi Housing Authority
P.O. Box 447
Biloxi, MS 39530

Bonneville Housing Authority
P.O. Box 368
Bonneville, MS 38829

Brookhaven Housing Authority
P.O. Box 641
Brookhaven, MS 39601

Canton Housing Authority
P.O. Box 77
Canton, MS 39046

Clarksdale Housing Authority
P.O. Box 908
Clarksdale, MS 38614

Collins Housing Authority
P.O. Box 931
Collins, MS 39428

Columbia Housing Authority
City Hall
Second St.
Columbia, MS 39429

Columbus Housing Authority
P.O. Box 648
Columbus, MS 39701

Mississippi Regional Housing Authority No. IV
P.O. Box 1064
Columbus, MS 39701

Corinth Housing Authority
P.O. Box 1003
Corinth, MS 38834

Tennessee Valley Regional Housing Authority No. 1
P.O. Box 1338
Corinth, MS 38834

Housing Authority – City of Forest
518 Fourth Ave., N.
Forest, MS 39074

South Delta Economic Development District, Inc.
P.O. Box 4626
Greenville, MS 38701

Housing Authority of Greenwood
c/o Frasier/Burgoon
P.O. Box 391
Greenwood, MS 38930

Gulfport Housing Authority
P.O. Box 59
Gulfport, MS 39501

Mississippi Regional Housing
    Authority No. VIII
Evergreen Station
P.O. Box 2347
Gulfport, MS 39501

Hattiesburg Housing Authority
P.O. Box 832
Hattiesburg, MS 39402

Hazelhurst Housing Authority
P.O. Box 572
Hazelhurst, MS 39083

Holly Springs Housing Authority
P.O. Box 550
Holly Springs, MS 38635

Itta Bena Housing Authority
Itta Bena Bank Building
Itta Bena, MS 38941

Iuka Housing Authority
P.O. Box 287
Iuka, MS 38852

Jackson Housing Authority
218 S. President St.
Jackson, MS 39201

Mississippi Regional Housing
    Authority No. VI
2041 Tivoli St.
Jackson, MS 39204

Redevelopment Authority City of
    Kosciusko
P.O. Box 723
Kosciusko, MS 39090

Laurel Housing Authority
P.O. Box 2245
Laurel, MS 39440

Long Beach Housing Authority
P.O. Drawer D
Long Beach, MS 39560

Louisville Housing Authority
P.O. Box 175
Louisville, MS 39339

Lumberton Housing Authority
P.O. Box 192
Lumberton, MS 39555

McComb City Housing Authority
P.O. Box 469
McComb, MS 39648

Mississippi Regional Housing
    Authority No. VII
P.O. Box 886
McComb, MS 39648

Summit Housing Authority
P.O. Box 886
McComb, MS 39648

Meridian Housing Authority
P.O. Box 870
Meridian, MS 39301

Mound Bayou Housing Authority
P.O. Box 565
Mound Bayou, MS 38762

Natchez Housing Authority
P.O. Box 1185
Natchez, MS 39120

Mississippi Regional Housing
    Authority No. V
P.O. Box 197
Newton, MS 39345

Okolona Housing Authority
P.O. Box 190
Okolona, MS 38860

Oxford Housing Authority
P.O. Box 488
Oxford, MS 38655

Pass Christian Authority
P.O. Box 530
Pass Christian, MS 39571

Choctow Housing Authority
Route 7
Box M 21
Philadelphia, MS 39350

Picayune Housing Authority
P.O. Drawer 40
Picayune, MS 39466

Pontotoc Housing Authority
P.O. Box 590
Pontotoc, MS 38863

Richton Housing Authority
P.O. Box 513
Richton, MS 39476

Sardis Housing Authority
13 Dewberry St.
Sardis, MS 38666

Senatobia Housing Authority
c/o Senatobia City Hall
Senatobia, MS 38668

Shelby Housing Authority
P.O. Box 272
Shelby, MS 38774

Starkville Housing Authority
P.O. Box 795
Starkville, MS 39759

Tupelo Housing Authority
P.O. Box 3
Tupelo, MS 38801

Vicksburg Housing Authority
Suite 203, Kaleel Building
Vicksburg, MS 39180

Walnut Housing Authority
P.O. Box 138
Walnut, MS 38683

Water Valley Housing Authority
Blackmur Drive
Water Valley, MS 38965

Waveland Housing Authority
500 Camille Circle
Waveland, MS 39576

Waynesboro Housing Authority
P.O. Box 22
Waynesboro, MS 39367

West Point Housing Authority
P.O. Box 158
West Point, MS 39773

Winona Housing Authority
P.O. Box 127
Winona, MS 38967

Yazoo City Housing Authority
P.O. Box 128
Yazoo City, MS 39194

MISSOURI

Alton Housing Authority
Box 381
City Hall
Alton, MO 65606

Anderson Housing Authority
Box 68
Anderson, MO 64831

Lanagan Housing Authority
Box 51
Anderson, MO 64831

Pineville Housing Authority
Box 51
Anderson, MO 64831

Southwest City Housing Authority
Box 51
Anderson, MO 64831

Aurora Housing Authority
Box 526
Aurora, MO 65605

Bernie Housing Authority
P.O. Drawer 210
Bernie, MO 63822

Bethany Housing Authority
P.O. Box 448
Bethany, MO 64424

Bloomfield Housing Authority
P.O. Box 6
Bloomfield, MO 63825

Boonville Housing Authority
506 Powell Court
Boonville, MO 65233

Branson Housing Authority
Box 629
Branson, MO 65516

Brookfield Housing Authority
A-1 Joyce Place
Brookfield, MO 64628

Brunswick Housing Authority
510 Adams St.
Box 125
Brunswick, MO 65236

Cameron Housing Authority
605 N. Walnut
Cameron, MO 64429

Campbell Housing Authority
Box 52
Campbell, MO 63933

Holcomb Housing Authority
Box 52
Campbell, MO 63933

Cardwell Housing Authority
P.O. Box 112
Cardwell, MO 63829

Carrollton Housing Authority
City Hall
Carrollton, MO 64633

Caruthersville Housing Authority
1119 Ward Ave.
Caruthersville, MO 63830

Chaffee Housing Authority
800 S. Main
Chaffee, MO 63740

Charleston Housing Authority
Box 67
Charleston, MO 63834

Chillicothe Housing Authority
320 Park Lane
P.O. Box 668
Chillicothe, MO 64601

Clarkton Housing Authority
c/o Executive Director
Clarkton, MO 63837

Clinton Housing Authority
7 Bradshaw Drive
Clinton, MO 64735

Colombia Housing Authority
1201 Paquin
Columbia, MO 65201

Dexter Housing Authority
208 Sayre
Dexter, MO 63841

Doniphan Housing Authority
City Hall
Doniphan, MO 63935

East Prairie Housing Authority
529 N. Lincoln
East Prairie, MO 63845

Eldon Housing Authority
City Hall
Eldon, MO 65026

Excelsior Springs Housing Authority
320 E. Excelsior St.
Excelsior Springs, MO 64024

Fayette Housing Authority
302 Villers Drive
Fayette, MO 65248

Flat River Housing Authority
City Hall
Flat River, MO 63601

Fredericktown Housing Authority
City Hall
Fredericktown, MO 63645

Fulton Housing Authority
P.O. Box 139
350 Sycamore St.
Fulton, MO 65251

Gainesville Housing Authority
City Hall
Gainesville, MO 65655

Gideon Housing Authority
Box 41
Gideon, MO 63848

Glasgow Housing Authority
508 Fourth St.
Glasgow, MO 65254

Grandin Housing Authority
City Hall
Grandin, MO 63943

Hannibal Housing Authority
100 N. Main St.
Hannibal, MO 63401

Hayti Housing Authority
Box 7
Hayti, MO 63851

Higginsville Housing Authority
13 W. 21st St.
Higginsville, MO

Hornersville Housing Authority
Box 167
Hornersville, MO 63855

Houston Housing Authority
Box 216
Houston, MO 65483

Illmo Housing Authority
Box 418
Illmo, MO 63754

Independence Housing Authority
210 S. Pleasant
Independence, MO 64050

Jefferson City Housing Authority
P.O. Box 1029
Jefferson City, MO 65101

Kansas City Housing Authority
1016 Locust
Kansas City, MO 64106

Kennett Housing Authority
Box 268
Kennett, MO 63857

Kirksville Housing Authority
P.O. Box 730
Kirksville, MO 63501

Lawson Housing Authority
Box 65
Lawson, MO 64062

Lebanon Housing Authority
P.O. Box 308
Lebanon, MO 65536

Lees Summit Housing Authority
111 S. Grand St.
Lees Summit, MO 64063

Lexington Housing Authority
City Hall
Lexington, MO 64067

Lilbourn Housing Authority
City Hall
Lilbourn, MO 63862

Malden Housing Authority
Box 395
Malden, MO 63863

Mansfield Housing Authority
City Hall
Mansfield, MO 67504

Marceline Housing Authority
P.O. Box 98
Marceline, MO 64658

Marionville Housing Authority
Box F
Marionville, MO 65705

Marshall Housing Authority
214 N. Lafayette
Marshall, MO 65340

Maryville Housing Authority
Baird Milling Co.
Maryville, MO 64468

Mexico Housing Authority
Box 484
Mexico, MO 65265

Milan Housing Authority
103½ N. Market St.
Milan, MO 63556

Moberly Housing Authority
Box 159
Moberly, MO 65270

Morehouse Housing Authority
City Hall
Morehouse, MO 63868

Mound City Housing Authority
Mound City, MO 64470

Mountain Grove Housing Authority
P.O. Box 571
Mountain Grove, MO 65711

Neosho Housing Authority
321 S. Hamilton St.
Neosho, MO 64850

Nevada Housing Authority
P.O. Box 541
Nevada, MO 64772

New Madrid Housing Authority
c/o Executive Director
New Madrid, MO 63869

Noel Housing Authority
Box 305
Noel, MO 64854

Oran Housing Authority
City Hall
Oran, MO 63771

Osceola Housing Authority
Box 385
Osceola, MO 64776

Plattsburg Housing Authority
Box 414
Plattsburg, MO 64477

Poplar Bluff Housing Authority
506 Hazel St.
Poplar Bluff, MO 63901

Portageville Housing Authority
Box 436
Portageville, MO 63873

Potosi Housing Authority
103 W. Citadel Drive
Potosi, MO 63664

Republic Housing Authority
681 E. Elm St.
Republic, MO 65738

Richland Housing Authority
Box 37
Richland, MO 65556

Richmond Housing Authority
302 N. Camden
Richmond, MO 64085

Rolla Housing Authority
c/o Executive Director
Rolla, MO 65401

St. Charles Housing Authority
118 Monroe
St. Charles, MO 63301

St. Joseph Housing Authority
323 N. Fifth St.
St. Joseph, MO 64501

Kinloch Housing Authority
5662 Carson Rd.
St. Louis, MO 63140

St. Louis County Housing Authority
20 S. Central
Suite 200
St. Louis, MO 63105

St. Louis Housing Authority
1221 Locust St.
St. Louis, MO 63103

Salem Housing Authority
615 McGrath Lane
Salem, MO 65560

Sedalia Housing Authority
400 W. Saline
Sedalia, MO 65301

Senath Housing Authority
Box 181
Senath, MO 63876

Sikeston Housing Authority
Box 829
Sikeston, MO 63801

Slater Housing Authority
14 Emerson Terrace
Slater, MO 65349

Smithville Housing Authority
161 Northview Heights
P.O. Box H
Smithville, MO 64089

Springfield Housing Authority
421 W. Madison Ave.
Springfield, MO 65806

Steele Housing Authority
200 Locust St.
Steele, MO 63877

Tarkio Housing Authority
218 Maple St.
Tarkio, MO 64491

Thayer Housing Authority
City Hall
Thayer, MO 65791

Tipton Housing Authority
City Hall
Tipton, MO 65081

Wardell Housing Authority
Box 7
Wardell, MO 63879

Webb City Housing Authority
Box 590
Webb City, MO 64870

Wellston Housing Authority
1804 Kienlen Ave.
Wellston, MO 63133

West Plains Housing Authority
Box 100
South Tower Apts.
West Plains, MO 65775

MONTANA

Anaconda Housing Authority
P.O. Box 1350
Anaconda, MT 59711

Chippewa Cree Housing Authority
Rocky Boy's Indian Reservation
Box Elder, MT 59521

Blackfeet Indian Housing Authority
P.O. Box 790
Browning, MT 59417

Butte Housing Authority
Administration Building
Silver Bow Homes
Butte, MT 59701

Crow Tribal Housing Authority
Crow Indian Reservation
Crow Agency, MT 59022

Glasgow Housing Authority
P.O. Box 1126
Glasgow, MT 59230

Great Falls Housing Authority
1500 Sixth Ave. S.
Great Falls, MT 59405

Fort Belknap Housing Authority
Fort Belknap Agency
Harve, MT 59526

Helena Housing Authority
Administration Building
Stewart Homes
Helena, MT 59601

Northern Cheyenne Housing Authority
Tribal Office Building
Lame Deer, MT 59043

Fort Peck Housing Authority
P.O. Box 1118
Poplar, MT 59255

Salish & Kootenai Housing Authority
Flathead Indian Agency
Ronan, MT 59864

Richland County Housing Authority
P.O. Box 271
Sidney, MT 59270

Whitefish Housing Authority
Box 547
Whitefish, MT 59937

NEBRASKA

Ainsworth Housing Authority
P.O. Box 214
Ainsworth, NB 69210

Albion Housing Authority
410 W. Church St.
Albion, NB 69210

Alma Housing Authority
710 Main St.
Alma, NB 68920

Ansley Housing Authority
c/o Executive Director
Ansley, NB 68814

Arapahoe Housing Authority
c/o Executive Director
Arapahoe, NB 68922

Auburn Housing Authority
1017 H St.
Auburn, NB 68305

Aurora Housing Authority
Crossroads Court Office
Aurora, NB 68818

Bassett Housing Authority
c/o Executive Director
Bassett, NB 68714

Bayard Housing Authority
c/o Executive Director
Bayard, NB 69334

Beatrice Housing Authority
Municipal Building
Beatrice, NB 68301

Beaver City Housing Authority
c/o Executive Director
Beaver City, NB 68926

Beemer Village Housing Authority
Box 302
Beemer, NB 68716

Benkelman Housing Authority
City Building
Benkelman, NB 69021

Bertrand Housing Authority
c/o Executive Director
Bertrand, NB 68927

Blair Housing Authority
758 S. 16th St.
Blair, NB 68008

Bloomfield Housing Authority
Bloomfield, NB 68718

Blue Hill Housing Authority
c/o Executive Director
Blue Hill, NB 68930

Bridgeport Housing Authority
P.O. Box 6
Bridgeport, NB 69336

Broken Bow Housing Authority
P.O. Box 504
Broken Bow, NB 68822

Burwell Housing Authority
P.O. Box 899
Burwell, NB 68823

Cairo Village Housing Authority
c/o Executive Director
Cairo, NB 68824

Cambridge Housing Authority
c/o Executive Director
Cambridge, NB 69022

Cedar Bluffs Housing Authority
c/o Executive Director
Cedar Bluffs, NB 68015

Central City Housing Authority
c/o Executive Director
Central City, NB 68826

Chadron Housing Authority
c/o Executive Director
Chadron, NB 69337

Chappell Housing Authority
c/o Executive Director
Chappell, NB 69129

Clarkson Housing Authority
P.O. Box 306
Clarkson, NB 68629

Clay Center Housing Authority
c/o Executive Director
Clay Center, NB 68933

Coleridge Housing Director
c/o Executive Director
Coleridge, NB 68727

Columbus Housing Authority
P.O. Box 473
Columbus, NB 68601

Cozad Housing Authority
Box 47
Cozad, NB 69130

Creighton Housing Authority
c/o Executive Director
Creighton, NB 68729

Crete Housing Authority
1600 Grove St.
Crete, NB 68333

Curtis Housing Authority
Box 204
Curtis, NB 69025

David City Housing Authority
P.O. Box 285
David City, NB 68632

Deshler Housing Authority
P.O. Box 427
Deshler, NB 68632

Doniphan Housing Authority
c/o Executive Director
Doniphan, NB 68832

Edgar Housing Authority
Box 266
Edgar, NB 68935

Emerson Housing Authority
c/o Executive Director
Emerson, NB 68733

Fairbury Housing Authority
P.O. Box 14
Fairbury, NB 68352

Fairmont Housing Authority
Box 158
Fairmont, NB 68354

Falls City Housing Authority
800 E. 21st St.
Falls City, NB 68355

Franklin Housing Authority
c/o Executive Director
Franklin, NB 68939

Fremont Housing Authority
2510 North Clarkson
Fremont, NB 68025

Friend Housing Authority
1027 Second St.
Friend, NB 68359

Genoa Housing Authority
Box 401
Genoa, NB 68640

Scotts Bluff County Housing Authority
89A Woodley Park Rd.
Gering, NB 69341

Gibbon Housing Authority
Box H
Gibbon, NB 68840

Gordon Housing Authority
109 N. Cornell St.
Gordon, NB 69343

Gothenburg Housing Authority
Box 486
Gothenburg, NB 69138

Hall County Housing Authority
804 N. Boggs Ave.
Grand Island, NB 68801

Grant Housing Authority
c/o Executive Director
Grant, NB 69140

Greeley Housing Authority
Kerry Kourt Apts.
Greeley, NB 68842

Gresham Housing Authority
c/o Executive Director
Gresham, NB 68367

Harrison Housing Authority
c/o Executive Director
Harrison, NB 69346

Harvard Housing Authority
c/o Executive Director
Harvard, NB 68944

Hay Springs Housing Authority
c/o Executive Director
Hay Springs, NB 69347

Hemingford Village Housing Authority
c/o Executive Director
Hemingford, NB 69348

Henderson Housing Authority
P.O. Box 25
Henderson, NB 68371

Hildreth Housing Authority
c/o Executive Director
Hildreth, NB 68947

Hooper Housing Authority
c/o Executive Director
Hooper, NB 68031

Humboldt Housing Authority
Community Building
Humboldt, NB 68376

Imperial Housing Authority
1013 Court St.
Imperial, NB 69033

Indianola Housing Authority
Box K
Indianola, NB 69034

Kearney Housing Authority
27th St. & Ave. 2
Kearney, NB 68847

Lexington Housing Authority
3rd & Monroe
Lexington, NB 68850

Lincoln Housing Authority
Box 5237
Lincoln, NB 68524

Loup City Housing Authority
Tenth & K Sts.
Loup City, NB 68853

Lynch Village Housing Authority
c/o Executive Director
Lynch, NB 68746

Lyons City Housing Authority
c/o Executive Director
Lyons, NB 68038

Omaha Tribal Housing Authority
Low-Rent Housing Office
Macy, NB 68039

Minden Housing Authority
P.O. Box 13
Minden, NB 68959

Nebraska City Housing Authority
Box 111
Nebraska City, NB 68410

Neligh Housing Authority
P.O. Box 48
Neligh, NB 68756

Nelson Housing Authority
c/o Executive Director
Nelson, NB 68961

Newman Grove Housing Authority
P.O. Box 100
Newman Grove, NB 68758

Niobrara Village Housing
Niobrara Valley Homes
Niobrara, NB 68760

Santee Sioux Tribal Housing Authority
Route No. 2
Niobrara, NB 68760

North Loup Housing Authority
c/o Executive Director
North Loup, NB 68859

North Platte Housing Authority
P.O. Box 1329
North Platte, NB 69101

Oakland Housing Authority
100 N. Aurora Ave.
Oakland, NB 68045

Omaha Housing Authority
711 N. 21st St.
Omaha, NB 68102

Ord Housing Authority
Parkview Village
Ord, NB 68601

Oshkosh Housing Authority
Mesa Vue
Oshkosh, NB 69154

Oxford Village Housing Authority
c/o Executive Director
Oxford, NB 68967

Pawnee City Housing Authority
Pawnee Village
Pawnee City, NB 68420

Pierce Housing Authority
c/o Executive Director
Pierce, NB 68767

Plattsmouth Housing Authority
801 Washington Ave.
Plattsmouth, NB 68048

Ravenna Housing Authority
1011 Grand Ave.
Ravenna, NB 68869

Red Cloud Housing Authority
Office in City Hall
Red Cloud, NB 68970

St. Edward Housing Authority
c/o Executive Director
St. Edward, NB 68660

St. Paul Housing Authority
c/o Executive Director
St. Paul, NB 68873

Sargent Housing Authority
Box 430
Sargent, NB 68874

Schuyler Housing Authority
712 F St.
Schuyler, NB 68661

Shelton Village Housing Authority
c/o Executive Director
Shelton, NB 68876

Stanton Housing Authority
P.O. Box 638
Stanton, NB 68779

Stromsburg City Housing Authority
c/o Executive Director
Stromsburg, NB 68666

Superior Housing Authority
c/o Executive Director
Superior, NB 51363

Sutherland Village Housing Authority
c/o Executive Director
Sutherland, NB 69165

Syracuse Housing Authority
990 Walnut
Syracuse, NB 68446

Tecumseh Housing Authority
Eighth & Broadway
Tecumseh, NB 68450

Tekamah Housing Authority
The Village
Tekamah, NB 68061

Tilden Housing Authority
c/o Executive Director
Tilden, NB 68782

Verdigre Housing Authority
c/o Executive Director
Verdigre, NB 68783

Wayne Housing Authority
409 Dearborn
Wayne, NB 68787

Weeping Water Housing Authority
City Hall
Weeping Water, NB 68463

Wilber Housing Authority
c/o Executive Director
Wilber, NB 68465

Winnebago Village Housing Authority
c/o Executive Director
Winnebago, NB 68071

Wood River Housing Authority
1413 Main St.
Wood River, NB 68883

Wymore Housing Authority
P.O. Box 93
Wymore, NB 68466

York Housing Authority
Box 447
York, NB 68467

NEVADA

Te-Moak Western Shoehone Housing
    Authority
2002 Idaho St.
P.O. Box 28
Elko, NV 89801

Clark County Housing Authority
Administrative Building — Victory
    Village
Henderson, NV 89015

Las Vegas Housing Authority
420 N. Tenth St.
Las Vegas, NV 89101

Lovelock Indian Housing Authority
Box 192
Lovelock, NV 89419

Moapa Indian Housing Authority
P.O. Box 4
Moapa, NV 89025

North Las Vegas Housing Authority
P.O. Box 4086
North Las Vegas, NV 89030

Reno Housing Authority
P.O. Box 969
Reno, NV 89504

Reno-Sparks Indian Housing Authority
34 Reservation Rd.
Reno, NV 89502

Dresslerville Housing Authority
Nevada Agency Branch of Housing
Stewart, NV 89437

Duck Valley Housing Authority
Nevada Branch of Housing
Stewart, NV 89437

Ely Housing Authority
Nevada Indian Agency
Stewart, NV 89437

Ft. McDermitt Housing Authority
Nevada Agency Branch of Housing
Stewart, NV 89437

Pyramid Lake Housing Authority
Nevada Agency Branch of Housing
Stewart, NV 89437

Walker River Housing Authority
Nevada Agency Branch of Housing
Stewart, NV 89437

Yerington Paiute Housing Authority
P.O. Box 489
Yerington, NV 89447

NEW HAMPSHIRE

Berlin Housing Authority
c/o Locator
Berlin, NH 03570

Claremont Housing Authority
45 Crescent St.
Claremont, NH 03743

Concord Housing Authority
40 S. Main St.
Concord, NH 03301

Dover Housing Authority
93 Pleasant View Circle
Dover, NH 03820

Exeter Housing Authority
P.O. Box 345
Exeter, NH 03833

Keene Housing Authority
105 Castle St.
Keene, NH 03431

Laconia Housing & Development
    Authority
25 Union Ave.
Laconia, NH 03246

Lancaster Housing Authority
c/o Housing Services Group
928 Mammoth Rd.
Manchester, NH 03104

Manchester Housing Authority
Housing Section
34 Fir St.
Manchester, NH 03101

New Hampshire State Housing
 Authority
1087 Elm St.
Room 102
Manchester, NH 03101

Nashua Housing Authority
114 W. Pearl St.
Nashua, NH 03060

Newmarket Housing Authority
Town Hall
Newmarket, NH 03857

Portsmouth Housing Authority
140 Court St.
Portsmouth, NH 03801

Rochester Housing Authority
Wellsweep Acres
Building No. 13
Rochester, NH 03867

Somersworth Housing Authority
42 Barlett Ave.
Somersworth, NH 03878

Lebanon Housing Authority
S. Main St.
West Lebanon, NH 03784

NEW JERSEY

Asbury Park Housing Authority
1004 Comstock St.
Asbury, NJ 07712

Atlantic City Housing Authority &
 Redevelopment
14 S. California Ave.
Atlantic City, NJ 08404

Bayonne Housing Authority
50 E. 21st St.
Bayonne, NJ 07002

Belmar Housing Authority
P.O. Box 90
Belmar, NJ 07719

Berkley Housing Authority
31 Park Ave.
Berkley Township, NJ 08721

Beverly Housing Authority
Magnolia & Front St.
Beverly, NJ 08010

Boonton Housing Authority
125 Chestnut St.
Boonton, NJ 07005

Brick Twp. Housing Authority
c/o Locator
Brick Twp., NJ 08723

Bridgeton Housing Authority
19 Maple Drive
Bridgeton, NJ 08302

Burlington Housing Authority
Col. Edw. B. Stone Villa
Burlington, NJ 08016

Camden Housing Authority
No. 1 Broadway
504 Commerce Building
Camden, NJ 08103

Cape May Housing Authority
319 Washington St.
Cape May, NJ 08204

Carteret Housing Authority
Bergen St.
Carteret, NJ 07008

Clementon Housing Authority
16 Berlin Rd.
Clementon, NJ 08021

Cliffside Park Housing Authority
663A Palisade Ave.
Cliffside Park, NJ 07010

Dover Housing Authority
5 E. Blackwell St.
Dover, NJ 07801

East Orange Housing Authority
18 Washington Place
East Orange, NJ 07018

Edgewater Borough Housing Authority
916 River Rd.
Edgewater, NJ 07020

Edison Township Housing Authority
Williard Dunham Drive
Edison, NJ 08817

Elizabeth Housing Authority
688 Maple Ave.
Elizabeth, NJ 07202

Englewood Housing Authority
9 West St.
Englewood, NJ 07631

Florence Township Housing Authority
Third & Eyre Sts.
Florence, NJ 08518

Fort Lee Housing Authority
Second Floor
320 Main St.
Fort Lee, NJ 07024

Franklin Township Housing Authority
1 Parkside St.
Franklin Township, NJ 08873

Freehold Borough Housing Authority
24 South St.
Freehold, NJ 07728

Garfield Housing Authority
71 Golden Age Court
Garfield, NJ 07026

Glassboro Housing Authority
Main & High Sts.
Levy Building
Glassboro, NJ 08028

Guttenberg Housing Authority
6900 Broadway
Guttenberg, NJ 07093

Bergen County Housing Authority
45 Essex St.
Hackensack, NJ 07601

Hackensack Housing Authority
170 Sussex St.
Hackensack, NJ 07601

Haddon Township Housing Authority
25 Wynnwood Ave.
Haddon Township, NJ 08108

Harrison Housing Authority
Harrison & Schuyler Aves.
Harrison, NJ 07021

Highland Borough Housing Authority
General Delivery
Highland, NJ 08904

Highlands Housing Authority
221 S. Sixth Ave.
Highlands, NJ 07732

Hightstown Housing Authority
131 Rogers Ave.
Hightstown, NJ 08520

Hoboken Housing Authority
400 Harrison St.
Hoboken, NJ 07030

Irvington Housing Authority
624 Nye Ave.
Irvington, NJ 07111

Jersey City Housing Authority
514 Newark Ave.
Jersey City, NJ 07308

Keansburg Borough Authority
1 Church St.
Keansburg, NJ 07734

Lakewood Housing Authority
483 Cedar Bridge Ave.
Lakewood, NJ 08701

Linden Housing Authority
c/o Locator
Linden, NJ 07036

Lodi Borough Housing Authority
De Vries Park
Lodi, NJ 07644

Long Branch Housing Authority
Garfield Court
Box 336
Long Branch, NJ 07740

Housing Authority — Township of
 Middletown
Daniel Towers, Oakdale Drive
Middletown, NJ 07748

Millville Housing Authority
P.O. Box 803
Millville, NJ 08332

Morristown Housing Authority
31 Early St.
Morristown, NJ 07960

Neptune Township Housing Authority
30 Ridge Ave.
Neptune, NJ 07753

Newark Housing Authority
57 Sussex Ave.
Newark, NJ 07103

New Brunswick Housing Authority
P.O. Box 110
New Brunswick, NJ 08901

Newton Housing Authority
32 Liberty St.
Newton, NJ 07860

North Bergen Township Authority
6121 Grand Ave.
North Bergen, NJ 07047

Ocean City Housing Authority
204 Fourth St.
Ocean City, NJ 08229

Orange Housing Authority
340 Thomas Blvd.
Orange, NJ 07050

Passaic Housing Authority
23 Aspen Place
Passaic, NJ 07055

Paterson Housing Authority
29 Harris Place
Paterson, NJ 07514

Penns Grove Borough Housing
    Authority
P.O. Box 527
Penns Grove, NJ 08069

Perth Amboy Housing Authority
881 Amboy Ave.
Perth Amboy, NJ 08861

Phillipsburg Housing Authority
502 Heclaman St.
Phillipsburg, NJ 08865

Plainfield Housing Authority
532 W. Third St.
Plainfield, NJ 07060

Pleasantville Housing Authority
140 N. Main St.
Pleasantville, NJ 07232

Princeton Borough Housing Authority
50 Clay St.
Princeton, NJ 08540

Rahway Housing Authority
498 Capobianco Plaza
Rahway, NJ 07065

Red Bank Borough Housing Authority
Evergreen Terrace
Red Bank, NJ 07701

Salem Housing Authority
205 Seventh St.
Salem, NJ 08079

South Amboy Housing Authority
Bayshore Drive
South Amboy, NJ 08879

Summit Housing Authority
71 Summit Ave.
Summit, NJ 07901

Trenton Housing Authority
P.O. Box 795
Trenton, NJ 08605

Union City Housing Authority
3911 Kennedy Blvd.
Union City, NJ 07087

Vineland Housing Authority
84 S. West Ave.
Vineland, NJ 08360

Weehawken Housing Authority
Municipal Building
Weehawken, NJ 07473

West New York Housing Authority
6100 Adams St.
West New York, NJ 07093

Wildwood Housing Authority
4400 New Jersey Ave.
Wildwood, NJ 08260

Woodbridge Township Housing
    Authority
10 Burns Lane
Woodbridge, NJ 07095

NEW MEXICO

Alamogordo Housing Authority
P.O. Box 336
Alamogordo, NM 88310

Albuquerque Housing Authority
Box 1293
Albuquerque, NM 87103

All Indian Pueblo Housing Authority
P.O. Box 14568, Station G
Albuquerque, NM 87103

Artesia Housing Authority
P.O. Box 1326
Artesia, NM 88210

Bayard Housing Authority
P.O. Box 768
Bayard, NM 88023

Bernalillo Housing Authority
Town Hall
Bernalillo, NM 87004

Central Housing Authority
Box 275
Central, NM 88026

Chama Housing Authority
c/o Executive Director
Chama, NM 87520

Cimmaron Housing Authority
c/o Executive Director
Cimmaron, NM 87714

Clayton Housing Authority
City Hall
Clayton, NM 88415

Clovis Housing Authority
P.O. Box 279
Clovis, NM 88101

Deming Housing Authority
c/o Executive Director
Deming, NM 88030

Jicarilla Apache Housing Authority
P.O. Box 486
Dulce, NM 87528

Espanola Housing Authority
City Hall
Espanola, NM 87532

Eunice Housing Authority
Box 1244
Eunice, NM 88231

Fort Sumner Housing Authority
Box 687
Fort Sumner, NM 88119

Gallup Housing Authority
Box 1334
Gallup, NM 87301

Pueblo of Laguna Housing Authority
P.O. Box 178
Laguna, NM 87026

Las Cruces Housing Authority
926 S. San Pedro
Las Cruces, NM 88001

Las Vegas Housing Authority
Box 1825
Las Vegas, NM 87702

San Miguel County Housing Authority
San Miguel Courthouse
Las Vegas, NM 87702

Lordsburg Housing Authority
300 E. Railroad Ave.
Lordsburg, NM 88045

Lovington Housing Authority
P.O. Box 785
Lovington, NM 88260

Maxwell Housing Authority
Box 341
Maxwell, NM 87728

Apache Mescalero Reservation
    Housing Authority
c/o Tribal Office
Mescalero, NM 88340

Raton Housing Authority
Box 482
Raton, NM 87740

Rudidoso Downs Housing Authority
Box 436
Rudidoso Downs, NM 88346

Rio Arriba County Housing Authority
Box 773
San Juan Pueblo, NM 87566

Nambe Pueblo Housing Authority
RFD No. 1, P.O. Box 117
Santa Fe, NM 87501

Northern Pueblo Housing Authority
500 W. San Francisco St.
Santa Fe, NM 87501

Santa Fe County Housing Authority
P.O. Box 3454
Sante Fe, NM 87501

Tesque Pueblo Housing Authority
RFD No. 1, P.O. Box 1
Santa Fe, NM 87574

Navajo Indian Housing Authority
c/o Executive Director
Shiprock, NM 87420

Springer Housing Authority
Box 207
Springer, NM 87747

Taos Housing Authority
Box 923
Taos, NM 87571

Truth or Consequences Housing
  Authority
408 Mcadoo St.
Truth or Consequences, NM 87901

Tucumcari Housing Authority
Box 730
Tucumcari, NM 88401

Wagon Mound Housing Authority
P.O. Box 1
Wagon Mound, NM 87752

Zuni Housing Authority
Zuni Tribal Council Building
Zuni, NM 87327

NEW YORK

Albany Housing Authority
20 Warren St.
Albany, NY 12202

Amsterdam Housing Authority
52 Division St.
Amsterdam, NY 12010

Auburn Housing Authority
Thornton Ave.
Auburn, NY 13021

Batavia Housing Authority
400 E. Main St.
Batavia, NY 14020

Beacon Housing Authority
1 Forrestal Hgts.
Beacon, NY 12508

Binghamton Housing Authority
150 Moeller St.
Binghamton, NY 13904

Buffalo Municipal Housing Authority
901 City Hall
Buffalo, NY 14202

Wilna Housing Authority
600 S. Washington St.
Carthage, NY 13619

Catskill Village Housing Authority
P.O. Box 362
Catskill, NY 12414

Cohoes Housing Authority
Garner St.
Cohoes, NY 12047

Corning Housing Authority
85 E. Market St.
Corning, NY 14830

Cortland Housing Authority
37 Port Watson St.
Cortland, NY 13045

Dunkirk Housing Authority
15 N. Main St.
Dunkirk, NY 14048

Islip Housing Authority
50 Irish Lane
East Islip, NY 11730

East Rochester Housing Authority
314 Main St.
East Rochester, NY 14445

Elmira Housing Authority
816 Roe Ave.
Elmira, NY 14905

Fort Edward Housing Authority
103 East St.
Fort Edward, NY 12828

Freeport Long Island Housing
  Authority
3 Buffalo Ave.
Freeport, Long Island, NY 11520

Geneva Housing Authority
10 Goodman St.
Geneva, NY 14456

Glen Cove Housing Authority
140 Glen Ave.
Glen Cove, NY 11542

Glens Falls Housing Authority
18 Warren St.
Glens Falls, NY 12801

Gloversville Housing Authority
Forest Hilltowers
Gloversville, NY 12078

North Hempstead Housing Authority
Pond Hill Road
Great Neck, NY 11020

Hempstead Village Authority
75 Laurel Ave.
Hempstead, NY 11550

Herkimer Housing Authority
315 N. Prospect St.
Herkimer, NY 13350

Oyster Bay Housing
355 Newbridge Rd.
Hicksville, NY 11801

Hornell Housing Authority
71 Church St.
Hornell, NY 14843

Hudson Housing Authority
City Hall
Hudson, NY 12543

Hudson Falls Housing Authority
220 Main St.
Hudson Falls, NY 12839

Huntington Housing Authority
5 Lowndes Ave.
Huntington Station, NY 11746

Ilion Village Housing Authority
56 Otsego St.
Ilion, NY 13357

Ithaca Housing Authority
113 S. Cayuga St.
Ithaca, NY 14850

Jamestown Housing Authority
Hotel Jamestown
Jamestown, NY 14701

Kenmore Housing Authority
Municipal Building
Kenmore, NY 14217

Kingston Housing Authority
Flatbush Ave.
Kingston, NY 12401

Lackawanna Municipal Housing
  Authority
52 Gates Ave.
Lackawanna, NY 14218

Liberty Housing Authority
Municipal Building
Liberty, NY 12754

Lockport City Housing Authority
45 Ontario St.
Lockport, NY 14094

Long Beach Housing Authority
City Hall
Long Beach, NY 11561

Malone Housing Authority
Alice Hyde Memorial Hospital
Malone, NY 12953

Massena Housing Authority
Victory Rd.
Massena, NY 13662

Mechanicville Housing Authority
John S. Moore Homes, Harris Ave.
Mechanicville, NY 12118

Hempstead Housing Authority
1701 Merrick Ave.
Merrick, NY 11566

Middletown Housing Authority
6-22 Sweezy Ave.
Middletown, NY 10940

Monticello Housing Authority
c/o Executive Director
Monticello, NY 12701

Montour Falls Housing Authority
Munich Office
408 W. Main St.
Montour Falls, NY 14865

Mount Kisco Housing Authority
Municipal Building
Mount Kisco, NY 10549

Mount Vernon Housing Authority
1 Eastchester Lane
Mount Vernon, NY 10550

Newark Housing Authority
114 E. Union
Newark, NY 14513

Newburgh Housing Authority
150 Smith St.
Newburgh, NY 12550

New Rochelle Housing Authority
c/o Executive Director
New Rochelle, NY 10304

New York City Housing Authority
250 Broadway
New York, NY 10007

Niagara Falls Housing Authority
720 Tenth St.
Niagara Falls, NY 14301

North Tarrytown Housing Authority
126 Valley St.
North Tarrytown, NY 10591

North Tonawanda Housing Authority
66 Central Lane
North Tonawanda, NY 14120

Norwich Housing Authority
Box 609
Norwich, NY 13815

Ogdensburg Housing Authority
232 Washington St.
Ogdensburg, NY 13669

Olean Housing Authority
132 N. Union St.
Olean, NY 14760

City of Oneida Housing Authority
226 Farrier Ave.
Oneida, NY 13421

Oneonta Housing Authority
11 Ford St.
Oneonta, NY 13820

Ossining Housing Authority
c/o Executive Director
Ossining, NY 10300

Peekskill Housing Authority
1001 Part St.
Peekskill, NY 10566

Plattsburgh Housing Authority
8 Tyrell Ave.
Plattsburgh, NY 12901

Port Chester Housing Authority
11 Weber Drive
Port Chester, NY 10573

Port Jervis Housing Authority
39 Pennsylvania Ave.
Port Jervis, NY 12771

Poughkeepsie Housing Authority
221 Smith St.
Poughkeepsie, NY 12601

Rensselaer Housing Authority
85 Aiken Ave.
Rensselaer, NY 12144

Rochester Housing Authority
5 Fitzhugh St., S.
Rochester, NY 14614

Rome Housing Authority
200 N. Levitt St.
Rome, NY 13441

St. Johnsville Housing Authority
Washington St.
St. Johnsville, NY 13452

Seneca Nation Housing Authority
Box 412
Salamanca, NY 14779

Saratoga Springs Housing Authority
Jefferson Terrace Management Building
Saratoga Springs, NY 12866

Schenectady Municipal Housing
  Authority
P.O. Box 932
Schenectady, NY 12301

Spring Valley Housing Authority
14 Union Rd.
Spring Valley, NY 10977

Romapo Housing Authority
Town Hall Route 59
Suffern, NY 10901

Oneida Housing Authority
114 S. Warren St.
Room 400
Syracuse, NY 13421

Syracuse Housing Authority
516 Burt St.
Syracuse, NY 13202

Tarrytown Housing Authority
Franklin Courts
Tarrytown, NY 10951

Troy Housing Authority
Taylor Apts. – Building 2
Troy, NY 12181

Tuckahoe Housing Authority
4 Union Place
Tuckahoe, NY 10707

Tupper Lake Housing Authority
Village Hall
Tupper Lake, NY 12986

Utica Municipal Housing Authority
509 Second St.
Utica, NY 13502

Watertown Housing Authority
454 Mill St.
Watertown, NY 13601

Watervliet Housing Authority
500 16th St.
Watervliet, NY 12189

Whitehall Housing Authority
c/o Executive Director
Whitehall, NY 12887

Greenburgh Housing Authority
9 Maple St.
White Plains, NY 10603

White Plains Housing Authority
223 Grove St.
White Plains, NY 10601

Woodridge Housing Authority
Box 655
Woodridge, NY 12789

Yonkers Municipal Housing Authority
P.O. Box 508
Yonkers, NY 10702

Yonkers Urban Renewal Agency
P.O. Box 508
Yonkers, NY 10702

NORTH CAROLINA

Ahoskie Housing Authority
City Hall
Ahoskie, NC 27910

Albemarle Housing Authority
Box 190
Albemarle, NC 28001

Andrews Housing Authority
Drawer C
Andrews, NC 28901

Asheboro Housing Authority
P.O. Box 267
Asheboro, NC 27203

Asheville Housing Authority
P.O. Box 1898
Asheville, NC 28802

Ayden Housing Authority
P.O. Box 482
Ayden, NC 28513

Beaufort Housing Authority
P.O. Box 390
Beaufort, NC 28516

Belmont Housing Authority
P.O. Box 984
Belmont, NC 28012

Benson Housing Authority
P.O. Box 308
Benson, NC 27504

Brevard Housing Authority
Cedar Crest Manor
Apt. A-1 W. Morgan St.
Brevard, NC 28712

Burlington Housing Authority
P.O. Box 2380
Burlington, NC 27215

Carthage Housing Authority
P.O. Box 524
Carthage, NC 28327

Chapel Hill Housing Authority
307 N. Columbia St.
Chapel Hill, NC 27514

Charlotte Housing Authority
200 W. Ninth St.
Charlotte, NC 28202

Qualla Housing Authority
P.O. Box 572
Cherokee, NC 28719

Concord Housing Authority
P.O. Box 382
Concord, NC 28025

Dunn Housing Authority
P.O. Drawer 1038
Dunn, NC 28334

Durham Housing Authority
P.O. Box 1726
533 E. Main St.
Durham, NC 27702

Edenton Housing Authority
P.O. Box 28
Edenton, NC 27932

Elizabeth City Housing Authority
P.O. Box 1485
Elizabeth City, NC 27909

Fairmont Housing Authority
P.O. Box 661
Fairmont, NC 28340

Farmville Housing Authority
172 Anderson Ave.
Farmville, NC 27828

Fayetteville Housing Authority
P.O. Box 710
Fayetteville, NC 28302

Forest City Housing Authority
12 Powell St.
Forest City, NC 28043

Gastonia Housing Authority
P.O. Box 2398
Gastonia, NC 28052

Eastern Carolina Reg. Housing
    Authority
P.O. Box 1315
Goldsboro, NC 27530

Goldsboro Housing Authority
P.O. Box 1403
Goldsboro, NC 27530

Graham Housing Authority
P.O. Box 89
Graham, NC 27253

Greensboro Housing Authority
P.O. Box 3115
Greensboro, NC 27402

Madison Housing Authority
c/o Locator
Greensboro, NC 27402

Greenville City Housing Authority
P.O. Box 1426
Greenville, NC 27834

Hamlet Housing Authority
P.O. Box 1188
Hamlet, NC 28345

Hendersonville Housing Authority
203 Justice St.
Hendersonville, NC 28739

Hertford Housing Authority
P.O. Box 166
Hertford, NC 27944

Hickory Public Housing Authority
P.O. Box 1515
Hickory, NC 28601

High Point Housing Authority
P.O. Box 1712
High Point, NC 27260

Hot Springs Housing Authority
P.O. Box 296
Hot Springs, NC 28743

Kings Mountain Housing Authority
201 McGill Court
Kings Mountain, NC 28086

Kinston Housing Authority
P.O. Box 674
Kinston, NC 28501

Laurinburg Housing Authority
P.O. Box 1637
Laurinburg, NC 28352

Lenoir Housing Authority
P.O. Box 659
Lenoir, NC 28645

Lexington Housing Authority
P.O. Box 1085
Lexington, NC 27292

Lincolnton Housing Authority
P.O. Box 753
Lincolnton, NC 28092

Lumberton Housing Authority
P.O. Drawer 701
Lumberton, NC 28358

Robeson County Housing Authority
Box 699
Lumberton, NC 28358

Marshall Housing Authority
c/o Executive Director
Marshall, NC 28753

Mars Hill Housing Authority
P.O. Box 186
Mars Hill, NC 28754

Maxton Housing Authority
P.O. Box 126
Maxton, NC 28364

Marshville Housing Authority
P.O. Box 804
Monroe, NC 28110

Monroe Housing Authority
P.O. Box 804
Monroe, NC 28110

Mooresville Housing Authority
P.O. Box 787
Mooresville, NC 28115

Morganton Housing Authority
P.O. Box 1053
Morganton, NC 28655

Mount Airy Housing Authority
P.O. Box 767
Mount Airy, NC 27030

Mount Gilead Housing Authority
P.O. Box 158
Mount Gilead, NC 27306

Murfreesboro Housing Authority
c/o Executive Director
Murfreesboro, NC 27855

Murphy Housing Authority
101 Beal Circle
Murphy, NC 28906

New Bern Housing Authority
P.O. Box 1486
New Bern, NC 28560

North Wilkesboro Housing Authority
P.O. Box 1371
North Wilkesboro, NC 28659

Oxford Housing Authority
P.O. Box 616
Oxford, NC 27565

Pembroke Housing Authority
P.O. Box 1053
Pembroke, NC 28372

Plymouth Housing Authority
Municipal Building
Plymouth, NC 27962

Raleigh Housing Authority
P.O. Box 28007
Raleigh, NC 27602

Randleman Housing Authority
606 South Main St.
Randleman, NC 27317

Roberson County Housing Authority
P.O. Box 31
Red Springs, NC 28377

Reidsville Housing Authority
246 Southwest Market St.
Reidsville, NC 27320

Roanoke Rapids Housing Authority
1025 Jackson St.
Roanoke Rapids, NC 27870

Robersonville Housing Authority
P.O. Box 988
Robersonville, NC 27871

Rockingham Housing Authority
P.O. Box 177
Rockingham, NC 28397

Rocky Mount Housing Authority
P.O. Box 4247
Rocky Mount, NC 27801

Roxboro Housing Authority
P.O. Box 496
Roxboro, NC 27573

Rowan County Housing Authority
P.O. Drawer
Salisbury, NC 28144

Salisbury Housing Authority
P.O. Box 159
Salisbury, NC 28144

Sanford Housing Authority
P.O. Box 636
Sanford, NC 27331

Selma Housing Authority
P.O. Box 584
Selma, NC 27576

Shelby Housing Authority
P.O. Box 1192
Shelby, NC 28150

Smithfield Housing Authority
P.O. Box 1058
Smithfield, NC 27577

Southern Pines Housing Authority
P.O. Box 1339
Southern Pines, NC 28387

Spruce Pine Housing Authority
P.O. Box 189
Spruce Pine, NC 28777

Star Housing Authority
c/o Executive Director
Star, NC 27356

Statesville Housing Authority
P.O. Box 187
Statesville, NC 28677

Tarboro Housing Authority
P.O. Box 1144
Tarboro, NC 27886

Thomasville Housing Authority
City Hall
Thomasville, NC 27360

Troy Housing Authority
201 Stanley St.
Troy, NC 27371

Valdese Housing Authority
P.O. Box 310
Valdese, NC 28690

Wadesboro Housing Authority
Box 211
Wadesboro, NC 28170

Mid-East Regional Housing Authority
P.O. Box 474
Washington, NC 27889

Washington Housing Authority
P.O. Box 1046
Washington, NC 27889

Waynesville Housing Authority
Drawer 1018
Waynesville, NC 28786

Whiteville Housing Authority
103M Westwood Ave.
Whiteville, NC 28472

Williamston Housing Authority
P.O. Box
Williamston, NC 27892

Wilmington Housing Authority
P.O. Box 3005
Wilmington, NC 28401

Wilson Housing Authority
P.O. Box 751
Wilson, NC 27894

Winston-Salem Housing Authority
901 Cleveland Ave.
Winston-Salem, NC 27101

Wake County Housing Authority
P.O. Box 368
Zebulon, NC 27597

NORTH DAKOTA

Turtle Mountain Housing Authority
Turtle Mountain Indian Agency
Belcourt, ND 58316

Burleigh County Housing Authority
P.O. Box 1881
Bismarck, ND 58501

Towner County Housing Authority
c/o Executive Director
Cando, ND 58324

Cooperstown Housing Authority
c/o Executive Director
Cooperstown, ND 58425

Devils Lake Housing Authority
Box 691
Devils Lake, ND 58301

Dunn County Housing Authority
Box 107
Dickinson, ND 58601

McKenzie County Housing Authority
P.O. Box 107
Dickinson, ND 58601

Stark County Housing Authority
P.O. Box 107
Dickinson, ND 58601

Fargo Housing Authority
P.O. Box 1030
Fargo, ND 58102

Fort Totten Housing Authority
c/o Bureau of Indian Affairs
Fort Totten, ND 58301

Standing Rock Housing Authority
c/o Executive Director
Fort Yates, ND 58000

Grafton Housing Authority
143 Eastwood Drive
Grafton, ND 58237

Grand Forks Housing Authority
Room 214
2 N. Third St.
Grand Forks, NC 58201

Mercer County Housing Authority
P.O. Box 507
Hazen, ND 58545

Stutsman County Housing Authority
1321 Gardenette Drive
Jamestown, ND 58401

Langdon Housing Authority
c/o Executive Director
Langdon, ND 58249

Morton County Housing Authority
306 Tenth Ave., NW
Mandan, ND 58554

Traill County Housing Authority
c/o Executive Director
Mayville, ND 58257

Benson County Housing Authority
c/o Executive Director
Minnewaukan, ND 58351

Minot Housing Authority
c/o Executive Director
Minot, ND 58701

Mott Housing Authority
c/o Executive Director
Mott, ND 58646

Eddy County Housing Authority
811 First Ave. North
New Rockford, ND 58356

Fort Berthold Housing Authority
Box 619
New Town, ND 58763

Rolette County Housing Authority
c/o Executive Director
Rolette, ND 58366

Rugby Housing Authority
City Hall
Rugby, ND 58368

Montrail County Housing Authority
c/o Executive Director
Stanley, ND 58784

Kidder County Housing Authority
c/o Executive Director
Steele, ND 58482

Barnes County Housing Authority
P.O. Box 567
Valley City, ND 58072

Pembina County Housing Authority
c/o Locator
Walhalla, ND 58282

Cass County Housing Authority
Box 511
West Fargo, ND 58078

Williston Housing Authority
1801 Eighth Ave. West
Williston, ND 58801

OHIO

Akron Housing Authority
180 W. Cedar St.
Akron, OH 44307

Ashtabula Metro Housing Authority
110 W. 44th St.
Ashtabula, OH 44004

Clermont Metropolitan Housing
  Authority
c/o Executive Director
Batavia, OH 45103

Stark Metropolitan Housing Authority
1800 W. Tuscarawas St.
Canton, OH 44708

Chillicothe Metropolitan Housing
  Authority
178 W. Fourth St.
Chillicothe, OH 45601

Cincinnati Metropolitan Housing
  Authority
16 W. Central Parkway
Cincinnati, OH 45210

Cleveland Metropolitan Housing
  Authority
1441 W. 25th St.
Cleveland, OH 44113

Cuyahoga Metropolitan Housing
  Authority
1441 W. 25th St.
Cleveland, OH 44113

Columbus Metropolitan Housing
  Authority
272 S. Gift St.
Columbus, OH 43215

Perry County Housing Authority
Route 1
Crooksville, OH 43731

Dayton Metropolitan Housing
  Authority
340 W. Fourth St.
Dayton, OH 45402

Columbia Metropolitan Housing
  Authority
325 Moore St.
East Liverpool, OH 43920

Butler Metropolitan Housing
  Authority
60 Hanover Drive
Hamilton, OH 45011

Huron Metropolitan Housing Authority
c/o Executive Director
Huron, OH 43602

Ironton Metropolitan Housing Authority
720 Washington St.
Ironton, OH 45638

Logan Metropolitan Housing Authority
c/o 198 Springhill Place
Logan, OH 43138

London Metropolitan Housing Authority
179 S. Main St.
London, OH 43140

Lorain Metropolitan Housing Authority
1730 Broadway
Lorain, OH 44052

Mansfield Metropolitan Housing Authority
45 W. Second St.
Mansfield, OH 44902

Martins Ferry Metropolitan Housing Authority
400 Center St.
Martins Ferry, OH 43935

Medina Metropolitan Housing Authority
221 N. State Rd.
Medina, OH 44256

Licking Metropolitan Housing Authority
38 First St.
Newark, OH 43055

Lake Metropolitan Housing Authority
200 W. Jackson St.
Painesville, OH 44077

Portsmouth Housing Authority
610 Fifth St.
Portsmouth, OH 45662

Ravenna Housing Authority
200 Main St.
Ravenna, OH 44266

Erie Metropolitan Housing Authority
128 Perry St.
Sandusky, OH 44870

Springfield Housing Authority
437 E. John St.
Springfield, OH 45505

Steubenville Metropolitan Housing Authority
815 N. Sixth St.
Steubenville, OH 43952

Toledo Metropolitan Housing Authority
P.O. Box 477
Toledo, OH 43601

Warren Housing Authority
700 Buckeye St., NW
Warren, OH 44485

Yellow Springs Metropolitan Housing Authority
1 Lawson St.
Yellow Springs, OH 45387

Youngstown Housing Authority
976 W. Federal St.
Youngstown, OH 44510

Zanesville Housing Authority
863 Durban Drive
Zanesville, OH 43701

OKLAHOMA

Ada City Housing Authority
P.O. Box 668
Ada, OK 74820

Afton Housing Authority
RR 2, Box 20 AHA
Afton, OK 74331

Anadarko Housing Authority
c/o Locator
Anadarko, OK 73005

Apache Tribe of Indians of Oklahoma
P.O. Box 309
Anadarko, OK 73005

Kiowa Tribe of Indians Housing Authority
P.O. Box 847
Anadarko, OK 73005

Antlers Housing Authority
105 NW Third St.
Antlers, OK 74523

Apache Housing Authority
P.O. Box 337
Apache, OK 73006

Chickasaw Nation Housing Authority
P.O. Box 997
Ardmore, OK 73401

Arnett Housing Authority
Town Hall
Arnett, OK 73832

Atoka Housing Authority
P.O. Box 80
Atoka, OK 74525

Beggs Housing Authority
P.O. Box 568
Beggs, OK 74421

Caddo Electric Cooperative Housing Authority
P.O. Box 70
Binger, OK 73009

Blair Housing Authority
Blair Enterprise Building
Blair, OK 73526

Boley Housing Authority
P.O. Box 25
Boley, OK 74829

Boswell Housing Authority
P.O. Box 310
Boswell, OK 74727

Bristow Housing Authority
1110 S. Chestnut
Bristow, OK 74010

Broken Bow Housing Authority
P.O. Box 177
Broken Bow, OK 74728

Cache Housing Authority
Box 267
Cache, OK 73527

Cement Housing Authority
P.O. Box 201
Cement, OK 73017

Cheyenne Housing Authority
Box 206
Cheyenne, OK 73628

Clayton Housing Authority
Box 8
Clayton, OK 74536

Cheyenne-Arapaho Housing Authority
Box 997
Clinton, OK 73601

Coalgate Housing Authority
P.O. Box 469
Coalgate, OK 74538

Comanche City Housing Authority
P.O. Box 207
Comanche, OK 73529

Commerce Housing Authority
P.O. Drawer 70
Commerce, OK 74339

Cyril Housing Authority
P.O. Box 435
Cyril, OK 73029

Drumright Housing Authority
Box 1114
Drumright, OK 74030

East Duke Housing Authority
Box 220
Duke, OK 73532

Eldorado Housing Authority
Box 293
Eldorado, OK 73537

Elk City Housing Authority
City Hall
Elk City, OK 73644

Enid Housing Authority
c/o Executive Director
Enid, OK 73100

Fort Cobb Housing Authority
Box 209
Fort Cobb, OK 73038

Fort Gibson Housing Authority
Box 426
Fort Gibson, OK 74434

Cookston Hills
P.O. Box 52
Gans, OK 74936

HOUSING 191

Geary Housing Authority
420 West Main
Geary, OK 73040

Caddo Indian Tribe Housing Authority
P.O. Box 167
Gracemont, OK 73042

Grandfield Housing Authority
P.O. Box 749
Grandfield, OK 73546

Granite Housing Authority
P.O. Box 248
Granite, OK 73547

Guthrie Housing Authority
Oak Park Addition
Guthrie, OK 73044

Haileyville Housing Authority
414 N. Tenth St.
Hartshorne, OK 74547

Hartshorne Housing Authority
P.O. Box 343
Hartshorne, OK 74547

Krebs Housing Authority
P.O. Box 343
Hartshorne, OK 74547

Heavener Housing Authority
P.O. Box 247
Heavener, OK 74937

Hobart Housing Authority
409 S. Broadway
Hobart, OK 73561

Holdenville Housing Authority
Box 150
Holdenville, OK 74848

Osage Indian Housing Authority
P.O. Box 517
Hominy, OK 74035

Choctaw Nation Housing Authority
Box G
Hugo, OK 74743

Hugo Housing Authority
Box 727
Hugo, OK 74743

Hydro Housing Authority
P.O. Box 422
Hydro, OK 73048

Idabel Housing Authority
Box 858
Idabel, OK 74745

Indiahoma Housing Authority
P.O. Box 157
Indiahoma, OK 73552

Keota Housing Authority
P.O. Box A
Keota, OK 74941

Langston Housing Authority
P.O. Box 90
Langston, OK 73050

Comanche Indian Housing Authority
Box 1671
Lawton, OK 73501

Lawton Housing Authority
620 E Ave.
Lawton, OK 73501

Kingston Housing Authority
Box 326
Madill, OK 73446

Madill Housing Authority
Box 326
Madill, OK 73446

Tishomingo Town Housing Authority
Box 326
Madill, OK 73446

Mangum Housing Authority
P.O. Box 394
Mangum, OK 73554

Konawa Housing Authority
P.O. Box 186
Maud, OK 74854

Maud Housing Authority
P.O. Box 246
Maud, OK 74854

Kiamichi Electric Co-op Housing
  Authority
P.O. Box 1233
McAlester, OK 74501

McAlester Housing Authority
526 E. Wichita
McAlester, OK 74501

Miami Housing Authority
205 B St., NE
Miami, OK 74354

Minco Housing Authority
P.O. Box 302
Minco, OK 73059

Muskogee Housing Authority
200 N. 40th St.
Muskogee, OK 74401

Newkirk Housing Authority
Box 316
Newkirk, OK 74647

Oilton Housing Authority
Box 176
Oilton, OK 74052

Oklahoma City Housing Authority
501 Couch Drive
Oklahoma City, OK 73102

Creek Nation Housing Authority
P.O. Box 297
Okmulgee, OK 74447

Osage County Housing Authority
P.O. Box 818
Pawhuska, OK 74056

City of Pawnee Housing Authority
P.O. Box 66
Pawnee, OK 74058

Pawnee Tribe of Oklahoma
P.O. Box 408
Pawnee, OK 74058

Picher Housing Authority
P.O. Box 188
Picher, OK 74360

Ponca City Housing Authority
P.O. Box 1450
Ponca City, OK 74601

Ponca Tribe Housing Authority
P.O. Box 1511
Ponca City, OK 74601

Prague Housing Authority
Box 366
Prague, OK 74864

Otoe-Missouri Tribal Authority
P.O. Box 141
Red Rock, OK 74651

Ringling Housing Authority
Box 20
Ringling, OK 73456

Roosevelt Housing Authority
Box 177
Roosevelt, OK 73564

Ryan Housing Authority
P.O. Box 352
Ryan, OK 73565

Sayre Housing Authority
Box 326
Sayre, OK 73622

Seiling Housing Authority
General Delivery
Seiling, OK 73663

Seminole City Housing Authority
Box 1253
Seminole, OK 74868

Absentee Shawnee Tribe Housing
  Authority
P.O. Box 425
Shawnee, OK 74801

Sac & Fox Indian Tribe Housing
  Authority
P.O. Box 1252
Shawnee, OK 74801

Shawnee Housing Authority
P.O. Box 1691
Shawnee, OK 74801

Snyder Housing Authority
300 E St.
Snyder, OK 73566

Housing Authority, Town of Sterling
P.O. Box 367
Sterling, OK 73567

Stigler Housing Authority
Box 33
Stigler, OK 74462

Stilwell Housing Authority
801 N. Fourth St.
Stilwell, OK 74960

Stratford Housing Authority
P.O. Box 310
Stratford, OK 74872

Stroud Housing Authority
718 W. Third St.
Stroud, OK 74079

Cherokee Nation Housing Authority
P.O. Box 794
Tahlequah, OK 74464

Talihina Housing Authority
P.O. Drawer C
Talihina, OK 74571

Housing Authority, Town of Temple
c/o D. Norman, Executive Director
P.O. Box 307
Temple, OK 73568

Terral Housing Authority
Box 70
Terral, OK 73569

Tipton Town Housing Authority
P.O. Box 369
Tipton, OK 73570

Tulsa City Housing Authority
P.O. Box 6369
Tulsa, OK 74106

Tuttle Housing Authority
Box S
Tuttle, OK 73089

Valliant Housing Authority
Box 391
Valliant, OK 74764

Walters Housing Authority
P.O. Box 452
Walters, OK 73572

Watonga Housing Authority
P.O. Box 28
Watonga, OK 73772

Waurika Housing Authority
Box 307
Waurika, OK 73573

Housing Authority, City of Waynoka
C B Unit 1
Box 1
Waynoka, OK 73860

Weleetka Housing Authority
Box 756
Weleetka, OK 74880

Wetumka Housing Authority
P.O. Box 425
Wetumka, OK 74883

Seminole Nation Housing Authority
P.O. Box 1481
Wewoka, OK 74884

Wewoka Housing Authority
P.O. Box 877
Wewoka, OK 74884

Wilburton Housing Authority
Box 238
Wilburton, OK 74578

Wister Housing Authority
P.O. Box a79
Wister, OK 74966

Wynnewood Housing Authority
806 E. Colbert
Wynnewood, OK 73098

Yale Housing Authority
P.O. Box 265
Yale, OK 74085

OREGON

Benton County Housing Authority
2223 Santiam Highway
Albany, OR 97321

Linn County Housing Authority
2223 Santiam Highway
Albany, OR 97321

Lane County Housing Authority
P.O. Box 907
Eugene, OR 97401

Umatilla County Housing Authority
P.O. Box 107
Hermiston, OR 97838

Washington County Housing Authority
245 SE Second Ave.
Hillsboro, OR 97123

Klamath Falls Housing Authority
621 Pine St.
Klamath Falls, OR 97601

Yamhill County Housing Authority
217 N. Adams St.
McMinnville, OR 97128

Jackson County Housing Authority
508 Edwards St.
Medford, OR 97501

Coos County Housing Authority
1700 Monroe
North Bend, OR 97459

North Bend Housing Authority
1700 Monroe St.
North Bend, OR 97459

Clackamas County Housing Authority
P.O. Box 70
Oregon City, OR 97045

Umatilla Reservation Housing
   Authority
P.O. Box 580
Pendleton, OR 97801

Portland Housing Authority
4400 NE Broadway
Portland, OR 97213

Douglas County Housing Authority
902 W. Stanton St.
Roseburg, OR 97470

Marion County Housing Authority
220 High St., NE
Salem, OR 97303

Polk County Housing Authority
204 SW Walnut Ave.
Salem, OR 97304

Salem Housing Authority
360 Church St., SE
Salem, OR 97301

Lincoln County Housing Authority
P.O. Box H
Toledo, OR 97391

Warm Springs Reservation Housing
   Authority
c/o Executive Director
Warm Springs, OR 97761

PENNSYLVANIA

Allentown Housing Authority
1339 Allen St.
Allentown, PA 18102

Altoona Housing Authority
1100 11th St.
Altoona, PA 16601

Beaver County Housing Authority
State Ave. & Toy St.
Beaver, PA 15009

Bethlehem Housing Authority
645 Main St.
Bethlehem, PA 18018

Indiana County Housing Authority
101 Morewood Terrace
Blairsville Boro, PA 15717

Tioga County Housing Authority
Borough Building
Blossburg, PA 15717

Somerset County Housing Authority
600 Kircher Place
Boswell, PA 15531

Berks County Housing Authority
16 S. Reading Ave.
Boyerstown, PA 19512

Bradford Housing Authority
2 Bushnell St.
Bradford, PA 16701

Butler County Housing Authority
P.O. Box 1917
Butler, PA 16001

Bradford County Housing Authority
c/o Executive Director
Canton, PA 17724

Carbondale Housing Authority
77 Main St.
Carbondale, PA 18407

Chester Housing Authority
6 W. Sixth St.
Chester, PA 19013

Clearfield County Housing Authority
P.O. Box 868
Clearfield, PA 16830

Connellsville Housing Authority
P.O. Box 762
Connellsville, PA 15425

Corry Housing Authority
126 Fourth Ave.
Corry, PA 16407

Potter County Housing Authority
Courthouse
Coudersport, PA 16915

Montour County Housing Authority
1 Beaver Place
Danville, PA 17821

Delaware County Housing Authority
1827 Constitution Ave.
Delaware Township, PA 19094

Bucks County Housing Authority
57 W. Court St.
Doylestown, PA 18901

Du Bois Housing Authority
16 Scribner Ave.
Du Bois, PA 15801

Easton Housing Authority
221 S. Fourth St.
Easton, PA 18042

Erie Housing Authority
606 Holland St.
Erie, PA 16501

Franklin City Housing Authority
11 Dale Ave.
Franklin, PA 16323

Harrisburg Housing Authority
351 Chestnut St.
Harrisburg, PA 17101

Hazelton Housing Authority
334 W. Birch St.
Hazelton, PA 18201

Westmoreland County Housing Authority
59 Lincoln Highway, E.
Jeannette, PA 15644

Johnstown Housing Authority
P.O. Box 419
Johnstown, PA 15907

Luzerne County Housing Authority
301 Market St.
Kingston, PA 18704

Armstrong County Housing Authority
100 N. Grant Ave.
Kittanning, PA 16201

Lancaster Housing Authority
333 Church St.
Lancaster, PA 17602

Lebanon County Housing Authority
400 S. Eighth St.
Lebanon, PA 17042

Carbon County Housing Authority
200 Interchange Rd.
Lehighton, PA 18235

Mifflin County Housing Authority
Lawler Place
Lewiston, PA 17044

Clinton County Housing Authority
710 Linden St.
Lock Haven, PA 17745

McKeesport Housing Authority
Ohio & Brownlee Sts.
McKeesport, PA 15132

Meadville Housing Authority
1120 Market St.
Meadville, PA 16335

Northumberland County Housing Authority
Milton Towers
50 Mahoning St.
Milton, PA 17847

Huntingdon County Housing Authority
G-1 Federal Drive
Mount Union, PA 17066

Nanticoke Housing Authority
100 Nanticoke Ave.
Nanticoke, PA 18364

Lawrence County Housing Authority
481 Neshannock Ave.
Box 268
New Castle, PA 16103

Oil City Housing Authority
1 Sycamore St.
Municipal Building
Oil City, PA 16301

Philadelphia Housing Authority
2012 Chestnut St.
Philadelphia, PA 19103

Allegheny County Housing Authority
429 Forbes Ave.
Pittsburgh, PA 15219

Pittsburgh Housing Authority
200 Ross St.
Pittsburgh, PA 15219

Pittston Housing Authority
Boulevard Towers on Kennedy Blvd.
Pittston, PA 18646

Montgomery County Housing Authority
Box 273
Pottstown, PA 19464

Pottsville Housing Authority
510 W. Norwegian St.
Pottsville, PA 17901

Schuylkill County Housing Authority
118 E. Norwegian St.
Pottsville, PA 17901

Jefferson City Housing Authority
RD No. 5
Punxsutawney, PA 15767

Jefferson County Redevelopment Authority
201 N. Jefferson St.
Punxsutawney, PA 15767

Reading Housing Authority
1301 Schuylkill Ave.
Reading, PA 19601

Elk County Housing Authority
109 N. Broad St.
Ridgway, PA 15853

Lackawanna County Housing Authority
506 Spruce St.
Scranton, PA 18503

Scranton Housing Authority
408 Adams Ave.
Scranton, PA 18510

Shamokin Housing Authority
415 E. Sunbury St.
Shamokin, PA 17872

Mercer County Housing Authority
335 Quinby St.
Sharon, PA 16146

Dauphin County Housing Authority
P.O. Box 7598
Steelton, PA 17113

Monroe County Housing Authority
1526 N. Fifth St.
Stroudsburg, PA 18360

Sunbury Housing Authority
725 Chestnut St.
Sunbury, PA 17801

Titusville Housing Authority
P.O. Box 103
Titusville, PA 16354

Fayette County Housing Authority
Bierer Wood Acres
Uniontown, PA 15401

Washington County Housing Authority
100 Crumrine Tower
Franklin St.
Washington, PA 15301

Franklin County Housing Authority
202 Ekder Ave.
Waynesboro, PA 17268

Green County Housing Authority
170 E. Greene St.
Waynesboro, PA 17268

Chester County Housing Authority
222 N. Church St.
West Chester, PA 19380

Wilkes-Barre City Housing Authority
Balt Blvd. & E. Northampton St.
Wilkes-Barre, PA 18702

Lycoming County Housing Authority
1600 Sherman St.
Williamsport, PA 17702

Williamsport City Housing Authority
143 W. Fourth St.
Room 209
Williamsport, PA 17701

York Housing Authority
449 E. King St.
York, PA 17404

RHODE ISLAND

Bristol Housing Authority
1014 Hope St.
Bristol, RI 02809

Central Falls Housing Authority
466 Hunt St.
Central Falls, RI 02863

Coventry Housing Authority
14 Manchester Circle
Coventry, RI 02816

Cranston Housing Authority
50 Birch St.
Cranston, RI 02905

Cumberland Housing Authority
1 Menden Rd.
Cumberland, RI 02864

East Providence Housing Authority
3663 Pawtucket Ave. Harbor View
East Providence, RI 02915

Burrillville Housing Authority
Ashton Court, Chapel St.
Harrisville, RI 02830

Jamestown Housing Authority
19 Pemberton Ave.
Jamestown, RI 02835

Johnston Housing Authority
8 Farand Circle
Johnston, RI 02919

Lincoln Housing Authority
10 Franklin St.
Lincoln, RI 02865

Newport Housing Authority
Park-Holm No. 1
Newport, RI 02840

North Providence Housing Authority
1073 Charles St.
North Providence, RI 02863

Pawtucket Housing Authority
214 Roosevelt Ave.
Pawtucket, RI 02862

Portsmouth Housing Authority
2368 E. Main Rd.
Portsmouth, RI 02871

Providence Housing Authority
263 Chad Brown St.
Providence, RI 02908

Smithfield Housing Authority
c/o Executive Director
Smithfield, RI 02828

South Kingstown Housing Authority
P.O. Box 6
Wakefield, RI 02883

Warren Housing Authority
Town Hall
Warren, RI 02885

Warwick Housing Authority
3070 W. Shore Rd.
Warwick, RI 02886

Westerly Housing Authority
8 Park View
Westerly, RI 02891

West Warwick Housing Authority
62 Robert St.
West Warwick, RI 02893

Woonsocket Housing Authority
547 Clinton St.
Woonsocket, RI 02895

SOUTH CAROLINA

Abbeville Housing Authority
212 Court Square
Abbeville, SC 29620

Aiken Housing Authority
P.O. Box 879
Aiken, SC 29803

Anderson Housing Authority
1-A Wil-Mary Building
Anderson, SC 29621

South Carolina Regional Housing
  Authority No. 3
P.O. Box 248
Barnwell, SC 29812

Beaufort Housing Authority
P.O. Box 1104
Beaufort, SC 29902

Bennettsville Housing Authority
P.O. Box 1154
Bennettsville, SC 29512

Charleston Housing Authority
20 Franklin St.
Charleston, SC 29402

Cheraw Housing Authority
Box 67
Cheraw, SC 29520

Clinton Housing Authority
City Hall
Clinton, SC 29325

Columbia Housing Authority
P.O. Box 4307
Columbia, SC 29204

Conway Housing Authority
2303 Leonard Ave.
Conway, SC 29526

Easley Housing Authority
401 E. First St.
Easley, SC 29640

Darlington Housing Authority
P.O. Box 1343
Florence, SC 29501

Florence Housing Authority
P.O. Box 1343
Florence, SC 29501

Fort Mill Housing Authority
110 Elliott St.
Fort Mill, SC 29715

Gaffney Housing Authority
Limestone Courts Management
  Building
Gaffney, SC 29340

Georgetown Housing Authority
P.O. Box 209
Georgetown, SC 29440

Greenville Housing Authority
511 Augusta St.
Greenville, SC 29605

Greenwood Housing Authority
P.O. Box 40
Greenwood, SC 29646

Greer Housing Authority
P.O. Box 413
Greer, SC 29651

Hartsville Housing Authority
P.O. Box 146
Hartsville, SC 29550

Kingstree Housing Authority
Box 157
Kingstree, SC 29556

Lake City Housing Authority
P.O. Box 1017
Lake City, SC 29560

Lancaster Housing Authority
P.O. Box 561
Lancaster, SC 29720

Laurens Housing Authority
P.O. Box 749
Laurens, SC 29360

South Carolina Regional Housing
  Authority No. 1
P.O. Box 326
Laurens, SC 29360

Marion Housing Authority
P.O. Box 224
Marion, SC 29571

Mullins Housing Authority
125 W. Wine St.
Mullins, SC 29574

Myrtle Beach Housing Authority
P.O. Box 1466
Myrtle Beach, SC 29577

Newberry Housing Authority
P.O. Drawer 538
Newberry, SC 29108

Rock Hill Housing Authority
P.O. Box 801
Rock Hill, SC 29730

Spartanburg Housing Authority
P.O. Box 2488
Spartanburg, SC 29302

Sumter Housing Authority
P.O. Box 1449
Sumter, SC 29150

Union Housing Authority
201 Porter St.
Union, SC 29379

Woodruff Housing Authority
Pinewood Court, Route 3
Woodruff, SC 29388

York Housing Authority
P.O. Box 500
York, SC 29745

SOUTH DAKOTA

Aberdeen Housing Authority
Box 807
Municipal Building
Aberdeen, SD 54701

Burke Housing & Redevelopment
  Commission
c/o Executive Director
Burke, SD 57523

Canton Housing & Redevelopment
    Commission
City Hall
123 S. Main St.
Canton, SD 57013

Clark Housing Authority
c/o Executive Director
Clark, SD 57225

De Smet Housing Authority
c/o Executive Director
De Smet, SD 57231

Cheyenne River Housing Authority
Cheyenne River Indian Reservation
Eagle Butte, SD 57625

Faulkton Housing Authority
c/o Executive Director
Faulkton, SD 57438

Crow Creek Housing Authority
Box 655
Fort Thompson, SD 27339

Hot Springs Housing & Redevelop-
    ment Commission
c/o Executive Director
Hot Springs, SD 57747

Howard Housing & Redevelopment
    Commission
Box K
Howard, SD 57349

Kennebec Housing & Redevelopment
    Commission
c/o Executive Director
Kennebec, SD 57544

Lake Andes Housing & Redevelop-
    ment Commission
c/o Executive Director
Lake Andes, SD 57356

Lake Norden Housing Redevelopment
    Commission
P.O. Box 216
Lake Norden, SD 57248

Lead Housing Authority
City Hall
Lead, SD 57754

Lemmon Housing Authority
c/o Executive Director
Lemmon, SD 57638

Lennon Housing & Redevelopment
    Commission
c/o Executive Director
Lennon, SD 57039

Lower Brule Housing Authority
Box 476
Lower Brule, SD 57548

Corson County Housing & Redevelop-
    ment Commission
c/o Executive Director
McLaughlin, SD 57642

Standing Rock Housing Authority
c/o Executive Director
McLaughlin, SD 57642

Madison Housing Redevelopment
    Authority
Drawer A
Madison, SD 57042

Martin Housing & Redevelopment
    Commission
Blackpipe State Bank
Martin, SD 57551

Millbank Housing Authority
902 E. Millbank Ave.
Millbank, SD 57252

Miller Housing & Redevelopment
    Commission
c/o Executive Director
Miller, SD 57362

Mitchell Housing Authority
115 W. Fourth Ave.
Mitchell, SD 57301

Murdo Housing & Redevelopment
    Commission
c/o Executive Director
Murdo, SD 57559

Parker Housing & Redevelopment
    Commission
c/o Executive Director
Parker, SD 57053

Pierre Housing Redevelopment
    Commission
222 E. Dakota Ave.
Pierre, SD 57501

Oglala Sioux Housing Authority
Box C
Pine Ridge, SD 57770

Pennington County Housing Authority
2040 W. Main
Suite 305
Rapid City, SD 57701

Pennington County Housing & Re-
    development Commission
801 San Francisco
Sixth District
Rapid City, SD 57701

Redfield Housing Redevelopment
    Commission
c/o Executive Director
Redfield, SD 57469

Rosebud Housing Authority
Tribal Building
Rosebud, SD 57570

Sioux Falls Housing & Renewal Office
100 N. Phillips Ave.
Sioux Falls, SD 57102

Sisseton Housing & Redevelopment
    Commission
c/o Executive Director
Sisseton, SD 57262

Sisseton Wahpeton Reservation
c/o Executive Director
Sisseton, SD 57262

Tyndall Housing Authority
c/o Executive Director
Tyndall, SD 57066

Viborg Housing Authority
c/o Executive Director
Viborg, SD 57070

Volga Housing & Redevelopment
    Authority
c/o Executive Director
Volga, SD 57071

Yankton Sioux Tribal Housing
    Authority
c/o Executive Director
Wagner, SD 57380

Watertown Housing Authority
c/o Executive Director
Watertown, SD 57201

Webster Housing Authority
c/o Executive Director
Webster, SD 57274

Wessington Springs Housing Authority
c/o Executive Director
Wessington Springs, SD 57382

TENNESSEE

Athens Housing Authority
P.O. Box 308
Athens, TN 37303

Polk County Housing Authority
Courthouse
Benton, TN 37307

Bolivar Housing Authority
729 Margan St.
Bolivar, TN 38008

Bristol Housing Authority
P.O. Box 3124
Bristol, TN 37620

Brownsville Housing Authority
P.O. Box 197
Brownsville, TN 38012

Chattanooga Housing Authority
P.O. Box 1486
Chattanooga, TN 37401

Clarksville Housing Authority
P.O. Box 603
Clarksville, TN 37040

Cleveland Housing Authority
P.O. Box 995
Cleveland, TN 37311

Clinton Housing Authority
825 McAdoo St.
Clinton, TN 37716

Columbia Housing Authority
P.O. Box 15
Columbia, TN 38401

Cookeville Housing Authority
P.O. Box 400
Cookeville, TN 38501

Covington Housing Authority
P.O. Box 88
Covington, TN 38019

Crossville Housing Authority
P.O. Box 425
Crossville, TN 38555

Dayton Housing Authority
P.O. Box 396
Dayton, TN 37321

Decherd Housing Authority
135 Cumberland View Homes
Decherd, TN 37324

Dickson Housing Authority
Evans Heights Apts.
Dickson, TN 37055

Dyersburg Housing Authority
P.O. Box 824
Dyersburg, TN 38024

Elizabethton Housing Authority
P.O. Box 189
Elizabeth, TN 37643

Erin Housing Authority
City Hall
Public Square
Erin, TN 37061

Erwin Housing Authority
P.O. Box 373
Erwin, TN 37650

Etowah Housing Authority
122 Circle Dr.
Etowah, TN 37331

Fayetteville Housing Authority
P.O. Box 593
Fayetteville, TN 37334

Franklin Housing Authority
P.O. Box 304
Franklin, TN 37064

Gallatin Housing Authority
P.O. Box 760
Gallatin, TN 37066

Portland Housing Authority
P.O. Box 760
Gallatin, TN 37066

South Carthage Housing Authority
P.O. Box 760
Gallatin, TN 37066

Gallaway Housing Authority
Box 106
Gallaway, TN 38036

Greeneville Housing Authority
P.O. Box 269
Greeneville, TN 37743

Harriman Housing Authority
P.O. Box 341
Harriman, TN 37748

Oak Ridge Housing Authority
P.O. Box 341
Harriman, TN 37748

Oliver Springs Housing Authority
P.O. Box 341
Harriman, TN 37748

Hartsville Housing Authority
P.O. Box 44
Hartsville, TN 37074

Hohenwald Housing Authority
323 Mill St.
Hohenwald, TN 38462

Humboldt Housing Authority
1828 Baum St.
Humboldt, TN 38343

Huntingdon Housing Authority
P.O. Box 532
Huntingdon, TN 38344

Jackson Housing Authority
P.O. Box 3188
Jackson, TN 38301

Jefferson City Housing Authority
707 Ellis St.
Jefferson, TN 37760

Jellico Housing Authority
1000 S. Main St.
Jellico, TN 37762

Johnson City Housing Authority
P.O. Box 59
Johnson City, TN 37601

Kingsport Housing Authority
P.O. Box 44
Kingsport, TN 37662

Knoxville Housing Authority
901 Broadway, NE
Knoxville, TN 37917

Lafayette Housing Authority
P.O. Box 116
Lafayette, TN 37083

Lafollette Housing Authority
P.O. Box 392
Lafollette, TN 37766

Lawrenceburg Housing Authority
P.O. Drawer C
Lawrenceburg, TN 38464

Lebanon Housing Authority
P.O. Box 187
Lebanon, TN 37087

Lenoir City Housing Authority
101 Oakwood Drive
Lenoir City, TN 37771

Lewisburg Housing Authority
744 Bark St.
Lewisburg, TN 37091

Lexington Housing Authority
100 Willow Courts
Lexington, TN 38351

Livingston Housing Authority
P.O. Box 98
Livingston, TN 38570

Loudon Housing Authority
c/o Executive Director
Loudon, TN 37774

Manchester Housing Authority
710 Butler Circle
Manchester, TN 37355

Martin Housing Authority
P.O. Box 143
Martin, TN 38237

Maryville Housing Authority
P.O. Box 428
Maryville, TN 37801

McKenzie Housing Authority
City Hall
McKenzie, TN 38201

McMinnville Housing Authority
301 Hardaway St.
McMinnville, TN 37111

Woodbury Housing Authority
301 Hardaway St.
McMinnville, TN 37111

Memphis Housing Authority
140 Adams Ave.
Memphis, TN 38103

Shelby County Housing Authority
140 Adams Ave.
Memphis, TN 38103

Milan Housing Authority
458 S. First St.
Milan, TN 38358

Millington Housing Authority
P.O. Box 55
Millington, TN 38053

Morristown Housing Authority
P.O. Box 497
Morristown, TN 37814

Mount Pleasant Housing Authority
Walton Circle
Mount Pleasant, TN 38474

Murfreesboro Housing Authority
P.O. Box 278
Murfreesboro, TN 37131

Nashville Housing Authority
P.O. Box 846
Nashville, TN 37202

Newbern Housing Authority
P.O. Box D
Newbern, TN 38059

Newport Housing Authority
203 Bowman Drive
Newport, TN 38721

Paris Housing Authority
P.O. Box 159
Paris, TN 38242

Parsons-Decaturville Housing
  Authority
P.O. Box 147
Parsons, TN 38363

Pulaski Housing Authority
606 Washington Heights
Pulaski, TN 38478

Ripley Housing Authority
101 Northcrest St.
Ripley, TN 38063

Rockwood Housing Authority
320 Evans Heights West
Rockwood, TN 37854

Rogersville Housing Authority
902 Locust St.
Rogersville, TN 37857

Savannah Housing Authority
515 Jefferson St.
Savannah, TN 38372

Sevierville Housing Authority
1200 Eastgate Homes
Sevierville, TN 37862

Shelbyville Housing Authority
P.O. Box 589
Shelbyville, TN 37160

Smithville Housing Authority
P.O. Box 12
Smithville, TN 37166

South Pittsburg Housing Authority
P.O. Box 231
South Pittsburg, TN 37380

Sparta Housing Authority
P.O. Box 419
Sparta, TN 38583

Springfield Housing Authority
P.O. Box 398
Springfield, TN 37172

Stanton Housing Authority
c/o Chairman
Stanton, TN 38069

Sweetwater Housing Authority
602 McCaslin Ave.
Sweetwater, TN 37874

Trenton Housing Authority
416 Lexington St.
Trenton, TN 38382

Tullahoma Housing Authority
212 Co-op Building
Tullahoma, TN 37388

Union City Housing Authority
P.O. Box 608
Union City, TN 38261

Waverly Housing Authority
Brookside Drive
Waverly, TN 37185

Winchester Housing Authority
P.O. Box 502
Winchester, TN 37398

TEXAS

Abeline Housing Authority
c/o Executive Director
Abeline, TX 79601.

Alamo Housing Authority
P.O. Box 445
Alamo, TX 78516

Alba Housing Authority
Box 219
Alba, TX 75410

Alice Housing Authority
Box 1407
Alice, TX 78332

Alpine Housing Authority
Box 843
Alpine, TX 79830

Alto Housing Authority
Box 473
Alto, TX 75925

Andrews Housing Authority
Box 395
Andrews, TX 79714

Anson Housing Authority
1225 Ave. J
Anson, TX 79501

Aransas Pass Housing Authority
Box 1109
Aransas Pass, TX 78336

Archer City Housing Authority
Box 334
Archer City, TX 76351

Aspermont Housing Authority
Box 545
Aspermont, TX 79502

Austin Housing Authority
P.O. Box 6159
Austin, TX 78702

Avery Housing Authority
P.O. Box 68
Avery, TX 75554

Avinger City Housing Authority
Box 176
Avinger, TX 75630

Baird Housing Authority
Box 1028
Baird, TX 79504

Ballinger Housing Authority
Ave. A & 13th St.
Ballinger, TX 76821

Balmorhea Housing Authority
Box 283
Balmorhea, TX 79718

Bandera Housing Authority
P.O. Box 896
Bandera, TX 78003

Bangs Housing Authority
P.O. Box 767
Bangs, TX 76823

Bartlett Housing Authority
City Hall
Bartlett, TX 76511

Bastrop Housing Authority
Box 707
Bastrop, TX 78602

Bay City Housing Authority
Box 1286
Bay City, TX 77414

Baytown Housing Authority
805 Nazro St.
Baytown, TX 77520

Beaumont City Housing Authority
Box 1312
Beaumont, TX 77704

Beckville Housing Authority
Box 97
Beckville, TX 75631

Beeville Housing Authority
Box 841
Beeville, TX 77418

Belton Housing Authority
Box 448
Belton, TX 76513

Cooperas Cove Housing Authority
Box 448
Belton, TX 76513

Rogers Housing Authority
P.O. Box 448
Belton, TX 76513

Big Sandy Housing Authority
City Hall
Big Sandy, TX 75755

Blooming Grove Housing Authority
P.O. Box 352
Blooming Grove, TX 76626

Bogata Housing Authority
Box 336
Bogata, TX 75417

Bells Housing Authority
Box 548
Bonham, TX 75418

Bonham Housing Authority
Box 548
Bonham, TX 75418

Ector Housing Authority
Box 548
Bonham, TX 75418

Howe Housing Authority
Box 548
Bonham, TX 75418

Leonard Housing Authority
Box 548
Bonham, TX 75418

Savoy Housing Authority
Box 548
Bonham, TX 75418

Tom Bean Housing Authority
Box 548
Bonham, TX 75418

Trenton Housing Authority
Box 548
Bonham, TX 75418

Whiteright Housing Authority
Box 548
Bonham, TX 75418

Wolfe City Housing Authority
Box 548
Bonham, TX 75418

Borger Housing Authority
903 Parkway
Borger, TX 79007

Brackettville Housing Authority
Box 371
Brackettville, TX 78832

Brady Housing Authority
Box 28
Brady, TX 76825

Breckenridge Housing Authority
911 North Payne St.
Breckenridge, TX 76024

Bremond Housing Authority
Box 198
Bremond, TX 76629

Brenham Housing Authority
Box 623
Brenham, TX 77833

Bridgeport Housing Authority
Box 486
Bridgeport, TX 76026

Bronte Housing Authority
Box 362
Bronte, TX 76933

Brownfield Housing Authority
218 W. Main St.
Brownfield, TX 79316

Brownsville Housing Authority
24 Elm St.
Brownsville, TX 78520

Brownwood Housing Authority
Box 143
Brownwood, TX 76801

Bryan Housing Authority
Box 605
Bryan, TX 77801

Bryson Housing Authority
Box 245
Bryson, TX 76027

Burkburnett Housing Authority
Box 937
Burkburnett, TX 76354

Burnet Housing Authority
c/o First State Bank
Burnet, TX 78611

Caldwell Housing Authority
P.O. Box 3
Caldwell, TX 77836

Calvert Housing Authority
P.O. Box 475
Calvert, TX 77837

Cameron Housing Authority
P.O. Box 549
Cameron, TX 76520

Canyon Housing Authority
Box 513
Canyon, TX 79015

Carrizo Springs Housing Authority
104 Fourth St.
Carrizo Springs, TX 78834

Celeste Housing Authority
P.O. Box 134
Celeste, TX 75423

Centerville Housing Authority
Box 35
Centerville, TX 75833

Childress Housing Authority
Box 722
Childress, TX 79201

Cisco Housing Authority
714 E. Tenth St.
Cisco, TX 76437

Clarendon Housing Authority
P.O. Box 945
Clarendon, TX 79226

Housing Authority, City of Clarksville
P.O. Box 621
Clarksville, TX 75426

Cleveland Housing Authority
801 Franklin St.
Cleveland, TX 77327

Clifton Housing Authority
P.O. Box 429
Clifton, TX 76634

Coleman Housing Authority
311 Commercial Ave.
Coleman, TX 76834

Colorado City Housing Authority
P.O. Box 1187
Colorado City, TX 79512

Comanche Housing Authority
Box 343
Comanche, TX 76442

Commerce Housing Authority
224 Durham Drive
Commerce, TX 75428

Como Housing Authority
Box 243
Como, TX 75431

Coolidge Housing Authority
Box 23
Coolidge, TX 76635

Cooper Housing Authority
Drawer 429
Cooper, TX 75432

Corpus Christi Housing Authority
Box 7008
Corpus Christi, TX 78415

Corsicana Housing Authority
Box 1090
Corsicana, TX 75111

Cotulla Housing Authority
Box 534
Cotulla, TX 78014

Crockett Housing Authority
Box 1052
Crockett, TX 75835

Crosbyton Housing Authority
Box 241
Crosbyton, TX 79322

Cross Plains Housing Authority
Box 487
Cross Plains, TX 76443

Crowell Housing Authority
Box 247
Crowell, TX 79227

Crystal City Housing Authority
P.O. Box 427
Crystal City, TX 78839

Cuero Housing Authority
Box 487
Cuero, TX 77954

Cumby Housing Authority
Box 278
Cumby, TX 75433

Daingerfield Housing Authority
Box J
Daingerfield, TX 75638

Dallas Housing Authority
2525 Lucas Drive
Dallas, TX 75219

Dawson Housing Authority
Box 156
Dawson, TX 76639

Dayton Housing Authority
Box 515
Dayton, TX 77535

Decatur Housing Authority
P.O. Box 218
Decatur, TX 76234

De Kalb Housing Authority
P.O. Box 297
De Kalb, TX 75559

De Leon Housing Authority
200 E. Navaro St.
De Leon, TX 76444

Del Rio Housing Authority
P.O. Drawer J
Del Rio, TX 78840

Denison Housing Authority
P.O. Box 447
Denison, TX 75021

Pottsboro Housing Authority
Box 447
Denison, TX 75021

Denton Housing Authority
215 E. McKinney
Denton, TX 76201

Deport Housing Authority
Box 127
Deport, TX 75435

Detroit Housing Authority
Box 139
Detroit, TX 75436

Devine Housing Authority
521 Rossville Rd.
Devine, TX 78016

Diboll Housing Authority
702 S. First St.
Diboll, TX 75941

Donna Housing Authority
P.O. Box 667
Donna, TX 78537

Dublin Housing Authority
201 May St.
Dublin, TX 76446

Eagle Pass Housing Authority
P.O. Box 844
Eagle Pass, TX 78852

Edcouch Housing Authority
Box 92
Edcouch, TX 78538

Eden Housing Authority
P.O. Box P
Eden, TX 76837

HOUSING 199

Edgewood Housing Authority
Drawer 4
Edgewood, TX 75117

Edingburg Housing Authority
P.O. Box 295
Edingburg, TX 78539

Edna Housing Authority
P.O. Box 698
Edna, TX 77957

El Campo Housing Authority
Box 107
El Campo, TX 77437

Eldorado Housing Authority
Box 453
Eldorado, TX 76936

Electra Housing Authority
Box 50
Electra, TX 76360

Elgin Housing Authority
114 N. Main St.
Elgin, TX 78621

El Paso Housing Authority
Box 9895
El Paso, TX 79989

Elsa Housing Authority
Box 98
Elsa, TX 78543

Ennis Housing Authority
Route 3
Box 200
Ennis, TX 75119

Falfurrias Housing Authority
Box 357
Falfurrias, TX 78355

Falls City Housing Authority
Box 145
Falls City, TX 78113

Caddo Mills Housing Authority
308 S. Washington St.
Farmersville, TX 75031

Blue Ridge Housing Authority
308 S. Washington St.
Farmersville, TX 75031

Farmersville Housing Authority
308 S. Washington St.
Farmersville, TX 75031

Ferris Housing Authority
Box 6972
Ferris, TX 75125

Flatonia Housing Authority
Box 152
Flatonia, TX 78941

Floresville Housing Authority
P.O. Box 6
Floresville, TX 78114

Floydada Housing Authority
302 E. Tennessee St.
Floydada, TX 79325

Fort Worth Housing Authority
Box 430
Fort Worth, TX 76101

Haltom City Housing Authority
2800 Moneda St.
Fort Worth, TX 76117

Franklin Housing Authority
Box 413
Franklin, TX 77856

Frisco Housing Authority
Box 264
Frisco, TX 75034

Gainesville Housing Authority
County Courthouse
Gainesville, TX 76240

Galveston Housing Authority
920 53rd St.
Galveston, TX 77550

Garrison Housing Authority
Box 142
Garrison, TX 75946

Gatesville Housing Authority
Box 52
Gatesville, TX 76528

Georgetown Housing Authority
P.O. Drawer 60
Georgetown, TX 78626

Gilmer Housing Authority
Box 397
Gilmer, TX 75644

Gladewater Housing Authority
Box 1009
Gladewater, TX 75647

Goldthwaite Housing Authority
Box 324
Goldthwaite, TX 76844

Gonzales Housing Authority
P.O. Box 43
Gonzales, TX 78629

Gorman Housing Authority
Box 158
Gorman, TX 76454

Granbury Housing Authority
503 Crockett
Granbury, TX 76048

Grandfalls Housing Authority
Box 152
Grandfalls, TX 79742

Grand Saline Housing Authority
City Hall
Grand Saline, TX 75140

Grandview Housing Authority
P.O. Box 366
Grandview, TX 76050

Granger Housing Authority
308 W. Davilla St.
Granger, TX 76530

Grapeland Housing Authority
Box 566
Grapeland, TX 75844

Grapevine Housing Authority
Box 307
Grapevine, TX 76051

Gregory Housing Authority
P.O. Drawer 267
Gregory, TX 78359

Housing Authority, City of Gregory
P.O. Box 206
Gregory, TX 78359

Groesbeck Housing Authority
P.O. Box 69
Groesbeck, TX 78359

Groveton Housing Authority
P.O. Box 385
Groveton, TX 75845

Gunter Housing Authority
Box 56
Gunter, TX 75058

Hale Center Housing Authority
Box 487
Hale Center, TX 79041

Hamilton Housing Authority
604 E. Henry
Hamilton, TX 76531

Hamlin Housing Authority
Box H
Hamlin, TX 79520

Harlingen Housing Authority
P.O. Box 1669
Harlingen, TX 78550

Haskell Housing Authority
Route 1,
Haskell, TX 79521

Hearne Housing Authority
Box 828
Hearne, TX 77859

Hemphill Housing Authority
Box 453
Hemphill, TX 75948

Henderson Housing Authority
817 W. Main St.
Henderson, TX 75652

Henrietta Housing Authority
Drawer 449
Henrietta, TX 76365

Hico Housing Authority
Box 314
Hico, TX 76457

Honey Grove Housing Authority
Box 224
Honey Grove, TX 75446

Houston Housing Authority
Box 2971
Houston, TX 77001

Hubbard Housing Authority
City Hall
Hubbard, TX 76648

Hughes Springs Housing Authority
P.O. Box 143
Hughes Springs, TX 76556

Huntington Housing Authority
Box 104
Huntington, TX 75949

Ingleside Housing Authority
Drawer Z
Ingleside, TX 78362

Itasca Housing Authority
Box 124
Itasca, TX 76055

Jefferson Housing Authority
Cypress Village
Jefferson, TX 75657

Johnson City Housing Authority
Box 225
Johnson City, TX 78636

Jourdanton Housing Authority
Box 485
Jourdanton, TX 78026

Junction Housing Authority
Box 26
Junction, TX 76849

Karnes City Housing Authority
Box 365
Karnes City, TX 78118

Kemp Housing Authority
Box 276
Kemp, TX 75143

Kenedy Housing Authority
Box 627
Kenedy, TX 78119

Poth Housing Authority
Box 299
Kenedy, TX 78119

Sinton Housing Authority
Box 299
Kenedy, TX 78119

Stockdale Housing Authority
P.O. Box 299
Kenedy, TX 78119

Three Rivers Housing Authority
P.O. Box 299
Kenedy, TX 78119

Yorktown Housing Authority
Box 299
Kenedy, TX 78119

Kerens Housing Authority
P.O. Box 97
Kerens, TX 75144

Kermit Housing Authority
City Hall
Kermit, TX 79745

Killeen Housing Authority
Box 125
Killeen, TX 76541

Kingsville Housing Authority
1000 Brown Villa
Kingsville, TX 78363

Kirbyville Housing Authority
Box 309
Kirbyville, TX 75956

Knox City Housing Authority
P.O. Box 235
Knox City, TX 79529

Kyle Housing Authority
Box 396
Kyle, TX 78640

Ladonia Housing Authority
Box 188
Ladonia, TX 75449

La Feria Housing Authority
Box 1366
La Feria, TX 78559

La Grange Housing Authority
Box 220
La Grange, TX 78945

Laredo Housing Authority
2000 San Francisco Ave.
Laredo, TX 78040

Levelland Housing Authority
1302 Ave. K
Levelland, TX 79336

Linden Housing Authority
Box 390
Linden, TX 75563

Ala-Coushata Independant Residence
    Housing Authority
Route 3
Livingston, TX 77351

Livingston Housing Authority
Box 872
Livingston, TX 77351

Llano Housing Authority
301 W. Main
Llano, TX 78643

Lockhart Housing Authority
Box 446
Lockhart, TX 78644

Lometa Housing Authority
Drawer 70
Lometa, TX 76853

Lone Oak Housing Authority
c/o Executive Director
Lone Oak, TX 75453

Loraine Housing Authority
Box 307
Loraine, TX 79532

Los Fresnos Housing Authority
P.O. Box 487
Los Fresnos, TX 78566

Lott Housing Authority
P.O. Box 336
Lott, TX 76656

Lubbock Housing Authority
515 N. Zenith
Lubbock, TX 79403

Luling Housing Authority
P.O. Box 229
Luling, TX 78648

Lytle Housing Authority
Box 603
Lytle, TX 78052

Mabank Housing Authority
Box 291
Mabank, TX 75147

Madisonville Housing Authority
601 S. Madison St.
Madisonville, TX 77864

Malakoff Housing Authority
Box M
Malakoff, TX 75148

Marble Falls Housing Authority
Box 668
Marble Falls, TX 78654

Marfa Housing Authority
P.O. Box 1138
Marfa, TX 79843

Marlin Housing Authority
Box 39
Marlin, TX 76661

Mart Housing Authority
Drawer 330
Mart, TX 76664

Mason Housing Authority
Box 3
Mason, TX 76856

Mathis Housing Authority
Box 425
Mathis, TX 78368

Maud Housing Authority
Box 73
Maud, TX 75567

McAllen Housing Authority
P.O. Box 970
McAllen, TX 78501

Housing Authority, City of Oglesby
Marblecrest Administration Building
McGregor, TX 76657

McGregor Housing Authority
Marblecrest Administration Building
McGregor, TX 76657

McKinney Housing Authority
1200 N. Tennessee St.
McKinney, TX 75069

McLean Housing Authority
P.O. Box 611
McLean, TX 79057

Memphis Housing Authority
P.O. Box 127
Memphis, TX 79245

Mercedes Housing Authority
P.O. Box 985
Mercedes, TX 78570

Meridan Housing Authority
City Hall
Meridan, TX 76665

Merkel Housing Authority
P.O. Box 417
Merkel, TX 79536

Mexia Housing Authority
701 N. Sherman
Mexia, TX 76667

Midland Housing Authority
P.O. Box 5576
Midland, TX 79701

Midlothian Housing Authority
City Hall
Midlothian, TX 76065

Mineral Wells Housing Authority
401 N. Oak St.
Mineral Wells, TX 76067

Mission Housing Authority
P.O. Box 747
Mission, TX 78572

Moody Housing Authority
Box 213
Moody, TX 76557

Mount Pleasant Housing Authority
Box 1051
Mount Pleasant, TX 75455

Mount Vernon Housing Authority
Box 554
Mount Vernon, TX 75457

Munday Housing Authority
Box 213
Munday, TX 76371

Naples Housing Authority
Box 6
Naples, TX 75568

New Boston Housing Authority
P.O. Box 806
New Boston, TX 75570

New Braunfels Housing Authority
Box 906
New Braunfels, TX 78130

Newcastle Housing Authority
Box 66
Newcastle, TX 76372

Newton Housing Authority
Box 626
Newton, TX 75966

Nixon Housing Authority
P.O. Box 447
Nixon, TX. 78140

Nocona Housing Authority
401 Laura St.
Nocona, TX 76255

Olney Housing Authority
Box 602
Olney, TX 79064

Olton Housing Authority
Box 651
Olton, TX 79064

Omaha Housing Authority
Box 667
Omaha, TX 75571

Orange City Housing Authority
P.O. Drawer C
Orange, TX 77630

Orange County Housing Authority
P.O. Drawer C
Orange, TX 77630

Overton Housing Authority
Box 373
Overton, TX 75684

Paducah Housing Authority
P.O. Box 759
Paducah, TX 79248

Paris Housing Authority
Box 688
Paris, TX 75460

Pearsall Housing Authority
211 S Oak ST.
Pearsall, TX 78061

Pecos Housing Authority
2313 Stafford St.
Pecos, TX 79772

Pharr Housing Authority
100 W. Polk Ave.
Pharr, TX 78577

Pineland Housing Authority
Box 266
Pineland, TX 75968

Pittsburg Housing Authority
Box 698
Pittsburg, TX 75686

Plano Housing Authority
Box 307
Plano, TX 75074

Pleasanton Housing Authority
Box 179
Pleasanton, TX 78064

Port Arthur Housing Authority
Box 727
Port Arthur, TX 77640

Port Isabel Housing Authority
P.O. Box 1196
Port Isabel, TX 78578

Port Lavaca Housing Authority
P.O. Drawer 7
Port Lavaca, TX 77979

Post Housing Authority
P.O. Box 143
Post, TX 79356

Poteet Housing Authority
P.O. Box 226
Poteet, TX 78065

Princeton Housing Authority
City Hall
Princeton, TX 75077

Quanah Housing Authority
P.O. Box 208
Quanah, TX 79252

Ranger Housing Authority
P.O. Box 58
Ranger, TX 76470

Rankin Housing Authority
Drawer 445
Rankin, TX 79778

Rising Star Housing Authority
Box 223
Rising Star, TX 76471

Robert Lee Housing Authority
P.O. Box 93
Robert Lee, TX 76945

Robstown Housing Authority
Box 986
Robstown, TX 78380

Roby Housing Authority
Box 147
Roby, TX 79543

Rochester Housing Authority
City Hall
Rochester, TX 79544

Rockwall Housing Authority
Box 397
Rockwall, TX 75087

Rosebud Housing Authority
Box 577
Rosebud, TX 76570

Rotan Housing Authority
Box 111
Rotan, TX 79546

Round Rock Housing Authority
c/o 214 E. Main
Round Rock, TX 78664

Royse City Housing Authority
c/o Executive Director
Royse City, TX 75089

Runge Housing Authority
Box 127
Runge, TX 78151

San Antonio Housing Authority
P.O. Drawer 1300
San Antonio, TX 78295

San Augustine Housing Authority
City Hall
San Augustine, TX 75972

San Benito Housing Authority
P.O. Box 1950
San Benito, TX 78586

Duval County Housing Authority
P.O. Box 95
San Diego, TX 78384

San Marcos Housing Authority
P.O. Box 725
San Marcos, TX 78666

San Saba Housing Authority
208 Wallace Ave.
San Saba, TX 76877

Santa Anna Housing Authority
Box 125
Santa Anna, TX 76878

Schertz Housing Authority
206-B Highway 78
Schertz, TX 78154

Schulenburg Housing Authority
Box 207
Schulenburg, TX 78956

Seagraves Housing Authority
Box 756
Seagraves, TX 79359

Sequin Housing Authority
Box 756
Sequin, TX 78155

Seymour Housing Authority
301 N. East St.
Seymour, TX 76380

Sherman Housing Authority
Box 1272
Sherman, TX 75090

Slaton Housing Authority
P.O. Box 327
Slaton, TX 79364

Smiley Housing Authority
Box 252
Smiley, TX 78159

Smithville Housing Authority
100 Valley View Drive
Smithville, TX 78957

Spearman Housing Authority
Box 607
Spearman, TX 79081

Spur Housing Authority
Box 687
Spur, TX 79370

Stamford Housing Authority
Box 1070
Stamford, TX 79553

Stanton Housing Authority
Box 866
Stanton, TX 79782

Strawn Housing Authority
Box 36
Strawn, TX 76475

Sweetwater Housing Authority
P.O. Box 1260
Sweetwater, TX 79556

Taft Housing Authority
223 Ave. C
Taft, TX 78390

Tahoka Housing Authority
Box 238
Tahoka, TX 79373

Talco Housing Authority
P.O. Box 365
Talco, TX 75487

Taylor Housing Authority
P.O. Box 672
Taylor, TX 76574

Teague Housing Authority
620 Main St.
Teague, TX 75860

Temple Housing Authority
700 W. Calhoun Ave.
Temple, TX 76501

Tenaha Housing Authority
Box 427
Tenaha, TX 75974

Texarkana Housing Authority
P.O. Box 5766
Texarkana, TX 75501

Texas City Housing Authority
Ninth St. & Fourth Ave. S
Texas City, TX 77590

Thorndale Housing Authority
Box 448
Thorndale, TX 76577

Throckmorton Housing Authority
Box 457
Throckmorton, TX 76083

Timpson Housing Authority
Box 357
Timpson, TX 75975

Tioga Housing Authority
Box 41
Tioga, TX 76271

Trinidad Housing Authority
Box 448
Trinidad, TX 75163

Trinity Housing Authority
Box 527
Trinity, TX 75862

Tulia Housing Authority
201 N. Maxwell
Tulia, TX 79088

Valley Mills Housing Authority
City Hall
Valley Mills, TX 76689

Van Housing Authority
P.O. Box 884
Van, TX 75790

Van Alstyne Housing Authority
Box 338
Van Alstyne, TX 75095

Vernon Housing Authority
Box 1780
Vernon, TX 76384

Victoria Housing Authority
1410 Crestwood Drive
Victoria, TX 77901

Waco Housing Authority
Box 978
Waco, TX 76703

Waelder Housing Authority
P.O. Box 7
Waelder, TX 78959

Waxahachie Housing Authority
208 Patrick St.
Waxahachie, TX 75165

Weatherford Housing Authority
City Hall
Weatherford, TX 76086

Wellington Housing Authority
719 West Ave.
Wellington, TX 79095

Weslaco Housing Authority
Box 92
Weslaco, TX 78596

Whitesboro Housing Authority
Box 430
Whitesboro, TX 76273

Whitney Housing Authority
P.O. Box 594
Whitney, TX 76692

Wichita Falls Housing Authority
Box 544
Wichita Falls, TX 76307

Windom Housing Authority
Box 996
Windom, TX 75492

Wink Housing Authority
Box 607
Wink, TX 79789

Winnsboro Housing Authority
Box 6
Winnsboro, TX 75494

Winters Housing Authority
110 S. Main
Winters, TX 79567

Woodville Housing Authority
803 S. Pecan
Woodville, TX 75979

Wortham Housing Authority
P.O. Box 265
Wortham, TX 76693

Yoakum Housing Authority
Box 450
Yoakum, TX 77995

UTAH

Ute Indian Tribal Housing Authority
c/o Uintah & Quray Agency
Ft. Duchesne, UT 84026

Ogden Housing Authority
P.O. Box 1639
Ogden, UT 84402

Salt Lake City Housing Authority
410 Arrow Press Square
Salt Lake City, UT 84101

Salt Lake County Housing Authority
2880 S. Main St.
Salt Lake City, UT 84115

VERMONT

Barre Housing Authority
14 Washington St.
Barre, VT 05641

Bennington Housing Authority
100 South St.
Bennington, VT 05201

Brattleboro Housing Authority
100 Melrose Terrace
Brattleboro, VT 05301

Burlington Housing Authority
230 St. Paul St.
Burlington, VT 05401

Montpelier Housing Authority
Montpelier, VT 05602

Vermont State Housing Authority
State Office Building
Montpelier, VT 05602

Rutland Housing Authority
6 Tremont St.
Rutland, VT 05701

Springfield Housing Authority
3 Lincoln St.
Springfield, VT 05056

Winooski Housing Authority
City Office Building
Winooski, VT 05404

VIRGINIA

Alexandria Redevelopment & Housing
    Authority
600 N. Fairfax St.
Alexandria, VA 22314

Bristol Redevelopment & Housing
    Authority
650 Quarry St.
Bristol, VA 24201

Charlottesville Housing Authority
P.O. Box 1405
Charlottesville, VA 22902

South Norfolk Redevelopment &
    Housing Authority
10 Admiral S. Rd.
Chesapeake, VA 23506

Danville Redevelopment & Housing
    Authority
651 Cardinal Place
Danville, VA 24540

Fairfax County Housing Authority
10530 Page Ave.
Fairfax, VA 22030

Franklin Housing & Redevelopment
    Authority
800 W. Second Ave.
Franklin, VA 23851

Hampton Redevelopment & Housing
    Authority
P.O. Box 280
Hampton, VA 23369

Harrisonburg Housing Authority
286 Kelley St.
Harrisonburg, VA 22801

Hopewell Redevelopment & Housing
    Authority
211 S. Seventh Ave.
Hopewell, VA 23860

Lynchburg Redevelopment & Housing
    Authority
P.O. Box 1298
Lynchburg, VA 24505

Newport News Housing Authority
P.O. Box 77
Newport News, VA 23607

Norfolk Redevelopment & Housing
    Authority
P.O. Box 968
Norfolk, VA 23501

Norton Redevelopment & Housing
    Authority
1104 Flanary Ave., SE
Norton, VA 24273

Petersburg Redevelopment & Housing
    Authority
Box 724
Petersburg, VA 23803

Portsmouth Redevelopment &
    Housing Authority
P.O. Box 1098
Portsmouth, VA 23705

Richmond Redevelopment & Housing
    Authority
P.O. Box 26887
Richmond, VA 23220

Roanoke Redevelopment & Housing
    Authority
2624 Salem Turnpike, NW
Roanoke, VA 24017

Suffolk Redevelopment & Housing
    Authority
Office of the City Manager
Suffolk, VA 23434

Waynesboro Redevelopment &
    Housing Authority
1700 New Hope Rd.
Waynesboro, VA 22980

Wytheville Redevelopment & Housing
    Authority
195 S. First St.
Wytheville, VA 24382

WASHINGTON

Anacortes Housing Authority
Eighth & Q Ave.
Anacortes, WA 98221

Bellingham Housing Authority
409 York St.
Bellingham, WA 98225

Bremerton Housing Authority
P.O. Box 631
Bremerton, WA 98310

Asotin Housing Authority
1212 Fair St.
Clarkston, WA 99403

Island County Housing Authority
P.O. Box 156
Couperville, WA 98239

Ellenburg Housing Authority
107 W. 11th St.
Ellenburg, WA 98926

Kittitas County Housing Authority
107 W. 11th St.
Ellenburg, WA 98926

Grant County Housing Authority
P.O. Box 296
Ephrata, WA 98823

Everett Housing Authority
14th & Poplar St.
Everett, WA 98201

Grays Harbor Cty. Housing Auth.
525 Eighth St.
Hoquiam, WA 98550

Kalama Housing Authority
P.O. Box 96
Kalama, WA 98625

Kelso Housing Authority
P.O. Box 599
Kelso, WA 98626

Kennewick Housing Authority
P.O. Box 6737
Kennewick, WA 99336

Swinomish Housing Authority
P.O. Box 322
Laconner, WA 98257

Snohomish County Housing Authority
4200 SW 196th
Lynnwood, WA 98036

Lummi Housing Authority
Lummi Indian Reservation
Marietta, WA 98268

Mountlake Terrace Housing Authority
Civic Center Building
Mountlake, WA 98043

Makah Housing Authority
P.O. Box 115
Neah Bay, WA 98357

Colville Indian Housing Authority
Box 150
Nespelem, WA 99155

Othello Housing Authority
334 N. Third Ave.
Othello, WA 99344

Pasco Housing Authority
P.O. Box 687
Pasco, WA 99301

Clallam County Housing Authority
2603 S. Francis St.
Port Angeles, WA 98362

Renton Housing Authority
P.O. Box 2316
Renton, WA 98055

Arlington Housing Authority
2112 Third Ave.
Seattle, WA 98121

King County Housing Authority
2112 Third Ave.
Seattle, WA 98121

Seattle City Housing Authority
825 Yesler Way
Seattle, WA 98104

Sedro Woolley Housing Authority
c/o Executive Director
Sedro Woolley, WA 98284

Spokane Indian Housing Authority
City Hall
Mayor's Office
Spokane, WA 99201

Sunnyside Housing Authority
P.O. Box 179
Sunnyside, WA 98944

Tacoma City Housing Authority
2302 Sixth Ave.
Tacoma, WA 98403

Quinaut Housing Authority
P.O. Box 1058
Taholah, WA 98587

Vancouver City Housing Authority
P.O. Box 2008
Vancouver, WA 98661

Yakima Nation Housing Authority
117 N. Second
Yakima, WA 98901

WEST VIRGINIA

Benwood Housing Authority
13th & High Sts.
Benwood, WV 26031

McMechen Housing Authority
13th & High Sts.
Benwood, WV 26031

Bluefield Housing Authority
Municipal Building
Bluefield, WV 24701

Buckhannon Housing Authority
Hinkle Drive
Buckhannon, WV 26201

Charleston Housing Authority
1809 Washington West
Charleston, WV 25321

Clarksburg Housing Authority
916 W. Pike St.
Clarksburg, WV 26301

Dunbar Housing Authority
1131 Dunbar Ave.
Dunbar, WV 25064

Elkins Housing Authority
P.O. Box 1030
Elkins, WV 26241

Fairmont Housing Authority
Deveny Building
Fairmont, WV 26554

Grafton Housing Authority
P.O. Box 428
Grafton, WV 26354

Huntington Housing Authority
P.O. Box 2183
Huntington, WV 25722

Keyser Housing Authority
440 Virginia St.
Keyser, WV 26726

Martinsburg Housing Authority
600 Horatio Gates Village
Martinsburg, WV 25401

Moundsville Housing Authority
501 Tenth St.
Moundsville, WV 26041

Mount Hope Housing Authority
P.O. Box 31
Mount Hope, WV 25880

Parkersburg Housing Authority
1901 Cameron Ave.
Parkersburg, WV 26101

Piedmont Housing Authority
P.O. Box 26
Piedmont, WV 26750

Point Pleasant Housing Authority
Second & Jones St.
Point Pleasant, WV 25550

South Charleston Housing Authority
P.O. Box 86
South Charleston, WV 25312

Spencer Housing Authority
601 Market St.
Spencer, WV 25276

Weirton Housing Authority
525 Cove Rd.
Weirton, WV 26062

Weston Housing Authority
P.O. Box 29
Weston, WV 26452

Wheeling Housing Authority
P.O. Box 6500
Wheeling, WV 26003

Williamson Housing Authority
P.O. Box 1758
Williamson, WV 25661

WISCONSIN

Abbotsford Housing Authority
120 Pine St.
Abbotsford, WI 54405

Albany Housing Authority
Albany, WI 53502

Algoma Housing Authority
145 Grand View Court
Algoma, WI 54201

Altoona Housing Authority
1303 Lynn Ave.
Altoona, WI 54720

Amery Housing Authority
118-120 Central St.
Amery, WI 54001

Antigo Housing Authority
Park View Manor
535 Third Ave.
Antigo, WI 54409

Appleton Housing Authority
525 N. Oneida St.
Appleton, WI 54861

Ashland Housing Authority
Box 841
422 W. Second St.
Ashland, WI 54806

Bad River Housing Authority
Route 2
Ashland, WI 54806

Barron Housing Authority
123 E. Franklin Ave.
Barron, WI 54812

Cumberland Housing Authority
c/o Executive Director
Barron, WI 54812

Red Cliff Chippewa Housing Authority
Route 1
Bayfield, WI 54814

Beloit Housing Authority
220 Portland Ave.
Beloit, WI 53511

Wisconsin Winnebago Housing
    Authority
c/o Executive Director
Black River Falls, WI 54615

Mohican Housing Authority
Route 1
Bowler, WI 54416

Brillion Housing Authority
City Hall
Brillion, WI 54110

Bruce Housing Authority
Box 65
Bruce, WI 54819

Chetek Housing Authority
Box 591
Chetek, WI 54728

Clintonville Housing Authority
71 Hughes St.
Clintonville, WI 54929

Wisconsin Potawatomi Housing
    Authority
c/o Executive Director
Crandon, WI 54520

Cross Plains Housing Authority
P.O. Box 235
Cross Plains, WI 53528

De Pere Housing Authority
850 Morning Glory Lane
De Pere, WI 54115

Edgerton Housing Authority
City Hall
Edgerton, WI 53534

Fond Du Lac Housing Authority
15 N. Marr St.
Fond Du Lac, WI 54935

Frederic Housing Authority
Farmers State Bank
Frederic, WI 54837

Grantsburg Housing Authority
Box 166
Grantsburg, WI 54840

Green Bay Housing Authority
604 City Hall
Green Bay, WI 54301

Greenwood Housing Authority
Box 8
Greenwood, WI 54437

Lac Courte Oreilles Housing Authority
c/o Executive Director
Haywood, WI 54843

Hurley Housing Authority
410 Third Ave., S.
Hurley, WI 54534

Hudson Housing Authority
1015 Second St.
Hudson, WI 54016

Jefferson Housing Authority
112 W. Dodge St.
Jefferson, WI 53549

Kaukauna Housing Authority
125 W. Tenth St.
Kaukauna, WI 54130

Kenosha Housing Authority
c/o Executive Director
Kenosha, WI 53104

Menominee County Housing Authority
c/o Executive Director
Keshena, WI 54135

Lac Du Flambeau Chippewa Housing
  Authority
Box 271
Lac Du Flambeau, WI 54538

Lacrosse Housing Authority
P.O. Box 1032
Lacrosse, WI 54601

Ladysmith Housing Authority
c/o Executive Director
Ladysmith, WI 54848

Lake Mills Housing Authority
101 Church St.
Lake Mills, WI 53551

Luck Housing Authority
Village Hall
Luck, WI 54853

Madison Housing Authority
703 Regent St.
Madison, WI 53701

Wisconsin State Housing Authority
14 N. Carroll St.
Madison, WI 53703

Manitowoc Housing Authority
1433 N. Sixth St.
Manitowoc, WI 54220

Marinette Housing Authority
1901 Hall Ave.
Marinette, WI 54143

Marshfield Housing Authority
606 S. Walnut Ave.
Marshfield, WI 54449

Mauston Housing Authority
City Hall
Mauston, WI 53948

Menomonie Housing Authority
P.O. Box 296
Menomonie, WI 54751

Merrill Housing Authority
215 Grand Ave.
Merrill, WI 54452

Milwaukee Housing Authority
734 N. Ninth St.
Milwaukee, WI 53212

Sakaogan Chippewa Housing Authority
c/o Executive Director
Mole Lake, WI 53200

Mondovi Housing Authority
156 S. Franklin St.
Mondovi, WI 54755

Monroe Housing Authority
Box 244
Monroe, WI 53566

Mosinee Housing Authority
City Hall
Mosinee, WI 54455

New London Housing Authority
301 E. Beacon Ave.
New London, WI 54961

New Richmond Housing Authority
c/o Executive Director
New Richmond, WI 54017

Oconto Housing Authority
407 Arbutus Ave.
Oconto, WI 54153

Oneida Housing Authority
Box 64
Oneida, WI 54155

Osceola Housing Authority
c/o Executive Director
Osceola, WI 54020

Oshkosh Housing Authority
100 Court St.
Oshkosh, WI 54901

Park Falls Housing Authority
City Hall
Park Falls, WI 54552

Plymouth Housing Authority
Room 203
City Hall
Plymouth, WI 53073

Prairie Du Chien Housing Authority
Box 325
Prairie Du Chien, WI 53821

Pulaski Housing Authority
Pulaski, WI 54160

Reedsville Housing Authority
c/o Executive Director
Reedsville, WI 54230

Rhinelander Housing Authority
411 W. Phillip St.
Rhinelander, WI 54501

Rib Lake Housing Authority
P.O. Box 248
Rib Lake, WI 54470

Rice Lake Housing Authority
Riverside Apts
423 Hatten Ave.
Rice Lake, WI 54868

Richland Center Housing Authority
No. 1 W. Seminary St.
Richland Center, WI 53581

River Falls Housing Authority
115 E. Elm St.
River Falls, WI 54022

Saulk City Housing Authority
806 Water St.
Saulk City, WI 53583

Shawano County Housing Authority
P.O. Box 502
Shawano, WI 54166

Shawano Housing Authority
City Hall
Shawano, WI 54266

Sheboygan Housing Authority
City Hall
Sheboygan, WI 53081

Shell Lake Housing Authority
Box 130
Shell Lake, WI 53871

South Milwaukee Housing Authority
P.O. Box 265
South Milwaukee, WI 53172

Sparta Housing Authority
P.O. Box 397
Sparta, WI 54656

Spooner Housing Authority
c/o Executive Director
Spooner, WI 54801

Stanley Housing Authority
124 West 4th Ave.
Stanley, WI 54768

Stevens Point Housing Authority
1300 Briggs St.
Stevens Point, WI 54481

Stratford Housing Authority
c/o Executive Director
Stratford, WI 54484

Superior Housing Authority
C-68 Park Place Homes
Superior, WI 54880

Thorp Housing Authority
c/o Morgan Plaza
Thorp, WI 54771

Tomah-Lacrosse Housing Authority
Box 292
Tomah, WI 55560

Viroqua Housing Authority
Viroqua, WI 54665

Washburn Housing Authority
Washburn, WI 54891

Watertown Housing Authority
c/o Executive Director
Watertown, WI 54300

Waukesha City Housing Authority
120 E. Corrina Blvd.
Waukesha, WI 53186

Wausau Housing Authority
500 Grand Ave.
Wausau, WI 54401

Wausaukee Village Housing Authority
c/o Executive Director
Wausaukee, WI 54177

Saint Croix Chippewa Housing
  Authority
Route 2
Webster, WI 54893

West Bend Housing Authority
475 Meadowbrook Drive
West Bend, WI 53095

Westby Housing Authority
204 Maple St.
Westby, WI 54667

Wisconsin Dells Housing Authority
Route 1
Indian Heights
Wisconsin Dells, WI 53965

Wisconsin Rapids Housing Authority
2521 Tenth St., S.
Wisconsin Rapids, WI 54494

Wittenberg Housing Authority
Webb St.
Wittenberg, WI 54499

Woodville Housing Authority
c/o Executive Director
Woodville, WI 54028

WYOMING

Casper Housing Authority
Wolcott & B
Casper, WY 82601

Cheyenne Housing Authority
P.O. Box 269
Cheyenne, WY 82001

Douglas Housing Authority
525 Oak St.
Douglas, WY 82633

Wind River Housing Authority
P.O. Box 327
Fort Washakie, WY 82514

Rock Springs Housing Authority
c/o Executive Director
Rock Springs, WY 82901

U.S. HOUSING DEVELOPMENTS FOR THE ELDERLY

Department of Housing and Urban Development
451 Seventh Street, SW
Washington, DC 20410
(202) 655-4000

ALABAMA

Birmingham Building Trade Towers
2021 Tenth Ave., S.
Birmingham, AL 35205

Fairhaven
1424 Montclair Rd.
Birmingham, AL 35201

Holy Comforter House
745 Walnut St.
Gadsden, AL 35901

Presbyterian Apartments
2003 Byrd Spring Rd., SW
Huntersville, AL 35802

John Knox Manor
4401 Narrow Lane Road
Montgomery, AL 36111

ALASKA

Gastineau Apartments
Juneau, AK 99801

ARIZONA

Allen Apartments, Inc.
117 S. Nobson
Mesa, AZ 85201

Citizens Towers
1200 S. Fifth Ave.
Phoenix, AZ 85003

Eastern Star Homes
4602 N. 24th St.
Phoenix, AZ 85016

Fellowship Towers
222 E. Indianola
Phoenix, AZ 85018

Hancox Desert Lodge
c/o John C. Lincoln Hospital
9211 N. Second St.
Phoenix, AZ 85020

Kivel Manor
3040 N. 36th St.
Phoenix, AZ 85018

Kivel Manor Addition
3020 N. 36th St.
Phoenix, AZ 85018

Orangewood (American Baptist
  Homes)
7550 N. 16th St.
Phoenix, AZ 85018

Phoenix Manor No. 1 and 2
2636 N. 41st Ave.
Phoenix, AZ 85009

Shangri La Apartments
2936 N. 36th St.
Phoenix, AZ 85018

Sharon Gardens (Villa Catalina)
3030 W. Culver
Phoenix, AZ 85009

Brownmoor Estates, Inc.
6125 E. Indian School Rd.
Scottsdale, AZ 85251

Hacienda de los Arcos
7500 E. Culver
Scottsdale, AZ 85257

Parkside Manor
6201 E. Exeter Blvd.
Scottsdale, AZ 85251

Amory Park Apartments
3833 E. Second St.
Suite 100
Tucson, AZ 85716

Campus Associates
2475 Haskell Rd.
Tucson, AZ 85716

Silver Bell Apartments
350 N. Silverbell Rd.
Tucson, AZ 85705

Sunhaven
4200 E. Tucson-Benson Highway
Tucson, AZ 85706

Tucson Green Valley Manor
U.S. 89 via Esperanza
Tucson, AZ 85716

Tucson House
1501 Miracle Mile Strip
Tucson, AZ 85705

ARKANSAS

Parkview Towers
1200 Commerce St.
Little Rock, AR 72202

Presbyterian Village
20th and Arch Sts.
Little Rock, AR 72206

CALIFORNIA

California Lutheran Homes
2400 S. Fremont Ave.
Alhambra, CA 91803

Quaker Retirement Center
2691 N. Lincoln Ave.
Altadena, CA 91002

Miracle Terrace
225 S. Western Ave.
Anaheim, CA 92804

Westlake Apartments
c/o Barker Management, Inc.
P.O. Box 148
Anaheim, CA 92805

Bakersfield Christian Towers
3015 Wilson Rd.
Bakersfield, CA 93304

Bellflower Friendship Manor
9603 E. Belmont St.
Bellflower, CA 90706

Bonnie Brae Terrace
2400 Carlmont Dr.
Belmont, CA 94002

Lawrence F. Moore Manor
(University Christian Church)
1909 Cedar St.
Berkeley, CA 94709

Strawberry Creek Lodge
1320 Addison St.
Berkeley, CA 94702

Del Rosa Plaza
444 N. Camden Drive
Beverly Hills, CA 90210

The Parkland
c/o Woodland Development Company
9090 Burton Way
Beverly Hills, CA 90211

Milias Apartments
1901 S. Bascom Ave.
Suite 353
Campbell, CA 95108

Carmel Valley Manor
P.O. Box 6087
Carmel, CA 93021

Community Congregational Tower
288 F St.
Chula Vista, CA 92010

Bonita Terrace
660 W. Bonita Ave.
Claremont, CA 91711

Claremont Village Green
630 W. Bonita Ave.
Claremont, CA 91711

Lakeside Haven
Konocti Harbor
Clear Lake, CA 95424

Cloverdale Senior Housing
c/o Grace Lutheran Church
890 Cloverdale Blvd.
Cloverdale, CA 95425

St. Timothy's Manor
415 S. Oleander Ave.
Compton, CA 90220

Bethel Towers of Costa Mesa
666 W. 19th St.
Costa Mesa, CA 92627

Marycrest Manor
10664 St. James Dr.
Culver City, CA 90230

Sunnyview Lutheran Home
2245 San Jose Stevens Creek Rd.
Cupertino, CA 95410

Fresno Village
1917 S. Chestnut Ave.
Fresno, CA 93702

Lutheran Village
1684 W. Shaw Ave.
Fresno, CA 93705

Matsen Towers
c/o Older Americans Housing, Inc.
1271 N. Wishon Ave.
Fresno, CA 93728

The Senior Citizens Village
1917 S. Chestnut Ave.
Fresno, CA 93702

Twilight Haven, Inc.
1717 S. Winery Ave.
Fresno, CA 93727

Ocean View Plaza
1001 Main St.
Half Moon Bay, CA 94019

Highland Park Haven
965 N. LaCienga Blvd.
Hollywood, CA 90028

The Concord
6900 Seville Ave.
Huntington Park, CA 90255

Lakeside Gardens
12219 Roberts Way
Lakeside, CA 92040

Monte Vista Lodge, Inc.
2211 Massachusetts St.
Lemon Grove, CA 92045

Hillcrest Gardens
550 Hillcrest Ave.
Livermore, CA 94550

Bethel Gardens
710 S. Ham Lane
Lodi, CA 95240

Creekside South
c/o Mr. Willard Collins
824 Mariposa Way
Lodi, CA 95240

American Gold Star Manor
P.O. Box 9025
Long Beach, CA 90810

Greenfair Towers II
c/o Retirement Housing Foundation
3844 Long Beach Blvd.
Long Beach, CA 90807

John Brown Towers
3737 Atlantic Avenue
Long Beach, CA 90807

Long Beach Brethen Manor
3333 Pacific Place
Long Beach, CA 90806

New Hope Home
1150 York St.
Long Beach, CA 90813

Pilgrim Towers North
3844 Long Beach Blvd.
Long Beach, CA 90807

Plymouth West
241 Cedar Ave.
Long Beach, CA 90802

Casa De Modesto
c/o Retirement Housing Foundation
3022 Salmon Dr.
Los Alamitos, CA 90720

Pioneer House
c/o Retirement Housing Foundation
3022 Salmon Dr.
Los Alamitos, CA 90720

Sun Valley Lodge
c/o Retirement Housing Foundation
3022 Salmon Dr.
Los Alamitos, CA 90720

The Beatitudes 1 and 2
c/o Retirement Housing Foundation
3022 Salmon Dr.
Los Alamitos, CA 90720

Trinity House
c/o Retirement Housing Foundation
3022 Salmon Dr.
Los Alamitos, CA 90720

California Teachers Association
c/o Bureau of Welfare CTA-SS
1125 W. Sixth St.
Los Angeles, CA 90017

Christ Unity Manor
635 Manhattan Place
Los Angeles, CA 90005

E. Victor Villa
555 W. 92nd St.
Los Angeles, CA 90044

Fairmont Terrace
4000 E. Fairmont St.
Los Angeles, CA 90063

First Community Senior Citizens
    Housing
3419 S. Central Ave.
Los Angeles, CA 90011

Good Shepherd Manor
3300 W. Vernon Ave.
Los Angeles, CA 90038

Los Angeles Home for the Armenian
    Aged
3732 W. 27th St.
Los Angeles, CA 90807

Meyler Park Apartments
425 S. Fairfax Ave.
Suite 300
Los Angeles, CA 90036

Mount Zion Towers
4817 S. Central Ave.
Los Angeles, CA 90011

Pilgrim Tower
1207 S. Vermont Ave.
Los Angeles, CA 90006

Progressive Home for the Elderly
7011 S. Figueron St.
Los Angeles, CA 90062

Redlands Village Green
c/o Bible Institute of Los Angeles
Los Angeles, CA 90001

Royal Oak Manor
1501 Wilshire Blvd.
Los Angeles, CA 90017

Wilshire Christian Towers
616 S. Normandie Ave.
Los Angeles, CA 90005

Peninsula Volunteer Properties
817 Partridge Ave.
Menlo Park, CA 94025

Community Church Retirement Center
40 Camino Alto
Mill Valley, CA 94941

Neighborhood Manor
1200 Woodrow Ave. at Tully Rd.
Modesto, CA 95350

Ralston Towers
P.O. Box 4075
Modesto, CA 95352

River Park Estates
Napa, CA 94558

Soroptimist Village
12657 Foster Rd.
Norwalk, CA 90650

Southland Lutheran Home
11701 Studebaker Rd.
Norwalk, CA 90650

Linda Glen
Soroptimist Satellite Senior Homes
1804 Franklin St.
Oakland, CA 94612

Otterheim Manor
5375 Manila Ave.
Oakland, CA 94618

President J. Monroe Manor
c/o Eskaton
7975 Capwell Dr.
Oakland, CA 94621

Printing Specialties Union
Retirement Center
2267 Telegraph Ave.
Oakland, CA 94612

St. Patrick's Terrace
Center & 12th Sts.
Oakland, CA 94607

Satellite Senior Homes
540 81st St.
Oakland, CA 94612

Satellite Senior Homes
3245 Sheffield Ave.
Oakland, CA 94602

Satellite Senior Homes
(St. Andrew's)
3250 San Pablo Ave.
Oakland, CA 94609

Westlake Christian Terrace
251 28th St.
Oakland, CA 94611

Eldorado
115 S. Clementine St.
Oceanside, CA 92054

Ontario Gardens
1900 S. Campus Ave.
Ontario, CA 91762

Adlai Stevenson House
455 E. Charleston Rd.
Palo Alto, CA 94306

Channing House
850 Webster St.
Palo Alto, CA 94301

The Concord
275 Cordova St.
Pasadena, CA 91106

Pleasanton Gardens
251 Kottinger Ave.
Pleasanton, CA 94566

Hospitality Home
c/o Indoor Sports Club, Inc.
1255 Val Vista St.
Pomona, CA 91766

Mt. San Antonio Gardens
(Congregational Homes)
900 W. Harrison Ave.
Pomona, CA 91767

The Sequoias
501 Portola Rd.
Portola Valley, CA 94025

Mayflower Gardens
65th and M Sts.
Quartz Hills, CA 93534

Auburn Palms
790 Bain Place
Redwood City, CA 90262

Casa de Redwood
413 Birch St.
Redwood City, CA 94062

The California Home for the Aged
19260 Sherman Way
Reseda, CA 91335

Mt. Rubidoux Manor
3993 Tenth St.
Riverside, CA 92501

The Plymouth Towers
3405-3455 Lemon St.
Riverside, CA 92501

Rose Garden Village, Inc.
3668 Adams St.
Riverside, CA 92504

Crosswood Apartments
c/o 350 University Ave.
Sacramento, CA 95825

Eastridge Apartments
c/o Trans-Pacific Industries
1620 35th Ave.
Sacramento, CA 95822

Henson Gardens
350 University Ave.
Sacramento, CA 95814

Ping Yuen Center
420 Eye St.
Sacramento, CA 95814

Sacramento Manor
7300 24th St. Bypass
Sacramento, CA 95822

Wong Center
333 J St.
Sacramento, CA 92103

Cathedral Arms
3955 Park Blvd.
San Diego, CA 92103

Grace Towers
3955 Park Blvd.
San Diego, CA 92103

Green Manor
2690 Escondido Ave.
San Diego, CA 93401

Luther Tower
1455 Second Ave.
San Diego, CA 92101

St. Paul's Manor
2635 Second Ave.
San Diego, CA 92103

St. Paul's Manor
2728 Sixth Ave.
San Diego, CA 92103

Wesley Terrace
5380 El Cajon Blvd.
San Diego, CA 92115

Westminster Manor
1730 Third Ave.
San Diego, CA 92101

Arcade Manor
1714 Stockton St.
San Francisco, CA 94133

Bethany Center Senior Housing
580 Capp St.
San Francisco, CA 94110

El Bethel Arms
497 Fulton St.
San Francisco, CA 94102

Jones Memorial Home
1975 Post St.
San Francisco, CA 94102

Jones Memorial Homes
1640 Steiner St.
San Francisco, CA 94115

Martin Luther Towers
25 California St.
San Francisco, CA 94111

Royal Adah Arms
1240 Fillmore St.
San Francisco, CA 94115

Salvation Army Apartments
101 Valencia St.
P.O. Box 3846
San Francisco, CA 94119

Vincentian Villa
1825 Mission St.
San Francisco, CA 94103

Western Park Apartments
1280 Laguana St.
San Francisco, CA 94115

Hidden Brooks Retirement Center
463 Wooster Ave.
San Jose, CA 95116

Hilltop Manor
198 S. Second St.
San Jose, CA 95113

Lincoln Glen Manor
1195 Clark St.
San Jose, CA 95125

Shrires Memorial Center
81 N. Second St.
San Jose, CA 95113

Town Park Towers
48 N. Third St.
San Jose, CA 95112

Fargo Senior Center
868 Fargo Ave.
San Leandro, CA 94579

Judson Terrace Homes
3000 Augusta St.
San Luis Obispo, CA 93401

Park Towers
700 Laurel Ave.
San Mateo, CA 94401

Pilgrim Plaza
120 N. San Mateo Drive
San Mateo, CA 94401

San Barbara Baptist Home, Inc.
(Valle Verde)
P.O. Box 3344
Santa Barbara, CA 93105

Liberty Tower
890 Main St.
Santa Clara, CA 95052

Valley Village
N. Winchester Rd. and Delores Ave.
Santa Clara, CA 95050

Garfield Park Village
721 Bay St.
Santa Cruz, CA 95060

Pacific Plaza
1431 Ocean Ave.
Santa Monica, CA 90401

Santa Monica Christian Towers
609 Arizona St.
Santa Monica, CA 90401

Santa Monica Christian Towers
1233 Sixth St.
Santa Monica, CA 90401

Westminster Towers
1112 Seventh St.
Santa Monica, CA 90403

Bethlehem Towers
801 Tupper St.
Santa Rosa, CA 95404

Seaside Civic League
Seaside, CA 93955

Bethel Lutheran Home
2280 Docery Ave.
Selma, CA 93662

Rotary Plaza
433 Alida Way
South San Francisco, CA 93702

Casa Manana Inn
3700 N. Sutter St.
Stockton, CA 95204

Lee Center
N/L Washington St. between
    Hunter and El Dorado Sts.
Stockton, CA 95202

Stockton Congregational Homes
(Plymouth Square)
Vine and Madison Sts.
Stockton, CA 95202

Golden West Manor
3510 W. Maricopa Ave.
Torrance, CA 90503

Village Garden Apartments
662 East St.
Tracy, CA 95376

Ascension Arms
301 Butte St.
Vallejo, CA 94590

Van Nuys Towers
14801 Sherman Way
Van Nuys, CA 91405

Ventura Town House
4848 Telegraph Rd.
Ventura, CA 94596

The Meadows
Visalia Senior Housing
1640 W. Mineral King Ave.
Visalia, CA 93277

Walnut Creek Manor
81 Mayhew Way
Walnut Creek, CA 94596

Park Towers
17250 Francisquito Ave.
West Covina, CA 91790

Quaker Homes
c/o 310 E. Philadelphia St.
Whittier, CA 90601

Whittier Lutheran Towers
7215 Bright Ave., S.
Whittier, CA 90602

COLORADO

Colorado Lutheran Home
8001 W. 71st Ave.
Arvada, CO 80002

Frasier Meadows Manor
350 Ponca Drive, Box 889
Boulder, CO 80302

Golden West Manor
1055 Adams Circle
Boulder, CO 80302

Presbyterian Manor
Arapahoe Ave. and 11th St.
Boulder, CO 80320

Royal Gorge Manor
1125 N. 15th St.
Canon City, CO 81212

BTC Apartments
416-423 East Kiowa
Colorado Springs, CO 80903

Pikes Peak Towers
1912 E. Lake Blvd.
Colorado Springs, CO 90810

Argonaut Apartments
233 E. Colfax
Denver, CO 80803

Broadway Baptist Housing
101 Grant St.
Denver, CO 80203

Campbell-Stone Memorial Residence
1295 Race St.
Denver, CO 80206

Central Church Housing
14th and High St.
Denver, CO 80209

DESCI
1901 E. 13th Ave.
Denver, CO 80206

Eden Manor
3405 W. 32nd Ave.
Denver, CO 80211

Francis Heights
2626 Osceola St.
Denver, CO 80212

Jewish Allied Housing
11 S. Adams
Denver, CO 80212

Juanita Nolasco Homes
4550 W. Ninth Ave.
Denver, CO 80204

Louisiana Manor
3128 W. Louisiana Ave.
Denver, CO 80219

Lutheran Apartments, Inc.
33 W. Third Ave.
Denver, CO 80223

Maltese Cross Manor
1590 Yates St.
Denver, CO 80204

Mentro Manor
1523 Quitman St.
Denver, CO 80204

Montview Manor
1980 Dahlia St.
Denver, CO 80220

NEDCO Elderly
933 E. 24th Ave.
Denver, CO 80205

NOCOLO BTC Housing, Inc.
1750 S. Federal Blvd.
Denver, CO 80219

Park Manor
Denver, CO 80201

Rocky Mountain Residences
1535 Franklin St.
Denver, CO 80218

Sunset Park
1865 Larimer St.
Denver, CO 80202

Tolstoi House, Inc.
1148 Vince St.
Denver, CO 80206

Tristate Buddhist Church Apts.
1255 19th St.
Denver, CO 80202

DMA Plaza 1
300 Remington St.
Ft. Collins, CO 80521

Colorado West Senior Citizens
2120 N. 10th St.
Grand Junction, CO 81501

Monterey Park Apartments
2120 N. 10th St.
Grand Junction, CO 81501

Bonnell Retirement Community
22nd St. and Eighth Ave.
Greeley, CO 80631

Geneva Village, Inc.
322 Colorado National Bank Building
Littleton, CO

Longmont Christian Housing
606 Pratt St.
Longmont, CO 80631

Big Thompson Manor
224 Monroe Ave.
Loveland, CO 80537

Park Central Apartments
1605 Moore Ave.
Pueblo, CO 81004

Presbyterian Towers
3504 Northridge
Pueblo, CO 81003

Pueblo BTC Apartments
242 N. Union
Pueblo, CO 81003

Highland West Apartments
c/o United Presbyterian
6340 W. 38th Ave.
Wheat Ridge, CO 80033

CONNECTICUT

Augustana Homes
850 Norman St.
Bridgeport, CT 06605

Inter-Church Residences, Inc.
3030 Park Ave.
Bridgeport, CT 06604

Merry Go Round Mews
38 Arch St., Bolling Place
Greenwich, CT 06830

New Milford Interfaith Housing
c/o the Veggo F. Larsen Co.
35 Worth Ave.
Hamden, CT 06518

Avery House
705 New Britain Ave.
Hartford, CT

Brotherhood Homes
Garden St. & Greenfield
Hartford, CT 06112

Capitol Towers
470 Broad St.
Hartford, CT 06106

Immanuel House
15 Woodland St.
Hartford, CT 06105

Montville Apartments
66 Montville St.
Hartford, CT 06120

St. Christopher Apartments
360 Main St.
Hartford, CT 06106

Tuscan Homes
66 Montville St.
Hartford, CT 06106

Vine Court
35 Vine Court
Hartford, CT 06112

West Hartford Fellowship Housing
250 Constitution Plaza
Hartford, CT 06103

Silver Pond
c/o Joseph Carabetta
60 Canyon Dr.
Meriden, CT 06450

Stoneycrest Towers
c/o Carabetta Rental Office
P.O. Box 240
Meriden, CT 06450

Newfield Towers
220 Newfield St.
Middletown, CT 06457

Fairbanks
201 Grand Ave.
New Haven, CT 06513

New Haven Jewish Community
    Council Housing
1050 Chapel St.
New Haven, CT 06510

Meadowbrook
Shephard Rd.
Norfolk, CT 06058

Davenport Residence
20 Drazen Dr.
North Haven, CT 06473

Kings Daughters & Sons Housing
168 East Ave.
Norwalk, CT 06851

Pilgrim Tower
25 Washington Court
Stamford, CT 06902

Quintard Manor
Quintard Terrace
Stamford, CT 06902

Nottingham Towers
23 Valentine Drive
Waterbury, CT 06708

Prospect Towers
c/o John A. Errichetti
P.O. Box 825
Waterbury, CT 06720

Savings Tower
45 N. Main St.
Waterbury, CT 06702

Waterbury First Church Housing
222 W. Main St.
Waterbury, CT 06702

Watergate
c/o Watergate Associates
P.O. Box 825
Waterbury, CT 06720

Brotherhood Homes
201 Auburn Rd.
West Hartford, CT 06119

DELAWARE

Church Home Foundation, Inc.
1010 Broom St.
Wilmington, DE 19806

Luther Towers
1201 N. Harrison St.
Wilmington, DE 19801

Terry Apartments
1002 W. 24th St.
Wilmington, DE 19802

Windsor Apartments
c/o Leon Weiner & Associates
Edgemart Building
4 Denny Road
Wilmington, DE 19809

DISTRICT OF COLUMBIA

Army Distaff Hall
6200 Oregon Ave., NW
Washington, DC 20015

FEDHAVEN
c/o 817 14th St., NW
Washington, DC 20005

Friendship Terrace
4201 Butterworth Place, NW
Washington, DC 20007

Green Valley Apartments
2412 Franklin ST., NE
Washington, DC 20018

The Roosevelt
2101 16th St., NW
Washington, DC 20009

FLORIDA

American Federation of Teachers
1675 NW Fourth Ave.
Boca Raton, FL 33432

Asbury Towers
P.O. Box 70
Bradenton, FL 33505

Bradenton Manor
2001 18th St., W.
Bradenton, FL 33505

Desoto Towers
1202 Manatee Ave.
Bradenton, FL 33505

Presbyterian Homes of Bradenton
6125 14th St., W.
Bradenton, FL 33507

Bayview Gardens, Inc.
2855 Gulf to Bay Blvd.
Clearwater, FL 33515

HOUSING

Prospect Towers
Chestnut & Myrtle Ave., S.
Clearwater, FL 33516

Sunshine Lake Apartments, Phase II
5915 Ponce De Leon Blvd.
Coral Gables, FL 33146

St. Andrews Towers
2644 NW 99th Ave.
Coral Springs, FL 33060

Louttit Manor
229 S. Ridgewood Ave.
Daytona Beach, FL 32014

College Arms Towers
Whitehair Building
Deland, FL 32720

Woodland Manor
740 N. Woodland Blvd.
Deland, FL 32730

Mease Manor, Inc.
Moore St. and New York Ave.
Dunedin, FL 33528

St. John's Village I
250 Oxford Rd.
Fern Park, FL 32730

Gateway Terrace
1943 Karen Drive
Ft. Lauderdale, FL 33304

Lakeshore Towers
Gainesville, FL 32601

Baptist Towers of Jacksonville
4100 LeBaron St.
Jacksonville, FL 32207

Campus Towers
1864 Kings Rd.
Jacksonville, FL 32209

Cathedral Manor
333 E. Ashley St.
Jacksonville, FL 32202

Cathedral Terrace
256 E. Church St.
Jacksonville, FL 32202

Cathedral Towers
601 N. Newnan St.
Jacksonville, FL 32202

Fannie E. Taylor Home for Aged
3927 Spring Park Rd.
Jacksonville, FL 32207

Florida Christian Home
1071 S. Edgewood Ave.
Jacksonville, FL 32205

Mount Carmel Gardens
5841 Mount Carmel Terrace
Jacksonville, FL 32216

Pablo Towers
115 S. Third St.
Jacksonville, FL 32250

Ridgecrest Baptist Villa
Phoenix Ave. and Ninth St.
Jacksonville, FL 32206

Riverside Presbyterian House
2020 Park St.
Jacksonville, FL 32204

Wesley Manor
State Road 13
Julington Creek, FL

Lakeland Presbyterian Apartments
Florida Ave. at Lake Morton Dr.
Lakeland, FL 33801

NALCREST
Lake Wales, FL 33853

Lake Worth Towers
1500 Lucerne Ave.
Lake Worth, FL 33460

Golden Age Village
P.O. Box 615
LeHigh Acres, FL 33936

Sunshine Villas
P.O. Box 356
LeHigh Acres, FL 33936

Sunshine Villas, Annex
P.O. Box 356
LeHigh Acres, FL 33936

Dowling Hall
Dowling Park
Live Oak, FL 32060

Trinity Towers
Strawbridge and Livingston
Melbourne, FL 32901

CTA Towers
1809 Brickell Ave.
Miami, FL 33129

Douglas Gardens
151 NE 52nd St.
Miami, FL 33137

Holy Comforter Senior Housing
150 SW 13th Ave.
Miami, FL 33135

Pine Woods
2001 E. Ridge Village Dr.
Miami, FL 33157

Bay Terrace
1250 West Ave.
Miami Beach, FL 33157

Four Freedoms House of Miami Beach
3800 Collins Ave.
Miami Beach, FL 33140

First Baptist Housing
414 E. Pine St.
Orlando, FL 32801

Hillcrest-Hampton
Hillcrest & N. Hampton
Orlando, FL 32803

Kinneret
515 S. Delaney Ave.
Orlando, FL 32801

Magnolia Towers
100 E. Anderson St.
Orlando, FL 32802

Orlando Central Towers
350 E. Jackson St.
Orlando, FL 32801

St. Elizabeths Gardens
801 NE 33rd St.
Pompano Beach, FL 33064

Presbyterian Home
P.O. Box 2258
Port Charlotte, FL 33950

Ft. Meyers Presbyterian Community
3800 50th Ave., S.
St. Petersburg, FL 33733

Lutheran Apartments
550 First Ave., S.
St. Petersburg, FL 33701

Menorah Center
58th St. & Burlington Ave., N.
St. Petersburg, FL 33710

Pinellas Knights Residences
550 Third Ave., & Fifth St.
St. Petersburg, FL 33060

Presbyterian Towers
430 Bay St. NE
St. Petersburg, FL 33701

Suncoast Manor
6909 Ninth St., S.
St. Petersburg, FL 33705

The Plaza Fifth Avenue, Inc.
441 33rd St., N.
St. Petersburg, FL 33713

Bram Towers
519 E. First St.
Sanford, FL 32771

Bethany Housing
1731 Redwood
Sarasota, FL 33581

Jefferson Center
930 N. Tamiami Trail
Sarasota, FL 33577

Heritage Presbyterian Housing
10200 122nd Ave., N.
Seminole, FL 33540

Miami Beach Marian Towers
17705 N. Bay Road
Sunny Isles, FL 33160

Lutheran Residences of S. Pasadena
6800 Park St., S.
South Pasadena, FL 32707

Florida Sunshine Apartments
Box 998
Tallahassee, FL 32304

CTA River Apartments
4504 N. Rome Ave.
Tampa, FL 33160

Florida Gulf Coast Apartments
816 W. Linebaugh Ave.
Tampa FL 32802

Haciendas De Ybor, Inc.
Palm Ave. & 17th St.
Tampa, FL 33602

Presbyterian Villas of Tampa
4011 S. Manhattan
Tampa, FL 33611

Tampa Baptist Manor
215 W. Grand Central Ave.
Tampa, FL 33606

Tampa Presbyterian Community
2909 Barcelona
Tampa, FL 33609

United Methodist Retirement Center
Harrison St. & Florida Ave.
Tampa, FL 33602

Tarpon Springs Manor
610 S. Mayo Dr.
Tarpon Springs, FL 33589

Christian Manor, Inc.
215 N. Congress Ave.
West Palm Beach, FL 33401

St. Andrew's Residences of the Palm Beaches
700 Harvey Building
West Palm Beach, FL 33401

Episcopal Catholic Apartments
656 Avenue L, NW
Winter Haven, FL 33880

First Christian Towers
Avenue A and Eighth St.
Winter Haven, FL 33880

The Plymouth
1550 Gay Drive
Winter Park, FL 32789

GEORGIA

Magnolia Manor
P.O. Box 346
Americus, GA 31709

S. Georgia Methodist Home for Aging
P.O. Box 246
Americus, GA 31709

Lanier Gardens
801 Riverhill Dr.
Athens, GA 30601

Whispering Pines
Whitehall Rd. and Venita Dr.
Athens, GA 30603

Baptist Towers
1900 Delowe Dr.
Atlanta, GA 30311

Big Bethel Towers
220 Auburn Ave., NE
Atlanta, GA 30303

Branan Towers
c/o Wesley Homes, Inc.
P.O. Box 15468
Atlanta, GA 30333

Budd Terrace
1833 Clifton Rd., NE
Box 15468
Atlanta, GA 30333

Calvin Court
479 E. Paces Ferry Rd., NE
Atlanta, GA 30308

Campbell-Stone Apartments
2911 Pharr Court, South, NW
Atlanta, GA 30305

Epworth Towers
3033 Continental Colony Parkway
Atlanta, GA 30331

Lakewood Christian Manor
c/o Georgia Christian Homes Rd.
2141 Springdale Rd., SW
Atlanta, GA 30315

Lutheran Towers
727 Juniper St. at Fourth
Atlanta, GA 30308

Wesley-Woods Towers
1825 Clifton Rd., NE
Atlanta, GA 30329

Wheat Street Charitable Foundation
375 Auburn Ave., NE
Atlanta, GA 30312

St. John's Towers
c/o Wesley Homes, Inc.
P.O. Box 15468
Atlanta, GA 30333

Christian Towers
1438 Church St.
Decatur, GA 30030

Clairmont Oaks
308 Clairmont Ave.
Decatur, GA 30030

Phillips Towers
218 E. Trinity Plaza
Decatur, GA 30030

St. Paul Apartments
753 College St.
Macon, GA 31201

Vineville Christian Towers
P.O. Box 248
Macon, GA 31202

Rose of Sharon
322 E. Taylor
Savannah, GA 31401

Baptist Village
P.O. Box 1100
Waycross, GA 31501

HAWAII

Kauluwela Elderly
c/o Aaron M. Chaney, Inc.
Box 212
Honolulu, HI 96810

Hale Mahaolu
Kane St.
Kahului, Maui, HI 96732

IDAHO

Boise Valley Sunset Homes
3115 Sycamore
Boise, ID 83703

ILLINOIS

Aurora Leland Senior Citizens Home
7 S. Island Ave.
Aurora, IL 60507

Parkside Manor
530 S. State St.
Belvidere, IL 61008

Cambridge Manor Apartments
S. Commons Housing for the Elderly
2651 S. Indiana Ave.
Chicago, IL 60616

Chicago Teachers Union Tower
134 N. LaSalle St.
Chicago, IL 60602

Country Club Apartments
6930 S. Shore Blvd.
Chicago, IL 60649

Drexel Square Apartments
811 E. Hyde Park
Chicago, IL 60615

Franciscan Tertiary Province of the Sacred Heart
1458 W. 51st St.
Chicago, IL 60609

Hollywood House
2150 N. Lincoln Park, W.
Chicago, IL 60602

Kenmore Housing for the Elderly
5209 N. Kenmore Ave.
Chicago, IL 60640

King Drive Apartments
48th and King Drive
Chicago, IL 60615

Pane Steward Apartments
c/o Peoples Consumer Coop.
4655 S. Michigan Ave.
Chicago, IL 60653

Self-Help Center
908 Argyle St.
Chicago, IL 60640

Ebenezer Prime Towers
Maple St.
Evanston, IL 60201

Immanuel Residences for the Elderly
6201 N. Kirkwood Ave.
Evergreen Park, IL 60646

New Mt. Morris Home for Aging
414 S. McKendrie
Mt. Morris, IL 61054

Naperville Elderly Homes
503 N. Washington St.
Naperville, IL 60540

Mayslake Village
1801 W. 35th St.
Oakbrook, IL 60523

Lutheran Home of Greater Peoria
7019 N. Galena Rd.
Peoria, IL 61614

Galena Park Terrace
5533 N. Galena Rd.
Peoria Heights, IL 61614

Skyrise Apartments
837 N. Main St.
Rockford, IL 61103

Big Meadow
100 Long Moor Rd.
Savanna, IL 61074

Shamel Manor
100 E. Edwards St.
Springfield, IL 62704

Marion Park
2126 Roosevelt Rd.
Wheaton, IL 60187

INDIANA

Bremen Manor
515 Whitlock St.
Bremen, IN 46615

Town and Garden Apartments
428 Pearl St.
Columbus, IN 47201

Horizon Homes
Burdette and Covert Aves.
Evansville, IN 47715

Northwest Indiana Methodist Home
1555 N. Main St.
Frankfort, IN 46014

Creencroft Central Manor
2000 S. 15th St.
Goshen, IN 46526

Village Towers Apartments
U.S. Highway 31, S.
Greenwood, IN 46142

Cambridge Square II
73rd St. and Township Line Rd.
Indianapolis, IN 46260

Hickory Village
c/o Hickory Village Apartments
P.O. Box 26292
Indianapolis, IN 46226

Indiana Retired Teachers Community
105 W. Market St.
Indianapolis, IN 46202

Plymouth Arms Apartments
P.O. Box 26292
Indianapolis, IN 46226

Wabash Senior Citizens Housing
10 N. Sixth St.
Terre Haute, IN 47801

IOWA

Friendship Home
North Division and Scott Sts.
Audubon, IA 50025

McBurney Apartments
116 Luick Lane, N.
Belmond, IA 50421

Geneva Corporation
Third St. & 5th Ave., SE
Cedar Rapids, IA 52401

Bluffs Towers
38 Pearl St.
Council Bluffs, IA 51501

Eventide Lutheran Home for the Aged
Missouri Synod
20th St.
Denison, IA 51442

Horace Mann Home for the Aged
(Heather Manor)
4025 Tonawanda Dr.
Des Moines, IA 50312

Plymouth Place
4111 Ingersoll Ave.
Des Moines, IA 50312

River Hills Apartments
700 E. Fifth St.
Des Moines, IA 50309

Wesley Acres
35th St. and Grand Ave.
Des Moines, IA 50309

United Manor
707 14th St.
DeWitt, IA 52742

Rotary Ann Home
Box 85
Eagle Grove, IA 50533

Prairie View Home
R.R. No. 3
Garner, IA 50438

Good Shepherd Retirement
 Apartments
302 Second St., NE
Mason City, IA 50401

Golden Buckle Home
500 E. Lake St.
Rockwell City, IA 50579

Franken Manor
2010 N. Main Ave.
Sioux Center, IA 51250

Martin Luther Home
5501 E. Gordon Dr.
Sioux City, IA 51106

Sunset Retirement Home
111 E. 20th St.
Spencer, IA 51301

Peace Haven
Box C
Walnut, IA 51577

Halycon House
1007 S. Iowa Ave.
Washington, IA 52353

Crestview Acres
916 Ashmorth Rd.
West Des Moines, IA 50265

KANSAS

Cross-Lines Retirement Center
1428 S. 32nd St.
Kansas City, KS 66102

Primrose Villa
2804 Sewell Ave.
Kansas City, KS 64104

Swan Manor
215 N. Broadway
La Cygne, KS 66040

Evangelical Village
9100 Park Ave.
Lenexa, KS 66215

Congregational Home
1203 W. 29th St.
Topeka, KS 66611

First Christian Church Apartments
1880 Gage Blvd.
Topeka, KS 66604

Landmark Plaza
1000 Kansas Ave.
Topeka, KS 66612

Presbyterian Manor
4712 W. Sixth St.
Topeka, KS 66606

American Baptist Estates
200 N. Meridian St.
Wichita, KS 67203

KENTUCKY

Lee County Housing for Elderly and
 Infirmed
P.O. Box 231
Beattyville, KY 41311

Hathaway Court
1200 Highway
Covington, KY 41011

Panorama Apartments
111 Brent Spence Square
Covington, KY 41011

Senior Citizens Home
c/o Baptist Church of Independence
 Inc.
Independence, KY 41051

Gerrard County Home for Aged
West Maple Ave.
Lancaster, KY 40444

Grayson Housing, Inc.
East Lake Dr.
Leitchfield, KY 42754

Christ Church Apartments
c/o Christ Church Episcopal
166 Market St.
Lexington, KY 40507

Emerson Center
2550 Garden Springs Dr.
Lexington, KY 40504

Laurel County Project for Elderly
Laurel County Fiscal Court
London, KY 40741

Baptist Towers
c/o Walnut Street Baptist Church
1101 S. Third St.
Louisville, KY 40203

Chapel House
949 S. Fifth St.
Louisville, KY 40203

Hillebrand House
1235 S. Third St.
Louisville, KY 40203

J.O. Blanton House
Fifth Street Hi-Rise
c/o William L. Higgins Management Co. Inc.
504 S. Sixth St.
Louisville, KY 40203

The Presbyterian Home for Senior Citizens
5906 Santa Rosa Dr.
Louisville, KY 40219

Trinity Towers
Third and Guthrie
Louisville, KY 40202

Wesley Manor
5012 E. Manslick Rd.
Louisville, KY 40219

Roosevelt House
2920 Yale Place
Owensboro, KY 42301

Jackson House
Ninth and Washington Sts.
Paducah, KY 42001

LOUISIANA

Arcadia Baptist Home
P.O. Box 599
Arcadia, LA 71001

Catholic-Presbyterian Apartments
655 North St.
Baton Rouge, LA 70802

Hicky Hills
c/o T.W. Alley, Jr.
P.O. Box 5044
Bossier City, LA 71010

Oak Woods Home for the Elderly
Handy Hill Road
Mer Rouge, LA 71261

Chateau de Villa
c/o William R. Boles
P.O. Box 7222
Monroe, LA 71201

Waskom Arms Apartments
c/o William R. Boles
P.O. Box 7222
Monroe, LA 71201

Christopher Homes
P.O. Box 51312
New Orleans, LA 70150

Monsignor Wynhoven Apartments
1624 National Bank of Commerce Building
New Orleans, LA 70112

The Volunteer Workers Association
717 Madeline St.
Rayville, LA 71269

The Evangeline
3875 Line Ave.
Shreveport, LA 71106

The Fountain
Fairfield and Mildred Sts.
Shreveport, LA 71101

Madison Parish Baptist Missionary Association
302 E. Washington St.
Tallulah, LA 71282

MAINE

Arch Project Beta
Capital Street Extension
Augusta, ME 04330

Sunset Manor
686 Broadway
Bangor, ME 04401

Elderly Home
512 Main St.
Madawaska, ME 04756

Ocean Pines
11th St. and Massachusetts Ave.
Old Orchard Beach, ME 04960

Deering Pavilion
880 Forest Ave.
Portland, ME 04103

Methodist Conference Home
39 Summer St.
Rockland, ME 04841

MARYLAND

Concord Apartments
2500 W. Belvedere Ave.
Baltimore, MD 21215

Harbor Center, Inc.
Christ Church Harbor Apartments
Charles & Hill Sts.
Baltimore, MD 21207

Marlbourough Apartments
c/o Midtown Contractors
1101 St. Paul St.
Suite 404
Baltimore, MD 21202

Memorial Apartments
301 McMechen St.
Baltimore, MD 21217

Nathan Hackerman Lodge
5713 Park Heights Ave.
Baltimore, MD 21215

St. James Terrace Apartments
809 N. Arlington Ave.
Baltimore, MD 21217

St. Mary's Roland View Towers (East)
3939 Roland Ave.
Baltimore, MD 21211

St. Mary's Roland View Towers (West)
3938 Roland Ave.
Baltimore, MD 21211

The Westminster House
542 N. Charles St.
Baltimore, MD 21201

St. John's Towers
505 Congress Ave.
Havre de Grace, MD 21078

Rebecca Apartments
10920 Connecticut Ave.
Kensington, MD 20795

Meridian Hill Apartments
1313 Southern Ave.
Oxon Hill, MD 20032

Bethany House
199 Rollins Ave.
Rockville, MD 20852

Friends House
17401 Norwood Rd.
Sandy Spring, MD 20860

Springvale Terrace
8505 Springvale Rd.
Silver Spring, MD 20910

United Church of Christ Home
8505 Springvale Rd.
Silver Spring, MD 20910

Takoma Tower
7051 Carroll Ave.
Takoma Park, MD 20012

Timber Ridge
P.O. Box 543
Westminster, MD 21157

MASSACHUSETTS

Fenway Housing for Elderly
1 Joy St.
Boston, MA 02108

Jewish Community II
40 Wallingford Rd.
Brighton, MA 02135

Union Towers
c/o Union Congregational Church
74 Commercial St.
East Braintree, MA 02184

Cape Cod United Church Homes
62 Locust St.
Falmouth, MA 02636

The Sundial
P.O. Box 503
Fitchburg, MA 01420

Bethany House
100 Water St.
Haverhill, MA 01830

First Church in Malden Homes
184 Pleasant St.
Malden, MA 02148

Salem Towers
280 Salem St.
Malden, MA 02148

Winslow Village
1500 Ocean St.
Marshfield, MA 02050

ABC Towers
P.O. Box 172
Melrose, MA 02176

Congregational Retirement Homes
200 W. Foster St.
Melrose, MA 02176

Jewish Comm. Housing for the Elderly
121 Monadnock Rd.
Newton, MA 02167

North Side Housing Corporation
20 Central St.
Peabody, MA 01960

Bradford Arms
383 North St.
Pittsfield, MA 01201

Fenno House
550 Hancock St.
Quincy, MA 02170

Quincy Point Congregational Church
  Homes
1000 Southern Artery
Quincy, MA 02169

Pulaski Heights
121 Chestnut St.
Springfield, MA 01103

Springfield Hobby Club Housing
128 Derryfield Ave.
Springfield, MA 01103

Colony Retirement Homes
485 Grove St.
Worcester, MA 06105

MICHIGAN

Lurie Terrace
600 W. Huron St.
Ann Arbor, MI 48103

Dunn Family Senior Citizens Homes
8400 Engleman Rd.
Centerline, MI 48015

Kiwanihome
430 S. Cochran Ave.
P.O. Box 22
Charlotte, MI 48113

New Life
P.O. Box 315
Clawson, MI 48017

Bishop Apartments
7404 Woodward Ave.
Detroit, MI 48202

Carmel Hall
2560 Woodward and Adelaide
Detroit, MI 48201

Cathedral Terrace
2700 Penobscot Building
Detroit, MI 48226

Federation Apartments
1624 Dime Building
Detroit, MI 48226

Independence Hall
17376 Wyoming Ave.
Detroit, MI 48221

LaBelle Towers
7404 Woodward Ave.
Detroit, MI 48202

Martin Luther King Housing Corp.
1132 Washington Blvd.
Detroit, MI 48226

Presbyterian Village of Detroit
25300 E. Seven Mile Rd.
Detroit, MI 48240

River Towers
7800 E. Jefferson
Detroit, MI 48240

Rochdale Court
1588 E. Lafayette
Detroit, MI 48207

Rochford Terrace
3387 Lawton St.
Detroit, MI 48203

St. Paul's Housing Corp.
11359 Dexter Blvd.
Detroit, MI 48205

The Apple Tree
13115 E. Jefferson
Detroit, MI 48215

Trenton Cooperative Apartments
7404 Woodward Ave.
Detroit, MI 48202

Detroit Baptist Manor
30251 W. Thirteen Mile Road
Farmington, MI 48024

Flint Heights Senior Citizens Apts.
1106 N. Dye Rd.
Flint, MI 48504

Flint Retirement Homes
814 E. Kearsley
Flint, MI 48502

Michigan Christian Home
1845 Boston, SE
Grand Rapids, MI 49506

Pilgrim Manor
2000 NE Leonard St.
Grand Rapids, MI 49508

Porter Hills Village
3500 E. Fulton St.
Grand Rapids, MI 49506

Capitol Grange Senior Citizens
  Housing Corp.
5878 Buena Parkway
Haslett, MI 48840

Chateau Cherry Hill
4300 Harrison Ave.
Inkster, MI 48141

Heritage Hills
c/o Golden Age Nonprofit Housing
  Corp.
2400 Partage St.
Kalamazoo, MI 49001

Trinity Park, Inc.
14800 Middlebelt Rd.
Livonia, MI 48154

Cleveland Manor
2200 Cleveland St.
Midland, MI 48640

Jefferson Towers
1077 Jefferson St.
Muskegon, MI 49443

Kiwanis Village of Owosso
City Club
Owosso, MI 48867

Clastonbury Manor
2187 Orchard Lake Rd.
Pontiac, MI 48053

American House
1900 N. Washington
Royal Oak, MI 48073

Royal Oak Cooperative Homes
Main & Sixth St.
Royal Oak, MI

Essex Manor
4000 Harold St.
Saginaw, MI 48001

Saginaw Westchester Village
4055 W. Michigan
Saginaw, MI 48101

Centrax Arms Apartments
c/o Advance Mortgage Corp.
23077 Greenfield Rd.
Southfield, MI 48075

Elmwood Park Plaza
c/o Elmwood Park Plaza, Inc.
2475 Lahser Rd.
Southfield, MI 48075

Elmwood Towers
21311 Civic Court Dr.
Box 267
Southfield, MI 48075

Seaway Tower
2475 Lahser Rd.
Southfield, MI 48075

The Normandy
20449 Ecorse Rd.
Taylor, MI 48180

Bethany Villa Housing Association
2601 John R
Troy, MI 48084

Bethany Villa No. 2
2601 John R
Troy, MI 48084

Wyandotte Apartments
2455 Biddle
Wyandotte, MI 48192

MINNESOTA

AFL-CIO Senior Courts
c/o Albert Lea Trades and Labor
  Assembly
404 E. Main St.
Albert Lea, MN 56007

St. Mark's Lutheran Home
400 15th Ave., SW
Austin, MN 55912

St. Mark's Lutheran Home Apts.
1401 Fourth St., SW
Austin, MN 55912

St. Luke's Lutheran Home
1219 S. Ramsey St.
Blue Earth, MN 56013

Park Lane Apartments
200 Park Lane
Buffalo, MN 55313

Retirement Center of Wright County
Third Ave., S. and Lake Blvd.
Buffalo, MN 55313

Grandview Christian Home
Second and Garland Ave., NW
Cambridge, MN 55008

Faith Haven
4901 Grand Ave.
Duluth, MN 55807

Gateway Tower, Inc.
14th Ave., W & Waterfront St.
Duluth, MN 55807

St. Ann's Home
330 E. Third St.
Duluth, MN 55805

"S" Elect Homes
801 E. Second St.
Duluth, MN 55805

Townview Villa
600 W. Second St.
Duluth, MN 55802

Rembrant of Edina
3434 Heritage Dr.
Edina, MN 55435

Riverview Apartments
400 Evans Ave.
Elk River, MN 55330

Augustana Apartments
118 S. Vine
Fergus Falls, MN 56537

Glenwood Retirement Home
719 SE Second St.
Glenwood, MN 56334

Hopkins Village Apartments
9 Seventh Ave., S.
Hopkins, MN 55343

Glorida Dei Manor
218 N. Holcomb St.
Litchfield, MN 55355

Lyon County Retirement Home
200 S. Fourth St.
Marshall, MN 56258

Ebenezer Towers
2545 Portland Ave.
Minneapolis, MN 55404

Edina Yorktown Towers
c/o Rainbow Development Company
625 E. 16th St.
Minneapolis, MN 55401

Heritage Homes, Inc.
7100 France Ave., S.
Minneapolis, MN 55419

Loring Towers
15 E. Grant St.
Minneapolis, MN 55403

Mt. Olivet Homes, Inc.
5517 Lyndale Ave., S.
Minneapolis, MN 55419

Oak Grove Tower
215 Oak Grove St.
Minneapolis, MN 55403

107 Uni Elderly
918 E. 22nd St.
Minneapolis, MN 55402

Brookside Manor
804 Benson Rd.
Montevideo, MN 56265

Elder's Home, Inc.
S. Tousely Ave. and Nowell St.
New York Mills, MN 56567

Northfield Retirement Center
(Lutheran Home of the Cannon Valley)
Cannon Valley Dr., W. of Cedar Ave.
Northfield, MN 55057

Community Memorial Home
Fourth and Center Sts.
Osakis, MN 56360

Hillside Gardens
419 Seventh St.
Proctor, MN 55810

Lincoln Square
c/o P.O. Box 319
Rochester, MN 55901

Rochester Manor
Rochester, MN 55901

Winona Square
c/o P.O. Box 319
Rochester, MN 55901

Good Shepherd Lutheran Home
Rushford, MN 55971

Central Towers
20 E. Exchange St.
St. Paul, MN 55101

Redeemer Arms
313 N. Dale St.
St. Paul, MN 55103

Wilder Residences Apartments
508 Humboldt
St. Paul, MN 55107

Estate Apartments
511 S. Fifth St.
St. Peter, MN 56082

Valley Home Society
Box 525
Thief River Falls, MN 56701

Sauer Memorial Home
1635 Service Drive
Winona, MN 55987

The Paul Watkins Memorial
  Methodist Home
175 E. Wabash St.
Winona, MN 55987

MISSISSIPPI

Santa Maria del Mar
305 E. Beach Blvd.
Biloxi, MS 39530

Seashore Manor
P.O. Box Y
Biloxi, MS 39533

Madonna Manor
559 Houston Ave.
Jackson, MS 39209

Villa Maria Retirement Apartments
921 Porter St.
Ocean Springs, MS 39564

Care Centers of Mississippi, Inc.
Chico Rd.
Pascagoula, MS 39567

Traceway Manor
2530 W. Main St.
Tupulo, MS 38801

MISSOURI

Wellington Arms
225 S. Meramec Ave.
Clayton, MO 63105

Good Shepherd Village
Concordia, MO 64020

Lutheran Good Shepherd Home
Third and West Sts.
Concordia, MO 64020

Baptist Towers
24 Highway and Jennings Rd.
Independence, MO 64056

Defenders Townhouse
Kansas City, MO 64141

KCEA Housing Foundation
c/o Kansas City Education Assn.
3142 Broadway
Kansas City, MO 64111

Nowlin Hall
1905 Hadesty
Kansas City, MO 64127

Paraclete Manor
4725 Prospect Ave.
Kansas City, MO 64130

Royal Tower Apartments
Tenth and McGee
Kansas City, MO 64106

John Calvin Manor
1005 W. Maple
Lee's Summit, MO 64063

Frank and Mary Bowen Memorial
  Residence
6140 Raytown Rd.
Raytown, MO 64133

Temple Heights Manor
5420 Blue Ridge Cutoff
Raytown, MO 64133

Santa Ana Apartments
3727 Ashby Rd.
St. Ann, MO 63074

Chariton Apartments
4249 Michigan Ave.
St. Louis, MO 63111

Council House
300 S. Grand Blvd.
St. Louis, MO 63103

Heritage House Redevelopment Corp.
c/o Olive St., between Ewing and Effingwell
St. Louis, MO 63103

Little Sisters of the Poor
3225 N. Florisant Ave.
St. Louis, MO 63108

Convenant House Apartments
c/o 6331 Delmar
University City, MO 63130

Parkview Towers
701-15 Westgate
University City, MO 63130

The Delcrest
8350 Delcrest
University City, MO 63130

MONTANA

Lutheran Retirement Home
3940 Rimrock Rd.
Billings, MT 59102

Sage Tower
917 N. 28th St.
Billings, MT 59101

Hillcrest Homes
Box 516
Bozeman, MT 59715

Skyline Lodge
Eighth Ave., NW & Fifth St., N.
Choteau, MT 59422

Horizon Lodge, Inc.
Box 1146
Mancoronel Building
Conrad, MT 59425

Hilltop Manor
Box 1027
Cut Bank, MT 59427

Grandview Apartments
1711 W. Merrill
Glendive, MT 59330

Eagles Manor
Ninth St. & 15th Ave., S.
Great Falls, MT 59401

Soroptimist Village
2200 Alder Drive
Great Falls, MT 59401

Penkay Eagles Manor
715 Fee St.
Helena, MT 59601

LaVatta Apartments
P.O. Box 75
Kalispell, MT 59901

Lewiston Eagles Manor
211 W. Janeaux
Lewiston, MT 59457

Miles City Eagles Manor
P.O. Box 1216
Miles City, MT 59301

Missoula Manor Homes
Central & Holborn
Missoula, MT 59801

Montana Pioneer Manors
120 E. Second Ave.
Plentywood, MT 59254

Richland Homes
P.O. Box 73
Sidney, MT 59270

NEBRASKA

Evangelical Lutheran Good Samaritan Society
1302 S. Ninth St.
Beatrice, NB 68310

Dome Creek Manor
1225 12th St.
Gering, NB 69314

Hasting Tower
721 First Ave.
Hastings, NB 68901

Methodist Memorial Homes
1319 Tenth Ave.
Holdredge, NB 68949

Clark Jeary Memorial Manor
60th & A Sts.
Lincoln, NB 68508

Gateway Manor
56th & O St.
Lincoln, NB 68508

Lincoln Manor
2626 N. 49th St.
Lincoln, NB 68504

Pioneer Housing Corp
12th & H Sts.
Lincoln, NB 68508

Tabitha Village
4720 Randolph St.
Lincoln, NB 68510

North Platte Odd Fellows Housing Corp.
Route 4
North Platte, NB 69101

Masonic Manor
52nd & Leavenworth Sts.
Omaha, NB 68106

OEA Manor
320 N. 22nd St.
Omaha, NB 68102

Skyline Manor
72nd & Military Ave.
Omaha, NB 68134

Veteran's Retreat
20th & Chicago Sts.
Omaha, NB 68102

Norfolk 100F Housing, Inc.
1201 Norfolk Ave.
Norfolk, NB 68701

NEVADA

Las Vegas Manor
Decatur & Vegas Dr.
Las Vegas, NV 89106

NEW HAMPSHIRE

United Church of Christ Retirement Community, Inc.
Concord, NH 03301

Nutfield Heights, Inc.
3 Boyd Ave.
Derry, NH 03038

NEW JERSEY

Best-of-Life Park
129 S. Virginia Ave.
Atlantic City, NJ 08404

Elliott House
1200 N. Indiana Ave.
Atlantic City, NJ 08401

Ocean Manor Apartments
New Hampshire Ave. at Broadwalk
Atlantic City, NJ 08401

Miriam Apartments
127 Hazell St.
Clifton, NJ 07015

Cooper Gate Apartments
780 Springdale Ave.
East Orange, NJ 07017

Acacia-Lumberton Manor
c/o R.O. Bernard
245 Forest Ave.
Glen Ridge, NJ 07028

Heath Village, Inc.
201 Main St.
Hackettstown, NJ 07840

Bethany Manor
2000 Florence Ave.
Hazlet, NJ 07730

Wesley Towers
444 Mt. Prospect Ave.
Newark, NJ 07194

G and View Terrace
23 E. Essex Ave.
Orange, NJ 07050

Dunrocen Residence Hall
Ridgewood Ave.
Paramus, NJ 07622

Governor Paterson Towers
225 20th Ave.
Paterson, NJ 07501

Governor Paterson Towers West
195 20th Ave.
Paterson, NJ 07501

Pitman Manor
Methodist Homes of New Jersey
535 North Oak
Pitman, NJ 08071

Trent Center Apartments
511-527 Greenwood Ave.
Trenton, NJ 08609

Trenton Lutheran Housing
189 S. Broad St.
Trenton, NJ 08608

Lions Center
3311 New Jersey Ave.
Wildwood, NJ 08260

NEW MEXICO

Encino House
609 Encino Place, NE
Albuquerque, NM 87106

Landsum Homes, Inc.
1508 Bryan Circle
Carlsbad, NM 88220

Kingdom of the Sun Retirement Center
Eighth and Buckeye
Deming, NM 88030

National Secretaries Association
    Retirement Center
P.O. Box 15004
Rio Rancho, NM 87114

Sunny Acres Senior Center
1414 S. Union
Roswell, NM 88201

Sunset 1600
1600 S. Sunset
Roswell, NM 88201

NEW YORK

Albany B'Nai B'rith
Senior Citizens Housing
Gideon Lodge No. 140
c/o 100 State Street
Albany, NY 12207

Ohav Shalom Senior
New Krumkill Road
Albany, NY

Lancaster Towers
4500 Vestal Parkway East
Binghamton, NY 13903

Shirley Court
3258 Main St.
Buffalo, NY 14214

Israel Senior Citizens Housing Corp.
19th & Seagirt Blvd.
Far Rockaway, NY 11691

Seagirt Village
19-25 Seagirt Blvd.
Far Rockaway, NY 11691

Gen. Douglas McArthur
    Senior Village
260 Clinton St.
Hempstead, NY 11550

Ithacare, Inc.
South Quarry St.
Ithaca, NY 14850

Harley Park Association
110 N. Third Ave.
Mt. Vernon, NY 10550

Middlewood
c/o BAI Management Corp.
80 N. Middletown Rd.
Nanuet, NY 10954

David Podell House
181 Henry St.
New York, NY 10002

Home of the Sages of Israel
25 Willett St.
New York, NY 10002

Morris Park Apartments
17 E. 124th St.
New York, NY 10035

The Bethel Methodist Home
19 Narragansett Ave.
Ossining, NY 10562

St. Marks Terrace
107 Chapel St.
Penn Yan, NY 10427

Beekman Tower
Beekman St. & Boyton Ave.
Plattsburgh, NY 12903

Saugerties Senior Housing
c/o Better Community Housing
    Development Fund
11 Elm St.
Saugerties, NY 12477

Historical Park Apartments
c/o Longley Jones Management Corp.
840 James St.
Syracuse, NY 13203

NORTH CAROLINA

Vanderbilt Apartments
75 Haywood St.
Asheville, NC 28801

The Methodist Retirement Homes
2616 Erwin Rd.
Durham, NC 27705

Ramblewood Apartments
P.O. Box 6309
Station B
Greenville, NC 27834

The Presbyterian Home, Inc.
201 Greensboro Rd.
High Point, NC 27260

Capital Towers
4812 Six Forks Roads
Raleigh, NC 27609

NORTH DAKOTA

Golden Valley Manor
Brinton Avenue & Near St.
Beach, ND 58621

Bethany Towers
1333 Third Ave., S.
Fargo, ND 58102

McLean Manor
Second Ave. & Fifth St., SE
Garrison, ND 58540

Harold S. Haaland Home
Tenth St. & Third Ave.
Rugby, ND 58368

Wishek Home for the Aged
Wishek, ND 58495

OHIO

Mennonite Memorial Home
410 W. Elm St.
Bluffton, OH 45817

Maplecrest Home for the Elderly
717 Rogers St.
Bucyrus, OH 44820

Eatondale North
4463 Glenhaven Rd.
Cincinnati, OH 45238

Hillrise Apartments
1500 Groesbeck Rd.
Cincinnati, OH 45224

Mt. Healthy Christian Home
c/o Christian Benevolent Association
    of Greater Cincinnati, Inc.
Cincinnati, OH

Queensgate II
Ninth & Central Ave.
Cincinnati, OH 45202

Reids Valley View Manor Apartments
1990 Westwood Northern Blvd.
Cincinnati, OH 45225

San Marco Apartments
1601-11 Madison Road
Cincinnati, OH 45206

SEM Ecumenical Manor Apartments
617 Vine St.
Cincinnati, OH 45215

Union Baptist Apartments
c/o R.E. Dietz Co.
225 E. Sixth St.
Cincinnati, OH 45202

Federation Towers
22nd St. & Scoville Ave.
Cleveland, OH 44104

Teamsters Housing
2070 E. 22nd St.
Cleveland, OH 44115

The Knickerbocker
c/o David G. Davies
1144 Union Commerce Building
Cleveland, OH 44115

Villa St. Rose
10900 Lake Ave.
Cleveland, OH 44102

Council Gardens
2501 Taylor Rd.
Cleveland Heights, OH 45218

Jaycee Arms Apartments
440 Dayton Towers Dr.
Columbus, OH

Lutheran Senior City
Johnstown Rd. & Parkview Ave., N.
Columbus, OH 43219

Rosa Park Apartments
1465 E. Broad St.
Columbus, OH 43205

Weldon Square Phase II
Fremont & Derrer Rds.
Columbus, OH 43204

Wesley Glen Retirement Center
5155 N. High St.
Columbus, OH 43214

Cathedral Apartments
2700 State Rd.
Cuyahoga Falls, OH 44223

Asbury Apartments
200 W. Fifth St.
Dayton, OH 45402

Brookview Place
4032 N. Main St.
Dayton, OH 45405

Golden Village
500 Scranton St.
Dayton, OH 45404

Jaycee Towers
440 Dayton Towers Dr.
Dayton, OH 45410

The Lakewoods
980 Wilmington Ave.
Dayton, OH 45420

London Town
300 Chelsea St.
Delaware, OH 43015

Foresthill Terrace Apartments
14030 Terrace Rd.
East Cleveland, OH 45212

Kentway Apartments
360 E. Summit St.
Kent, OH 44240

Heritage Manor
State Route No. 53
Kenton, OH 43326

Lake Shore Towers
12506 Edgewater Dr.
Lakewood, OH 44107

Westerly III
c/o Lakewood Sr. Citizens Inc.
14300 Detroit Ave.
Lakewood, OH 44107

Firelands Retirement Centers, Inc.
2019 E. Erie Ave.
Lorain, OH 44052

Rotary Towers
400 Delaware Ave.
Marion, OH 43302

Windsor Manor Apartments
207 Windsor Court
Marysville, OH 43040

Luther House
SOM Center Rd.
Mayfield Heights, OH

Schnurmann House
1223-1227 Drury Court
Mayfield Heights, OH

Villa Serena
6800 Mayfield Rd.
Mayfield Heights, OH

Glenview
RD No. 3
Montpelier, OH 43543

Firelands Retirement Centers, Inc.
Oberlin, OH 44074

Independence Place
Independence Rd. & Ames Ave.
Parma Heights, OH 45229

The Educator
9275 N. Church Dr.
Parma Heights, OH 45229

Elm House
230 Elm St.
Perrysburg, OH 44454

Richwood Apartments
235 Grove St.
Richwood, OH 43344

Viewpoint
P.O. Box 1101
Sandusky, OH 44870

Crestview of Ohio
Monroe St. & Harroun Rd.
Sylvania, OH 43560

Kiwanis Manor Apartments
7 W. Market St.
Tiffin, OH 44883

Ashland Manor
310-318 W. Woodruff Ave.
Toledo, OH 43624

Madonna Homes
722 Huron St.
Toledo, OH 43604

The Westmoor
1001 N. Byrne Rd.
Toledo, OH 43607

Terrace Ridge Apartments
1312 McKaig Ave.
Troy, OH 45373

First Community Village
1800 Riverside Drive
Upper Arlington, OH 43221

Sugar Grove Square
530 S. State St.
Westerville, OH 43081

College Hills Retirement Village
P.O. Box 762
Wooster, OH 44691

Worthington Villa
814 Hartford St.
Worthington, OH 43805

Eldercrest Apartments
8 Ridgeview Lane
Youngstown, OH 44514

Mapleview Terrace
1356 Athena Lane
Zanesville, OH 43701

OKLAHOMA

Cordell Christian Home
1400 N. College St.
Cordell, OK 73632

Evangelical Lutheran Good Samaritan Home
330 Randlett
Hobart, OK 73651

Cedar Crest Manor, Inc.
1700 Fort Sill Blvd.
Lawton, OK 73501

Kate Frank Manor
S. 33rd St.
Muskogee, OK 74401

Superbia Senior Citizens Village
Oklahoma City, OK

Woodcrest Apartments
4901 E. Reno
Oklahoma City, OK 73117

Mansion House
c/o Eighth Floor
Mobil Building
Tulsa, OK

Pythian Manor
6568 E. 21st Place
Tulsa, OK 74129

Sheridan Terrace
585 N. Memorial
Tulsa, OK 74115

Terrace View Apartments
1729 S. Denver
Tulsa, OK 74119

OREGON

Forest Glen Senior Residence
P.O. Box 726
Canyonville, OR 97417

Samaritan Village
285 N. 35th St.
Corvallis, OR 97330

Eugene Good Samaritan Center
Severson Memorial Home
3500 Hillyard St.
Eugene, OR 97405

Ya-Po-Ah Terrace
135 E. Sixth St.
Eugene, OR

Conifer No. 314
Royal & Stevens St.
Medford, OR 97501

Rose Villa
13505 SE River Rd.
Milwaukie, OR 97222

Mt. Angel Tower
Mt. Angel, OR 97362

Friendsview Manor
1301 E. Fulton St.
Newburg, OR 97132

Labor Center Retirement Apartments
318 Portland Labor Center
201 SW Arthur St.
Portland, OR 97201

Marshall Union Manor
2020 NW Northup St.
Portland, OR 97210

Pisgah Home Colony
7511 SE Henry
Portland, OR 97206

Terwilliger Plaza, Inc.
2545 SW Terwilliger Blvd.
Portland, OR 97201

The Village
c/o North Pacific Homes, Inc.
18001 SE Powel Blvd.
Portland, OR 97236

Westmorland's Manor
6404 SE 23rd Ave.
Portland, OR 97202

Capital Manor
1955 Dallas Highway
Salem, OR 97304

Willamette Lutheran Home, Inc.
7693 Wheatland Rd., NE
Salem, OR 97303

PENNSYLVANIA

Episcopal House
524 Walnut St.
Allentown, PA 18101

Phoebe Apartments
1901 Linden St.
Allentown, PA 18104

B'nai B'rith Apartments
Third & Chestnut Sts.
Harrisburg, PA 17101

Presbyterian Apartments
322 N. Second St.
Harrisburg, PA 17101

Parkview Towers Apartments
111 Caroline St.
Munhall, PA 15120

Riverside Apartments
125 W. North St.
New Castle, PA 16101

Jefferson Apartments
1514 W. Marshall St.
Norristown, PA 19401

Ascension Manor
911 N. Franklin St.
Philadelphia, PA 19123

Brith Sholom House
3939 Conshohocken
Philadelphia, PA 19131

Casa Enrico Fermi
1300 Lombard St.
Philadelphia, PA 19147

Econ-Toland Apartments
Queen Lane & New Hall Sts.
Philadelphia, PA 19144

Elks National Retirement Center
c/o 1522 N. 16th St.
Philadelphia, PA 19121

Four Freedoms House of Philadelphia
6101 N. Morris St.
Philadelphia, PA 19144

Fraternal Order of Police
Senior Citizens Apartments
1336 Spring Garden St.
Philadelphia, PA 19123

Guild House
711 Spring Garden St.
Philadelphia, PA 19123

Marshall L. Shepard Village
642 N. 31st St.
Philadelphia, PA 19104

Phillip Murray House
4 N. 11th St.
Philadelphia, PA 19107

Sidney Hillman Apartments for the Elderly
22 S. 22nd St.
Philadelphia, PA 19103

Stephen Smith Towers
1030 Belmont Ave.
Philadelphia, PA 19104

York House, Inc.
York Road & Somerville Ave.
Philadelphia, PA 19141

York House South
c/o Home for the Jewish Aged
5301 Old York Road
Philadelphia, PA 19141

Auba Senior Citizens Apartments
2700 Centre Ave.
Pittsburgh, PA 15204

Episcopal Residences
4001 Penn Ave.
Pittsburgh, PA 15224

Grant Towers
c/o Grant Tower Associates
643 Liberty Ave.
Pittsburgh, PA 15222

Riverview Apartments
234 McKee Place
Pittsburgh, PA 15213

Riverview Phase II
Browns Hill Rd.
Pittsburgh, PA 15217

Episcopal House of Reading
Washington & Ninth Sts.
Reading, PA 19601

PUERTO RICO

La Egida
c/o Puerto Rico Teachers Association
P.O. Box 1088
Hato Rey, PR 00917

LaCiudad Del Retiro
Nuevo, PR

Altergarten Las Teresas
Rio Piedras, PR 00923

Multifamiar Trigo
c/o Trigo Housing Inc.
GPO Box 927
San Juan, PR

Clinica Dr Pila
1205 Ponce de Leon Ave.
Santurce, PR 00907

Hogar Camelitano
c/o P.O. Box 3264
Santurce, PR 00907

Residencias Los Jardines
c/o Banco de San Juan
Ponce de Leon Ave.
Santurce, PR 00907

RHODE ISLAND

1890 House
c/o Robert R. Forcier
505 Riogua Ave.
Coventry, RI 02816

Mt. Vernon Apartments
2352 Mendon Rd.
Cumberland, RI 02864

Trustees of Methodist Faith and Welfare Services
67 Howland Ave.
East Providence, RI 02814

Spring Villa Apartments
c/o Chris Jodie Realty
P.O. Box 957
Pawtucket, RI 02862

Charlesgate Square
c/o Davenport Associates, Inc.
15 Westminister St.
Providence, RI 02903

Charles Place
460 Charles St.
Providence, RI 02904

Huntington Towers
Benedict St.
Providence, RI

Olney Tower
One Valley St.
Providence, RI 02907

Parks Place
9 Parkis Ave.
Providence, RI 02907

Waterview Apartments
c/o Urban Housing Corp.
170 Westminister St.
Providence, RI 02903

SOUTH CAROLINA

Episcopal Diocesan Housing
175 Market St.
Charleston, SC 29401

Christopher Towers
1805 Devine St.
Columbia, SC 29201

Finley House
2100 Blossom St.
Columbia, SC 29205

SOUTH DAKOTA

Morning Manor
Alcester, SD 57001

Chamberlain Home for the Elderly
16th Ave. & Main St.
Chamberlain, SD 57325

Kingsbury Memorial Manor
Lloyd & Walters Ave.
Lake Preston, SD 57249

Wesley Acres
1115 W. Havens Ave.
Mitchell, SD 57301

Eastview Apartments
3400 E. 11th St.
Sioux Falls, SD 57103

Luther Manor
38th & Lake Ave, South
Sioux Falls, SD 57105

Pioneer Memorial Manor
930 Tenth St.
Spearfish, SD 57783

TENNESSEE

Jaycee Tower 2
Gateway at W. Ninth St.
Chattanooga, TN 37402

St. Barnabas Apartments Inc.
307 W. Seventh St.
Chattanooga, TN 37407

The Towers
500 W. Ninth St.
Chattanooga, TN 37402

Cleveland Towers
c/o North Cleveland Church of God
335 11th St., NE
Cleveland, TN 37311

Appalachian Christian Village
2012 Sherwood Dr.
Johnson City, TN 37601

Christian Home for the Aged
2012 Sherwood Dr.
Johnson City, TN 37601

Crestridge Apartments
Longview Road, NW
Knoxville, TN 37919

Presbyterian Homes of Tennessee
2829 Kingston Pike
Knoxville, TN 37919

Town View Towers
Townview Drive
Knoxville, TN 37915

Asbury Acres
Sevierville Pike, US 411
Maryville, TN 37801

Ascension Towers
961 Getwell Road
Memphis, TN 38111

Lutheran Towers
274 Highland Street
Memphis, TN 38111

Wesley Highland Towers
400 S. Highland
P.O. Box 11601
Memphis, TN 38111

Chippington Tower
Berkley Dr.
Nashville, TN

Greenhills Apartments
2209 Abbott Martin Rd.
Nashville, TN 37215

Leah Rose Senior Citizens
1900 Acklen Ave.
Nashville, TN 37212

Presbyterian Apartment, Inc.
115 Woodmont Blvd.
Nashville, TN 37205

Trevecca Towers
60 Lester Ave.
Nashville, TN 37210

Trevecca Towers No. 2
60 Lester Ave.
Nashville, TN 37210

Wedgewood Towers
12th Ave. S., at Wedgewood
Nashville, TN

TEXAS

Abilene Manor
302 N. Cypress St.
Abilene, TX 79601

Abilene North Manor
Willis and Vogel
Abilene, TX 79601

Arlington Villa
2601 Randol Mill Rd.
Arlington, TX 76010

Rebekah Baines Johnson Center
21 Waller St.
Austin, TX 78702

St. James House of Baytown, Inc.
Baker Rd.
Baytown, TX 77520

Crestview, Inc.
505-A E. 27th St.
Bryan, TX 77801

Casa de Oro Apartments
c/o First Assembly of God Church
3401 S. Alameda
Corpus Christi, TX 78412

"4600 Ocean Drive"
Corpus Christi, TX 78412

The Briarwood
1200-1300 Williams Drive
Corpus Christi, TX 78411

Autumn Leaves, Inc.
1010 Emerald Isle
Dallas, TX 75218

Blanton Gardens
4829 W. Lawther Dr.
Dallas, TX 75218

Dorchester House
911 St. Joseph St.
Dallas, TX 75216

Forest Dale Apartments
11851 High Dale
Dallas, TX 75216

Presbyterian Village, Inc.
550 Ann Arbor
Dallas, TX 75216

Pythian Manor
2719 E. Illinois
Dallas, TX 75216

The Fairmont
3500 Fairmont St.
Dallas, TX 75219

Tyler Street Manor
922 W. Ninth St.
Dallas, TX 75208

Wedgewood
Wedglea Dr.
Dallas, TX 75211

Fairhaven
2400 Bell Ave.
Denton, TX 76201

Christian Homes, Inc.
4600 Boat Club Rd.
Fort Worth, TX 76135

Normandale Place
8713 S. Normandale St.
Fort Worth, TX 76116

Wesleyan Homes, Inc.
Twelfth St. at Church
Georgetown, TX 78626

Clarewood House
7400 Clarewood Dr.
Houston, TX 77036

Heights Towers
P.O. Box 7417
Houston, TX 77008

Independence Hall
Airline Dr. at Burress St.
Houston, TX 77022

McCardell Square
2801 Conti St.
Houston, TX 77020

Woodland Christian Towers
607 E. Rogers St.
Houston, TX 77022

Hilltop Village
P.O. Box 671
Kerrville, TX 78028

St. Francis Village
Lake Benbrook, TX 76126

Golden Age Homes, Inc.
P.O. Box 870
Lockhart, TX 78644

Homestead Apartments
5401 56th St.
Lubbock, TX 79414

Westlake Apartments
2601 York Ave.
Lubbock, TX 79407

Midland Presbyterian Homes
Illinois and Kessler
Midland, TX 79701

First Christian Tower Apartments.
813 W. Eighth St.
Plainview, TX 79072

Rio Concho Manor
401 Rio Concho Dr.
San Angelo, TX 76903

Granada Hotel
311 S. St. Mary's St.
San Antonio, TX 78204

Morningside Manor, Inc.
602 Babcock Rd.
San Antonio, TX 78201

Walnut Manor
4718 Camino Dorado
San Antonio, TX 78233

Wedgewood Apartments
6701 Blanco Rd.
San Antonio, TX 78216

Regis Hotel
400 Austin St.
Waco, TX 76701

Stillwell Memorial Residence
Lake Air
Waco, TX 76710

Wesley Manor
P.O. Box 114
Weslaco, TX 78596

UTAH

Fellowship Manor
2334 Monroe Blvd.
Ogden, UT 84401

Alben Apartments
1810 S. Main St.
Salt Lake City, UT 84115

Friendship Manor
1559 S. 15th St., E.
Salt Lake City, UT 84105

Wasatch Manor
525 S. Second St., E.
Salt Lake City, UT 84102

VERMONT

Vernon Retirement Home
Vernon Advent Christian Home, Inc.
Vernon, Vermont 05354

VIRGINIA

Vinson Hall
6251 Old Dominion Dr.
McLean, VA 22101

Cogic Memorial Home for the Elderly
740 Goff St.
Norfolk, VA 23504

Lakewood Plaza
c/o Lakewood Plaza Associates
P.O. Box 12612
Norfolk, VA 23502

The John Knox Home
Colonial Ave. at Princess Ann Rd.
Norfolk, VA

Fellowship Home
11450 N. Shore Dr.
Reston, VA 22070

Interfaith Housing
800 North H St.
Richmond, VA 47374

Friendship Manor
c/o 3312 Oakland Blvd.
Roanoke, VA 24012

Shenandoah Homes, Inc.
5300 Hawthorne Rd., NW
Roanoke, VA 24012

WASHINGTON

Deer Park Apartments
c/o Ericks Realty, Box E
Deer Park, WA 99006

Wesley Terrace
816 S. 216th St.
Des Moines, WA 98188

Cottonwood Spring
c/o N.A. Medley
21636 SE 20th
Issaquah, WA 98027

Campus Towers
1767 20th St.
Longview, WA 98632

Bayview Manor
11 W. Aloha St.
Seattle, WA 98118

Council House
1501 17th Ave.
Seattle, WA 98144

Four Freedoms House of Seattle
747 N. 145th St.
Seattle, WA

Hilltop House
1005 Terrace St.
Seattle, WA 98104

Kawabe Memorial House
221 18th Ave. S.
Seattle, WA 98144

Lutheran Retirement Home of Greater
  Seattle, Inc.
6720 E. Green Lake Way, N.
Seattle, WA 98103

Norse Home, Inc.
5311 Phinney Ave., N.
Seattle, WA 98103

Northhaven, Inc.
11045 Eighth Ave., NE
Seattle, WA 98125

Park Shore
c/o Presbyterian Ministries Inc.
1630 43rd Ave., E.
Seattle, WA

The Camelia House
1357-23-31 32nd Ave., NE
Seattle, WA

Theodora Home
6559 35th St., NE
Seattle, WA 98105

Cathedral Plaza
W. 1023 Riverside Ave.
Spokane, WA

Hamilton House
E. 902 Boone Ave.
Spokane, WA 99202

Pines Village
N. 512 Pines Rd.
Spokane, WA 99206

Regal Village
c/o Robert Moe
508 Paulsen Building
Spokane, WA 99201

Ritzville Apartments 2
c/o A&F Development
915 W. Second
Spokane, WA 99204

Riverview Lutheran Home
1801 Upright Dr., E.
Spokane, WA 99207

Rockwood Manor
c/o Spokane Methodist Homes, Inc.
2903 E. 25th Ave.
Spokane, WA 99203

Golden Opportunity Living
  Development
S. 18th & Union
Tacoma, WA 98405

Harborview Properties, Inc.
919 Fawcett Ave., S.
Tacoma, WA 98402

Smith Towers
515 Washington St.
Vancouver, WA 98650

Brookhaven
130 Bryant Ave.
Walla Walla, WA 99362

Mike Foye Home
Seventh & Alder Sts.
Walla Walla, WA 99362

Warm Beach Manor
Route 1, Box 120
Warm Beach, WA

Wenatchee Immanuel Baptist Homes
512 Terminal St.
Wenatchee, WA 98801

Yakima First Baptist Homes
515 E. Yakima Ave.
Yakima, WA 98901

WEST VIRGINIA

West Virginia Homes, Inc.
23 Brooks St.
Charleston, WV 25301

Friendship Homes
P.O. Box 75
Morgantown, WV 26505

Windsor Hotel
Main St. at 12th St.
Wheeling, WV 26003

16
In-Home Services

Living in their own homes is a great desire of many older people. In-home services can help make this possible. Some older persons with chronic conditions need regular, continuing help with preparing meals, keeping the house tidy, and personal grooming. For others, help is needed only temporarily; for example, while recovering from an illness or while the person who usually gives care is unable to do so.

Many older people may be quite able to handle normal household tasks, but need help with heavier chores such as washing walls, moving furniture, cleaning gutters, and taking down storm windows. Accidents that permanently disable people often occur because homes lack minor necessary repairs.

Homemaker-Home Health Aide Services

Homemaker service in many communities provides an alternative to institutionalization for individuals in need of personal assistance. Usually sponsored or coordinated by a visiting nurse association, welfare department, or other social agency, Homemaker service can be useful to all persons without regard to income, social status, or other arbitrary limitation.

A Homemaker is usually a mature woman with skills in home management and instinctive understanding of human behavior. She usually has some basic training in simple home care of the sick, but she is not a substitute for professional personnel such as a nurse or social worker. Neither is she a maid.

With professional supervision by nurses or social workers, Homemakers have helped many individuals to remain in familiar home surroundings. Even where an older person does not live alone, a Homemaker's services can lessen the stress on the person's usual caretaker, thereby avoiding unnecessary institutionalization and making life happier for the whole family.

Home Health Aides are paraprofessionals who meet a variety of out-of-hospital health needs. They are sometimes part of Homemaker service personnel or part of health-service teams. Before Medicare was passed, very few health insurance programs provided coverage for home health services and there were relatively few Homemaker-Home Health Aide agencies. By 1970, however, 2,300 home health agencies had qualified to participate in the Medicare program. Studies indicate that physicians and patients who use Homemaker-Home Health services like them. Most professionals agree that there should be more such agencies offering a greater variety of in-home services.

Because a Homemaker-Home Health Aide is likely to be called into a home in time of crisis, and frequently will be substituting her judgment for that of the older person in her care, the training, reliability, and basic common sense of the worker must be assured by the sponsor of the service.

Many agencies and independent groups provide Homemaker-Home Health Aide service. Any such service should be officially recognized by local health and welfare councils, visiting nurse associations, state welfare or social-service departments, and state and local health departments.

The National Council of Homemaker-Home Health Aide Services, Inc. is presently developing accreditation standards for Homemaker-Home Health Aide agencies.

Other Home Services

Many communities have devised other organized ways to help older people to care for themselves and their households.

Earlham, Iowa, has shown that a small rural town can successfully provide home services economically to its senior citizens. Since 1963, the Earlham Care Program has provided Homemakers to help with cleaning and cooking, and handymen to replace light bulbs, mow lawns, make small repairs, and put up storm windows for the winter.

In Washington state, STEP (Service to Elderly Persons) coordinates a program in which teenagers perform heavy household and gardening tasks. They move furniture, wash walls, mow lawns, spade gardens, and help with other lifting chores.

Elder-Care, one of the SOS programs (Senior Opportunities and Services) funded by the Office of Economic Opportunity, includes housecleaning, marketing, meal preparation, and home repairs in its neighborhood service system for senior citizens in Jasper, Alabama. Older persons employed by the Community Action Agency in Jasper provide these services.

Community Activities for Senior Arkansans (CASA), sponsored by the Farmer's Union and funded by AOA and the U.S. Department of Labor, used local senior citizens to provide in-home services. They repaired screens, steps, and porches; brought in wood for a blind man; and cooked for the sick. Aides said they gained as much from this project as the people they helped.

Repairs-on-Wheels is a volunteer service in Westmoreland County, Pennsylvania. Minor repairs are made to the homes of senior citizens who are not physically able to do it themselves. No federal or state funds are used.

When institutionalization can be avoided, the social benefits to both the individual and the community are enormous. While precise figures on alternative costs are not available from most programs, the State of Nevada, which analyzed its costs after 2 years of Homemaker service, states that its department of welfare saved over $43,000 the first year of operation and $65,000 the second year. It realized significant savings even for clients who received extremely high amounts of service. For instance, one woman was maintained in her own home at a total cost of $5,314.48. The alternative — nursing-home care — would have cost $8,400.

New Jersey and Wisconsin have also analyzed the cost of Homemaker service and found substantial savings over alternative care costs. (See Home Health Agencies, Chapter 13; Homemaker-Home Health Aides, Chapter 14.)

17
Legal Services

The Legal Services Corporation is a private corporation established and funded by Congress to provide legal assistance to the poor. In addition to the assistance provided for the elderly by legal services programs in general, the corporation funds the National Senior Citizens Law Center in Los Angeles, which provides general legal services directly to elderly citizens. The address of the law center follows:

National Senior Citizens Law Center
1709 W. Eighth Street
Los Angeles, CA 90017
(213) 483-3990
Contact: Paul Nathanson, Executive Director

The Corporation also finances the Council of Elders in Boston, Legal Services for the Elderly Poor in New York, and the Senior Citizens Project of California Rural Legal Assistance in San Francisco.

This Chapter contains a list of the Legal Services' National Research and Technical Assistance Centers and the regional legal services offices of the National Senior Citizens Law Center.

LEGAL SERVICES

NATIONAL RESEARCH & TECHNICAL ASSISTANCE CENTERS

National Housing & Economic
 Development Law Project
Earl Warren Legal Institute
University of California
2313 Warring St.
Berkeley, CA 94704
(415) 642-2826

National Health Law Program
10995 Le Conte Ave.
Los Angeles, CA 90024
(213) 825-7601

National Senior Citizens Law Center
1709 W. Eighth St.
Los Angeles, CA 90017
(213) 483-3990

Youth Law Center
Western States Project
693 Mission St.
Seventh Floor
San Francisco, CA 94105
(415) 495-6420

Indian Law Backup Center
Native American Rights Fund
1506 Broadway
Boulder, CO 80302
(303) 447-8760

Legal Action Support Project
Bureau of Social Science Research
1990 M Street, NW
Washington, DC 20036
(202) 223-4300

Legal Services Training Program
Columbus School of Law
Catholic University of America
Washington, DC 20017
(202) 832-3900

Mental Disability Legal Resource
 Center
ABA 1800 M Street, NW
Washington, DC 20036
(202) 331-2240

Migrant Legal Action Program
1910 K St., NW
Washington, DC 20006
(202) 785-2475

National Health Law Program
2000 P St., NW
Washington, DC 20036
(202) 452-8050

National Housing & Economic Development Law Project
2000 P St., NW
Washington, DC 20036
(202) 452-8050

National Legal Aid and Defender
 Association
2100 M St., NW
Washington, DC 20037
(202) 452-0620

National Paralegal Institute
2000 P St., NW
Washington, DC 20036
(202) 872-0655

National Resource Center on Correctional Law & Legal Services
1705 De Sales St., NW
Washington, DC 20036
(202) 331-2290

Technical Assistance Project
National Legal Aid & Defender Assn.
2100 M St., NW
Washington, DC 20037
(202) 452-0620

National Clearinghouse for Legal Services
500 N. Michigan Ave.
Chicago, IL 60611
(312) 943-2866

National Consumer Law Center, Inc.
11 Beacon St.
Boston, MA 02108
(617) 523-8010

Harvard Center for Law & Education
14 Appian Way
Larsen Hall
Cambridge, MA 02138

National Juvenile Law Center
St. Louis University School of Law
3642 Lindell Blvd.
St. Louis, MO 63108
(314) 533-8868

Center on Social Welfare Policy & Law
95 Madison Ave.
New York, NY 10016
(212) 679-3709

National Employment Law Project
423 W. 118th St.
New York, NY 10027
(212) 866-8591

REGIONAL LEGAL SERVICE OFFICES

REGION I (Connecticut, Maine, Massachusetts, New Hampshire, Rhode Island, Vermont)
Legal Services Corp.
Boston Regional Office
11 Beacon St.
Boston, MA 02108
(617) 223-4093

REGION II (New York, Puerto Rico, Virgin Islands)
Legal Services Corp.
New York Regional Office
10 E. 40th St.
New York, NY 10016
(212) 826-5745

REGION III (Delaware, District of Columbia, Maryland, Pennsylvania, New Jersey)
Legal Services Corp.
Philadelphia Regional Office
101 N. 33rd St.
Philadelphia, Pennsylvania 19104
(215) 596-6104

REGION IV (Michigan, Ohio, Virginia, West Virginia)
Until a regional office location is named, legal services offices in Michigan and Ohio are temporarily assigned to Region V, and offices in Virginia and West Virginia are temporarily assigned to Region III.

REGION V (Illinois, Indiana, Iowa, Kansas, Minnesota, Missouri, Nebraska, North Dakota, South Dakota, Wisconsin)
Legal Services Corp.
Chicago Regional Office
310 South Michigan Ave.
Chicago, IL 60604
(312) 353-0350

REGION VI (Alabama, Arkansas, Florida, Georgia, Kentucky, Louisiana, Mississippi, North Carolina, South Carolina, Tennessee)
Legal Services Corp.
Atlanta Regional Office
615 Peachtree St., NE
Atlanta, GA 30308
(404) 526-3049

REGION VII (Arizona, Colorado, New Mexico, Oklahoma, Texas, Utah)
Legal Services Corp.
Denver Regional Office
209 16th St.
Denver, CO 80202
(303) 327-3306

REGION VIII (California, Nevada)
Legal Services Corp.
San Francisco Regional Office
690 Market St.
San Francisco, CA 94104
(415) 556-6952

REGION IX (Alaska, Hawaii, Idaho, Micronesia, Montana, Oregon, Washington, and Wyoming)
Legal Services Corp
Seattle Regional Office
1321 Second Ave.
Seattle, WA 98101
(206) 442-0593

OFFICE OF LEGAL SERVICES CORP.

ALABAMA

Legal Aid Society of Birmingham
713 N. 18th St.
Birmingham, AL 35203
(205) 322-6665
Contact: Marvin Campbell

Legal Aid Society of Madison County
102 Clinton Ave., W.
Huntsville, AL 35801
(205) 536-9645
Contact: J. Norman Bradley, Jr.

ALASKA

Alaska Legal Services Corp.
524 W. Sixth St.
Anchorage, AK 99501
(907) 272-9431
Contact: Loyette Goodell

ARIZONA

Pinal and Gila Counties Legal Aid Society
115 S. Main St.
Coolidge, AZ 85228
(602) 723-5419
Contact: J. Warren Wright

Coconino County Legal Aid
19 E. Phoenix St.
Flagstaff, AZ 86001
(602) 774-0653
Contact: Douglas Meiklejohn

Maricopa County Legal Aid Society
Maricopa County Migrant Legal Services
Farmworker Division
1831 W. Buckeye Rd.
Phoenix, AZ 85007
(602) 254-6121
Contact: Martin Solomon

Papago Legal Services
P.O. Box 246
Sells, AZ 85634
(602) 383-2221
Contact: Larry Garcia

Legal Aid Society of the Pima County Bar Association
377 S. Meyer
Tucson, AZ 85701
(602) 623-6260
Contact: David M. Cherry

DNA – People's Legal Services, Inc.
P.O. Box 306
Window Rock, AZ 86515
(602) 871-4151
Contact: Peterson Zah

ARKANSAS

Legal Aid Bureau of Pulaski County, Inc.
1520 Broadway
Little Rock, AR 72202
(501) 376-3423
Contact: William H. Howell

Jackson County Legal Services Program
P.O. Box 623
Newport, AR 72112
(501) 523-2312
Contact: Robert B. Lamb

CALIFORNIA

Berkeley Neighborhood Legal Services
1810 Sixth St.
Berkeley, CA 94710
(415) 841-9274
Contact: Robert L. Valencia

National Housing & Economic Development Law Project
University of California School of Law
Earl Warren St.
Berkeley, CA 94704
(415) 642-2826
Contact: Alvin Hirshen (Housing Section)
Arthur Blaustein (Economic Section)

Greater Bakersfield Legal Assistance, Inc.
703 Sumner St.
Bakersfield, CA 93305
(805) 325-5943
Contact: Richard G. Fathy

Southeast Legal Aid Center
1331 E. Compton Blvd.
Compton, CA 90221
(213) 638-6194
Contact: Randall Lyons

Fresno County Legal Services, Inc.
1221 Fulton Mall
Fresno, CA 93721
(209) 485-9880
Contact: Brett Dorian

The Legal Aid Foundation of Long Beach
4790 E. Pacific Highway
Long Beach, CA 90804
(213) 434-7421
Contact: Toby J. Rothschild

Legal Aid Foundation of Los Angeles
1550 W. Eighth St.
Los Angeles, CA 90017
(213) 487-3310
Contact: Charles E. Jones

National Health Law Program
10995 Le Conte Ave.
Los Angeles, CA 90024
(213) 825-7601
Contact: Stanton J. Price

National Senior Citizens Center
1709 W. Eighth St.
Los Angeles, CA 90017
(213) 483-3990
Contact: Paul S. Nathanson

Western Center on Law and Poverty
1709 W. Eighth St.
Los Angeles, CA 90017
(213) 483-1491
Contact: Daniel M. Luevano

Merced Legal Services Association
1812 L St.
P.O. Box 1310
Merced, CA 95340
(209) 723-5466
Contact: Eleanor M. Chassey

Stanislaus County Legal Assistance, Inc.
925 J St.
P.O. Box 3291
Modesto, CA 95353
(209) 524-6212
Contact: Lanny Sundell

Napa County Legal Assistance Agency
1795 Third St.
Napa, CA 94558
(707) 255-4933
Contact: Larry E. Mowinckel

California Indian Legal Services, Inc.
477 15th St.
Oakland, CA 94612
(415) 465-0320
Contact: George Forman

Legal Aid Society of Alameda County
1815 Telegraph Ave.
Oakland, CA 94612
(415) 451-9261
Contact: Clifford C. Sweet

Legal Aid Association of Ventura County
P.O. Box 259
631 Cooper Rd.
Oxnard, CA 93030
(805) 483-2417
Contact: Richard A. Weinstock

San Fernando Valley Neighborhood Legal Services
13327 Van Nuys Blvd.
Pacoima, CA 91331
(213) 896-5211
Contact: Mrs. Aviva K. Bobb

Legal Aid Society of Pasadena
Citizens Bank Building
Pasadena, CA 91101
(213) 795-3233
Contact: Frederick T. Kamminga

Shasta County Legal Aid Society
1370 West St.
Redding, CA 96001
(916) 241-3565
Contact: Wilson Curle

Legal Aid Society of San Mateo County
2221 Broadway
Redwood City, CA 94063
(415) 365-8411
Contact: Peter Reid

Contra Costa Legal Services Foundation
337 Tenth St.
Richmond, CA 94801
(415) 233-9954
Contact: Eugene M. Swann

Community Legal Services Riverside County
3615 Main St.
Riverside, CA 92501
(714) 683-7108
Contact: William D. Schuetz

Legal Aid Society of Sacramento County
1235 A St.
Sacramento, CA 95814
(916) 444-6760
Contact: Don Greisman

Legal Aid Society of San Diego, Inc.
Granger Building
964 Fifth Ave.
San Diego, CA 92101
(714) 232-4725
Contact: Gregory Knoll

California Rural Legal Assistance
1212 Market St.
San Francisco, CA 94102
(415) 864-2752
Contact: Richard Baca

San Francisco Neighborhood Legal Assistance Foundation
1095 Market St.
San Francisco, CA 94103
(415) 626-3811
Contact: Thomas J. Mack

Youth Law Center
693 Mission St.
San Francisco, CA 94105
(415) 495-6420
Contact: Peter B. Sandman

Community Legal Services
210 S. First St.
San Jose, CA 95103
(408) 998-5200
Contact: Stephen Manley

Legal Aid Society of Marin County
710 C Street
San Rafael, CA 94901
(415) 454-8085
Contact: Richard A. Hirsch

Legal Aid Society of Orange County
1932 W. 17th St.
Santa Ana, CA 92706
(714) 835-8806
Contact: John P. McDonald

Legal Aid Society of Monterey County
1070 Columbus Ave.
Seaside, CA 93955
(408) 394-8571
Contact: Patrick M. Ford

Legal Aid Society of San Joaquin
  County
110 N. San Joaquin St.
Stockton, CA 95202
(209) 466-0213
Contact: John W. Coyne

Tulare County Legal Services
  Association
147½ South K St.
Tulare, CA 93274
(209) 686-1763
Contact: John Higgins

Legal Services Foundation of
  Mendocino & Lake Counties
280 N. Oak St.
Ukiah, CA 95482
(707) 462-1471
Contact: Michael S. Zola

Solano County Legal Assistance
  Agency
902 Marin St.
Vallejo, CA 94950
(707) 643-0054
Contact: Armando A. Zavala

Legal Aid Society of Santa Cruz
  County, Inc.
P.O. Box 1166
Watsonville, CA 95076
(408) 724-2253
Contact: Peter Schilla

COLORADO

Indian Law Center
Native American Rights Fund
1506 Broadway
Boulder, CO 80302
(303) 447-8760
Contact: Bruce Green

Pikes Peak Legal Services
13 E. Vermijo
Colorado Springs, CO 80903
(303) 471-0380
Contact: Loa E. Bliss

Colorado Migrant Legal Services at
  Colorado Rural Legal Services,
  Inc.
1644 Emerson St.
Denver, CO 80218
(303) 831-7751
Contact: Theron P. O'Connor

Colorado Rural Legal Services, Inc.
1644 Emerson St.
Denver, CO 80218
(313) 831-7751
Contact: Arthur S. Lucero

Legal Aid Society of Metropolitan
  Denver
912 Broadway
Denver, CO 80203
(303) 573-9313
Contact: Max B. Rothman

Pueblo County Legal Services, Inc.
100 S. Main
Pueblo, CO 81003
(303) 545-6686
Contact: Albert G. Davis

CONNECTICUT

Neighborhood Legal Services, Inc.
524 Albany St.
Hartford, CT 06112
(203) 278-6850
Contact: Director

Neighborhood Legal Services, Inc.
Farmworkers Division
524 Albany St.
Hartford, CT 06112
(202) 278-6850
Contact: Alan Rom

Middlesex County Legal Assistance
  Association, Inc.
55 William St.
Middletown, CT 06457
(203) 347-7237
Contact: Richard F. Kelly

Legal Aid Bureau of New Britain, Inc.
111 Franklin Square
New Britain, CT 06050
(203) 225-8678
Contact: Elliot Ginsberg

New Haven Legal Assistance
  Association, Inc.
265 Church St.
New Haven, CT 06510
(203) 777-7601
Contact: Elizabeth R. Rindskopf

Legacy, Inc.
87 Main St.
Norwich, CT 06360
(203) 889-1365
Contact: Ralph U. Bergman

Fairfield County Legal Services, Inc.
342 Atlantic St.
Stamford, CT 06901
(203) 348-9216
Contact: Roger E. Koontz

Waterbury Legal Aid & Reference
  Service, Inc.
61 Field St.
Waterbury, CT 06702
(203) 756-8074
Contact: Norman Johnson

Tolland-Windham Legal Assistance
  Program, Inc.
746 Main St.
Willimantic, CT 06226
(203) 423-8425
Contact: Douglas M. Crockett

DELAWARE

Community Legal Aid Society, Inc.
204 W. Seventh St.
Wilmington, DE 19801
(302) 655-7351
Contact: Peter M. Siegel

DISTRICT OF COLUMBIA

Antioch School of Law
1624 Crescent Place, NW
Washington, DC 20009
(202) 265-9500
Contact: Mrs. Jean Camper Cahn

Legal Action Support Project
Bureau of Social Science Research, Inc.
1990 M St., NW
Washington, DC 20036
(202) 223-4300
Contact: Dr. Leonard H. Goodman

Legal Services Training Program
Columbus School of Law
Catholic University of America
Washington, DC 20064
(202) 832-3900
Contact: Richard E. Carter

Migrant Legal Action Program
1910 K St., NW
Washington, DC 20006
(800) 424-8800
Contact: Raphael Gomez

National Clients Council
1910 K St., NW
Washington, DC 20006
(202) 833-9434
Contact: Bernard Veney

National Legal Aid and Defender
  Association Management
  Assistance Project
2100 M St., NW
Washington, DC 20037
(202) 452-0620
Contact: Frank Jones

National Paralegal Institute
2000 P St., NW
Washington, DC 20036
(202) 872-0655
Contact: William Fry

National Senior Citizen's Law Center
910 17th St., NW
Washington, DC 20006
(202) 872-1404
Contact: James Lanigan

Neighborhood Legal Services Program
Barrister Building
635 F St., NW
Washington, DC 20004
(202) 628-9161
Contact: Willie Cook

Reginald Heber Smith Community
  Lawyer Fellowship Program
Harvard University·
1343 H St., NW
Washington, DC 20005
(202) 737-3755
Contact: Glenn E. Carr

Urban Institute
2100 M St., NW
Washington, DC 20037
(202) 223-1950
Contact: Joseph Wholey

FLORIDA

Volusia County Legal Services, Inc.
356 S. Beach St.
Daytona Beach, FL 32014
(904) 255-6573
Contact: Reginald Moore

Florida Rural Legal Services
51 N. Flagler
Homestead, FL 33030
(305) 248-5775
Contact: David Lillesand

Duval County Legal Aid Association, Inc.
205 E. Church St.
Jacksonville, FL 32202
(904) 356-8375
Contact: Paul C. Doyle

Legal Services of Greater Miami, Inc.
395 NW First St.
Miami, FL 33128
(305) 379-0822
Contact: Howard W. Dixon

Florida Legal Services, Inc.
308 E. Park Ave.
Tallahassee, FL 32301
(904) 222-5788
Contact: Robert Travis

Law, Inc. of Hillsborough County
1155 E. Cass
Tampa, FL 33602
(813) 223-2525
Contact: Julius L. Williams

GEORGIA

Atlanta Legal Aid Society, Inc.
153 Pryor St., SW
Atlanta, GA 30303
(404) 524-5811
Contact: Robert Dokson

Georgia Legal Services Program, Inc.
15 Peachtree St., NE
Atlanta, GA 30303
(404) 656-6021
Contact: John Cromartie

HAWAII

Legal Aid Society of Hawaii
1164 Bishop St.
Honolulu, HI 96817
(805) 536-4302
Contact: Anthony P. Locricchio

IDAHO

Idaho Legal Aid Services, Inc.
104½ S. Capitol Blvd.
Boise, ID 83702
(208) 345-0106
Contact: Warren Derbidge

ILLINOIS

Commerce Clearinghouse, Inc.
4025 W. Peterson
Chicago, IL 60646
(312) 267-9010
Contact: Robert C. Bartlett

Cook County Legal Assistance Foundation, Inc.
19 S. LaSalle St.
Chicago, IL 60603
(312) 263-2267
Contact: Kermit B. Coleman

Illinois Migrant Legal Assistance Project
Legal Assistance Foundation of Chicago
1212 N. Ashland
Chicago, IL 60622
(312) 489-6797
Contact: Bruce Goldsmith

Legal Assistance Foundation of Chicago
343 S. Dearborn St.
Chicago, IL 60604
(312) 922-5625
Contact: James Weill

National Clearinghouse for Legal Services, Inc.
500 N. Michigan Ave.
Chicago, IL 60611
(312) 943-2866
Contact: Mary Ader

Greater Peoria Legal Aid Society
100 Admans St.
Peoria, IL 61602
(309) 674-9831
Contact: John E. Carlson

Land of Lincoln Legal Assistance Foundation
516 E. Monroe
Springfield, IL 62701
(217) 544-7493
Contact: Martin Mendelsohn

Legal Referral Bureau of Lake County, Inc.
11 S. County St.
Waukegan, IL 60085
(312) 662-6925
Contact: Doug Grimes

INDIANA

Legal Aid of Fort Wayne, Inc.
402 E. Main St.
Fort Wayne, IN 46802
(219) 743-7351
Contact: Solomon Lowenstein

Legal Aid Society of Gary
31 E. Fifth Ave.
Gary, IN 46404
(219) 886-3161
Contact: Phyllis Senegal

Legal Services Organization of Indianapolis, Inc.
107 N. Pennsylvania
Indianapolis, IN 46202
(317) 639-4151
Contact: Norman P. Metzger

Legal Aid Society of Saint Joseph County, Inc.
204 S. William St.
South Bend, IN 46619
(219) 287-1056
Contact: Richard Hill

IOWA

Legal Aid Society of Polk County, Iowa
102 E. Grand Ave.
Des Moines, IA 50309
(515) 282-8375
Contact: Robert C. Oberbillig

Dubuque Area Legal Services Agency
630 Fischer Building
Dubuque, IA 52001
(319) 588-4655
Contact: Paul E. Kempter

Hawkeye Legal Service Society
225 Gilbert St.
Iowa City, IA 52240
(319) 351-6570
Contact: Thomas H. McMurray

Black Hawk County Legal Aid Society
708 First National Building
Waterloo, IA 50703
(319) 235-7008
Contact: Charles Hoffman

KANSAS

Wyandotte County Legal Aid Society, Inc.
907 N. Seventh St.
Kansas City, KS 66101
(913) 621-0200
Contact: Dwight Henderson

Legal Aid Society of Topeka, Inc.
121 E. Sixth St.
Topeka, KS 66603
(913) 354-8531
Contact: Roger L. McCollister

Legal Aid Society of Wichita, Inc.
104 S. Broadway
Wichita, KS 67202
(316) 265-9681

KENTUCKY

Legal Aid Society of Louisville
315 S. Fifth St.
Louisville, KY 40202
(502) 584-1254
Contact: Kurt Berggren

Northeast Kentucky Legal Services Program, Inc.
320 E. Main St.
Morehead, KY 40351
(606) 784-8921
Contact: William B. Maines

Appalachian Research and Defense
  Fund
P.O. Box 152
Prestonsburg, KY 41653
(606) 886-3877
Contact: John Rosenberg

LOUISIANA

Legal Aid Society of Baton Rouge
2303 Government St.
Baton Rouge, LA 70806
(504) 387-5173
Contact: Howard Bushey

Southwest Louisiana Legal Services
  Society, Inc.
2225 Moeling St.
P.O. Box 3002
Lake Charles, LA 70601
(318) 436-3308
Contact: Stephen A. Berniard

New Orleans Legal Assistance Corp.
226 Carondelet St.
New Orleans, LA 70130
(504) 523-1297
Contact: Galen Brown

Caddo-Bossier Legal Aid Society
508 Ricou-Brewster Building
Shreveport, LA 71101
(318) 222-7186
Contact: J. Waddy Tucker

Delta Legal Services, Inc.
506 E. Green St.
Tallulah, LA 71282
(318) 574-3271
Contact: George Spencer

MAINE

Pine Tree Legal Assistance, Inc.
178 Middle St.
Portland, ME 04111
(207) 774-8211
Contact: Susan Calkins

MARYLAND

Legal Aid Bureau
341 N. Calvert St.
Baltimore, MD 21202
(301) 539-5340
Contact: Charles Dorsey

MASSACHUSETTS

Boston Legal Assistance Project
27 School
Boston, MA 02108
(617) 742-8930
Contact: William J. McNally

Massachusetts Law Reform Institute
2 Park Square
Boston, MA 02116
(617) 482-0890
Contact: Allan G. Rodgers

National Consumer Law Center
One Court St.
Boston, MA 02108
(617) 523-8010
Contact: Mark Budnitz

Cambridge & Somerville Legal Services
24 Thorndike St.
Cambridge, MA 02139
(617) 492-5520
Contact: Allan Rader

Harvard Center for Law and Education
Harvard University
14 Appian Way
Cambridge, MA 02138
(617) 495-4666
Contact: Robert Pressman

North Suffolk Legal Assistance
  Association, Inc.
279 Broadway
Chelsea, MA 02150
(617) 884-7568
Contact: Allen H. Roffman

Legal Services for Cape Cod & Islands,
  Inc.
138 Winter St.
Hyannis, MA 02601
(617) 775-7021
Contact: James J. Wechsler

Merrimack Valley Legal Services, Inc.
45 Merrimack St.
Lowell, MA 01852
(617) 458-1465
Contact: Maxa Berid

Neighborhood Legal Services, Inc.
31 Exchange St.
Lynn, MA 01901
(617) 599-7730
Contact: David Kerman

Onboard Legal Services, Inc.
18 S. Water St.
New Bedford, MA 02744
(617) 996-8576
Contact: John M. Stellato

Council of Elders
280 Martin Luther King Jr. Blvd.
Roxbury, MA 02119
(617) 442-4000
Contact: John Green

New England Farmworkers Council
3502 Main St.
Springfield, MA 01107
(413) 736-4525
Contact: Bruce Young Candelaria

Western Massachusetts Legal Service,
  Inc.
791 State St.
Springfield, MA 01109
(413) 781-7814
Contact: Victor Geminiani

Central Massachusetts Legal Services,
  Inc.
306 Main St.
Worcester, MA 01608
(617) 752-3718
Contact: John J. Bush

MICHIGAN

Washtenaw County Legal Aid Society,
  Inc.
212 E. Huron St.
Ann Arbor, MI 48108
(313) 665-6181
Contact: Michael B. Bixby

Legal Aid Society of Calhoun County
37 Capital Ave., NE
Battle Creek, MI 49014
(616) 965-3951
Contact: William L. Coash

Michigan Migrant Legal Assistance
  Project, Inc.
102 S. Mechanic St.
Berrien Springs, MI 49103
(616) 471-2819
Contact: Richard Feferman

Michigan Legal Services, Inc.
220 Bagley Ave.
Detroit, MI 48226
(313) 964-4130
Contact: Alan W. Houseman

Wayne County Neighborhood Legal
  Services
2222 Woodward Ave.
Detroit, MI 48201
(313) 964-4610
Contact: James Jackson Jr.

Legal Services of Eastern Michigan
Genessee Bank Building
Flint, MI 48503
(313) 234-2621
Contact: Gary Kolb

Legal Aid Society of Grand Rapids
  & Kent County
1208 McKay Tower
Grand Rapids, MI 49502
(616) 451-2504
Contact: Robert Munroe

The Greater Lansing Legal Aid Bureau,
  Inc.
300 N. Washington Ave.
Lansing, MI 48933
(517) 484-7773

Macomb County Legal Aid Bureau
Macomb County Building
Mount Clemens, MI 48043
(313) 463-1597
Contact: Thomas L. Buller

Muskegon-Oceana Legal Aid Bureau,
  Inc.
427 W. Western
Muskegon, MI 49440
(616) 726-5085
Contact: Bruce Krueger

Oakland County Legal Aid Society
Connally's National Bank Building
10 W. Huron
Pontiac, MI 48058
(313) 332-9175
Contact: Mrs. Dorothy L. Cottrell

Berrien County Legal Services Bureau, Inc.
901 Port St.
St. Joseph, MI 49085
(616) 983-6363
Contact: Edward M. Yampolsky

Upper Peninsula Legal Services, Inc.
416 Ashmun St.
Sault St. Marie, MI 49783
(906) 632-3361
Contact: William J. James

MINNESOTA

Legal Aid Society of Minneapolis
501 Park Ave.
Minneapolis, MN 55415
(612) 332-1441

Legal Assistance of Ramsey County, Inc.
370 Selby St.
St. Paul, MN 55102
(612) 222-5863
Contact: Richard A. Kaplan

MISSISSIPPI

Coahoma Legal Aid, Inc.
130 Desoto Ave.
Clarksdale, MS 38614
(601) 627-7896
Contact: Carl Montgomery

Community Legal Services
413 S. President St.
Jackson, MS 39205
(601) 948-6752
Contact: Joe Ragland

North Mississippi Rural Legal Services
P.O. Box 826
Oxford, MS 38614
(601) 234-2918
Contact: Wilhelm Joseph

MISSOURI

Legal Aid & Defender Society of Greater Kansas City
15 W. Tenth St.
Suite 1113
Kansas City, MO 64105
(816) 474-6750

Legal Aid Society of the City & County of St. Louis
4030 Chouteau St.
St. Louis, MO 63110
(314) 533-3000
Contact: David Lander

National Juvenile Law Center
St. Louis University School of Law
3642 Lindell Blvd.
St. Louis, MO 63108
(314) 533-8868
Contact: Paul Piersma

MONTANA

Montana Legal Services Association
601 Power Block
Helena, MT 59601
(406) 442-9830
Contact: Neil Haight

NEBRASKA

Legal Aid Society of Lincoln, Inc.
800 Anderson Building
116 N. 12th St.
Lincoln, NB 68508
(402) 435-2161
Contact: David Piester

Legal Aid Society of Omaha/Council Bluffs, Inc.
700 Farnam Building
1613 Farnam St.
Omaha, NB 68102
(402) 348-1060
Contact: Ward R. Johnson

Panhandle Legal Services, Inc.
701 E. Overland
P.O. Box 605
Scottsbluff, NB 69361
(308) 632-4734
Contact: Donald E. Sanders

NEVADA

Clark County Legal Services Program
900 W. Bonanza
Las Vegas, NV 89106
(702) 648-6970
Contact: James O. Porter

Washoe County Legal Aid Society
150 N. Center St.
Reno, NV 89501
(702) 648-2695
Contact: Charles R. Zeh

NEW HAMPSHIRE

New Hampshire Legal Assistance
88 Hanover St.
Manchester, NH 03101
(603) 668-2900
Contact: George Charles Bruno

NEW JERSEY

Cape Atlantic Legal Services, Inc.
1421 Atlantic Ave.
Atlantic City, NJ 08401
(609) 348-4208
Contact: Charles M. Middlesworth, Jr.

Camden Regional Legal Services, Inc.
Point and Pearl Sts.
Camden, NJ 08102
(609) 964-2010
Contact: Barney Hamlin

Union County Legal Services Corp.
1034 E. Jersey St.
Elizabeth, NJ 07201
(201) 354-4340
Contact: Donald T. Smith

Bergen County Legal Services Association
53 Main St.
Hackensack, NJ 07601
(201) 487-2166
Contact: Richard S. Semel

Hudson County Legal Services Corp.
628 Newark Ave.
Jersey City, NJ 07306
(201) 792-6363
Contact: Timothy K. Madden

Essex-Newark Legal Services Project, Inc.
463 Central Ave.
Newark, NJ 07107
(201) 485-3800
Contact: Harris David

Newark Legal Services Project
Essex-Newark Legal Services Project, Inc.
449 Central Ave.
Newark, NJ 07107
(201) 484-4010
Contact: Clinton Lyons

Middlesex County Legal Services Corp.
335 George St.
New Brunswick, NJ 08901
(201) 745-9600
Contact: Melville D. Miller, Jr.

Essex Legal Services Project, Inc.
81 Main St.
Orange, NJ 07050
(201) 672-3838
Contact: Robert L. Doris, Jr.

Passaic County Legal Aid Society, Inc.
5 Colt St.
Paterson, NJ 07505
(201) 525-4068
Contact: Harold Hoffman

Somerset-Sussex Legal Services
60 Millstone Rd.
Somerset, NJ 08873
(201) 545-6243
Contact: Joseph Lipofsky

Ocean-Monmouth Legal Services
27 Washington St.
Toms River, NJ 08753
(201) 341-2727
Contact: Jane B. Cordo

Mercer County Legal Aid Society
440 E. State St.
Trenton, NJ 08608
(609) 695-6249
Contact: Alice A. Costello

NEW MEXICO

Legal Aid Society of Albuquerque, Inc.
1015 Tijeras, NW
Albuquerque, NM 87101
(505) 247-4158
Contact: Michael B. Browde

Sandoval County Legal Services, Inc.
602 Camino Del Pueblo
Bernalillo, NM 87004
(505) 867-2348
Contact: William Torrington

Northern New Mexico Legal Services
322 Montezuma St.
Sante Fe, NM 87501
(505) 758-2219
Contact: Albert V. Gonzales

Zuni Legal Aid & Defender Society
Pueblo of Zuni
P.O. Box 368
Zuni, NM 87327
(505) 782-4426
Contact: Bruce Boynton

NEW YORK

Legal Aid Society of Albany, Inc.
79 N. Pearl St.
Albany, NY 12207
(518) 462-6765
Contact: Lawrence F. Klepper

Orleans Legal Aid Bureau, Inc.
20-A E. Bank St.
Albion, NY 14411
(716) 589-5652
Contact: John Cebula

Broome Legal Assistance Corp.
30 Fayette St.
Binghampton, NY 13901
(607) 723-7966
Contact: Seymour Nathanson

Neighborhood Legal Services, Inc.
1490 Jefferson Ave.
Buffalo, NY 14204
(716) 883-3640
Contact: Marilyn Dixon-Zahm

Chautauqua County Legal Services, Inc.
307 Central Ave.
Dunkirk, NY 14048
(716) 366-3934
Contact: Terry C. Duro

Chemung County Neighborhood Legal Services, Inc.
403 E. Third St.
Elmira, NY 14901
(607) 734-1647
Contact: Thomas S. Dubel

Nassau County Law Services Committee, Inc.
285 Fulton Ave.
Hempstead, NY 11550
(516) 292-8100
Contact: Leonard S. Clark

Monroe County Legal Assistance Corp.
Mid-Hudson Valley Legal Services Project
34 South St.
Middletown, NY 10940
(914) 343-0831
Contact: William Crain

Center on Social Welfare Policy & Law
95 Madison Ave.
New York, NY 10016
(212) 679-3709
Contact: Henry A. Freedman

Community Action for Legal Services, Inc.
335 Broadway
New York, NY 10013
(212) 966-6600
Contact: Marttie Thompson

Legal Aid Society of Rockland County, Inc.
2 Congers Rd.
New York, NY 10956
(914) 634-3627
Contact: Douglas Good

Legal Services for the Elderly Poor
2095 Broadway
New York, NY 10023
(212) 595-1340
Contact: Jonathan A. Weiss

National Employment Law Project
423 W. 118th St.
New York, NY 10027
(212) 866-8591
Contact: Walker Thompson

Niagara County Legal Aid Society, Inc.
302 Portage Rd.
Niagara Falls, NY 14302
(716) 284-8831
Contact: William Loncto

Greater Upstate Law Project
80 W. Main St.
Rochester, NY 14614
(716) 454-6500
Contact: Steven L. Brown

Monroe County Legal Assistance Corp.
80 W. Main St.
Rochester, NY 14614
(716) 325-2520
Contact: David C. Levin

Onondaga Neighborhood Legal Services, Inc.
633 S. Warren
Syracuse, NY 13202
(315) 475-3127
Contact: Douglas A. Eldridge

Legal Aid Society of Oneida County, Inc.
505 Mayro Building
Utica, NY 13501
(315) 732-2131
Contact: Robert B. Salzman

Westchester Legal Services, Inc.
56 Grand St.
White Plains, NY 10601
(914) 761-9200
Contact: Norman B. Lichtenstein

NORTH CAROLINA

Legal Aid Society of Mecklenburg County
404 E. Trade St.
Charlotte, NC 28202
(704) 376-1608
Contact: Terence Roche

Durham Legal Aid Society
353 W. Main St.
Durham, NC 27702
(919) 688-6396
Contact: Denison Ray

Legal Aid of Forsyth County
202 W. Third St.
Winston-Salem, NC 27101
(919) 725-0836
Contact: Thorns Craven

NORTH DAKOTA

Society for Legal Aid
15 S. 21st St.
Fargo, ND 58102
(701) 232-4495
Contact: Maurice E. Garrison

North Dakota Legal Services, Inc.
P.O. Box 217
New Town, ND 58763
(701) 627-4719
Contact: Judith A. Atkinson

OHIO

Summit County Legal Aid Society
34 S. High St.
Akron, OH 44308
(216) 535-4191
Contact: Richard M. Landis

Ohio Migrant Legal Action
105 N. Main St.
Bowling Green, OH 43402
(419) 352-4625
Contact: Marvin H. Feingold

Stark County Legal Aid Society
306 Market Ave., N.
Canton, OH 44702
(216) 456-8361
Contact: Robert Wachunas

The Legal Aid Society of Cincinnati
2400 Reading Rd.
Cincinnati, OH 45202
(513) 241-9400
Contact: Terry Lawson

Legal Aid Society of Cleveland, Inc.
2108 Payne Ave.
Cleveland, OH 44114
(216) 861-6242
Contact: C. Lyonel Jones

Legal Aid & Defender Society of Columbus
241 S. High St.
Columbus, OH 43215
(614) 224-8374
Contact: Caroline Watts

Ohio State Legal Services Association
8 E. Broad St.
Columbus, OH 43215
(614) 221-2668
Contact: Franklin A. Martens

Legal Aid Society
117 S. Main St.
Dayton, OH 45402
(513) 228-8104
Contact: Christine Lobas Magee

Legal Aid Society of Lorain County, Inc.
401 Broad St.
Elyria, OH 44035
(216) 322-5116
Contact: Robert L. Leece

Butler County Legal Assistance Association
Rentschler Building
Hamilton, OH 45011
(513) 894-7664
Contact: Waren G. Bisdorf

Allen County Legal Services Association
311 E. Market St.
Lima, OH 45801
(419) 224-9070
Contact: David A. Little

Tuscarawas Valley Legal Services Association
151 N. Broadway
New Philadelphia, OH 44663
(216) 343-5012
Contact: John M. Smith

Licking County Legal Aid Society, Inc.
38 S. Third St.
Newark, OH 43055
(614) 345-0850
Contact: Kenneth B. Schumaker

Scioto County Legal Aid Association
1104 Kinney's Lane
Portsmouth, OH 45662
(614) 354-2508 or (614) 353-1607
Contact: Leonard Berkeley

Advocates for Basic Legal Equality (ABLE)
740 Spitzer Building
Toledo, OH 43604
(419) 255-0814
Contact: R. Michael Frank

Toledo Legal Aid Society
One Stranahan Square
Toledo, OH 43614
(419) 244-8345
Contact: Earl H. Staelin

Mahoning County Legal Assistance Association
804 Central Tower Building
Youngstown, OH 44503
(216) 744-3196
Contact: Thomas P. Lorden

OKLAHOMA

Southwest Oklahoma Legal Aid Council, Inc.
213 W. Walnut
Altus, OK 73521
(405) 482-7431
Contact: Suzanne Mollison

Delaware & Adair Counties Legal Services Program
P.O. Box 390
Jay, OK 74346
(918) 253-4980
Contact: Brad Scheer

The Legal Aid Society of Oklahoma County, Inc.
200 N. Harvey St.
Oklahoma City, OK 73102
(405) 272-9461
Contact: Stanley Foster

Tulsa County Legal Aid Society, Inc.
630 W. Seventh St.
Tulsa, OK 74127
(918) 584-3338
Contact: Byron S. Matthews

OREGON

Lane County Legal Aid Services, Inc.
1309 Willamette St.
Eugene, OR 97401
(503) 342-6056
Contact: Mervyn II. Loya

Legal Aid Service Multnomah Bar Association
310 SW Fourth Ave.
Portland, OR 97204
(503) 224-4086
Contact: Paul J. Kelly

Marion-Polk Legal Aid Service, Inc.
1244 State St.
Salem, OR 97301
(503) 581-5265
Contact: Michael Friel

PENNSYLVANIA

Delaware County Legal Assistance Association
410 Welsh St.
Chester, PA 19013
(215) 874-8421
Contact: David A. Scholl

Bucks County Legal Aid Society
95 E. State St.
Doylestown, PA 18901
(215) 345-6176
Contact: David Tilove

Pennsylvania Legal Services Center
112 Market St.
Harrisburg, PA 17101
(717) 787-2338
Contact: Rand Bragg

Cambria County Office of Legal Aid, Inc.
415 Main St.
Johnstown, PA 15901
(814) 536-8917
Contact: Edward R. Schellhammer

Central Pennsylvania Legal Services
53 N. Duke St.
Lancaster, PA 17602
(717) 397-4236
Contact: J. Richard Gray

Community Legal Services, Inc.
Juniper & Locust Sts.
Philadelphia, PA 19107
(215) 735-6101
Contact: Laurence M. Lavin

Neighborhood Legal Services Association
535 Fifth Ave.
Pittsburgh, PA 15219
(412) 281-1662
Contact: R. Stanton Wettick

Lackawanna County Legal Aid & Defender Association
129 N. Washington Ave.
Scranton, PA 18503
(717) 342-0184
Contact: Eugene F. Smith

Southwest Pennsylvania Legal Services
80 E. Beau St.
Washington, PA 15301
(412) 225-6170
Contact: Robert Brenner

Luzerne County Legal Services Association, Inc.
211 S. Main St.
Wilkes-Barre, PA 18701
(717) 825-8567
Contact: F. Charles Petrillo

PUERTO RICO

Puerto Rico Migrant Legal Services
Calle Hatillo No. 6
Hato Rey, PR 00928
(809) 765-5354
Contact: Salvadore Tio

San Juan Legal Services, Inc.
Edificio Ballester Office No. 301
Paseo Covadonga, Puerto de Tierra
San Juan, PR 00902
(809) 724-3521
Contact: Miguel E. Herrero Frank

RHODE ISLAND

Rhode Island Legal Services, Inc.
56 Pine St.
Providence, RI 02903
(401) 274-2652
Contact: John J. Donohue

SOUTH CAROLINA

Neighborhood Legal Assistance
  Program
119 Spring St.
Charleston, SC 29403
(803) 722-8474
Contact: David B. Richardson

Neighborhood Legal Assistance
  Program
119 Spring St.
Charleston, SC 29403
(803) 722-0107
Contact: Cleveland Stevens

Legal Aid Service Agency
1519 Gervais St.
P.O. Box 1056
Columbia, SC 29202
(803) 779-3310
Contact: Edward A. Harter, Jr.

Legal Services Agency of Greenville
  County, Inc.
135 S. Main St.
Greenville, SC 29601
(803) 233-2779
Contact: Willie T. Smith, Jr.

SOUTH DAKOTA

South Dakota Legal Services
P.O. Box 148
Mission, SD 57555
(605) 856-4444
Contact: Terry L. Pechota

Black Hills Legal Services, Inc.
502 Omaha St.
Rapid City, SD 57701
(605) 342-7171
Contact: Michael A. Wolff

TENNESSEE

Legal Aid Society of Chattanooga
Georgia Ave. at McCallie
Chattanooga, TN 37402
(615) 266-8188
Contact: James Bradley

Legal Aid Clinic
University of Tennessee Law School
1505 W. Cumberland Ave.
Knoxville, TN 37902
(615) 974-2331
Contact: Gerald Becker

Memphis & Shelby County Legal
  Services
46 N. Third St.
Memphis, TN 38103
(901) 526-5132
Contact: A.C. Wharton

Legal Services of Nashville, Inc.
607 Sudekum Building
Nashville, TN 37219
(615) 244-6317
Contact: Walter Cotten Kurtz

TEXAS

Legal Aid & Defenders Society of
  Travis County
1713 E. Sixth St.
Austin, TX 78702
(512) 476-6321
Contact: Paul Rich

Legal Aid Society of Nueces County
921 N. Chaparral St.
Corpus Christi, TX 78401
(512) 883-8223
Contact: Gilbert Rodriguez

Dallas Legal Services Foundation, Inc.
912 Commerce St.
Dallas, TX 75202
(214) 742-1631
Contact: Sylvia Demarest

Texas Rural Legal Aid, Inc.
216 N. Closner
Edinburg, TX 78539
(512) 787-9978
Contact: David Hall

El Paso Legal Assistance Society
109 N. Oregon St.
El Paso, TX 79901
(915) 544-3022
Contact: Israel Galinao

Tarrant County Legal Aid Foundation
201 E. Belknap
Ft. Worth, TX 76102
(817) 334-1435
Contact: Robert Byrd

Houston Legal Foundation
609 Fannin
Houston, TX 77002
(713) 225-0321
Contact: Henry W. McCormick

Laredo Legal Aid Society, Inc.
1104 Victoria
Laredo, TX 78040
(512) 722-7581
Contact: A.A. Figueroa, Jr.

Bexar County Legal Aid Association
203 W. Nueva St.
San Antonio, TX 78207
(817) 227-0111
Contact: Frank Christian

Waco-McLennan County Legal Aid
210 W. Waco Dr.
Waco, TX 76707
(817) 752-5596
Contact: James Lamb

UTAH

Weber County Legal Aid Services, Inc.
453 24th St.
Ogden, UT 84401
(801) 392-9431
Contact: Paul D. Vernieu

Salt Lake County Bar Legal Services
216 E. Fifth, S.
Salt Lake City, UT 84111
(801) 328-8891
Contact: E. Barney Gesas

VERMONT

Vermont Legal Aid, Inc.
192 Bank St.
Burlington, VT 05401
(802) 863-2781
Contact: John A. Dooley, III

VIRGINIA

Charlottesville-Albermarle Legal Aid
  Society
420 Third St., NE
Charlottesville, VA 22901
(804) 293-3109, -5131
Contact: David M. Levy

Smyth-Bland Legal Aid Society
204 W. Main St.
Marion, VA 24354
(804) 783-8300
Contact: Richard Money

Neighborhood Legal Aid Society
300 E. Clay St.
Richmond, VA 23241
(804) 643-0218
Contact: John Levy

Legal Aid Society of Roanoke Valley
702 Shenandoah Ave., NW
Roanoke, VA 24016
(703) 344-2088
Contact: Henry Woodward

WASHINGTON

Northwest Washington Legal Services
1712½ Hewitt Ave.
Everett, WA 98201
(206) 258-2681
Contact: Steven Randels

Seattle-King County Legal Aid Bureau
618 Second Ave.
Seattle, WA 98104
(206) 464-5911
Contact: Greg Dallaire

Spokane County Legal Services
W. 246 Riverside Ave.
Spokane, WA 99201
(509) 838-3671
Contact: Norman Rosenberg

Pierce County Legal Assistance
  Foundation
744 Market St.
Tocoma, WA 98402
(206) 572-4343
Contact: Thomas G. Bruce

WEST VIRGINIA

Appalachian Research & Defense Fund
1116-B Kanawha Blvd., E.
Charleston, WV 25301
(304) 344-9687
Contact: Milton Dale

Legal Aid Society of Charleston
1026 Quarrier St.
Charleston, WV 25301
(304) 343-4481
Contact: Edwin McClellan

West Virginia Legal Services Plan
State Capitol Building
Charleston, WV 25305
(304) 348-8980
Contact: David Cecil

North Central West Virginia Legal
    Aid Society
356 Spruce St.
Morgantown, WV 26505
(304) 296-3100
Contact: Larry Starcher

Mingo County Legal Services
P.O. Box 1519
Williamson, WV 25661
(304) 235-1452
Contact: James Martin

WISCONSIN
Milwaukee Legal Services, Inc.
211 W. Kilbourn Ave.
Milwaukee, WI 53203
(414) 278-7722
Contact: Steven Steinglass

Wisconsin Judicare
811 N. First Ave.
Wausau, WI 54401
(715) 842-1681
Contact: John M. Wiley

WYOMING
Legal Aid Services, Inc.
Odd Fellows Building
136 S. Walcott
Casper, WY
(307) 235-2786
Contact: Curtis L. Harden

Legal Services for Laramie County,
    Inc.
1810 Pioneer St.
Cheyenne, WY 82001
(307) 634-1566
Contact: Ron Arnold

Wind River Legal Services
P.O. Box 247
Fort Washakie, WY 82514
(307) 255-8290
Contact: Steven Avery

CALIFORNIA RURAL LEGAL ASSISTANCE (CRLA)

California Rural Legal Assistance
National Senior Citizens Law Project
942 Market St.
San Francisco, CA 94102
(415) 989-3966

Branch Offices

California Rural Legal Assistance
651 Main St.
El Centro, CA 92243
(714) 353-0220
Contact: James Gonzales

California Rural Legal Assistance
7891-D Westwood Drive
Gilroy, CA 95020
(408) 842-8271
Contact: Rubin Lopez

California Rural Legal Assistance
422 Healdsburg Ave.
Healdsburg, CA 95448
(707) 433-4429
Contact: Jerry Wilhelm

California Rural Legal Assistance
529 South D St.
Madera, CA 93637
(209) 674-5671
Contact: Chris Hamilton

California Rural Legal Assistance
818 D St.
Marysville, CA 95901
(916) 742-5191
Contact: Michael Weisz

California Rural Legal Assistance
335 Perkins St.
McFarland, CA 93250
(805) 792-2157
Contact: Tom Olmos

California Rural Legal Assistance
1900 K St.
Sacramento, CA 95814
(916) 446-7901
Contact: Alex Saldamando

Senior Citizens of CRLA
1900 K St.
Sacramento, CA 95814
(916) 446-7904
Contact: Ralph Abascal

California Rural Legal Assistance
328 Cayuga St.
Salinas, CA 93901
(408) 424-2201
Contact: Tim MacCarthy

California Rural Legal Assistance
126 W. Mills St.
Santa Maria, CA 93454
(805) 922-4563
Contact: Mike Stern

COMMUNITY ACTION FOR LEGAL SERVICES (CALS)
(New York)

Bronx Legal Services Corp.
579 Courtland Ave.
Bronx, NY 10451
(212) 993-6251
Contact: Donald Grajales

Landlord/Tenant Unit of South Bronx
Legal Services (Bronx Corp. B)
579 Courtland Ave.
Bronx, NY 10451
(212) 993-8200
Contact: Fred Levine

Bedford Stuyvesant Community Legal
    Services, Corp.
1368 Fulton St.
Brooklyn, NY 11216
(212) 638-7816
Contact: Lester Evans

Brooklyn Legal Services Corp.
260 Broadway
Brooklyn, NY 11211
(212) 782-6195
Contact: Richard S. Panebianco

Brooklyn Legal Services Corp.
152 Court St.
Brooklyn, NY 11201
(212) 855-8003
Contact: John C. Gray, Jr.

CALS – Brooklyn Office
130 Clinton St.
Brooklyn, NY 11201
(212) 522-1923
Contact: Steven M. Bernstein

Queens Legal Services Corp.
89-02 Sutphin Blvd.
Jamaica, NY 11435
(212) 657-8611
Contact: Mark H. Spires

Harlem Assertion of Rights Legal
    Services, Inc.
35 W. 125th St.
New York, NY 10027
(212) 369-4100
Contact: Kirkland Taylor

Legal Aid Society
11 Park Place
New York, NY 10007
(212) 227-2755
Contact: Kalman Finkel

Manhattan Legal Services Corp.
170 E. 116th St.
New York, NY 10029
(212) 427-0693
Contact: Louis B. York

Mobilization for Youth Legal Services,
    Inc. (MFY)
214 E. Second St.
New York, NY 10009
(212) 777-5250
Contact: George C. Stewart

18
Medicare and Medicaid

MEDICARE

Medicare is a health insurance program under Social Security that helps millions of Americans 65 and older, and many disabled people under 65, to pay the high cost of health care. It has two parts — hospital insurance and medical insurance.

The hospital-insurance part of Medicare helps pay for inpatient hospital care and for certain follow-up care after you leave the hospital. The medical-insurance part of Medicare helps pay for doctor's services, outpatient hospital services, and many other medical items and services not covered under hospital insurance.

Who qualifies for Medicare? Practically everyone 65 or older is eligible for Medicare. Also, the following people under 65 are eligible:

Disabled people who have been entitled to Social Security benefits for two consecutive years or more.
People insured under Social Security who need dialysis treatments or a kidney transplant because of permanent kidney failure.
Wives, husbands, or children of insured people may also be eligible if they need kidney dialysis or a transplant.

Everyone 65 or older who is entitled to monthly Social Security or Railroad Retirement benefits gets hospital insurance automatically without paying monthly premiums. You don't have to retire to get hospital-insurance protection. If you keep working after you are 65, you'll have this protection if you have worked long enough under Social Security or Railroad Retirement.

The following chart shows how many quarters of coverage are needed for hospital insurance:

Year You Reach 65	Quarters of coverage needed*
1974	21 (20 for women)
1975	24 (21 for women)

*Quarters of coverage are counted in 3-month periods — January-March, April-June, July-September, October-December. In general, you get credit for a quarter of coverage if you are paid wages of $50 or more in that quarter. Four quarters are counted for any year in which a person has $400 or more in net earnings from self-employment or cash wages from farm work.

People 65 or older who are not automatically entitled to hospital insurance can buy this protection. The premium is $40 a month. To buy hospital insurance, you will also have to enroll and pay the monthly premium for medical insurance.

To find out whether you are eligible for Medicare and to make sure you get the full protection of Medicare starting with the month you reach 65, please check with your Social Security office about 2 or 3 months before you reach 65. If you are now receiving monthly Social Security checks, you will be contacted by mail a few months before you are 65.

If you are a disabled person who has been entitled to Social Security disability benefits for two consecutive years or more, you will get hospital insurance automatically. You will receive information about Medicare in the mail.

If you are a widow, 50 years of age or older, and have been severely disabled at least 2 years but haven't filed a claim based on your disability (because you were getting Social Security checks as a mother caring for young or disabled children), you should contact your Social Security office to see if you're eligible for medicare. Medicare for disabled people begins with the 25th month they've been entitled to monthly benefits. People who receive railroad disability annuities or retirement benefits because of a disability should contact a Railroad Retirement office about the special requirements they must meet to get Medicare.

If you or your dependent needs kidney dialysis or a kidney transplant, you may be eligible for Medicare. Coverage can begin either the first day of the month that follows at least two full calendar months of dialysis treatment or, if earlier, upon admission to a hospital for kidney transplant surgery. You can get further information from any Social Security office.

Hospital insurance benefits. Your hospital insurance helps the cost of medically necessary covered services for the following care:

Up to 90 days of inpatient care in any participating hospital in each benefit period.*
For the first 60 days, it pays for all covered services after the first $92.
For the 61st day through the 90th day, it pays for all covered services except for $23 a day.
Care in a psychiatric hospital has a lifetime limit of 190 inpatient days.

You also have a "reserve" of 60 additional inpatient hospital days. You can use these extra days if you ever need more than 90 days of hospital care in any benefit period. Each reserve day you use permanently reduces the total number of reserve days you have left. For each of these additional days you use, hospital insurance pays for all covered services except for $46 a day.

Medicare hospital insurance also provides for up to 100 days of care in each benefit period in a participating skilled-nursing facility, a specially qualified facility, which is staffed and equipped to furnish skilled-nursing care, skilled rehabilitation care, and many related health services. Hospital insurance pays for all covered services for the first 20 days and all but $11.50 a day for up to 80 more days if the following five conditions are met:

You have been in a hospital at least 3 days in a row before your transfer to the skilled nursing facility.
You are transferred to the skilled-nursing facility because you require care for a condition that was treated in the hospital.
You are admitted to the facility within a short time after you leave the hospital, generally within 14 days.
A doctor certifies that you need, and you actually receive, skilled-nursing or skilled-rehabilitation services on a daily basis, and the facility's utilization review committee does not disapprove your stay.

*A benefit period is a way of measuring your use of services under Medicare's hospital insurance. Your first benefit period starts the first time you enter a hospital after your hospital insurance begins. When you have been out of a hospital (or other facility primarily providing skilled nursing or rehabilitation services) for 60 days in a row, a new benefit period starts the next time you go into a hospital. There is no limit to the number of benefit periods you can have.

Up to 100 home health "visits" in each benefit period from a participating Home Health Agency during the 12 months after your discharge from a hospital or skilled-nursing facility are covered if all six of the following conditions are met:

You were in a participating hospital for at least 3 days in a row.
The home health care is for further treatment of a condition that was treated in the hospital or skilled-nursing facility.
The care you need includes part-time skilled-nursing care, physical therapy, or speech therapy.
You are confined to your home.
A doctor determines you need home health care and sets up a home health plan for you within 14 days after your discharge from a hospital or participating skilled-nursing facility.
The home health agency providing services is participating in Medicare.

What services are covered? Covered services in a hospital or skilled-nursing facility include the cost of room and meals (including special diets) in semiprivate accommodations (two to four beds), regular nursing services, and services in an intensive-care unit of a hospital. They also include the cost of drugs, supplies, appliances, equipment, and any other services ordinarily furnished to inpatients of the hospital or skilled-nursing facility in which you are treated.

What services are not covered? Hospital inusrance is basic protection against the high cost of illness after you are 65 or while you are severely disabled, but it will not pay all of your health-care bills. No payment will be made for:

Services or supplies that are not necessary for the diagnosis or treatment of an illness or injury.
Doctor bills. (They are, however, covered if you have medical insurance.)
Private-duty nurses.
Cost of the first 3 pints of blood needed during a benefit period while you are an inpatient in a hospital or skilled-nursing facility.
Convenience items requested by you, such as a telephone or television in your room.
Care a patient may get in a hospital or skilled-nursing facility when the main reason for the patient's admission or stay is his (or her) need for help with such things as bathing, eating, dressing, walking, or taking medicine at the right time.

Medical insurance. Medical insurance under Medicare helps pay for doctors' services and a number of other medical services and supplies not covered by hospital insurance. People who want medical insurance pay a monthly premium.

How to get medical insurance protection. Nearly all people who become entitled to hospital insurance are automatically enrolled for medical insurance. If you can be enrolled automatically for medical insurance, you will receive information in the mail about 3 months before you become entitled to hospital insurance. The information you receive will tell you exactly what to do if you do not want medical insurance.

Automatic enrollment for medical insurance, however, does not apply to people living in Puerto Rico or in foreign countries or to people who continue to work past age 65. These people sign up for medical insurance if they want it.

Medical insurance has a 7-month initial enrollment period. This period begins 3 months before the month you become eligible for medical insurance and ends 3 months after that month. If you turn down medical insurance and then decide you want it after your 7-month initial enrollment period ends, you can sign up during the general enrollment period, January 1 through March 31 of each year. If you enroll during a general enrollment period, however, your protection won't start until the following July, and your premium will be 10 percent higher for each 12-month period you could have been enrolled but were not.

If you decide to cancel your medical insurance, your coverage and premium payments will stop at the end of the calendar quarter following the quarter that your written cancellation notice is received by the Social Security Administration. You can reenroll in medical insurance only once after canceling your protection.

Medical insurance benefits. Medical insurance will help pay for the following services:

Physicians' services, no matter where you receive them in the United States — in a doctor's office, hospital, home, or elsewhere — including medical supplies usually furnished by a doctor in the office, services of the office nurse, and drugs the doctor administers as part of his treatment, which you cannot administer yourself. There is a limit on payment for covered psychiatric services furnished outside a hospital.

Physicians' services outside the United States are covered only if they are furnished in connection with covered care in a foreign hospital.

Outpatient hospital services in an emergency room or an outpatient clinic of a hospital for both diagnosis and treatment.

Up to 100 home health "visits" each calendar year, if the following four conditions are met:

You need part-time skilled-nursing care or physical speech therapy.

A doctor determines you need the services and sets up a plan for home health care.

You are confined to your home.

The home health agency providing services is participating in Medicare.

These visits are in addition to the posthospital visits you get if you have hospital insurance.

Also provided for are outpatient physical therapy and speech pathology services, whether or not you are homebound, furnished under the supervision of participating hospitals, skilled-nursing facilities, or home health agencies; or approved clinics, rehabilitation agencies, or public health agencies under a plan established and periodically reviewed by a doctor.

Medicare also covers:

A number of other medical and health services prescribed by your doctor such as diagnostic services; X-ray or other radiation treatments; surgical dressings, splints, casts, braces; artificial limbs, and eyes; certain colostomy-care supplies; and rental or purchase of medically necessary durable medical equipment such as a wheelchair or oxygen equipment for use in your home.

Certain ambulance services.

Limited services by chiropractors.

Home and office services by licensed and certified physical therapists, with certain payment limitations.

How much does medical insurance pay for these services? Each year, as soon as your covered medical expenses go over $60 (the annual deductible), medical insurance will pay 80 percent of the "reasonable charges" for all covered services you have for the rest of the year regardless of the number of bills you have. ("Reasonable charges" are determined by the Medicare carrier — the organization selected by the Social Security Administration to handle medical insurance claims in the area where you receive services.)

There are four exceptions to this general rule.

Laboratory and radiology services by doctors while you are an inpatient of a hospital are paid at 100 percent without your meeting the $60 deductible.

Home health services are paid at 100 percent after the $60 annual deductible.

Payment for services of independent physical therapists is limited to a maximum of $80 a year.

Payment for physicians' psychiatric services outside a hospital is limited to a maximum of $250 a year.

Medical insurance does not cover some services or supplies, for example:

Services or supplies that are not necessary for the diagnosis or treatment of an illness or injury.

Routine physical checkups.

Prescription drugs and patent medicines.

Glasses and eye examinations to fit glasses.

Hearing aids and examinations for hearing aids.

Immunizations.

Dentures and routine dental care.

Orthopedic shoes.

Personal comfort items.

The first 3 pints of blood you receive in each calendar year.

For further information, call any Social Security Office listed in the white pages of your telephone directory under United States Government.

MEDICAID

Medicaid is for certain needy and low-income people:

- the aged (65 or older)
- the blind
- the disabled
- members of families with dependent children.

Some states also include, at state expense, other needy and low-income people.

Medicaid, which varies from state to state, is now in 49 states, the District of Columbia, Guam, Puerto Rico, and the Virgin Islands. Arizona does not have a Medicaid program.

Medicaid pays for at least these services:

- inpatient hospital care
- outpatient hospital services
- other laboratory and X-ray services
- skilled-nursing facility services
- physicians' services
- screening, diagnosis, and treatment of children under 21
- home-health-care services
- family-planning services.

In many states, Medicaid pays for such additional services as dental care, prescribed drugs, eyeglasses, clinic services, intermediate-care-facility services, and other diagnostic, screening preventive, and rehabilitative services.

Medicaid can pay what Medicare does not pay for people who are eligible for both programs.

Medicaid can pay the $104, which Medicare does not pay in each benefit period for eligible people. Also, Medicaid can pay the first $60 per year of medical-care costs and, for eligible people, can pay what Medicare does not pay of the remaining reasonable charges.

The federal government contributes from 50 percent (to the richest state) to 78 percent (to the state with the lowest *per capita* income) of medical-care costs for needy and low-income people who are aged, blind, disabled, under 21, or members of families with dependent children. States pay the remainder, often with help from local governments.

Medicaid is run by state governments within federal guidelines. The Medical Services Administration of the Social and Rehabilitation Service of the U.S. Department of Health, Education and Welfare is responsible for federal aspects of Medicaid.

Medicaid insists on high standards, supports development of needed facilities, encourages innovation in medical-care delivery, and requires review of care. In addition, Medicaid (1) requires that medical services be available to all eligible people in a state, and (2) trains and employs neighborhood people as community health workers.

Discrimination Prohibited. Title VI of the Civil Rights Act of 1964 states: "No person in the United States shall, on the ground of race, color, or national origin, be excluded from participation in, be denied the benefit of, or be subjected to discrimination under any program or activity receiving Federal financial assistance." Medicaid must be operated in compliance with this law.

Listed herein are the local offices in each state that administer Medicaid. Write or call them to determine if you are eligible for Medicaid coverage.

MEDICAID

Medical Services Administration
Social and Rehabilitation Service
330 C Street, SW
Washington, DC 20201
(202) 245-0111
Contact: Edward Palder

REGIONAL OFFICES

ALABAMA (Region IV)

Alabama Department of Public Health
State Office Building
Montgomery, AL 36130
(205) 832-3120

Alabama Department of Public Health
2500 Fairlane Drive
Montgomery, AL 36130
(205) 277-2710

ALASKA (Region X)

Department of Health & Social Service
Juneau, AK 99811
(907) 465-3355

ARIZONA (Region IX)

Department of Health Services
1740 W. Adams St.
Phoenix, AZ 85001
(602) 271-3387

ARKANSAS (Region IV)

Arkansas Social Services
Medical Care Division
P.O. Box 1437
Little Rock, AR 72203
(501) 371-1806

CALIFORNIA (Region IX)

Medi-Cal Division
Department of Health
714 P St.
Sacramento, CA 95814
(916) 445-6141

COLORADO (Region VIII)

Division of Medical Assistance
Department of Social Services
1575 Sherman Ave.
Denver, CO 80203
(303) 892-3031

CONNECTICUT (Region I)
Department of Social Services
110 Bartholomew Ave.
Hartford, CT 06106
(203) 566-3435

DELAWARE (Region III)
Department of Health & Social Services
Delaware State Hospital
New Castle, DE 19720
(302) 421-6011

Department of Health & Social Services
P.O. Box 309
Wilmington, DE 19899
(302) 571-3131

DISTRICT OF COLUMBIA (Region III)
Department of Human Resources
1350 E St., NW
Washington, DC 20004
(202) 629-5443

Department of Human Resources
500 First St., NW
Washington, DC 20001
(202) 629-6601

Department of Human Resources
614 H St., NW
Washington, DC 20001
(202) 737-7672

FLORIDA (Region IV)
Department of Health & Rehabilitation Services
1322 Winewood Blvd.
Tallahassee, FL 32301
(904) 487-2380

GEORGIA (Region IV)
Georgia Department of Human Resources
State Office Building
Atlanta, GA 30334
(404) 655-5680

Georgia Department of Human Resources
618 Ponce de Leon Ave.
Atlanta, GA 30308
(404) 894-4328

HAWAII (Region IX)
Dept. of Social Service & Housing
P.O. Box 339
Honolulu, HI 96809
(808) 548-6260

IDAHO (Region X)
Department of Health & Welfare
Statehouse
Boise, ID 83720
(208) 964-3556

ILLINOIS (Region V)
Department of Public Aid
316 S. Second St.
Springfield, IL 62706
(217) 782-1211

Department of Public Aid
931 E. Washington St.
Springfield, IL 62763
(217) 782-0506

INDIANA (Region V)
State Department of Public Welfare
100 N. Senate Ave.
Indianapolis, IN 46204
(317) 633-6650

IOWA (Region VIII)
Bureau of Medical Services
Iowa Dept. of Social Service
Lucas State Office Building
Des Moines, IA 50319
(515) 281-3359

KANSAS (Region VII)
State Department of Social Welfare
State Office Building
Topeka, KS 66612
(913) 296-3271

KENTUCKY (Region V)
Department of Human Resources
Highway 127, S.
Frankfort, KY 40601
(502) 564-4321

LOUISIANA (Region VI)
Louisiana Health & Human Resources Administration
P.O. Box 44215
Baton Rouge, LA 70804
(504) 389-5796

MAINE (Region I)
Department of Human Services
Statehouse
Augusta, ME 04330
(207) 289-2736

MARYLAND (Region III)
Dept. of Health & Mental Hygiene
201 W. Preston St.
Baltimore, MD 21201
(301) 383-2600

MASSACHUSETTS (Region I)
Department of Public Welfare
600 Washington St.
Boston, MA 02111
(617) 727-6190

Massachusetts Commission for the Blind
110 Tremont St.
Boston, MA 02108
(617) 727-5580

MICHIGAN (Region V)
Citizens Services Administration
Michigan Dept. of Social Services
300 S. Capitol Ave.
Lansing, MI 48926
(517) 374-9080

MINNESOTA (Region V)
Department of Public Welfare
Centennial Office Building
658 Cedar St.
St. Paul, MN 55101
(612) 296-2766

Medical Assistance Program
690 N. Roberts St.
St. Paul, MN 55118
(612) 296-7554

MISSISSIPPI (Region IV)
Mississippi Medicaid Commission
2906 N. State St.
Jackson, MS 39216
(601) 354-7464

MISSOURI (Region VII)
Bureau of Medical Services
Department of Social Services
Broadway State Office Building
Jefferson City, MO 65101
(314) 751-2500

MONTANA (Region VIII)
Medical Assistance Bureau
Dept. of Social & Rehabilitation Service
P.O. Box 1723
Helena, MT 59601
(406) 587-3952

NEBRASKA (Region VIII)
Medical Services
State Department of Public Welfare
1526 K St., Fourth Floor
Lincoln, NB 68508
(402) 471-2384

NEVADA (Region IX)
Department of Human Resources
505 E. King St.
Carson City, NV 89710
(702) 885-4730

Medical Care Section
251 Jeanell Dr.
Carson City, NV 89710
(702) 885-4775

NEW HAMPSHIRE (Region I)
Department of Health & Services
8 Loudon St.
Concord, NH 03301
(603) 271-3331 or 271-3332

NEW JERSEY (Region II)

Department of Institutions & Agencies
135 W. Hanover
Trenton, NJ 08625
(609) 292-3717

Division of Medical Assistance &
   Health Services
New Jersey Dept. of Institutions &
   Agencies
324 E. State St.
Trenton, NJ 08608
(609) 292-7110

NEW MEXICO (Region VI)

State Welfare Agency
Health & Social Services Department
P.O. Box 2348
Santa Fe, NM 87501
(505) 476-2188

NEW YORK (Region II)

Division of Medical Assistance
New York State Dept. of Social
   Services
1450 Western Ave.
Albany, NY 12203
(518) 457-3775

NORTH CAROLINA (Region IV)

Medical Services Section
Department of Human Resources
325 N. Salisbury St.
Raleigh, NC 27611
(919) 829-2060

NORTH DAKOTA (Region VIII)

Medical Services
Social Service Board of North Dakota
State Capitol Building
Bismarck, ND 58501
(701) 224-2321

OHIO (Region V)

Division of Medical Assistance
Department of Public Welfare
30 E. Broad St.
Columbus, OH 43215
(614) 466-2365

OKLAHOMA (Region VI)

Medical Services Division
Department of Institutions
Social & Rehabilitation Service
P.O. Box 25352
Oklahoma City, OK 73125
(405) 521-3801

OREGON (Region X)

Medical Assistance Unit
Public Welfare Division
Department of Human Resources
400 Public Service Building
Salem, OR 97310
(503) 378-3694

PENNSYLVANIA (Region III)

Bureau of Medical Assistance
Department of Public Welfare
Health & Welfare Building
Harrisburg, PA 17120
(717) 787-7362

PUERTO RICO (Region II)

Department of Health
P.O. Box 9342
Santurce, PR 00908
(809) 722-2050

Department of Health
P.O. Box 10037
Caparra Heights Station
Rio Piedras, PR 00922
(809) 765-9941

RHODE ISLAND (Region I)

Department of Social & Rehabilitative
   Services
600 New London Ave.
Cranston, RI 02920
(401) 464-2174

SOUTH CAROLINA (Region IV)

Division of Medical Assistance
State Dept. of Social Services
P.O. Box 1520
Columbia, SC 29202
(803) 758-3244

SOUTH DAKOTA (Region VIII)

Division of Social Welfare
Department of Medical Services
State Office Building, No. 1
Pierre, SD 57501
(605) 224-3495

TENNESSEE (Region V)

Department of Public Health
344 Cordell Hull Building
Nashville, TN 37219
(615) 741-3644

Department of Public Health
Middle Tennessee Chest Disease
   Hospital
Ben Allen Rd.
Nashville, TN 37206
(615) 741-7221

TEXAS (Region VI)

Department of Public Welfare
John H. Reagan Building
Austin, TX 78701
(512) 475-3575

UTAH (Region VIII)

Office of Medical Services
Department of Social Services
211 State Capitol
Salt Lake City, UT 84111
(801) 533-5038

VERMONT (Region I)

Department of Social Welfare
State Office Building
4 E. State St.
Montpelier, VT 05602
(802) 828-3441

VIRGINIA (Region III)

Medical Assistance Program
State Department of Health
109 Governor St.
Richmond, VA 23219
(804) 786-7933

WASHINGTON (Region X)

Office of Medical Assistance
Department of Social & Health Services
Olympia, WA 98504
(206) 753-0526

WEST VIRGINIA (Region III)

Division of Medical Care
Department of Welfare
1900 Washington St.
Charleston, WV 25305
(304) 348-8990

WISCONSIN (Region V)

Wisconsin Department of Health &
   Social Service
One W. Wilson St.
Madison, WI 53702
(608) 226-3681

WYOMING (Region VIII)

Medical Assistance Services
Division of Health & Social Services
Department of Health & Social
   Services
State Office Building
Cheyenne, WY 82001
(307) 777-7533

19
Mental Health Centers

In a unique approach to treating and preventing mental illness, the National Institute of Mental Health is helping communities across the country develop mental-health centers where people with emotional problems can get comprehensive and continuing treatment in their home communities.

Centers are planned and run by people in the community, with initial help from the federal government in the form of construction and staffing grants. To be eligible for such support, a center must offer the essential direct services of inpatient and outpatient care, partial hospitalization (day, night, or weekend care), around the clock emergency services, and the indirect services of consultation and education to community agencies, physicians, clergy, teachers, and so on.

Additional services such as rehabilitation, training research and evaluation, central administrative services, and special services for specific patient groups (i.e., the elderly) are provided by almost all the centers.

Each center listed here serves a distinct community ranging in size from 75,000 to 200,000 persons.

ALABAMA

Calhoun-Cleburn
331 E. Eighth St.
Anniston, AL 36201
(205) 236-3403

University of Alabama Comprehensive
1700 Seventh St.
Birmingham, AL 35233
(205) 934-5171

Western Alabama
1912 Eighth Ave.
Birmingham, AL 35202
(205) 324-9571

North Central Alabama
401 Grant St., SE
Decatur, AL 35601
(205) 355-6091

West Alabama
Highway 80 East
Demopolis, AL 36732
(205) 289-2410

Wiregrass Comp.
Prevatte Rd. & Ross Clark Circle
Dothan, AL 36301
(205) 794-9013

Muscle Shoals
635 W. College St.
Florence, AL 35630
(205) 764-3431

Cherokee-Etowah-DeKalb
901 Goodyear Ave.
Gadsden, AL 35903
(205) 492-7800

Marshall-Jackson
P.O. Box 457
Guntersville, AL 35976
(205) 582-2956

Northwest Alabama Comp.
Airport Rd.
Route 1
Hamilton, AL 35570
(205) 921-2186

Huntsville-Madison Comprehensive
218 Randolph Ave., SE
Huntsville, AL 35801
(205) 539-3754

Mobile
2400 Gordon Smith Dr.
Mobile, AL 36617
(205) 473-4423

East Alabama Comprehensive
1930 Pepperell Parkway
Opelika, AL 36801
(205) 745-6223

Clay-Randolph-Talladega
15 N. Hightower Ave.
Sylacauga, AL 35150
(205) 249-2865

Community Mental Health Center of
 Bibb-Pickens-Tuscaloosa
 Counties
2012 Eighth St.
Tuscaloosa, AL 35401
(205) 345-1600

ALASKA

Gateway
3134 Tongass Ave.
Ketchikan, AK 99901
(907) 225-4135

Kodiak Island Borough
P.O. Box 712
Kodiak, AK 99615
(907) 486-5742

ARIZONA

Northern Arizona Comprehensive
Guidance Center Inc.
2501 N. Fourth St.
Flagstaff, AZ 86001
(602) 774-5097

Phoenix South
5 N. Eighth Ave.
Phoenix, AZ 85007
(602) 257-9339

The Camelback Hospital
6411 E. Thomas
Phoenix, AZ 85018
(602) 947-6353

Tucson East
4455 E. Fifth St.
Tucson, AZ 85711
(602) 881-0520

Tucson Southern Counties Mental
Health Services Inc.
1935 S. Sixth Ave.
Tucson, AZ 85713
(602) 623-6194

ARKANSAS

North Central Arkansas
P.O. Box 2578
Batesville, AR 72501
(501) 793-2339

South Arkansas Regional Health
Center
490 W. Faulkner St.
El Dorado, AR 71730
(501) 862-5491

Western Arkansas Counseling &
Guidance Center
910 S. 12th St.
Fort Smith, AR 72901
(501) 785-4263

East Arkansas Regional
307 Valley Dr.
Helena, AR 72342
(501) 338-7461

Ouachita Regional Counseling
124 Rugg St.
Hot Springs, AR 71901
(501) 624-7111

George W. Jackson
2920 McClellan Dr.
Jonesboro, AR 72401
(501) 972-4000

Greater Little Rock Comprehensive
4313 W. Markham St.
Little Rock, AR 72201
(501) 666-0961

Human Services Center of West
Central Arkansas
507 W. Second St.
Russellville, AR 72801
(501) 968-1298

Delta Counseling & Guidance Center
204 W. College
Monticello, AR 71655
(501) 367-6202

Ozarks Regional
P.O. Box 209
Mountain Home, AR 72653
(501) 425-6439

Southeast Arkansas
2500 Rike Drive
Pine Bluff, AR 71601
(501) 534-1834

Ozark Guidance Center
712 Maple Ave.
Springdale, AR 72764
(501) 751-7052

Texarkana Regional Mental Health–
Mental Retardation Center
409 Texas Blvd.
Texarkana, Arkansas-TX 75501
(214) 793-4655

CALIFORNIA

Kern View Community Mental Health
Center & Hospital
3600 San Dimas St.
Bakersfield, CA 93301
(805) 327-7621

Peninsula Hospital
1783 El Camino Real
Burlingame, CA 94010
(415) 697-4061

Community Hospital of the Monterey
Peninsula
P.O. Box HH
Carmel, CA 93921
(408) 624-5311

Didi Hirsch
4760 S. Sepulveda Ave.
Culver City, CA 90230
(213) 390-6693

North County
48 Southgate Ave.
Daly City, CA 94015
(415) 873-1800

Fresno Community Hospital
Fresno & R Sts.
Fresno, CA 93721
(209) 233-0911

South Santa Clara County
287 Leavesley Rd.
Gilroy, CA 95020
(408) 842-0251

Marin
250 Bon Air Rd.
Greenbrae, CA 94904
(415) 461-9100

Hemet Valley Hospital District
1116 E. Latham Ave.
Hemet, CA 92343
(714) 658-9434

Golden State
11505 Kagel Canyon St.
Lake View Terrace, CA 91342
(213) 896-1161

Cedars-Sinai
8730 Alden Dr.
Los Angeles, CA 90048
(213) 652-5000

Central City
4211 S. Avalon Blvd.
Los Angeles, CA 90011
(213) 232-4111

Gateways Hospital
1891 Effie St.
Los Angeles, CA 90026
(213) 666-0171

Kedren
7760 S. Central Ave.
Los Angeles, CA 90001
(213) 587-9161

Martin Luther King Jr.
General Hospital
12012 Compton Ave.
Los Angeles, CA 90059
(213) 537-4541

Resthaven Psychiatric Hospital
765 W. College St.
Los Angeles, CA 90012
(213) 626-8241

West Valley
14195 S. Capri Dr.
Los Gatos, CA 95030
(408) 379-7020

South County Mental Health Services
799 Willow Rd.
Menlo Park, CA 94025
(415) 364-5600

Scenic General Hospital
803 Scenic Dr.
Modesto, CA 95390
(209) 524-1251

San Fernando Valley
9017 Reseda Blvd.
Northridge, CA 91324
(213) 885-7788

East Oakland
499 Fifth St.
Oakland, CA 94607
(415) 534-8055

Oxnard Regional Mental Health Center
— Center for Problems in Living
620 South D St.
Oxnard, CA 93030
(805) 487-5511

Desert Hospital
P.O. Box 1627
Palm Springs, CA 92262
(714) 325-1417

North County
270 Grant Ave.
Palo Alto, CA 94306
(408) 321-2141

Pasadena
56 Waverly Dr.
Pasadena, CA 91105
(213) 795-8471

Kings View
11490 So Rio Vista Ave.
Reedley, CA 93654
(209) 638-3655

Ingleside
7500 E. Hellman Ave.
Rosemead, CA 91770
(213) 288-1160

East Sacramento County Mental
 Health Service
2315 Stockton Blvd.
Sacramento, CA 95817
(916) 453-2974

North Sacramento
2315 Stockton Blvd.
Sacramento, CA 95817
(916) 453-2974

Sutter Hospitals
5275 F St.
Sacramento, CA 95819
(916) 452-3271

Bayview
SF General Hospital
San Francisco, CA 94110
(415) 648-8200

District V
1351 24th Ave.
San Francisco, CA 94122
(415) 982-3732

Mission
1665 Mission St.
San Francisco, CA 94103
(415) 558-2564

Northeast
511 Columbus Ave.
San Francisco, CA 94133
(415) 441-4283

Westside
2201 Sutter St.
San Francisco, CA 94115
(415) 563-7710

Central
2221 Enborg Lane
San Jose, CA 95126
(408) 286-5442

East Valley
1989 McKee Rd.
San Jose, CA 95116
(408) 926-2900

San Jose
77 N. 15th St.
San Jose, CA 95112
(408) 292-4697

San Luis Obispo
2180 Johnson Ave.
San Luis Obispo, CA 93401
(805) 543-1500

Central County Mental Center
3700 Edison St.
San Mateo, CA 94402
(415) 573-3571

Santa Barbara County
4444 Calle Real
Santa Barbara, CA 93105
(805) 964-6713

St. John's Hospital
1328 22nd St.
Santa Monica, CA 90404
(213) 829-5465

Simi-Conejo Regional
2003 Royal Ave.
Simi Valley, CA 93065
(805) 527-6430

El Camino
660 S. Fair Oaks Ave.
Sunnyvale, CA 94086
(408) 732-2760

Olive View Medical Center
14445 Olive View Dr.
Sylmar, CA 91342
(213) 367-2231

Emanuel Hospital
825 Delbon Ave.
Turlock, CA 95380
(209) 634-9151

Ventura
300 Hillmont Ave.
Ventura, CA 93003
(805) 648-6181

Woodland Memorial Hospital
1325 Cottonwood St.
Woodland, CA 95695
(916) 662-3961

COLORADO

San Luis Valley Comp.
1015 Fourth St.
Alamosa, CO 81101
(303) 589-3671

Mental Health Center of Boulder
 County, Inc.
1333 Iris Ave.
Boulder, CO 80302
(303) 443-8500

Adams County
4371 E. 72nd Ave.
Commerce City, CO 80022
(303) 287-8001

Arapahoe
4857 S. Broadway
Denglewood, CO 80110
(303) 761-0620

Bethesda
4400 E. Iliff Ave.
Denver, CO 80222
(303) 758-1514

Malcolm X Center
2222 E. 18th Ave.
Denver, CO 80206
(303) 320-6840

Northwest Denver Comprehensive
W. Eighth Ave. & Cherokee St.
Denver, CO 80204
(303) 693-7377

Colorado West Regional
829 Grand Ave.
Glenwood Springs, CO 81601
(303) 945-5933

Weld Mental Health Center Inc.
1220 11th Ave., Suite 304
Greeley, CO 80631
(303) 353-3686

Jefferson County
9808 W. Cedar Ave.
Lakewood, CO 80226
(303) 238-0536

Midwestern Colorado Mental Health
 Center Inc.
428 Main St.
Montrose, CO 81401
(303) 249-9694

Spanish Peaks
401 Michigan Ave.
Pueblo, CO 81004
(303) 544-6373

CONNECTICUT

Greater Bridgeport Community Mental
 Health Center
1635 Central Ave.
Bridgeport, CT 06610
(203) 384-1711

Connecticut
34 Park St.
New Haven, CT 06508
(203) 772-3300

Central Connecticut
91 Northwest Dr.
Plainville, CT 06062
(203) 747-6801

Stamford-Darien-New Canaan-
 Greenwich-Stamford Hospital
Shelburne & W. Broad
Stamford, CT 06902
(203) 327-1234

The Charlotte Hungerford Hospital &
 Psychiatric Clinic
540 Litchfield St.
Torrington, CT 06790
(203) 489-0441

DELAWARE

Sussex County
Beebe Hospital
Lewes, DE 19720
(302) 645-6211

Southern New Castle County
10 Central Ave.
New Castle, DE 19720
(302) 421-8373

DISTRICT OF COLUMBIA

Area A
3246 P St., NW
Washington, DC 20007
(202) 333-2653

Area B
1125 Spring Rd., NW
Washington, DC 20010
(202) 629-4027

Area C
1905 E St., SE
Washington, DC 20003
(202) 626-5365

Area D Community Mental Health Center
St. Elizabeth Hospital – Dix Pavilion
2700 Martin Luther King Ave., SE
Washington, DC 20032
(202) 562-4000

FLORIDA

The Mental Health Center of Polk County Inc.
1745 Highway 17, S.
Bartow, FL 33830
(813) 533-3141

Manatee County
818 13th St., W.
Bradenton, FL 33505
(813) 746-6909

Volusia County
P.O. Box 1990
Daytona Beach, FL 32015
(904) 255-0161

South County
2300 Seacrest Blvd.
Delray Beach, FL 33444
(305) 832-0470

Lake Sumter
117 Magnolia Ave.
Eutis, FL 32726
(904) 357-4161

Indian River Community Mental Health Center Inc.
800 Ave. H
Fort Pierce, FL 33450
(305) 464-8111

North Central Florida
606 SW Third Ave.
Gainesville, FL 32601
(904) 376-5364

Jackson Memorial Hospital
1700 NW Tenth Ave.
Miami, FL 33136
(305) 371-9611

Marion-Citrus
2022 SW Pine Ave.
Ocala, FL 32670
(904) 629-8893

Orange Memorial Hospital
1416 S. Orange Ave.
Orlando, FL 32806
(305) 241-2411

Northwest Florida Mental Health Center Inc.
600 N. Cove Blvd.
Panama City, FL 32401
(904) 769-2407

Escambia County Inc.
1201 W. Hemandez St.
Pensacola, FL 32501
(904) 433-3081

Brevard County Community Mental Health Center's Inc.
1770 Cedar St.
Rockledge, FL 32955
(305) 636-5641

Apalachee Community Mental Health Services Inc.
805 N. Gadsden St.
Tallahassee, FL 32303
(904) 224-9633

Hillsborough
5707 N. 22nd St.
Tampa, FL 33610
(813) 237-3914

Northwest Florida Mental Health Center Inc.
St. Joseph's Hospital
3001 W. Buffalo Ave.
Tampa, FL 33607
(813) 877-8161

Palm Beach County
1041 45th St.
West Palm Beach, FL 33407
(305) 844-9741

Winter Haven Hospital
200 Ave. F., NE
Winter Haven, FL 33880
(813) 294-4238

GEORGIA

Albany Area
520 N. Jefferson St.
Albany, GA 31701
(912) 439-4140

Northeast Georgia
797 Cobb St.
Athens, GA 30604
(404) 542-8890

Atlanta South Central
1039 Ridge Ave., SW
Atlanta, GA 30315
(404) 688-1350

Northside Hospital
1000 Johnson Ferry Rd., NE
Atlanta, GA 30342
(404) 252-7300

Augusta Area Mental Health Center – University Hospital
1350 Walton Way
Augusta, GA 30902
(404) 722-2615

North Central Georgia
1407 Burleyson St.
Dalton, GA 30720
(404) 226-6141

Central Dekalb
440 Winn Way
Decatur, GA 30030
(404) 292-5231

South Central Georgia
2121 Bellevue Rd.
Dublin, GA 31021
(912) 272-2051

Northwest Georgia
c/o Hutcheson Memorial Tri-County Hospital
Fort Oglethorpe, GA 30741
(404) 861-1416

North Georgia
315 S. Enota Dr.
Gainesville, GA 30501
(404) 536-6681

Middle Georgia
770 Hemlock St.
Macon, GA 31201
(912) 745-0411

Clayton
15 SW Upper Riverdale Rd.
Riverdale, GA 30274
(404) 471-4111

Comprehensive Mental Health Center for Chatham County
2 E. Henry St.
Savannah, GA 31405
(912) 944-2022

John D. Archbold Memorial Hospital
Mimosa Dr. & Gordon Ave.
Thomasville, GA 31792
(912) 226-4121

South Health District
2206 Williams St.
Valdosta, GA 31601
(912) 247-3491

HAWAII

Kalihi-Palama
810 N. Vineyard Blvd.
Honolulu, HI 96817
(808) 847-1156

Queen's Medical Center
1301 Punchbowl St.
Honolulu, HI 96813
(808) 538-9011

Windward
45-700 Keaahala Rd.
Kaneohe, HI 96744
(808) 247-2148

Kauai
3040 Umi St.
Lihue, HI 96766
(808) 245-4378

Maui Mental Health Service
121 Mahalani St.
Wailuku, HI 96793
(808) 244-3747

IDAHO

Idaho Department of Health & Welfare
Region IV
1477 N. Orchard St.
Boise, ID 83704
(208) 384-3510

Idaho Department of Health & Welfare
Region III
P.O. Box 988
Caldwell, ID 83605
(208) 459-7456

Idaho Department of Health & Welfare
Region I
315 Wallace Ave.
Coeur D'Alene, ID 83814
(208) 667-6406

Eastern Idaho
140 E. 25th St.
Idaho Falls, ID 83401
(208) 523-9100

Idaho Department of Health & Welfare
Region II
412 Sixth St.
Lewiston, ID 83501
(208) 746-2651

Gateway
421 Memorial Drive
Pocatello, ID 83201
(208) 233-6170

Idaho Department of Health & Welfare
Region V
638 Addison Ave., W.
Twin Falls, ID 83301
(208) 734-4000

ILLINOIS

Kane-Kendall County
30 S. Stolp Ave.
Aurora, IL 60504
(312) 897-0584

Community Mental Health Program at
the Medical Center
1601 W. Taylor St.
Chicago, IL 60612
(312) 341-8411

Edgewater-Uptown
1004 W. Wilson Ave.
Chicago, IL 60640
(312) 769-0205

Garfield Park Community Mental
Health Inc.
9 S. Kedzie Ave.
Chicago, IL 60612
(312) 722-7900

Northside Community Mental Health
Center—Northwestern University
Medical School
303 E Chicago Ave.
Chicago, IL 60611
(312) 649-8050

Ravenswood Hospital Medical Center
4550 N. Winchester Ave.
Chicago, IL 60640
(312) 878-4300

St. Mary of Nazareth
1120 N. Leavitt St.
Chicago, IL 60622
(312) 292-5420

Ben Gordon
637 S. First St.
DeKalb, IL 60115
(815) 756-4875

St. Clair County
358 N. 88th St.
East St. Louis, IL 62205
(618) 322-0847

Fulton & McDonough Counties
301 E. Jefferson St.
Macomb, IL 61455
(309) 833-2191

South Cook County Mental Health
Service
205th & Cicero Sts.
Matteson, IL 60443
(312) 333-0006

Proviso Township
1440 W. North Ave.
Melrose Park, IL 60160
(312) 681-2324

Lasalle County
305 W. Jefferson St.
Ottawa, IL 61350
(815) 434-4727

Mental Health for West Central Illinois
West Central University
Quincy, IL 62301
(217) 223-0535

Rock Island & Mercer Counties
2701 17th St.
Rock Island, IL 61201
(309) 793-1000

Illinois River Valley Community
Mental Health Center
St. Margaret's Hospital
600 E. First St.
Spring Valley, IL 63622
(815) 663-2611

INDIANA

South Central Mental Health
Foundation
640 S. Rogers
Bloomington, IN 47401
(812) 339-1691

Quinco Consulting Center
2075 Lincoln Park Dr.
Columbus, IN 47201
(812) 379-2341

Oaklawn
2600 Oakland Ave.
Elkhart, IN 46514
(219) 294-3551

Southwestern Indiana Mental Health
Center Inc.
415 Mulberry St.
Evansville, IN 47713
(812) 423-7791

Community Hospital of Indianapolis
Inc.
1500 N. Ritter Ave.
Indianapolis, IN 46219
(317) 353-5411

Midtown Community Mental Health
Center
Marion County General Hospital
960 Locke St.
Indianapolis, IN 46202
(317) 630-7621

Southern Indiana–Mental Health &
Guidance Center Inc.
207 W. 13th St.
Jeffersonville, IN 47130
(812) 283-4491

Regional Mental Health Center
3500 S. Lafountain St.
Kokomo, IN 46901
(317) 453-0702

Laporte County
1304 Jefferson Ave.
Laporte, IN 46350
(219) 362-2145

Saint Joseph County Inc.
711 E. Colfax
South Bend, IN 46617
(219) 233-5123

Katherine Hamilton Mental Health
Center Inc.
620 Eighth Ave.
Terre Haute, IN 47804
(812) 232-0361

Comprehensive Community Mental
Health Center
520 S. Seventh St.
Vincennes, IN 47591
(812) 885-3291

Five County
703 S. Buffalo St.
Warsaw, IN 46580
(219) 267-7169

IOWA

Pottawattamie
719 S. Main St.
Council Bluffs, IA 51501
(712) 328-2609

Scott County Inc.
1441 W. Central Park Ave.
Davenport, IA 52804
(319) 326-6491

Polk County East
1301 Center St.
Des Moines, IA 50309
(515) 285-6781

Polk County West
1301 Center St.
Des Moines, IA 50309
(515) 243-4294

Dubuque
James & Peabody Sts.
Dubuque, IA 52001
(319) 588-8400

Northwest Iowa
1120 First Ave.
Spencer, IA 51301
(712) 446-2337

KANSAS

East Central Kansas
501½ Commercial St.
Emporia, KS 66801
(316) 342-0548

High Plains
201 E. Seventh St.
Hays, KS 67601
(913) 628-8251

Sekan
614 Professional Building
Independence, KS 67301
(316) 331-1748

Wyandotte County Mental Health & Guidance Center Inc.
Eaton at 36th Ave.
Kansas City, KS 66103
(913) 831-9500

Johnson County Northeast Mental Health Center–Mission
6000 Lamar Ave.
Mission, KS 66202
(913) 384-1100

Prairie View
E. First St.
Newton, KS 67114
(316) 283-2400

Johnson County Southwest
539 E. Santa Fe
Olathe, KS 66061
(913) 384-1100

Shawnee Community Mental Health Corporation Inc.
1615 W. Eighth St.
Topeka, KS 66606
(913) 234-2120

North Sedgwick County
1801 E. Tenth St.
Wichita, KS 67214
(316) 268-8251

South Wichita-Sedgwick County
3620 E. Sunnybrook St.
Wichita, KS 67210
(316) 268-8251

KENTUCKY

Lansdown Comprehensive Care Center
P.O. Box 790
Ashland, KY 41101
(606) 325-9657

Cumberland River Board Inc.
Doctor's Park
Corbin, KY 40701
(606) 528-7010

Northern Kentucky Comprehensive Care Center - Region 7A
430 Garrett St.
Covington, KY 41011
(606) 491-1022

Southern Bluegrass Comprehensive Care Center
1086 Greenleaf Plaza
Danville, KY 40422
(606) 236-4245

North Central Comprehensive Care Center - Region V
50 Pub Square
Elizabethtown, KY 42701
(502) 769-1304

Bluegrass West Comprehensive Care Center
404 Ann St.
Frankfort, KY 40601
(502) 223-2182

Barren River Comprehensive Care Center
1006 Glenview Drive
Glasgow, KY 42141
(502) 651-6882

Cumberland River Center
Mounted Route No. 1
Harlan, KY 40831
(606) 573-1624

Upper Kentucky River Regional Mental Health - Mental Retardation Comprehensive Care Center
Lincoln Hotel Building
Hazard, KY 41701
(606) 436-5761

Pennyroyal Regional Mental Health Center
735 North Drive
Hopkinsville, KY 42240
(502) 886-5163

Bluegrass East Comprehensive Care Center
201 Mechanic St.
Lexington, KY 40507
(606) 254-3844

Hikes Point
3717 Taylorsville Rd.
Louisville, KY 40220
(502) 459-5166

Three Rivers
3418 Frankfort Ave.
Louisville, KY 40207
(505) 245-0291

Waverly Mental Health Center - Area D
1901 Outer Loop
Louisville, KY 40219
(502) 361-3332

West Central
600 S. Preston St.
Louisville, KY 40201
(502) 587-7629

Comprehend Inc. Region 8 Mental Health - Mental Retardation Comprehensive Care Center
16 E. Third St.
Maysville, KY 41056
(606) 564-4016

Cave Run Comprehensive Care Center
325 E. Main St.
Morehead, KY 40351
(606) 784-6416

Northern Kentucky Comprehensive Care Center
718 Columbia St.
Newport, KY 41071
(606) 491-6510

Green River Comprehensive Care Center
311 W. Second St.
Owensboro, KY 42301
(502) 683-0278

Western Kentucky
1530 Lone Oak Rd.
Paducah, KY 42001
(502) 442-7121

Mountain Comprehensive Care Center
205 N. Arnold Ave.
Prestonsburg, KY 41653
(606) 886-3887

Lake Cumberland Comprehensive Care Center
129 S. Main St.
Somerset, KY 42501
(606) 679-1137

LOUISIANA

Margaret Dumas Memorial
3843 Harding Blvd.
Baton Rouge, LA 70807
(504) 389-5901

Bogalusa
619 Willis Ave.
Bogalusa, LA 70427
(504) 735-8286

Donaldsonville
412 Iberville St.
Donaldsonville, LA 70346
(504) 473-7901

Hammond
Highway 51 South
Hammond, LA 70401
(504) 345-2160

Terrebonne Mental Health Center & LaFourche Mental Health Clinic
500 Legion Ave.
Houma, LA 70360
(504) 876-6010

Acadiana
400 St. Julian St.
Lafayette, LA 70501
(318) 233-7500

Lake Charles
4105 Kirkman St.
Lake Charles, LA 70601
(318) 477-3563

St. Tammany
900 Wilkerson St.
Mandeville, LA 70448
(504) 626-8555

Monroe Regional
4800 S. Grand St.
Monroe, LA 71201
(318) 325-9605

Charity Hospital at New Orleans & Tulane University School of Medicine
1532 Tulane Ave.
New Orleans, LA 70140
(504) 523-3381

Chartres
417 Bienville St.
New Orleans, LA 70130
(504) 389-5792

New Orleans Mental Health Foundation Inc.
1040 Calhoun St.
New Orleans, LA 70118
(504) 899-8282

Pontchartrain
1190 Florida Ave.
New Orleans, LA 70119
(504) 944-6711

Touro Infirmary
1401 Foucher St.
New Orleans, LA 70115
(504) 897-3311

Region II Mental Health Center
Ruston Mental Health Clinic
P.O. Box 1006
Ruston, LA 71270
(318) 255-0535

Tallulah Mental Health Clinic
P.O. Box 109
Tallulah, LA 71282
(318) 574-1713

MAINE

The Counseling Center
43 Illinois Ave.
Bangor, ME 04401
(207) 947-0366

Aroostook Mental Health Services Inc.
c/o Community General Hospital
Green St.
Fort Fairfield, ME 04742
(207) 472-3511

Tri-County Mental Health Services Inc.
106 Campus Ave.
Lewiston, ME 04240
(207) 783-9141

Maine Medical Center
22 Bramhall St.
Portland, ME 04102
(207) 871-2187

Penobscot Bay Medical Center
Diamond Hill
Rockport, ME 04856
(207) 236-4393

York County Counseling Services Inc.
200 Main St.
Saco, ME 04072
(207) 282-5976

Kennebec Valley
North St.
Waterville, ME 04901
(207) 873-2136

MARYLAND

Inner City
25 S. Calvert St.
Baltimore, MD 21202
(301) 383-2045

Provident
1900 Eutaw Place
Baltimore, MD 21217
(301) 523-7671

Comprehensive Community Mental Health Center No. 2 of Prince George's County
9171 Central Ave.
Capital Heights, MD 20021
(301) 350-3100

Southwestern
10 Winters Lane
Catonsville, MD 21228
(301) 788-8681

Community Mental Health Center of Prince George's County No. 1
Prince George's General Hospital
Cheverly, MD 20785
(301) 341-2290

Regional Health
Willow Brook Rd.
Cumberland, MD 21502
(301) 722-3010

Upper Montgomery
18101 Prince Phillip Drive
Olney, MD 20832
(301) 774-7800

Takoma Park–Silver Spring
7600 Carroll Ave.
Takoma Park, MD 20012
(301) 891-7303

Eastern Regional Health Center
Ridge Rd. at Kennedy Expressway
Towson, MD 21237
(301) 494-2731

MASSACHUSETTS

Boston State Hospital
591 Morton St.
Boston, MA 02124
(617) 436-6000

Boston University Commonwealth of Massachusetts
Treatment Training & Research Center
720 Harrison Ave.
Boston, MA 02118
(617) 262-4200

Erich Kindemann
Government Center
Boston, MA 02114
(617) 727-7100

Massachusetts Center
74 Fenwood Rd.
Boston, MA 02115
(617) 734-1300

Tufts
49 Bennet St.
Boston, MA 02111
(617) 482-2800

Cambridge–Somerville Mental Health & Retardation Center
9 Sacramento St.
Cambridge, MA 02138
(617) 491-2960

Concord Area
Old Rd. to Nine Acre Corner
Concord, MA 01742
(617) 369-1400

Dr. John C. Corrigan
49 Hillside St.
Fall River, MA 02720
(617) 678-2901

The Greater Framingham
25 Evergreen St.
Framingham, MA 01701
(617) 879-7111

Gardner-Athol
13 Elm St.
Gardner, MA 01440
(617) 632-8548

Franklin-Hampshire Area
164 High St.
Greenfield, MA 01301
(413) 772-0211

Mystic Valley
186 Bedford St.
Lexington, MA 02173
(617) 861-0890

Dr. Harry C. Solomon
391 Varnum Ave.
Lowell, MA 01854
(617) 454-8851

Greater Lynn
500 Lynnfield St.
Lynn, MA 01904
(617) 598-8800

Newton-Wellesley-Weston
76 Eldridge St.
Newton, MA 02158
(617) 969-5197

Community Care Center, Inc.
85 Hillman St.
Springfield, MA 01103
(413) 736-3668

Metropolitan-Beaverbrook
475 Trapelo Rd.
Waltham, MA 02154
(617) 894-4300

MENTAL HEALTH CENTERS

MICHIGAN

Mid-Michigan
300 S. Warwick
Alma, MI 48801
(517) 463-4971

Northeast Michigan Mental Health Center Inc.
1521 W. Chisholm St.
Alpena, MI 49707
(517) 356-2161

Washtenaw County
2929 Plymouth Rd.
Ann Arbor, MI 48105
(313) 761-9830

Calhoun-Branch Community Health Services Board
197 N. Washington Ave.
Battle Creek, MI 49017
(616) 965-3908

Bay-Arenac
1908 Columbus Ave.
Bay City, MI 48706
(517) 893-5511

Model Neighborhood
3455 Woodward Ave.
Detroit, MI 48201
(313) 833-9750

Northeast Guidance Center
17000 E. Warren St.
Detroit, MI 48224
(313) 886-7923

Southwest Detroit
2343 12th St. at Fisher
Detroit, MI 48216
(313) 962-3830

Greater Flint
420 W. Fifth Ave.
Flint, MI 48503
(313) 767-7630

North Kent County
1542 Bradford St., NE
Grand Rapids, MI 45903
(616) 456-3985

Borgess Hospital
1521 Gull Rd.
Kalamazoo, MI 49001
(616) 383-7000

Ingham Medical
401 W. Greenlawn Ave.
Lansing, MI 48910
(517) 372-8460

St. Lawrence Hospital
1201 W. Oakland St.
Lansing, MI 48915
(517) 372-7900

Six Area Coalition
2075 Fort St.
Lincoln Park, MI 48146
(313) 382-6776

Community Mental Health Center
425 Fisher St.
Marquette, MI 49855
(906) 225-1181

Midland-Gladwin
4005 Orchard Dr.
Midland, MI 48640
(517) 631-2320

Muskegon County
1092 Holton Rd.
Muskegon, MI 49443
(616) 744-1651

West Oakland
140 Elizabeth Lake Rd.
Pontiac, MI 48053
(313) 338-7241

Port Huron Hospital
1001 Kearney St.
Port Huron, MI 48060
(313) 982-8511

Saginaw County
111 S. Michigan Ave.
Saginaw, MI 48602
(517) 752-4178

Riverwood
2611 Morton Ave.
St. Joseph, MI 49085
(616) 983-7781

MINNESOTA

Bethany Lutheran Home for Children Human Development Center
Ninth St. & 40th Ave.
Duluth, MN 55807
(218) 624-0193

Hennepin County Mental Health/ Mental Retardation Area Program
527 Park Ave.
Minneapolis, MN 55404
(612) 348-8010

Zumbro Valley
2100 E. Center St.
Rochester, MN 55901
(507) 288-1873

Central Minnesota
1321 13th St.
St. Cloud, MN 56301
(612) 252-5010

Northwestern
120 Labree Ave., S.
Thief River Falls, MN 57601
(218) 749-2881

Range Mental Health Center Inc.
624 S. 13th St.
Virginia, MN 55792
(218) 749-2881

West Central Community Services Center Inc.
1125 Sixth St., SE
Willmar, MN 56201
(612) 235-4613

MISSISSIPPI

Comprehensive Center for Mental Health
864 Ritchie Ave.
Clarksdale, MS 38614
(601) 627-7267

Delta Community Mental Health Services
1654 E. Union St.
Greenville, MS 38701
(601) 335-5274

Region VI Community Mental Health- Mental Retardation Center
P.O. Box 1505
Greenwood, MS 38930
(601) 453-6211

Gulf Coast
4514 15th St.
Gulfport, MS 39501
(601) 982-8811

Pine Belt Regional Mental Health- Mental Retardation Complex
830 S. Gloster St.
Tupelo, MS 38801
(601) 842-2133

Regional Mental Health Complex
P.O. Box 902
Starkville, MS 39759
(601) 323-9261

MISSOURI

Saint Francis
825 Goodhope St.
Cape Girardeau, MO 63701
(314) 334-4461

Mid-Missouri
803 Stadium Rd.
Columbia, MO 65201
(314) 499-2511

Mark Twain
109 Virginia St.
Hannibal, MO 63401
(314) 361-4970

Northeastern Jackson County
1505 W. Truman Rd.
Independence, MO 64050
(816) 252-2430

Ozark
2808 Picher St.
Joplin, MO 64801
(417) 781-2410

Western Missouri
600 E. 22nd St.
Kansas City, MO 64108
(816) 471-3000

Southeast Missouri
1301 First St.
Kennett, MO 63857
(314) 888-4522

Southeastern Jackson County
769 Tudor Rd.
Lee's Summit, MO 64063
(816) 524-7300

East Central Missouri
700 E. Monroe St.
Mexico, MO 65265
(314) 581-1785

Tri-County
2900 Hospital Dr.
North Kansas City, MO 64116
(816) 842-8555

Lutheran Medical Center
2639 Miami St.
St. Louis, MO 63118
(314) 772-1456

Malcolm Bliss
1420 Grattan St.
St. Louis, MO 63104
(314) 241-7238

MONTANA

South Central Montana Regional
1245 N. 29th St.
Billings, MT 59101
(406) 252-5658

Southwestern Montana Regional
Silver Bow Annex
Continental Drive
Butte, MT 59701
(406) 723-3447

Northcentral Montana Comprehensive
Holiday Shopping Center
Great Falls, MT 59403
(406) 761-2100

Eastern Montana Regional
Executive Building
Miles City, MT 59301
(406) 232-1687

Western Montana Regional
2829 Fort Missoula Rd.
Missoula, MT 59801
(406) 543-5177

NEBRASKA

Mid-Nebraska
914 Baumann Dr.
Grand Island, NB 68801
(308) 382-1943

South Central
Hastings Regional CTR
Hastings, NB 68901
(402) 463-2471

Lancaster County
134 S. 13th St.
Lincoln, NB 68508
(402) 475-4208

Great Plains
221 S. Jeffers St.
North Platte, NB 69101
(308) 532-4050

Douglas County Hospital
4102 Woolworth Ave.
Omaha, NB 68105
(402) 348-7000

Immanuel
6901 N. 72nd St.
Omaha, NB 68122
(402) 572-2121

Panhandle Mental Health Center &
  Mental Retardation Facility
4110 Ave. D
Scottsbluff, NB 69361
(308) 635-3171

NEVADA

Las Vegas
6101 W. Charleston Blvd.
Las Vegas, NV 89102
(702) 870-7211

NEW HAMPSHIRE

Northern New Hampshire Mental
  Health System Inc.
Washington St.
Conway, NH 03818
(603) 447-3347

Dartmouth-Hitchcock
9 Maynard St.
Hanover, NH 03755
(603) 643-4000

Greater Manchester
401 Cypress St.
Manchester, NH 03103
(603) 668-4111

Community Council of Nashua
7 Prospect St.
Nashua, NH 03060
(603) 889-6147

NEW JERSEY

The Community Center for Mental
  Health Inc.
2 Park Ave.
Dumont, NJ 07628
(201) 385-4400

Elizabeth General Hospital
925 E. Jersey St.
Elizabeth, NJ 07201
(201) 289-8600

Hunterdon Medical Center
Route No. 31
Flemington, NJ 08822
(201) 782-2121

Hackensack Hospital
66 Hospital Place
Hackensack, NJ 07601
(201) 487-4000

St. Mary
308 Willow Ave.
Hoboken, NJ 07030
(201) 792-3300

Christ Hospital
176 Palisades Ave.
Jersey City, NJ 07306
(201) 653-1220

Jersey City Medical Center
50 Baldwin Ave.
Jersey City, NJ 07304
(204) 451-9800

Cumberland County Guidance Center
RD No. 1
Carmel Rd.
Millville, NJ 08332
(609) 825-6810

Jersey Shore Medical Center
1945 Corlies Ave.
Neptune, NJ 07753
(201) 775-5500

Mount Carmel Guild
17 Mulberry St.
Newark, NJ 07102
(201) 624-2405

New Jersey Medical School
65 Bergen St.
Newark, NJ 07107
(201) 456-4683

South Newark/Irvington
201 Lyons Ave.
Newark, NJ 07112
(201) 926-7026

Passaic–Clifton–St. Mary's Hospital
200 Pennington Ave.
Passaic, NJ 07055
(201) 473-2565

Paterson Community Mental Health
  Center Inc.
137 Ellison St.
Paterson, NJ 07505
(201) 881-7700

Raritan Bay
570 Lee St.
Perth Amboy, NJ 08861
(201) 442-1666

Rutgers Community Mental Health
  Center
Rutgers Medical School
Piscataway, NJ 08854
(201) 564-4338

Central Bergen Community Health
  Mental Center Inc.
289 Market St.
Saddlebrook, NJ 07652
(201) 265-8200

South Amboy Memorial Hospital
540 Bordentown Ave.
South Amboy, NJ 08879
(201) 721-1000

Gloucester County
404 Tatum St.
Woodbury, NJ 08096
(609) 845-8050

NEW MEXICO

Bernalillo County
2600 Marble Ave., NE
Albuquerque, NM 87106
(505) 265-3511

Southwest
575 N. Main St.
Las Cruces, NM 88001
(505) 526-6604

Alcoholism Center
1413 Chavez St.
Las Vegas, NM 87701
(505) 425-9511

NEW YORK

St. Mary's Hospital at Amsterdam
427 Guy Park Ave.
Amsterdam, NY 12010
(518) 842-1900

Cayuga County
146 North St.
Auburn, NY 13021
(315) 253-0341

Lincoln
781 E. 142nd St.
Bronx, NY 10454
(212) 993-4500

Bedford Stuyvesant
289 Lewis Ave.
Brooklyn, NY 11221
(212) 574-7200

Brookdale Hospital
Brookdale Plaza & Linden Blvd.
Brooklyn, NY 11212
(212) 240-5661

Maimonides
4802 Tenth Ave.
Brooklyn, NY 11219
(212) 854-7373

Buffalo General Hospital
80 Goodrich St.
Buffalo, NY 14203
(716) 845-4131

Nassau County Medical Center
2201 Hempstead Turnpike
East Meadow, NY 11544
(516) 542-2604

Warren/Washington Community
    Mental Health Center of
    Glens Falls Hospital
100 Park St.
Glens Falls, NY 12801
(518) 793-5148

Orange County Community Mental
    Health Center at Arden Hill
    Hospital
Harriman Dr.
Goshen, NY 10924
(914) 294-5441

Queens Hospital
82-68 164th St.
Jamaica, NY 11432
(212) 990-2927

Metropolitan
1900 Second Ave.
New York, NY 10029
(212) 369-7900

Soundview-Throgs Neck
2527 Glebe Ave.
New York, NY 10461
(212) 430-8907

Washington Heights-West Harlem
558 W. 158th St.
New York, NY 10032
(212) 781-5000

Niagara Falls Memorial Medical Center
621 Tenth St.
Niagara Falls, NY 14302
(716) 278-4536

Oswego County
74 Bunner St.
Oswego, NY 13126
(315) 342-4660

Rockland County
Sanatorium Rd.
Pomona, NY 10907
(914) 354-0200

Dutchess County
230 North Rd.
Poughkeepsie, NY 12601
(914) 485-9715

Convalescent Hospital for Children
2075 Scottsville Rd.
Rochester, NY 14623
(716) 436-4442

Genesee Center
224 Alexander St.
Rochester, NY 14067
(716) 263-5250

Rochester Center
1425 Portland Ave.
Rochester, NY 14621
(716) 544-5220

University of Rochester
260 Crittenden Blvd.
Rochester, NY 14642
(716) 275-3129

North Richmond
55 Austin Place
Staten Island, NY 10304
(212) 390-1315

Rensselaer County
2215 Burdette Ave.
Troy, NY 12180
(518) 274-3000

Mercy Hospital of Watertown
218 Stone St.
Watertown, NY 16301
(315) 785-2135

Nassau Center for Emotionally
    Disturbed Children
72 S. Woods Rd.
Woodbury, NY 11797
(516) 921-7650

NORTH CAROLINA

Blue Ridge
356 Biltmore Ave.
Asheville, NC 28801
(704) 254-2331

Alamance-Caswell Area
1946 Martin St.
Burlington, NC 27215
(919) 228-1727

Orange-Person-Chatham
310 W. Franklin St.
Chapel Hill, NC 27514
(919) 929-4723

Mecklenburg County
501 Billingsley Rd.
Charlotte, NC 28211
(704) 374-2191

Piedmont Area
102 Church St., NE
Concord, NC 28025
(704) 786-5146

Smoky Mountain
P.O. Box 2784
Cullowhee, NC 28723
(704) 293-9281

Cumberland County Mental Health
    Center
Cape Fear Valley Hospital
Owen Drive
Fayetteville, NC 28304
(919) 323-0601

Gaston County
Court Ave.
Gastonia, NC 28052
(704) 867-4411

Wayne County
715 E. Ash St.
Goldsboro, NC 27530
(919) 735-4331

Guilford County
300 N. Edgeworth St.
Greensboro, NC 27401
(919) 373-3630

Catawba County
346 Third Ave., NW
Hickory, NC 28601
(704) 328-5361

Southeastern Regional
209 W. 28th St.
Lumberton, NC 28358
(919) 738-5261

Neuse Clinic
2000 Neuse Blvd.
New Bern, NC 28560
(919) 638-4171

Sandhills Mental Health Center Inc.
P.O. Box 24
Pinehurst, NC 28374
(919) 295-6853

W.H. Trentman Mental Health Center
    of Wake County
2921 Holston Lane
Raleigh, NC 27610
(919) 291-6238

Halifax County
701 Jackson St.
Roanoke Rapids, NC 27870
(919) 537-6174

Edgecomb-Nash
369 Falls Rd.
Rocky Mount, NC 27801
(919) 537-6174

Tri-County
165 Mahaley Ave.
Salisbury, NC
(704) 633-3616

Lee-Harnett
130 Carbonton Rd.
Sanford, NC 27330
(919) 775-4129

Johnson County
Highway 301
Smithfield, NC 27577
(919) 934-5121

Tideland
1308 Highland Dr.
Washington, NC 27889
(919) 946-8061

Wilson-Greene
1709 Tarboro St. SW
Wilson, NC 27893
(919) 291-8021

NORTH DAKOTA

Southeast Mental Health &
  Retardation Center
700 First Ave., S.
Fargo, ND 58102
(701) 237-4513

Northeast Mental Health &
  Retardation Center
509 S. Third St.
Grand Forks, ND 58201
(701) 775-0525

South Central Mental Health &
  Retardation Center
1521 Business Loop, E.
Jamestown, ND 58401
(701) 252-2641

Memorial Mental Health &
  Retardation Center
1007 NW 18th St.
Mandan, ND 58544
(701) 663-6575

North Central Mental Health &
  Retardation Center
140 Souris Dr.
Minot, ND 58701
(701) 839-7665

OHIO

Akron Child Guidance Center &
  Portage Path
312 Locust St.
Akron, OH 44302
(216) 762-0591

Central Community Health
  Board
921 Curtis St.
Concinnati, OH 45206
(513) 281-1051

North Central Hamilton County
1720 Section Rd.
Cincinnati, OH 45241
(513) 531-6633

Community Guidance & Human
  Services Center
3740 Euclid Ave.
Cleveland, OH 44115
(216) 431-7774

Southeast Cleveland
12100 Kinsman Rd.
Cleveland, OH 44120
(216) 283-8444

West Side Community Mental Health
  Task Force Inc.
6601 Detroit Ave.
Cleveland, OH 44102
(216) 281-2660

Columbus Area Center
1515 E. Broad St.
Columbus, OH 43205
(614) 252-0711

North Central Community Mental
  Health & Retardation Services of
  Franklin County
9 W. Buttles Ave.
Columbus, OH 43215
(614) 228-2900

Southwest Community Mental Health
  & Retardation Center
854 W. Town St.
Columbus, OH 43222
(614) 224-4024

Fallsview
330 Broadway, E.
Cuyahoga Falls, OH 44221
(216) 929-8301

Good Samaritan
1425 W. Fairview Ave.
Dayton, OH 45406
(513) 278-2612

Tuscarawas Valley
201 Hospital Dr.
Dover, OH 44622
(216) 343-3311

Gallia, Jackson, & Meigs Counties
Springvalley Plaza
Gallipolis, OH 45631
(614) 446-4950

Marymount Hospital
12300 McCracken Rd.
Garfield Heights, OH 44125
(216) 581-0500

Northwest
718 W. Market St.
Lima, OH 45801
(419) 229-4050

Shawnee
25th & Elmwood Dr.
Portsmouth, OH 45662
(614) 354-2804

Clark County
1345 N. Fountain Blvd.
Springfield, OH 45501
(513) 399-7121

Jefferson County
St. John's Heights
Steubenville, OH 43952
(614) 264-1644

Child & Adult
1001 Covington St.
Youngstown, OH 44510
(216) 747-2601

Muskingum
2845 Bell St.
Zanesville, OH 43701
(614) 454-9766

OKLAHOMA

Jim Taliaferro
602 SW 38th St.
Lawton, OK 73501
(405) 321-4880

Carl Albert
P.O. Box 579
McAlester, OK 74502
(405) 321-4880

Central State
909 E. Alameda St.
Norman, OK 73069
(405) 321-4880

Bi-State Mental Health Foundation
1500 N. Sixth St.
Ponca City, OK 74601
(405) 762-6627

Tulsa
1620 E. 12th St.
Tulsa, OK 74120
(918) 582-2131

OREGON

Lane County
1857 University St.
Eugene, OR 97403
(503) 342-5717

Eastern Oregon
P.O. Box A
Pendleton, OR 97801
(503) 276-3229

PENNSYLVANIA

Altoona Hospital
700 Howard Ave.
Altoona, PA 16603
(814) 946-2141

Muhlenberg Medical Center
Schoenersville Rd.
Bethlehem, PA 18017
(215) 865-0711

Irene Stacy
112 Hillvue Dr.
Butler, PA 16001
(412) 287-0791

MENTAL HEALTH CENTERS

Holy Spirit Hospital
N. 21st St.
Camp Hill, PA 17011
(717) 761-0202

Franklin-Fulton County
Professional Arts Building
Chambersburg, PA 17201
(717) 264-5410

Geisinger Medical Center
North Academy Ave.
Danville, PA 17821
(717) 275-6396

Clearfield-Jefferson Mental Health/
 Mental Retardation and DA
 Programs
100 Hospital Ave.
DuBois, PA 15801
(814) 371-2200

Monroe, Carbon, & Pike Counties
206 E. Brown St.
East Stroudsburg, PA 18301
(717) 421-2901

Hamot
118 E. Second St.
Erie, PA 16507
(814) 453-6081

St. Vincent Hospital
232 W. 25th St.
Erie, PA 16512
(814) 459-4000

Centerville Clinic
Route 1
Fredericktown, PA 15333
(412) 757-6801

Westmoreland Hospital
532 W. Pittsburg St.
Greensburg, PA 15601
(412) 836-2911

Harrisburg Hospital
South Front St.
Harrisburg, PA 17101
(717) 782-5716

Hazelton-Nanticoke
130 W. Broad St.
Hazelton, PA 18201
(717) 735-7590

South Hills Health System
1800 West St.
Homestead, PA 15120
(412) 462-2000

Conemaugh Valley Memorial Hospital
1086 Franklin St.
Johnstown, PA 15905
(814) 536-6671

Latrobe Area
W. Second Ave.
Latrobe, PA 15650
(412) 539-9711

Meadville City Hospital
751 Liberty St.
Meadville, PA 16335

Lawrence County
25½ N. Mercer St.
New Castle, PA 16101
(412) 658-3578

Albert Einstein Community Mental
 Health & Mental Retardation
 Center
York & Tabor Rds.
Philadelphia, PA 19141
(215) 457-7800

Episcopal Hospital
Front St. & Lehigh Ave.
Philadelphia, PA 19125
(215) 426-8000

Hahnemann
314 N. Broad St.
Philadelphia, PA 19102
(215) 568-0860

Hall-Mercer Community Mental Health
 & Mental Retardation Center of
 Penn Hospital
Eighth & Spruce Sts.
Philadelphia, PA 19106
(215) 289-3461

Jefferson
Health Science Center
130 S. Ninth St.
Philadelphia, PA 19107
(215) 829-0791

Nazareth Hospital
2601 Holme Ave.
Philadelphia, PA 19152
(215) 331-8000

North Central Philadelphia
3701 N. Broad St.
Philadelphia, PA 19140
(215) 226-5000

Northeast
Roosevelt Blvd. & Adams Ave.
Philadelphia, PA 19124
(215) 743-1600

Philadelphia Psychiatric Center
4900 Wyalusing Ave.
Philadelphia, PA 19131
(215) 878-7100

West Philadelphia Community Mental
 Health Consortium Inc.
P.O. Box 8076
Philadelphia, PA 19101
(215) 387-5000

St. Francis
45th St. off Penn Ave.
Pittsburgh, PA 15201
(412) 622-4545

Western Psychiatric Institute & Clinic
3811 O'Hara St.
Pittsburgh, PA 15261
(412) 624-2300

Venango County
P.O. Box 1048
Oil City, PA 16301
(814) 676-1871

Beaver County
176 Virginia Ave.
Rochester, PA 15074
(412) 775-5208

Robert Packer Hospital
Guthrie Square
Sayre, PA 18840
(717) 888-6666

Child Guidance
1822 Mulberry St.
Scranton, PA 18501
(717) 346-6573

Fayette County
Federal Bank Building
Uniontown, PA 15401
(412) 437-1201

Crozer-Chester Medical Center
15th & Upland Ave.
Upland, PA 19013
(215) 874-9611

Luzerne-Wyoming County Mental
 Health Center Number One
103 S. Main St.
Wilkes-Barre, PA 18701
(717) 823-2155

Divine Providence
1100 Grampian Blvd.
Williamsport, PA 17701
(717) 326-4191

PUERTO RICO

Aguadilla
Yumet Ave.
P.O. Box 1006
Aguadilla, PR 00603
(809) 891-1586

Arecibo
Arecibo District Hospital
Arecibo, PR 00612
(809) 878-3535

Bayamon
Victory Shopping Center
Bayamon, PR 00619
(089) 786-3620

Caguas
Sub-Regional Hospital
Caguas, PR 00625
(809) 744-1711

Carolina
Fernandez Juncos No. 56
Carolina, PR 00630
(809) 769-9024

Cayey
Hospital T.B.
Jose De Diego Ave.
Cayey, PR 00633
(809) 767-9222

Fajardo
Celis Aguilero St. at A R Barcelo St.
Fajardo, PR 00648
(809) 723-6323

Humacao
Avenida Cruz Ortiz Stella
Humacao, PR 00661
(809) 852-1076

Manati
MacKinley, No. 113
Manati, PR 00701
(809) 854-2435

Mayaguez
c/o Mayaguez Medical Center
Mayaguez, PR 00708
(809) 832-1768

Ponce
Ponce Psychiatric Hospital
Ponce, PR 00731
(809) 842-8223

RHODE ISLAND

Newport County
Friendship St.
Newport, RI 02840
(401) 846-6400

Northern Rhode Island
115 Cass Ave.
Woonsocket, RI 02895
(401) 767-3211

SOUTH CAROLINA

Anderson-Oconee-Pickens
200 McGee Rd.
Anderson, SC 29621
(803) 224-2105

Coastal Empire
125 S. Ribaut Rd.
Beaufort, SC 29902
(803) 524-3378

Charleston Area
30 Lockwood Dr.
Charleston, SC 29401
(803) 577-2300

Columbia Area
1618 Sunset Dr.
Columbia, SC 29203
(803) 758-3595

Pee Dee
Route 2
Florence, SC 29501
(803) 662-1401

Greenville Area Community Mental
  Health Center and Marshall I
  Pickens Hospital
715 Grove Rd.
Greenville, SC 29605
(803) 242-8001

Beckman Center
Phoenix & Alexander Sts.
P.O. Box 70
Greenwood, SC 29646
(803) 223-8331

York-Chester-Lancaster
103 Sedgewood Dr.
Rock Hill, SC 29730
(803) 327-2012

Spartanburg Area
149 E. Wood St.
Spartanburg, SC 29303
(803) 585-0366

Santee-Wateree
215 N. Magnolia St.
Sumter, SC 29150
(803) 775-9364

SOUTH DAKOTA

Northeastern
P.O. Box 82
Aberdeen, SD 57401
(605) 225-1010

Inter-Agency Mental Health Services
800 E. 21st St.
Sioux Falls, SD 57101
(605) 339-8179

TENNESSEE

Bristol Regional
26 Midway St.
Bristol, TN 37620
(615) 968-1561

Columbia Area
308 W. Seventh St.
Columbia, TN 38401
(616) 388-6653

Plateau
Burgess Falls Rd.
Cookeville, TN 38501
(615) 858-3171

Jackson
238 Summar Drive
Jackson, TN 38301
(901) 424-8751

Wautauga Area
109 W. Wautauga Ave.
Johnson City, TN 37601
(615) 928-6545

Helen Ross McNabb Center
1520 Cherokee Trail
Knoxville, TN 37920
(615) 637-9711

Northeast
593-95 Vandalia St.
Memphis, TN 38112
(901) 327-7391

Whitehaven-Southwest
1264 Wesley Dr.
Memphis, TN 38116
(901) 332-6050

Dede Wallace
700 Craighead Ave.
Nashville, TN 37204
(615) 385-1418

Meharry
1005 18th Ave.
Nashville, TN 37208
(615) 327-6608

The Regional Mental Health Center of
  Oak Ridge
240 W. Tyrone Rd.
Oak Ridge, TN 37830
(615) 482-1076

Multi-County
1803 N. Jackson St.
Tullahoma, TN 37388
(615) 455-3476

TEXAS

Amarillo
2103 W. Sixth St.
Amarillo, TX 79175
(806) 376-4431

Austin-Travis County
1430 Collier St.
Austin, TX 78704
(512) 447-4141

Southeast Travis County
1430 Collier St.
Austin, TX 78704
(512) 447-4141

Central Brazos Valley
405 W. 28th St.
Bryan, TX 77801
(713) 822-7326

Nueces County Mental Health/Mental
  Retardation Community Center
1611 Fifth St.
Corpus Christi, TX 78404
(512) 888-5541

District V
329 E. Colorado
Dallas, TX 75203
(214) 943-2122

District VI
721 S. Peak St.
Dallas, TX 75223
(214) 826-2170

Presbyterian Hospital
8200 Walnut Hill Lane
Dallas, TX 75231
(214) 369-4111

Tropical Texas Center
1425 S. Ninth St.
Edinburg, TX 78539
(512) 383-0121

El Paso Center
4821 Alameda Ave.
El Paso, TX 79905
(915) 532-6961

Gulf Coast Regional Mental Health–
  Mental Retardation Center
Angleton Mental Health Group Home
1124 24th St.
Galveston, TX 77550
(713) 763-2373

Gulf Coast Regional Mental Health–
  Mental Retardation Center
Texas City–Lamarque Group Home
1124 24th St.
Galveston, TX 77550
(713) 763-2373

Mid-Houston
2909 Louisiana St.
Houston, TX 77006
(713) 526-1267

West End Neighborhood Health Center
190 Heights Blvd.
Houston, TX 77007
(713) 222-4311

Kingsville
Kleberg County Courthouse
Kingsville, TX 78363
(512) 592-4386

Laredo Mental Health Center
(Rio Grande Area III)
508 Main St.
Laredo, TX 78040
(512) 723-2926

Lubbock Regional
1210 Texas Ave.
Lubbock, TX 79401
(806) 763-4213

Permian Basin Community Centers
3701 N. Big Spring
Midland, TX 79701
(915) 683-5591

Odessa
204 16th St.
Odessa, TX 79760
(915) 333-3265

Central Plains Comprehensive
  Community
2601 Dimmitt Rd.
Plainview, TX 79072
(806) 296-2726

Greater West Texas
244 N. Magdalen St.
San Angelo, TX 76901
(915) 655-5674

Bexar County Mental Health–Mental
  Retardation Center — Southeast
3721 S. Presa St.
San Antonio, TX 78210
(512) 532-4288

Bexar County Mental Health–Mental
  Retardation Center — Southwest
2415 W. Southcross
San Antonio, TX 78211
(512) 924-1411

Northwest San Antonio
4502 Medical Drive
San Antonio, TX 78284
(512) 696-6217

Central Counties Center
Two N. Fourth St.
Temple, TX 76501
(617) 778-4841

Regional Center for East Texas
305 S. Broadway
Tyler, TX 75701
(214) 597-1351

Heart of Texas
1401 N. 18th St.
Waco, TX 76703
(817) 752-3451

Wichita Falls
1800 Rose St.
Wichita Falls, TX 76301
(817) 322-1196

UTAH

Davis County
55 S. Main St.
Farmington, UT 84025
(801) 867-2211

Murray-Jordan-Tooele Mental Hygiene
  Center
5130 S. State St.
Murray, UT 84107
(801) 262-8416

Weber-Morgan County
350 Healy St.
Ogden, UT 84401
(801) 399-8384

Four Corners
61 N. Second, E.
Price, UT 84501
(801) 637-2358

Timpanogos
1161 E. 300, N.
Provo, UT 84601
(801) 373-7393

Granite
156 Westminster Ave.
Salt Lake City, UT 84115
(801) 487-5841

Salt Lake
807 E. South Temple
Salt Lake City, UT 84102
(801) 328-0361

VERMONT

Southeastern Vermont
18 The Square
Bellows Falls, VT 05101
(802) 463-4589

Champlain Valley Mental Health
  Council
260 College St.
Burlington, VT 05401
(802) 862-6514

Lamoille County Mental Health
  Services Inc.
Box 611 Washington Highway
Morrisville, VT 05661
(802) 888-4635

Northeast Kingdom Mental Health
  Service Inc.
60 Broadview Ave.
Newport, VT 05855
(802) 334-7951

Southwest Region
78 S. Main St.
Rutland, VT 05701
(802) 775-2381

VIRGINIA

Mt. Vernon Center
8119 Holland Rd.
Alexandria, VA 22306
(703) 451-1246

Woodburn Center
3340 Woodburn Rd.
Annandale, VA 22003
(703) 573-0523

Planning District I
P.O. Box 537
Big Stone Gap, VA 24219
(703) 523-1366

Planning District 13
P.O. Box 56
Boydton, VA 23917
(804) 738-6189

Blue Ridge
1602 Gordon Ave.
Charlottesville, VA 22902
(804) 295-2161

Chesterfield County
P.O. Box 92
Chesterfield, VA 23832
(804) 748-1421

Planning District IX
West Davis St.
Culpeper, VA 22701
(703) 825-8284

Riverside Hospital
J. Clyde Morris Blvd.
Newport News, VA 23601
(804) 596-3081

Psychiatric Institute
721 Fairfax Ave.
Norfolk, VA 23507
(703) 622-7968

Maryview Hospital
3636 High St.
Portsmouth, VA 23707
(703) 399-5211

Roanoke Area
920 S. Jefferson St.
Roanoke, VA 24016
(703) 345-9841

City of Virginia Beach
Pembroke 3
Virginia Beach, VA 23462
(804) 490-0583

WASHINGTON

Eastside
2253 140th St., NE
Bellevue, WA 98004
(206) 747-9000

Cascade Islands
1135 Mount Baker Highway
Bellingham, WA 98225
(206) 676-8455

Mid-Columbia
1175 Gribble
Richland, WA 99352
(509) 943-9104

Harborview
326 Ninth Ave.
Seattle, WA 98104
(202) 223-3411

Highline–West Seattle
922 SW 151st St.
Seattle, WA 98166
(206) 433-5750

Seattle Mental Institute
1605 17th Ave.
Seattle, WA 98122
(206) 329-5400

Tacoma-Pierce County
P.O. Box 5007
Tacoma, WA 98405
(206) 597-8207

WEST VIRGINIA

Fayette-Monroe-Raleigh-Summers Mental Health Council
P.O. Box 1759
Beckley, WV 25801
(304)252-8651

Appalachian
Wilmoth & Yokum St.
Elkins, WV 26241
(304) 636-3232

Reg. II
P.O. Box 8069
Huntington, WV 25705
(304) 525-7851

Logan-Mingo Area
206 Dingess St.
Logan, WV 25601
(304) 752-6320

Eastern Panhandle
212 S. College St.
Martinsburg, WV 25401
(304) 263-8954

Valley Comp. Community Mental Health Center, Inc.
603 E. Brockway Ave.
Morgantown, WV 26505
(304) 296-1731

Southern Highlands
12th St. Extension
Princeton, WV 24740
(304) 425-9543

Northern Panhandle
2121 Eoff St.
Wheeling, WV 26003
(304) 234-8671

WISCONSIN

North Central
Beaser Ave. & Maple Lane
Ashland, WI 54806
(715) 682-2382

Lakeland Counseling Center of Walworth County
P.O. Box 290
Elkhorn, WI 53121
(414) 723-5400

Fond Du Lac County
459 E. First St.
Fond Du Lac, WI 54935
(414) 921-5480

Brown County
1320 Mahon Ave.
Green Bay, WI 54301
(414) 468-1136

Mississippi River Services Center
Independence Medical Development Building
Independence, WI 54747
(715) 985-3104

Milwaukee County Mental Health Centers
9191 Watertown Plank Rd.
Milwaukee, WI 53226
(414) 257-7490

Sauk, Juneau, & Richland Counties
710 N. Webb Ave.
Reedsburg, WI 53959
(608) 524-4391

Marathon County Health Care Center
1100 Lakeview Dr.
Wausau, WI 54401
(715) 842-1636

WYOMING

Southeast Wyoming
2322 Evans Ave.
Cheyenne, WY 82001
(307) 634-4487

Fremont Counseling Service
195 N. Fourth St.
Lander, WY 82520
(307) 332-2231

Northern Wyoming
1221 W. Fifth St.
Sheridan, WY 82801
(307) 674-4405

ORGANIZATIONS RECEIVING INITIATION AND DEVELOPMENT GRANTS

ALABAMA

Mobile Mental Health Center Inc.
P.O. Box 1524
Mobile, AL 36601

ARIZONA

Santa Cruz Family Guidance Center
Nogales, AZ 85621

ARKANSAS

Delta Counseling & Guidance Center Inc.
Drew County Memorial Hospital
100 Jefferson
P.O. Box 731
Monticello, AR 71655

Ozarks Regional Mental Health Center Inc.
Baxter County Health Department
Mountain Home, AR 72653

North Central Arkansas Mental Health Clinic Inc.
Third & Hazel St.
Newport, AR 72112

Community Mental Health Program of ARVAC Inc.
301 S. Boulder
Russellville, AR 72801

CALIFORNIA

East Los Angeles Health Task Force
4457 E. Telegraph Rd.
Los Angeles, CA 90023

FLORIDA

Pinellas County Mental Health Board & Adult Mental Health Clinic of Pinellas County
6170 Central Ave.
Saint Petersburg, FL 33706

GEORGIA

Laurens County Department of Public Health
P.O. Box 1226
Dublin, GA 31021

IDAHO

South Central Idaho Mental Health Center Inc.
112 East C St.
P.O. Box 548
Shoshone, ID 83352

INDIANA

Mental Health Foundation of Monroe County Inc.
640 S. Rogers
P.O. Box 1149
Bloomington, IN 47401

Community Mental Health–Mental Retardation Center
285 Bielby Rd.
Lawrenceburg, IN 47025

MICHIGAN

Detroit-Wayne County Community Mental Health Services Board
1800 Kales Building
Detroit, MI 48226

MISSISSIPPI

Region VI Mental Health–Mental
  Retardation Commission
P.O. Box 547
Greenwood, MS 38930

Southwest Mississippi Mental Health–
  Mental Retardation Commission
  Region II
P.O. Box 230
Magnolia, MS 39652

Region VII Mississippi Mental Health–
  Mental Retardation Commission
305 University Dr.
Starkville, MS

Region XII Mississippi Mental Health–
  Mental Retardation Commission
  of Mental Health & Mental
  Retardation
P.O. Box 205
Sumrall, MS 39482

NEW JERSEY

Atlantic Area Guidance Center
13 N. Hartford Ave.
Atlantic City, NJ 08401

Community Mental Health Center
  Area 40
Mount Carmel Guild
17 Mulberry St.
Newark, NJ 07102

NEW MEXICO

Rio Del Norte Planning Committee Inc.
437 Onate St., NW
Espanola, NM 87532

OHIO

Community Guidance & Human
  Services Planning Committee
1368 E. 55th St.
Cleveland, OH 44103

Franklin County Mental Health &
  Retardation Board
233 S. High St.
Columbus, OH 43215

Day-Mont-West Mental Health Corp.
P.O. Box 223
Roosevelt Station
Dayton, OH 45408

TENNESSEE

University of Tenessee College of
  Medicine
Department of Psychiatry
42 N. Dunlap St.
Memphis, TN 38103

TEXAS

City Health Department
P.O. Box 550
Crystal City, TX 78839

VIRGINIA

Richmond Subarea A-1 Community
  Mental Health Center
c/o Richmond County Mental Health/
  Mental Retardation Services
  Board
701 E. Franklin St.
Richmond, VA 23219

20 National Alliance of Businessmen

The National Alliance of Businessmen (NAB) was formed by presidential mandate in 1968 and has been supported by every administration since its founding. It now has operating units in 130 cities throughout the country — each supported by government, labor, education, and leading companies. Its main objective is to open the job market to a broad category of disadvantaged people.

NAB's responsibility has been expanded to include Vietnam-era veterans, the handicapped, ex-offenders, and needy youth. It's primary mission is to make the business community aware that meaningful employment is the best solution for many of our most pressing national problems, and to encourage young people to secure the best possible education.

The real work at NAB is done by account executives. These are either executives who are on loan from major corporations or *retired* executives serving on a volunteer basis. Retired executives are nonsalaried, but they are compensated for commuting costs from out of town. They are trained and given background information at NAB headquarters. A major part of their time is spent face to face with business executives in the field.

Following is a list of the local NAB offices across the country. If you are interested in volunteering your time, contact them.

REGIONAL OFFICES

ALABAMA

c/o Central Bank & Trust Co.
935 Daniel Building
Birmingham, AL 35233
(205) 254-1696
Contact: King Sparks

c/o Aluminum Co. of America
1509 Government St. 501
Mobile, AL 36604
(205) 690-2166
Contact: Robert C. Knauer

ALASKA

121 W. Fireweed Ln. 240
Anchorage, AK 99503
(907) 272-9479
Contact: Kevin Pat Parnell

ARIZONA

c/o Phoenix Advisory Board
111 W. Monroe St., Room 720
Phoenix, AZ 85003
(602) 261-4901
Contact: R.T. Bob Bartlett

ARKANSAS

c/o Union National Bank
512 Continental Building
Little Rock, AR 72701
(501) 378-5378
Contact: William T. Prince, III

CALIFORNIA

J.C. Penney Co.–Retired
2101 K St., Mall
Bakersfield, CA 93301
(805) 327-8665
Contact: Arthur J. Boehning

12139 Mt. Vernon Ave.
Colton, CA 92324
(714) 825-1490
Contact: Metro. Director

c/o Shofner Insurance Agency
2220 Tulare St.
Fresno, CA 93721
(209) 266-2032
Contact: William J. Shofner

c/o Southern California Gas. Co.
450 N. Grand Ave.
Los Angeles, CA 90012
(213) 626-5121
Contact: William A. Wilson

2218 Webster St.
Oakland, CA 94612
(415) 839-9460
Contact: C.L. Johnson

c/o IBM Corp.
1 City Blvd., W.
Orange, CA 92668
(714) 547-5923
Contact: Ramon Diaz

c/o Bank of America
2322 J St.
Sacramento, CA 95816
(916) 440-3151
Contact: Clint Ekbom

c/o General Dynamics/Convair
861 Sixth Ave.
San Diego, CA 92101
(714) 234-2296
Contact: Dennis Nelson

NATIONAL ALLIANCE OF BUSINESSMEN

c/o Management Council
433 California St.
San Francisco, CA 94104
(415) 421-9660
Contact: Arthur L. Fine

c/o ITT Cannon Electric
666 E. Dyer Rd.
Santa Ana, CA 92702
(714) 557-7835
Contact: Stuart Steinhauer

c/o Lockheed Missiles & Space
P.O. Box 251
Santa Clara, CA 95052
(408) 249-0501
Contact: B.A. Bud Martin

Colonel USAF Ret.
3868 State St.
Santa Barbara, CA 93105
(805) 687-6481
Contact: H. Ben Walsh

COLORADO

c/o Looart Press Inc.
111½ E. Pikes Peak
Colorado Springs, CO 80903
(303) 636-3331
Contact: Daniel F. Looney

c/o Johns-Manville
Building 5WI Greenwood Pla.
Denver, CO 80217
(303) 770-1000
Contact: William J. Christman

CONNECTICUT

c/o Bridgeport Chamber of Commerce
180 Fairfield Ave.
Bridgeport, CT 06604
(203) 333-0176
Contact: William L. Hawkins

c/o Hartford Chamber of Commerce
250 Constitution Plaza
Hartford, CT 06103
(203) 525-4451
Contact: Paul E. Gradwell

c/o Chamber of Commerce
195 Church St.
New Haven, CT 06510
(203) 562-5194
Contact: Walter J. Coleman

c/o Chamber of Commerce
32 N. Main
Waterbury, CT 06702
(203) 757-0701
Contact: Richard J. Giesbrant

DELAWARE

c/o Diamond State Telephone
300 Delaware Ave.
Wilmington, DE 19801
(302) 571-6106
Contact: Robert E. Davis

DISTRICT OF COLUMBIA

c/o Peat Marwick Mitchell & Co.
1129 20th St., NW
Washington, DC 20036
(202) 833-8190
Contact: Michael A. Freedman

FLORIDA

c/o Southern Bell Telephone
4019 Woodcock Dr.
Jacksonville, FL 32207
(904) 791-3511
Contact: R. Bruce Black, Jr.

2500 SW Third Ave.
Miami, FL 33129
(305) 854-0787
Contact: Metro. Director

c/o Southern Bell
3191 Maguire Blvd. R180
Orlando, FL 32803
(305) 894-1851
Contact: Fred C. Bush

c/o Vince Whibbs Pontiac
3401 Navy Blvd.
Pensacola, FL 32507
(904) 433-7671
Contact: Henry Delong

c/o Montgomery Wards & Co.
300 31st St., N.
St. Petersburg, FL 33713
(813) 893-3500
Contact: Guy Chapman

GEORGIA

c/o Federal Reserve Bank
235 Peachtree, NE
Atlanta, GA 30303
(404) 526-6347
Contact: Anna Grace Green

c/o Georgia Business & Industry
  Association
181 Washington St., SW
Atlanta, GA 30303
(404) 659-4444
Contact: James N. Parkman

c/o Partner
801 Broad St.
Augusta, GA 30902
(404) 722-5532
Contact: Robert E. Stagg

c/o Lockheed-Georgia Co.
86 S. Cobb Dr.
Marietta, GA 30063
(404) 424-4838
Contact: Hugh L. Gordon

HAWAII

c/o Business Community
200 N. Vineyard Blvd.
Honolulu, HI 96817
(808) 536-6922
Contact: L.D. McLaurin

ILLINOIS

c/o Illinois Bell Telephone Co.
6 N. Michigan Ave.
Chicago, IL 60602
(312) 346-0941
Contact: James R. Wadsworth

c/o Peoria Area Bus. & Ind.
301 SW Adams St.
Peoria, IL 61602
(309) 674-9343
Contact: David H. Steinbach

c/o The Quaker Oats Co.
Quaker Rd.
Rockford, IL 61105
(815) 964-4671
Contact: Edward P. Cunningham

INDIANA

c/o Chamber of Commerce
826 Ewing St.
Fort Wayne, IN 46802
(219) 742-1361
Contact: Don Petruccelli

c/o Indiana Bell Telephone
504 Broadway
Gary, IN 46402
(219) 886-2359
Contact: Donald Duran

c/o Citizens Gas & Coke Utility
320 N. Meridian St.
Indianapolis, IN 46204
(317) 632-1316
Contact: James D. Calhoun

c/o South Bend–Mishawaka Chamber
  of Commerce
320 W. Jefferson
South Bend, IN 46624
(219) 234-0051
Contact: Joseph A. Sanders

IOWA

800 High St.
Des Moines, IA 50307
(515) 283-2161
Contact: Monroe Colston

KANSAS

c/o Garvey Industries Inc.
111 W. Douglas
Wichita, KS 67202
(316) 261-5397
Contact: Steven Overstreet

KENTUCKY

1015 W. Chestnut St.
Louisville, KY 40203
(502) 584-2403
Contact: Victor L. Priebe

LOUISIANA

c/o Chamber of Commerce
109 Industrial Parkway
Lafayette, LA 70501
(318) 232-0562
Contact: Bill J. Center

c/o IBM
2025 Canal St.
New Orleans, LA 70112
(504) 821-2887
Contact: Gary W. December

c/o Southmoor Insurance Agency Inc.
P.O. Box 30001
Shreveport, LA 71130
(318) 226-5009
Contact: Robert G. Scott

MAINE

c/o Dead River Co.
324 Harlow St.
Bangor, ME 04401
(207) 945-6434
Contact: Carl E. Delano

c/o Portland Chamber of Commerce
142 Free St.
Portland, ME 04101
(207) 772-2811
Contact: Carl F. Brown

MARYLAND

1100 N. Eutaw St.
Baltimore, MD 21201
(301) 728-2383
Contact: James J. Kotmair, Jr.

c/o Hercules Inc.
141 Baltimore St.
Cumberland, MD 21502
(301) 724-8833
Contact: George L. Baker

c/o Mack Trucks, Inc.
138 E. Antietam St.
Hagerstown, MD 21740
(301) 797-5800
Contact: Roger Keller

MASSACHUSETTS

c/o Honeywell Information Systems
50 Federal St.
Boston, MA 02110
(617) 482-6513
Contact: Leroy L. Gragwell

176 Church St.
Lowell, MA 01852
(617) 459-0113
Contact: Metro. Director

422 Mt. Pleasant St.
New Bedford, MA 02746
(617) 996-3395
Contact: Francis I. Lawler

c/o Quarbin Industries, Inc.
25 Harrison Ave.
Springfield, MA 01103
(413) 781-4187
Contact: Edward R. Irwin

21A Cummings Park
Woburn, MA 01801
(617) 935-8430
Contact: Richard C. Wells

c/o Guaranty Bank & Trust
370 Main St.
Worcester, MA 01608
(617) 753-2991
Contact: Bernard W. McCarthy

MICHIGAN

c/o Michigan Employment Security
  Commission
1200 Sixth St.
Detroit, MI 48226
(313) 237-0130
Contact: Robert J. Walters

444 Church St.
Flint, MI 48502
(313) 232-0196
Contact: William A. Washington

c/o Import Motors Ltd.
1133 Michigan St., NE
Grand Rapids, MI 49503
(616) 451-8358
Contact: Eugene C. Naylor

c/o Borgess Hospital
438 W. South St.
Kalamazoo, MI 49006
(616) 342-0254
Contact: John Isaia

505 W. Washtenaw St.
Lansing, MI 48933
(517) 371-1610
Contact: Metropolitan Director

107 S. Washington
Saginaw, MI 48605
(517) 753-6361
Contact: Robert M. Houghton

MINNESOTA

c/o Superwood Corp.
205 Sellwood Building
Duluth, MN 55802
(218) 722-3363
Contact: John Nordstrom

c/o General Mills
628 Nicollet Mall
Minneapolis, MN 55402
(612) 333-2317
Contact: Robert W. Callaghan

c/o First National Bank of St. Paul
Fourth Robert & Minn. Sts.
St. Paul, MN 55101
(612) 291-5000
Contact: Russell H. Johnson

370 Wabasha St.
St. Paul, MN 55102
(612) 222-5561
Contact: Metropolitan Director

MISSISSIPPI

c/o Business Community
733 N. State St.
Jackson, MA 39201
(601) 355-6468
Contact: A.P. Fatherre

MISSOURI

c/o IBM
114 W. 11th St.
Kansas City, MO 64105
(816) 374-2536
Contact: Jerry Ray

c/o St. Louis Community & Growth
  Association
710 N. 12th St.
St. Louis, MO 63101
(314) 421-2234
Contact: Harry R. Cole

NEBRASKA

c/o Northwestern Bell Telephone Co.
4470 Farnam St.
Omaha, NB 68131
(402) 551-3090
Contact: William J. Cavel

NEW JERSEY

c/o Monmouth–Orange County
  Development Council
601 Bangs Ave.
Asbury Park, NJ 07712
(201) 776-6670
Contact: Robert M. Benham

c/o New Jersey State Employment
  Service
1800 Davis St.
Camden, NJ 08104
(609) 962-6501
Contact: Joseph F. Driscoll

c/o Jersey County Chamber of
  Commerce
One Exchange Place
Jersey City, NJ 07302
(201) 547-7487
Contact: James M. Cederdahl

c/o Greater Newark Chamber of
  Commerce
50 Park Place
Newark, NJ 07102
(201) 642-2713
Contact: Michael J. Derogatis

c/o OPT. Industries, Inc.
300 Red School Lane
Phillipsburg, NJ 08865
(201) 538-4100
Contact: Jerome Potash

c/o Rockwell International Corp.
28 W. State St.
Trenton, NJ 08608
(609) 396-2323
Contact: Merlin Smith

c/o Chamber of Commerce
655 Amboy Ave.
Woodbridge, NJ 07095
(201) 634-8770
Contact: Roger W. Johnson

NATIONAL ALLIANCE OF BUSINESSMEN

NEW MEXICO
c/o Sandia Laboratories
111 Carlisle Blvd. SE
Albuquerque, NM 87106
(505) 266-5963
Contact: M.A. McCutchan

NEW YORK
3 Computer Dr.
Albany, NY 12205
(518) 458-7406
Contact: George L. Johnson

c/o General Electric Co.
19 Chenango St.
Binghamton, NY 13901
(607) 722-4274
Contact: Francis L. Kattell

c/o Gibraltar Steel
290 Main St.
Buffalo, NY 14202
(716) 855-3633
Contact: Richard O'Brien

c/o Sperry Rand Corp.
25 S. Service Rd.
Jericho, NY 11753
(516) 333-9373
Contact: Arthur E. Savigne

c/o Macys Department Store
380 Madison Ave.
New York, NY 10017
(212) 573-9500
Contact: Richard Cukor

25 North St.
Rochester, NY 14604
(716) 232-2600
Contact: Edward Croft

c/o Hall & McChesney, Inc.
P.O. Box 591
Syracuse, NY 13201
(315) 422-3131
Contact: Hendrix Teneyck

c/o Special Metals Corp.
209 Elizabeth St.
Utica, NY 13501
(315) 724-3151
Contact: Gordon Hathaway

NORTH CAROLINA
c/o North Carolina National Bank
500 E. Morehead St.
Charlotte, NC 28202
(704) 372-4491
Contact: Al Graham

c/o Western Electric
P.O. Box 6978
Greensboro, NC 27405
(919) 275-0783
Contact: Edith Brann

NORTH DAKOTA
c/o IBM
321 N. Fourth St.
Fargo, ND 58102
(701) 293-5830
Contact: Bruce W. Furness

OHIO
c/o East Ohio Gas Co.
150 E. Market St.
Akron, OH 44308
(216) 253-4434
Contact: Louis C. Brown

c/o Cincinnati Bell Telephone
309 Vine St.
Cincinnati, OH 45202
(513) 381-3160
Cohtact: Eugene W. Scroggin

c/o Greater Cleveland Growth
  Association
1375 Euclid Ave.
Cleveland, OH 44115
(216) 861-6100
Contact: Theodore Small

c/o Rockwell International
8 E. Long St.
Columbus, OH 43215
(614) 224-9154
Contact: Robert Hadden

c/o Ohio Bureau of Employment
  Service
225 S. Main St.
Dayton, OH 45402
(513) 228-4145
Contact: Wallace C. Johnston

c/o Ohio Bureau Employment Service
707 Broadway
Lorain, OH 44052
(216) 224-2228
Contact: Glorida L. Phillips

c/o Owen Corning Fiberglas
P.O. Box 309
Toledo, OH 43691
(419) 476-7588
Contact: Ronald W. (Skip) Allan

2026 South Ave.
Youngstown, OH 45502
(216) 744-5201
Contact: Metropolitan Director

OKLAHOMA
c/o Southwestern Marketing System
4801 Classen Blvd.
Oklahoma City, OK 73118
(405) 840-3243
Contact: Carroll Emberton

c/o Gulf Oil Co.
2651 E. 21st St.
Tulsa, OK 74114
(918) 747-3636
Contact: Joe Stokes

OREGON
c/o Eugene Realty
P.O. Box 185
Eugene, OR 97401
(503) 485-8574
Contact: Delbert Hill

c/o Aluminum Company of America
921 SW Washington
Portland, OR 97205
(503) 226-4063
Contact: Harry F. Godges

c/o Union Pacific Railroads
921 SW Washington
Portland, OR 92705
(503) 221-3291
Contact: Douglas D. McDaniel

PENNSYLVANIA
c/o Pennsylvania Power & Light Co.
1411 Union Blvd.
Allentown, PA 18103
(215) 435-9025
Contact: John F. Ward

114 Walnut St.
Harrisburg, PA 17101
(717) 233-5796
Contact: Kathryn M. Close

c/o U.S. National Bank
427 Swank Building
Johnstown, PA 15901
(814) 536-6211
Contact: Harold E. Trevenen

c/o Lancaster Area Manufacturers
  Association
30 W. Orange St.
Lancaster, PA 17604
Contact: Dean Keller

3 Penn Center Plaza
Philadelphia, PA 19102
(215) 665-0254
Contact: E. Dale Foster

c/o Allegheny Conference —
  Community Development
911 Penn Ave.
Pittsburgh, PA 15222
(412) 565-2762
Contact: Richard P. Bell

c/o National Central Bank
443 Wash St.
Reading, PA 19603
(215) 376-4879
Contact: David Hoffman

c/o Dentsply International
35 N. George
York, PA 17405
(717) 854-5596
Contact: James D. Quickel

PUERTO RICO
c/o Arthur Andersen & Co.
G.P.O. Box 2399
San Juan, PR 00936
(809) 764-2669
Contact: Jose Reinaldo Lugo

RHODE ISLAND
Two Jackson Walkway 1
Providence, RI 02903
(401) 521-4747
Contact: Anne Garberg

SOUTH CAROLINA

252 Building
Greenville, SC 29607
(803) 233-2020
Contact: John M. Scott, Jr.

SOUTH DAKOTA

c/o Northwestern Bell
101 W. Ninth St.
Sioux Falls, SD 57102
(605) 338-0851
Contact: John H. Brehmer

TENNESSEE

c/o Whalum Co.
P.O. Box 224
Memphis, TN 38101
(901) 523-8091
Contact: Harold Whalum

TEXAS

c/o Rockwell International —
    Collins Division
1507 Pacific Ave.
Dallas, TX 75201
(214) 749-7161
Contact: Alfred L. Nash

c/o Chamber of Commerce
P.O. Box 682
El Paso, TX 79944
(915) 533-5434
Contact: Jack I. Hamilton

c/o Lone Star Gas Co.
819 Taylor St.
Fort Worth, TX 76102
(817) 334-2061
Contact: Bob Jernigan

c/o Tenneco Inc.
3637 W. Alabama St.
Houston, TX 77027
(713) 627-9600
Contact: Lois B. Parsons

c/o Conroy Court–South Square
3355 Cherry Ridge
San Antonio, TX 78230
(512) 344-9738
Contact: Thomas Perkins

UTAH

c/o Granite School District — Retired
10 Exchange P.
Salt Lake City, UT 84111
(801) 328-4825
Contact: Mr. Alma H. Dalebout

VIRGINIA

c/o First Virginia Bank of Tidewater
5 Koger Executive Center
Norfolk, VA 23502
(804) 461-9396
Contact: Keith N. Lindgren

c/o Richmond Chamber of Commerce
201 E. Franklin St.
Richmond, VA 23219
(804) 782-2708
Contact: Carlion P. Moffatt

c/o Eli Lilly & Co.
2823 Williamson Rd., NE
Roanoke, VA 24012
(703) 982-6286
Contact: M. Ann Cummings

WASHINGTON

c/o Boeing Co.
2200 Sixth Ave.
Seattle, WA 98121
(206) 622-2391
Contact: John T. Codling

c/o Tacoma Business Community
302 Broadway Terrace Building
Tacoma, WA 98402
(206) 593-6521
Contact: Genevieve Tucker

WEST VIRGINIA

c/o E. I. Du Pont De Nemours & Co.
901 W. Du Pont Ave.
Belle, WV 25015
(304) 949-4313
Contact: John E. Talman

c/o Kentucky Power Co.
P.O. Box 2845
Huntington, WV 25728
(304) 529-6069
Contact: J.E. Runyon

WISCONSIN

c/o Lacrosse Area
710 Main St.
Lacrosse, WI 54601
(608) 784-4880
Contact: Michael Cordes

c/o First Federal Savings & Loan
    Association
615 E. Washington Ave.
Madison, WI 53703
(608) 255-9222
Contact: Dennis J. Oloughlin

c/o Metropolitan Milwaukee
    Association of Commerce
828 N. Broadway
Milwaukee, WI 53202
(414) 273-3000
Contact: Hilda Heglund

300 Fifth St.
Racine, WI 53403
(414) 632-6114
Contact: Victor C. Tannehill

c/o Fleming Shoe Store
122 W. Court
Richland Center, WI 53581
(608) 647-3410
Contact: Robert Fleming

21 National Nutrition Program

The National Nutrition Program for Older Americans (NPOA), operated by the Administration on Aging, is designed to provide inexpensive, nutritionally sound meals to older Americans, particularly those with low incomes or otherwise in greatest need. The nutrition program is authorized by Title VII of the Older Americans Act of 1965 (P.L. 89-73), as amended (P.L. 92-258, P.L. 93-29, P.L. 93-351, and P.L. 94-135).

The Problem

In addition to promoting better health among older Americans through improved nutrition, education, counseling, and the limited delivery of health services, the nutrition program helps reduce the isolation of older persons by offering them an opportunity to participate in community activities and to combine food and friendship. The 1972 amendments to the Older Americans Act stated the situation:

> "...Many older persons do not eat adequately because (1) they cannot afford to do so; (2) they lack the skills to select and prepare nourishing and well-balanced meals; (3) they have limited mobility, which may impair their capacity to shop and cook for themselves; and (4) they have feelings of rejection and loneliness which obliterate the incentive necessary to prepare and eat a meal alone. These and other physiological, psychological, social and economic changes that occur with aging result in a pattern of living which causes malnutrition and further physical and mental deterioration."

The Response

To meet this situation, there have been established throughout the country NPOA projects that provide at least one hot meal a day, at least 5 days a week, to Americans 60 and over and their spouses of any age. The meal must provide one-third of the Recommended Dietary Allowances as established by the Food and Nutrition Board, National Research Council-National Academy of Sciences in 1974. The U.S. Department of Agriculture provides a stipulated value of donated foods for each meal that the NPOA serves.

Provision of meals in group settings is emphasized. Meal sites include schools, churches, community centers, senior citizens' centers, public housing, and other public and nonprofit facilities where other supportive services may also be available. Outreach programs identify those older persons most in need. Escort and transportation services to bring participants to NPOA project sites are also part of the package the program provides.

Although the nutrition program by law is not a home-delivered-meal activity, it does provide home-delivered meals to regular participants who from time to time are unable to attend the meal service site. Currently, about 13 percent of all meals served are home-delivered.

The Older Americans Act recognizes the need for a network of supportive services, including health services, information and referral, escort services, health and welfare counseling, and consumer education. The NPOA project sites act as centers of activity, attracting older persons to a place where, in addition to a nourishing meal, they have the opportunity to receive these services, as well as advice on such important matters as legal rights, housing, shopping assistance, aging as a process, income maintenance, and crime prevention. They also have the opportunity for socialization and recreation and for volunteer service to others. Under the terms of the 1973 amendments to the Older Americans Act, states are encouraged to make nutrition program projects part of the system of services coordinated through area agencies on aging.

An important part of the nutrition program is health and nutrition education, designed to promote attention to all health needs, including good nutrition. Such education makes older persons and project staff and volunteers aware of the relative values of food and its contribution to health and well-being, and thereby can influence selection, purchase, and preparation.

Administration

In each state, the nutrition program is administered by the state agencies on aging, unless another agency is designated by the governor and approved by the commissioner on aging. The administering agency makes grants or contracts with public and nonprofit agencies, institutions, and organizations for actual provision and delivery of meals. Information concerning administration of the program is available from the state agencies on aging. (See Chapter 3, Area Agencies on Aging.)

Who Receives Services?

An NPOA project must serve primarily low-income persons 60 years of age and over and their spouses and other older Americans who are determined to be in greatest need. The state also must ensure that awards are made to initiate projects to serve minority, native American, and limited-English-speaking individuals, at least in proportion to their numbers within the state. Meal sites must be located in urban areas that have heavy concentrations of target-group older Americans and in rural areas that have high proportions of eligible older persons.

No one may be turned away from a meal for inability to pay, and there is no means test. However, all participants are given an opportunity to pay all or part of the cost of a meal. The NPOA project councils, all of which contain participant majorities, establish either a contribution schedule based on resources or a single flat sum as a guide to the size of contributions. Participants determine for themselves what they are able to contribute. Contributions are received in such a manner that the amount contributed is known only to the participant contributor.

A comprehensive list of nutrition-sites follows.

NPOA SITES

ALABAMA

District IV Nutrition Project
700 Olintard
Anniston, AL 36201

Nutrition Program for Elderly
2112 11th Ave.
Birmingham, AL 35203

Positive Maturity Nutrition Program
360C Eighth Ave., S.
Birmingham, AL 35222

Fuller Life Meals Program
P.O. Box 269
Camden, AL 36726

Tarcog Nutrition Program for Aging
Central Bank
Huntsville, AL 35801

Nutrition Program Sail
P.O. Box 1665
Mobile, AL 36601

Harvest
303 Washington Ave.
Montgomery, AL 36101

Food and Fun For Senior Citizens
P.O. Box 2603
Muscle Shoals, AL 35660

West Alabama Plan & Development Council
P.O. Box 28
Tuscaloosa, AL 34501

ALASKA

Anchorage Senior Citizens Center
135 E. Eighth St.
Anchorage, AK 99501

Alaskaland VII
P.O. Box 2707
Fairbanks, AK 99701

Southeast Nutrition Program
529 Gold
Juneau, AK 99801

ARIZONA

Bisbee-Douglas Nutrition
314 Tenth St.
Douglas, AZ 85607

Nacog Nutrition Project
119 E. Aspen
Flagstaff, AZ 86001

Services for Senior Citizens
250 E. Cedar
Globe, AZ 85501

Leap Nutrition Project
302 W. Washington
Phoenix, AZ 85003

Maricopa County Nutrition Project
4645 E. Washington St.
Phoenix, AZ 85034

Ticson Nutrition Project
102 N. Plummer
Tucson, AZ 85719

Navajo Nation Nutrition
Aged Blind Disabled Program
Window Rock, AZ 86515

Operation Food For Friends
P.O. Box 929
Yuma, AZ 85364

ARKANSAS

White River Planning & Development District
P.O. Box 2396
Batesville, AR 72501

West Arkansas Planning & Development District
523 Garrison Ave.
Fort Smith, AR 72901

Northwest Arkansas Development District
P.O. Box 668
Harrison, AR 72601

West Central Arkansas Planning & Development District
P.O. Box 1558
Hot Springs, AR 71901

East Arkansas Planning District
P.O. Box 1403
Jonesboro, AR 72401

Southwest Arkansas Planning & Development District
P.O. Box 767
Magnolia, AR 71753

Central Arkansas Planning & Development District
5111 John Kennedy Blvd.
N. Little Rock, AR 72116

SE Arkansas Economic Development District
P.O. Box 6806
Pine Bluff, AR 71601

Senior Citizens Services Texarkana Inc.
Texarkana, AR 75501

CALIFORNIA

Hub City Buyers Clubs Senior Citizens Program
1112 N. Sante Fe Ave.
Compton, CA 90221

Imperial County Senior Power Nutrition Program
143 S. Sixth St.
El Centro, CA 92243

Tri-City Senior Concern
17696 Foothill Blvd.
Fontana, CA 92335

Fresno-Madera County Senior Citizens Nutrition Program
2100 Tulare St.
Fresno, CA 93721

Long Beach CEO SOS Nutrition Program
853 Atlantic Ave.
Long Beach, CA 90813

Casa Maravilla Senior Citizens
4950 E. Floral Dr.
Los Angeles, CA 90022

City of La Recreation & Parks
200 N. Main St.
Los Angeles, CA 90012

Hot Meals for the Elderly
2230 W. Jefferson Blvd.
Los Angeles, CA 90018

Kosher Meals for the Elderly
7711 Melrose
Los Angeles, CA 90036

Program of Retired Citizens
1450 W. Venice Blvd.
Los Angeles, CA 93721

Senior Citizens Action Program
4865 E. First St.
Los Angeles, CA 90022

Napa Valley Dining Club
4215 Soland Ave.
Napa, CA 94558

Pasadena Nutrition Program Seniors
717 N. Lake Ave.
Pasadena, CA 91104

Superior California Senior Service
P.O. Box 924
Red Bluff, CA 96080

Senior Citizens Nutrition Project
621 Middlefield Road
Redwood City, CA 94063

ITCC Indian Health & Nutrition Program
2969 Fulton Ave.
Sacramento, CA 95821

San Diego County Nutrition Project
1955 Fourth Ave.
San Diego, CA 92101

Kimochi Sfissei Project
1581 Webster St.
San Francisco, CA 94115

Missions Rebels Senior Citizens Nutrition Program
2700 16th St.
San Francisco, CA 94103

Satellite Food Service
1280 Laguna St.
San Francisco, CA 94115

Western Addition Senior Citizens Service Center
1453 Fillmore St.
San Francisco, CA 94115

Nutrition & Service Project
55 W. Younger Ave.
San Jose, CA 95114

Project TLB
201 S. Sullivan
Santa Ana, CA 92704

Santa Barbara Bi-County Senior Meals
735 State St.
Santa Barbara, CA 93101

RHAAC SOS Nutrition Program
9836 S. Jersey Ave.
Santa Fe Spring, CA 90670

Golden Circle Dining Clubs
1617 Terrace Way
Santa Rosa, CA 95404

Full Activity Center Program
114 S. Sutter St.
Stockton, CA 95202

Meals for Seniors
411 E. Kern Ave.
Tulare, CA 93274

First Christian Church
35 Indiana St.
Vallejo, CA 94590

MIG Nutrition Needs of Elderly
3147 Loma Vista Rd.
Ventura, CA 93041

COLORADO

San Luis Valley Nutrition
1202 San Juan
Alamosa, CO 81101

Delta Montrose Nut Project
126 E. Fourth
Delta, CO 81416

Seniors Nutrition Program
1865 Larimer St.
Denver, CO 80202

Trinity Services Corp.
1820 Broadway
Denver, CO 80202

Mesa County Nutrition Program
P.O. Box 2390
Grand Junction, CO 81501

Pueblo Nutrition Program
314 E. Seventh
Pueblo, CO 81003

CONNECTICUT

Greater Bridgeport Elderly
115 Main St.
Bridgeport, CT 06601

Southwestern Connecticut Nutrition
850 Norman St.
Bridgeport, CT 06705

Quinebaug Valley Senior Citizens
P.O. Box 108
Brooklyn, CT 06234

Danbury Area Elderly Nutrition
261 Main St.
Danbury, CT 06810

Mana Team
256 Main St.
Derby, CT 06418

CRT Elderly Nutrition Program
358 C Main St.
Hartford, CT 06120

Southeast Connecticut Elderly Nutrition
One Sylvandale Rd.
Jewert City, CT 06351

Office of Urban Affairs
8 Hughes Place
New Haven, CT 06511

Central Connecticut Elderly Nutrition
91 Northwest Dr.
Plainville, CT 06062

Nutritious Meals for Elderly
140 Main St.
Torrington, CT 06750

CNVR Elderly Nutrition
20 E. Main St.
Waterbury, CT 06702

DELAWARE

Manna Nutrition Program
126 W. Division St.
Dover, DE 19901

Cheer Nutrition Program
10001 Middleford Rd.
Seaford, DE 19973

New Castle County Nutrition
2920 Duncan Rd.
Wilmington, DE 19808

Serve Nutrition Program
1901 Market St.
Wilmington, DE 19802

DISTRICT OF COLUMBIA

Friendship House Nutrition Program
619 D St., SE
Washington, DC 20003

Keen
1225 Maple View Place, SE
Washington, DC 20020

Life at Sixty Clubs
3308 14th St., NW
Washington, DC 20010

Open Older People Eating Nutrition
Mount Saint Albans
Washington, DC 20016

SNACC
1424 16th St., NW
Washington, DC 20036

FLORIDA

Manatee Nutrition Project for Elderly
912 Seventh Ave., E.
Bradenton, FL 33505

Seniors Nutritional Aid Program
Holiday Office Center
Cocoa Beach, FL 32931

Central Dining Program
524 S. Beach St.
Daytona Beach, FL 33926

Walton County Congregate Meals
P.O. Box 692
Defuniak, FL 32433

Service Agency for Seniors
1300 S. Andrews Ave.
Ft. Lauderdale, FL 33316

Lee County Congregate Meals
3308 Canal
Fort Myers, FL 33901

Seminole Hot Meal Program
6073 Stirling Rd.
Hollywood, FL 33024

Community Involvement & Nutrition
  Service Program
1093 W. Sixth St.
Jacksonville, FL 32209

Monroe County Nutrition Program
600 White St.
Key West, FL 32931

Polk County Nutrition Program
1234 E. Lime St.
Lakeland, FL 33801

Community Action-Agency
Senior Centers for Dade County, Inc.
395 NW First St.
Miami, FL 33131

Geriatric Nutrition Program
819 SW 12th Ave.
Miami, FL 33130

Nutrition Program for Elderly
1515 NW Seventh St.
Miami, FL 33125

Senior Centers Nutrition Program
1407 NW Seventh St.
Miami, FL 33125

JVS Nutritional Project
920 Alton Rd.
Miami Beach, FL 33139

Marion County Nutrition Program
515 SW Second St.
Ocala, FL 32670

Orange County Nutrition Activity
  Program
410 Woods Ave.
Orlando, FL 32805

Nutrition Program for the Elderly in
  Bay County
416 Jenks Ave.
Panama City, FL 32401

Escameia County Congregate Meals
23 North St.
Pensacola, FL 32593

Palm Beach County Nutrition Project
301 Broadway
Riviera Beach, FL 33404

St. John's County Citizens Advisory
  Council on Aging
City Building
St. Augustine, FL 32084

The Neighborly Center Inc.
1450 Fourth St., S.
St. Petersburg, FL 33701

Candelight Dining
P.O. Box 1795
Sarasota, FL 33578

Leon Conghone-Del-Meals Program
2330 Office Plaza, E.
Tallahassee, FL 32304

Senior Citizens Nutrition Program
2103 N. Rome Ave.
Tampa, FL 33607

GEORGIA

Southwest Area Nutrition Project
600 N. Davis St.
Albany, GA 31701

Northeast Georgia Nutrition Project
305 Research Rd.
Athens, GA 30601

Atlanta Region Nutrition Project
100 Peachtree St., NW
Atlanta, GA 30303

CSRA Nutrition Project
Box 2800
Augusta, GA 30904

Lower Chattahoochee Nutrition
  Program
900 Linwood Blvd.
Columbus, GA 31902

Georgia Mountains Nutrition Project
P.O. Box 1720
Gainesville, GA 30501

Upper Ocmilgee Nutrition Project
Box 133
Jackson, GA 30233

North Georgia Nutrition Project
Box 530
Jasper, GA 30143

Middle Georgia Nutrition Project
789 Main St.
Macon, GA 31201

Coosa Valley Nutrition Project
P.O. Drawer H
Rome, GA 30161

Coastal Nutrition Project
6606 Abercorn Ext.
Savannah, GA 31405

Coastal Plain Nutrition Project
Box 1645
Valdosta, GA 31601

HAWAII

Hawaii County Nutrition Program
34 Rainbow Dr.
Hilo, HI 96720

ACFSC Congregate Dining Corp.
623 S. Beretania St.
Honolulu, HI 96813

Kauai–Good-Life Congregate Meal
P.O. Box 111
Lihue, HI 56766

Maui County Nutrition Project
200 S. High St.
Wailuka, HI 96793

IDAHO

Ada-Elmore Nutrition Project
1455 N. Orchard
Boise, ID 83704

North Idaho Nutrition Project
P.O. Box 1300
Coeur D'Alene, ID 83814

Forward Hol
405 S. Wardwell
Emmett, ID 83617

Shoshone-Bannock Nutrition Project
P.O. Box 306
Fort Hall, ID 83203

Eastern Idaho Nutrition Project
P.O. Box 1098
Idaho Falls, ID 83401

Noon-Ta-Kehse-Nim Ne-Mee-Poom
P.O. Box 305
Lapwai, ID 83540

North Central Idaho Nutrition Project
P.O. Box 268
Lewiston, ID 83501

Southeast Idaho Nutrition Project
1356 N. Main
Pocatello, ID 83201

South Central Idaho Nutrition Project
P.O. Box 1238
Twin Falls, ID 83301

ILLINOIS

Food Facts and Fun
3512 McArthur Blvd.
Alton, IL 62002

Fulton County Elderly Nutrition
  Program
175 White Court
Canton, IL 61520

Golden Goose Nutrition Project
940 N. Oakland Ave.
Carbondale, IL 62901

NATIONAL NUTRITION PROGRAM 267

Wabash Area Development Inc.
Box 392
Carmi, IL 62821

White County Nutrition Project
205 E. Robinson
Carmi, IL 62821

Project Bread
311 S. Elm St.
Centralia, IL 62801

East Central Illinois Nutrition Program
Eastern Illinois University
Charleston, IL 61920

Chicago Nutrition Program for Older Adults
330 S. Wells St.
Chicago, IL 60606

Dupage County Nutrition Program
19 S. LaSalle St.
Chicago, IL 60603

Illinois Senior Nutrition Program
1415 N. Park Dr.
Chicago, IL 60610

Nutrition Project for Elderly
875 N. Dearborn St.
Chicago, IL 60606

Suburban Cook County Elderly Nutrition Program
600 S. Michigan Ave.
Chicago, IL 60605

Senior Adult Meal Service
100 N. Franklin St.
Danville, IL 61832

Senior Citizens Nutritional Program
1306 N. Warren
Decatur, IL 62526

Food Feeding Our Older
145 Fisk Ave.
DeKalb, IL 60115

The Gold Plate Program Perry County
325 N. Linden
Duquoin, IL 62832

Golden Circle
206 S. Willow
Effingham, IL 62401

Golden Circle Activity Center
Box 178
Elizabethtown, IL 62931

New Horizons for Golden American
320 N. Kellogg
Galesburg, IL 61401

Embarras River Basin Program
Box 307
Greenup, IL 62428

Marshall Stark Woodford Nutrition
St. Marys Community Center
Henry, IL 61537

Bread of Love Nutrition Program
314 Finley
Jacksonville, IL 62650

Illinois Valley Senior Citizen Nutrition Program
P.O. Box 431
Jerseyville, IL 62052

Nutrition Project for the Elderly
27 S. Chicago St.
Joliet, IL 60436

Kankakee County Congregate Feeding
258 E. Court St.
Kankakee, IL 60901

Kewanee-Senior Citizens Center
314 N. Tremont St.
Kewanee, IL 61443

Lawrence County Nutrition Program
1407 State St.
Lawrence, IL 62439

Nutrition Feeding Program for the Elderly
128 Pine St.
Lincoln, IL 62656

Guad County Senior Citizens Program
730 E. Clinton Ave.
Monmouth, IL 61462

Smiles Nutrition Program
415 Blache
Mounds, IL 62964

Jefferson County Senior Citizens Nutrition Program
811 Casey
Mt. Vernon, IL 62864

Older Americans Nutrition Program
Rural Route 1
Oglesby, IL 61438

Tazewell County Nutrition Services Program
243 Derby St.
Pekin, IL 61554

Elderly Nutrition Program
711 W. McDean St.
Peoria, IL 61065

Project Meals
Box 522
Quincy, IL 62301

Whiteside County Golden Meals
457 Garden Circle
Rockfalls, IL 61071

Meet Eat Nutrition Program for Elderly
304 N. Main St.
Rockford, IL 61101

Congregate Program for Older Persons
1823 Second Ave.
Rock Island, IL 61201

Sang County Nutrition Project for Elderly
1315 S. Eighth St.
Springfield, IL 62703

L.C.C.S. Nutrition Program
4 S. Genessee St.
Waukegan, IL 60085

Wit and Wisdom Center Franklin
502 E. Main St.
West Frankfort, IL 62896

INDIANA

Dearborn County Social Council
P.O. Box 157
Dillsboro, IN 47018

Southwest Indiana Regional Council on Aging
528 Main St.
Room 307
Evansville, IN 47708

Allen County Council on Aging
227 E. Washington Blvd.
Fort Wayne, IN 46802

Clinton County Council on Aging Program
252 S. Second
Frankfort, IN 46041

LCEO, Inc.
5518 Calumet St.
Hammond, IN 46320

Indianapolis Nutrition for Seniors
155 E. Market St.
Indianapolis, IN 46204

Title VII Nutrition Program for Elderly
317 E. Fifth St.
New Albany, IN 47150

Older Americans Service Corp.
Box 206
Orleans, IN 47452

Miami County Y.M.C.A.
Sixth & Wabash
Peru, IN 46970

Elderly Nutrition Program
121 W. Main St.
Portland, IN 47371

The Eatin' Nutrition Site
306 S. Tenth St.
Richmond, IN 47374

Title VII Nutrition Project
710 N. Ewing
Seymour, IN 47274

Real Services
P.O. Box 1835
South Bend, IN 46634

West Council In Nutrition for the Poor Elderly
P.O. Box 627
Terre Haute, IN 47808

Regional Council on Aging, Inc.
19 N. Fourth St.
Vincennes, IN 47591

IOWA

Area X Area Agency on Aging
Congregate Meal Program
6301 Kirkwood Blvd., SW
Cedar Rapids, IA 52406

Area XIII Agency on Aging
409 First National Bank Building
Council Bluffs, IA 51501

Area XIV Nutrition Program
215 N. Elm St.
Creston, IA 50801

Great River Bend AAA Nutrition
105 S. Main St.
Davenport, IA 52801

Central Iowa Nutrition Program
104½ E. Locust St.
Des Moines, IA 50309

Northeast Iowa Area Agency on Aging
Title VII Nutrition Program
Dubuque Building
Dubuque, IA 52001

Wooden Moccasin
300 S. 18th St.
Estherville, IA 51334

Pioneer Trail Nutrition Project
500 College Dr.
Mason City, IA 50401

Southeast Central Iowa Area Agency on Aging
Indian Hills Community College
Ottumwa, IA 52501

Nutrition Program for the Elderly
P.O. Box 447
Sioux City, IA 51102

Hawkeye Valley Title VII Project
P.O. Box 690
Waterloo, IA 50704

KANSAS

South Central Kansas Area Agency on Aging
P.O. Box 1122
Arkansas City, KS 67005

Southwest Kansas Area Agency on Aging
1802 Jones
Garden City, KS 67846

Northwest Kansas Area Agency on Aging
208 E. Seventh St.
Hays, KS 67801

Northeast Kansas Area Agency on Aging
P.O. Box 56
Hiawatha, KS 66434

Southeast Kansas Area Agency on Aging
201 S. Ninth St.
Humboldt, KS 66748

Wyandotte Leavenworth County Area Agency on Aging
701 N. Seventh St.
Kansas City, KS 66101

North Central Flint Hills Area Agency on Aging
425 Pierre St.
Manhattan, KS 66502

Mid-American Council on Aging
5311 Johnson Dr.
Mission, KS 66205

Capitol Area Agency on Aging
215 E. Seventh
Topeka, KS 66603

Central Plains Area Agency Aging
455 N. Main
Wichita, KS 67202

KENTUCKY

Nutrition Program for the Elderly
814 State St.
Bowling Green, KY 42101

Northern Kentucky Project
629 Madison Ave.
Covington, KY 41011

Licking Valley Nutrition Program
2358 W. Water St.
Flemingsburg, KY 41041

Greem River Nutrition Project
223½ Main St.
Henderson, KY 40601

Bluegrass Community Services
2057 Regency Circle
Lexington, KY 40503

Metropolitan Social Services
216 S. Fifth St.
Louisville, KY 40202

Country Gathering
P.O. Box U
Olive Hill, KY 41164

Gateway Senior Citizens
Box 36
West Liberty, KY 41472

Community Action Council
P.O. Box 748
Whitesburg, KY 41858

LOUISIANA

South Louisiana Nutrition Program
515 Edwards St.
Abbeville, LA 70510

Rapides Nutrition Program
1319 Bush Ave.
Alexandria, LA 71301

Baton Rouge Congregate Nutrition Program
1961 Government St.
Baton Rouge, LA 70806

St. Taffany Parish Senior Nutrition Project
P.O. Box 171
Covington, LA 70433

Washington Parish Nutrition Project
P.O. Box 214
Franklinton, LA 70438

North Central Nutrition Project
P.O. Box 326
Homer, LA 71040

Acadiana Food & Friends Project
103 Zim Circle
Lafayette, LA 70501

Elderly Nutrition Program Cal Parish
P.O. Box 3049
Lake Charles, LA 70601

Ouachita Nutrition Programs
1209 Oliver St.
Monroe, LA 71201

Succor & Supportive Services
P.O. Box 944
Natchitoches, LA 74157

Nutrition Programs — Jefferson & Orleans
333 St. Charles
New Orleans, LA 70130

Allen Parish Nutrition Program
P.O. Box 728
Oakdale, LA 71463

Iberville Ascension Project
413 Placuemine
Placuemine, LA 70764

Tangi-Nutrition Program
142 S. Eighth St.
Ponchatcula, LA 70454

Cadoo Bossier Nutrition Program for the Aging
705 Grand Ave.
Shreveport, LA 71101

Terrebonne-LaFourche Nutrition Project
306 Tetreau St.
Thibodalx, LA 70301

Acadiani Food & Friends Program
P.O. Box 312
Ville Platte, LA 70586

MAINE

Central Senior Citizen Association
P.O. Box 484
Augusta, ME 04330

Meals for Maine Inc.
890 Hammond St.
Bangor, ME 04401

Western Maine Meals for the Elderly
65 Central Ave.
Lewiston, ME 04240

Cumberland-York Senior Citizens Council
142 High St.
Portland, ME 04101

Forget Me Not Meals
P.O. Box 1286
Presque Isle, ME 04769

MARYLAND

Eating Together in Baltimore
City Hall Office of Mayor
Baltimore, MD 21202

Senior Citizens Diners Club
9171 Central Ave.
Capitol Heights, MD 29027

Uppershore Title VII Nutrition Program
P.O. Box 248
Centerville, MD 21617

Senior Citizens Congregate Meals Program
206 Paca St.
Cumberland, MD 21802

Food and Friends
520 N. Market St.
Frederick, MD 21701

Anne-Arundel County Nutrition Program for the Elderly
6652 Shelly Rd.
Glen Burnie, MD 21661

Title VII Nutrition Program
25 W. Franklin St.
Hagerstown, MD 21740

Title 7 Nutrition Program for the Elderly
Court House
Leonardtown, MD 20650

Nutrition for the Elderly
14 Maryland Ave.
Rockville, MD 20850

Mac Nutrition Program
Pine Bluff State Hospital
Salisbury, MD 21801

Nutrition Program for the Elderly
121 W. Susquehanna Ave.
Towson, MD 21204

Harford-Carroll Nutrition Program
West End School
Schoolhouse Ave.
Westminister, MD 21157

MASSACHUSETTS

Southwest Boston Senior Nutrition Program
4258 Washington St.
Boston, MA 02131

C & Rop Regional Nutrition Program
161 School St.
Chicopee, MA 01013

Area III Elderly Nutrition Project
222 Bowdoin St.
Dorchester, MA 02122

Fall River-Westport Nutrition Project
1197 Robeson St.
Fall River, MA 02720

Cape Ann Senior Meals
94 Main St.
Gloucester, MA 01930

Franklin City Nutrition Project
39 Federal St.
Greenfield, MA 01301

Cape Islands Home Care
146 Main St.
Hyannis, MA 02601

Montachusett Nutrition Project
305 Whitney St.
Leominster, MA 01453

Lynn Regional Nutrition Project
75 Union St.
Lynn, MA 01902

Malden Action Inc.
341A Forest St.
Malden, MA 02148

Elderly Nutrition Program
725 Pleasant St.
New Bedford, MA 02740

Berkshire County Nutrition Project
246 North St.
Pittsfield, MA 01201

Chelsea Revere Winthrop Home Care Corp.
453 Broadway
Revere, MA 02151

Boston Two Nutrition Project
55 DiMock St.
Roxbury, MA 02119

Senior Citizen Home Care Corp. Nutrition Project
249 Elm St.
Somerville, MA 02144

Home Care Corp. Nutrition Program for the Elderly
1414 State St.
Springfield, MA 01109

Merrimack Valley Title VII
57 River Rd.
West Andover, MA 01810

MICHIGAN

Memca Nutrition Program
275 Bagley St.
Alpena, MI 59707

Lake County Meals Program
St. Ann's Church
Baldwin, MI 49304

Region 3 Senior Nutrition Program
P.O. Box 1026
Battle Creek, MI 49016

Bay City Senior Citizens Food Programs
902 N. Madison
Bay City, MI 48706

St. Joseph County Food Program
Court House Annex
Centerville, MI 49033

Cut Wayne County Nutrition
1150 Griswold
Detroit, MI 48226

Food & Friendship Project
1151 Taylor
Herm Kiefer Hospital
Detroit, MI 48202

Men Delta Schft Title XII
225 N. 21st
Escanaba, MI 49829

GLS Senior Citizen Food Service
601 S. Saginaw St.
Flint, MI 48502

Gladwin Senior Citizen Food Program
Box 41
Gladwin, MI 48624

Kent County Elderly Nutrition Project
300 Montoe, NW
Grand Rapids, MI 49502

Baraga Houghton Kewenaw County Area Agency
P.O. Box 420
Hancock, MI 49930

Dickinson-Iron County Nutrition Program
107 Fourth Ave.
Iron River, MI 49935

Gogebic Optonagon Senior Citizen Nutrition Project
216 W. Ayer
Ironwood, MI 49938

Nutrition Program for the Elderly
401 S. Mechanic St.
Jackson, MI 49204

Senior Services Inc.
616 Locust St.
Kalamazoo, MI 49007

Kalkaska Happy Days Club
P.O. Box 415
Kalkaska, MI 49646

Ingham County Senior Citizens Nutrition Project
P.O. Box 1406
Lansing, MI 48904

Alger-Marquette Senior Citizens Diners
600 Al Tamont St.
Marquette, MI 49855

Outer Monroe Nutrition Program for the Aging
105 Front St.
Monroe, MI 48161

Macomb County Seniors Nutrition Project
59 N. Walnut
Mt. Clemens, MI 48043

Isalellagratiot Senior Citizen Power
County Building
Mt. Pleasant, MI 48858

Muskegon Senior Nutrition Service Aging
445 Ada Ave.
Muskegon, MI 49442

Senior Citizen Nutrition Program
196 Oakland Ave.
Pontiac, MI 48058

St. Clair County Senior Citizens Nutrition Program
502 Quay St.
Port Huron, MI 48060

Saginaw County Nutrition Program for the Aged
1537 S. Washington
Saginaw, MI 48601

Berrien County Senior Citizen Nutrition Program
305 Lake Blvd.
St. Joseph, MI 49085

Chip-Luce-Mack Nutrition Program
519 Ashmun St.
Sault Ste. Marie, MI 49783

Montcalm County Nutrition Program for the Aged
P.O. Box 435
Stanton, MI 48858

Northwest Michigan Senior Citizen Nutrition Program
313 Rose St.
Traverse City, MI 49684

MINNESOTA

Senior Citizens Nutrition Program
Sixth and Oak
Carver, MN 55315

Elderly Nutrition Program
P.O. Box 217
Cass Lake, MN 56633

Senior Meals and Activities
114 S. Main St.
Crookston, MN 56716

Duluth Seniors Dinner Program
206 W. Fourth St.
Duluth, MN 55802

Senior Citizens Nutrition Program
104 Second St., SE
Little Falls, MN 56345

Nutrition Program for Elderly
321 Liberty St.
Mankato, MI 56001

Nutrition Program for the Elderly
438 W. Main
Marshall, MN 56258

Congregate Dining Project
430 Oak Grove
Minneapolis, MN 55403

Nutrition Program for the Elderly
Courthouse
Montevideo, MN 56265

Nutrition and Program Centers
Holiday Mall
Moorhead, MN 56560

Headwaters Nutrition Project
Box 312
Park Rapids, MN 56479

Olmsted County Nutrition Program
22 N. Broadway
Rochester, MN 55901

Semcac Senior Nutrition Program
Box 547
Rushford, MN 55971

Nutrition Centers Program
810 St. Germain
St. Cloud, MN 56301

Senior Nutrition Program
630 Laurel Ave.
St. Paul, MN 55104

Arrowhead Elderly Nutrition Project
Sixth St. and Third Ave. S.
Virginia, MN 55792

Senior Citizens Nutrition Program
Courthouse
Willmar, MN 56201

MISSISSIPPI

Nutrition & Social Services for the Elderly
P.O. Box 642
Booneville, MS 38829

North Delta Nutrition Program for the Elderly
P.O. Box 1244
Clarksdale, MS 38614

Fellowship Food Centers
161 Maple St.
Columbus, MS 39701

South Delta Nutrition Program for the Elderly
Route 1
Box AB52
Greenville, MS 38701

Title VII Nutrition Project for the Elderly
1020 Third Ave.
Gulfport, MS 39501

Central Mississippi Nutrition Program for the Elderly
2675 River Ridge Rd.
Jackson, MS 39216

Mississippi Regional Housing Authority No. 5
P.O. Box 197
Newton, MS 39345

North Central Nutrition Program for the Elderly
P.O. Box 668
Winona, MS 38967

MISSOURI

Northwest Area Nutrition Program
Courthouse Building
Albany, MO 64402

Southeast Missouri Area Agency on Aging Nutrition Project
23 N. Middle
Cape Girardeau, MO 63701

Mid-East Area Agency on Aging
555 Brentwood Blvd.
Clayton, MO 63105

Central Missouri Nutrition Project
909 University
Columbia, MO 65201

Mid-American Regional Council
20 W. Ninth St.
Kansas City, MO 64105

Northeast Missouri Area Agency on Aging
P.O. Box 186
Kirksville, MO 63501

St. Louis Area Agency on Aging
560 Delmar Blvd.
St. Louis, MO 63101

Southwest Area Agency on Aging
1824 S. Stewart St.
Springfield, MO 65804

MONTANA

Deer Lodge County Council on Aging
921 E. Park
Anaconda, MT 59711

The Seniors Dinners Program
3300 Second Ave., N.
Billings, MT 59101

Butte Senior Citizens Diners Club
107 E. Granite
Butte, MT 59701

Action for Eastern Montana
Haggnston Building
Glendive, MT 59330

Hill County Council for Aging
Senior Nutrition Program
Box 711
Havre, MT 59501

RKY Montana Development Council
P.O. Box 721
Helena, MT 59601

Western Montana Nutrition Program
944 S. Main
Kalispell, MT 59901

NEBRASKA

Northwest-Northeast Senior Citizen Nutrition
Box 746
Chadron, NB 69337

Nutrition Program for Hall County Seniors
107½ W. Fourth
Grand Island, NB 68801

Adams County Nutrition Program for the Elderly
619 N. St. Joseph Ave.
Hastings, NB 68091

Service & Activity for Independent Living
2022 Ave A.
Kearney, NB 68847

Senior Diners
411 S. 13th
Lincoln, NB 68508

Eastern Nebraska Human Services Agency
855 S. 72 St.
Omaha, NB 68114

Western Nebraska Area Agency on Aging Nutrition Program
Nebraska Western College
Scottsbluff, NB 69361

Project Rural Alive
P.O. Box 10
Walthill, NB 68067

Nutrition Program for Older Indians
P.O. Box 238
Winnebago, NB 68071

NEVADA

Happy Hour Hot Meals
901 Beverly Dr.
Carson City, NV 89701

Elko Keen Age Happy Meals
Box 1638
Elko, NV 89801

White Pine Nutrition Program
P.O. Box 326
Ely, NV 89301

Fallon Nevada Meals on Wheels
310 E. Court St.
Fallon, NV 89406

Mineral County Care & Share
Box 1058
Hawthorne, NV 89415

Clark County Meals on Wheels
727 N. Main St.
Las Vegas, NV 89701

Numega
Rural Delivery
Nixon, NV 89424

Duck Valley Meals for the Elderly
P.O. Box 219
Owyhee, NV 89832

Lincoln Nutrition for Seniors
Box 118
Panaca, NV 89402

Care & Share
2075 W. Seventh St.
Reno, NV 89503

Lyon Food Fun and Fellowship
Box 421
Yerington, NV 89447

NEW HAMPSHIRE

North Country Senior Meals
69 Willard St.
Berlin, NH 03570

Nutrition West
109 Pleasant St.,
Claremont, NH 03743

Elderly Feeding Program/
    Rockingham County
93 N. State St.
Concord, NH 03301

Group Site Meals for the Elderly
653 Main St.
Laconia, NH 03246

Elderly and Nutritional Service
201 Main St.
Nashua, NH 08060

Strafford County Nutrition Program
Bartlett Ave.
Somersworth, NH 03878

NEW JERSEY

South Monmouth County Nutrition
    Project
510 Grand Ave.
Asbury, NJ 07960

Atlantic County Nutrition Project
2322 Pacific Ave.
Atlantic, NJ 08410

Camden County Nutrition Project
915 Haddon Ave.
Camden, NJ 08103

Cape May County Nutrition Project
Crest Haven Road
Cape May, NJ 08210

Passaic County Nutrition Project
1 Westervelt Place
Clifton, NJ 07011

Union County Nutrition Project
208 Commerce Place
Elizabeth, NJ 07201

Hunterdon County Nutrition Project
79 Main St.
Flemington, NJ 08822

North Hudson Nutrition Project
6907 Bergenline Ave.
Guttenberg, NJ 07093

Bergen County Nutrition Project
57 Main St.
Hackensack, NJ 07601

Irvington Nutrition Project
Municipal Building
Civic Square
Irvington, NJ 07111

Jersey City Nutrition Project
30 Baldwin Ave.
Jersey City, NJ 07304

Essex County Nutrition Project
Midland Ave. & Portland Pl.
Montclair, NJ 07042

Morris County Nutrition Project
32 Washington St.
Morristown, NJ 07960

Burlington County Nutrition Project
42 Grant St.
Mount Holly, NJ 08060

Newark Nutrition Project
2 Cedar St.
Newark, NJ 07102

Middlesex County Nutrition Project
51 Livingston Ave.
New Brunswick, NJ 08901

Sussex County Nutrition Project
62 Main St.
Newton, New Jersey 07860

Paterson Nutrition Project
185 Carroll St.
Paterson, NJ 07501

Warren County Nutrition Project
Municipal Building
Corliss Ave.
Phillipsburg, NJ 08865

Cumberland County Nutrition Project
P.O. Box 308
Rosenhayn, NJ 08320

Gloucester County Nutrition Project
Gloucester County College
Sewell, NJ 08080

Somerset County Nutrition Project
County Administration Building
Somerville, NJ 08876

Ocean County Nutrition Project
1500 Church Road
Toms River, NJ 08753

Mercer County Nutrition Project
Donnelly Hospital
2300 Hamilton
Trenton, NJ 08619

NEW MEXICO

Metropolitan Nutrition Project
1202 Edith Blvd., NE
Albuquerque, NM 87102

McKinley County Nutrition Project
P.O. Box 70
Gallup, NM 87301

Dona Ana County Hot Meals Program
410 S. Valley Dr.
Las Cruces, NM 88001

Joy Nutrition Project
737 E. Alameda
Rosewell, NM 88201

Senior Citizens Nutrition Project
P.O. Box 4455
Santa Fe, NM 87501

Senior Citizens Program of Taos Rio
    Arriba
P.O. Box FF
Taos, NM 87571

NEW YORK

Low Cost Meals for the Elderly
25 Delaware Ave.
Albany, NY 12210

Meals for the Elderly
25 Church St.
Amsterdam, NY 12010

Elderberry Dinner Club
309 W. Morris St.
Bath, NY 14810

Noontimers Dinner Club
309 W. Morris St.
Bath, NY 14810

Broome County Nutrition Program
County Office Building
Binghamton, NY 13902

Nutrition Project of ECOA
55 Franklin St.
Rath Building
Buffalo, NY 14202

St. Lawrence Nutrition Project
County Office Building
Canton, NY 13617

Nutrition Program for Seniors
1 Old Country Rd.
Carle Place, NY 11514

Greene Columbia Nutrition Program
465 Main St.
Catskill, NY 12414

Cortland Nutrition Program
25 Court St.
Cortland, NY 13045

Senior Meals Program
129 Main St.
Delhi, NY 13753

Essex County Nutrition Program
Town Hall Building
Elizabethtown, NY 12932

Chemung County Nutrition Project
703 John St.
Elmira, NY 14901

Fulton County Meals for Elderly
Old Court House
Fonda, NY 12068

Senior Nutrition Center
H Lee Dennison Center
Hauppauge, NY 11787

Area Nutrition Program
104 Washington St.
Herkimer, NY 13350

Secoco Dinner Program
431 Warren St.
Hudson, NY 12534

Nutrition for Elderly Tompkins County
225 S. Aulton St.
Ithaca, NY 14850

Hot Meals for the Elderly
286 Wall St.
Kingston, NY 12401

Nutrition for the Elderly
Warren County Municipal Center
Lake George, NY 12845

Project Echo
200 Erie St.
Little Valley, NY 14755

Niagara Nutrition for Elderly
Civil Defense Building
Lockport, NY 14094

Lewis County Nutrition Program
7660 State St.
Lowville, NY 13367

Wayne Cap Nutrition Program
Route 31
Lyons, NY 14489

Franklin Nutrition Program
8 E. Main St.
Malone, NY 12953

Title VII Luncheon Club
County Office Building
Mayville, NY 14757

Sullivan Senior Citizens Meals
Sullivan County Office Building
Monticello, NY 12701

Orange County Nutrition Project
234 Van Ness St.
Newburgh, NY 12550

Senior Nutrition Project
7 Elmwood Ave.
New City, NY 10956

New York City Nutrition Program
250 Broadway
New York, NY 10007

Chenango County Nutrition Project
6 Turner St.
Norwich, NY 13815

Nutrition Program for the Elderly
United Seneca Elders
Box 2
Oneida, NY 14521

Snack Project
109 N. Main
Oneida, NY 13421

Nutrition Program for the Aging
2 Mitchell St.
Oneonta, NY 13820

Oswego Nutrition Program
110 W. Sixth St.
Oswego, NY 13126

Project Dinner Bell
68 North Ave.
Owego, NY 13827

Clinton County Nutrition Program
229 S. Catherine St.
Plattsburgh, NY 12901

Nutrition Program for Elderly
236 Main St.
Poughkeepsie, NY 12601

Monroe County Nutrition Program
375 Westfall Rd.
Rochester, NY 14620

Saratoga County Nutrition Service
1 Franklin Sq.
Saratoga, NY 12866

Nutrition Program for the Elderly
30 North Berry St.
Schenectady, NY 12305

Rensselaer County Nutrition Service
Kennedy Towers
Troy, NY 12180

Nutrition Program
800 Park Ave.
Utica, NY 13501

Calories and Conservation
400 N. Main St.
Warsaw, NY 14564

Nutrition Project Jefferson for the Aging
175 Arsenal St.
Watertown, NY 13601

Schuyler County Nutrition Program
112 Sixth
Watkins Glen, NY 14891

Food and Nutrition Project
S. Brooklyn Ave.
Wellsville, NY 14895

Westchester County Nutrition Program
827 County Office Building
White Plains, NY 10601

NORTH CAROLINA

LHND-OR-SKY Nutrition Program
P.O. Box 2175
Asheville, NC 28802

Carteret Nutrition Program
P.O. Drawer 90
Beaufort, NC 28516

Yadkin Valley Elderly Nutrition Program
P.O. Box 328
Boonville, NC 27011

Feeding Program for the Elderly
243½ E. Front St.
Burlington, NC 27215

Mecklenburg County Nutrition Program
720 E. Fourth St.
Charlotte, NC 27606

Cherokee Senior Citizens Lunch
P.O. Box 427
Cherokee, NC 28719

Cadarrus County Nutrition Program
P.O. Box 707
Concord, NC 28205

Region M Nutrition Program
801 Arsenal Ave.
Fayetteville, NC 28305

Gaston County Nutrition Project
508 W. Main St.
Gastonia, NC 28052

Wayne Nutrition Program for the Elderly
300 N. Virginia St.
Goldsboro, NC 27530

Mountain-Project Nutrition Program
Route 1
Hayesville, NC 28786

Kerr Tar Regional Nutrition Project
P.O. Box 1500
Henderson, NC 27536

Nutrition Program for the Elderly
1076 College Ave.
Lenoir, NC 28645

Davidson County Nutrition Program
P.O. Box 389
Lexington, NC 27292

Lumber River Nutrition Project
P.O. Box 955
Lumberton, NC 28358

Union County Nutrition Program
P.O. Box 218
Monroe, NC 28110

Title VII Nutrition Project
P.O. Box 669
Newton, NC 28650

Nutrition Program for the Elderly
Box 12276
Research Triangle, NC 27709

Need Nutrition Program
P.O. Box 307
Rocky Mount, NC 27801

Rowan County Nutrition Project
1300 W. Bank St.
Salisbury, NC 28144

Hot Meals for the Elderly
224 N. Greene St.
Snow Hill, NC

Region N Nutrition Program
728 Main St.
Troy, NC 27371

Mid-East Regional Program for Elderly
P.O. Box 1218
Washington, NC 27889

Senior Citizens Nutrition Program
104 W. Smith St.
Whiteville, NC 28472

Broc Elderly Nutrition Program
P.O. Box 756
Wilkesboro, NC 28697

Senior Citizens Nutrition Program
601 N. Main St.
Winston Salem, NC 27101

NORTH DAKOTA

Meals N' More
107 E. Bowen Ave.
Bismarck, ND 58501

Senior Meals & Services
Highway 20 North
Devils Lake, ND 58301

Fargo Senior Commission on Aging
914 Main Ave.
Fargo, ND 58102

Grand Forks Nutrition Project for
   the Elderly
1600 Fifth Ave. N.
Grand Forks, ND 58201

James River Senior Citizens Center,
   Inc.
Box 1092
Jamestown, ND 58401

Mandan Golden Age Services
104 Third Ave. NW
Mandan, ND 58554

Minot Commission on Aging, Inc.
505 First Ave. Building
Minot, ND 58701

Barnes County Cares
P.O. Box 1066
Valley City, ND 58072

OHIO

Summit County Nutrition Program
80 W. Center St.
Akron, OH 44308

Ashtabula County Nutrition Program
4538 172 Main Ave.
Ashtabula, OH 44004

Start County Nutrition Program
618 Second St.
Canton, OH 44703

PSA No. 1 Nutrition Project
1428 Vine St.
Cincinnati, OH 45210

Cuyahoga County Title VII Nutrition
1276 W. Third St.
Cleveland, OH 44113

Central Ohio Title VII
181 S. Washington Blvd.
Columbus, OH 43215

Montgomery County Nutrition
   Program
P.O. Box 105
Dayton, OH 45402

Gala
1070 S. Jackson St.
Defiance, OH 43512

Scope Nutrition Program
535 N. Barron
Eaton, OH 45320

COAD Nutrition Project
516 Nernon St.
Ironton, OH 45638

District 3 Elderly Nutrition Project
322 N. Main St.
Lima, OH 45802

Columbiana County Nutrition Project
110 Nelson Ave.
Lisbon, OH 44432

Lorain County Title VII Program
1536 30th St.
Lorain, OH 44055

District 5 Nutrition Program
50 Elymyer Ave.
Mansfield, OH 44903

Belmont County Nutrition Program
Box 381
Martins Ferry, OH 43935

Seniors Nutrition Program
1100 Kenton St.
Springfield, OH 45505

Lucas County Senior Nutrition
1810 Madison Ave.
Toledo, OH 44004

Champaign Logan-Shelby County
   Nutrition Program
Champaign County Court House
Urbana, OH 43078

Trumbull County Nutrition Program
303 Mahoning Ave., NW
Warren, OH 44483

Science Nutrition Program
110 E. Market St.
Washington, OH 43160

Mahoning County Nutrition Program
25 W. Rayen Ave.
Youngstown, OH 44503

OKLAHOMA

Southern Oklahoma Nutrition
   Program
P.O. Box 3125
Ardmore Air Park, OK 73401

Comanche County Nutrition Program
   for the Aged
P.O. Box 5338
Lawton, OK 73501

Nutrition Program Elderly Congregate
   Sites
200 N. Walker
Oklahoma City, OK 73102

East Oklahoma Nutrition Service for
   the Aged
P.O. Box 1367
Muskogee, OK 74401

Creek County Nutrition Project
Creek County Courthouse
Sapulpa, OK 74066

Pattawatomie County Council
Nutrition for Senior Citizens
Tenth and Harrison Sts.
Shawnee, OK 74801

Tulsa Area Nutrition Project
200 Civic Center
Tulsa, OK 74103

Kiamechi Area Nutrition Program
East Oklahoma State College
Box K
Wilburton, OK 74578

OREGON

District 4 Nutrition for the Elderly
240 NW Sixth
Corvallis, OR 97330

Lane County Elderly Nutrition
170 E. 11th Ave.
Eugene, OR 97401

Loaves and Fishes
530 E. Main
Medford, OR 97501

Loaves & Fishes
1817 NE 17th Ave.
Portland, OR 97212

District 3 Nutrition for Elderly
215 Front St., NE
Salem, OR 97310

PENNSYLVANIA

Lehigh County Nutrition for the
   Elderly
523 Hamilton St.
Allentown, PA 18101

Huntington Bedford Fulton Area
  Agency on Aging
Box 46
Bedford, PA 18822

Columbia Monitor Nutrition Program
587 E. Fifth St.
Bloomsburg, PA 17815

Cumberland County Nutrition Project
35 E. High St.
Carlisle, PA 17013

Delaware County Nutrition Program
150 W. Fifth St.
Chester, PA 19063

Clearfield County Nutrition Project
315 E. Markes St.
Clearfield, PA 16830

Bucks County Nutrition Program
Nesuaniny Manor Center
Doylestown, PA 18901

Northampton County Nutrition
  Program for the Elderly
15 N. Second St.
Easton, PA 18042

Erie County Nutrition Project
Erie County Courthouse
Erie, PA 16501

Meals Together Elderly Nutrition
  Project
Box 7
Exton, PA 19341

Adams County Title VII Nutrition
  Project
P.O. Box 205
Gettysburg, PA 17335

Westmoreland County Nutrition
  Program
Courthouse Main St.
Greensburg, PA 15601

Dauphin County Congregate Meals
128 Walnut
Harrisburg, PA 17101

Meals on Wheels — Blair Co. Inc.
516 Allegheny St.
Hollidaysburg, PA 16648

Wayne Monroe & Pike County
  Nutrition Program
314 Tenth St.
Honesdale, PA 18431

Area Agency on Aging
County Court House
Indiana, PA 15701

Carbon County Nutrition Program
  for the Elderly
Courthouse Annex
Jim Thorpe, PA 18009

Senior Activities Center
444 Main St.
Johnstown, PA 15901

Senior Citizens Nutrition Project
33 N. Duke St.
Lancaster, PA 17602

Lebanon County Nutrition Project
Municipal Building
Lebanon, PA 17042

Mifflin-Juniata Nutrition Project
Mifflin-Juniata Area Agency on Aging
Courthouse
Mifflintown, PA 17059

Nutrition Program for the Elderly
  —Pike County
Court House
Milford, PA 18337

Mon Valley Health Welfare County
Eastgate 8
Monessen, PA 15062

Susquehanna County Nutrition Project
Court House
Montrose, PA 18801

Senior Adult Lunch Club
24 E. Oak St.
Norristown, PA 19401

Philadelphia Nutrition Program
1317 Filbert St.
Philadelphia, PA 19107

Allegheny County Nutrition Program
429 Forbes Ave.
Pittsburgh, PA 15219

Nutrition Program of Beaver & Butler
  Counties
5940 Baum Building
Pittsburgh, PA 15206

Nutrition Program for the City of
  Pittsburgh
200 Ross St.
Pittsburgh, PA 15219

Schuylkill County Nutrition Program
  for the Elderly
Second & Laurel Blvd.
Pottsville, PA 17901

Franklin County Nutrition Project
Quincy United Methodist
Box 217
Quincy, PA 17247

Berks County Nutrition Program for
  the Elderly
756 Penn St.
Reading, PA 19602

PSA VI Nutrition Program
Elk County Courthouse
Ridgeway, PA 15853

Lycoming Clinton Bi-County
  Nutrition Program
P.O. Box 1118
Saloma, PA 17767

Lackawanna Nutrition Program for
  the Elderly
YWCA Building
Jefferson Ave.
Scranton, PA 18503

N. Humberland County Nutrition
  Project
235 W. Spruce St.
Shambkin, PA 17872

Somerset County Office for Aging
147 E. Union St.
Somerset, PA 15501

Tri-City Nutrition Project
Senior Citizen Ave.
Towonoa, PA 18848

Luz-Wyo County Nutrition for Elderly
54 W. Union St.
Wilkes-Barre, PA 18701

York County Nutrition Program
750 Kelly Dr.
York, PA 17405

PUERTO RICO

Senior Citizens Center
James Madison Urb
Caguas, PR 00625

Senior Citizens Center
Public Urb Garcia Benitez
Caguas, PR 00625

Senior Citizens Center
Public Urb Juan J. Garcia
Caguas, PR 00625

Senior Citizens Center
Public Urb Benigno Garcia
Cayey, PR 00633

Senior Citizens Center
Palmer St. No. 22
Guavama, PR 00654

Senior Citizens Center
Box 2
Isabela, PR 00662

Senior Citizens Center
Box 791
Jaylya, PR 00668

Senior Citizens Center
Box 511
Las Piedras, PR 00671

Senior Citizens Center
Bo Mediania Alta
Box R
Loiza, PR 00672

Senior Citizens Center
Las Mesas Branch
Mayaguez, PR 00708

Senior Citizens Center
80 Achiote
Naranjito, PR 00719

Asociacion Benefica
Avenida Hostos No. 170
Ponce, PR 00731

Senior Citizens Center
Caimito Branch
Rio Piedras, PR 00654

Services for Senior Citizens
Human Resources Dept.
Box 43
San Juan, PR 00930

Project Hope Nutrition Program
Box 9472
Santurce, PR 00924

Senior Citizens Center
BO Espinosa
Vega Alta, PR 00762

Senior Citizens Center
Bo Pugnado Afuera
Vega Baja, PR 00763

RHODE ISLAND

Senior Meal Project
30 Rolf St.
Cranston, RI 02910

Senior Inn Inc.
474 Broadway
Pawtucket, RI 02860

Project Hope
300 Hartford Ave.
Providence, RI 02909

Eastshore Elderly Nutrition Program
100 Bullocks Point Ave.
Riverside, RI 02915

Warwick Community Action Inc.
389 Greenwich Ave.
Warwick, RI 02886

Senior Services Inc.
100 Front St.
Woonsocket, RI 02895

SOUTH CAROLINA

Nutrition Program for Elderly
127 Greenville St., SW
Aiken, SC 29801

Meals for Elderly & Lonely Citizens
2714 N. Main St.
Anderson, SC 29621

Nutrition Program for the Elderly
P.O. Box 343
Charleston, SC 29402

Central Mid Region Planning County
Dutch Square Blvd.
Columbia, SC 29210

Waccamaw Region Older Adults
    Nutrition
P.O. Box 671
Conway, SC 29526

Nutrition Program for the Elderly
HWY 17 C
Fidgeland, SC 29936

Pee Dee Region Nutrition Project
Coit St.
Florence, SC 29501

Congregate Dining Nutrition Program
P.O. Box 3105
Greenville, SC 29611

Food & Fellowship for Senior Citizens
Box 777
Laurens, SC 29360

Orangeburg County Council on Aging
    Nutrition Program
P.O. Box 1301
Orangeburg, SC 29115

York County Council on Aging
    Nutrition Project
120 Hampton St.
Rock Hill, SC 29730

Congregate Dining
168 Oakland Ave.
Spartanburg, SC 29302

Wateree Community Action Agency
225 W. Liberty St.
Sumter, SC 29150

SOUTH DAKOTA

Area IV Senior Nutrition Project
709 S. Penn
Aberdeen, SD 57401

Cheyenne Meals Program for the
    Elderly
Culture Center
Eagle Butte, SD 57625

District 3 Pilot Nutrition Program
P.O. Box 6
Lake Andes, SD 57356

Food for Aging for Individuals on the
    Reservation
Community Action Agency
Lower Brule, SD 57548

Food for Aging Indians on the
    Reservation
Lower Brule Sioux Tribe
Lower Brule, SD 57548

District 1 Nutrition Project for the
    Elderly
P.O. Box 268
Madison, SD 57042

Meals for the Elderly
P.O. Box 311
Martin, SD 57551

Meals Program for the Elderly
220 Omaha
Rapid City, SD 57701

District 11 Nutrition Project
132 S. Dakota Ave.
Sioux Falls, SD 57102

TENNESSEE

Southeastern Tennessee Nutrition
    Project for the Elderly
10 Newby St.
Chattanooga, TN 37402

Upper Cumberland Nutrition Program
    for the Elderly
P.O. Box 713
Cookeville, TN 38501

Nutrition Program for Seniors over 60,
    Southwestern District
225 W. Main St.
Henderson, TN 38340

Program on Aging
908 W. Maple
Johnson City, TN 37601

Greater Knoxville Senior Nutrition
    Program
318 Winona
Knoxville, TN 37917

Nutrition Program for the Elderly
P.O. Box 63
Martin, TN 38237

Memphis Delta Development District
    Nutrition Program
85 N. Cleveland
Memphis, TN 38111

Mid Cumberland Elderly Nutrition
    Project
501 Union St.
Nashville, TN 37219

South Center Nutrition for the Elderly
Motlow College
Tullahoma, TN 37368

TEXAS

Abilene Nutrition Project
555 Walnut
Abilene, TX 79604

East Texas Nutrition Project
Henderson County Junior College
Athen, TX 75751

Austin Travis County Nutrition
    Program
P.O. Box 1088
Austin, TX 78767

Senior Opportunity Service Program
P.O. Box 1049
Beeville, TX 78102

Years for Profit Nutrition
308 W. 28 St.
Bryan, TX 77801

Nueces County Nutrition Project
P.O. Box 9277
Corpus Christi, TX 78408

Dallas County Nutrition Program
Carter Towers
Dallas, TX 75208

El Paso County Nutrition Program
4824 Alberta
El Paso, TX 79905

Tarrant County Nutrition Program
1000 Macon
Fort Worth, TX 76102

Harris County Senior Citizens Program
406 Caroline
Houston, TX 77002

Deep East Texas Nutrition Program
272 E. Lamar St.
Jasper, TX 75951

East Texas Nutrition Project
Citizens Bank Building
Kilgore, TX 75662

Texas Tech Nutrition Program
Texas Tech University
Lubbock, TX 79409

Amigos Del Valle
606 W. Sam Houston
Pharr, TX 78577

Southeastern Texas Nutrition Project
920 Dequeen Blvd.
Port Arthur, TX 77660

South Texas Nutrition Project
420 E. Main St.
Rio Grande, TX 78582

Graysca County Senior Luncheon Action
P.O. Box 1295
Sherman, TX 75090

San Patricio County Nutrition Program
111 North Oden
Sinton, TX 78387

Cass Morris Red River County Nutrition
1510 Plum
Texarkana, TX 75501

Smith County Nutrition Program
4202 S. Broadway
Tyler, TX 75701

Jackson Lavaga Dewitt County
P.O. Box
Victoria, TX 77901

McClennan County Nutrition Project
1101 Washington
Waco, TX 76701

North Texas Nutrition Project
P.O. Box 1655
Wichita Falls, TX

UTAH

Davis County Senior Nutrition Program
Davis County Courthouse
Farmingham, UT 84025

Weber County Nutrition Program
650 25th St.
Ogden, UT 84401

Hot Meals for Seniors
27 E. Second, S.
Price, UT 84501

SCS Nutrition
1775 S. Dakota Lane
Provo, UT 84601

Washington County Nutrition Program
Box O
St. George, UT 84770

Nutrition Title VII Project
2033 S. State
Salt Lake City, UT 84115

VERMONT

Central Vermont Nutrition Project
289 N. Main St.
Barre, VT 05641

Comprehensive Service for Seniors
139 Main St.
Battleboro, VT 05301

Bennington County Nutrition Project
River Rd.
Bennington, VT 05257

ECVA Nutrition Program
Box 327A
Bradford, VT 05033

Nutrition for the Elderly
100 Dorset St.
Burlington, VT 05401

Northeast Kingdom Senior Services
Box 121
Lyndonville, VT 05851

Rutland County Nutrition Project
24½ Center St.
Rutland, VT 05701

VIRGINIA

Nutrition Program for Eastern Shenandoah
Box 316
Accomac, VA 23301

Nutrition Program for the Elderly
418 Fourth St., NE
Charlottesville, VA 22901

Pcca Senior Nutrition Project
P.O. Box 936
Chatham, VA 24531

Title VII Nutrition Program
10½ E. Main St.
Christiansburg, VA 24073

Nutrition Services
138 S. Main St.
Culpeper, VA 22701

Senior Citizens Nutrition Program
P.O. Box 22
Cumberland, VA 23040

Senior Nutrition Project
7309 Arlington Blvd.
Falls River, VA 22042

Rappahannock Nutrition Project
1101 Caroline St.
Fredericksburg, VA 22401

Northwest Nutrition & Social Program
1 W. Main St.
Front Royal, VA 22630

Senior Nutrition Activity Center
Cessa Madison College
Harrisburg, VA 22801

Nutrition Program for the Elderly
P.O. Box 1207
Lebanon, VA 24266

Nutrition Project
Patrick Henry Hospital
Newport News, VA 23602

Nutrition Project for Southeastern Virginia
9 Koger Executive Center
Norfolk, VA 23502

Nutrition Program
1032 Virginia Ave.
Norton, VA 24273

Gillfield-Crater Nutrition Program
Gill & Perry Sts.
Petersburg, VA 23803

Capital Area Nutrition Project
6 N. Sixth St.
Richmond, VA 23220

Nutrition Program
401 Campbell Ave., SW
Roanoke, VA 24016

Senior Nutrition Project
P.O. Box 7
Wytheville, VA 24382

WASHINGTON

G.H. Senior Nutrition Project
215½ E. Market St.
P.O. 181
Aberdeen, WA 93520

Meals for Older Americans of Whatem County
314 E. Holly St.
Bellingham, WA 98225

Kitsap County Senior Chuckwagon Club
605 Washington St.
Bremerton, WA 98366

Lewis County Senior Nutrition Program
Courthouse
Chehalis, WA 98532

Title VII Nutrition Program
3402 112 St., SW
Everett, WA 98204

Senior Citizen Nutrition Project
P.O. Box 1844
Omak, WA 98841

Caljef County Senior Citizens Nutrition
215½ S. Lincoln
Port Angeles, WA 98362

Benton-Franklin Nutrition Program
650 George Washington Way
Richland, WA 99352

Seattle-King County Nutrition Project
313½ First, S.
Seattle, WA 98104

Nutrition Project Title VII
W. 1115 Mallon Ave.
Spokane, WA 99201

Title VII Nutrition Project
306 S. Seventh
Tacoma, WA 98402

Chelan-Douglas "Senior Meals"
105 S. Wenatchee Ave.
Wenatchee, WA 98801

WEST VIRGINIA

Raleigh County Nutrition Program
431 S. Fayette Ave.
Beckley, WV 25801

Mercer County Nutrition Program
Box 3185
Bluewell, WV 24701

Multi County Nutrition Program
Box 3228
Charleston, WV 25332

Tri County Nutrition Program
418 Ben St.
Clarksburg, WV 26301

North Central Nutrition Program
208 Adams St.
Fairmont, WV 26554

South Western Nutrition Program
1139 Fourth Ave.
Huntington, WV 25701

Logan County Nutrition Program
Box 1346
Logan, WV 25601

Eastern West Virginia Nutrition
    Program
120 S. Main St.
Moorefield, WV 26836

West Central Elderly Feeding Project
Box 227
Parkersburg, WV 26101

Nicholas County Nutrition Program
611 Church St.
Summerville, WV 26651

Onio County Nutrition Program
329 McClain Building
Wheeling, WV 26003

WISCONSIN

Buffalo County Nutrition Program
Courthouse
Alma, WI 54610

Barron County Nutrition Program
330 E. La Salle St.
Barron, WI 54812

Pepin County Nutrition Program
Courthouse
Durano, WI 54736

Eau Claire County Nutrition Program
720 Second Ave.
Eau Claire, WI 54701

Fond du Lac County Nutrition Program
Courthouse
Fond du Lac, WI 54935

Great Lakes Intertribal Council
P.O. Box 5
Lac Du Flambeau, WI 54538

Rusk County Nutrition Program
Rusk County Courthouse
Ladysmith, WI 54848

Grant County Nutrition Program
111 S. Jefferson St.
Lancaster, WI 53815

Dane County Nutrition Services
1245 E. Washington Ave.
Madison, WI 53703

Milwaukee County Nutrition Program
901 N. Ninth St.
Milwaukee, WI 53233

Clark County Nutrition Program
Clark County Courthouse
Neillsville, WI 54456

Oconto County Nutrition Program
Courthouse
Oconto, WI 54153

Winnebago County Nutrition Program
448 Algoma Blvd.
Oshkosh, WI 54901

Sheboygan County Nutrition Program
615 N. Sixth St.
Sheboygan, WI 53081

Douglas County Nutrition Program
Courthouse
Superior, WI 54880

Bayfield County Nutrition Program
Courthouse
Washburn, WI 54891

Marathon County Nutrition Project
212 River Drive
Wausau, WI 54401

Trempealeau County Nutrition
    Program
Trempealeau County Courthouse
Whitehall, WI 54773

Wood County Nutrition Program
400 Market St.
Wisconsin Rapids, WI 54494

WYOMING

Laramie County Senior Center Nutri-
    tion Program
P.O. Box 269
Cheyenne, WY

Linta Senior Citizens Project
Box 728
Evanston, WY 82930

Nutrition Project for the Elderly
Laramie Senior Center
101 Ivanson
Laramie, WY 82070

Sheridan Senior Nutrition Program
P.O. Box 2011
Sheridan, WY 82801

22
Nursing Homes

Nursing homes are subject to a variety of local, state, and federal regulations, both as to facilities and staff. In most cases, the administrator is required to be licensed, and there are requirements as to staffing or services by physicians, nurses, pharmacists, and other professionals. In order to check on particular establishments, contact the local and state health authorities and the nearest Medicare headquarters.

The National Center for Health Statistics, a federal agency, publishes a list of all nursing homes in the United States having more than three beds. The current directory, in four volumes, lists 21,218 homes and gives the following information: Name of home, address, type of ownership (individual, corporation, nonprofit, state government, etc.), number of beds, ages of patients accepted, and sex of patients accepted.

The volumes are broken down as follows:

1. Northeast: HEW publication (HRA) 76-20001. Covers Connecticut, Maine, Massachusetts, New Hampshire, New Jersey, New York, Pennsylvania, Rhode Island, Vermont.
2. North Central: HEW publication (HRA) 76-20002. Covers Illinois, Indiana, Iowa, Kansas, Michigan, Minnesota, Missouri, Nebraska, North Dakota, Ohio, South Dakota, Wisconsin.
3. South: HEW publication (HRA) 76-20003. Covers Alabama, Arkansas, Delaware, District of Columbia, Florida, Georgia, Kentucky, Louisiana, Maryland, Mississippi, North Carolina, Oklahoma, South Carolina, Tennessee, Texas, Virginia, West Virginia.
4. West: HEW publication (HRA) 76-20004. Covers Alaska, Arizona, California, Colorado, Hawaii, Idaho, Montana, Nevada, New Mexico, Oregon, Utah, Washington, Wyoming.

Further information about this directory may be obtained from the National Center for Health Statistics, Office of Scientific & Technical Information, Parklawn Building, Rockville, MD 20852. Include the publication number with your inquiry.

The American Health Care Association is the largest federation of nursing homes. It is composed of 50 state associations whose members represent 7,800 facilities and more than 600,000 beds — one-half of all nursing home beds in the United States. The address of the national headquarters is:

American Health Care Association
1200 15th St., NW
Washington, DC 20005
(202) 833-2050

The state associations, in alphabetical order, follow.

STATE HEALTH-CARE ASSOCIATIONS

ALABAMA
Alabama Nursing Home Association
660 Adams Ave.
Montgomery, AL 36104
(205) 265-1996

ALASKA
Alaska State Hospital Association
Nursing Home Committee of Alaska
State Hospital Association
5531 Arctic Blvd.
Anchorage, AK 99502
(907) 277-1633

ARIZONA
Arizona Association of Health Care
  Facilities
512 W. Stella Lane
Phoenix, AZ 85013
(602) 279-2915

NURSING HOMES

ARKANSAS
Arkansas Nursing Home Association
University Tower Building
Little Rock, AR 72204
(501) 664-7311

CALIFORNIA
California Association of Health
  Facilities
1401 21st St.
Sacramento, CA 95814
(916) 444-7600

COLORADO
Colorado Health Care Association
The Silver State Savings Building
1500 Grant St.
Denver, CO 80203
(303) 861-8228

CONNECTICUT
Executive Secretary
Connecticut Association of Extended
  Care Facilities
Arterburn Convalescent Hospital
53 Morningside Dr.
Milford, CT 06460
(203) 933-2535

DELAWARE
Delaware Health Care Facilities
  Association
3600 Silverside Rd.
Wilmington, DE 18810
(302) 998-0181

DISTRICT OF COLUMBIA
District of Columbia Health Facilities
  Association
Mar Salle Convalescent Center
2131 O St., NW
Washington, DC 20037
(202) 785-2577

FLORIDA
Executive Vice President
Florida Nursing Home Association
821 N. Highland Ave.
Orlando, FL 32803
(305) 843-3820

GEORGIA
Georgia Nursing Home Association
3250 Memorial Dr.
Decatur, GA 30032
(404) 284-8700

HAWAII
Long Term Care Division of the
  Hospital Association of Hawaii
Maunalani Hospital
5113 Maunalani Circle
Honolulu, HI 96816
(808) 732-0771

IDAHO
Idaho Health Facilities Inc.
527 Memorial Dr.
Pocatello, ID 83201
(208) 232-8956

ILLINOIS
Illinois Health Care Association
1728 S. Sixth St.
Springfield, IL 62703
(217) 528-6455

INDIANA
Indiana Health Care Association
Illinois Building
17 W. Market St.
Indianapolis, IN 46204
(317) 636-6406

IOWA
Health Facilities Association of Iowa
4010 Woodland Plaza
P.O. Box 236
West Des Moines, IA 50265
(515) 225-0666

KANSAS
Kansas Nursing Home Association
1301 Topeka Blvd.
Topeka, KS 66612
(913) 233-3343

KENTUCKY
Kentucky Association of Health Care
  Facilities
Delson Apts.
Collins Lane
Frankfort, KY 40601
(502) 875-1500

LOUISIANA
Louisiana Nursing Home Association
1933 Wooddale Blvd.
Baton Rouge, LA 70806
(504) 927-3518

MAINE
Maine Association of Nursing Homes
99 Western Ave.
Augusta, ME 04330
(207) 623-1975

MARYLAND
Health Facilities Association of
  Maryland
10400 Connecticut Ave.
Kensington, MD 20795
(301) 933-5550

MASSACHUSETTS
Massachusetts Federation of Nursing
  Homes, Inc.
Dedham Office Park
886 Washington St.
Dedham, MA 02026
(617) 326-8967

MICHIGAN
Executive Vice President
Health Care Association of Michigan
300 S. Capitol Ave.
Lansing, MI 48933
(517) 371-1700

MINNESOTA
Minnesota Association of Health Care
  Facilities
2850 Metro Dr.
Minneapolis, MN 55420
(612) 854-2844

MISSISSIPPI
Mississippi Nursing Home Association
4444 N. State St.
Jackson, MS 39206
(601) 362-2527

MISSOURI
Missouri Nursing Home Association
107 Adams St.
Jefferson City, MO 65101
(314) 635-9283

MONTANA
Montana Nursing Home Association
P.O. Box 908
Helena, MT 59601
(406) 442-1432

NEBRASKA
Nebraska Health Care Association
Box 30247
Lincoln, NB 68503
(402) 435-3551

NEVADA
Nevada Association of Health
  Facilities, Inc.
365 West A St.
Fallon, NV 89406
(702) 423-6551

NEW HAMPSHIRE
New Hampshire Association of
  Licensed Nursing Home and
  Related Facilities
Hillsborough County Nursing Home
Rural Route 2
Goffstown, NH 03045
(603) 669-2119

NEW JERSEY
New Jersey Association of Health
  Care Facilities
332 W. State St.
Trenton, NJ 08618
(609) 989-8200

NEW MEXICO
New Mexico Health Care Facilities Association
El Castillo Retirement Residences
250 E. Alameda
Sante Fe, NM 87501
(505) 988-2877

NEW YORK
New York State Health Facilities Association, Inc.
203 Loew Building
Syracuse, NY 13202
(315) 422-3806

NORTH CAROLINA
North Carolina Health Care Facilities Association
111 Corcoran St.
Durham, NC 27701
(919) 682-6200

OHIO
Ohio Health Care Association
1550 W. Fifth Ave.
Columbus, OH 43212
(614) 488-0711

OKLAHOMA
Oklahoma State Nursing Home Association
200 NE 28th St.
Oklahoma City, OK 73105
(405) 521-0941

OREGON
Oregon Health Care Association
801 NE 28th Ave.
Portland, OR 97232
(503) 233-5373

PENNSYLVANIA
Health Care Facilities Association of Pennsylvania
111 Erford Rd.
Camp Hill, PA 17011
(717) 232-6631

RHODE ISLAND
Rhode Island State Nursing Home Association
1150 New London Ave.
Cranston, RI 02920
(401) 463-8044

SOUTH CAROLINA
South Carolina Nursing Home Association
2804 Augusta Rd.
West Columbia, SC 29169
(803) 796-5035

SOUTH DAKOTA
South Dakota Association of Health Care Facilities, Inc.
1820 W. 41st St.
Sioux Falls, SD 57105
(605) 339-2071

TENNESSEE
Tennessee Health Care Association
P.O. Box 11113
Nashville, TN 37211
(615) 834-6520

TEXAS
Texas Nursing Home Association
6225 U.S. Highway 290 E.
Austin, TX 78723
(512) 453-7204, Ext. 64

UTAH
Utah Nursing Home Association
707 E. Fifth, S.
Salt Lake City, UT 84102
(801) 363-1131

VERMONT
Vermont Nursing Home Association
DeGoesbriand Unit
Burlington, VT 05401
(802) 863-4917

VIRGINIA
Virginia Nursing Home Association
4615 W. Broad St.
Richmond, VA 23230
(804) 353-9101

WASHINGTON
Washington State Health Facilities Association
1818 Westlake Ave.
Seattle, WA 98109
(206) 284-6474

WEST VIRGINIA
West Virginia Nursing Home Association
College Parkway
Parkersburg, WV 26101
(304) 428-2330

WISCONSIN
Wisconsin Association of Nursing Homes
123 W. Washington Ave.
Madison, WI 53703
(608) 257-0125

WYOMING
Wyoming Association of Licensed Nursing Homes
West Park County Nursing Home
707 Sheridan Ave.
Cody, WY 82414
(307) 587-4211

23
Outreach Services

One of the major problems faced by older people is loneliness. More often than not, they are withdrawn from the social life of the community because of infirmities of age, which limit their physical activities, or simply because they feel that they just don't belong any more.

Consequently, it is often desirable and necessary to seek out older people to make sure they know what services are available and where they can call for help. This kind of program, often called "Outreach," can be organized by almost any group or agency with volunteers who have some special training, in much the same way that Medicare Alert sought out older people to tell them about Medicare when that program began.

Outreach volunteers can be older people themselves. Often, they are the most effective. Some communities pay outreach workers for time and services; all communities should pay for transportation and other expenses.

Sometimes outreach can be provided by active senior centers through the establishment of satellite neighborhood centers. These neighborhood offshoots can draw previously isolated older people into neighborhood activity.

Project FIND (Friendless, Isolated, Needy, or Disabled), conducted from August 1967 through November 1968 by the National Council on Aging and the Office of Economic Opportunity, made surveys of 12 communities, using aides who ranged in age from 50 to 85. The aides found isolated persons and referred those who needed help to services available in the community. If needed services were not available, the aides tried to secure volunteer help, especially when the need was severe. One of the significant discoveries of FIND was that many persons eligible for Social Security were not receiving it. The fact that 28,079 referrals were made to existing services, and that 24,124 unavailable services were needed, clearly establishes a reason for outreach.

In some places, television and radio programs — for, about, and by older people — have provided a special kind of outreach. Some of these maintain a telephone-answering service or include in their programming persons who will answer questions on the air. Because the older viewers have confidence in the programs, even extremely isolated individuals do seek and accept information, which they would resist or not seek from a social agency that was strange to them. An aggressive campaign to make people aware of the program's existence is essential to the success of this type of program.

Outreach should be considered as part of every program established for older persons. Often those who need service most are least likely to be aware of potential assistance. These people are not usually reached by standard mass-media communication channels. Cut off from their communities by high costs and almost complete lack of transportation, they must be actively sought out and personally invited to participate in programs.

24
Preretirement Planning

The subject of retirement and retirement planning is becoming of increasing interest to Americans. In 1970, a total of 20.1 million men and women — one in 10 — in the United States were age 65 or older. During this century, the population above 65 years of age has more than doubled (from 4.1 percent in 1900), while the number increased more than sixfold (from 3 million), because of general population growth. Furthermore, given present birth and death rates, absolute numbers in the older population are expected to increase 46 percent to 29 million by the year 2000. This figure would represent 10.6 percent of the total population. Also, it should be remembered that persons may retire from the working world before age 65, some as early as age 62, 60, or even 55.

There are various sources of information for persons interested in retirement planning, i.e., persons approaching retirement themselves, professionals or students in the field of aging or social programs, community colleges planning to offer courses in the subject, and other concerned individuals and groups. This chapter, while not pretending to be a complete resource list, offers some suggestions as to where ideas, information, and materials may be obtained.

Administration on Aging (AOA)

Under the Older Americans Act of 1965, the HEW Administration on Aging (AOA) sponsors programs that benefit the elderly throughout the country. In all states and in nearly 500 communities, there have been designated agencies on aging, which act as advocates for the elderly and coordinate activities on their behalf. Individuals approaching retirement age would be well advised to contact their state agency on aging, which can provide information on available programs and services for older persons and can refer them to the nearest area agency.

The AOA National Clearinghouse on Aging also makes available various publications in the field of aging. The bibliographies, *Words on Aging* and *More Words on Aging*, list various retirement-planning materials from a number of sources. Also of interest are *Handle Yourself with Care* (safety tips for older persons), the *Fitness Challenge* (on exercises and physical fitness), and *You, the Law, and Retirement* (legal information). *To Find the Way to Opportunities and Services for Older Americans* tells how to find what is available for the elderly in their own communities. *Facts about Older Americans* is a folder describing the retirement-age population.

Single copies of these publications may be obtained from the Administration on Aging, Washington, DC 20201, or from the U.S. Government Printing Office, Washington, DC 20402. Also, *Aging*, a magazine published by AOA, provides information on programs, national developments, legislation, research, and new publications in the field of aging. Published 10 times a year, a subscription costs $5.05 from the Government Printing Office. Single copies are available from the AOA as long as the supply lasts.

Organizations

National Retired Teachers Association (NRTA) and American Association of Retired Persons (AARP). NRTA and AARP, companion organizations that have been in the field of retirement planning for some years, offer a broad range of services, programs, and publications for older persons. Their series of retirement-preparation booklets, which are "designed to help you enjoy more fully your life today and to be better prepared for tomorrow," cover such topics as health, safety, law, psychology, money, management, consumerism, crime, jobs, housing, moving, home repairs, food, hobbies, and even pets. NRTA and AARP also publish *Modern Maturity* magazine and *NRTA Journal* for their respective members.

Members of NRTA and AARP must be 55 years or older. Information about services, publications, and membership can be obtained from NRTA/AARP national headquarters at 1909 K St., NW, Washington, DC 20049. The telephone number is (202) 872-4700. The national office can also refer inquirers to local NRTA/AARP chapters (or see list in Chapter 2). Also, AARP offers, through its Action for Independent Maturity (AIM) division, retirement-planning seminars and training programs for employers and other organizations and groups. The person to contact is AIM Director, Clifton W. Fichtner, at the preceding address, or by telephone at (202) 872-4852.

AIM publishes a magazine, *Dynamic Maturity,* for persons still in the preretirement years.

National Council on Aging. Industrial gerontology, which is a discipline within the field of gerontology, studies middle-aged and older persons in the working world and examines the impact of age on one's lifework or career. The National Council on Aging's Institute of Industrial Gerontology has designed and implemented preretirement planning programs for various groups nationally and focuses on the subject in its quarterly journal, *Industrial Gerontology.* The 1974-75 winter issue of the journal was devoted entirely to various aspects of retirement, including an article, "Re-Evaluating the Need for Retirement Preparation Programs," which should be of interest to those planning programs for retirees. The journal costs $20 a year or $6 an issue and can be ordered from the National Council on Aging, 1828 L Street, NW, Washington, DC 20036. Telephone: (202) 223-6250. Further information is available from Thomas Bradley, Associate Director, National Council on Aging.

Institute of Life Insurance. The Institute of Life Insurance has recently entered the field of preretirement planning. With the help of the University of Chicago, the institute held a seminar on the subject in 1971. Publications on pensions, life and health insurance, and other pertinent topics are available from the institute at 277 Park Avenue, New York, NY 10017. Telephone: (212) 922-3000.

Colleges and Universities

A number of colleges and universities are now interested in the field of aging in general, and offer several services and materials on preretirement planning. Among the people and programs to contact are:

University of Chicago, Industrial Relations Center. The center provides seminars and programs on retirement preparation for businesses and industries throughout the United States, and has developed a set of integrated program materials for this purpose. A brochure describing the services offered is available from Marvin Veronee, Director of Retirement Studies, University of Chicago, Industrial Relations Center, 1225 E. 60th Street, Chicago, IL 60637. Telephone: (312) 753-2081.

University of Michigan-Wayne State Institute of Gerontology. One of the foremost organizations in the field of gerontology and the first to offer an educational program for older people, the Wayne State Institute of Gerontology conducts studies and provides consultation as a basis for developing preretirement programs; develops pilot educational programs; holds courses for discussion leaders and trainers in the retirement education field; and evaluates retirement and preretirement programs. In addition, the institute produces and makes available such materials as a leader's manual, a booklet entitled *Preparation for Retirement* for use in programs, and 16-millimeter sound films dealing with various retirement situations. The institute has developed pilot programs for the United Auto Workers and the Chrysler-UAW Pension Plan, among others. More information can be obtained from the codirectors of the institute, Harold R. Johnson and Charles Parrish, at 520 E. Liberty, Ann Arbor, MI 48108. Telephone: (313) 764-3493.

Drake University, College of Continuing Education, Preretirement Planning Center. Following a 3-year demonstration (research) grant for retirement planning aimed at the 50-to-65 age group, the Preretirement Planning Center has continued and expanded its program. A seven-session course is offered both to the community at large and through in-plant programs in business and industry in the Des Moines area. Followup courses are planned to focus on special topics of interest. The center also offers intensive 3-day trainer-training seminars for professionals.

Publications on all programs are available upon request from the director, Dr. Donald L. Bowman. The address is Drake University, Des Moines, IA 50311. Telephone: (515) 271-2184.

University of Southern California, Ethel Percy Andrus Gerontology Center. The Andrus Center is conducting a full-scale research project, funded by HEW's Office of Education, designed to test three existing models of preretirement education against various community groups and to develop a new model from these. Attitudinal change about aging and retirement will be explored. Prior to this, USC mainly did preretirement training in the Los Angeles area, both on and off campus. The project, directed by Virginia Boyack, is aimed at adding new dimensions — social and psychological — to the previous emphasis on economic aspects of retirement. The school has a packet of materials available on request. Contact Ms. Boyack or Dr. Paul A. Kerschner, Associate Director, Andrus Gerontology Center, University of Southern California, Los Angeles, CA 90007. Telephone: (213) 746-6040.

Unions

Labor unions, too, take a keen interest in helping their members prepare for the cessation of their working years, not only through emphasis on pensions and similar benefits, but also frequently through preretirement planning. Two unions with specific programs in this area are the United Auto Workers and the Steelworkers of America.

United Auto Workers. In 1964, the Chrysler Corporation of Detroit and the United Automobile Workers instituted a preretirement counseling program for Chrysler employees, with the assistance of the Institute of Gerontology, University of Michigan. Between 1965 and 1973, an estimated 15 percent of the active employees over age 53 participated, many with their spouses, in seven 2-hour sessions on living arrangements, health, legal affairs, Social Security and Medicare, retirement benefits, financial planning, and leisure time. Information about the program is available from Arthur Hughes, International Union, UAW, Solidarity House, 8000 E. Jefferson, Detroit, MI 48214. Telephone: (313) 926-5491.

United Steelworkers of America. The United Steelworkers began preretirement planning activities for members in 1956, aided by the University of Chicago's Industrial Relations Center. The union has now developed 10 video cassette presentations of 30 minutes each on topics of interest to retirees. Through the union's 24 district offices, the 150 copies of the cassettes are loaned out, mainly for presentation to the membership. A simpler, less expensive program is being prepared on 35-millimeter color slides covering similar retirement topics, with an accompanying narrative. For further information, contact James C. O'Brien, Director, Department of Older and Retired Workers, United Steelworkers of America, AFL-CIO, 815 16th Street, NW, Washington, DC 20006. Telephone: (202) 838-6929.

Government

Federal Government. It is estimated that some 223,000 federal employees are eligible to retire in the next 5 years. A recent General Accounting Office survey on preretirement counseling programs in federal agencies drew a response from 255 personnel offices, of which 162 reported that they provided literature or limited counseling and 83 offered from 6 to 44 hours of counseling (both individual and group) to potential retirees.

To ascertain the need for and effectiveness of retirement-planning programs, the U.S. Civil Service Commission conducted a study of the reactions and attitudes of a sample of recent retirees and employees eligible for retirement. As a result, the commission is encouraging and assisting federal agencies to make retirement-planning programs available to employees who wish to participate. It has also developed a course for agency retirement advisers, who will in turn conduct retirement-planning courses or provide individual preretirement advice. For more information on the study and subsequent programs, contact the Director, Personnel Management Training Center, Bureau of Training, U.S. Civil Service Commission, Washington, DC 20415. Telephone: (202) 632-5638.

Chicago Mayor's Office for Senior Citizens. One of the first priorities of the Chicago Mayor's Office for Senior Citizens (established in 1956) is preretirement planning. Focused on business and industry in the city of Chicago, the office conducts regular workshops and seminars, for employees and employers, ranging from luncheon meetings to more elaborate programs. Presently, the office is concentrating on small business. The program is supported by city funds and operates within the municipality. A newly reprinted booklet, *How to Organize a Retirement Program,* and other material for persons interested in preretirement planning are available. Contact Robert J. Ahrens, Director, Mayor's Office for Senior Citizens, 330 S. Wells, Chicago, IL 60606. Telephone: (312) 744-5770.

25 Publications

This chapter lists publications that are of interest to older people. They are listed in the following order: organization-sponsored, other publications (by subject matter), and magazines.

ORGANIZATION-SPONSORED PUBLICATIONS

ACTION FOR INDEPENDENT MATURITY (AIM)
1909 K Street, NW
Washington, DC 20049

These publications are free to members:

AIM's Guide for Dynamic Fitness

AIM's Guide to Financial Security

AIM's Guide to Home and Personal Security

AIM's Guide to Housing Security

AIM's Guide to Legal Affairs

AIM's Guide to Leisure Years on Being Alone

Outline of AIM Retirement Planning Seminar (Descriptions Booklet)

ADMINISTRATION ON AGING
U.S. Dept. of HUD
Superintendent of Documents
Washington, DC 20403

All AOA publications listed are free.

AOA Fact Sheet: Administration on Aging

AOA Fact Sheet: Alternatives to Institutional Living

AOA Fact Sheet: Employment and Volunteer Opportunities for Older People

AOA Fact Sheet: National Nutrition Program for the Elderly

AOA Fact Sheet: Retirement Housing for Older Adults

AOA Fact Sheet: Transportation Projects Serving the Elderly

AOA: Federal Focal Point for Action for Older Americans

Basic Concepts of Aging: A Programmed Manual

Brighter Vistas–Church Programs for Older People

Consumer Guide for Older People

Designs for Action for Older Americans: A Centralized Comprehensive Program

Designs for Action for Older Americans: Employment Referral

Designs for Action for Older Americans: Group Volunteer Service

Designs for Action for Older Americans: Psychiatric Care

Designs for Older Americans: What Churches Can Do

Estimates of Size and Characteristics of Older Population in 1974 with Projections to Year 2000 (statistical memo No. 31)

Facts about Older Americans (1975)

Facts and Figures on Older Americans No. 1: Measuring Adequacy of Income (1971)

Facts and Figures on Older Americans No. 2: The Older Population Revisited (1971)

Facts and Figures on Older Americans No. 3: Income and Poverty in 1970 – Advance Report (1971)

Facts and Figures on Older Americans No. 4: Federal Outlays in Aging – FY 1967-72 (1971)

Facts and Figures on Older Americans No. 5: An Overview (1971)

Facts and Figures on Older Americans No. 6: State Trends – 1950 to 1970 (1971)

Facts and Figures on Older Americans No. 7: Income and Poverty in 1972 – Advance Report (1973)

Facts and Figures on Older Americans No. 8: Poverty by State and Ethnic Group, 1969– (1973)

Facts and Figures on Older Americans No. 9: The Older American Indian Population-Geographic Distribution

Facts and Figures on Older Americans No. 10: Cumulative Index to Facts and Figures on Older Americans – No. 1 thru 9

Facts and Figures on Older Americans No. 11: Income and Poverty in 1973

Fitness Challenge – in the Later Years

Guide for In-Service Training for Developing Services for Older People

285

Guidelines for a Telephone Reassurance Service

Handle Yourself with Care

Handle Yourself with Care: Instructor's Guide for an Accident Prevention Course for Older Americans

Home Delivered Meals: A Selected Annotated Bibliography

Home Delivered Meals Program for the Elderly — A Demonstration

Homemaker–Health Aide Service Training Manual

Homes for the Aged: Supervision and Standards — A Report on the Legal Situation in European Countries

Indicators of the Status of the Elderly in the United States

Information and Referral Centers: A Functional Analysis (1972)

Information and Referral Services: Information Giving and Referral

Information and Referral Services: Reaching Out

Information and Referral Services: The Resource File

I&R Program Configuration: A Guide for Statewide Planning

Let's End Isolation

More Words on Aging

Nutrition and Aging: A Selected Annotated Bibliography 1964–1972

Nutrition Education in Group Meals for the Aged

The Older Americans Act of 1965, as Amended and Related Acts

Older Americans and Community Colleges: An Overview

Older Americans Are a National Resource

Packaging Materials for Home-Delivered Meals: A Study

Para Encontrar El Camino (To Find the Way to Opportunities and Services for Older Americans)

Partnership for Older Americans (1973)

Project Helping Wheels

Protective Services for the Aged

Public Information Activities for State and Area Agencies on Aging

The Senior Citizen Paralegal: An Advocate for the Elderly Poor

Symposium: Nutrition and Aging

To Find the Way to Opportunities and Services for Older Americans

Toward a Declaration of Rights and Obligations of Older Americans

Transportation and Aging: Selected Issues

Transportation for the Elderly: The State of the Art

1971 White House Conference on Aging Publications Report: Toward a National Policy on Aging — Volume I

1971 White House Conference on Aging Report: Toward a National Policy on Aging — Volume II

Post White House Conference on Aging Reports (1973)

Words on Aging

A Work Study Program in Social Gerontology

You, the Law, and Retirement

ANDRUS GERONTOLOGY CENTER
University of Southern California
University Park
Los Angeles, CA 90007

About Aging: A Catalog of Films (88 pp., $3.00)

Aging: Prospects and Issues (211 pp., $4.00)

Americans in Middle Years (54 pp., $3.00)

Community Services and the Black Elderly (46 pp., $2.00)

Dealing With Death (71 pp., $2.50)

Drugs and the Elderly (96 pp., $3.00)

Older Volunteer Training Program (44 pp., $2.00)

Releasing the Potential of the Older Volunteer (88 pp., $3.50)

Sexuality and Aging (92 pp., $3.00)

Technical Bibliographies on Aging (set of nine, $18)

The Psychosocial Needs of the Aged (84 pp., $2.50)

Time on Our Hands: The "Problem" of Leisure (73 pp., $2.50)

NATIONAL RETIRED TEACHERS ASSOCIATION
AMERICAN ASSOCIATION OF RETIRED PERSONS
P.O. Box 2400
Long Beach, CA 90801

These publications are free to members.

NRTA-AARP Legislative Objectives

On Being Alone

Tax Facts for Older Americans

Your New Social Security and Medicare Benefits

Your Retirement Anti-Crime Guide

Your Retirement Consumer Guide

Your Retirement Food Guide

Your Retirement Health Guide

Your Retirement Hobby Guide

Your Retirement Home Guide

Your Retirement Home Repair Guide

Your Retirement Job Guide

Your Retirement Legal Guide

Your Retirement Moving Guide

Your Retirement Pet Guide

Your Retirement Psychology Guide

Your Retirement Safety Guide

Your Retirement Widowhood Guide

EMPLOYMENT

Books

Answers to Your Everyday Money Questions ($1.95)
Lorraine L. Blair
Henry Regnery Co.
180 N. Michigan Ave.
Chicago, IL 60601

How to Make Big Money at Home in Your Spare Time ($2.95)
Scott Witt
Parker Publishing Co.
Nyack, NY 10794

Planning Your Financial Future: Investments, Insurance, Wills ($6.50)
U.S. News & World Report
P.O. Box 951
Hicksville, NY 11802

Sylvia Porter's Money Book ($14.95)
Sylvia Porter
Doubleday Co., Inc.
245 Park Ave.
New York, NY 10017

The New York Times Guide to Personal Finance ($6.95 hardcover, $3.50 paperback)
Sal Nuccio
Harper & Row
10 E. 53rd St.
New York, NY 10022

Booklets

Contemporary Crafts Marketplace ($13.95, plus $0.40 shipping)
R.R. Bowker
Order Dept.
P.O. Box 1807
Ann Arbor, MI 48106

A Directory of Franchising Organizations ($2.50)
Pilot Books
347 Fifth Ave.
New York, NY 10016

Not Quite Ready to Retire ($1.25)
MacMillan, Inc.
Front & Brown Sts.
Riverside, NJ 08075

Small Business Bibliographies (free)
Small Business Administration (local)
or write to:
Small Business Administration
Publications Division
1030 15th St., NW
Washington, DC 20416

Starting and Managing a Small Business of Your Own ($1.35)
Superintendent of Documents
Government Printing Office
Washington, DC 20402

OTHER PUBLICATIONS

Tax Benefits for Older Americans (free)
Available from local offices of the Internal Revenue Service

Tax Information on Individual Retirement Savings Program (free)
Available from local offices of the Internal Revenue Service

FINANCIAL

Booklets

Consumer Information (free)
Public Documents Distribution Center
Pueblo, CO 81009

Guide to Financial Security (free)
AIM
1909 K St., NW
Washington, DC 20049

Money Management Booklets (set $3.50)
Money Management Institute
Household Finance Corp.
Prudential Plaza
Chicago, IL 60601

Books

Consumer Reports Buying Guide ($1.95)
Consumer Union
256 Washington St.
Mt. Vernon, NY 10550

That We May Eat: 1975 Yearbook of Agriculture ($7.30)
Government Printing Office
Washington, DC 20402

HEALTH

Books

Aging with Honor and Dignity ($8.50)
Mina Field
Charles C. Thomas Publishers
301 E. Lawrence Ave.
Springfield, IL 62703

Complete Illustrated Book of Better Health ($17.95)
Richard J. Wagman
J.G. Ferguson Co.
6 N. Michigan Ave.
Chicago, IL 60602

Let's Talk about Food ($2.00)
Philip White
American Medical Association
535 N. Dearborn St.
Chicago, IL 60610

The Modern Family Health Guide ($9.95)
Morris Doubleday & Co., Inc.
227 Park Ave.
New York, NY 10017

Nutrition and Physical Fitness ($10)
Jean Bogart
W.B. Saunders Co.
218 W. Washington Square
Philadelphia, PA 19105

Booklets

Eating Right for Less ($1.75, plus $0.25 postage)
Consumers Union
Dept. JA-41
Orangeburg, NY 10962

Fitness Challenge of the Later Years ($0.75)
Superintendent of Documents
Government Printing Office
Washington, DC 20402

Food Guide for Older Folks ($0.40)
Superintendent of Documents
Government Printing Office
Washington, DC 20402

Guide to Home and Personal Security (free)
Action for Independent Maturity
1909 K St., NW
Washington, DC 20049

Guide for Dynamic Fitness
Action for Independent Maturity
1909 K St., NW
Washington, DC 20049

Handle Yourself with Care ($0.40)
Superintendent of Documents
Government Printing Office
Washington, DC 20402

Your Retirement Food Guide (free)
American Association of Retired Persons
1909 K St., NW
Washington, DC 20049

Your Retirement Health Guide (free)
American Association of Retired Persons
1909 K St., NW
Washington, DC 20049

Your Retirement Safety Guide (free)
American Association of Retired Persons
1909 K St., NW
Washington, DC 20049

HOUSING

Booklets (free)

Guide to Housing Security
Action for Independent Maturity
1909 K St., NW
Washington, DC 20049

Social Security Benefits Outside the U.S., No. 609
Superintendent of Documents
Government Printing Office
Washington, DC 20204
(202) 541-3000

Tips on Mobile Home Selection
Mobile Home Manufacturers Institute
14650 Lee Rd.
Chantilly, VA 22021

Where to Retire on a Small Income
Norman D. Ford
Harian Publications
1000 Prince St.
Greenlawn, NY 11740

Books

America's 50 Safest Cities ($8.95)
David Franke
Arlington House Publishers
165 Huguenot St.
New Rochelle, NY 10801

Cabins and Vacation Homes ($2.45)
Sunset Books
Menlo Park, CA 94025

Florida Condominium Directory
  ($4.95, plus $0.50 shipping)
Trend House
P.O. Box 2350
Tampa, FL 33601

Guide to Retirement Living ($3.95)
Rand McNally & Co.
39 S. LaSalle
Chicago, IL 60603

National Directory of Housing for Older People ($5.50)
National Council on the Aging
1828 L St., NW
Washington, DC 20036

National Directory of Retirement Residences ($9.95)
Frederick Fell, Inc.
386 Park Ave., S.
New York, NY 10016

Woodall's Mobile Home and Park Directory ($5.95)
Woodall Editors
500 Hyacinth Place
Highland Park, IL 60035

LEGAL

Booklets

AIM's Legal Guide (free)
Action for Independent Maturity
1909 K St.
Washington, DC 20049

If You Should Die — Can Your Wife Take Over? ($3.95)
Stoney Brook Publishing Co.
186 Main St.
West Chelmsford, MA 01863

Law and the Courts: Layman's Handbook of Legal Procedures ($0.50)
American Bar Association
1155 E. 60th St.
Chicago, IL 60637

Legal Profession in the United States ($0.50)
American Bar Foundation
1155 E. 60th St.
Chicago, IL 60637

You — The Law — And Retirement ($0.70)
Administration on Aging
Superintendent of Documents
Government Printing Office
Washington, DC 20402

Books

Everything You've Always Wanted to Know about the Law (but Couldn't Afford to Ask) ($1.75)
Edward Colby
Books for Better Living
Division of American Art Enterprises, Inc.
21322 Lassen St.
Chatsworth, CA 91311

Intelligent Woman's Guide to Future Security ($4.95)
Luis Kutner
Dodd, Mead & Co.
79 Madison Ave.
New York, NY 10016

Lawyers for People of Moderate Means: Some Problems of Availability of Legal Services ($5.00)
Barlow Christensen
American Bar Foundation
1155 E. 60th St.
Chicago, IL 60637

The Family Legal Advisor ($10.70)
Alice K. Helm, Editor
Greystone Press
225 Park Ave., S.
New York, NY 10003

What Everyone Needs to Know about Law ($6.50)
U.S. News & World Report
2300 N St., NW
Washington, DC 20007

MENTAL HEALTH

Booklets

Marriage and Love in the Middle Years ($0.35)
James A. Peterson
Public Affairs Pamphlets
381 Park Ave., S.
New York, NY 10016

Mental Illness: A Guide for the Family ($0.80)
National Association for Mental Health
1800 N. Kent St.
Suite 200
Arlington, VA 22209

Retirement Roles and Activities
Superintendent of Documents
Government Printing Office
Washington, DC 20402

Books

Getting Older and Staying Young ($8.95)
D.D. Stonecypher
W.W. Norton & Co., Inc.
500 Fifth Ave.
New York, NY 10036

Retirement in American Society ($12.50)
Gordon F. Streib & Clement J. Schneider
Cornell University Press
124 Roberts Place
Ithaca, NY 14850

The Aged, The Family and the Community ($13.50)
Minna Field
Columbia University Press
562 W. 113 St.
New York, NY 10025

RECREATION

Books

Contemporary Crafts Marketplace ($13.95, plus $0.40 shipping)
R.R. Bowker
Order Dept.
P.O. Box 1807
Ann Arbor, MI 48106

Crafts and Hobbies ($3.95)
Garry Winter, Editor
Arco
219 Park Ave., S.
New York, NY 10003

Hobbies: A Complete Introduction to Crafts, Collections, Nature Study and Other Life-Long Pursuits ($9.95)
Alvin Schwartz
Simon & Schuster, Inc.
630 Fifth Ave.
New York, NY 10022

How to Pass the High School Equivalency Examination ($4.95)
Henry Regnery Co.
180 N. Michigan Ave.
Chicago, IL 60601

Retire to Action: A Guide to Voluntary Service ($5.95)
Julietta K. Arthur
Abingdon Press
201 Eighth Ave., S.
Nashville, TN 37203

Booklets

A Guide to Books on Recreation (free)
National Recreation & Park Association
1601 N. Kent
Arlington, VA 22209

Guide to Leisure Years
Action for Independent Maturity
1909 K St., NW
Washington, DC 20049

AAHA Washington Report (Semimonthly)
American Association of Homes for the Aging
374 National Press Building
Washington, DC 20045
(202) 347-2000

AARP News Bulletin (11/year)
American Association of Retired Persons
1909 K St., NW
Washington, DC 20049
(202) 872-4700

AAUP (quarterly)
American Association of University Professors
One Dupont Circle
Washington, DC 20036
(202) 466-8050

Abstracts for Social Workers (quarterly)
National Association of Social Workers, Inc.
1425 H St., NW
Washington, DC 20005
(202) 628-6800

Action (bimonthly & May)
American Society for Personnel Administrators
19 Church St.
Berea, OH 44107
(216) 234-2500

Administrative Management (monthly)
Geyer-McAllister Publication, Inc.
51 Madison Ave.
New York, NY 10010
(212) 689-4411

Adult Leadership (monthly)
Adult Education Association of the U.S.A.
810 18th St., NW
Washington, DC 20006
(202) 347-9574

AEA Dateline (monthly)
Adult Education Association of the U.S.A.
810 18th St., NW
Washington, DC 20006
(202) 347-9574

AFB Newsletter (quarterly)
American Foundation for the Blind, Inc.
15 W. 16th St.
New York, NY 10011
(212) 924-0420

Transition — A Guide to Retirement ($0.55)
Superintendent of Documents
Government Printing Office
Washington, DC 20402

MAGAZINES

AFB Washington Report (bimonthly)
American Foundation for the Blind, Inc.
15 W. 16th St.
New York, NY 10011
(212) 924-0420

Affirmative Action Register (monthly)
Affirmative Action Personnel Registry
10 S. Brentwood Blvd.
St. Louis, MO 63105
(314) 863-1711

AFL-CIO Free Trade Union News (monthly)
American Federation of Labor & Congress of Industrial Organizations
Dept. of International Affairs
815 16th St., NW
Washington, DC 20006
(202) 637-5000

AFL-CIO News (weekly)
American Federation of Labor & Congress of Industrial Organizations
815 16th St., NW
Washington, DC 20006
(202) 637-5000

Age of Achievement (monthly)
Barbara Krohn, Editor & Publisher
835 Securities Building
Seattle, WA 98110
(206) 622-3538

AGHE Newsletter (quarterly)
Association for Gerontology in Higher Education
One Dupont Circle, NW
Washington, DC 20036
(202) 659-4898

Aging (monthly)
Administration on Aging
Superintendent of Documents
Government Printing Office
Washington, DC 20204
(202) 541-3000

Aging International (quarterly)
NRTA-AARP International Activities Dept.
1909 K St., NW
Washington, DC 20049
(202) 872-4700

AHEA Action (weekly)
American Home Economics Associations
2010 Massachusetts Ave., NW
Washington, DC 20036
(202) 833-3100

Turn Your Ideas into Dollars ($2.00)
Pilot Books
347 Fifth Ave.
New York, NY 10016

AHCA Weekly Notes (weekly)
American Health Care Association
1200 15th St., NW
Washington, DC 20005
(202) 833-2050

American College of Nursing Home Administration Newsletter (monthly)
American College of Nursing Home Administrators
8641 Colesville Rd., Suite 409
Silver Springs, MD 20910
(301) 589-9070

American Geriatrics Society Newsletter (9/year)
American Council on Consumer Interests
162 Stanley Hall
University of Missouri
Columbia, MO 65201
(314) 882-4450

American Geriatrics Society Newsletter (monthly)
American Geriatrics Society
10 Columbus Circle
New York, NY 10019
(212) 582-1333

American Health Association Journal (bimonthly)
American Health Care Association
1200 15th St., NW
Washington, DC 20005
(202) 833-2050

American Journal of Public Health (monthly)
American Public Health Association
1015 18th St., NW
Washington, DC 20036
(202) 463-4574

American Medical News (weekly)
American Medical Association
535 N. Dearborn St.
Chicago, IL 60610
(312) 751-6013

AOA Fact Sheet (monthly)
U.S. Administration on Aging
Superintendent of Documents
Government Printing Office
Washington, DC 20204
(202) 541-3000

AOA Program Instruction (Irregularly)
U.S. Administration on Aging
Superintendent of Documents
Government Printing Office
Washington, DC 20204
(202) 541-3000

Aspects of Aging (bimonthly)
Central Bureau for the Jewish Aging
31 Union Square, W.
New York, NY 10003
(212) 924-5454

Bulletin of the National Conference on Social Welfare (quarterly)
National Conference on Social Welfare
22 W. Gay St.
Columbus, OH 43215
(614) 221-4469

California Pioneer Teacher (quarterly)
California Retired Teachers Association
1716 Jefferson St.
Napa, CA 94558
(707) 255-7311

Center Report (bimonthly)
Center for the Study of Aging and Human Development
Duke University
Durham, NC 27710
(919) 684-8111

Challenge (monthly)
U.S. Department of Housing & Urban Development
Superintendent of Documents
U.S. Government Printing Office
Washington, DC 20204
(202) 541-3000

Chapter News (quarterly)
AARP
1909 K St., NW
Washington, DC 20049
(202) 872-4700

Choice (monthly)
Retirement Choice Magazine Company Ltd.
100 Riverview Center
Middletown, CT 06457
(203) 347-6933

Civil Rights Digest (quarterly)
U.S. Commission on Civil Rights
1121 Vermont Ave.
Washington, DC 20425
(202) 254-6600

Consumer Education Forum (quarterly)
American Council on Consumer Interests
162 Stanley Hall
University of Missouri
Columbia, MO 65201
(314) 882-4450

Consumer News (semimonthly)
U.S. Office of Consumer Affairs
330 Independence Ave., SW
Washington, DC 20201
(202) 245-6296

COPH Bulletin (quarterly)
National Congress of Organization for the Physically Handicapped, Inc.
7611 Oakland Ave.
Minneapolis, MN 55423
(612) 861-2162

Current Housing Reports Housing Vacancies (irregularly)
U.S. Department of Commerce
Bureau of the Census
14th St. between Constitution Ave. & E St., NW
Washington, DC 20230
(202) 783-9200

Dialogue: A Staff Publication of NRTA-AARP (monthly)
AARP-NRTA
1909 K St., NW
Washington, DC 20049
(202) 872-4700

Dynamic Maturity
Action for Independent Maturity
American Association of Retired Persons
1909 K St., NW
Washington, DC 20049
(202) 872-4700

Education Commission of the State Bulletin (monthly)
Education Commission of the States
300 Lincoln Tower Building
1860 Lincoln St.
Denver, CO 80203
(303) 893-5200

Family Health (monthly)
American Medical Association
535 N. Dearborn St.
Chicago, IL 60610
(312) 751-6013

FHC Newsbriefs (quarterly)
Foundation for Cooperative Housing
1001 15th St., NW
Washington, DC 20005
(202) 737-3411

Florida's Health (monthly)
Florida State of Health Office
P.O. Box 210
Jacksonville, FL 32201
(904) 725-5430

Forty Plus of Washington (monthly)
Forty Plus of Washington
1718 P St., NW
Washington, DC 20036
(202) 387-1582

Good Neighbor (monthly)
American National Red Cross
17th & D Sts., NW
Washington, DC 20006
(202) 737-8300

Gray Panther Network (monthly)
Gray Panthers
3700 Chestnut St.
Philadelphia, PA 19104
(215) 382-6644

Hastings Center Report (bimonthly)
Institute of Society, Ethics & the Life Sciences
Hastings College
Hastings, NB 68901
(402) 463-2402

Home Health News & Review (weekly)
National Association of Home Health Agencies
10 Columbus Circle
New York, NY 10019
(212) 582-1022

Housing Affairs Letter (weekly)
Community Development Services, Inc.
1319 F. St., NW
Washington, DC
(202) 638-6113

HUD Newsletter (weekly)
U.S. Dept. of Housing & Urban Development
451 Seventh St., NW
Washington, DC 20410
(202) 655-4000

In Common (monthly)
Common Cause
2030 M St., NW
Washington, DC 20036
(202) 833-1200

Interaction (monthly)
ACTION
1201 Connecticut Ave., NW
Washington, DC 20036
(202) 293-7625

Inter Dependent (monthly)
United Nations Association of the U.S.A.
345 E. 46th St.
New York, NY 10017
(212) 697-3232

Journal of Community Health (quarterly)
Behavioral Publications
72 Fifth Ave.
New York, NY 10011
(212) 243-6000

Journal of Geriatric Psychiatry (semiannual)
Boston Society of Gerontological Psychiatry
90 Forest Ave., NW
Boston, MA 01021
(617) 965-4260

Journal of Gerontological Nursing (monthly)
Charles B. Slack, Inc.
301 E. Lawrence Ave.
Springfield, IL 62703
(217) 789-8980

Journal of Gerontology (bimonthly)
Gerontological Society
One Dupont Circle
Washington, DC 20036
(202) 659-4698

Journal of Home Economics (monthly)
American Home Economics Association
2010 Massachusetts Ave., NW
Washington, DC 20036
(202) 833-3100

Journal of Housing (11/year)
National Association of Housing & Redevelopment Officials
2600 Virginia Ave., NW
Washington, DC 20037
(202) 333-2020

Journal of Leisure Research (quarterly)
National Recreation & Park Association
1601 N. Kent St.
Arlington, VA 22209
(703) 525-0606

Journal of Long Term Care Administration (quarterly)
American College of Nursing Home Administration
4650 E. West Highway
Washington, DC 20014
(301) 652-8384

Journal of Nutrition (monthly)
American Institute of Nutrition
9650 Rockville Rd.
Bethesda, MD 20014
(301) 530-7050

Journal of Rehabilitation (bimonthly)
National Rehabilitation Association
1522 K St., NW
Washington, DC 20005
(202) 659-2430

Journal of the American Geriatrics Society (monthly)
American Geriatrics Society
10 Columbus Circle
New York, NY 10019
(212) 582-1333

Just Economics (monthly)
Movement for Economic Justice
1609 Connecticut Ave., NW
Washington, DC 20009
(202) 462-4200

Kennedy Institute Quarterly Report (quarterly)
The Joseph & Rose Kennedy Institute for the Study of Human Reproduction & Bioethics
3520 Prospect St.
Washington, DC 20007
(202) 625-2371

Manpower (monthly)
U.S. Employment & Manpower Administration
Superintendent of Documents
Government Printing Office
Washington, DC 20204
(202) 541-3000

Mature Years (quarterly)
United Methodist Church
1200 Davis St.
Evanston, IL 60201
(312) 869-4550

Medicare-Medicaid (weekly)
Commerce Clearing House
4025 W. Paterson
Chicago, IL 60646
(312) 236-2350

Memo from the National Institute of Senior Citizens (10/year)
National Council on the Aging, Inc.
1828 L St., NW
Washington, DC 20036
(202) 223-6250

Memorandum (irregularly)
U.S. Senate Special Committee on Aging
The Capitol
Washington, DC 20510
(202) 224-3121

Modern Maturity (bimonthly)
American Association of Retired Persons
215 Long Beach Blvd.
Long Beach, CA 90802
(213) 432-5781

Money (monthly)
Time, Inc.
Time & Life Building
New York, NY 10019
(212) 556-3060

Monitor (bimonthly)
Center for Community Change
1000 Wisconsin Ave., NW
Washington, DC 20007
(202) 338-6310

Monthly Catalog of Government Publication (monthly)
Superintendent of Documents
U.S. Government Printing Office
Washington, DC 20204
(202) 541-3000

Monthly Labor Review (monthly)
U.S. Bureau of Labor Statistics
Superintendent of Documents
U.S. Government Printing Office
Washington, DC 20204
(202) 541-3000

More Life for Your Years (monthly)
American Medical Association
Department of Education
535 N. Dearborn St.
Chicago, IL 60610
(312) 751-6013

NARC's Government Report (monthly)
National Association for Retarded Citizens
2709 Ave. E, East
Arlington, TX 76011
(817) 261-4961

NARFE Newsletter (irregularly)
National Association of Retired Federal Employees
1533 New Hampshire Ave., NW
Washington, DC 20036
(202) 234-0832

NASW News (8/yearly)
National Association of Social Workers
1425 H St., NW
Washington, DC 20005
(202) 628-6800

National Council for Homemaker-Home Health Aide Services Inc., News (5/year)
National Council for Homemaker-Home Health Aide Services Inc.
67 Irving Pl.
New York, NY 10003
(212) 674-4990

National Journal Reports (monthly)
Government Research Corp.
1730 M St., NW
Washington, DC 20036
(202) 833-8000

National Voluntary Organization for Independent Living for the Aged Newsletter (monthly)
National Council on Aging
1828 L St., NW
Washington, DC 20036
(202) 223-6250

Nation's Health (monthly)
American Public Health Association
1015 18th St., NW
Washington, DC 20036
(202) 467-5000

New England Journal of Medicine (weekly)
Massachusetts Medical Society
10 Shattuck St.
Boston, MA 02115
(617) 734-9800

New Outlook for the Blind (irregularly)
American Foundation for the Blind, Inc.
15 W. 16th St.
New York, NY 10011
(212) 924-0420

News 'n' Views (monthly)
Council Center for Senior Citizens
National Council of Jewish Women
One W. 47th St.
New York, NY 10036
(212) 674-8010

Normative Aging Study Newsletter (2/year)
Boston Veterans Administration Outpatient Clinic
John F. Kennedy Federal Building
Boston, MA 02203
(617) 223-3080

NRTA-AARP Legislative Report (bimonthly)
NRTA-AARP
1909 K St., NW
Washington, DC 20049
(202) 872-4700

NRTA Journal
National Retired Teachers Association
215 Long Beach Blvd.
Long Beach, CA 90801
(213) 236-3996

NRTA News Bulletin (11/Yearly)
National Retired Teachers Association
1909 K St., NW
Washington, DC 20049
(202) 872-4700

Nursing Homes (monthly)
Cogswell House, Inc.
222 Wisconsin Ave.
Lake Forest, IL 60045
(312) 295-2959

Of Consuming Interest (weekly)
Federal State Reports
Superintendent of Documents
U.S. Government Printing Office
Washington, DC 20204
(202) 541-3000

Older Worker Specialist (bimonthly)
National Council on the Aging
(Institute of Industrial Gerontology)
1828 L St., NW
Washington, DC 20036
(202) 223-6250

Parks & Recreation (monthly)
National Recreation & Park Association
1601 N. Kent St.
Arlington, VA 22209
(703) 525-0606

Personnel (bimonthly)
American Management Association
135 W. 50th St.
New York, NY 10020
(212) 584-8100

Personnel Journal (monthly)
Personnel Journal, Inc.
1131 Olympic Blvd.
Santa Monica, CA 90404
(213) 451-8724

Personnel Literature (monthly)
U.S. Civil Service Commission Library
1900 E St.
Washington, DC 20415
(202) 655-4000

Personnel Policy Briefs (semimonthly)
Management Information Center, Inc.
P.O. Box 357
Miami, FL 33145
(305) 576-0522

Pension & Finance Planning News (quarterly)
Institute of Life Insurance
277 Park Ave.
New York, NY 10017
(212) 922-3000

Perspective on Aging (bimonthly)
National Council on Aging, Inc.
1828 L St., NW
Washington, DC 20036
(202) 223-6250

Playtime (monthly)
Playtime
Sterling, VA 22170
(703) 450-5177

Prevent Blindness News (2/year)
National Society for the Prevention of Blindness
79 Madison Ave.
New York, NY 10016
(212) 684-3505

Public Health Reports (monthly)
U.S. Health Resources Administration
5600 Fishers Lane
Rockville, MD 20852
(301) 443-2525

Public Personnel Management (bimonthly)
Internation Personnel Management Association
1313 E. 60th St.
Chicago, IL 60637
(312) 947-2570

Public Welfare (quarterly)
American Public Welfare Association
1155 16th St., NW
Washington, DC 20036
(202) 833-9250

Re: Action (quarterly)
B'nai B'rith Commission on Community Volunteer Services
1640 Rhode Island Ave., NW
Washington, DC 20036
(202) 393-5284

Retirement Letter (monthly)
Phillips Publishing, Inc.
8401 Connecticut Ave.
Washington, DC 20015
(202) 652-5522

Retirement Life (monthly)
National Association of Retired Federal Employees
1533 New Hampshire Ave., NW
Washington, DC 20036
(202) 234-0832

Roll Call (weekly)
Roll Call, Inc.
428 Eighth St., SE
Washington, DC 20003
(202) 546-3080

RS Monthly Benefit Statistics (irregularly)
Superintendent of Documents
Government Printing Office
Washington, DC 20204
(202) 541-3000

Second Spring (bimonthly)
Adult Benevolent Association
810 18th St., NW
Washington, DC 20006
(202) 234-9574

Senior Citizens News (bimonthly)
National Council of Senior Citizens
1511 K St., NW
Washington, DC 20005
(202) 783-6850

Sight Saving Review (quarterly)
National Society for the Prevention of Blindness, Inc.
79 Madison Ave.
New York, NY 10016
(212) 684-3505

Social & Rehabilitation Record (monthly)
U.S. DHEW — Social & Rehabilitation Service
Superintendent of Documents
U.S. Government Printing Office
Washington, DC 20204
(202) 541-3000

Social Forces (quarterly)
University of North Carolina
Chapel Hill, NC 27514
(919) 933-3061

Social Security Bulletin (monthly)
U.S. DHEW Social Security Administration
Superintendent of Documents
Government Printing Office
Washington, DC 20204
(202) 541-3000

Social Security Rulings (bimonthly)
Superintendent of Documents
Government Printing Office
Washington, DC 20204
(202) 541-3000

Social Work
National Association of Social Workers
1425 H St., NW
Washington, DC 20005
(202) 689-9771

Southern Living (monthly)
Progressive Farmer Co.
P.O. Box 523
Birmingham, AL 35201
(205) 870-4440

State Government (quarterly)
Council of State Governments
Iron Works Pike
Lexington, KY 40511
(606) 252-2291

Statistical Summary of VA Activities (monthly)
U.S. Veterans Administration
Information Service
810 Vermont Ave., NW
Washington, DC 20420
(202) 393-4120

Synagogue Aging (monthly)
Synagogue Council of America
432 Park Ave., S.
New York, NY 10016
(212) 686-8670

The Retired Officer (monthly)
Retired Officers Association
1625 Eye St., NW
Washington, DC 20006
(202) 783-8755

Unemployment Insurance (monthly)
Commerce Clearing House
4025 W. Paterson
Chicago, IL 60646
(312) 236-2350

United Retirement Newsletter
    (monthly)
United Business Service
210 Newburg St.
Boston, MA 02116
(617) 267-8855

Volta Review (monthly)
Alexander Graham Bell Association
3417 Volta Place, NW
Washington, DC 20007
(202) 337-5220

Voluntary Action Leadership
    (quarterly)
National Center for Voluntary Action
1785 Massachusetts Ave., NW
Washington, DC 20036
(202) 797-7800

Voluntary Action News (bimonthly)
National Center for Voluntary Action
1785 Massachusetts Ave., NW
Washington, DC 20036
(202) 797-7800

Volunteer Leader
American Hospital Association
840 N. Lake Shore Dr.
Chicago, IL 60611
(312) 645-9400

Volunteer News (monthly)
Andrus Gerontology Center
University of Southern California
University Park
Los Angeles, CA 90007
(213) 746-6060

Washington Notes (irregularly)
The National Assembly of National
    Voluntary Health & Social
    Welfare Organizations
345 E. 46th St.
New York, NY 10017
(212) 490-2900

Washington Report (semimonthly)
Chamber of Commerce of U.S.
1615 H St., NW
Washington, DC 20062
(202) 659-6000

*Washington Report on Long Term
    Care* (weekly)
McGraw-Hill Publishing Co.
1221 Avenue of the Americas
New York, NY 10019
(212) 997-1221

Word from Washington (irregularly)
National Conference on Public
    Employees Retirement System
1390 Logan
Denver, CO 80203
(303) 534-1203

Worklife
U.S. Employment & Manpower
    Administration
200 Constitution Ave.
Washington, DC 20210
(202) 523-6050

26 Publishers

The following list of publishers is by no means all-inclusive, but those listed do publish many books and periodicals in the field of aging. The authors consider these among the most prolific publishers in the field.

Administration on Aging
Department of Health, Education & Welfare
Washington, DC 20201

AIM
1909 K St., NW
Washington, DC 20049

American Association of Retired Persons
1909 K St., NW
Washington, DC 20049

Andrus Gerontology Center
University of Southern California
University Park
Los Angeles, CA 90007

Baywood Publishing Company, Inc.
43 Central Dr.
Farmingdale, NY 11735

Black Aging
P.O. Box 8522
Durham, NC 27707

McGraw-Hill Publishing Co.
1221 Avenue of the Americas
New York, NY 10021

National Council on the Aging
1828 L St., NW
Washington, DC 20036

National Retired Teachers Association
215 Long Beach Blvd.
Long Beach, CA 90802

Social Security Administration
Department of Health, Education & Welfare
6401 Security Blvd.
Baltimore, MD 21235

Superintendent of Documents
Government Printing Office
Washington, DC 20204

Charles C Thomas Publishing Co.
301 E. Lawrence Ave.
Springfield, IL 62703

University of Florida Press
Gainesville, FL 32601

University of Michigan Press
615 E. University
Ann Arbor, MI 48106

University of Minnesota Press
2037 University Ave., SE
Minneapolis, MN 55414

University of Missouri Press
107 Swallow Hall
Columbia, MO 65201

27 Recreation

In many parts of the country, municipal or county recreation departments sponsor senior centers with varied programs, including arts and crafts, dramatic and musical groups, hobby clubs, special events such as picnics and outings, and many other activities.

Older Americans Act

The Older Americans Act has placed responsibility for planning, development, and coordination of federally funded programs for the elderly in each state upon the state agency on aging designated by the governor. The state agency can often provide information about local recreational programs for the elderly or refer inquiries to the area agencies on aging, which have been set up within the states, usually where there are concentrations of older people. (See Chapter 31, State Agencies on Aging.)

Several publications relating to leisure time activities for the elderly are available from the Administration on Aging, Washington, DC 20201. Some examples are:

"The Fitness Challenge" (exercises for senior citizens)
"Recommended for Action: Retirement Roles and Activities"
"AOA Fact Sheet: Employment and Volunteer Activities for Older People"

Other sources from which information may be obtained concerning recreational and leisure activities for the elderly are listed below.

National Park Service

The National Park Service, U.S. Department of Interior, offers to persons 62 years of age and older a Golden Age Pass, which enables the holder to pay a reduced price to any park that charges a fee. The pass may be obtained by older person who presents proof of age at any national park. The National Park Service also has recognized the special needs of handicapped and infirm persons and has published the *National Park Guide for the Handicapped* (catalog No. GPO I-29.9-2H19), which may be obtained from the Superintendent of Documents, Government Printing Office, Washington, DC 20402.

Library of Congress

Through its Blind and Visually Handicapped Division, the Library of Congress offers services for persons with a visual handicap. Special materials can be provided to any person who is certified by a competent authority to be unable to use conventional print material. Braille publications, cassettes, talking books on phonodiscs, and open-reel tapes may be selected. These are obtainable through regional and subregional libraries. In most cases, local public libraries can provide information, or contact may be made with the Blind and Visually Handicapped Division, 1291 Taylor St., NW, Washington, DC 20011.

National Recreation and Parks Association

The National Recreation and Parks Association (1601 N. Kent Street, Arlington, VA 22209) has three publications for sale, two of them prepared for use by personnel conducting recreation programs for the elderly or handicapped, and a third for older persons themselves. These are:

Management Aid Number 88, Recreation in Nursing Homes ($2.75)
Group Work with the Aged ($9.50)
There's Gold in Your Golden Years ($4.95)

National Organizations

There are four national organizations representing older persons that have local units in many parts of the country. The local units schedule meetings and plan activities that often include recreational or social components. Information can be obtained from the national headquarters of these groups, which are the National Retired Teachers Association and:

> American Association of Retired Persons
> 1901 K Street, NW
> Washington, DC 20005
>
> National Council of Senior Citizens
> 151 K Street, NW
> Washington, DC 20005
>
> National Association of Retired Federal Employees
> 1533 New Hampshire Avenue, NW
> Washington, DC 20036

Volunteer Opportunities

Many older Americans may wish to utilize their leisure by contributing their services to day-care centers, hospitals, schools, and other agencies. They can do this by offering to help a particular agency, or by contacting the volunteer office of their local health and welfare council. Here, too, the state or area agency on aging may be able to provide information. Also, the federal agency, ACTION, sponsors Older American Volunteer Programs, including Foster Grandparents (FGP), Retired Senior Volunteer Program (RSVP), and Service Corps of Retired Executives and Active Corps of Executives (SCORE/ACE). Information about local sites of these programs may be obtained from:

> ACTION
> 806 Connecticut Ave., NW
> Washington, DC 20525
> (202) 393-3111

Reduced Fares and Admissions

In some areas, reduced fees for admission to movies and other forms of recreation, and reduced fares for transportation are in effect for older persons, at least at certain times. Again, the state and area agencies on aging are the appropriate sources of information on this. (In addition, see Chapter 33, Transportation.)

28
Revenue Sharing (Dollars for the Aged)

The federal revenue sharing law provides that one-third of general revenue-sharing monies be distributed directly to states and two-thirds to local governments. State governments may spend this money in any legal way they choose, but the law provides that money sent to local communities is to be spent on either lawful capital expenditures or for operating and maintenance expenses in any of eight priority categories, including "social services to the aged and poor."

However, revenue-sharing dollars will not be spent for the elderly unless local organizations and older citizens' groups press their governors, mayors, county commissioners, and township trustees for a fair share of the funds. Interested persons and groups should get together and try to agree on a common approach to state and local officials, who determine how the money is to be spent. In fact, the legislation requires that local government include citizen participants in planning for use of these funds. Such participation would give older persons an opportunity to consider their community's entire budget, not just the revenue sharing allocation.

Federal regulations and other explanatory literature on revenue sharing are available from the Office of Revenue Sharing, Department of the Treasury, 2401 E St., NW, Washington, DC 20226. Telephone: (202) 634-5191. The director of the office is Graham W. Watt.

Also, the National Council on Aging, 1828 L Street, NW, Washington, DC 20036, publishes a useful 46-page booklet, "Revenue Sharing and the Elderly: How to Play and Win." It is available by mail at $2.85 per copy, postpaid.

29
Senior Centers

Senior Centers offer companionship, counseling, medical care, recreation, education, and most of all a community and a chance to get back into the mainstream.

Often, these centers are the only organizations in a community to which older Americans can belong. Besides the area agencies on aging, the senior centers are often the only places older Americans can turn to for information on transportation discounts, recreation, education, employment, health, home service, and so on.

There are literally thousands of senior centers in the United States, and we do not have the space to list all of them in this book; however, we have listed all the state agencies on aging. Call or write to your state agency, and ask for the senior center that is the closest to your community.

Membership fees to these clubs is minimal, and often it is free.

For the location of a senior center near you, call or write:

National Council on the Aging, Inc.
National Institute of Senior Centers
1828 L St., NW
Washington, DC 20036
(202) 223-6250

The institute publishes a directory of all senior centers in the United States, which you can order from the preceding address. The cost is $10 per copy.

30
Shows and Conventions

In this chapter, some of the annual conferences dealing with subjects important to the elderly are listed. Naturally, we could not list all such conferences because many are one-time affairs. If you are interested in attending these conventions, contact the appropriate organization or association listed in Chapter 4, Associations and Organizations.

CONFERENCES

CALIFORNIA

Psychological Support Systems for the
    Dying
University of California Extension
Berkeley, CA 94720
Meeting: Annual

A Preretirement Planning Conference
University Park
Los Angeles, CA 90007
Meeting: Annual

Congress of the International Senior
    Citizens Association
11753 Wilshire Blvd.
Los Angeles, CA 90025
Meeting: Annual

American Geriatrics Society
18102 Irvine Blvd.
Tustin, CA 92680
Meeting: Annual

DISTRICT OF COLUMBIA

American Association of Homes for
    the Aging
374 National Press Building
Washington, DC 20045
Meeting: Annual

American Association of Retired
    Persons
1909 K St., NW
Washington, DC 20006
Meeting: Biennial

American Health Care Association
1200 15th St., NW
Washington, DC 20005
Meeting: Annual

American Podiatry Association
20 Chevy Chase Circle, NW
Washington, DC 20015
Meeting: Annual

Association for Gerontology
1 Dupont Circle
Suite 520
Washington, DC 20036
Meeting: Annual

Association of Homes for the Aging
1050 17th St., NW
Washington, DC 20036
Meeting: Annual

Congress in Social Gerontology
425 13th St., NW
Washington, DC 20004
Meeting: Annual

Council on the Aging, Inc.
1828 L St., NW
Washington, DC 20036
Meeting: Annual

Economics of Aging Committee
400 Sixth St., SW
Washington, DC 20201
Meeting: Annual

Federal Council on the Aging Meeting
400 Sixth St., SW
Washington, DC 20201
Meeting: Annual

Federal Council on Aging
400 Sixth St., SW
Washington, DC 20201
Meeting: Annual

Federal Council on Aging
400 Sixth St., SW
Washington, DC 20201
Meeting: Quarterly

Gerontological Society
One Dupont Circle
Washington, DC 20036
Meeting: Annual

Long-Term Care Administration
4650 E. West Highway
Washington, DC 20014
Meeting: Annual

National Council on Aging
1828 L St., NW
Washington, DC 20036
Meeting: Annual

National Retired Teachers Association
    & American Association of
    Retired Persons
1909 K St., NW
Washington, DC 20049
Meeting: Annual

Public Health Association
1015 18th St., NW
Washington, DC 20036
Meeting: Annual

Rights of Older Americans Committee
400 Sixth St., SW
Washington, DC 20201
Meeting: Annual

Senior Services Committee
Donohoe Building
400 Sixth St., SW
Washington, DC 20201
Meeting: Annual

FLORIDA

Southern Conference on Gerontology
807 Seagle Building
Gainesville, FL 32601
Meeting: Annual

Aging Conference
Eckerd College
St. Petersburg, FL 33733
Meeting: Annual

Transportation for Elderly & Handicapped Conference
Florida State University
Tallahassee, FL 32306
Meeting: Annual

Mid-Life Work & Learning Options Conference
University of South Florida
Tampa, FL 33620
Meeting: Biennial

GEORGIA

American Geriatrics Society
c/o Dr. Robert B. Greenblatt
Medical College of Georgia
Augusta, GA 30902
Meeting: Annual

HAWAII

Hawaii Governor's Conference on Aging
1149 Bethal St.
Room 311
Honolulu, HI 96813
Meeting: Annual

ILLINOIS

Conference on Aging
200 S. Third St.
Belleville, IL 62221
Meeting: Annual

Aging Conference
3300 W. Peterson Ave.
Chicago, IL 60659
Meeting: Annual

Great Lakes Senior Citizens Conference
721 N. La Salle St.
Chicago, IL 60610
Meeting: Annual

IOWA

Conference on Preretirement Planning
Drake University
Des Moines, IA 50311
Meeting: Annual

INDIANA

Governor's Conference on Aging
215 N. Senate Ave.
Indianapolis, IN 46202
Meeting: Annual

Indiana Senior Citizens Association
155 E. Market St.
Indianapolis, IN 46204
Meeting: Annual

Kirkpatrick Memorial Workshop on Aging
Ball State University
Muncie, IN 47306
Meeting: Annual

KENTUCKY

Council on Aging & Kentucky Gerontological Society
University of Kentucky
Lexington, KY 40506
Meeting: Annual

MARYLAND

American Geriatrics Society & Baltimore City Hospitals
Baltimore City Hospital
Baltimore, MD 21223
Meeting: Annual

Department of Psychology
University of Maryland
College Park, MD 20742
Meeting: Annual

MICHIGAN

Institute of Gerontology Conference
543 Church St.
Ann Arbor, MI
Meeting: Annual

Later Life Conference
University of Michigan
Ann Arbor, MI 48109
Meeting: Annual

MISSOURI

Catholic Hospital Association
1438 S. Grand Blvd.
St. Louis, MO 63104
Meeting: Annual

Elderly Living in Single Rooms Conference
3550 Lindell Blvd.
St. Louis, MO 63103
Meeting: Biennial

MONTANA

Montana Governor's Conference on Aging
Aging Services Bureau
P.O. Box 1723
Helena, MT 59601
Meeting: Annual

Governor's Conference on Aging
944 S. Main St.
Kalespell, MT 59901
Meeting: Annual

NEBRASKA

American Aging Conference
University of Nebraska Medical Center
Omaha, NB 68108
Meeting: Annual

NEW HAMPSHIRE

Older Women Alone Conference
5 Market St.
Portsmouth, NH 03801
Meeting: Annual

Women in Transition
5 Market St.
Portsmouth, NH 03801
Meeting: Annual

NEW JERSEY

Preretirement Conference
Convent Station
Morristown, NJ 07961
Meeting: Annual

NEW YORK

American Geriatrics Society
10 Columbus Circle
New York, NY 10019
Meeting: Annual

Geriatrics Society
10 Columbus Circle
New York, NY 10019
Meeting: Annual

Meeting of Gerontological Society with American Geriatrics Society
1 Dupont Circle
Washington, DC 20036
or
10 Columbus Circle
New York, NY 10019
Meeting: Annual

Homemaker–Home Health Aide Services Council
67 Irving Place
New York, NY 10003
Meeting: Annual

International Council on Social Welfare
345 E. 46th St.
New York, NY 10017
Meeting: Annual

National Accreditation Council for Agencies Serving the Blind & Visually Handicapped
79 Madison Ave.
New York, NY 10016
Meeting: Annual

National Retirement Show
527 Madison Ave.
New York, NY 10022
Meeting: Annual

Women in Mid-Life Crisis Conference
Cornell University
Ithaca, NY 14853
Meeting: Irregularly

NORTH CAROLINA

Daycare for Older Adults
Duke University Medical Center
Box 3003
Durham, NC 27710
Meeting: Annual

OREGON

Conference on Justice & Older Americans
10525 SE Cherry Blossom Dr.
Portland, OR 97216
Meeting: Annual

TEXAS

Effective Psychotherapy
Texas Medical Center
Houston, TX 77025
Meeting: Annual

VIRGINIA

Society of Consultant Pharmacists
2300 Ninth St., S.
Arlington, VA 22204
Meeting: Annual

WASHINGTON

The Rights & Responsibilities of the Older Person Conference
Community Services Division
P.O. Box 1788
Olympia, WA 98504
Meeting: Annual

WISCONSIN

In-Home Services Conference
926 N. Sixth St.
Milwaukee, WI 53203
Meeting: Annual

National Geriatrics Society
212 W. Wisconsin Ave.
Milwaukee, WI 53203
Meeting: Annual

31
State Agencies on Aging

State agencies on aging can supply information about federal and state programs for the aging (i.e., Social Security, Supplementary Security Income, food stamps, meals, Medicare, Medicaid, and jobs) and can often help older persons interpret requirements for eligibility and help them approach the proper agencies. The state agencies also advise and inform the elderly about housing, transportation, counseling, homemaker-home health aides, and other important services.

All the state agencies on aging are listed in this chapter.

STATE AGENCIES ON AGING

State Commission on Aging
740 Madison Ave.
Montgomery, AL 36130
(205) 832-6640

Office on Aging
Department of Health & Social Services
Juneau, AK 99802
(907) 586-6153

Bureau on Aging
Department of Economic Security
548 E. McDowell
Phoenix, AZ 85004
(602) 271-4446

Office on Aging
Seventh & Gaines
Little Rock, AR 72202
(501) 371-2441

Office on Aging
Health & Welfare Agency
455 Capitol Mall
Sacramento, CA 95814
(916) 322-3887

State Department of Social Services
Division of Services for the Aging
1575 Sherman St.
Denver, CO 80203
(303) 892-2651

Department of Aging
90 Washington St.
Hartford, CT 06115
(203) 566-2480

Division of Aging
Department of Health & Social Services
2413 Lancaster Ave.
Wilmington, DE 19805
(302) 571-3481

Office of Services to the Aged
Department of Human Resources
Minsey Building
1329 E. St., NW
Washington, DC 20004
(202) 638-2406

Program Office of Aging & Adult Services
1323 Winewood Blvd.
Tallahassee, FL 32301
(904) 488-2650

Office of Aging
Department of Human Resources
47 Trinity Ave.
Atlanta, GA 30308
(404) 894-5333

Commission on Aging
1149 Bethel St.
Honolulu, HI 96813

Office on Aging
Statehouse
Boise, ID 83720
(208) 964-3833

Department on Aging
2401 W. Jefferson St.
Springfield, IL 62706
(217) 782-5773

Commission on the Aging & the Aged
Graphic Arts Building
215 N. Senate Ave.
Indianapolis, IN 46202
(317) 633-5948

Commission on the Aging
415 Tenth St.
Des Moines, IA 50319
(515) 281-5187

Services for the Aging Section
Division of Social Services
Social and Rehabilitation Services Department
State Office Building
Topeka, KS 66612
(913) 296-4986

Aging Branch
Center for Aging & Community Services Development
Department for Human Resources
403 Wapping St.
Frankfort, KY 40601
(502) 564-6930

Bureau of Aging Service
Division of Human Resources
Health & Social Rehabilitation Services Administration
P.O. Box 44282
Capital Station
Baton Rouge, LA 70804
(504) 389-2172

STATE AGENCIES ON AGING

Bureau of Maine's Elderly
Department of Human Services
State House
Augusta, ME 04333
(207) 622-6171

Office on Aging
State Office Building
301 W. Preston St.
Baltimore, MD 21201
(301) 383-2100

Executive Office of Elder Affairs
Department of Elder Affairs
120 Boylston St.
Boston, MA 02116
(617) 727-7751

Office of Services to the Aging
3500 N. Logan St.
Lansing, MI 48909
(517) 373-8230

Governor's Citizens Council on Aging
Metro Square Building
Seventh & Roberts Sts.
St. Paul, MN 55101
(612) 296-2544

Council on Aging
510 George St.
Jackson, MS 39216
(601) 354-6590

Office of Aging
Department of Social Services
Broadway State Office Building
P.O. Box 570
Jefferson City, MO 65101
(314) 751-2075

Commission on Aging
300 S. 17th St.
Lincoln, NB 68509
(402) 471-2307

Division of Aging
Department of Human Resources
505 E. King St.
Carson City, NV 89710
(702) 885-4210

Council on Aging
14 Depot St.
Concord, NH 03301
(603) 271-2751

Division on Aging
Department of Community Affairs
363 W. State St.
Trenton, NJ 08625
(609) 292-3765

State Commission on Aging
408 Galisteo St.
Sante Fe, NM 87501
(505) 827-5258

Office for the Aging
N.Y. State Executive Department
855 Central Ave.
Albany, NY 12206
(518) 457-7321

Office for the Aging
2 World Trade Center
New York, NY 10047
(212) 488-6405

Department for Aging
Department of Human Resources
213 Hillsborough St.
Raleigh, NC 27603
(919) 829-3983

Aging Services
Social Services Board
State Capitol Building
Bismarck, ND 58505
(701) 224-2577

Commission on Aging
34 N. High St.
Columbus, OH 43215
(614) 466-5500

Special Unit of Aging
Department of Institutions
Social and Rehabilitation Services
Box 25352
Oklahoma City, OK 73125
(405) 521-2281

Program on Aging
Human Resources Department
772 Commercial St., SE
Salem, OR 97310
(503) 378-4728

Office for the Aging
Department of Public Welfare
510 House & Welfare Building
Harrisburg, PA 17120
(717) 787-5350

Gericulture Commission
Department of Social Services
Apartado 11697
Santurce, PR 00908
(809) 722-2429

Department of Community Affairs
Division on Aging
150 Washington St.
Providence, RI 02903
(401) 528-1000

Commission on Aging
915 Main St.
Columbus, SC 29201
(803) 758-2576

Office on Aging
Department of Social Services
State Office Building
Illinois St.
Pierre, SD 57501
(605) 224-3656

Commission on Aging
S & P Building
306 Gay St.
Nashville, TN 37201
(615) 741-2056

Governor's Committee on Aging
Southwest Tower
211 E. Seventh St.
Austin, TX 78711
(512) 475-2717

Division of Aging
Department of Social Services
345 S. Sixth, E.
Salt Lake City, UT 84102
(801) 328-6422

Office on Aging
Department of Human Resources
81 River St.
Montpelier, VT 05602
(802) 828-3471

Office on Aging
830 E. Main St.
Richmond, VA 23219
(804) 786-7894

Office on Aging
Department of Social & Health Services
P.O. Box 1788
Olympia, WA 98504
(206) 753-2502

Commission on Aging
State Capitol
Charleston, WV 25305
(304) 348-3317

Division on Aging
Department of Health & Social Services
State Office Building
1 W. Wilson St.
Madison, WI 53702
(608) 266-2536

Aging Services
Department of Health & Social Services
Division of Public Assistance & Social
   Services
Hathaway Building
Cheyenne, WY 82002
(307) 777-7561

32
Telephone Reassurance

Many older people who live alone fear that they may fall or be taken suddenly ill and be unable to call for help. After a woman died in just such a situation, the first telephone reassurance project was started in Michigan.

Telephone reassurance provides daily telephone contact for older people who might otherwise have no outside contact for long periods of time.

Persons receiving telephone reassurance are called at a predetermined time each day. If the person does not answer, help is immediately sent to his or her home. In the event of no answer, a neighbor, relative, or nearby police or fire station is usually asked to make a personal check. Such details are worked out when a person begins receiving the service.

Telephone services have been credited with saving many lives by dispatching medical help in time. In one case, an alert caller noticed a slight slurring of speech in a client she talked with regularly. Although the client reported no difficulties, the caller reported the slurred speech to her supervisor who sent someone to check the situation personally. The client had suffered a heart spasm and was rushed to the hospital — in time.

Telephone reassurance generally costs little and can be provided by callers who range from teenagers to older people themselves. They are sponsored by a variety of organizations and agencies, such as women's clubs and police departments. For example, in Nassau County, New York, residents of a home for the aged make calls to older people who live alone. In Florida, 102 older persons who cannot leave their homes are called daily by 42 senior center members.

In Albuquerque, New Mexico, a hospital auxiliary and the Business and Professional Women's Club make daily calls. In Nebraska, the State Federation of Women's Clubs sponsors telephone reassurance. And, in Ohio, six different churches cooperate in sponsoring a telephone program.

Another type of telephone service, which has been outstandingly popular, is provided in Davenport, Iowa. Called "Dial-a-Listener," it provides a telephone number for an older person to call if he or she just wants to talk. Ten elderly professional people are the listeners.

For information on the telephone reassurance program in your area, contact the state or area agency on aging.

33
Transportation Projects Serving the Elderly

Inadequate transportation is one of the major problems confronting older Americans. Many older people, due to physical disabilities or limited funds, cannot rely on private automobiles to meet their transportation needs. These same conditions may also preclude or limit their use of mass-transit systems. Moreover, there may be no public transportation available in their area.

Yet, it is precisely those elderly Americans who find it difficult to get around who have the greatest need for transportation. It is they who must shop regularly for food, medicine, and other essentials, or visit the doctor for treatment, or drop by the senior center for a hot meal and some companionship.

The U.S. Department of Transportation, the Administration on Aging, the General Services Administration, and many communities and civic organizations either now offer, or are experimenting with, various forms of assistance to help meet the transportation needs of America's older population.

DOT Programs

The U.S. Department of Transportation (DOT) and the Administration on Aging, under a joint working agreement, have pledged mutual cooperation and coordination in helping meet the transportation needs of older people in urban areas.

Under Section 16(b) (2) of the Urban Mass Transportation Act of 1964 as amended, $22 million is available in fiscal year 1976 for capital assistance grants and loans to private and nonprivate corporations and associations to help them provide transportation services for the elderly and the handicapped in urban areas.

The National Mass Transportation Act of 1974 includes a number of provisions that may aid older riders. The act requires that any public transit system receiving capital assistance funds from the Urban Mass Transportation Administration (UMTA) charge half the fare or less for the elderly. For the first time, it also permits UMTA to fund operating expenses and authorizes $500 million for transportation capital expenditures in nonurbanized areas.

Other programs administered by UMTA include research-and-development grants to test innovative approaches to transportation problems, and funding for capital assistance, the acquisition of vehicles, and other needed equipment. For further information, contact either the state agency on aging or the Administrator, Urban Mass Transportation Administration, U.S. Department of Transportation, 400 Seventh St., SW, Washington, DC 20590.

The Federal Aid Highway Act of 1973 as amended (P.L. 93-87, Section 147, Title I) provides for a public-transportation demonstration program designed to encourage the development, improvement, and use of public mass-transportation in rural areas. The program is administered by the Federal Highway Administration of DOT. Applicants for these demonstration funds must be either public agencies or public-purpose (nonprofit) agencies or corporations, preferably with state or areawide responsibilities.

Although the program is designed for demonstrations for the general rural public, one criterion for project selection by the Federal Highway Administration is that the transportation system be adaptable to the needs of the elderly and handicapped. Congress has appropriated $15 million for this grant program in fiscal year 1976.

Organizations and agencies interested in rural demonstration projects can contact their state's department of transportation or agency on aging for information regarding the status of this program and possibilities for support.

AOA Programs

There are several other avenues of assistance that can be used to provide transportation services to the elderly.

Under Title III of the Older Americans Comprehensive Services Amendments, which authorizes support for state and community programs, the Administration on Aging (AOA) awards grants to the designated state agencies on aging to assist state and local agencies in the development of comprehensive and coordinated services to the elderly. The designated state agency can identify potential sources of funding for transportation, provide advice on how best to plan for and implement a project, and coordinate efforts with other agencies and organizations that might be involved in planning and supporting transportation projects.

The state agency can also advocate the use of existing transportation services on behalf of the elderly and help in efforts to secure revenue-sharing funds to establish transportation projects for the elderly. Under certain limited circumstances, the state agency or possibly the AOA can provide direct project funding.

The commissioner on aging has conducted a comprehensive study and survey of the transportation problems of older Americans with a view to finding practical solutions for improving transportation for older people. These findings were submitted to the president and Congress on January 1, 1975. A how-to-do-it guide on transportation for the elderly, "Planning Handbook: Transportation Services for the Elderly," has recently been published by AOA. (See Chapter 1 for address.)

Other Programs

Many states and local areas operate diverse transportation projects ranging from the relatively inexpensive, informal use of volunteer drivers in small towns and rural areas to the use of sophisticated demand-responsive or regularly scheduled transit vehicles, often designed to meet their patrons' special needs.

Free or reduced fares on public transportation vehicles are enabling the elderly in many parts of the country to travel during midday, night, and weekend hours. All public transit operators in Pennsylvania, for example, participate in the state's free-fare program, which is subsidized by the Pennsylvania lottery. Many areas that permit older people to ride free during offpeak transit hours also offer reduced (but not free) fares during rush hours.

Demonstration Projects

A number of transportation projects around the country are showing what can be done for older Americans with good management, local support, and adequate funding. Listed herein are but a few examples of demonstration programs serving a variety of purposes and funded by various sources.

In California. "Whistlestop Wheels" in Marin County provides transportation for elderly, ill, and handicapped residents via demand-responsive van service plus a large volunteer driver pool. Although parts of the county are served by public transportation, this consists primarily of commuter bus service to San Francisco.

The "Whistlestop Wheels" program not only transports senior citizens and those of all ages who are handicapped or need medical care — it also supports a variety of service and charitable organizations. The senior-citizens component provides free transportation to evening meals at senior centers throughout the county. It also offers a group shopper-shuttle service, which picks up groups from various housing projects at specified times.

The 12-vehicle operation is sponsored by the Marin County Transit District.

In Florida. A project in St. Petersburg called TOTE (Transportation of the Elderly) provides service to the elderly and handicapped where little or none existed before. Eligible riders have access to specially equipped minibuses that offer door-to-door service, nominal fares (35 cents and 60 cents), and transportation by advance reservation, weekly subscription, or telephone request, as well as charter service.

TOTE, which began in 1972 with a planning phase to determine what would best serve the needs of the elderly and handicapped, is cosponsored by the UMTA, the DOT, the Florida Department of Transportation, and the City of St. Petersburg. It serves 30,000 people in the heart of the city, where every third person is 60 or older.

By identifying its target population (everyone must register for TOTE) and catering to their special needs with well-designed buses, good service, and a range of options, TOTE has developed a successful strategy for upgrading its customers' usefulness to themselves and to the community.

In Illinois. In Chicago, the YMCA, with the AOA's demonstration-grant support, set up the Senior Citizens Mobile Service. In a 3-year demonstration, the mobile service provided transportation to 1,606 different seniors on 30,403 trips. A total of 48 different agencies participated through referrals and requests for service.

Appointments for trips were scheduled a day ahead, and the central office was able to communicate with the van driver by two-way radio, allowing last-minute changes and emergencies to be handled.

Many persons have said that they feel 10 to 15 years younger as a result of the service. Some were able to go beyond their immediate neighborhoods for the first time in their lives. Many made enduring friendships during their rides together.

Although the demonstration-grant funds for this project have ended, the mobile service is continuing operation with local funding. The Martin Luther King Urban Progress Center was impressed enough to give $20,000 toward the project's continuation.

In Missouri. OATS — Older Adult Transportation Service — is a personal membership, door-to-door bus network operating in more than 80 of Missouri's 114 counties. Over 10,000 people are enrolled in OATS, which is a nonprofit corporation serving the elderly and medically handicapped. They pay a moderate annual membership fee plus a per-mile contribution for distance traveled.

Although the 48-bus system is rapidly growing into a statewide network, routes and schedules and certain policies are determined at the local level by county committees composed of volunteers. An additional 500 volunteers across the state regularly call or are called by OATS subscribers needing transportation. In fact, OATS management has stated that the expanding service could not exist without its heavy reliance on volunteers in a variety of roles.

OATS is sponsored by the Missouri State Office of Aging.

In nine Missouri counties, a variety of United States Government surplus vehicles serve the transportation needs of all ages including older people. Some vehicles are available on call; others run a regular route. Operating costs of the system are built into the budget of the Community Action Agency (Office of Economic Opportunity). Paid staff members and volunteers, including senior citizens, run the service. The welfare department pays for persons on public assistance. Riders in better financial circumstances who use the service sometimes make financial contributions. The Community Action Agency is presently considering converting this service into a transportation cooperative owned and operated by an incorporated membership group of rider-consumers.

In Nebraska. In Lincoln, a senior handi-bus provides mobility to handicapped and older persons, who reside in the city and the surrounding Lancaster County, who have no other transportation means, are physically isolated, and need to get the medical facilities, employment, and other essential activities.

The City of Lincoln's Areawide Model Project on Aging (now an Area Agency on Aging), working in conjunction with the city-owned public transportation system, incorporated the senior handi-bus into the Lincoln Public Transportation System in June 1972. Later, the system was expanded with UMTA capital assistance funds to include the nonelderly handicapped. Six radio-dispatched passenger vans operate door-to-door; four have hydraulic wheelchair lifts. Riders reserve their trips 24 hours in advance, with buses dispatched according to the daily reservation schedule. Whenever reservations exceed system capacity, priority is given to medical and employment needs.

In Rhode Island. Senior Citizen's Transportation, Inc. (SCT) is a statewide system of free transportation for the elderly. The 30 radio-equipped vehicles in the SCT fleet are available through a dial-a-ride arrangement 5 days a week. The three most popular uses of the service are for medically related purposes, shopping and recreational trips. SCT is funded in part through the Model Project Program, Section 308, as amended.

South Providence, Rhode Island, once a thriving area with grocery stores, banks, and doctor's offices in every block or two, has lost many of its stores, banks, and doctors in recent years. To help approximately 2,000 older persons still living there to do their shopping and reach services in other parts of town, a station wagon was purchased by the Rhode Island Division on Aging. It averages 12 calls a day. Most trips are to doctor's offices, clinics, and hospitals, but many people use this service to go grocery-shopping. One trip usually serves several people at a time.

In Virginia. In November 1975, a new private nonprofit transportation agency was established in Roanoke, VA, to unify existing human-service transportation services into a single coordinated system. To achieve this, Project RADAR (Roanoke Agencies Dial-A-Ride) will pool the existing resources, equipment, and personnel of participating social-service agencies. Some 22 agencies in the city have documented the need for this type of service and their willingness to participate. The service components of the system includes demand response, scheduled routes, special charter trips, and general transportation planning and implementation activities. The system is already providing transportation for some agencies, that is, to and from Title VII nutrition sites in the city.

More Transportation Services

Private Cars. Volunteers driving private cars have given older citizens of South Routt County, Colorado, a choice of services and opportunities that were once closed to them for lack of public transportation. In this high country, with low temperatures and lots of snow, even a few miles is a very long distance. No accessible public transportation exists.

Because a number of the small communities lack medical services, many of the trips are to doctors' offices. Other trips take senior citizens to polling places. In one instance, after almost a lifetime of residence in this country, three volunteer rides to Denver made it possible for an elderly woman to receive her United States citizenship. With it, she was able to qualify for Medicare.

Funded by the Colorado state agency on aging, with local sponsorship by the Visiting Nurse Association, this project is opening many additional opportunities for older citizens as their communities become more aware of them and their needs.

In four rural counties of Pennsylvania, STRIDE (Small Transportation Required in Developing Economy) serves the need of all age groups including the elderly. It, too, uses privately owned vehicles.

These vehicles, however, are not necessarily driven by their owners. Some persons drive their own cars to work in the morning and instead of parking them where they would be idle, turn them over to STRIDE drivers. The cars are returned to their owners at the end of the workday. Funded by the Office of Economic Opportunity,

STRIDE has a board of directors and neighborhood councils in each community.

Texas "Roadrunner" Volunteers, Inc., a group in Austin, Texas, which calls upon nursing-home residents, leased a station wagon and a small buss primarily to take the patients on needed trips. When it was found that many former volunteer-visitors had dropped out of the program because they no longer felt able to drive their own cars, "Roadrunners" provided their transportation and they were again able to donate their services to the community.

Reduced Fares. At least 50 cities with public transportation systems have experimented with reducing fares for older people during nonrush hours.

In July 1973, Pennsylvania became the first state in the nation to effect a statewide free-fare program for senior citizens. Seventy-seven transit operators participate in the highly successful project. In some — but not all — areas, fares are reduced even during rush hours.

In several instances, reduced fares have not only made life happier for older citizens, but have increased ridership to the point of increasing transit companies' total revenues.

The small town of Commerce, California, provides free bus service to people of all ages within its city limits and to a major shopping center outside the city. Buses run every half-hour. No one has to walk more than a block from any point in the 8-square-mile community to a bus stop.

Any organization with membership composed of at least 60 percent Commerce city residents may schedule two free chartered bus trips per year to any destination within 50 miles of the city. Organizations, including three senior citizens organizations, use the free bus to go to ball games, museums, plays, and other events. Commerce, a suburb of Los Angeles, has a population of 10,000 people. Total cost of the five-bus system is $100,000 per year.

To sign up for any of the transportation programs just mentioned that are in your community, contact the organization directly or call your area agency on aging and request information on the procedure to follow to receive transportation.

If these programs are not operating in your state, get in touch with the state's department of transportation, the senior center, and the state agency on aging, and ask what transportation programs are available in your community.

Senior Center Bus Services. Some Senior Centers provide a bus that runs between the members' homes and the centers.

In Prince Georges County, Maryland, a sprawling suburban area, buses stop at designated points to pick up groups of senior center members. The same buses sometimes take members on tours or sightseeing trips away from the centers.

"Dial-a-Bus" is a system operated by the Little House Senior Center in Menlo Park, California. Center members may have a standing reservation, or they may phone in by noon of the day they wish to ride. A 12-passenger bus is driven along three regular routes by Little House members. In addition to regular runs, the bus is used for group outings and regular visits to four convalescent homes in the area where Little House members entertain the residents.

There is no charge for this bus service, but Little House estimates it costs 60 cents a person per ride, which includes gas, insurance, and amortization of the vehicle. Many members contribute funds for the minibus operation.

STATE DEPARTMENTS OF TRANSPORTATION

ALABAMA
Department of Transportation
11 S. Union St.
Montgomery, AL 36104
(205) 832-5440

ALASKA
Department of Transportation
Third St.
Douglas, AK 99824
(907) 364-2121

ARIZONA
Department of Transportation
206 S. 17th Ave.
Phoenix, AZ 85007
(602) 261-7011

CALIFORNIA
Department of Transportation
1120 N St.
Sacramento, CA 95814
(916) 445-2201

CONNECTICUT
Department of Transportation
20 Wolcott Hill Rd.
Wethersfield, CT 06109
(203) 566-3477

DELAWARE
Department of Transportation
Highway Department Administration Building
Dover, DE 19901
(302) 678-5711

DISTRICT OF COLUMBIA
Department of Transportation
415 12th St., NW
Washington, DC 20004
(202) 628-6000

FLORIDA
Department of Transportation
605 Suwannee St.
Tallahassee, FL 32304
(904) 488-8772

GEORGIA
Department of Transportation
No. 2 Capitol Square
Atlanta, GA 30334
(404) 656-5200

HAWAII
Department of Transportation
869 Punchbowl St.
Honolulu, HI 96813
(808) 548-3205

IDAHO
Department of Transportation
3311 W. State St.
Boise, ID 83707
(208) 384-3699

ILLINOIS
Department of Transportation
2300 S. Dirkesen Parkway
Springfield, IL 62764
(217) 782-2276

INDIANA
Department of Transportation
100 N. Senate Ave.
Indianapolis, IN 46204
(317) 633-5816

IOWA
Department of Transportation
State Capitol
Des Moines, IA 50319
(515) 296-1101

KANSAS
Department of Transportation
State Office Building
Topeka, KS 66612
(913) 296-3461

KENTUCKY
Department of Transportation
High & Clinton Sts.
Frankfort, KY 40601
(502) 564-4890

LOUISIANA
Department of Transportation
P.O. Box 44245
Baton Rouge, LA 70804
(504) 389-5112

MAINE
Department of Transportation
State Office Building
Augusta, ME 04330
(207) 289-2551

MARYLAND
Department of Transportation
Baltimore-Washington International
Airport, MD 21240
(301) 768-9520

MASSACHUSETTS
Department of Transportation
One Asburton Place
Boston, MA 02108
(617) 727-7680

MICHIGAN
Department of Transportation
425 W. Ottowa
Lansing, MI 48904
(517) 373-2090

MINNESOTA
Department of Transportation
State Highway Building
St. Paul, MN 55155
(612) 296-3000

MISSISSIPPI
Department of Transportation
Woolfolk State Office Building
Northwest St.
Jackson, MS 39205
(601) 354-6594

MISSOURI
Department of Transportation
119 W. Capitol Ave.
Jefferson, MO 65101
(314) 751-2551

MONTANA
Department of Transportation
E. Sixth Ave. & Roberts St.
Helena, MT 59601
(406) 449-2482

NEBRASKA
Department of Transportation
S. Junction US 77 & N-2
Lincoln, NB 68509
(402) 477-6012

NEVADA
Department of Transportation
1263 S. Stewart St.
Carson City, NV 89701
(702) 885-5440

NEW HAMPSHIRE
Department of Transportation
85 Loudon Rd.
Concord, NH 03301
(603) 271-3734

NEW JERSEY
Department of Transportation
1035 Parkway Ave.
Trenton, NJ 08625
(609) 292-3535

NEW MEXICO
Department of Transportation
1120 Cerrillos Rd.
Sante Fe, MN 87503
(505) 983-0100

NEW YORK
Department of Transportation
1220 Washington Ave.
Albany, NY 12226
(518) 457-4422

NORTH CAROLINA
Department of Transportation
1 S. Wilmington St.
Raleigh, NC 27611
(919) 829-7384

NORTH DAKOTA
Department of Transportation
Capitol Grounds
Bismarck, ND 58501
(701) 224-2500

OHIO
Department of Transportation
25 S. Front St.
Columbus, OH 43215
(614) 469-6600

OKLAHOMA
Department of Transportation
200 NE 21st St.
Oklahoma City, OK 73105
(405) 521-2631

OREGON
Department of Transportation
State Highway Building
Salem, OR 97310
(503) 378-6388

PENNSYLVANIA
Department of Transportation
1220 Transportation & Safety Building
Harrisburg, PA 17120
(717) 787-5574

PUERTO RICO
Department of Transportation
Box 3909 GPO
San Juan, PR 00936
(809) 725-5840

RHODE ISLAND
Department of Transportation
State Office Building
Providence, RI 02903
(401) 277-2481

SOUTH CAROLINA
Department of Transportation
State Highway Building
Columbia, SC 29202
(803) 758-2716

SOUTH DAKOTA
Department of Transportation
East Broadway
Pierre, SD 57501
(605) 224-3265

TENNESSEE
Department of Transportation
Sixth Ave. N. & Deaderick St.
Nashville, TN 37219
(615) 741-3011

TEXAS
Department of Transportation
11th & Brazos Sts.
Austin, TX 78701
(512) 475-2081

UTAH
Department of Transportation
603 State Office Building
Salt Lake City, UT 84114
(801) 533-4000

VERMONT
Department of Transportation
133 State St.
Montpelier, VT 05602
(802) 828-2657

VIRGINIA
Department of Transportation
1221 E. Broad St.
Richmond, VA 23219
(809) 774-1301

WASHINGTON
Department of Transportation
Franklin & Maple Park
Olympia, WA 98504
(206) 753-6170

WEST VIRGINIA
Department of Transportation
1900 Washington St., E.
Charleston, WV 25305
(304) 348-3456

WISCONSIN
Department of Transportation
4802 Sheboygan Ave.
Madison, WI 53702
(608) 266-1113

WYOMING
Department of Transportation
State Highway Office Building
Cheyenne, WY 82001
(307) 777-7471

34
YMCA and YWCA

Both the Young Men's Christian Association (YMCA) and the Young Women's Christian Association (YWCA) have programs for the elderly in many of their community branches. You can discover what programs are available by calling the branch nearest you. The phone number and address of all community branches can be found in either the white or yellow pages of the telephone directory.

YMCA

Examples of programs in some branches of the YMCA are the Cardiovascular Health Institute, club programs, and post-cardiac rehabilitation.

YWCA

Examples of programs in some branches of the YWCA are exercise programs, nutrition programs, physical fitness programs, retired senior volunteers, senior citizens' swimming programs, senior citizens' trips, "serendipity" tours, vacations for senior citizens, and "The Aging Process: Exploring Stages of Growth and Change."

NATIONAL HEADQUARTERS

Young Men's Christian Association
291 Broadway
New York, NY 10017
(212) 374-2000
Contact: Robert W. Harlan

Young Women's Christian Association
600 Lexington Ave.
New York, NY 10022
(212) 753-4700
Contact: Elizabeth Steel Genne